MANAGERIAL ECONOMICS

JAMES G. MULLIGAN
University of Delaware

MANAGERIAL ECONOMICS
STRATEGY FOR PROFIT

ALLYN AND BACON
BOSTON ▪ LONDON ▪ SYDNEY ▪ TORONTO

Series Editor: Cary Tengler
Cover Administrator: Linda Dickinson
Composition Buyer: Linda Cox
Manufacturing Buyer: William Alberti
Editorial-Production Services: Barbara Willette
Text Designer: Melinda Grosser for *silk*
Cover Designer: Lynda Fishbourne
Production Administrator: Kathy Smith

Copyright © 1989 by Allyn and Bacon
A Division of Simon & Schuster
160 Gould Street
Needham Heights, Massachusetts 02194-2310

Library of Congress Cataloging-in-Publication Data

Mulligan, James Gregory.
    Managerial economics.

    Includes index.
    1. Managerial economics. I. Title.
HD30.22.M86   1989   658.1'5   88-7389
ISBN 0-205-11711-2

Printed in the United States of America

10 9 8 7 6 5 4 3 2   92 93

CONTENTS

PREFACE

A managerial economics book must give the reader an appreciation of the great value of economic reasoning in solving business problems. Few readers of a managerial economics book plan on becoming economists. They need an accessible but insightful analysis of problems they are likely to encounter. Creative application of economic principles and reasoning is vital to successful use of economic tools in commerce on any level. Information and technique can give no viable solution without creative application. Not content with the available books on this subject, I chose to write *Managerial Economics: Strategy for Profit* to demonstrate the importance of the application of economic reasoning.

I want the nonspecialist reader to have the opportunity to think as an economist does when analyzing problems. The best way to do this is to practice within a series of realistic settings that require economic reasoning. By following this approach, the reader will be better equipped for solving problems and for creating profitable commercial endeavors.

The book follows the everyday activities of four fictional entrepreneurs and firms that depend on economic analysis to solve their business problems. There are over 150 additional applications, mostly drawn from recent professional journal articles that directly relate the theory to existing problems.

The reader should not be forced to rely on applications alone, however. There are also graphical explanations and numerical problems using basic algebra that provide rigorous theoretical support. Readers without a calculus background will not be at a disadvantage, as mathematical explanations and problems are based on nothing more difficult than the algebraic solution of two equations with two unknowns. In addition, the numerical problems are tied to the graphical examples. Key terms are clearly defined in the text, and the definitions are indicated by a symbol in the margin for easy reference.

Above all, this is meant to be an economically based guide for entrepreneurs and managers. The book will serve as a primer for many problems that demand specialized skills and techniques of analysis. These will help the reader in learning how to formulate the relevant questions and knowing what to do next. The book will provide a means of beginning to develop economic analysis skills.

The first five chapters form the theoretical base for the rest of the book. The reader can proceed to any other chapter or part of a chapter after reading the first five chapters. Although the remainder of the book (Chapters 6–18) is in five parts, the reader should follow his or her interests in choosing topics and not feel constrained by the structure.

Some readers will be most interested in pricing strategies (Part II), since price theory is a major focus of economic analysis. Others may wish to emphasize techniques such as statistical estimation, risk analysis, and capital budgeting (Part V) and supplement their study by choosing among the other more applied chapters. Readers who are interested in organizational issues will want to concentrate on Part III, while those with an interest in policy will find Part IV especially helpful. The typical reader will sample topics from all parts of the book.

In addition to the emphasis on applications in every chapter, there are topics that are not usually found in other managerial economics books. There is an entire chapter on information costs and the promotion of product quality (Chapter 9). One chapter provides a consistent, unified discussion of pricing strategies when facing competitors (Chapter 7). There are two chapters on the organization of the firm emphasizing the importance of transactions costs in choosing between vertical integration and market-based contractual arrangements (Chapters 10 and 12). Although other books include short sections on antitrust and regulatory policy, this book has separate chapters on antitrust, regulation, and trade policy (Chapters 13, 14, and 15). These three chapters expose the reader to the importance of economic reasoning in effective policy making.

Principal Features

The book differs from other books on the same subject in the following ways:

1. The economic concepts are introduced by four fictional entrepreneurs who face realistic problems requiring economic analysis. The four entrepreneurs appear throughout the book.
2. There are over 150 applications drawn mostly from recent journal articles.
3. There are over 60 numerical problems tied to the graphical explanations to enhance the analytical explanations. These problems use linear relationships and simple algebra.

4. The following are additional applied topics that are not usually found in other books. These applications demonstrate the extensive role of economic reasoning in business decision making.

a. A chapter on pricing strategies when facing competition, including such topics as pricing to deter entry, collusion, and contestable markets.

b. A chapter on information costs and the promotion of product quality, including such topics as search costs, the role of advertising and brand names, choice of a product's characteristics, and regulation of quality.

c. A chapter on the transaction-cost theory of firm organization and a companion chapter on contractual-based vertical arrangements such as exclusive territories, exclusive dealing, resale price maintenance, and franchising.

d. A chapter on international trade, including such topics as the motivation for trade and the effects of protectionist trade policies.

Consistency with Other Managerial Economics Books

While this book offers the reader the new features listed above, it includes the topics that are traditionally found in a managerial economics book.

1. There is a thorough discussion of demand, production, and cost theory in Chapters 2, 3 and 4.

2. Chapter 5 covers the benchmark market structures of perfect competition, monopoly, and monopolistic competition.

3. Chapter 6 provides a unified treatment of monopoly pricing, including price discrimination, metering, and peak load pricing along with markup pricing and incremental analysis.

4. Chapter 8 provides a thorough discussion of multiproduct pricing, including the new topic of mixed bundling of a competitive good with a monopolized good.

5. Chapter 11 covers transfer pricing and the allocation of output across plants.

6. There is extensive coverage of managerial techniques for solving economic problems. Chapter 16 contains three separate sections on demand estimation, the estimation of cost functions, and forecasting. The reader can pursue any one or all three of these topics. The emphasis in this chapter is the application of these techniques and the underlying economic rationale for the use of each technique.

7. Chapters 17 and 18 provide detailed coverage of risk analysis and capital budgeting that extend the theoretical discussions of Chapters 2 through 5. Chapter 17 contains a practical entrepreneurial problem that increases in complexity throughout the chapter.

In summary, this book remains faithful to the traditional topics offered by a managerial economics book, while changing the emphasis toward an applied, problem-solving approach. The abundance of applications in each chapter and the entirely new chapters will leave no doubt as to the practical value of economic reasoning.

Acknowledgments

This book has been a collaborative effort with Lois Jackson Mulligan. We would like to thank economics editor Cary Tengler, the production staff of Allyn and Bacon, Inc., especially Kathy Smith, our copy editor Nancy Blodget, and production coordinator Barbara Willette for their help. We appreciated the comments and helpful suggestions from those economists who have reviewed parts or all of the book and from the many students who have used material from the book in their classes. The reviewers include David Black, Michael Staten, Anita Schwarz, Jack Carter, and William Latham of the University of Delaware; Wayne Carroll of the University of Wisconsin at Eau Claire; David Round of the University of Adelaide in Adelaide, Australia; William Stewart of the Ecole Superieure de Commerce in Lyon, France; Paul Seidenstat of Temple University; Clifford Hawley of West Virginia University; Sharon Levin of the University of Missouri at St. Louis; and James Simpson of the Office of Management and the Budget.

MANAGERIAL ECONOMICS

INTRODUCTION

1

Managers constantly make decisions that affect the economic vitality of firms. Some successful managers may simply be lucky, basing their decisions on hunches. Others may be equipped with a special ability to formulate innovative plans and make sound judgments. In other words, luck is not always an ingredient in successful decision making. This book offers assistance to managers who are interested in removing some of the hoping and guesswork from their decision-making process.

The economic environment affects all firms and managers, and vice versa. Managers are more likely to be successful if they understand how their actions affect the market and how market forces affect the firm. A *market* is a collection of buyers and sellers of similar products. For example, there are distinct markets for wheat, pianos, cameras, and trash bags.

This book focuses on what economists currently know about the market in which managers must operate. While every market situation is likely to be unique, managers will find that some of the economic principles discussed in this text are directly related to their own current or future situations. While one course in managerial economics will not make anyone an economist, a course such as this one should provide a foundation in the economic principles that affect decisions in business administration, marketing, accounting, finance, operations research, and other related business fields.

A managerial economics course provides the opportunity to isolate critical economic principles that appear often in varied business situations. By its very nature, economics focuses on the underlying reasons for the occurrence of economic phenomena. It is not an exact science, with tables and formulas that managers can turn to for answers to all their business problems. Instead, economics provides a logical framework for approaching a business problem rationally. Since managers face problems that have economic implications, they will better understand the solutions to these problems if they have a basic knowledge of the economics involved.

The Objectives of the Firm

Let us concentrate our attention on the firm. Managerial economics is an application of economic theory and methodology to problems faced by the firm. Since the firm's decisions have an economic impact not only on itself, but on our entire society, it will be useful to start with a theory of the firm's behavior.

Throughout most of the book we will assume that the owners of a firm are intent on maximizing their own wealth by maximizing the wealth of the firm. The owners assign to the managers of the firm the task of achieving this objective. Wealth maximization is the maximization of profits over the life of the firm.

Although we will assume for the time being that wealth maximization is the owners' objective, we will consider alternative assumptions in detail. We will also consider the possibility that managers may choose to deviate from the owners' wishes and pursue objectives that enrich the managers at the expense of the owners.

A firm accumulates wealth by earning revenues in excess of costs. Every department of the firm has an impact on the firm's wealth. The marketing department focuses its attention primarily on sales. The finance department concentrates on attracting the lowest-cost source of capital. The production department focuses on the firm's costs. These concerns overlap. For example, marketing efforts incur costs, while production decisions affect the quality of the product and customers' interest in purchasing it.

Constrained Wealth Maximization

The firm does not have unlimited resources to solve its wealth-maximization problem. The wealth-maximization decision of the firm is a constrained-maximization problem. That is, while the firm is attempting to maximize its wealth, it must do so subject to several constraints. How the firm solves this problem depends on the specific set of constraints that it faces. The firm must contend with constraints imposed by the market, the limits of available technology, uncertainty about the future, and the legal environment.

The market affects the firm's access to resources and forces the firm to provide products that consumers want. Through the market the firm must contend with its competitors and potential competitors. Available technology may limit the amount of output that the firm can hope to achieve from any given level of input. The legal environment constrains the firm's behavior via antitrust laws, regulations, and restrictive trade policies.

Uncertainty results from the cost of acquiring information. Firms must inform themselves regarding the demand for their products, their costs, and the performance of their employees in order to make rational business decisions. Since consumers also face information costs in determining product quality, firms must devise methods for communicating the quality of their products to consumers.

Given these constraints, the firm must choose its output and input levels, prices, product quality, product mix, advertising levels, and internal organizational structure. All of these decisions affect the wealth of the firm. Even though the people making these decisions have their primary expertise in areas such as engineering, accounting, finance, law, business administration, and operations research, they will be making economic decisions. The firm's success will depend on how well each manager understands the nature and impact of each constraint on the overall profitability of the firm.

The Impact of Economic Reasoning

Among business executives there is a growing awareness of the advantages of an economic understanding of business problems. Although a 1969 survey showed that apparently only 63 of 1,900 U.S. corporations were using economic analysis to model their firm's market environment, the situation changed quickly. As early as 1974, Professor Thomas H. Naylor of Duke University and Daniel R. Gattis of Minton Amick and Associates of Raleigh, North Carolina, were reporting that 73 percent of U.S. corporations were using economic analysis to form corporate planning models while another 15 percent were developing a model.[1]

The 1974 survey found that there was a strong need for economic planning owing to such concerns as the uncertainty of the market environment due to fluctuations in input and output prices, the growing importance of international trade, and the changing role of government policy toward business. The survey found that the interdependence among the departments of a firm demands a more systematic approach to the firm's decision making.

Economic modeling of the firm allows managers to explore several alternatives before making a commitment and increases their understanding of the market environment. In the Naylor-Gattis survey, 78 percent of the managers considered the ability to explore other alternatives as the major benefit of economic analysis in the firm's decision making.

More recent surveys confirm these findings. For example, Professor Guisseppi Forgionne of Drexel University found in 1982 that almost 80 percent of managers believed that the benefits of economic analysis justified the costs. Over 85 percent reported that economic analysis allowed them to interpret data effectively, nearly 70 percent said that economic analysis forced them to define the problem clearly and concisely, and two-thirds thought that it highlighted relevant policy implications and ramifications.[2]

This book will expose you to numerous economic concepts. You will have an opportunity to see how you can apply them realistically. Chapters 2, 3, and 4 provide the elements of the theories of demand, production, and

---

[1] Thomas H. Naylor and Donald R. Gattis. "Corporate Planning Models." *California Management Review* XVIII, No. 4 (Summer 1976):69–79.

[2] Guisseppi A. Forgionne. "Economic Tools Used by Management in Large American-Operated Corporations." *Business Economics* (April 1984):5–14.

cost, respectively. Chapter 5 completes the discussion of basic tools. It also provides a reference for the remaining chapters. Chapter 5 also describes the structure and behavior of the firm in the two extreme market cases—perfect competition and monopoly—and provides a basis for analyzing the variations of these two structures found in actual markets. In the last thirteen chapters we will expand the theories developed in Chapters 2–5.

The most extensively researched area of economics concerns pricing strategies, which will be considered in Chapters 6–8. We will begin with single-product pricing. Topics will include markup pricing, price discrimination (that is, market segmentation), metering, tied sales, incremental pricing, and peak-load pricing. We will extend the pricing rules to the sale of more than one type of product. The multiproduct firm must consider the effects that the output and price of each of its products has on the sales of its other products.

Market forces constrain firms' behavior. Firms must compete with both small and large firms. The firm can attempt to coexist peacefully or take direct action to either drive competitors out of the market or to prevent potential competitors from entering the market. We will analyze the economic principles of several market structures and pricing strategies.

Executives often bemoan competition based solely on price and actively pursue nonprice methods to differentiate their products from those of their competitors. In Chapter 9 we will explore the economic theory behind nonprice competitive methods and the choice of product attributes by the firm. Our emphasis will be on strategies for promoting the firm's product in a market environment of incomplete information about product quality.

Once a firm chooses the characteristics of its product, it must develop strategies to convince customers in advance that the product actually does possess these characteristics. We will discuss an economic theory that emphasizes the importance of brand names, advertising, and warranties in overcoming the informational costs of assuring product quality.

In Chapters 10–12 we will consider a longer list of important organizational issues. We will go inside the firm and discuss the economic justification for the size and structure of firms. By focusing on the advantages and disadvantages of the market as the supplier of inputs, we will make a distinction between the market and the firm as the most efficient solver of specific economic problems. We will also consider problems owners may have in convincing managers to carry out their wishes. Without sufficient control by owners, managers may pursue counterobjectives, which could impede the owners' goal of wealth maximization.

Since a large firm may operate at many levels in the vertical production chain, it must establish procedures for setting the prices of inputs it produces and uses itself. The firm must also decide how to allocate output among its various production units. While some manufacturers provide their own distribution and retail functions for their products, others rely on other firms for these services. Economic theory offers an understanding of the common distributional strategies of franchising, exclusive territories, and exclusive dealing. These options will be contrasted with direct ownership of distribution and retail firms by manufacturers.

Although we will analyze the government's impact on firms throughout, there are three chapters that deal exclusively with the government's impact on business decisions. We will emphasize the effects of antitrust, regulatory, and international trade policies on the firm's market environment. No firm can escape the effect of government policy. Trade policy affects most firms. Even though a firm may not be an exporter or a direct competitor with firms from other countries, it will normally use inputs affected by international trade.

Chapters 6–15 need not be covered in sequence. Although these ten chapters fit into three related parts (Pricing and Product Promotion Strategies, Organization of the Firm, and Government Policy), you may read the chapters in any order without loss of continuity or understanding. Although there are topics that cross the boundaries of the chapters, the explanations are self-contained.

Chapters 16–18 consider techniques that will help managers implement the economic reasoning emphasized in earlier chapters. Managers and other staff members commonly employ statistical estimation, forecasting, risk analysis, and capital-budgeting techniques in making their decisions. These techniques help managers analyze data in an economically logical manner. These chapters may be read once you have completed Chapters 2–5. Since risk-analysis and capital-budgeting techniques are closely interrelated, you should read Chapter 17 (Risk Analysis) before Chapter 18 (Capital Budgeting).

While the topics in this text do not exhaust the subject of managerial economics, they do provide an opportunity for you to practice problem solving through economic reasoning. At the very least, you will gain an appreciation for the value of this approach. You cannot solve economic problems by consulting tables with predetermined formulas and solutions. You must develop a way of thinking that you can apply to unique problems as they develop. This text will give you the opportunity to perfect your thinking process and develop your problem-solving skills.

Selected References

Baumol, William J. "What Can Economic Theory Contribute to Managerial Economics?" *American Economic Review, Papers and Proceedings* (May 1961):142–6.

Beasley, W. Howard. "Can Managerial Economics Aid the Chief Executive Officer?" *Managerial and Decision Economics* 2 (September 1981):129–132.

Forgionne, Guisseppi A. "Economic Tools Used by Management in Large American Operated Corporations." *Business Economics* (April 1984):5–17.

Friedman, Milton. "The Methodology of Positive Economics." In *Essays in Positive Economics.* Chicago: University of Chicago Press, 1953.

Jensen, Michael C., and Meckling, William H. "Theory of the Firm: Managerial Behavior, Agency Costs and Ownership Structure." *Journal of Financial Economics* 3 (1976):305–360.

Machlup, Fritz. "Theories of the Firm: Marginalist, Behavioral, Managerial." *American Economic Review* 57 (March 1967): 1–33.

Whitman, Marina. "Economics from Three Perspectives." *Business Economics* (January 1983): 20–24.

Appendix: Mathematical Review

You can understand all mathematically related discussions in this text if you have a basic knowledge of high school algebra and geometry. In Chapter 2 there will be one optional discussion based on the calculus of first derivatives. If you are not familiar with calculus, you can omit this section without loss of continuity. In this appendix we will consider briefly the graphing of straight lines, the determination of slopes, the solution of two equations in two unknowns, and the first derivative of a function in one variable.

Graphing of a Straight Line

You will need to know the relationship between the mathematical form of an equation and the graph of the equation. For example, assume we are interested in graphing the equation

$$Y = 100 - 2X.$$

We could choose either variable Y or X to appear on the vertical axis of our graph. By custom one normally places Y, the dependent variable, on the vertical axis.

There are several ways of plotting this equation. One could choose values of X and Y that satisfy the equation and plot these points. Since it is a straight line, one needs only two points. We could determine where this line would cross the Y and X axes, if, in fact, it crosses both. In this case, when X is 0, Y must be 100. When Y is 0, X must be 50. Figure 1-1 (p. 8) shows the line.

If the constant term, 100, were to increase to 200, this line would now cross the Y-axis at 200. It would cross the X-axis at 100. Since the only change would be an increase in the constant term, the new line would be parallel to the first one. This happens because -2, the coefficient of the X variable, is the slope of the line, which in this case does not change. The **slope** of a line is the change in Y divided by the change in X, or in symbols,

$$\text{Slope} = \Delta Y / \Delta X,$$

where Δ means "change in."

For example, if the equation were

$$Y = 200 - 2X,$$

any increase in X by one unit would make Y decrease by 2. This happens regardless of the starting values of X and Y. For example, if X were 10, Y would be 180. If X were to increase to 11, Y would drop to 178, a change of -2.

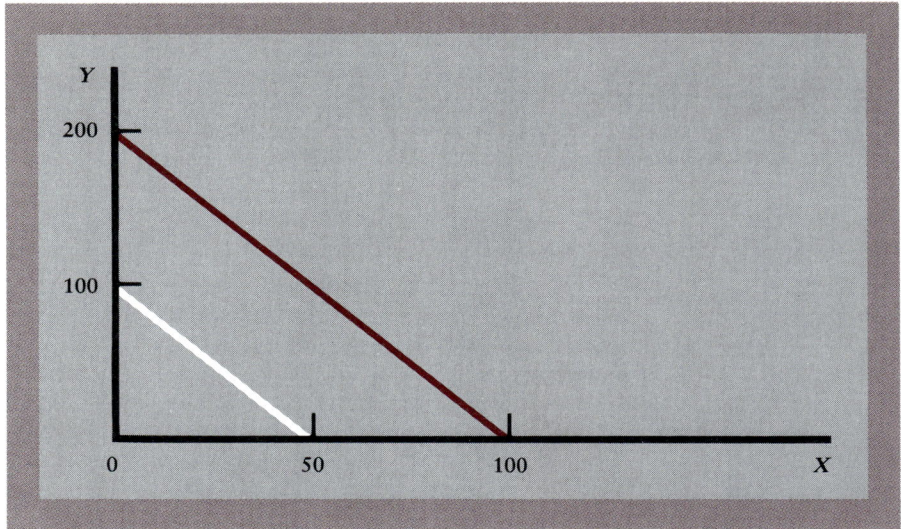

FIGURE 1-1 ▪ Slope of a straight line. The equation $Y = 100 - 2X$ intercepts the Y-axis at Y equal to 100 and intercepts the X-axis at X equal to 50. The slope is the change in Y divided by the change in X. For a straight line the slope equals the value of the coefficient of the X variable. In this case the slope is -2. A change in the Y-intercept term from 100 to 200 shifts the straight line outward. Since there was no change in the slope, the two lines are parallel.

Slopes of Nonlinear Curves

To determine the slope of a nonlinear equation precisely, we must use calculus. While we will discuss derivatives later, we will now consider a graphical technique for determining the slope. In Figure 1-2 there is a nonlinear relationship between Y and X. Since the curve is nonlinear, the slope varies as one moves along the cruve. Since we are aware that a straight line has the same slope at every point on the line, we can approximate the slope of a curve at a particular point by drawing a line that is tangent to the curve at that point.

For example, in Figure 1-2 the straight line is tangent to the nonlinear curve at point a. A line is tangent to a curve if it has the same slope as the curve at the one point that they share. If we moved the line slightly lower, it would cross the curve in two places—at either side of point a. If we moved it higher, it would not have any points in common with the curve.

At point a in Figure 1-2 the slope of the straight line touching the curve approximates the slope of the curve at that point. Since the straight line passes through the coordinates for X and Y at $(0, 5)$ and $(20, 10)$, the slope of the line is the difference in the Y values divided by the difference in the X values. The change in Y is $10 - 5$, or 5, while the change in X is $20 - 0$, or 20. The change in Y divided by the change in X (that is, the slope of the line) is $5/20$, or 0.25.

Since the curve becomes flatter as X increases, all points to the right of a will have slopes less than 0.25, and all points to the left of a will have slopes greater than 0.25. We could approximate these slopes using the same method.

Two Equations in Two Unknowns

The solution to several economic problems will involve the common point of two economic lines, such as a demand curve and a supply curve. Since we can represent a line by an equation, we will be able to determine these common points by using the equations. For example, let us assume that we have the following two equations:

$$Y = 100 - 2X \quad \text{and} \quad Y = 50 + 3X.$$

There are two equivalent methods for solving for X and Y. First of all, we could write each equation with one of the variables isolated on the left-hand side. As written, the equations have Y on the left-hand side. Since Y equals Y, it must follow that

$$100 - 2X = 50 + 3X.$$

Solving for X yields X equal to 10. By substituting for X in both original equations, we find that Y must be 80.

Sometimes you might find it easier to solve for X and Y by beginning with one equation placed immediately above the other.

$$2X + Y = 100$$

$$3X - Y = -50$$

By multiplying both sides of one or both equations by whatever numbers necessary, we would want to create a situation such as that shown above. Here we have one of

FIGURE 1-2 ▪ **Slopes of nonlinear curves.** A straight line that is tangent to a curve has the same slope as the curve at the point of tangency. In this case the straight line and the curve have the same slope at point a. The slope of the line equals $(10 - 5)/(20 - 0) = 5/20 = 0.25$.

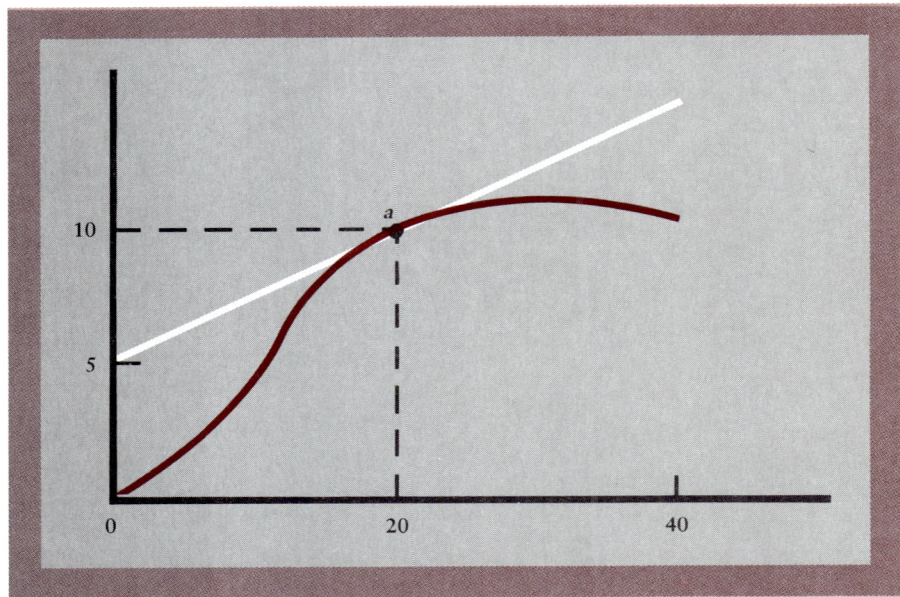

the variables, Y, with a coefficient of $+1$ in one equation and a coefficient of -1 in the other equation. By adding the two equations we eliminate the Y variable, yielding

$$5X = 50 \quad \text{or} \quad X = 10.$$

Your choice of methods will depend on the equations. Both methods work regardless of the nature of the equations, but one approach may be faster than the other for a given situation. Note that we could have solved for both X and Y by plotting both lines on a graph, as shown in Figure 1-3. The solution for X and Y will occur where both lines cross. As expected, Figure 1-3 shows the crossing point to occur where X is 10 and Y is 80.

Derivative of an Equation with One Variable

There is one optional section in the text that requires the knowledge of first derivatives. While this section is not essential, it will be useful to you if you can follow the basic logic of the explanation. The only technique from calculus that you need to know is the first derivative.

Let us assume that we have a general equation of the form

$$Y = aX^b + c,$$

FIGURE 1-3 ▪ **Two equations in two unknowns: a graphical solution.** The two straight lines have one point in common. The intersection of the two lines occurs at the point where the values of X and Y are the same as the values determined by the mathematical procedure involving two equations and two unknowns.

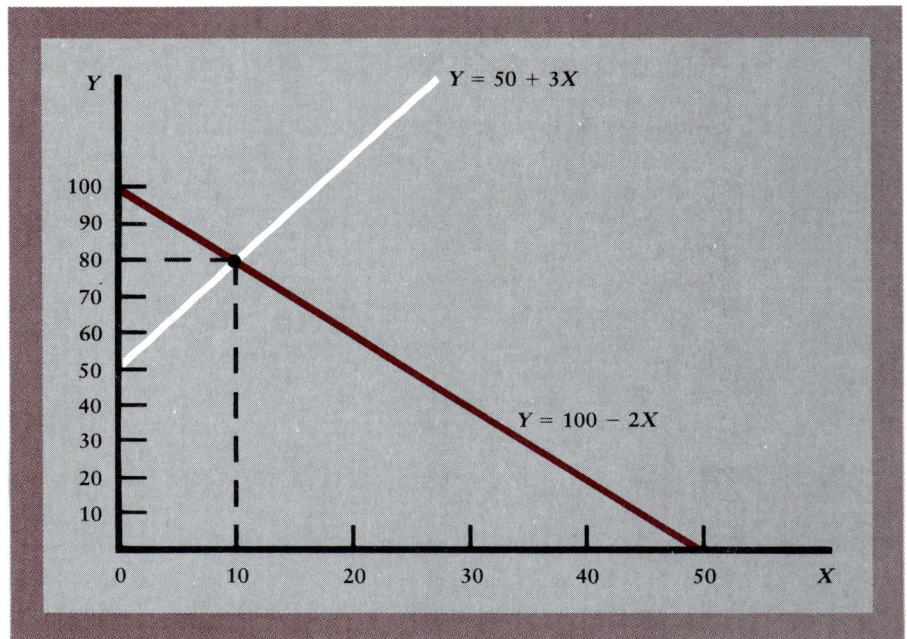

where a, b, and c are constants. The first derivative, dY/dX, will take the form

$$dY/dX = abX^{b-1}.$$

Note that the derivative of a constant term is 0.

If a were 4, b were 6, and c were 3, the equation would be

$$Y = 4X^6 + 3$$

and the first derivative, dY/dX, would be

$$dY/dX = 24X^5.$$

The first derivative would represent the slope of a curve with Y on the vertical axis and X on the horizontal axis. In the case of a straight line, such as $Y = 100 - 2X$, the first derivative would be -2, since the derivative of a constant term is 0 and the derivative of $-2X$ would be -2.

Although we can determine the slope of a straight line without calculus, calculus is especially useful for determining the slopes of nonlinear curves. Since in the preceding example the first derivative is a function of X, the slope will vary as X varies. To determine the slope at any point we would substitute the value of X into the equation. For example, the slope of the curve at X equal to 2 would be $24(2)^5$, or 768.

BASIC ECONOMIC
BACKGROUND

In this part of the book we concentrate on the fundamentals of demand, production, and cost theory. We start in Chapter 2 with the foundations of demand theory. The quantity of a good that consumers want at any point in time depends on several factors, such as consumers' income and the price of the good. We will develop the relationship between the quantity demanded of a good and the important factors influencing this decision.

In Chapter 3 we consider the technical relationship between the quantity of inputs and the quantity of output produced by the firm. Although all firms are unique to some degree, we will establish production relationships that are common to all firms. The technical production relationship forms the basis of the link between a firm's costs and its output level.

Chapter 4 formally develops the relationship between costs and output. We will consider several different cost concepts at the beginning of the chapter. We will then see how the relevant cost for each managerial application depends on the specific situation. While firms may pursue other objectives, we will concentrate on profit maximization as the primary concern of most firms starting in Chapter 4. A profit-maximizing firm must consider input and output prices in addition to the technical relationship between inputs and output when choosing the optimal amount of inputs for each output level.

P A R T

I

Chapter 5 analyzes the importance of the market environment. While profit-maximizing firms prefer control over the market, market forces do not always offer this opportunity. We will consider two extreme market situations. We begin with perfect competition, a market in which firms have no power to set price or distinguish their product from that of their competitors. We next consider monopoly markets. If a firm has a monopoly, it faces no competition and can choose its profit-maximizing output and price without fear of other firms challenging its market position. These markets will provide benchmarks for comparing other, more probable market environments that have aspects of both extreme market conditions.

While these four basic chapters contain several direct applications of the theory developed in each chapter, they also provide a basic theoretical foundation for the remainder of the book. The remaining chapters extend the basic theory to a wide range of day-to-day problems faced by managers. Once you have mastered the basic theory in the next four chapters, you will be able to go to any of the remaining chapters in whatever order you please.

DEMAND THEORY

2

MARKET VERSUS
FIRM DEMAND

THE IMPORTANCE
OF TIME

The Effect of Time on
Other Elasticities

Time as a Demand Factor

OTHER APPLICATIONS
OF THE
ELASTICITY CONCEPT

Advertising

Gas-Mileage Elasticity
of Demand

Many entrepreneurs start new businesses because of their personal interest in a specific product or type of service. For example, someone opening a restaurant for the first time may have a passion for cooking, or at least for eating. However, there are many economic aspects to the restaurant business that have little to do with cooking. Unless the new owner is aware of these other factors and the economic impact they have on the financial well-being of a new firm, the owner may soon be specializing in cooking at home.

Most important, the firm must offer a product or service that interests consumers. The firm's success depends on its ability to identify the types of customers interested in the product and the degree of their interest. In this chapter we will concentrate on the theoretical relationship between the quantity that customers want of a firm's product and the factors that influence them in making this decision. Starting in Chapter 5 we will explore extensions of the basic demand theory presented here. In Chapter 16 we will continue the discussion by considering several statistical issues related to the demand theory.

Before we can solve complex problems we must feel comfortable with each of the elements of the economic analysis that we will employ. In this chapter we will look at the elements of demand theory and form a framework for solving more complicated problems later. We will start by analyzing the factors that influence a consumer's decision to purchase a firm's product. We will then determine how to measure the impact these factors have on the revenues earned by the firm.

Demand

Rather than wrestle with complex demand-related problems now, we will start with the basics—the problems that a manager or owner faces when determining the interest customers have in the company's product. To introduce the concepts of demand theory we will follow the fortunes of a new owner who needs information concerning the demand for his product. While this person's problems may appear to be simple at first, they will evolve in complexity as we pursue them in greater detail through the course of this book.

Let us begin by meeting Rocky Sanders, who has recently purchased the Poobell Plastic Trash Bag Company. Although Rocky has worked for various companies, he is relatively new to the trash bag business. Since he believes that Poobell is already producing the bags efficiently, he intends to focus his attention on the marketing of his product.

Rocky needs to know what the demand is for his trash bags. The term **demand** refers to the relationship between the quantity of the product that customers would like to purchase during a given period of time and the factors that influence the amount desired. Rocky's focus is on both the demand for his own product and the overall market demand for products similar to his own.

The total demand for Rocky's bags is a summation of the demands of all of his customers. These customers comprise individual consumers as well as other firms. While most of the demand is from individual consumers who purchase goods for their own use at home, Rocky sells some of what he produces to other firms, to be used as inputs in the production of their own goods. For example, landscaping firms buy his bags to retain moisture in the rootballs of the trees they sell to their customers.

Derived Demand

The theory of demand for inputs evolves from an analysis of the firm's production process, which reveals the value of the product to the firm relative to alternative inputs. For example, how many plastic bags a landscaping firm wants depends on the demand for its trees, shrubs, and bushes. This type of demand is called a derived demand, since it is derived from the demand for the firm's own product—in this case, landscaping services. A **derived demand** represents the demand coming from customers who use the product as an input in the production of their own products. We will discuss the theory of derived demand in much greater detail in Chapter 4.

Consumer Demand

Economists base the theory of consumer demand on the assumption that consumers maximize their utility. **Utility** is a measure of the well-being or level of satisfaction of consumers, and depends on the quantities of goods bought by the consumers.

In attempting to maximize utility, consumers make decisions concerning the purchase of products subject to various constraints, such as their income and the prices of the products they purchase. This theory suggests that an individual's preference or taste for the product, the person's income, and prices all have an impact on the consumer's ultimate decision of how much of a particular good to buy.

In addition, firms such as Poobell Plastic Trash Bag Company may be able to influence customers' preferences through their advertising and product-design efforts. By determining the effect of each of these factors on the quantity demanded of the good, the firms are in a better position to target the product to specific groups and direct their advertising efforts.

The Demand Function

Up to this point we have described demand in general terms only. We can just as easily specify the demand relationship for Poobell bags as follows:

$$Q_x = f(P_x, P_y, I, A, T),$$

where Q_x is the quantity demanded of bags, P_x is the price of bags, P_y is the price of a competitor's bags, I is a measure of the income of the potential customers, A is the amount of advertising expenditures by the firm, and T represents the tastes of potential customers. The **quantity demanded** is the specific amount of the good desired, given a specific level of each of the demand factors. By expressing the demand relationship this way, we are assuming that the factors listed inside the parentheses have an effect on the quantity demanded of trash bags. This expression shows that Q_x is a function of, or is dependent on, all of the factors listed within the parentheses.

Which demand factors are important depends on the specific product. For example, average annual snowfall and population density are important factors in the demand for snowmobiles. The current exchange rate between the U.S. dollar and the Greek drachma and the fear of potential terrorist attacks affect the demand for airline tickets to Athens by American tourists. Largely due to terrorist attacks in Greece and other European countries, the number of American tourists visiting Greece in 1986 fell to 206,000, as compared to 466,000 in 1985.

2-1	Please pass the salt

APPLICATION

The demand for salt depends on several factors. Salt regulates the body's temperature and chemistry. Without enough salt one can feel tired, nauseous, dehydrated, or can even die. The need for salt varies depending on one's physical condition. For example, when a woman is pregnant she requires more salt than she would normally.

Derek Denton has suggested that at one time salt shortages in Borneo, Indonesia, and the Amazon may have increased the demand for cannibalism in these areas. The salt from the victims may have been a substitute for salt from other scarcer sources, such as fish. In more modern civilizations scientists find that urban dwellers appear to consume more salt. This may be partly due to the fact that salt helps the adrenal glands perform more effectively in relieving stress. Thus, people with stressful jobs may need more salt.

However, excess use of salt may lead to high blood pressure, heart attacks, and strokes. As people become more aware of the potentially harmful effects of salt, they may develop tastes for low-salt potato chips, butter, and tuna fish. This increased awareness of the benefits of a low-salt diet is correlated with consumers' educational levels. People with more education are more likely to be aware of the health risks of excess salt consumption and to have less demand for salt than the less-informed.

Regardless of the price of salt or salty foods, we would thus expect that the demand for salt would have to do with people's physical needs, which vary considerably.

Source: Derek Denton, "The Most-Craved Crystal: Why Humans Consume Salt in Such Excess." *The Sciences* (November–December 1986). The Sciences, Nov.–Dec. 1986 issue, by The New York Academy of Sciences.

While you might find information on most of the important demand factors for most products, it is difficult to quantify tastes. For example, given the environment of their homeland, Saudi Arabians may not have developed a taste for skiing and therefore may not demand as many snow skis as Northern Europeans, even if other demand factors, such as price and income, are the same. Even if they moved to Northern Europe, some Saudi Arabians still might have little interest in skiing.

While there may be a difference in tastes between these two groups of people, the most important demand factor is probably the difference in average daily temperature, which can be quantified. Unless you can find a measurable proxy for a specific taste factor (such as temperature as a proxy for skiing preferences, or per cent of the population living in urban areas for a country's preference for salt), you unfortunately must omit the taste factor from the specification of the demand function. Consider the following example.

| 2-2 | Going my way |

APPLICATION   The reason for significant differences in demand may depend on noneconomic factors. For example, despite little difference between the cost of cremation and the cost of more traditional forms of interment, there are significant variations in the percentages of people choosing cremation in European countries.

In 1987 only 3 percent of French body disposals were cremations. Cremation is equally unpopular in Spain. On the other hand, in 1985, 67 percent of the British dead were cremated. In Denmark it was 62 percent, while in Sweden it was 56 percent.

The significant factor here is religion. Great Britain, Denmark, and Sweden are mostly Protestant nations. France and Spain are mostly Catholic. In half-Catholic Germany, less than 20 percent of the dead are cremated.

This information suggests that religion greatly influences people's preferences for burial or cremation. From this information we cannot be sure whether Catholics have a strong personal distaste for cremation or whether they are behaving more out of custom, tradition, or religious belief. Nevertheless, a firm considering starting or expanding a cremation business should take into account the importance of the religious composition of the market. The Catholic percentage of the population may serve as a proxy for the underlying personal preferences associated with religion that influence the demand for cremation.

The Demand Equation

Let us now return to Rocky Sanders. Once Rocky has decided which variables to include in the demand function for his trash bags, he must choose the proper functional form. Although the choice of functional form is often difficult in practice, we will assume at this point that Rocky can represent the demand function as a linear equation. We will wait until Chapter 16 to consider the merits of nonlinear functional forms.

We will concentrate on the basic economic concepts of demand and then turn to the more advanced statistical issues later. Once an owner such as Rocky understands these principles, he can better apply them to an analysis of his own company's data. Assume that the demand for Poobell trash bags in thousands of boxes per week, (Q_0), is a linear function of the following factors: price in dollars per box, (P_0); price of Plenz Bags, the leading competitor, in dollars per box, (P_1); and average family income of residents in the market area in thousands of dollars, (I). Represented by a linear equation, the function would be

$$Q_0 = a + bP_0 + cP_1 + dI,$$

where the coefficients a, b, c, and d are parameters, or constants. Once the coefficients are known, you can determine the effects of changing any of the variables specified in the equation. We have omitted other possible demand factors, such as advertising expenditures, to simplify the explanation. You can use the same basic analysis regardless of which factors you include in the demand equation.

| 2-1 | The demand equation |

NUMERICAL EXAMPLE

Assume that we know the values of the coefficients to be as follows: a is 82, b is -50, c is 5, and d is 10. We can now rewrite the linear equation as

$$Q_0 = 82 - 50P_0 + 5P_1 + 10I.$$

We can determine the effects of a change in any of the variables in this equation. For example, assume that P_1 and I do not change. Since the coefficient of P_0 is constant at 50 and Q_0 is in thousands of boxes, a one-dollar increase in the price of Poobell bags decreases the quantity demanded by 50 times 1000, or 50,000 boxes.

If we know the expected values of income, the price of Plenz bags, and the price of Poobell bags, we can predict the quantity demanded of Poobell bags. For example, if P_0 is \$4.00, P_1 is \$3.60, and I is \$30.00, the equation predicts that Q_0 will be 200,000, as follows:

$$Q_0 = 82 - 50(4) + 5(3.60) + 10(30)$$
$$= 82 - 200 + 18 + 300$$
$$= 200.$$

As long as we are confident that the coefficients will not change with changes in values of the variables, the equation will provide useful information about the interest in Poobell bags.

The Demand Curve

A firm must set a price for its product. No matter what the firm uses as its rationale for choosing its price, the choice of price will affect the quantity of the product the firm sells and the revenues and profits the firm earns. Although we must delay our discussion of optimal price until Chapter 5, at this point we need to determine what happens to quantity demanded and revenues as the firm adjusts its price. Since price is a critical factor for the firm, economists attach considerable importance to its role in the firm's decision-making process. To emphasize the role of price, economists use a demand curve, a convenient graphical tool for analyzing simple economic problems. A **demand curve** is a graphical representation of the relationship between the price and the quantity demanded of the good, assuming all other demand factors remain constant as price and quantity demanded change.

Let us return to Rocky and create a demand curve for his trash bags. We will simulate the effects of changing the price of Rocky's bags by assuming that the values of all other factors remain unchanged.

2-2   **Demand curve**

NUMERICAL
EXAMPLE

If we again assume that P_1 equals \$3.60 and I equals \$30, the equation in Numerical Example 2-1 becomes

$$Q_0 = 82 - 50P_0 + 5P_1 + 10I$$
$$= 82 - 50P_0 + 5(3.6) + 10(30)$$
$$= 400 - 50P_0.$$

By substituting values for the price of the competing product and average family income, we have reduced the equation to a linear relationship between Q_0 and P_0. Figure 2-1 represents this relationship graphically. When graphed in this way, the demand function becomes a demand curve.

Figure 2-1 shows how quantity demanded changes with adjustments in price, assuming all other demand factors remain constant.[1] Economists call this movement a change in the quantity demanded. A **change in the quantity demanded** is a movement along a demand curve as the price changes. All other demand factors remain constant.

A change in any other factor causes the demand curve to shift to a new location. This represents a change in demand, since the quantity demanded at each price of Poobell bags is different than before. A **change in demand** involves the shifting of the demand curve to a new location due to a change in at least one of the demand factors other than the price of the good. Refer to Figure 2-1 for examples of a change in the quantity demanded and a change in demand.

---

[1] Notice that the graph shows P_0 on the vertical axis and Q_0 on the horizontal axis. Since P_0 is the variable under Rocky's control, mathematicians would prefer that we place the dependent variable (the quantity demanded of trash bags) on the vertical axis, and the independent variable (the price) on the horizontal axis. The reversal in this case is the result of a misconception at the turn of this century as to the causal relationship between price and quantity demanded. Despite the fact that this misconception has now been clarified, the axis reversal for price and quantity has remained as a convention.

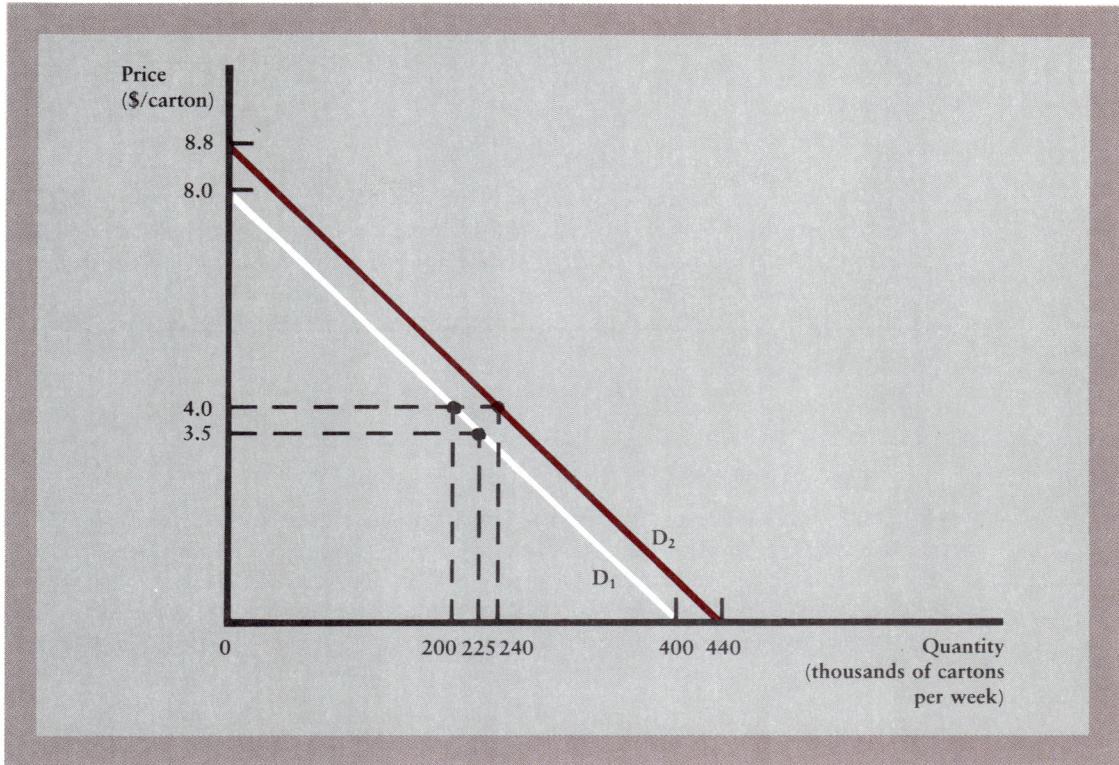

Price
($/carton)

8.8
8.0

4.0
3.5

D₂

D₁

0   200 225 240   400 440   Quantity
(thousands of cartons
per week)

FIGURE 2-1 ▪ **The demand for Poobell's trash bags.** The demand curve, $Q_0 = 400 - 50P_0$, has a price intercept of 8.0 and a quantity-demanded intercept of 400. Any change in P_0 results in a movement along the demand curve. A change in a demand factor other than P_0 causes the demand curve to shift to the right or left. For example, a change in income caused the demand curve, D_1, to shift to the right, to D_2. The new equation, $Q_0 = 440 - 50P_0$, has a price intercept of 8.8 and a quantity-demanded intercept of 440.

| 2-3 | **Changes in quantity demanded and demand** |

NUMERICAL EXAMPLE

If all other factors remain constant, a change in the price of a box of Poobell bags from \$4.00 to \$3.50 produces a change in the quantity demanded from 200,000 to 225,000 boxes per week. Since this involves a movement along the demand curve, it is a change in the quantity demanded.

Continue to assume that the price of the competitor's trash bags, P_1, stays at \$3.60. If average family income increases by \$4,000 to \$34,000, the equation will now have a constant term that is 40 higher than the previous one.

$$Q_0 = 82 - 50P_0 + 5P_1 + 10I$$
$$= 82 - 50P_0 + 5(3.6) + 10(34)$$
$$= 82 - 50P_0 + 18 + 340$$
$$= 440 - 50P_0.$$

The demand curve corresponding to the new equation, D_2, will be to the right of the previous demand curve. At $4.00 per box, the quantity demanded will now be 240,000 boxes. A drop in the average family income would shift the demand curve to the left.

Elasticities of Demand

While knowledge of the demand function is useful in and of itself, you could use this information to determine even more about the demand relationship by calculating elasticities of demand. An **elasticity of demand**, e_X, is the percentage change in the quantity demanded of the product resulting from a 1 percent change in a demand factor X, holding all other demand factors constant. In mathematical notation the elasticity would equal

$$e_X = \frac{\%\Delta Q}{\%\Delta X}$$
$$= \frac{\frac{\Delta Q}{Q} \times 100}{\frac{\Delta X}{X} \times 100}$$
$$= \frac{\Delta Q}{\Delta X} \times \frac{X}{Q},$$

where Δ represents a change in the variable, Q is quantity demanded of the product, and X is the amount of the demand factor. Note that we must multiply both the numerator and the denominator by 100 to convert the changes in Q and X into percentages. Since 100 appears in both the numerator and the denominator, the two values of 100 cancel each other out in the final expression.

The elasticity of demand is a useful measure of the responsiveness of the quantity demanded to the change in each of the demand factors. While we will concentrate on changes in the price of Rocky's product, customers' incomes, and prices of alternative products, we could calculate an elasticity for any demand factor that can be measured.

Rocky can use the information he learns about the elasticities to make better plans for future sales. For example, assume that Rocky reads in the *Farmer's Almanac* that the average weekly rainfall this coming summer is going to be 10 percent greater than last year's. He might like to know what effect this change in rainfall will have on sales of his trash bags.

Since more rain means that people's lawns will grow faster, Rocky expects that people will need more trash bags to cope with the extra grass clippings. If rainfall is a significant factor in the demand for trash bags, Rocky will benefit by knowing the elasticity due to an expected change in future rainfall. We can predict Rocky's sales more accurately if we know this elasticity.

Rocky should also consider how responsive customers will be to a change in his price. For example, he knows that a decrease in price increases the number of bags that he will sell, but he is not sure whether the revenue he will earn will increase or decrease. Since a price decrease lowers the amount of revenue per unit sold, he must know whether or not the extra quantity sold will offset the effects of the lower price. We will soon find out that he can use an elasticity to answer that question as well.

Methods for Measuring the Elasticity of Demand

Rather than continue to catalog the usefulness of specific elasticities, let us discuss two techniques for measuring any elasticity. Whether we are interested in the elasticity of demand due to a change in income, rainfall, or price, we will be able to use both of these methods for finding a numerical value for the elasticity that interests us. There are two methods for determining any demand elasticity: the arc method and the point method. Which method one chooses depends on what information is available. Although we will see later how the two relate to each other, we will start with the arc method.

Arc Method We mentioned earlier that Rocky might be interested in calculating the expected impact on quantity demanded of trash bags due to a 10 percent increase in the average weekly rainfall. The arc method provides an approximate answer. Let us assume that Rocky has only the following information: the quantity demanded of his bags equals 220,000 boxes when the average weekly rainfall is 1 inch, and equals 260,000 boxes when the average weekly rainfall increases to 3 inches. Assume that the values of all other variables do not change.

Since Rocky must rely on only two observations of both the quantity demanded and the rainfall, he will have to use an approximation, called the arc method, to obtain an average value of the elasticity due to the change in rainfall from 1 to 3 inches. The **arc method** approximates the effect of a relatively large change in the demand factor. The approximation formula is as follows:

$$e_X = \frac{\%\Delta Q}{\%\Delta X}$$

$$= \frac{\dfrac{\Delta Q}{Q} \times 100}{\dfrac{\Delta X}{X} \times 100}$$

$$= \frac{\Delta Q}{\Delta X} \times \frac{X}{Q}$$

$$= \frac{Q_2 - Q_1}{X_2 - X_1} \times \frac{\dfrac{X_2 + X_1}{2}}{\dfrac{Q_2 + Q_1}{2}}.$$

By using the arc method, one can approximate the change in Q and the change in X by computing the difference in the two observations of each variable. The average of X divided by an average of Q replaces X/Q in the elasticity of demand definition. By using an average instead of the starting values of X and Q, the arc method creates an average value of the elasticity across the range of values for both X and Q.

2-4	Arc method

NUMERICAL EXAMPLE Rocky knows that the quantity demanded of his trash bags will be 260,000 when the average rainfall is 3 inches and 220,000 when the average rainfall is 1 inch. We assume that all other demand factors remain constant and that we have no further information about the demand relationship. We will use R in place of X in the arc method formula to represent average rainfall per week. The arc method formula will now be

$$e_R = \frac{Q_2 - Q_1}{R_2 - R_1} \times \frac{\dfrac{R_2 + R_1}{2}}{\dfrac{Q_2 + Q_1}{2}}$$

$$= \frac{260,000 - 220,000}{3 - 1} \times \frac{\dfrac{3 + 1}{2}}{\dfrac{260,000 + 220,000}{2}}$$

$$= \frac{40,000}{2} \times \frac{2}{240,000}$$

$$= \frac{1}{6} = .1667.$$

We could use this estimate of the rainfall elasticity to predict the impact of a 1 percent change in the average rainfall on the quantity demanded of his trash bags. Since the elasticity is 0.1667, a 1 percent increase in rainfall would result in a 0.1667 percent increase in the quantity demanded, assuming all other factors remain constant. A 10 percent increase in the average rainfall would suggest a 10×0.1667 percent, or 1.667 percent, increase in the quantity demanded of Rocky's trash bags.

The arc method provides an average for a wide range of values for the demand factor. In Rocky's example, the observations on quantity demanded correspond to a change in rainfall from 1 to 3 inches. Rocky has to assume that any 1 percent change in average rainfall within the range of 1 to 3 inches will have a 0.1667 percent effect on quantity demanded, regardless of what the average rainfall was before the 1 percent increase.

If Rocky is interested in knowing the elasticity with a greater degree of precision, he must know $\Delta Q/\Delta R$ at the point of the change. In a graph of Q versus R, $\Delta Q/\Delta R$ would be the slope of the curve. The slope will change at each point on the curve, unless the curve is a straight line. We would use the point method to make this calculation.

Point Method The **point method** is simply the arc method applied to an infinitesimal change in the demand factor. This method depends on knowledge of the precise value of the percent change in quantity demanded divided by the precise value of the percent change in the demand factor. Unlike the arc method, it is not an approximation. The formula is the same as the formula for the general definition of an elasticity with the actual value of the starting point used for X/Q.

To use the point method, we need to know exactly what $\Delta Q/\Delta R$ is for an extremely small change in R.

| 2-5 | Point method |

NUMERICAL
EXAMPLE

Assume that Rocky has more precise information about the effect of rainfall on the demand for his bags. Instead of knowing the quantity demanded for two values of average weekly rainfall, he knows exactly how much the quantity demanded will change with a one-unit change in rainfall. For example, assume that he knows that $\Delta Q/\Delta R$ equals 10 when Q equals 220 and R equals 1. We could substitute these values directly into the elasticity formula as follows:

$$\frac{\% \Delta Q}{\% \Delta R} = \frac{\Delta Q}{\Delta R} \times \frac{R}{Q}$$

$$= 10 \times \frac{1}{220}$$

$$= \frac{10}{220}$$

$$= 0.0455.$$

In this case a 1 percent increase in the average rainfall would cause a 0.0455 percent increase in the quantity demanded.

While the point method is always preferable, you may have to compromise and use the arc method when data are limited.

The Own-Price Elasticity of Demand

The most commonly calculated elasticity is the own-price elasticity of demand. The **own-price elasticity of demand**, e_p, is the percentage change in the quantity demanded of a good resulting from a 1 percent change in the price of the good. In mathematical notation, this is written as

$$e_p = \frac{\% \Delta Q}{\% \Delta P} = \frac{\Delta Q}{\Delta P} \times \frac{P}{Q},$$

where Q is the quantity demanded of the good and P is the price of the good.

The own-price elasticity of demand tells us what would happen to quantity demanded if the price were changed. This elasticity can be calculated by using either the point or the arc method.

2-6

Own-price elasticity of demand

NUMERICAL
EXAMPLE

Assume that all we know about the demand relationship for Poobell trash bags is that when the price is $4.00, quantity demanded is 220,000 boxes of bags, and when the price is $3.50, quantity demanded is 245,000 boxes. In this case we do not know whether the demand curve is a straight line or not. We could use the arc method to provide an approximation of the elasticity between these two values on the demand curve. The arc method formula in this case is

$$e_d = \frac{\% \text{ change in } Q}{\% \text{ change in } P}$$

$$= \frac{Q_b - Q_a}{P_b - P_a} \times \frac{\dfrac{P_b + P_a}{2}}{\dfrac{Q_b + Q_a}{2}}.$$

If we replace Q_b with 245,000, Q_a with 220,000, P_b with 3.5, and P_a with 4, the own-price elasticity of demand becomes

$$e_p = \frac{245,000 - 220,000}{3.5 - 4} \times \frac{\dfrac{3.5 + 4}{2}}{\dfrac{245,000 + 220,000}{2}}$$

$$= -50,000 \times \frac{3.75}{232,500}$$

$$= -0.806.$$

This indicates that a 1 percent increase in the price of Rocky's trash bags would result in a 0.806 percent decrease in the quantity demanded of his bags, assuming all other factors remain constant.

Now let us assume instead that Rocky actually knew that the equation of the demand curve was

$$Q = 420 - 50P_0,$$

where Q is in thousands of boxes. He could have determined the own-price elasticity when P_0 was equal to a specific price as follows:

Assume that P_0 equals 4. Then

$$Q = 420 - 50P_0 = 420 - 200 = 220.$$

Note that no matter what value is chosen for P_0, Q will always decrease by 50 as P_0 increases by one more unit. This is due to the coefficient of -50 in front of the P_0 term. The coefficient of the price variables, -50, will thus equal $\Delta Q/\Delta P_0$, and e_p will be as follows:

$$e_p = \frac{\Delta Q}{\Delta P_0} \times \frac{P_0}{Q}$$

$$= -50 \times \frac{4}{220}$$

$$= -\frac{200}{220} = -0.909.$$

Since $\Delta Q/\Delta P_0$ will always be -50 along this straight-line demand curve, we could determine the elasticity at each point on the curve by substituting the corresponding values of P_0 and Q at each point into this formula in place of 4 and 220, respectively.

This own-price elasticity provides useful information to policymakers, as well as managers. Consider the following example.

APPLICATION Local regulatory authorities decide how telephone companies may charge their customers for local calls. Until the early 1980s, most companies charged customers a flat monthly fee regardless of the number of calls made. However, responding to criticism that the no-cost additional calls lead to wasteful use of telephone capacity, regulators have been trying to determine consumers' reactions to a per-use charge of the telephone.

Several studies have been done on the effects of different pricing strategies on telephone use. For example, consider Rand Corporation's analysis of an experiment conducted by General Telephone and Electronics (GTE) from 1975 to 1979 in three central Illinois cities: Jacksonville, Clinton, and Tuscola.

The researchers estimated the effects of changing the company's pricing policy from the monthly fixed fee to a per-use charge. GTE tried two types of user charges: a per-call charge and a per-minute charge. For example, starting in June of 1979, all private-party customers had to pay 2.5 cents per call and 1 cent per minute for a local call. Between September 1977 and June 1979, the per-call and per-minute charges differed among the three cities. Prior to September 1977, all customers paid the flat monthly fee.

Changes in the per-call charge and the per-minute charge affect both the number of calls and the length of calls. While controlling for such factors as the possibility that customers would switch to multiparty lines in response to a change in per-use charges, the researchers were able to estimate the elasticities due to the change in the per-call and per-minute fees. They determined that the elasticity of demand for calls due to a change in the price per call was -0.076. The elasticity of demand for calls due to a change in the price per minute was -0.055. The elasticity of demand for minutes per call was -0.109 due to a change in the price per minute and -0.086 due to a change in the price per call.

These elasticities are low. These customers did not make large percentage changes in their quantity demanded of calls and the length of their calls in response to the change in the price of making calls. Regulators are currently conducting these experiments in other geographical areas to determine the sensitivity of these elasticities to other demand factors, such as the size of households and family income level. Since there would be an increased cost due to measuring the number of calls and the duration of each call, regulators want to be sure of the overall benefits of a full-scale, mandatory change in telephone pricing before making substantial changes in pricing policy.

Source: Rolla Edward Park, Bruce M. Wetzel, and Bridger M. Mitchell, "Price Elasticities for Local Telephone Calls." *Econometrica* 51, No. 6 (November 1983):1699–1731. The Econometric Society.

Own-Price Elasticity of Demand Along a Straight-Line Demand Curve

Since we can calculate an arc elasticity with less information than is needed to determine a point elasticity, you might wonder why we should bother gathering enough information to calculate point elasticities at each point along the demand curve. In this section we will see how the point elasticity reveals more detailed and useful information about consumers' behavior.

Although the arc method provides useful information, it cannot offer the precision that comes with the point estimates. For example, although the slope of a straight line does not change as one moves along the line, the own-price elasticity does change. Since the arc method provides only an average value, you would not know how much the point elasticity varied between the two points you had chosen.

As one moves down the demand curve toward the Q-axis, the value of P decreases, while the value of Q increases. Recall that the elasticity formula is

$$e_d = \frac{\Delta Q}{\Delta P} \times \frac{P}{Q}.$$

The elasticity will range from zero, where the straight-line demand curve crosses the Q-axis, to minus infinity ($-\infty$), where it crosses the P-axis. When the demand curve crosses the P-axis, Q is zero. Since the elasticity formula has the value of Q in the denominator, dividing by zero will yield an elasticity of negative infinity. Since P is zero at the other end of the demand curve, the elasticity at that point is zero.

Figure 2-2 (p. 32) defines the range of the own-price elasticity of demand, e_p, along a straight-line demand curve as shown in the following chart.

Range of own-price elasticity along the demand curve

Perfectly elastic	$e_p = -\infty$	
Elastic	$-\infty < e_p < -1$	*e airline*
Unit elastic	$e_p = -1$	
Inelastic	$-1 < e_p < 0$	*salt.*
Perfectly inelastic	$e_p = 0$	

At the midpoint between the origin and the points where the demand curve crosses each axis, the own-price elasticity of demand is -1. You can see this in the following numerical example.

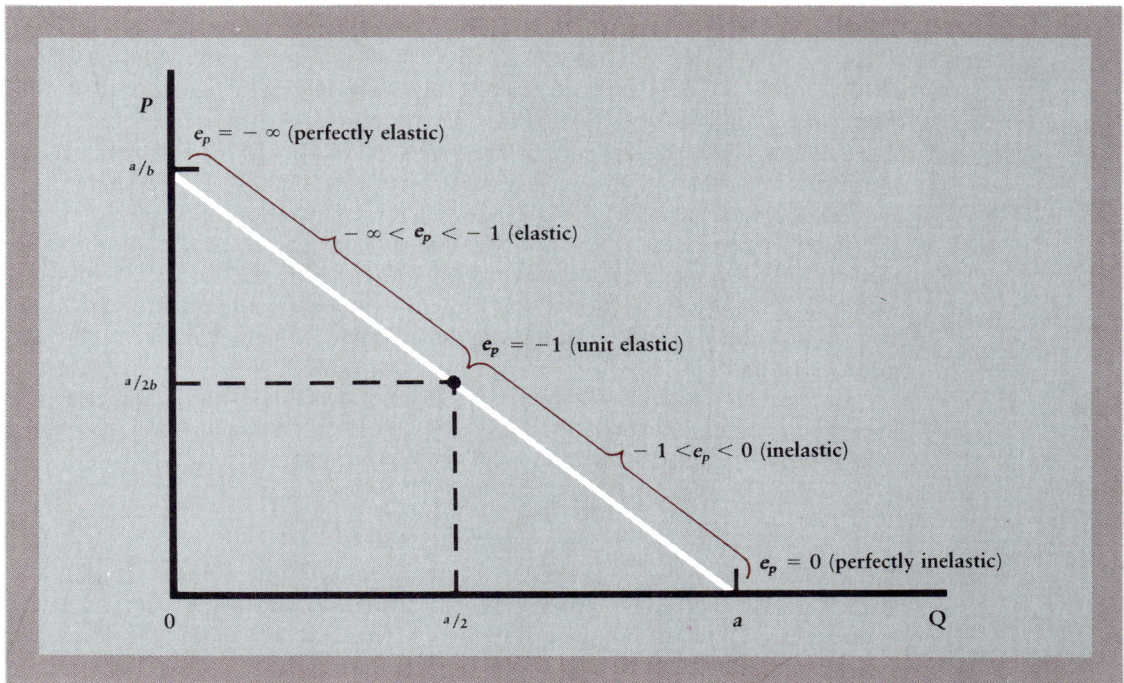

FIGURE 2-2 ▪ **Elasticity along a straight-line demand curve.** The own-price elasticity of demand varies from $-\infty$ to 0 along a straight-line demand curve. The demand curve has the equation $Q = a - bP$, where a and b are constants. The price intercept is a/b and the quantity-demanded intercept is a. The demand curve has an elasticity of -1 at the midpoint $(a/2b, a/2)$. The demand curve is perfectly elastic at the price-intercept point and perfectly inelastic at the quantity-demanded intercept. The demand curve is elastic between the price intercept and the midpoint, and inelastic between the midpoint and the quantity-demanded intercept.

2-7   **Elasticity at the midpoint**

NUMERICAL
EXAMPLE

Assume that the demand equation is

$$Q = 150 - 2P.$$

The P-intercept term is 75 and the Q-intercept term is 150. The midpoints are 37.5 for P and 75 for Q. Since $\Delta Q/\Delta P$ remains constant at -2, the own-price elasticity at the midpoint is

$$-2 \times \frac{37.5}{75} = -1.$$

Extreme Cases

Figure 2-3 shows two extreme cases: perfectly elastic and perfectly inelastic demand curves. In part (a) of the figure, the demand curve is horizontal. If the demand curve is horizontal, the response to a price change is infinite. For example, a slight increase in price from P would result in a decrease in quantity demanded to zero. The horizontal demand curve is therefore perfectly elastic.

If customers felt that Poobell trash bags were no different from any other company's bags, and Poobell had a relatively small share of the market, Rocky would face a perfectly elastic demand curve. If he raised his price above that of his competitors, no one would buy his bags. If he lowered his price, he could sell all he wanted to sell. Since he would be a small supplier relative to the overall size of the market, he could already sell all he wanted to at the market price. He would have no incentive to lower his price in this case.

The vertical demand curve in Figure 2-3(b) is perfectly inelastic. In this case the quantity demanded is constant regardless of the price. Since any change in price will have no effect on the quantity demanded, the own-price

FIGURE 2-3 ▪ **Perfectly elastic and perfectly inelastic demand.** The perfectly elastic demand curve in (a) has a slope of 0, while the perfectly inelastic demand curve in (b) has an infinite slope.

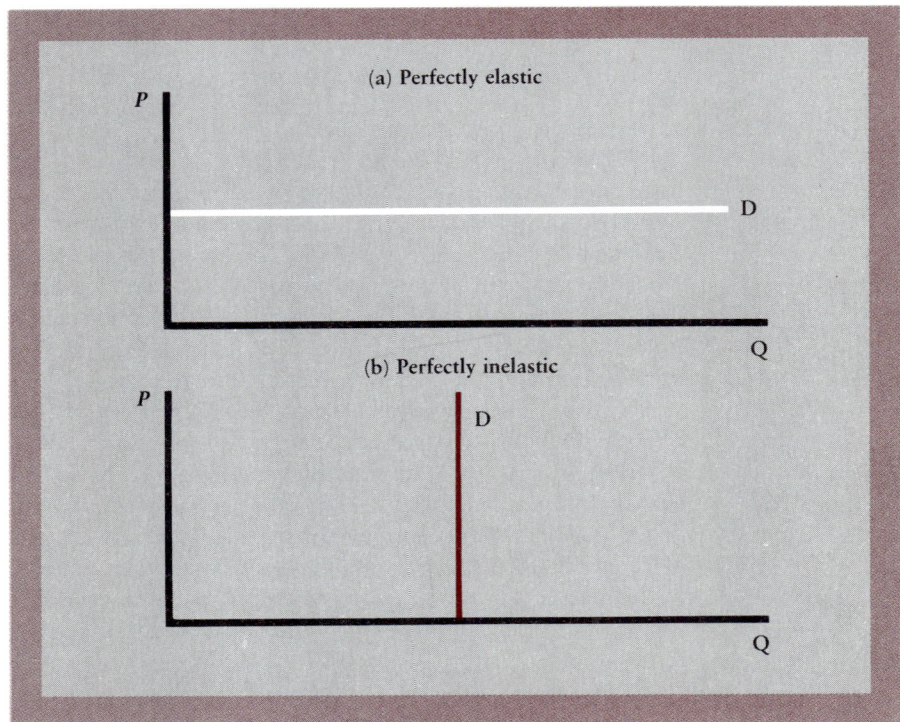

(a) Perfectly elastic

(b) Perfectly inelastic

elasticity will be zero. It is unlikely that Rocky could find a way to make the demand for his trash bags perfectly inelastic. However, assume that Rocky's cardiologist tells Rocky he has only one month to live unless he agrees to have a heart transplant operation. Rocky's demand for surgery might be an example of perfectly inelastic demand, at least up to some price, since he would probably pay almost any price for the operation.

A vertical demand curve is rare. Consider the following example.

| 2-4 | Am I covered? |

APPLICATION   Health care consumes a larger percentage of resources in the United States than in any other country in the world. For years policymakers have been trying to devise a system for checking the growth rate in this industry. Many researchers feel that a major contributor to the demand for health care is the prevalence of comprehensive insurance coverage. When consumers have comprehensive insurance, they do not pay an additional charge for each use they make of a medical facility or physician. Many experts contend that this type of insurance encourages people to overuse the system.

Some analysts also suggest that consumers do not even pay attention to the price of comprehensive insurance; that is, they have perfectly inelastic demand curves for health insurance. Professor Charles E. Phelps of the University of Rochester and Dr. M. Susan Marquis of Rand Corporation suggest otherwise. They estimated demand for supplementary health insurance for 1326 families who participated in an experimental study of the effects of various health coverage plans.

Dr. Marquis and Professor Phelps evaluated data from the Rand Health Insurance Experiment. The study used families from four metropolitan and two rural sites. Seventy percent participated in the study for three years, while the rest participated for five years. The sample was representative of families whose members were under sixty-two years of age, with some minor exceptions due to income and military affiliation. Each family received an experimental insurance plan that varied in terms of the share the family had to pay and the limit on the out-of-pocket expenses for health care.

After completing their participation in the study, the 1326 families received hypothetical offers to purchase supplementary insurance. The two researchers based their analysis on the families' responses to these offers. Results showed that the price elasticity of demand for full supplementary insurance was -0.6 at the current average price of insurance; that is, a 1 percent increase in the price of health insurance would result in an average decrease of 0.6 percent in the amount of coverage desired. This result suggests that the demand curve for health insurance is inelastic but not perfectly inelastic.

Source: M. Susan Marquis and Charles E. Phelps, "Price Elasticity and Adverse Selection in the Demand for Supplementary Health Insurance." *Economic Inquiry* XXV (April 1987):299–313.

Elasticity and Total Revenue

The own-price elasticity shown in Figure 2-2 is not the only thing that varies along the straight-line demand curve. In moving along a negatively sloped demand curve, you should note that both the price and quantity demanded change. The changes in price and quantity demanded affect total revenue. **Total revenue** from the sale of a good equals the price of the good times the quantity purchased.

Now that you know that the own-price elasticity of demand varies along the demand curve, you can relate this own-price elasticity of demand to total revenue at each point on the demand curve. First, we must establish how total revenue varies along a demand curve.

Table 2-1 (p. 36) shows a demand relationship between price and quantity demanded for discrete changes in price. Table 2-1 includes total revenue for each price and quantity. For example, when the price is $10, no one wants the good and total revenue will be zero. If the price is $9, the firm will sell only one unit and total revenue will be $9. At a price of $8, the firm will sell two units and total revenue will be $16.

By lowering the price from $10 to $9, the firm increases sales by one unit and total revenue by $9. By lowering the price to $8, the firm sells two units for a total revenue of $16. The change in total revenue from selling the second unit is

$$\$16 - \$9 = \$7.$$

The change in total revenue due to a one-unit change in output is called **marginal revenue** (*MR*). In notation, this is represented as

$$MR = \frac{\Delta TR}{\Delta Q}.$$

Table 2-1 shows the marginal revenue at each output level. Note that the firm must lower its price in order to sell additional units of the good. Total revenue increases as we lower the price to $5. Below $5, total revenue becomes smaller again.

In general, total revenue increases and then decreases as we move down a linear demand curve. While lowering the price of the good reduces the revenue earned by the firm per unit of the good, lowering the price encourages consumers to buy more of the good. A lower price and a larger number of goods sold affect the firm's revenues in opposite ways. Marginal revenue combines these two opposing effects on total revenue. We will soon compare these opposing forces in more detail.

First let us see the effects of a change in price on total revenue more clearly by considering a continuous demand curve. Figure 2-4 shows the relationship between total revenue and the own-price elasticity of demand along the corresponding demand curve. Just as in Table 2-1, total revenue reaches a peak at the midpoint of the demand curve and then declines with

TABLE 2-1 ▪ Total and marginal revenue

Price	Quantity	Total Revenue	Marginal Revenue
10	0	0	
9	1	9	9
8	2	16	7
7	3	21	5
6	4	24	3
5	5	25	1
4	6	24	−1
3	7	21	−3
2	8	16	−5
1	9	9	−7
0	10	0	−9

further movement down the demand curve. Note that at the point of maximum revenue, the slope of the total revenue curve must equal zero. The slope of the total revenue curve will be marginal revenue.

Figure 2-4 shows the marginal revenue corresponding to all other output levels. Note that the two components of total revenue—price and quantity demanded—move in opposite directions. For example, if Rocky were to lower the price of his trash bags, he would receive less revenue from each box sold, but he would sell more boxes. Whether his total revenue increased or decreased would depend on whether the lower price or the higher quantity sold dominated.

Recall that the own-price elasticity of demand equals the percentage change in quantity demanded divided by the percentage change in price. If the percentage change in price is greater than the percentage change in quantity demanded, the denominator is greater than the numerator, making the elasticity less than 1 in absolute value. Remember that this occurs on the inelastic portion of the demand curve. If the percentage change in quantity is greater than the percentage change in price, the opposite occurs: the elasticity is greater than 1 in absolute value. This corresponds to the elastic portion of the demand curve.

You can now put together the effects of the change in price and the change in quantity demanded. For example, if Rocky wants to lower his price and he is on the elastic portion of his demand curve, he knows that the percentage decrease in price will not be as large as the percentage increase in quantity demanded. As a result, a drop in price will increase total revenue. If he were on the inelastic portion of the demand curve, the opposite would occur: a drop in price would decrease his total revenue, since the percentage decrease in price would dominate the percentage increase in quantity demanded. Since the elasticity equals -1 at the midpoint of the demand curve, the percentage change in price must equal the percentage change in quantity demanded. Any small movement from this point would have no effect on his total revenue, and his marginal revenue would be zero.

Since you should be concerned about the effect a change in your price will have on your total revenue, you will always want to know on which side of the unit-elastic point you are operating. As we see in Figure 2-4, if you are on the inelastic portion of the demand curve and you lower the price, you will cause your revenue to drop. If you are on the elastic portion and you lower your price, your revenue increases.

FIGURE 2-4 ▪ **Relationship between elasticity and total revenue.** Total revenue increases at a decreasing rate as price decreases along the elastic portion of the demand curve. At the unit elastic point, total revenue is at a maximum and marginal revenue is 0. Lowering price over the inelastic portion of the demand curve decreases total revenue, since marginal revenue is negative.

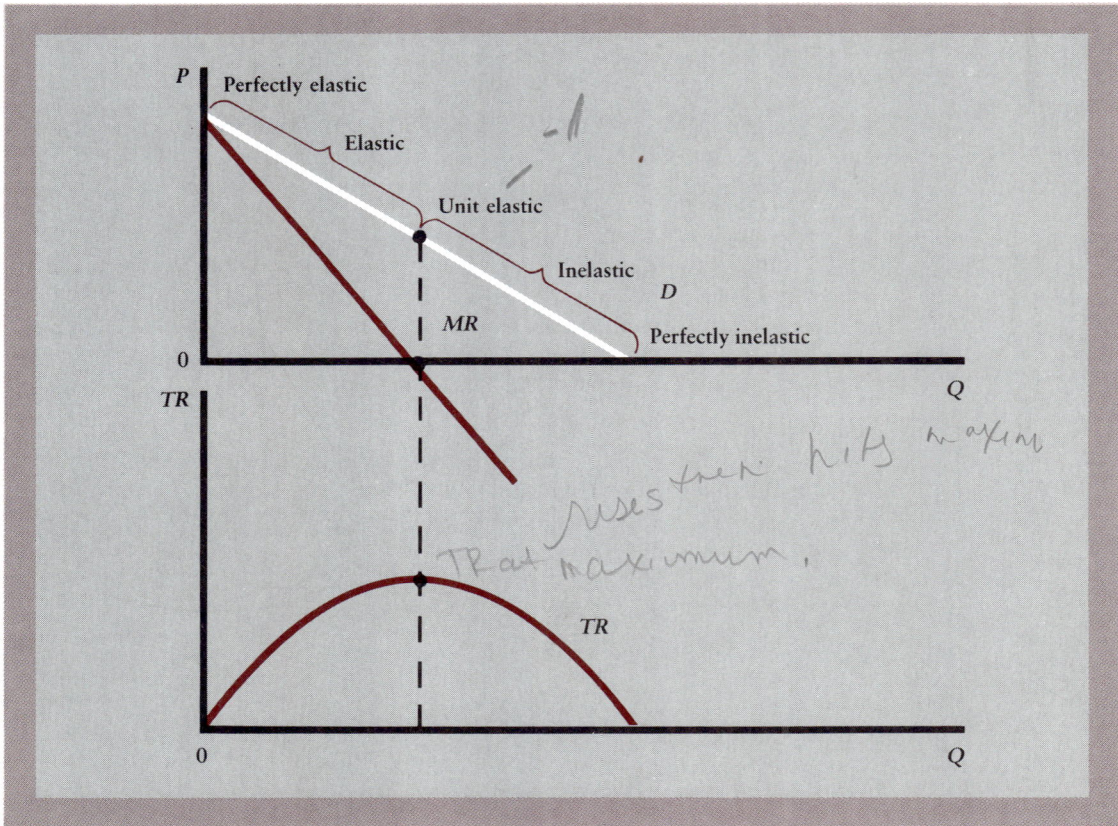

NUMERICAL EXAMPLE

By using calculus you can calculate precisely the relationship between elasticity and marginal revenue. If the demand equation is a straight line, it will have an equation of the form

$$P = a - bQ \tag{1}$$

or equivalently,

$$Q = \frac{a}{b} - \frac{P}{b}. \tag{2}$$

Recall that the elasticity formula is

$$\frac{\%\,\Delta Q}{\%\,\Delta P} \quad \text{or} \quad \frac{\Delta Q}{\Delta P} \times \frac{P}{Q}.$$

Since $\Delta Q/\Delta P$ is an approximation for dQ/dP, the elasticity is

$$\frac{dQ}{dP} \times \frac{P}{Q}.$$

The expression dQ/dP equals $-1/b$, which is the coefficient of the P term in the demand equation (2): $Q = a/b - P/b$. By substituting $-1/b$ for dQ/dP, the own-price elasticity of demand now becomes

$$e_p = \frac{dQ}{dP} \times \frac{P}{Q} = -\frac{1}{b} \times \frac{P}{Q}.$$

The inverse of this expression is

$$\frac{1}{e_p} = -\frac{bQ}{P}. \tag{3}$$

Recall that marginal revenue is the change in total revenue resulting from a one-unit change in Q. This is the same as the derivative of total revenue with respect to a change in quantity, $d(TR)/dQ$. Since total revenue equals PQ, total revenue will in this case equal

$$PQ = (a - bQ)Q = aQ - bQ^2.$$

The derivative of this expression with respect to Q will be

$$MR = \frac{dTR}{dQ} = a - 2bQ,$$

which has the same form as the equation for the demand curve, with one exception: the slope is twice as large in absolute value.[2] We can rewrite the equation for marginal revenue as

$$MR = a - 2bQ = (a - bQ) - bQ. \qquad (4)$$

Note from equation (1) that $a - bQ$ is the same as P, and from equation (3), that $-bQ = P/e_p$. We can substitute these identities into equation (4) to obtain

$$MR = (a - bQ) - bQ = P + \frac{P}{e_d} = P(1 + e_d).$$

Marginal revenue is therefore equal to $P(1 + 1/e_d)$. We can use this relationship to check the placement of the marginal revenue curve in Figure 2-4. For example, when P equals MR, $1/e_d$ must be zero and e_d must be minus infinity. When MR is zero, both $1/e_d$ and e_d must equal -1.

Income Elasticity of Demand

All other elasticities can be calculated by using the same procedures described for calculating the own-price elasticity of demand—that is, either the arc method or the point method. While one can calculate an elasticity for any quantifiable demand factor, the income elasticity of demand provides especially useful information. The **income elasticity of demand** is the percentage change in quantity demanded resulting from a 1 percent change in income:

$$e_I = \frac{\% \Delta Q}{\% \Delta I} = \frac{\Delta Q}{\Delta I} \times \frac{I}{Q},$$

where Q is the quantity demanded of the good and I is a measure of the income of consumers (for example, average family income).

For instance, information about the income elasticity of demand could be of use to Rocky's mother, Mrs. Sanders, who owns several local day-care centers. Mrs. Sanders has observed that the children at the centers are well-dressed and come mostly from middle- and upper-income families. She could find out how responsive the demand for her day-care services is to different family income levels. This would be important to her if she were considering expanding into a new location.

---

[2] Note that the demand equation is $P = a - bQ$, while the equation for marginal revenue is $MR = a - 2bQ$. Both linear equations have the same intercept term, a, on the vertical axis, while the slope of the marginal-revenue equation, $-2b$, is twice the slope of the demand equation.

Assume that you know that the demand equation for day care at one of her centers is

$$Q = 55 - P + 3I,$$

where Q is the number of children using the center each week, P is the weekly price in dollars, and I is the average family income in thousands of dollars. Assume also that the average family income of people living near a prospective day-care center is \$30,000, while the average income for families living near her existing centers is \$25,000. When family income is \$25,000, the demand equation becomes

$$Q = 55 - P + 3(25)$$
$$= 130 - P.$$

FIGURE 2-5 ▪ **The effect of a change in income on demand.** A change in income shifts the demand curve to the right or left. In this case an increase in income shifted the demand curve to the right. If price remains constant at \$60, quantity demanded will increase from 70 to 85.

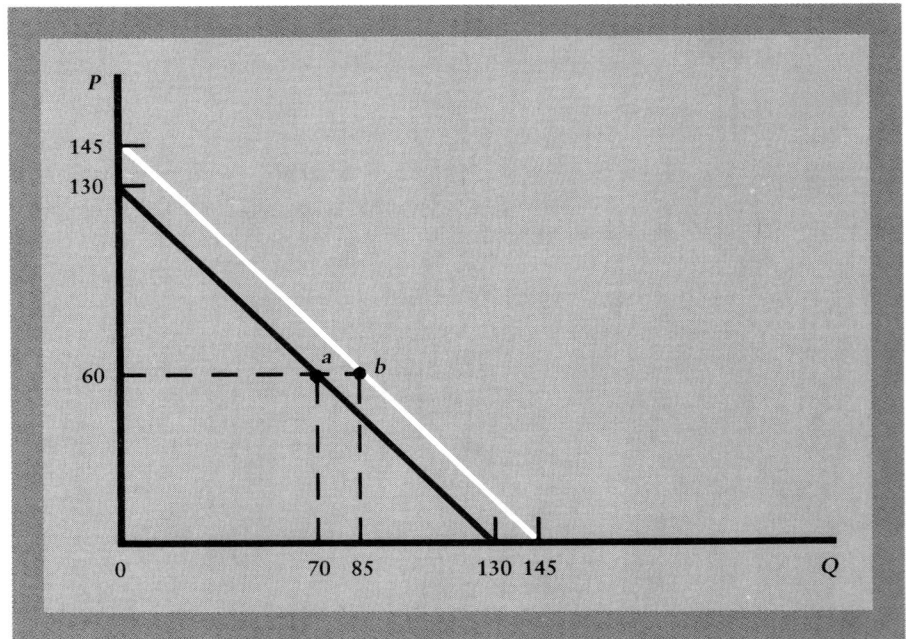

At an income of $30,000, the demand equation is

$$Q = 55 - P + 3(30)$$
$$= 145 - P.$$

Figure 2-5 shows the effect of the change in income as a shift in the demand curve for day care. Depending on the information available about the relationship between Q and I, this elasticity could be calculated by either the arc or the point method.

In this example, you have enough information to calculate the income elasticity of demand using either the arc or the point method. In order to use the arc method, you must know the value of the quantity demanded at each of two income levels. In this example you know this once you know P. For example, when P is $60 per week, quantity demanded increases from 70 to 85 children per week as family income increases from $25,000 to $30,000. This is shown in Figure 2-5 as a movement from point a to point b. Remember that by calculating the income elasticity, you assume all other demand factors are constant, including the price of the good.

Using the arc-method formula, you can determine the income elasticity over the $25,000 to $30,000 income range to be

$$e_I = \frac{Q_b - Q_a}{I_b - I_a} \times \frac{\dfrac{I_b + I_a}{2}}{\dfrac{Q_b + Q_a}{2}}$$

$$= \frac{85 - 70}{30,000 - 25,000} \times \frac{\dfrac{30,000 + 25,000}{2}}{\dfrac{85 + 70}{2}}$$

$$= \frac{15}{5,000} \times \frac{27,500}{77.5}$$

$$= 1.0645.$$

Since the income elasticity is 1.0645, a 1 percent increase in average family income would increase the number of children demanding services at the day-care center by 1.0645 percent.

We can obtain more precise measures of this elasticity by calculating point elasticities at different income levels. We know that the coefficient of the income term of a linear demand equation is equal to $\Delta Q/\Delta I$. Since the coefficient is 3 in this case, a $1,000 increase in the average family income increases the quantity demanded by 3 children per week. If P remains constant at $60, we know from before that Q will be 70 when I is 25.

Substitute these numbers into the point elasticity formula.

$$e_I = \frac{\Delta Q}{\Delta I} \times \frac{I}{Q}$$

$$= 3 \times \frac{25}{70}$$

$$= 1.071.$$

At I equal to 30 and P still equal to \$60, Q is 85. The income elasticity of demand at this point is

$$e_I = \frac{\Delta Q}{\Delta I} \times \frac{I}{Q}$$

$$= 3 \times \frac{30}{85}$$

$$= 1.057.$$

Normal and Inferior Goods

The income elasticity reveals how responsive the demand curve is to changes in income. In Numerical Example 2-9, the income elasticity was positive, since an increase in income resulted in an increase in quantity demanded. This is an example of a normal good. If quantity demanded decreases, the good is considered an inferior good. This difference can be summarized as follows:

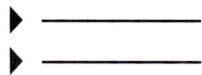

$e_I > 0$ **Normal good**

$e_I < 0$ **Inferior good**

$e_I = 0$ No relationship to income

The classification of a good as either normal or inferior depends not only on the characteristics of the product but also on the income level of the consumer. For example, individuals with low incomes may consider used clothing to be a normal good. For people with a higher income, any increase in income might be spent on new clothing to replace used clothing in their wardrobes, making used clothing an inferior good. High-income people may never have purchased used clothing. An increase in their income may have no effect on used-clothing purchases. As another example, in most developing countries, people with higher incomes smoke more cigarettes. In the United States, people with higher incomes smoke fewer cigarettes.

Most new products in a developed economy are normal goods. Information about the income elasticity is useful in determining which income group might be most receptive to the firm's marketing efforts and how the market is likely to respond to changes in purchasing power in future time periods. For example, knowledge of the income elasticity could help Mrs. Sanders forecast the effects on the demand for her centers due to a change in a government tax policy that would affect consumer income.

The normal-good classification can be subdivided into two groups based on the income elasticity's relationship to 1. If the elasticity exceeds 1, a 1 percent increase in income results in a greater than 1 percent increase in the demand for the firm's product. For example, if the income elasticity is 2.5, a 1 percent increase in income results in a 2.5 percent increase in the demand for the product.

Since the elasticity is calculated by holding the prices of all products constant, the firm is capturing a proportionally greater share of the increase in income when the income elasticity is greater than 1 ($e_I > 1$). These types of goods are called **luxury goods.** Examples might be memberships in exclusive clubs, dinners at restaurants, and purchases of imported beers.

If the proportional increase is less than 1 ($e_I < 1$), the product is a **necessity good,** at least as far as the consumers are concerned. Since the money spent on most basic foods, such as bread and milk, becomes a smaller percentage of overall expenditures with increases in income, most basic foods are considered necessities. Less essential foods, such as lobsters and imported caviar, are more likely to be considered luxuries.

Rocky might find this distinction useful for finding the appropriate market for his plastic bags. He is not sure who buys his bags. If the typical customer has a higher income, he may want to adjust his advertising to reach these people. If he finds that his sales do not vary as people's incomes increase over time, he might want to diversify by offering a high-quality designer plastic bag.

If Mrs. Sanders opens another day-care center, the income elasticity might help her determine how large a facility to rent or build in the new neighborhood. If the income elasticity is slightly greater than 1, she might expect that increases in family income will result in a slightly greater percentage increase in the quantity demanded for her center's services.

| 2-5 | **Here's looking at you, mate** |

APPLICATION Australians are among the world leaders in per capita consumption of beer. They have also become interested in wine. Since the 1950s Australians have been increasing their consumption of wine at the same time that their high-quality wines from the southeastern area of the country have been earning a growing international reputation. The increase in their consumption of wine has been at the expense of beer consumption, as the overall percentage of their budget allocated to alcoholic beverages has not significantly changed.

Professor Kenneth W. Clements of the University of Western Australia and Professor Lester W. Johnson of Macquarie University have studied the evolution of the demand for beer and wine, along with the demand for spirits, such as whiskey and rum. They analyzed Australian data covering the period from 1955 to 1977. They found that the average beer consumption per capita increased by approximately 1.2 percent per year, while wine consumption increased by 4.5 percent and spirits by 2.2 percent.

Throughout the time period, Australians spent approximately 6 percent of their budget on alcoholic beverages. Although beer consumption increased, the share of beer expenditures in the overall alcohol category declined from 76 percent to 66 percent, while wine consumption rose from 8.6 percent to 18.6 percent during the time period. The spirits share remained relatively constant at approximately 16 percent of the alcoholic-drink budget.

They determined that the income elasticity for the consumption of the entire group was essentially 1; that is, a 1 percent increase in income led to a 1 percent increase in the consumption of alcoholic beverages. The distribution among the three types differed: 0.80 for beer, 0.75 for wine, and 1.91 for spirits. While all three were normal goods, beer and wine were found to be necessities, and spirits, a luxury, since the income elasticity exceeded 1. In Australia at that time, the typical consumer of spirits did have an upper-level income. The own-price elasticities were −0.36 for beer, −0.43 for wine, and −0.74 for spirits—all three in the inelastic range. The own-price elasticity for the entire group of alcoholic beverages was −0.6.

Although the researchers had several objectives for their study, they were particularly interested in finding out why wine consumption increased faster than beer consumption did. They found three reasons. First, since the income elasticity of wine was greater than the income elasticity of beer, the increase in income favored wine consumption more than it did beer consumption.

Second, the rise in the price of beer relative to the price of wine encouraged some consumers to switch from beer to wine. And thirdly, the Australian government increased its tax on beer more than on wine. The higher tax on beer relative to the tax on wine has the same effect as a higher price of beer relative to the price of wine: a switch from beer to wine on the part of consumers.

Clements and Johnson concluded that there was a strong annual trend away from beer and towards wine, which was independent of income and price. The researchers suggested three reasons for the shift in national preference away from beer to wine: an influx of Southern European migrants with a stronger tradition of wine drinking than beer consumption, a change in demographic structure due to the post-World War II baby boom, and marketing and packaging innovations for wine. Due to data limitations, they were unable to calculate elasticities for these demand factors.

Source: Kenneth W. Clements and Lester W. Johnson, "The Demand for Beer, Wine, and Spirits: A Systemwide Analysis." *Journal of Business* 56, No. 3 (July 1983):273–304. © by the University of Chicago.

Cross-Price Elasticity of Demand

Since the price of other products generally has some impact on the demand for a firm's own goods, it would be useful to know precisely how to determine this effect. We can measure this effect by calculating another elasticity. Let us now consider this problem for Rocky's company. The price of the competitor's bags, Plenz plastic bags, directly influences the market demand for Poobell trash bags. Another less obvious factor might be the price of lawn fertilizer. That is, if the price of lawn fertilizer increases, home owners may choose to use less fertilizer, and less fertilizer means less active lawns and less demand for trash bags.

One can determine the importance of such influences by calculating cross-price elasticities. The **cross-price elasticity of demand** shows the effect of a price change of a good on the quantity demanded of another good. In mathematical notation, this is expressed as

$$e_{12} = \frac{\% \Delta Q_1}{\% \Delta P_2}$$

$$= \frac{\Delta Q_1}{\Delta P_2} \times \frac{P_2}{Q_1},$$

where Q_1 is the quantity demanded of the first good, P_1 is the price of the first good, and P_2 is the price of the second good. The formula shows the effect of a 1 percent change in the price of the second good on the quantity demanded of the first good.

The sign of the cross-price elasticity of demand is important. If an increase in the price of a product, such as Plenz bags, resulted in a rightward shift in the demand curve for Poobell bags, the quantity demanded would increase for Poobell bags and the two goods would be called substitutes. An increase in the price of lawn fertilizer most likely would shift the demand curve for trash bags to the left, decreasing the demand for trash bags, and we would call these two goods complements. In the case of substitutes, the cross-price elasticity of demand is positive, and in the case of complements, it is negative. This can be summarized mathematically as follows:

> **Substitutes:** $e_{12} > 0$
>
> **Complements:** $e_{12} < 0$.

2-6	**Can I get to New Jersey from here?**

APPLICATION   On March 20, 1986, the federal government initiated a one-way toll experiment for the westbound lanes of the Verrazano Narrows Bridge connecting Staten Island and Brooklyn, New York. The government was interested in reducing the time motorists spent commuting from Staten Island to New York City during the morning rush hours. By eliminating the eastbound toll and doubling the westbound toll, motorists faced only one toll stop per day. The westbound toll for cars rose from $1.75 to $3.50, while the truck tolls doubled to between $8 and $24, depending on the size of the truck.

The Port Authority of New York studied the impact of the new tolls on the Holland Tunnel linking New York City with New Jersey. They estimated that truck traffic near the tunnel rose from nine hundred to eleven hundred— an increase of 22 percent—during a typical three-hour afternoon period. Studies were conducted both before and after the new tolls went into effect. Total westbound traffic through the tunnel, including cars, increased by 3 percent.

The Triborough Bridge and Tunnel Authority, which operates the Verrazano Narrows Bridge, estimated that it would lose $5.3 million in 1986 due to a drop-off of 1.6 percent of total traffic (that is, both eastbound and westbound traffic). According to city transportation officials, truckers bound for New Jersey or Staten Island began choosing alternate routes through Manhattan, even though these routes were less direct. The Holland Tunnel is free going west—the reverse of the Verrazano Narrows Bridge.

If there had been no change in other factors influencing the traffic near the Holland Tunnel, the federal government could have used this experimental data to calculate the cross-price elasticity of demand due to the change in the price of using the bridge. Since a doubling of the price (that is, a 100 percent increase) caused a 3 percent increase in tunnel traffic, the cross-price elasticity for all traffic would be 3%/100%, or 0.03.

Since few car drivers found avoiding the price increase worth the longer drive through Manhattan, most of the diverted vehicles were trucks. Assuming that the Port Authority's estimates were correct, the cross-price elasticity of the quantity demanded of the Holland Tunnel due to truck traffic would be 22%/100%, or 0.22.

Recall, however, that we are *assuming* that there was no change in other factors that might have affected the demand truckers had for use of the Holland Tunnel. For example, westbound traffic through the tunnel might have increased during 1986 because of the Fourth of July/Statue of Liberty celebrations or the sharp drop in gasoline prices during early 1986. Even without the higher bridge toll, the tunnel traffic figures might have been higher than those for 1985. Unless we correct for these other effects, we might overestimate the full impact of the higher westbound toll.

From this analysis we may conclude that the government could accomplish its objective of increasing the rate of flow of commuter traffic by using the new toll structure for cars only. The new system does not appear to affect car drivers' choice of route. By retaining the toll at both ends of the bridge for trucks, the government could reduce the flow of truck traffic through the tunnel. The government was still analyzing the problem when this book went to press.

Market Versus Firm Demand

An understanding of the cross-price elasticities is important to firms when there are alternatives to the firm's product or service. As shown in the previous example, the cross-price elasticity indicates how sensitive one's demand curve is to the competitors' pricing strategy.

In Rocky's case, if the cross-price elasticity of demand between Plenz and Poobell trash bags is a large positive number, the two products are close substitutes and Rocky might want to reconsider the nature of the market. A **market** is a collection of buyers and sellers of similar products. He might find it more useful to consider the market to be all plastic trash bags, regardless of manufacturer.

Many companies belong to trade associations, which estimate demand functions from data supplied by members. There are trade associations for a wide range of goods, including textiles, cardboard boxes, cement, and many other commodities. These associations not only compile statistics, but they actively promote the market demand for their members' products through advertising. For example, dairy and poultry trade associations sponsor cooking contests and local advertising campaigns. United States textile and clothing trade associations appeal to patriotism in their advertisements by encouraging Americans to buy American-made clothing and textile products.

2-7   A flexible market

APPLICATION

In 1953 the District Court of Delaware heard a case brought by the Justice Department against E.I. Du Pont de Nemours and Company. The Justice Department alleged that Du Pont had monopolized the market for cellophane. While everyone agreed that Du Pont held exclusive rights to market cellophane in the United States, the court decided in favor of Du Pont!

The relevant antitrust law in this case was the Sherman Act. To be convicted of monopolization under the Sherman Act, a company must have a large share of the market and must be intent on monopolizing. The court dismissed the case because Du Pont did not have a large share of the relevant market! The case hinged on how the market was defined.

Although a market is defined as a collection of buyers and sellers of similar products, there may not always be complete agreement on what products should be included in each market. For example, Du Pont purchased the United States rights to cellophane from a French company. Du Pont then licensed another U.S. company to produce some cellophane, and the two companies made all the cellophane sold in the United States. Defining the market as all buyers and sellers of cellophane in the United States would have given Du Pont control over the entire market. The court chose instead to define the market as flexible packaging materials, which included all other wrapping materials, such as polyethylene film and aluminum wrap. Du Pont had no more than a 20 percent share of this market, which the court considered too low to constitute a monopoly. In reaching this conclusion, the court accepted evidence showing the sensitivity of Du Pont's sales to the prices of alternative materials.

Since the cross-price elasticities were relatively large, the polyethylene film, aluminum wrap, and other wrapping materials were close substitutes. The court agreed that the relevant market for this case should include all products that were close substitutes for cellophane. The Supreme Court upheld this decision in 1961.

Source: U.S. v. E.I. Du Pont de Nemours, 366 U.S. 316 (1961).

The courts have also used cross-price elasticities to define markets in merger cases. While we will consider the government's position toward mergers in more detail in Chapter 13, we can see in the following application another example of how the courts have relied on the cross-price elasticity.

2-8

The Supreme Court puts its foot down

APPLICATION   The Justice Department prosecuted the merger between Brown Shoe Company and Kinney because it feared there was a growing concentration of market power in the hands of a few firms in the United States. The Brown Shoe Company case represents an unusual situation in the history of merger cases because of the relatively small market shares involved. With the merger, the new company would have had, at most, 4.5 percent of the United States manufacturing and retail markets.

The Brown Shoe Company argued that it did not compete directly with Kinney. Brown supplied mainly mid-priced men's shoes, and Kinney sold mostly lower-priced women's shoes. Since they were not direct competitors, they felt that a merger between them would not have increased the concentration of market power for the products they sold. Despite this claim, the Justice Department countered with estimates of positive cross-price elasticities in several metropolitan areas of the country, which suggested that the two companies *were* direct competitors. Due to this cross-price elasticity evidence and a fear of rising market power in this industry, the Supreme Court ruled against the merger in 1962.

Source: U.S. v. Brown Shoe Company, 370 U.S. 294 (1962).

The Importance of Time

Time may influence the quantity demanded in two ways. First of all, the value of other elasticities may be dependent upon the amount of time that passes between the change in the demand factor and the change in quantity demanded. Secondly, the waiting time itself may be a demand factor.

The Effect of Time on Other Elasticities

The magnitude of any elasticity depends on the amount of time that passes between the change in the demand factor and the observed change in quantity demanded. For example, an increase in the price of gasoline has an immediate impact on gasoline consumption. The effect of the increased price on consumption two years later might be quite different.

2-9

APPLICATION

A slow response to OPEC

In the early 1970s the Organization of Petroleum Exporting Countries (OPEC) reduced oil production significantly and caused a sudden, large increase in the price of petroleum products. The own-price elasticity of demand for petroleum was highly inelastic at that time. The own-price elasticity of demand became more elastic as time passed, however, as more substitutes became available and customers altered their consumption habits.

The high price of oil spurred activity in many areas. At the time of the price increase, electric utility companies in the United States were heavily dependent upon oil. During the 1970s these companies began converting to coal and nuclear-power units. They also built firing units (that is, production facilities) that could use more than one fuel, increasing the companies' flexibility in response to changes in the relative prices of different fuels. Automobile manufacturers increased production and sales of smaller, more fuel-efficient automobiles. Home owners installed insulation. Companies invested in research and other efforts aimed at fuel conservation. All of these adjustments affected both the location and the elasticity of the demand curve for petroleum. In general, as time passes and alternatives become more available, the own-price elasticity of demand of a product or service becomes more elastic.

Time as a Demand Factor

Time itself may be a demand factor. For example, how long we must wait to see a physician or to be admitted into a hospital may affect our demand for medical care. There have been numerous studies of this phenomenon, and we will review one in the following application.

49

APPLICATION

In this chapter prices and income have been given a dominant role in the demand function. Depending upon the nature of the product or service, there may be other demand factors that are even more important. In Application 2-4 we saw that the widespread use of comprehensive health insurance makes the out-of-pocket cost of a visit to a physician or hospital essentially zero for many Americans. When the price of a service is not a deciding factor, there must be other ways of rationing the service. Several analysts believe that the time a patient spends traveling to an appointment at the hospital or doctor's office is such a factor.

Hospital administrators have been very concerned with this issue, since it affects the demand for their hospitals' services. Marjorie McGuirk and Frank Porell of the University of Wisconsin at Milwaukee analyzed data on inpatient trips to twenty-nine hospitals located in Allegheny County, Pennsylvania during the year 1975. Allegheny County includes Pittsburgh and is a mostly urban area. The researchers concentrated on four types of hospital services: medical-surgical, obstetric-gynecological (OB-GYN), pediatric, and psychiatric.

They used estimates of travel time from the patient's community to the hospital as a demand factor in the choice of hospital. Although they had additional objectives for their study, they calculated the time elasticity of demand for their sample and concluded that most of the time elasticities were greater than 1 in absolute value. In other words, a 1 percent increase in travel time lowered the percentage of patients choosing a particular hospital by more than 1 percent.

Despite the presence of many hospitals in the county area, the researchers concluded that most patients chose hospitals close to their homes. They found differences relative to service type. For example, patients going for psychiatric care were less sensitive to travel time. Not surprisingly, OB-GYN travel time elasticities were much higher, even though the researchers had combined two patient types into this one category.

The researchers controlled for both travel time and distance in their study. Although it is difficult to separate the two effects, they determined that time is of more concern to patients than actual distance traveled. The results of this study suggest to policymakers that improved access to hospitals, resulting in less travel time, may be an alternative to building more facilities closer to patients' homes. Travel time appears to be important enough to warrant careful consideration in hospital planning.

Source: Marjorie A. McGuirk and Frank W. Porell, "Spatial Patterns of Hospital Utilization: The Impact of Distance and Time." *Inquiry* 21 (Spring 1984):84–95.

Other Applications of the Elasticity Concept

As was mentioned earlier, we could calculate an elasticity for any demand factor. To complete this discussion we will look at two more examples that demonstrate the use of elasticities. While they do not exhaust all the possibilities of using elasticities, they do serve as examples of how to solve a wide range of problems.

Advertising

Advertising can greatly influence the demand for a firm's product. While Chapter 9 will concentrate on the role of advertising in economic decision-making, we note here that a firm could calculate an advertising elasticity. This information is useful in evaluating the potential of an advertising effort.

Normally we associate an advertising campaign with an attempt to increase customers' interest in a firm's product. A successful campaign shifts the demand curve to the right. However, in some cases, advertising may be used to discourage consumption, as we see in the following application.

2-11	Ten fun ideas for when the lights are out

APPLICATION

Following the oil embargo of 1973, government regulators initiated programs and advertising campaigns to help reduce the use of electricity. Professors David Kaserman and John Mayo of the University of Tennessee were interested in measuring the impact of this conservational advertising on the demand for electricity by home owners.

The researchers used data from thirty-four electric utilities in the northeastern United States from 1974 through 1979. They had information on the price of electricity, the price of natural gas, the price of fuel oil, per capita income, heating degree days, cooling degree days, and the dollar amount of advertising.

They determined that the advertising elasticity of demand was only -0.018; that is, a 10 percent increase in advertising expenditures resulted in only a 0.18 percent decrease in quantity demanded. The own-price elasticity of demand was -0.760. The income elasticity was 0.507 and the cross-price elasticity due to a change in the price of natural gas was -0.171.

From this analysis they concluded that advertising did not have much of an impact on the consumption habits of consumers. They also determined that, since the own-price elasticity was in the inelastic range, consumers did not decrease their consumption significantly with an increase in the price of electricity.

Source: David L. Kaserman and John W. Mayo, "Advertising and the Residential Demand for Electricity." *Journal of Business* 58, No. 4 (1985):399–408. © by the University of Chicago.

Gas-Mileage Elasticity of Demand

In our discussion of the effects of time on other elasticities of demand, we mentioned that many American consumers switched from large to small automobiles. Part of the reason for this switch was the United States Government's insistence on higher average-mileage performance for cars built in the United States.

2-12

APPLICATION

Around the world on a tank of gas

In the 1970s and early 1980s the United States Government considered two basic policy approaches aimed at reducing the consumption of gasoline and thereby reducing the country's dependence on foreign gasoline. The government increased excise taxes and instituted higher mileage standards for new automobiles, both of which should, in theory, have led to lower consumption of gasoline. Professor Roger Blair of the University of Florida, Professor David Kaserman of the University of Tennessee, and Dr. Richard Tepel of Oak Ridge National Laboratory used monthly data from Florida from 1967 to 1976 to test the importance of both approaches.

While the increase in price by way of the increase in excise tax had an unambiguous effect on the quantity demanded, the higher mileage standards had two opposing effects: lower per-mile consumption of gasoline, on the one hand, and more driving on the part of motorists, due to the lower cost per extra mile, on the other hand. They estimated that the own-price elasticity of gasoline demand was -0.412 and the income elasticity was 0.278. The mileage-efficiency elasticity of demand was -0.703. This means that a 10 percent increase in the average mileage-performance standard of the typical car resulted in a 7 percent drop in gasoline consumption.

Source: Roger D. Blair, David L. Kaserman, and Richard Tepel, "The Impact of Improved Mileage on Gasoline Consumption." *Economic Inquiry* XXII (April 1984):209–17.

Summary

In this chapter we have analyzed several issues related to the demand for a firm's product. Knowledge of the nature of the demand function faced by a firm enables the firm to design its marketing efforts more effectively. The manager must give careful attention to factors that affect the demand for the firm's product.

Given data on the firm's output and these demand factors, the manager can calculate the impact these factors have on sales. A useful measure of this impact is the elasticity of demand. Although we focused on the elasticities due to changes in price and income, one could calculate an elasticity for any of the demand factors.

While elasticities reveal information on the sensitivity of the quantity demanded to changes in the demand factors, one can also relate elasticities to other important information. For example, the own-price elasticity of demand is directly related to changes in revenue received by the firm at each output level.

This chapter provided a basic background in the concept of demand. Starting in Chapter 5, we will match the demand for a firm's product to the costs of producing it. At that point we will consider several strategies for maximizing a firm's profits, all of which will depend on the specific demand faced by the firm. The statistical issues related to estimating demand equations and elasticities will be delayed until Chapter 16.

Important Terms

Demand (p. 17)
Derived Demand (p. 17)
Utility (pp. 17–18)
Quantity Demanded (p. 18)
Demand Curve (p. 21)
Change in the Quantity Demanded (p. 22)
Change in Demand (p. 22)
Elasticity of Demand (p. 24)
Arc Method (p. 25)
Point Method (p. 27)
Own-Price Elasticity of Demand (p. 28)

Total Revenue (p. 35)
Marginal Revenue (p. 35)
Income Elasticity of Demand (p. 39)
Normal Good (p. 42)
Inferior Good (p. 42)
Luxury Good (p. 43)
Necessity Good (p. 43)
Cross-Price Elasticity of Demand (p. 45)
Substitutes (p. 45)
Complements (p. 45)
Market (p. 47)

Selected References

Blair, Roger D.; Kaserman, David L.; and Tepel, Richard C. "The Impact of Improved Mileage on Gasoline Consumption." *Economic Inquiry* XXII (April 1984):209–17.

Brookshire, David S.; Coursey, Don L.; and Schulze, William D. "The External Validity of Experimental Economics Techniques: Analysis of Demand Behavior." *Economic Inquiry* XXV (April 1987): 239–50.

Clements, Kenneth W. and Johnson, Lester W. "The Demand for Beer, Wine, and Spirits: A Systemwide Analysis." *The Journal of Business* 56, No. 3 (July 1983):273–304.

Hamilton, James L. "The Demand for Cigarettes: Advertising, the Health Scare, and the Cigarette Advertising Ban." *Review of Economics and Statistics* 54 (November 1972):401–11.

Hogarty, Thomas F. and Elzinga, Kenneth G. "The Demand for Beer." *Review of Economics and Statistics* 54 (May 1972):195–98.

Kaserman, David L. and Mayo, John W. "Advertising and the Residential Demand for Electricity." *The Journal of Business* 58 (October 1985):399–408.

Lancaster, Kelvin J. *Consumer Demand: A New Approach.* New York: Columbia University Press (1971).

Marquis, M. Susan and Phelps, Charles E. "Price Elasticity and Adverse Selection in the Demand for Supplementary Health Insurance." *Economic Inquiry* XXV (April 1987):299–313.

McGuirk, Marjorie A. and Porell, Frank W. "Spatial Patterns of Hospital Utilization: The Impact of Distance and Time." *Inquiry* 21 (Spring 1984):84–95.

Park, Rolla Edward; Wetzel, Bruce M.; and Mitchell, Bridger M. "Price Elasticities for Local Telephone Calls." *Econometrica* 51, No. 6 (November 1983):1699–1731.

Pitt, Mark M. "Food Preferences and Nutrition in Rural Bangladesh." *The Review of Economics and Statistics* LXV, No. 1 (February 1983):105–14.

Suits, Daniel B. "The Elasticity of Demand for Gambling." *Quarterly Journal of Economics* 93 (February 1979):155–62.

Problems

1. Larry, Ann, and Frank constitute the entire market for chicken. Larry's demand function is

$$Q_1 = 50 - P$$

for price less than or equal to $50. For $P > 50$, his demand is 0. Ann's demand function is

$$Q_2 = 100 - 2P$$

for price less than or equal to $50. For $P > 50$, her demand is 0. Frank's demand function is

$$Q_3 = 100 - 4P$$

for price less than or equal to $25. For $P > 25$, his demand is 0.

(a) How much chicken does each person demand when the prices are $0, $10, $25, $50, and $75?

(b) What is the total market demand at these prices?

(c) Graph each individual's demand curve and construct the market demand curve.

2. Casa della Maison Restaurant is planning a sweatshirt advertising promotion. Limited sales data from a few sweatshirt sales of a prototype of the design indicate that

$$Q = 2000 - 200P,$$

where Q is sweatshirt sales and P is price.

(a) How many sweatshirts could the restaurant sell at $5 each?

(b) What price would it have to charge to sell 1,500 sweatshirts?

(c) At what price would sweatshirt sales equal zero?

(d) Plot the demand, marginal revenue, and total revenue curves.

(e) Calculate the point price elasticity of demand at a price of $7.50.

(f) At what price would the point price elasticity of demand be -1?

3. The demand for Ravenswood Parcel Service's guaranteed six-hour delivery of regular-sized envelopes is given by the following equation:

$$X = 5 - 0.5P_x + 0.0005I + 2P_y,$$

where X is the number of envelopes delivered, P_x is the price in dollars per envelope, I is average disposable income of the serviced population in dollars, and P_y is the dollar-per-envelope price of a competitor's overnight service.

(a) Determine the point own-price elasticity of demand of X when I equals 10,000, P_x equals 2, and P_y is 1.

(b) What happens to total revenue if P_x increases slightly? Why?

(c) Determine the own-price elasticity of demand due to a change in P_x from 1 to 3. Assume that I equals 100 and P_y equals 1.

4. Scarpia Office and Stationery Supplies estimates that the demand function for its pewter letter openers is given by the following equation:

$$Q = 7 - 0.5P_Q + 2P_Y + 0.01I + 0.02A,$$

where Q is the quantity demanded of the firm's letter openers, P_Q is the price of the letter opener, P_Y is the price of another firm's product, I is the income per capita, and A is the dollar value of the firm's advertising effort.

(a) Assume that P_Y equals 2, I is 1,000, and A equals 400. Calculate the elasticity of the demand curve for a change in P_Q from 40 to 20.

(b) Assume that the firm is considering the change in price mentioned in part (a). The firm is only concerned about the impact of the change on the firm's total revenue. What advice would you offer the firm?

(c) What would your advice be if the change in the price of X is very small?

5. Assume that the following is the demand equation for Sacks Hammers:

$$Q_x = 10,000 - 200P_x + 0.1Y + 0.5A - 200P_w,$$

where Q_x is the quantity demanded of hammers per month, P_x is the price of one hammer in dollars, Y is the average income of the people likely to buy the hammers, A is the advertising budget per month in dollars, and P_w is the price of a large sheet of $\frac{3}{4}$-inch plywood. The price of $\frac{3}{4}$-inch plywood is a proxy for wood products. Assume that P_x is 5, Y is 15,000, A is 5,000, and P_w is 10.

(a) Calculate the elasticities for each of the variables.

(b) Plot the demand curve for Sacks Hammers.

(c) Show what happens to the demand curve in part (b) if P_w increases to 15.

6. Buzz Plonk, owner of Plonk Package Store, is considering reducing the prices on his private-label vodka. Assume that the elasticity of demand for this vodka is -1.5. His wholesale purchase price for the vodka is $5 per quart. He currently sells it for $10 per quart.

(a) What will happen to his revenue if he lowers the price of vodka?

(b) Would you recommend this price reduction?

Answer questions 7–12 with true, false, or uncertain. Be prepared to provide an explanation for each of your answers.

7. The demand function $Q = 150/P$ is inelastic at all prices.

8. If one raises prices along an inelastic portion of the demand curve, total revenue increases.

9. If one calculates the own-price elasticity of demand with the arc method, using

the two points where a straight-line demand curve crosses the price and quantity axes, the elasticity equals -1.

10. The elasticity of a demand curve is constant as long as the slope of the curve is constant.

11. If the own-price elasticity of demand is -0.8, the firm will increase its revenue by raising its price.

12. If the cross-price elasticity of demand between two products is $+25$, the two products are close substitutes.

PRODUCTION THEORY

3

Profit-maximizing managers must be aware of their cost structures. Costs depend on both the price of inputs and the amount of output that these inputs can produce. While ultimately we are interested in the cost of producing the firm's output, we will concentrate first on the technical (engineering) relationship between the firm's inputs and outputs. We will completely ignore the influence of costs at this time. In the next chapter we will introduce input prices in order to determine the lowest-cost combination of inputs.

Conceptually, we can characterize a firm as a collection of inputs that produces output. While the relationship between inputs and outputs may be unique for each firm, all production processes have certain principles in common. In order to focus on these common characteristics, we will start with a general specification of a production relationship, which is called a production function.

Production Functions

A **production function** is a table, graph, or mathematical expression that reveals the maximum output that a given set of inputs can produce. In functional notation the production function for a simple process with one product, Q, and two inputs, X and Y, is

$$Q = f(X, Y).$$

The function $Q = f(X, Y)$ is a general expression. The actual expression depends upon the nature of the production process. We will start with simple production processes in order to insure that you are comfortable with the basic principles of production theory. A solid understanding of these fundamentals will make the study of more complex and realistic applications, beginning in Chapter 5, much easier.

First let us analyze a simplified production process. For example, assume that we want to analyze the production function for Verte Tree Company, a small tree-trimming firm. For mathematical simplicity assume that the company uses only two inputs: laborers and large, mobile, tree-trimming machines. The owner, Harry Sampson, asks a consulting firm to send a representative to construct some graphs showing what he could produce with different combinations of inputs. The consulting firm gives Phyllis Steene the assignment.

As background information, Phyllis first shows Harry the various ways in which she could characterize his production process. For example, Table

3-1 shows a representative production relationship between an output, Q, and two inputs, X and Y. By presenting the production relationship in this manner, we are assuming that the inputs are available only in increments of one unit. For example, X equal to 3.5 is not possible.

Notice that by moving from the lower left of the table to the upper right, output generally increases as both input levels increase. The numbers for such a table would come from the specific production relationship under consideration. The data from Table 3-1 could be plotted on a three-dimensional graph, such as Figure 3-1 (p. 60), where output is measured by the height of the blocks. Each block represents the maximum output at the corresponding input levels of X and Y.

Before we analyze this specific production function in greater detail, let us consider the following example.

TABLE 3-1 ▪ A production table for two inputs

Y										
10	210	530	630							
9	260	570	720	750						
8	280	590	780	830	880					
7	270	570	795	875	900	880	850			
6	250	550	775	840	880	870	840	780		
5	210	500	730	800	840	860	820	760		
4	170	420	620	690	740	760	770	750	700	600
3	110	320	440	500	550	580	590	590	570	520
2	60	150	250	320	370	410	430	440	420	330
1	20	50	100	130	150	170	180	170	150	120
0	1	2	3	4	5	6	7	8	9	10 X

FIGURE 3-1 ▪ **The production possibilities set.** The *X*- and *Y*-axes measure the quantities of the two inputs. The inputs are available in integer amounts only. The height, or third dimension, of the graph measures the output associated with each combination of inputs.

We'll have a nine-pounder, please

Normally, we think of production relationships in terms of the production of manufactured goods, but we can apply the concept of a production function to the production of any type of output, including services, education, and even newborn babies! For example, Professors Mark Rosenzweig of the University of Minnesota and T. Paul Schultz of Yale University specified a multiple-input production function for a newborn's birth weight.

Previous medical research showed a strong relationship between a newborn's weight and the baby's future health and development. Since there is significant variability in birth weight, Professors Rosenzweig and Schultz hypothesized that an expectant mother might be able to choose inputs that could influence the weight and future health of her baby. They hypothesized that birth weight was a function of several inputs, including the number of months before the mother's first prenatal visit to a doctor, the number of cigarettes she smoked per day while pregnant, the order of the birth among her total number of births, and her age.

The researchers analyzed data on 9,000 live births to married couples between 1967 and 1969. They concluded that most of the inputs did significantly influence a newborn's weight. For example, the typical smoker smoked 14 cigarettes per day during her pregnancy and produced a baby who was 7 percent lighter than the average baby of a nonsmoker. The researchers concluded that the optimal age for the mother was 24 years. At 20 years of age the mother produced a baby with a 4.4 percent lower birth weight. Babies with mothers 30 years of age had 6.7 percent lower birth weights.

The mother's age had an additional impact. The researchers found that a mother who had her fourth child at age 30 produced a heavier baby than a 20-year-old woman giving birth to her fourth child. They also determined that lower birth weights for black babies than for white babies, shown in previous studies, was due to shorter gestation periods for black babies. The researchers discovered that prenatal care leads to longer gestation periods and heavier babies. They suggested that a policy promoting earlier prenatal care for black mothers may help solve the problem of lower birth weights.

Source: Mark R. Rosenzweig and T. Paul Schultz, "Estimating a Household Production Function: Heterogeneity, the Demand for Health Inputs, and Their Effects on Birth Weight." *Journal of Political Economy* 91, No. 5 (1983):723–46. © by the University of Chicago.

Short Run versus Long Run

Throughout the rest of the book we make a distinction between the short run and the long run. The *short run* is a time period that is not long enough for the firm to be able to adjust the amount of all of its inputs. In other words, the amount of at least one input remains fixed. The *long run* is a time sufficiently long for the firm to be able to adjust the amount of all of its inputs. We will find this distinction especially useful in simplifying the problems faced by the firm. We start with an analysis of the short run.

The Short Run

Let us look more closely at the production function for the Verte Tree Company. In the short run we know that the amount of at least one input is fixed. We will assume in Harry Sampson's case that in the short run the number of machines, Y, is fixed. If Harry were interested, Phyllis could determine the impact on output of varying the numbers of laborers while holding the number of machines constant.

Marginal Product

▶ _____ **Marginal product** is the additional output that a firm can produce by using one additional unit of an input while holding the amount of the other inputs constant. The marginal product of input X, MP_X, equals the change in the output of good Q divided by the change in X. In mathematical notation we have

$$MP_X = \frac{\Delta Q}{\Delta X},$$

when all other inputs are held constant.

3-1	Marginal product

GRAPHICAL
EXPLANATION

Although Harry is interested in the amount of output that a given level of inputs will generate, he also cares how much the output will change if he decides to add more laborers to his work force. He may find that additional units of an input do not have the same incremental effect on output that the first units did.

When thinking about the effects of changing an input, such as laborers, in unit increments, it helps to imagine someone walking up stairs, where the height of each step is the level of output. Most people walking up stairs take the steps one at a time and measure the height of the next step relative to the last step, rather than relative to the bottom of the staircase. It is often useful to think of the production function in the same manner.

In Figure 3-1, if Y represents the tree-trimming machines, we can hold Y constant at three units, and X can represent the number of laborers. By varying X from 0 to 10 in increments of one unit, output increases as X

increases up to the point where X is 7. Output remains at 590 when X is both 7 and 8. For X greater than 8, output starts to decline with additional units of X.

Diminishing Marginal Product

As mentioned earlier, all production functions have certain characteristics in common. For example, Harry should expect that by adding more laborers while holding the number of machines constant, he will eventually reach a point where the marginal product of laborers will diminish. While marginal product may increase for relatively lower levels of the input, marginal product will decrease eventually. It may even become negative for relatively large amounts of the input.

In Figure 3-1, since X is changing by one unit at a time, the height of each step relative to the previous step represents marginal product—that is, the incremental change in output for a one-unit change in X. In Figure 3-1, marginal product increases as X increases from 0 to 2 when Y is held constant at 3. Increasing marginal product is a possible but uncommon occurrence.

You may recall seeing the Chaplinesque character in a recent IBM television commercial that showed how computer systems could help organize a cake-baking and decorating business. In the commercial the owner of the firm tries to operate an assembly line of cakes in need of decorating and packaging. Unfortunately, the system gets out of control and all the cakes fall on the floor. In this case the addition of one other worker at the other end of the conveyor belt could have added more in marginal product than the first worker did.

Although additional workers can space themselves evenly along an assembly line and perhaps increase overall output, the incremental increase in output eventually diminishes given the fixed nature of the equipment used in the production process. In the end there may be so many workers that they get in each other's way, causing output to decrease as more workers are added. For example, in Figure 3-1, if Y is constant at 3, the incremental increase in output becomes smaller for X between 2 and 7. Once X exceeds 8, the change in output is negative.

Total-Product Curve

Although in Figure 3-1 the firm can adjust input levels only in increments of whole units, it could adjust some inputs continuously. For example, gasoline can be used in increments as small as a drop. Figure 3-2 shows a general production relationship between an input and an output, given that the firm can adjust the input, X, continuously while holding the levels of all other inputs constant. In the graph, output increases steadily at an increasing rate until it reaches X_1, the inflection point on the curve. The **inflection point** indicates a reverse in the direction of the change of the slope of a curve. For example, for increases in X to the left of X_1, the slope is increasing. To the right of X_1 an increase in X corresponds to a decrease in the slope, resulting in a progressively flatter curve.

Output reaches a peak at X_2 and declines for increases in X to the right of X_2. The curve representing the continuous relationship between output and an input is called the total-product curve. The **total-product curve** is a continuous graphical representation of the relationship between the amount of output and the amount of one input, holding the amounts of all other inputs constant.

Marginal-Product Curve

Since Harry can hire workers for any continuous increment of time, such as $6\frac{1}{2}$ hours per day, the continuous graphs are more appropriate than tables for his operation. Since he can vary the amount of laborers continuously, he can construct a marginal-product curve from information provided by the total-product curve.

Assume that Figure 3-2 represents the total-product curve for Harry's company. The input that he is considering changing is the number of laborer hours per day. Below the total-product curve in Figure 3-2 is a graph of marginal product that corresponds to the total-product curve.

Recall that the marginal product is the change in output resulting from a one-unit change in input. Since the slope of the total-product curve equals the change in total product due to a change in the quantity of the input, the slope of the total-product curve must be the marginal product. The **marginal-product curve** shows the relationship between the level of the input and the marginal product of that unit of the input on a graph.

3-2	**Marginal-product curve**

GRAPHICAL EXPLANATION

There are two important benchmarks for the slope of Harry's total-product curve and for marginal product: the inflection point at X_1 and the maximum value of Q at X_2. The slope of the total-product curve increases up to X_1 and decreases to the right of X_1. The slope (and thus the marginal-product curve) reaches its maximum value at X_1. This is shown in the lower graph in Figure 3-2. At X_2 total product reaches its peak and the slope is zero. Since the slope is zero, marginal product is zero at this point. To the right of this point marginal product becomes negative.

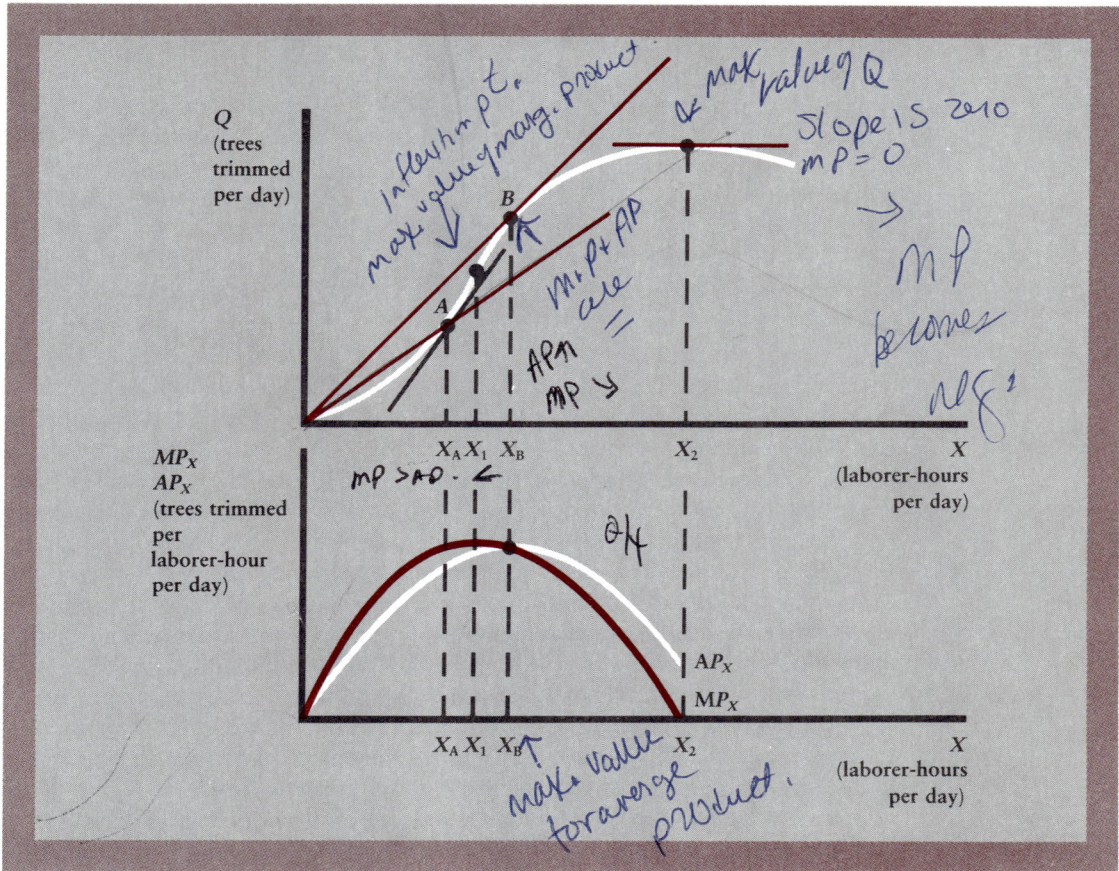

FIGURE 3-2 ■ Total-, marginal-, and average-product curves. The top graph shows the continuous relationship between the amount of output and the amount of input. The lower graph shows the corresponding marginal-product and average-product curves. The inflection point at X_1 on the total-product curve corresponds to the maximum value of marginal product (that is, the slope of the total-product curve). The maximum point on the total-product curve occurs at X_2. Since the slope of the total-product curve is 0 at X_2, marginal product equals 0 at X_2. The slope of a line drawn from the origin to a point on the total product curve has the same value as the average product at that point. The maximum value for average product occurs at X_B. At this point average product and marginal product have the same value. To the left of B, marginal product exceeds average product. To the right of B, marginal product is less than average product.

Average-Product curve

Average product is another useful measure of output. **Average product, AP_X,** equals the amount of output divided by the amount of the input—that is,

Q/X. We call the graphical representation of average product and its corresponding input level an **average-product curve**. The average-product curve tells how productive each worker is on the average.

For any continuous total-product curve there is a set relationship between the corresponding average- and marginal-product curves. Consider the following graphical explanation.

The average-product curve versus the marginal-product curve

GRAPHICAL EXPLANATION

The average-product curve can be constructed by analyzing the slope of a straight line drawn from the origin to a point on the total-product curve. Since it is a straight line, you can determine its slope by using any two points on the line.

For example, in Figure 3-2, choose the origin and the point where the line crosses the total-product curve at point A. The slope of this line is simply $(Q_A - 0)/(X_A - 0)$, or Q_A/X_A. Since average product is Q_A/X_A by definition, the slope of the line from the origin to a point on the total-product curve is always equal to the average product at that point.

Since a line drawn tangent to the total-product curve has the same slope as the curve at the point of tangency, we can compare marginal and average product by comparing the slope of a tangent line with the slope of a line drawn from the origin to the tangency point. For example, since at A the line drawn from the origin is flatter than a line drawn tangent to the curve at A, average product is less than marginal product at point A.

Since at point B the line from the origin is indistinguishable from a line drawn tangent to the total-product curve, marginal product and average product are equal at B. You can see the relationship between marginal and average product at the bottom of Figure 3-2.

To the right of X_B, average product exceeds marginal product. To the left of X_B, marginal product exceeds average product. Average product reaches a maximum at X_B, since a line drawn from the origin always has a flatter slope (that is, lower average product) by passing through any other point on the total-product curve.

A more productive meal

APPLICATION

Nutritionists are interested in the biological relationship between a person's nutritional intake and work performance. Economists also are interested in this relationship and the role that economic incentives play in an individual's choice of diet. In a recent study, Professor John Strauss of Yale University found a specific relationship between food intake and productivity for farmers in Sierra Leone, a small West African country.

He assumed that each agricultural household farmed subject to a production function of agricultural output and inputs, such as labor hours, caloric intake of workers, fixed capital, and land cultivated. By specifying the production function in this way, he was able to measure the direct impact of caloric intake on the output of the farm.

He analyzed data from a survey of households in the 1974–75 cropping year (May through April). Included in the data set was information on the production and purchase of 196 foods eaten by the farmers. Using conversion tables he calculated the caloric intake for each worker on the farm.

Figure 3-3 shows a total-product curve from the study. The curve relates the input of calories to output per hour of labor. The important input for the

FIGURE 3-3 ▪ **Total-product curve (Sierra Leone farmers).** The vertical axis provides a relative measure of output per worker for the Sierra Leone farmers. The total-product curve indicates that increases in caloric intake per day increase productivity. There is, however, diminishing marginal product over the observed range of caloric intake.

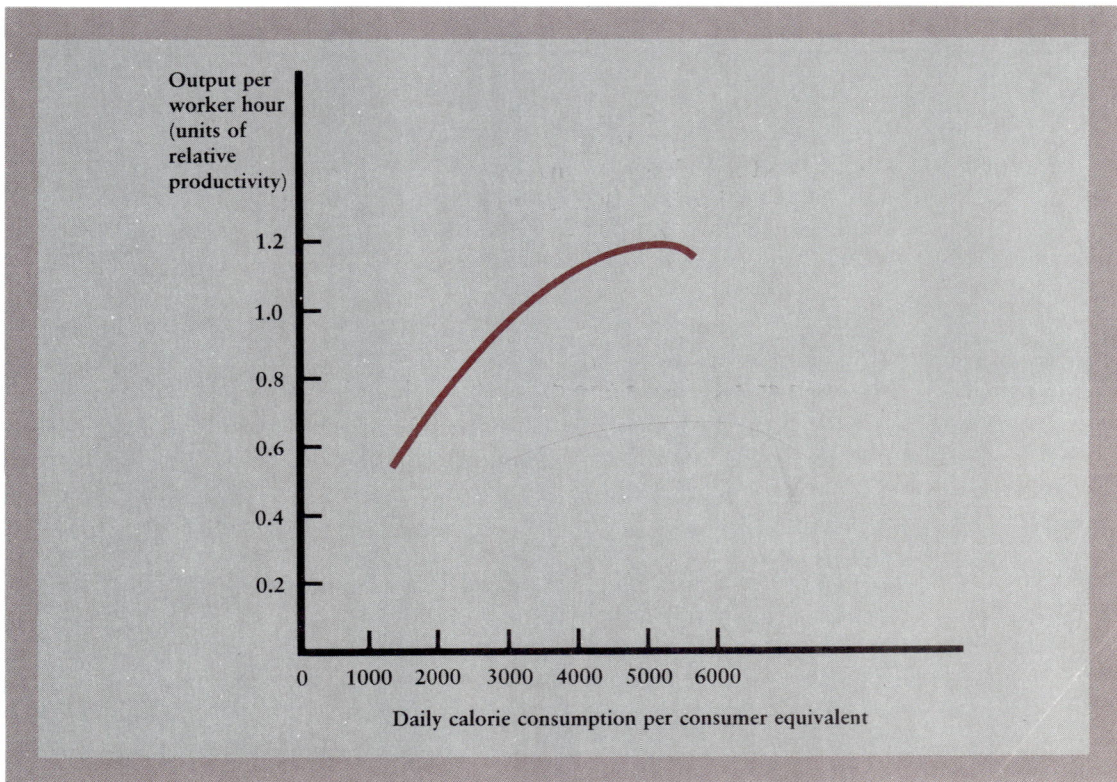

study—daily calorie consumption per person—is on the horizontal axis. The graph shows how caloric intake affects the productivity of one hour of worker effort.

Note that this total-product curve has a positive but declining slope. The declining slope indicates diminishing marginal productivity of caloric consumption per day. Efficiency units reached a peak at 5,200 calories per day. Increases in calories beyond 5,200 had a negative marginal effect on productivity.

To further illustrate the impact of increasing the caloric input per day, Professor Strauss calculated an output elasticity. He defined this elasticity as the percentage increase in efficiency units due to a 1 percent increase in caloric consumption. For example, at the average intake for the group with the lowest one-third consumption of calories (that is, 1,500 calories per day), the output elasticity was 0.49 (that is, a 1 percent increase in caloric intake increased productivity by 0.49 percent). The elasticity decreased steadily at higher caloric levels. At a caloric intake of 4,500 calories per day (that is, the average intake for the one-third highest calorie group), the elasticity was only 0.12. At the peak of the total product curve the elasticity would be zero.

Source: John Strauss, "Does Better Nutrition Raise Farm Productivity?" *Journal of Political Economy* 94, No. 2(1986):297–320. © by the University of Chicago.

It is important to distinguish between average and marginal product. As we will see later on, most economic decisions depend on an understanding of the marginal effects of the proposed action rather than on the average effects. Although we will return to this distinction often, consider the following example.

3-3   I have more important things to do at home

APPLICATION

As we saw earlier, economists have applied production theory to a wide range of issues. Professors Charles R. Link and James G. Mulligan of the University of Delaware looked at the relationship between marginal and average products in the production of learning by elementary-school students in the United States. There continues to be an active debate in this country about the advantages of lengthening the school year and increasing the time per day students spend studying mathematics and reading.

Production theory predicts that eventually there will be diminishing returns from increasing the amount of math and reading instruction. These researchers analyzed data from a random sample of approximately 118,000 United States elementary-school students during the 1977–78 school year to determine the extent of these diminishing returns.

They assumed that higher test scores on standardized mathematics and reading tests depended on a number of important inputs: the time spent studying the subject, the participation of parents, and the efforts and abilities of teachers. Although, on the average, students who received more instruction improved their test scores more than those receiving less instruction, the marginal product of an additional hour of math or reading instruction per day was essentially zero at the levels of instruction they were receiving.

By specifying the relationship between achievement and the inputs as a production function, the researchers were able to provide a structure for analyzing a large amount of educational data. Once organized this way, the data led to an interesting conclusion. While lengthening the school year may lead to improvements in educational attainment, lengthening the school day does not seem to be worth the effort.

Source: Charles R. Link and James G. Mulligan, "The Merits of a Longer School Day." *Economics of Education Review 5*, No. 4 (1986):373–81.

The Long Run

Now let us consider what Harry could do in the long run when both of his inputs are variable. He could choose combinations of the two inputs (workers and tree-trimming machines) to produce his tree-trimming jobs. Let us describe the choices available to him, and in the next chapter we will determine exactly which combination he should select.

Input Substitution

Harry may have greater flexibility in adjusting his labor force, but given enough time he could alter the number of machines as well. Assume that Harry rents his machines. According to his rental contract, he can adjust the hours of machine time continuously, as long as he reserves them a few days in advance.

Since most of his work is scheduled well enough in advance to plan the use of machines and workers with certainty, he wants to see what options he has concerning the mix of machines and laborers to be used on his upcoming jobs. If both inputs can be adjusted continuously, he can construct a curve, called an isoquant, that will show all combinations of laborers and machines for a specific number of tree-trimming jobs. An **isoquant** stands for "equal" (*iso-*) "quantity" (*quant*) and represents all combinations of two inputs that can produce the same level of output without any waste of inputs.

Figure 3-4 (p. 70) represents the substitution possibilities for the Verte Tree Company. Assume that the tree company plans to trim ten large trees per day using three laborers per day (X). Since Harry does not wish to use any more tree-trimming machines (Y) than necessary, he determines that his production process requires at least seven machines. These machines can run unattended for periods of time, due to advances in technology incorporated into the machines by the manufacturer.

The company could use fewer machines, but it would need more laborers to complete the same number of jobs per day. For example, at X equal to 4, it would take only five units of Y to produce ten units of Q. We could continue this experiment for all values of X until we had created a set of X and Y combinations that were capable of completing ten jobs per day. We could repeat the same exercise for every possible quantity. For example, to trim fourteen trees, Harry would need more machines (Y) for every number of laborers (X) than he would need for an output of ten trees.

Figure 3-4 shows several additional isoquants representing the minimum combinations of X and Y necessary to produce each of these output levels.

FIGURE 3-4 ▪ **Isoquants.** Harry can trim ten trees per day using various combinations of laborers and machines. For example, he can use four laborers and five machines, or, if he wants to produce the same output level with only three laborers, he must increase the number of machines to seven. These are only two of an infinite number of possible combinations.

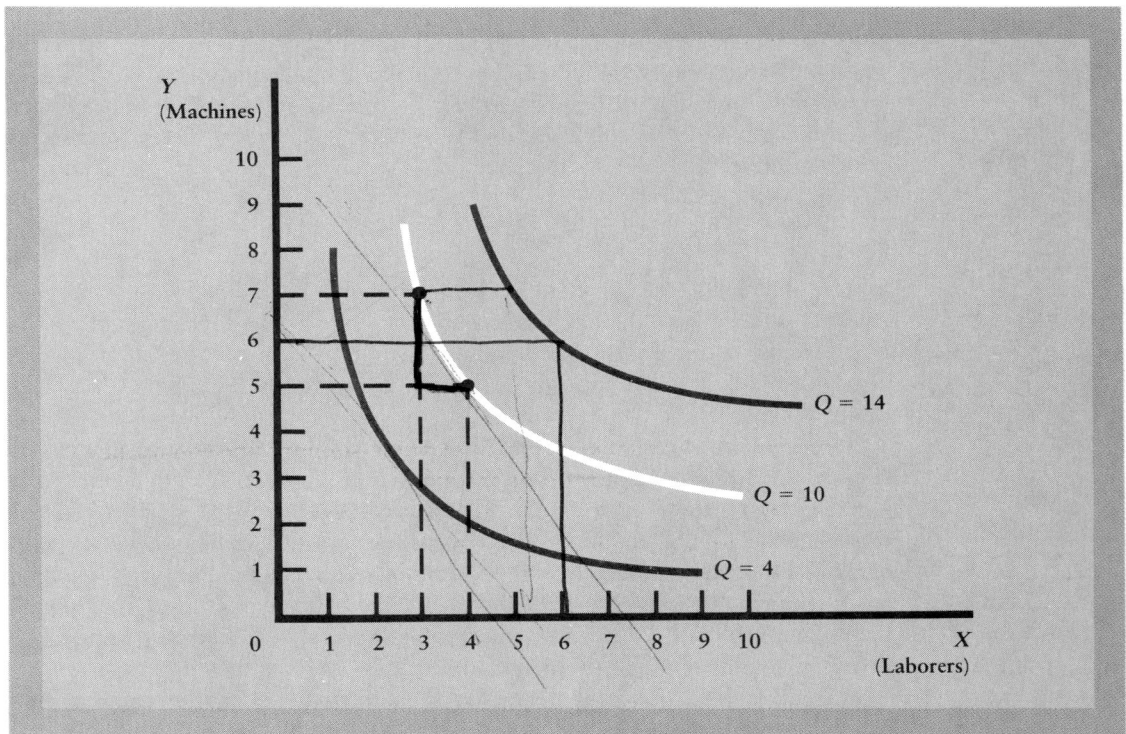

By plotting all of the isoquants, we can fully characterize the production process for an output produced by two inputs.

We could generalize this approach by using mathematical equations to represent choices among more than two inputs. Graphical examples beyond the two-input case are not feasible. Although most production processes employ more than two inputs, it is often useful to isolate the substitution possibilities between pairs of inputs.

Marginal Rate of Technical Substitution

The slope of an isoquant shows how much one input can be reduced by the one-unit increase of the second input, while holding output constant. Economists use a special term to represent the absolute value of the slope of the isoquant: **marginal rate of technical substitution** (MRTS), which we denote as

$$MRTS = \left| \frac{\Delta Y}{\Delta X} \right|$$

The marginal rate of technical substitution is directly related to the marginal products of both of the inputs. The isoquant in Figure 3-5 (p. 72) has a negative slope: that is, $\Delta Y / \Delta X$ is negative. As one moves along an isoquant, the quantity of output stays constant while the amounts of X and Y move in opposite directions. For example, when X increases and Y is held constant, output increases by $\Delta X \times \Delta Q / \Delta X$. The effect of a change in Y on Q is $\Delta Y \times \Delta Q / \Delta Y$. The sum of the two effects on Q must offset one another to be on the same isoquant.

Since, by definition, $\Delta Q / \Delta X$ is the marginal product of X and $\Delta Q / \Delta Y$ is the marginal product of Y,

$$(\Delta X \times MP_X) + (\Delta Y \times MP_Y) = 0$$

and

$$-\frac{\Delta Y}{\Delta X} = \frac{MP_X}{MP_Y}.$$

Since the absolute value of the slope of an isoquant line equals the MRTS, MRTS will also equal the ratio of the marginal products: MP_X / MP_Y.

If the firm is operating where the marginal products of X and Y decrease with increases in the quantities of both X and Y, the isoquants will be strictly convex to the origin. A curve is **strictly convex** if a line drawn tangent to the curve lies to the lower left of the curve. Notice that if X increases and Y decreases, the numerator decreases due to the decrease in MP_X. The denominator increases due to the movement back up the marginal-product curve for Y with a decrease in Y. The total effect is a decrease in the value of the marginal rate of technical substitution (MRTS). At the limit of very large X,

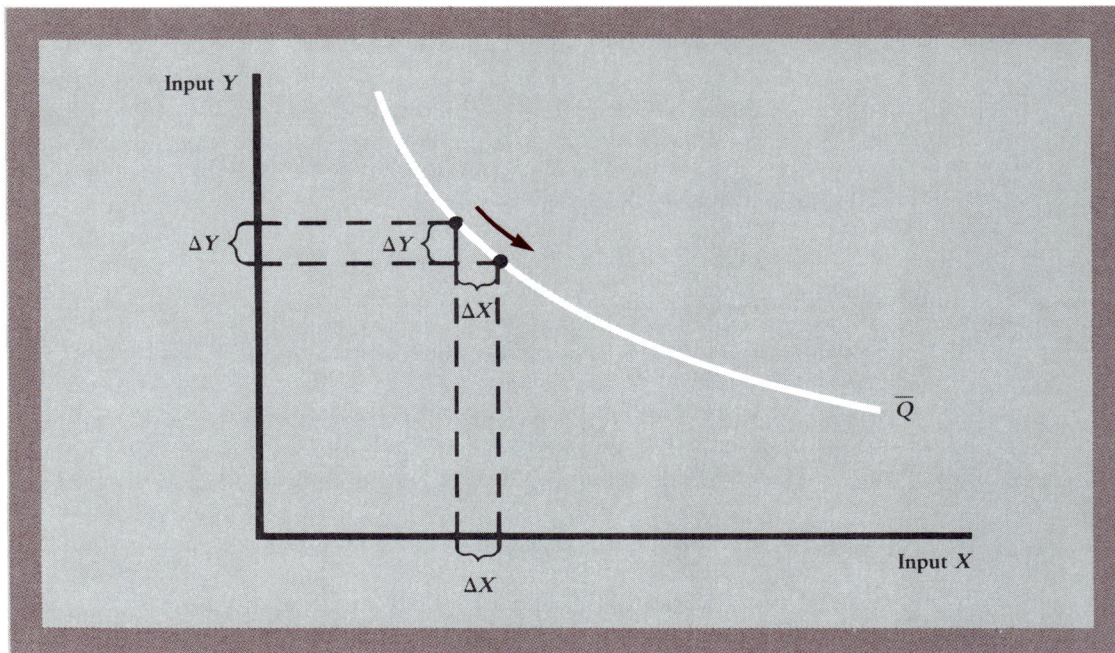

FIGURE 3-5 ▪ Movement along an isoquant. By moving along an isoquant we must offset the effects of a change in one input by a change in the amount of the second input. In this case, we are decreasing the amount of input Y and increasing the amount of input X as we move to the lower right along the isoquant.

MRTS approaches zero. The opposite occurs with an increase in Y and a corresponding decrease in X. In the limit the *MRTS* approaches infinity. For example, the isoquants in Figure 3-4 were strictly convex.

3-4 | **A technical solution**

APPLICATION Mikhail Gorbachev became the leader of the Soviet Union in 1985 and soon began announcing his intent to improve the economic condition of the Soviet Union. Despite skepticism in the West, Mr. Gorbachev indicated that he wanted to reduce the arms race and focus his country's resources on economic growth. Starting in 1987 Mr. Gorbachev responded to American suggestions for mutually verifiable reductions in nuclear arms. The discussions concentrated on the reductions of short- and long-range nuclear weapons based in Europe.

At the time of these discussions, the Western Allies were very concerned about the predominant strength of Eastern Bloc conventional forces. Western analysts estimated that in 1987 the Soviet Union had substantially more troops and tanks within striking distance of Western Europe than the Western Allies had within striking distance of the Soviet Union. The United States and its allies have a relatively larger proportion of nuclear weapons and other advanced technology (for example, aircraft with nuclear capability) than of conventional troops, and have relied on this. The Soviet Union has relied more heavily on conventional troops. The isoquants shown in Figure 3-6 will help us understand this choice.

In the figure we have a simplified picture of both alliances' choices. The vertical axis measures the number of conventional forces, while the horizontal axis measures the number of nuclear weapons. While there is variety within each category, the graphical approach simplifies the story to avoid our having to use a more mathematical expression to analyze the alliances' choices among more than two inputs.

Although we will have to wait until the next chapter for a procedure for determining each alliance's preferred mix of inputs, the isoquants indicate that there are more ways of achieving the same objective (such as national defense). For example, if NATO chooses to maintain the same level of defense,

FIGURE 3-6 ▪ **National defense.** Countries and alliances produce national defense with a variety of inputs. The plan to reduce nuclear weapons will lower the overall level of national defense, unless the countries substitute more conventional forces to offset the reduction in nuclear weapons. The slope of the isoquants depends on the technical relationship between these inputs. According to some observers, a reduction in nuclear weapons would require sizable increases in conventional forces to assure the same level of national defense. This argument suggests that the isoquants may be steeply sloped.

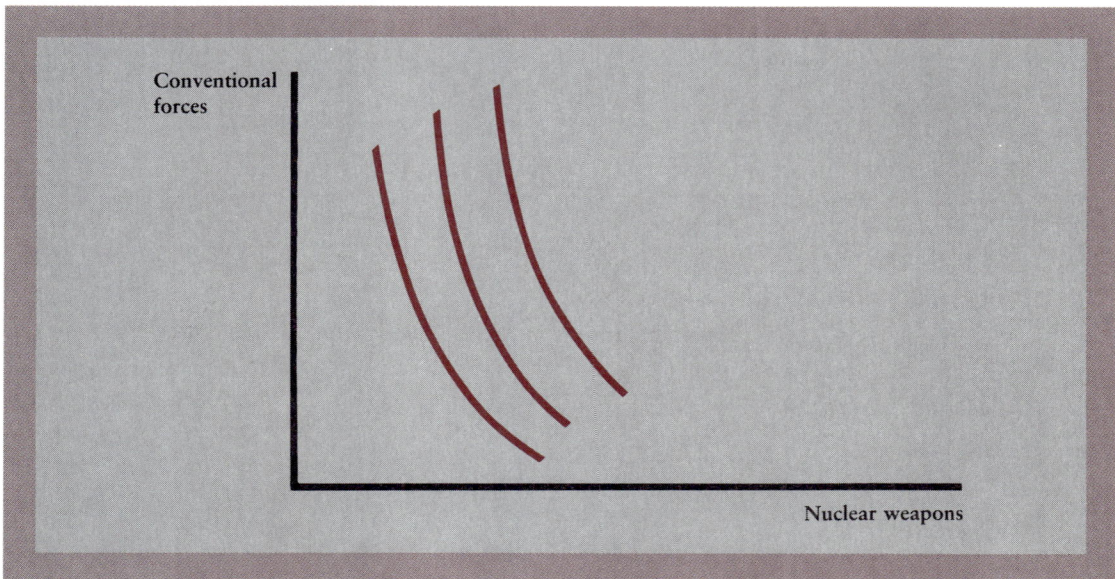

it must increase its level of conventional forces to replace the loss of nuclear weapons. The marginal rate of technical substitution indicates the tradeoff between nuclear and conventional forces at each point on a given isoquant. Most people hope that both alliances will find a way of moving to an isoquant closer to the origin.

Perfect Substitutes and Complements

Not all isoquants look like those in Figures 3-4 and 3-5. If they are straight lines, the slope is the same at all X, Y combinations and the two goods are

FIGURE 3-7 ▪ **Perfect substitutes and perfect complements.** If two goods are perfect substitutes, the slope of the isoquants is constant and the isoquants are straight lines at every input combination. If two goods are perfect complements, there are no substitution possibilities, and the firm must always use inputs in the same proportion, such as four wheel rims for every car body.

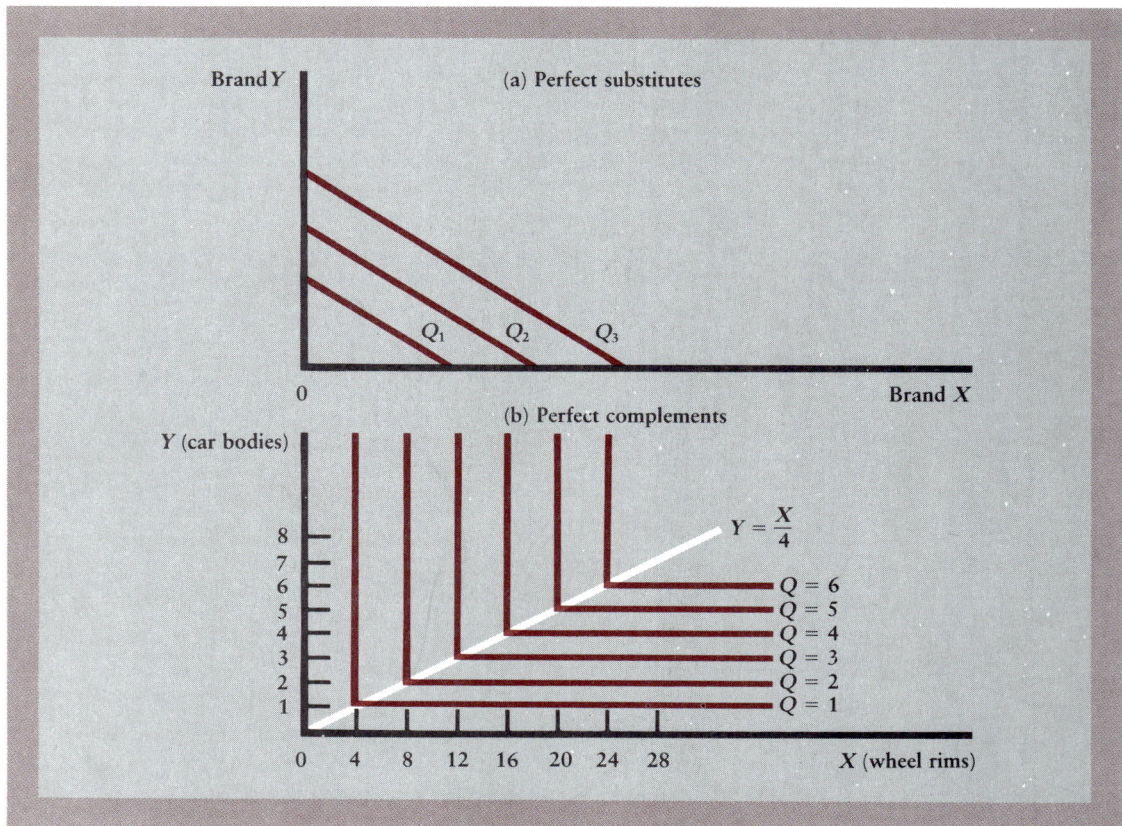

perfect substitutes. Figure 3-7(a) shows some straight-line isoquants. For example, a transportation company might consider two brands of gasoline, X and Y, to be perfect substitutes, as long as they have the same octane ratings.

Figure 3-7(b) shows some perfect complements—in this case, wheel rims and car bodies. Two goods are **perfect complements** if a firm uses the inputs in the same proportion regardless of the output level. For example, most automobiles require four wheel rims and one car body to perform properly. The addition of fewer than four more wheel rims will make the marginal product of an additional car body equal to zero. The isoquants will be L-shaped, with the kink in the isoquant occurring where the proportion of wheel rims to car bodies is 4 to 1.

Returns to Scale

Harry has often wondered whether his company was too small to operate efficiently. By carefully determining the nature of his isoquants, he can answer this question. He can use the information about his production process to determine the impact on his output rate of a proportional increase in both of his inputs.

The effect that the proportionate increase in all inputs has on output is a question of returns to scale. A firm changes its scale when it increases all of its inputs in fixed proportion. Average output per unit of inputs can do one of three things: increase, decrease, or stay the same. For example, if by doubling inputs, the firm doubles its output rate, it experiences **constant return to scale.** If output were to more than double as inputs doubled, there would be **increasing returns to scale.** If output were to less than double, there would be **decreasing returns to scale.**

Figure 3-8 (p. 76) shows the effect of a doubling of both the number of laborers and the number of machines from X_1 and Y_1 to X_2 and Y_2. Since both laborers and machines are twice as large as before, the two inputs are in the same proportion. In Figure 3-8 doubling the inputs has resulted in more than a doubling of output from 28 to 60. This is an example of increasing returns to scale. By doubling both inputs again to X_3 and Y_3, the firm experiences an output rate of 100, which is less than twice the output rate of 60. This is an example of decreasing returns to scale over this input range.

Figure 3-8 shows that returns to scale can vary over the range of possible outputs of the firm. In Chapter 4 we will extend the returns to scale concept to a company's cost function. We will add information about input prices to that of the production function and see how different scales of operation impact a firm's costs.

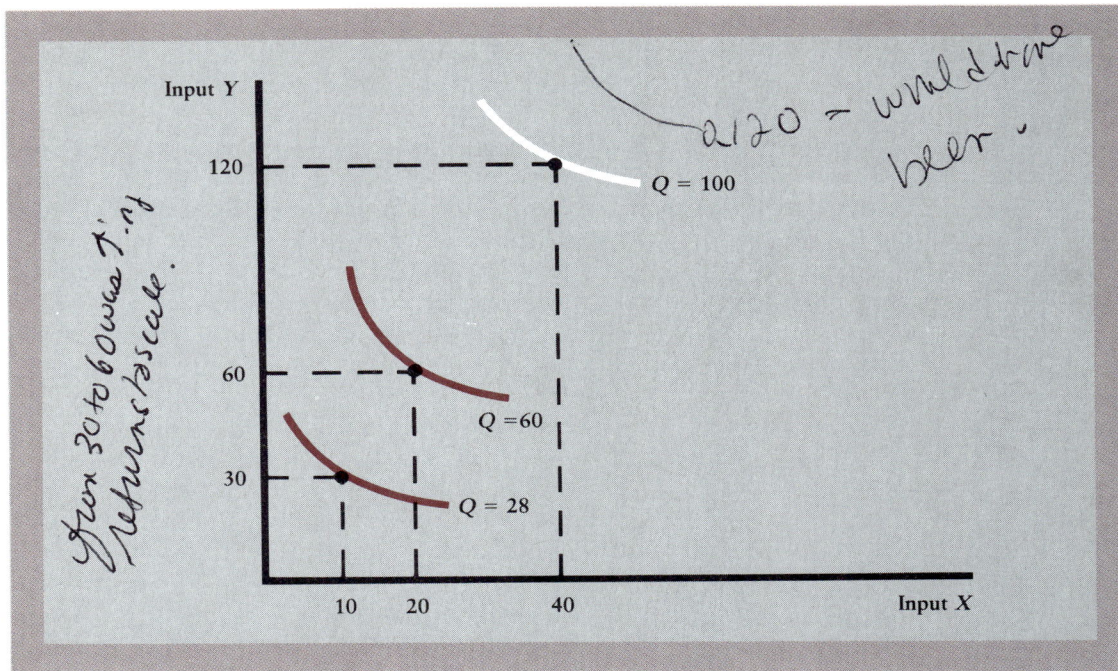

Handwritten notes on figure:
- *a 1 20 → wandd trive beer.*
- *from 30 to 60 wua T. ng returns to scale.*

FIGURE 3-8 ▪ **Scale economies.** Doubling the level of Y from 30 to 60 and the level of X from 10 to 20 more than doubles output. In this case there are increasing returns to scale. A further doubling of the level of the inputs increases output from 60 to 100. Since output is not doubled, there are decreasing returns to scale over this range of output.

3-1	Returns to scale

NUMERICAL
EXAMPLE

We can determine the extent of scale economies directly from the equation of the production function. For example, assume that the production function is as follows:

$$Q = 10X^{0.4}Y^{0.6}.$$

By the definition of scale economies we must increase both X and Y in the same proportion and observe whether output increases in the same proportion. Assume that we multiply both X and Y by a constant, a. For example, let a equal 2. We will use the constant, a, to show the generality of the result.

Assume that we start with X_1 and Y_1 units of the inputs. These inputs produce Q_1 units of the output; that is,

$$Q_1 = 10X_1^{0.4}Y_1^{0.6}.$$

Now multiply the inputs by the constant, a, so that X_2 equals aX_1 and Y_2

equals aY_1. We now have

$$Q_2 = 10X_2^{0.4}Y_2^{0.6}$$

Substitute for both X_2 and Y_2.

$$Q_2 = 10(aX_1)^{0.4}(aY_1)^{0.6}$$
$$= 10a^{0.4}X_1^{0.4}a^{0.6}Y_1^{0.6}$$
$$= 10a^{(0.4+0.6)}X_1^{0.4}Y_1^{0.6}$$
$$= a^{1.0}(10X_1^{0.4}Y_1^{0.6})$$
$$= aQ_1.$$

Since Q_2 equals aQ_1, this production function exhibits constant returns to scale. By multiplying the inputs by a, we increase output in the same proportion. This result depends critically on the exponents of the inputs in the production function. In this case the two exponents, 0.4 and 0.6, added up to 1. If the sum of the exponents had been a number less than 1, there would have been decreasing returns to scale (that is, output would have increased by less than a times the original output). If the sum of the exponents had been greater than 1, there would have been increasing returns to scale.

| 3-5 | **The answer lies in the exponents** |

APPLICATION Economists call the type of production function used in Numerical Example 3-1 a Cobb-Douglas production function. This mathematical representation appeared first in an article written by an economist, P.H. Douglas, and a statistician, C.W. Cobb. Professor Douglas used the specification several times in his efforts to measure the productivity of the U.S. economy.

Economists have used the Cobb-Douglas production function to estimate production relationships for firms, industries, and even countries. Professor Douglas's first work appeared in 1924. He studied the substitution possibilities and scale economies of the U.S. economy.

He assumed the economy used two inputs: capital and labor. Using data from each year between 1899 and 1922, he determined that the exponent for the capital variable was 0.75 and the exponent for the labor variable was 0.25. Since the two exponents added up to 1, he concluded that there were constant returns to scale for the economy. Since Professor Douglas's initial study, most work on a national level has led to the same conclusion concerning economies of scale.

Professor J.R. Maroney used industry data from 1967 for a similar study. He found only three U.S. industries that did not exhibit constant returns to scale: food and beverages, furniture, and chemicals. Even these three industries had exponents that added up to approximately 1: 1.07 for food and beverages, 1.11 for furniture, and 1.09 for chemicals.

More recently, researchers using more general specifications of industry production functions and more sophisticated statistical techniques have continued to find a general absence of further scale economies at current output levels. Firms appear to exhaust scale economies at lower levels of output than their current levels of production.

Sources: Paul H. Douglas, *The Theory of Wages*. New York: The Macmillan Company (1924). J.R. Maroney, "Cobb-Douglas Production Functions and Returns to Scale." *Western Economic Journal* 6, No. 1 (December 1967):39–51.

A Change in Technology

The production function represents the maximum output possible from a set of inputs, given the current level of technology. As time passes new ideas lead to technical change. Technical change causes the isoquants to change their location on the graph. For example, if technological change led to a doubling of output at all possible input levels, the isoquants would look the same as before, but the output level for each combination of inputs would be twice as much as before.

Changes in technology also usually favor the use of one input over another. In this case the marginal rate of technical substitution (that is, the absolute value of the slope of the isoquant) changes. If we have information on the nature of the production function, we can plot the isoquants at different time periods to measure the impact of the change in technology. As we will see in the next chapter, a change in technology that alters the marginal rate of technical substitution causes a firm to alter the proportion of the inputs it uses.

3-6 **Shifty curves**

APPLICATION Professors Finn Førsund and Lennert Hjalmarsson measured the impact of technological change on the isoquants for the Swedish cement industry. As a part of their study, they constructed isoquants showing the substitution possibilities in the short run between labor and fuel for each year from 1955 to 1979 for one large Swedish cement company.

The cement company produced cement in kilns. The capacity output of each kiln differed depending on the technology inherent to the kiln. The kilns also differed in the amounts of fuel and labor they required to produce cement. Since there were different types of kilns at the company, the company could vary the amounts of labor and energy used by using different kilns. There would continue to be substitution possibilities as long as the company was not operating at its capacity.

In the next chapter we will see how a firm chooses a combination of inputs based on the prices of each input. In the cement example, the choice of kiln depended on the cost of labor relative to fuel. For example, if fuel had become less expensive relative to labor, the firm would have moved its output to kilns that used fuel more intensively.

At this point we will only focus on the isoquants and how they changed over the course of the study. Figure 3-9 shows an example of isoquants with the amount of fuel per ton of cement on the vertical axis and the number of worker-hours per ton of cement on the horizontal axis. There are two sets of isoquants for three different output levels. Although each set belongs on its own separate graph, superimposing both sets of isoquants on the same graph shows how a change in technology can affect the isoquants. In this case the change in technology has both moved the isoquants closer to the origin and made the slope of the isoquants steeper (that is, the *MRTS* is a large number).

Figure 3-9 illustrates the main findings of the study on Swedish cement. Over time the introduction of new kilns with new technology caused the

FIGURE 3-9 ■ **A change in technology.** This figure shows two sets of isoquants from two different years (1955 and 1979). The change in technology between 1955 and 1979 resulted in greater output given the same amount of the inputs (that is, a movement of the isoquants closer to the origin) and change in the slope of the isoquants.

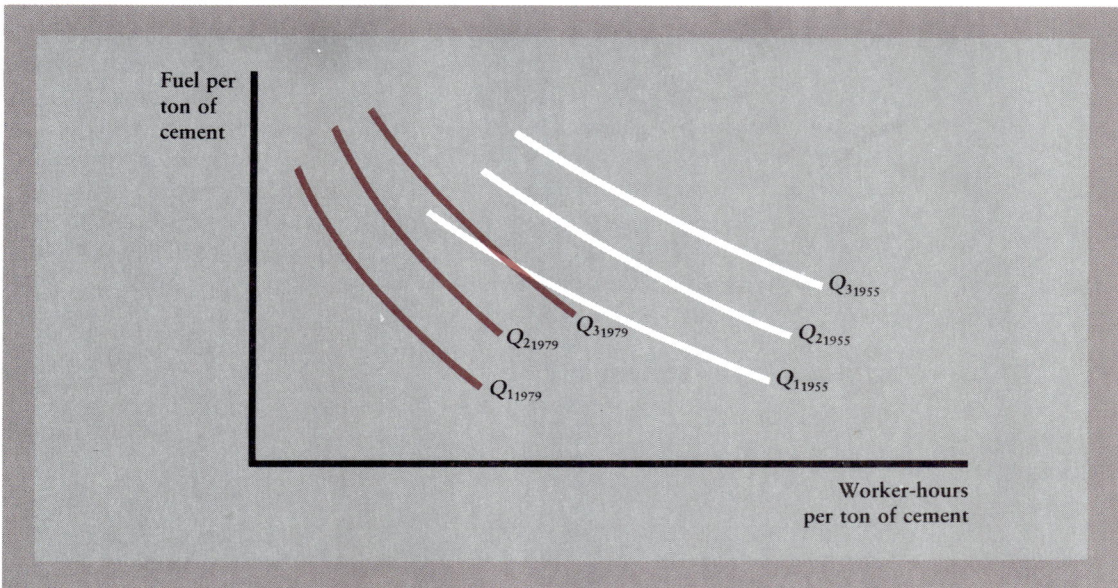

isoquants to become steeper (that is, there was a decrease in the possibility for substitution between fuel and labor). There was also a substantial productivity gain. Recall that we would show a change in technology by renumbering the isoquants to reflect a higher output for the same level of inputs. In this case the average amount of labor required to produce the same amount of cement decreased by 67 percent from 1955 to 1979. The amount of energy required dropped by 17 percent.

This change in productivity showed that new kilns used fuel more intensively than labor while lowering the amount of both inputs needed to produce the same level of output. The Swedish cement company's production function changed in two ways. First, there was an overall increase in productivity. Second, the slope of the isoquants changed, favoring a higher proportional use of energy than labor at each output level.

Source: Finn R. Førsund and Lennart Hjalmarsson, "Technical Progress and Structural Change in the Swedish Cement Industry 1955–1979." *Econometrica* 51, No. 5 (September 1983):1449–67. The Econometric Society.

Summary

In this chapter we considered the relationship between a firm's output and its inputs. We used a production function to represent this relationship. The production function is a useful way of characterizing a production relationship. It can help analyze issues such as the choice of a farmer's diet, the length of the school day, and the mix of fuel and labor in the production of cement.

We stressed the importance of determining the marginal effect on output of a one-unit change in the input. This will be a useful concept to remember when we consider the firm's costs. Most economic decisions depend on the marginal effects of those decisions. Unfortunately, many people concentrate on the average effects. It is essential to understand the difference between marginal and average effects.

We concluded the chapter with a discussion of scale economies and technological change. We looked at both concepts in relation to isoquants. Next, we will expand both concepts to include the effect of scale and technology on input prices. In Chapter 4 we will add the price of each input to the information on the firm's production function. With input prices and the production function we will be able to derive all of the firm's cost curves. The shape of these cost curves will depend directly on the shape of the product curves derived in this chapter.

Important Terms

Production Function (p. 58)

Marginal Product (p. 62)

Inflection Point (p. 63)

Total-Product Curve (p. 64)

Marginal-Product Curve (p. 64)

Average Product (pp. 65–66)

Average-Product Curve (p. 66)

Isoquant (p. 69)

Marginal Rate of Technical Substitution (p. 71)

Strictly Convex (p. 71)   Constant Return to Scale (p. 75)
Perfect Substitutes (p. 75)   Increasing Returns to Scale (p. 75)
Perfect Complements (p. 75)   Decreasing Returns to Scale (p. 75)

Selected References

Douglas, Paul H. "Are There Laws of Production?" *American Economic Review* 38 (March 1948):1–41.

Gold, Bela. "Changing Perspectives on Size, Scale, and Returns: An Interpretive Survey." *Journal of Economic Literature* 19 (March 1981):5–33.

Johnston, J. "An Economic Study of the Production Decision." *Quarterly Journal of Economics* 75 (1961):234–61.

Kendrick, John W. and Vaccara, Beatrice N., eds. *New Developments in Productivity Measurement and Analysis.* Chicago: University of Chicago Press (1980).

Link, Charles R. and Mulligan, James G. "The Merits of a Longer School Day." *Economics of Education Review* 5, No. 4 (1986):373–81.

Rees, Albert. "Improving Productivity Measurement." *American Economic Review* 70 (May 1980):340–42.

Rosenzweig, Mark R. and Schultz, T. Paul. "Estimating a Household Production Function: Heterogeneity, the Demand for Health Inputs, and Their Effects on Birth Weight." *Journal of Political Economy* 91, No. 5 (1983):723–46.

Strauss, John. "Does Better Nutrition Raise Farm Productivity?" *Journal of Political Economy* 94, No. 2 (1986):297–320.

Problems

1. (a) If the production function for Grow's Low-Cal Cheeseburgers is

$$Q = 10Y + 2X,$$

calculate the marginal rate of substitution (*MRTS*) when Y equals 25 and X equals 50.

(b) At what output levels would the *MRTS* be greater than it is at Y equal to 25 and X equal to 50?

2. The production function for the Sal Fussen Sport Shoe, Q, is

$$Q = X^{0.5}Y^{0.5}.$$

(a) What is the average productivity of X and Y?

(b) Graph the average product of Y curve when X equals 100.

(c) For this particular function, one can show that $MP_x = \frac{1}{2}AP_x$ and $MP_y = \frac{1}{2}AP_y$. What is the *MRTS* when X is 100 and Q is 10?

(d) Sketch the $Q = 10$ isoquant.

3. The Kowshmare Mattress Company makes its mattresses by using combinations of two inputs. Assume that the firm operates to the right side of the inflection point on the total-product curves of both inputs. Show what the isoquants must look like for this production process. Be sure to prove why they look the way they do.

4. Determine the returns to scale for the following production functions.

(a) $Q = 25X^{0.5}Y^{0.5}$

(b) $Q = 10X^{0.4}Y^{0.4}$

(c) $Q = 15X^{0.4}Y^{0.7}$

(d) $Q = 12X^{0.3}Y^{0.3}Z^{0.4}$

5. Assume that the production process for Madame Sybell's Palm-Reading Service depends on only one input: Madame Sybell's time. The total number of successful palm readings per day is given by the following production function:

$$Q = 100H^{0.5},$$

where Q is the number of successful palm readings per day and H is the number of hours Madame Sybell spends reading palms each day.

(a) Graph the relationship between Q and H.

(b) What is Madame Sybell's average productivity? Graph the average-product curve.

(c) The marginal-product curve equals

$$MP = 50H^{-0.5}.$$

Graph this relationship and compare the marginal-product curve to the average-product curve.

(d) How would you justify the shapes of these curves?

6. Assume that two inputs are perfect complements. What do the marginal-product curves look like for these two inputs?

Answer questions 7–12 with true, false, or uncertain.

7. As long as the marginal product is constant for at least one of two inputs, the isoquants will be straight lines.

8. If the slope of the total-product curve is always positive, but decreases as the amount of the input increases, the marginal-product curve will lie below the average-product curve.

9. The marginal-product curve crosses the average-product curve at the maximum point on the marginal-product curve.

10. If the total-product curve does not reach a maximum point, marginal product will not be a decreasing function of the input.

11. A production function can exhibit both diminishing marginal product and constant returns to scale.

12. If two goods are perfect substitutes, the $MRTS$ equals 1.

COST THEORY

4

DERIVED DEMAND FOR AN INPUT

PROFIT-MAXIMIZING OUTPUT

BREAKEVEN ANALYSIS
Determination of the Breakeven Output
The Choice of Technology

The main objective of this chapter is the derivation of cost functions that are consistent with the production theory of the preceding chapter. The cost of producing a firm's output depends on input prices and the specification of the production function. Before deriving a specific cost function, we must be aware of several cost concepts.

As we will see, the definition of cost depends on the specific problem that the firm must confront. We will start by relating each of the cost concepts to the problems faced by the new owner of a firm. As a simplified example, we will consider each concept as it relates to an entrepreneur's decision to start a restaurant.

Once we have determined the relevant cost, we will construct a cost function. The cost function relates cost to output, based on the assumption that the firm uses its inputs in an economically efficient manner. We will then use information about the production function and input prices to determine the cost-minimizing choice of inputs for each level of output.

Cost minimization is not the only objective of the firm, however. The firm must also determine its output level. The profit-maximizing firm must solve both of these problems by not only minimizing the cost of producing any given output level, but also choosing the output level that maximizes its profits.

We can approach the profit-maximization decision from two equivalent directions: We can determine either the input levels that maximize profits or the output level that maximizes profits. Since the production function relates inputs to outputs, once we know either the input levels or the output level we know the other as well.

At the end of the chapter we will discuss a simple technique often used by managers to determine the amount of a product or service that they must produce to cover their costs. This technique is also very useful when a firm is trying to decide whether to adopt a new machine or a technologically advanced production process.

The Relevant Cost

Consider the following dilemma of a potential restaurant owner, Blanche Mayzone. Blanche is a manager at a popular continental-style restaurant located in a downtown area. She must decide whether to open a restaurant of her own or continue working as a manager.

Blanche makes $20,000 per year as manager. She owns two houses, one of which she recently inherited. She plans to convert one house into her restaurant. She has been renting the house to a family at the market rate of $500 per month. Since Blanche likes her job as manager, she has decided not to open a restaurant unless she can improve her financial status. In order to make a sound judgment, she estimates all of the costs of opening a restaurant and all of the benefits she expects from the new venture.

Blanche expects to pay $80,000 to renovate the house. Most of the money would go toward outfitting the kitchen. She also expects to spend $5,000 in legal fees fighting a law suit to be brought by her tenants for illegal eviction. Although her lawyer has assured her that the eviction case has no merit, she knows she will still have to absorb these costs. She also has to pay $3,000 to hire a consulting firm to work out the necessary rezoning procedures.

Since she is unsure of the success of the venture, Blanche chooses to rent all of her tables, chairs, linens, china, and other equipment from a restaurant supply company for $15,000 per year. She never was particularly adept at cooking, so she will also have to hire a chef in addition to a serving and reception staff. The expected total labor cost will be $70,000 per year.

She expects to rely primarily on the Forbye Produce and Meat Company for her ingredients, which will cost approximately $200,000 annually. Liquor will cost $100,000 per year. Yearly costs of utilities and other supplies will be approximately $30,000. Given all of these costs, Blanche has to make a number of important decisions, not the least of which is whether or not to open the restaurant.

Opportunity Costs

Before starting a new business, an entrepreneur such as Blanche Mayzone must consider one of the most important cost concepts: opportunity costs.

> **Opportunity cost** is the value forgone by the entrepreneur by not taking advantage of the next best alternative.

In Blanche's case there are several opportunity costs, such as her job as a restaurant manager, the rent from the house to be converted into her restaurant, and the lost return on any financial investment she might make in her restaurant. The cost of the first two forgone opportunities would be $20,000 per year in salary and $500 per month in rental income, for a total of $26,000 the first year.

Assuming she had no better alternative for employment and was charging the market rate for rent, this amount of money would be the value of her next best alternative. We must know the expected interest rate in order to determine an opportunity cost for any money that she invests. For example, assuming a 10 percent interest rate, the $8,000 fees and the $80,000 renovation charges would mean $8,800 in forgone interest each year.

A new owner is not the only one who must be aware of opportunity costs. For example, there are opportunity costs associated with every decision made by governments on behalf of their people. John Walker has observed how costly some government decisions can be, as we see in the following application.

4-1

Your choice: A day at the Redwood National Park or a cruise around the world

APPLICATION

In his article, Mr. Walker argues that governments make major political decisions while sometimes ignoring the opportunity costs of these decisions to taxpayers. More specifically, he feels that the United States Government should have made a better estimate of the opportunity cost of creating the Redwood National Park in 1968 and expanding it in 1977.

Mr. Walker recounts testimony made by Barney Dowdle before Congress in 1977. According to this testimony, the park recorded 4,770 visitor-days in 1976. The trees were worth $5,000 to $10,000 each, while the land and timber were worth $40,000 per acre, based on the future revenue expected from harvesting. Using this and other information, Mr. Dowdle determined that the cost per visitor-day was $5,000 per year in 1976.

According to Mr. Walker, there is no evidence of any additional benefit to society beyond the value to park visitors. Claims that the park would halt erosion in the area were not substantiated, according to the author. The expansion in 1977 added over 15,000 acres to the park. Mr. Walker notes that the park was not near capacity before the expansion, so that the additional cost raised the opportunity cost to nearly $15,000 per visitor-day per year—just enough for a world cruise.

Mr. Walker's analysis does ignore one other potentially important factor. Even though some citizens might never visit the park, they may be willing to pay a small sum of money each year to guarantee that the park will be there if they ever decide to visit it. For example, if the opportunity cost was $15,000 per visitor-day and there were 4,770 visitor-days per year, the opportunity cost of the park would have been $71,550,000 per year. If 100,000,000 U.S. citizens (less than half the U.S. population at the time) expressed an interest in paying to guarantee the survival of the park, the cost would only be 71.55 cents per paying citizen per year.

Source: John L. Walker, "Tall Trees, People, and Politics: The Opportunity Cost of the Redwood National Park." *Contemporary Policy Issues* (March 1984):22–29.

Explicit Versus Implicit Costs

Primarily for tax purposes and to be accountable to shareholders, accountants have developed rules for recording a company's costs. They prefer to treat some costs differently than others. For example, Blanche will have well-documented annual costs, as shown here:

Forebye's Produce and Meats	$200,000
Liquor	100,000
Labor	70,000
Utilities and miscellaneous expenses	30,000
Equipment rental	15,000
Total	$415,000

These are examples of explicit costs, which are easily justifiable by canceled checks or receipts. On the other hand, it is more difficult to quantify noncash implicit costs. **Explicit costs** are easily documented, out-of-pocket expenses, such as wages and cost of materials and utilities. **Implicit costs** are the costs of inputs supplied by the owners of the firm. The implicit costs will be the opportunity costs of these inputs to the owners.

In Blanche's case, the opportunity cost of her time and the use of her house will be implicit costs, since she will not pay herself for the use of these inputs. She will use the salary that she forgoes by leaving her job as the true cost of her time when deciding to open the restaurant.

The rental value of unique properties, such as the house used for the restaurant, is also difficult to discover without market-determined values of similar properties. In addition, Blanche will lose the annual return on the money paid for renovation and for legal and consulting fees. She will know the opportunity cost of this money at the time she pays the fees, but its value will fluctuate over time, depending on interest rates. Interest rates also depend on the amount of risk an individual is willing to take when investing. If Blanche has to borrow the money to finance the renovations and fees, the interest charges will be explicit costs.

Business Versus Economic Costs

Business costs include all explicit, or out-of-pocket, expenses. **Economic costs** include all explicit and all implicit expenses. This distinction is important. Economists are concerned with the reasons for people's behavior. In this case we want to know whether or not Blanche should open a restaurant. If she can cover only her explicit costs, she will be worse off by opening the restaurant. Let's pursue this distinction by introducing economic profits.

Business Versus Economic Profits

Blanche's ultimate objective as a new entrepreneur will be economic profits, which are not the same as business profits. **Business profits** equal the difference between total revenue and total business cost. **Economic profits** equal the difference between total revenue and total economic cost. When company officials discuss their profits, they normally are referring to business profits. To them profits represent revenues in excess of their explicit costs. These profits amount to a return on the assets invested in the company by the company's owners. If Blanche's revenues were $500,000 per year, she would make an annual business profit of

$$\$500,000 - \$415,000 = \$85,000.$$

However, an expected business profit of $85,000 does not provide enough information concerning the decision to open the restaurant. This decision depends on the potential for economic profits. A company that does not make an economic profit would be better off switching to the next best alternative.

Since Blanche would lose approximately $34,800 per year in opportunity costs associated with her job, house, and financial investment, she would need to cover these costs as well as her explicit costs. Thus, her economic profits would be

$$\$500,000 - \$415,000 - \$34,800 = \$50,200.$$

Given that she expects to make economic profits, Blanche should go ahead and open the restaurant.

Sunk Costs

Until now we have implicitly assumed that there is little risk in Blanche's endeavor. In fact, however, opening a restaurant is a risky venture. Most restaurants do not stay in business for long. For example, even if Blanche's restaurant does well for a few years, another restaurant could open nearby and reduce her revenues.

When opening a new business, one must also consider the cost of going out of business. By renting her equipment, Blanche would not face the problem of selling it if she had to leave the business. The money spent on fees to rezone her house for commercial purposes may be recoverable, as long as someone buying the business does not have in mind an alternative location unencumbered with zoning restrictions. The remodeling cost may be recoverable, depending upon the demand for that style of restaurant. If the restaurant has not been successful partly due to its decor, a new owner may place no value on it. If unrecoverable, the original decorating cost would be a sunk cost. The legal fees for evicting the tenants would also be a sunk cost. Sunk costs are nonrecoverable costs.

While sunk costs represent a potential loss that should be considered before opening a new business, they are also important in guiding pricing decisions. For example, if Blanche buys her wine in large orders to save on transportation and handling costs, she might see the value of her inventory fluctuate with the market changes in wine prices, since a considerable amount of time would pass between orders.

For example, in 1983 the United States dollar was worth about eight French francs. By the beginning of 1985 the exchange rate had risen to almost eleven French francs per dollar. If Blanche had been in business in 1983 and had purchased wines whose cost reflected the less favorable exchange rates, she would have seen the value of her inventory drop during the next two years.

Although she may have paid $5 for a bottle of wine in 1983 that she could have purchased in 1985 for $3, she should have considered the cost of the wine in 1985 to be $3 for her pricing decisions. The difference of $2 per bottle represents a sunk cost. We will return to the subject of sunk costs in Chapter 7.

Incremental Costs

Blanche knew that she would likely be asked to sell some of her products on a take-out basis, but she had made no immediate plans to formalize this sideline, preferring instead to consider each order individually. In weighing each of these requests, she needed a clear understanding of her relevant costs.

One night at the restaurant, Blanche met a customer who spent most of her time traveling. She was en route to a surprise visit to her parents' house, which was 150 miles away. She had not visited her parents recently and wanted to do something special for them. After supper at the restaurant, she decided to call other relatives living near her parents to arrange a banquet for the next night in her parents' honor.

The guest offered Blanche a take-it-or-leave-it offer of $25 per four-course take-out meal for twenty people. If Blanche refused the offer, the guest was going to make arrangements with a restaurant closer to her parents' home. Blanche would normally charge $30 per person for such a meal. Her decision should depend on her costs. The relevant costs in this situation are her incremental costs, which are those expenses that are directly related to the number of units sold.

Consider the incremental costs of selling these twenty dinners. If the restaurant were operating at less than full capacity, there would be no need to increase the physical size of the restaurant to meet this order. However, she might have to pay her staff overtime and order additional ingredients, both of which would be included in her incremental costs. The cost of the facilities would not be an incremental cost, since she would absorb that cost whether she took the order or not.

Blanche should also think about whether someone locally might hear about the cut-rate price and demand a similar discount. Since the customer was only passing through and would not likely be in the area again for some time, Blanche could dismiss this potential problem. She would have to add these effects to her incremental costs only to the extent that the sale would force her to lower her prices to other customers.

While Blanche would prefer to charge a higher price for her dinners, the $25 price would probably entice her to make the sale, as long as it exceeded her incremental cost. Anything she made in excess of her incremental cost would go toward covering her fixed costs.

Short-Run Versus Long-Run Costs

It is useful to distinguish between short-run and long-run costs. As business conditions change, companies consider making adjustments in their output levels. How their costs change depends on the time it takes to make the adjustment.

Most of our attention during the rest of the book will be focused on the short-run and long-run decisions that profit-maximizing firms must make. Realistically, there is a middle ground between these two extremes, when a firm can adjust inputs by incurring adjustment costs in addition to the normal price of the input. For example, if Blanche were to run out of veal one night, she could pay extra to have someone from Forbye's Produce and Meats make an unscheduled delivery.

While figuring adjustment costs is not difficult, it does involve a level of mathematics beyond the requirements of this text. Therefore, we will concentrate on short-run and long-run problems, such as the decision to accommodate an increase in the number of customers served at the restaurant. For example, Blanche could stay open later at night, employing her staff for more hours per day. In this case, she would be making a short-run decision, since she would not need to vary all of her inputs.

In the long run, she could increase her volume of business by expanding into another building with a second kitchen. Given enough time, she could consider the lowest-cost means of accommodating a larger clientele. The actual amount of time necessary to adjust all inputs would depend on the specific application. If another house were available to purchase, Blanche would be limited only by the time it would take for renovations. If she had to build a new facility, she might have to wait for a longer period of time.

Long-Run Cost Minimization

Before we can consider profit-maximization behavior on a more general level, we need to discuss the importance of cost minimization. When a firm faces several input options, it must base its decision on a consistent framework. Let's return to the story of Phyllis Steene, Harry Sampson, and the Verte Tree Company.

Due to a general increase in the demand for workers in the area, Harry has had to increase the hourly wage he pays in order to insure that he has enough workers for his tree-trimming jobs. Although he knows that in the short run he can only adjust the number of workers he employs in response to the wage increase, he wants Phyllis to help him decide on a long-run strategy. He wants to know whether he should consider using a higher proportion of tree-trimming machines to workers than he currently uses.

For mathematical simplicity, continue to assume that the company trims its trees using combinations of only two inputs: workers (input X) and machines (input Y). Harry can choose any combination of these two inputs along a given isoquant. While the output level remains constant along an isoquant, the total cost of using these inputs changes. If the number of trees clipped is a function of inputs X and Y, the total cost (TC) of producing any given level of output is

$$TC = P_X X + P_Y Y,$$

where P_X and P_Y are the prices of X and Y, respectively.

Before going much further, let us assume that TC remains constant and that Harry has no control over the price of X and Y The only choice available to him is the number of machines and workers to use. The TC equation then becomes a straight line, which we can rewrite as follows:

$$Y = \frac{TC}{P_Y} - \left(\frac{P_X}{P_Y}\right)X.$$

TC/P_Y is the Y-intercept term, while $-P_X/P_Y$ is the slope. This line is called an **isocost line**, which is a graphical representation of all combinations of two inputs that a firm can purchase for a specific amount of money, given fixed prices for the two inputs. In Harry's case, it represents all combinations of X and Y that he can purchase for a fixed amount of money.

Exactly how many trees Verte Tree Company clips depends on the demand for these jobs, as well as the cost of trimming a tree. Regardless of how many trees are clipped, Harry will want to minimize the cost of trimming each one.

Cost minimization occurs when a firm chooses the least costly input combinations.

GRAPHICAL
EXPLANATION
Figure 4-1 shows several isoquants and isocost lines. Given a specific output, such as twenty trimmed trees per day, the firm chooses the input combination that minimizes the cost of clipping twenty trees. The isocost line shows the cost of the various input combinations. Since the slope of the isocost line is dependent only on the relative price ratio of the two inputs, changes in total cost result in a parallel shift of the isocost line.

Since increases in total cost shift the isocost line to the right, Harry should

FIGURE 4-1 ▪ Long-run cost minimization. The isocost lines cross the Y-axis at a value of Y equal to TC/P_Y and cross the X-axis at a value of X equal to TC/P_X. If the input prices remain constant, a change in total cost will shift the isocost line. At TC_3 the firm is spending too much money to produce twenty units of output, and at TC_1 it is spending too little. At TC_1 the firm cannot purchase enough inputs to produce twenty units of output. At TC_2 the firm can produce twenty units of output by using X^* units of input X, and Y^* units of input Y. At this point the firm maximizes its output for its expenditure of TC_2. Equivalently, it minimizes its cost of producing twenty units of output.

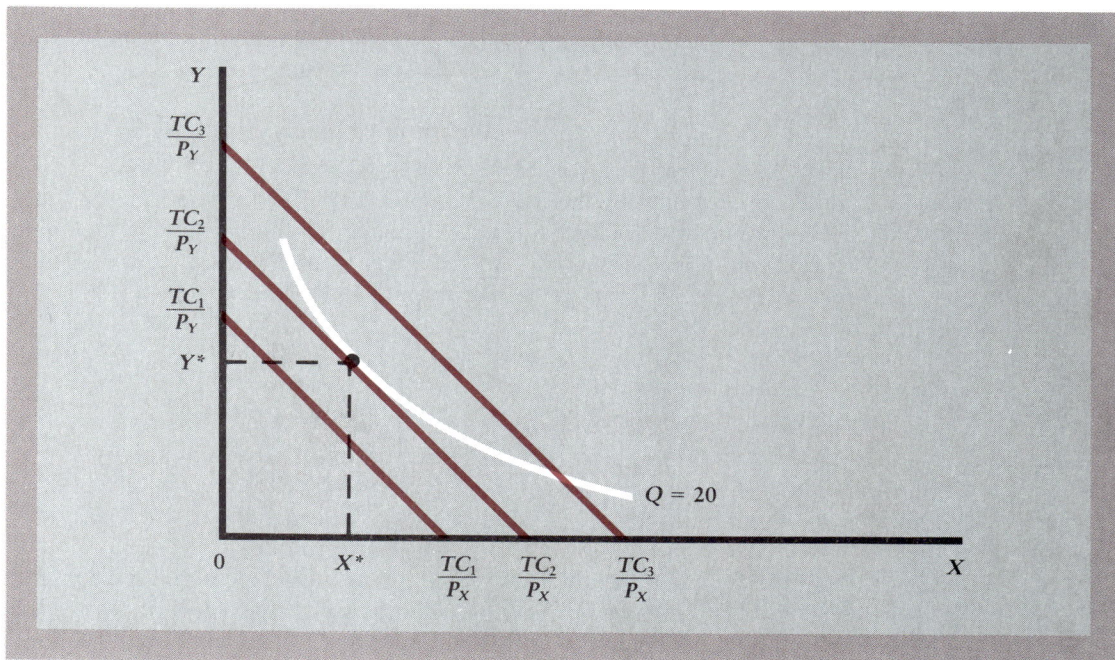

prefer the input combination which has an isocost line passing through it closest to the origin. For Q equal to 20, the input combination (X^*, Y^*) meets this criterion. Any other input combination would have an isocost line passing through it to the right of the curve going through the point (X^*, Y^*).

Since, at (X^*, Y^*), the isocost line is tangent to the isoquant for twenty trees of output, the two lines have the same slope. As noted earlier, Phyllis assumes that Harry has no control over what he pays his workers and what he pays for use of a machine, so the slope of the isocost line, $-P_X/P_Y$, is always the same, regardless of the output level of the firm. Since the slope of the isocost line is $-P_X/P_Y$ and the slope of the isoquant is $-MRTS$, $MRTS$ equals P_X/P_Y at the cost-minimizing input levels.

While cost minimization means that costs are kept to a minimum for a given output level, it also means maximizing output for a given cost. For example, assume that the least costly combination of workers and machines needed to trim twenty trees costs Harry a total of $500 a day. This is the same as saying that if Harry attempted to maximize his output, given $500 to spend, the company could clip no more than twenty trees.

By increasing its expenditures on inputs at current prices, the firm can produce more output. An increase in expenditures shifts the isocost line to the right. By shifting the isocost line to the right, one can locate all of the cost-minimizing input combinations for any number of trees that Harry chooses to trim. Recall that this is a long-run problem, so there is sufficient time to vary all of these inputs without incurring any adjustment costs. By connecting all the tangencies with a curve, Phyllis creates the firm's expansion path. An **expansion path** is a collection of cost-minimizing combinations of inputs corresponding to each possible output level of a firm, given a fixed ratio of the input prices. There is a different expansion path for each input price ratio.

Figure 4-2 (p. 94) shows the expansion path for the Verte Tree Company. As long as the input prices remain in the same ratio, Harry will choose input combinations where the $MRTS$ is the same. The expansion path shows whether the company will increase the amount of one input relative to the second input as output increases. If the expansion path is a straight line such as the one in Figure 4-2, the company will use X and Y in the same proportion at all output levels. If the expansion path is not a straight line, the company will alter the proportion of X and Y at different output levels.

Recall that the $MRTS$, the absolute value of the slope of the isoquant, is equivalent to the ratio of the marginal products of the two inputs. Since the isocost line and the isoquant have the same slope along the expansion path, P_X/P_Y equals MP_X/MP_Y. Rearranging terms yields

$$\frac{MP_X}{P_X} = \frac{MP_Y}{P_Y}.$$ (1)

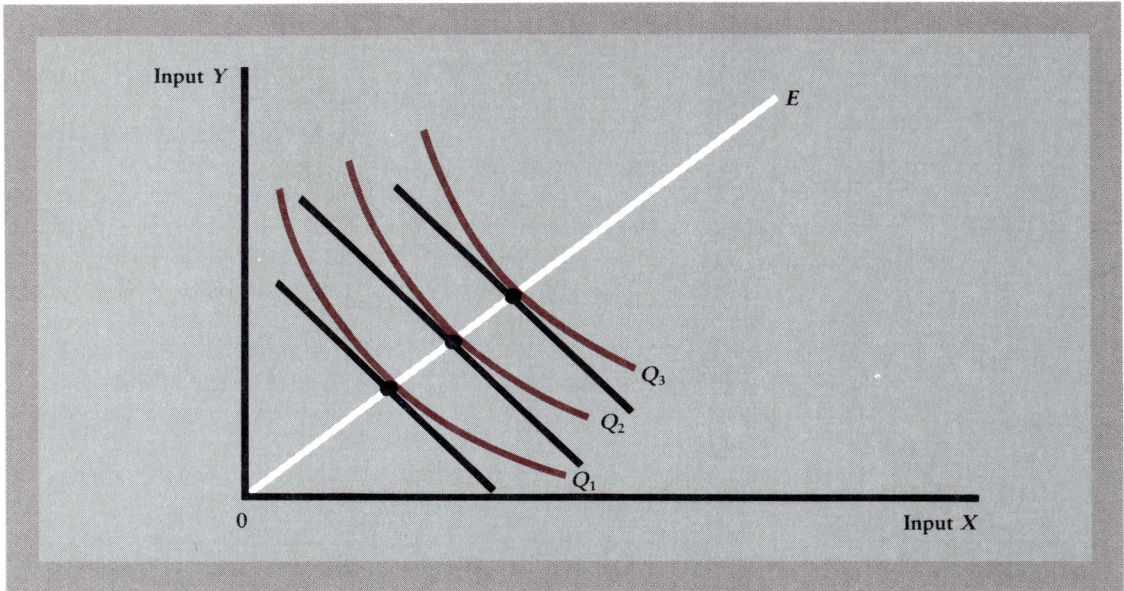

FIGURE 4-2 ▪ Expansion path. By increasing its expenditures, the firm can produce increasing amounts of the output. The expansion path connects all the cost-minimizing input combinations corresponding to the different output levels. The expansion path could be a straight line, as shown, or it could be nonlinear. The slope of the expansion path depends on the technical nature of the production function.

This cost-minimizing condition states that the last dollar spent on a worker must yield the same additional output as the last dollar spent on the machine. For example, if P_X is $1, P_Y is $2, and the marginal product of the last unit of X is 2 units of output, the cost-minimizing firm would be getting 4 units of additional output from the last unit of Y. Otherwise, the firm would not be minimizing cost. For example, if MP_Y were only 3 instead of 4, the firm would be using too much Y and not enough X.

| 4-1 | **Cost-minimization choice of two inputs** |

NUMERICAL
EXAMPLE

Assume that the production function for the Verte Tree Company is as follows:

$$Q = 10X^{0.4}Y^{0.6}.$$

Assume also that the price of X is $2 and the price of Y is $4. Given these prices, we want to know the equation for the firm's expansion path. Once we know this equation, we can determine the optimal combination of X and Y for each output level.

From the previous discussion we know that the firm is on its expansion path when

$$\frac{MP_X}{P_X} = \frac{MP_Y}{P_Y}.$$

The marginal product of X for this production function is[1]

$$MP_X = 10(0.4)X^{-0.6}Y^{0.6}.$$

The marginal product of Y is

$$MP_Y = 10(0.6)X^{0.4}Y^{-0.4}.$$

We can rearrange equation (1) as follows:

$$\frac{MP_X}{MP_Y} = \frac{P_X}{P_Y}.$$

In this case substituting for MP_X and MP_Y gives us

$$\frac{10(0.4)X^{-0.6}Y^{0.6}}{10(0.6)X^{0.4}Y^{-0.4}} = \frac{2}{4}.$$

Rearranging terms, we have

$$\frac{2Y}{3X} = \frac{2}{4}$$

or

$$Y = \frac{3X}{4}.$$

In this case the expansion path is a straight line. Y will always equal three-fourths of the amount of X when the firm minimizes its costs. To determine the exact amounts of X and Y we must know the output level.

4-2	**A legal substitution**

APPLICATION   Schools that train paralegals have promoted their graduates as potential substitutes for lawyers. Given the relative increase in lawyers' salaries in recent years, we would expect that law firms could save money by shifting to a

---

[1] Since the production function is not a linear equation, we cannot determine the equation for marginal product without using calculus. Since the formal derivation of the marginal-product equation for this numerical example is a side issue, we will ignore it and concentrate instead on determining the equation for the expansion path, assuming that we already know the equations for the marginal products of both inputs.

greater reliance on paralegals for background work and paperwork normally done by lawyers.

Professor Robert Feinberg of Pennsylvania State University found some initial evidence that supported this claim. For example, he reported that the number of paralegals increased by 135 percent between 1972 and 1977, while the number of lawyers increased by only 41 percent. The share of law firms' cost due to paralegals almost doubled from 3.7 to 6.7 percent during the same time period. Since the cost share of salaried associate lawyers stayed constant, Professor Feinberg speculated that the paralegal schools' claims may have had some support.

He tested this hypothesis more systematically using data from the 1977 Census of Service Industries for law partnerships in sixty-five large metropolitan areas. He based his statistical test on the isoquant and isocost analysis that we have used in this chapter. He wanted to see whether law firms used more paralegals and fewer lawyers when the relative price of paralegals decreased.

He determined that there was actually little possibility of substitution between attorneys and paralegals. For example, an increase in lawyers' salaries did not lead to a significant increase in the number of paralegals that the typical firm hired. Surprisingly, there was significant substitution among paralegals, legal secretaries, and clerks in response to changes in relative salaries of these employees.

He also noted that other researchers have found that New York City law firms use their paralegals in many different ways. For the most part, the New York firms use their paralegals for clerical work, despite the claims of the paralegal schools. This evidence suggests that if you want to do interesting legal work, you might have to go to law school after all.

Source: Robert M. Feinberg, "Paralegals and Substitution Among Labor Inputs in the Law Firm." *The Journal of Industrial Economics* XXXIII (September 1984):99–104.

Short-Run Cost Curves

If Harry orders tree-triming machines, he may not have enough time to change the number of machines ordered in response to an unexpected change in the demand for his services. If the number of machines available to him is fixed, he will have to rely on extra workers to meet an increase in demand. This becomes a short-run problem for Harry.

In the short run, Harry is unable to vary all inputs freely. At the end of this chapter we will derive the curve expressing Harry's derived demand for the variable input: workers. But first, let's consider what Harry's costs look like if he chooses to adjust his output level in the short run.

GRAPHICAL
EXPLANATION

Figure 4-3 shows the possible input combinations for producing output given that the number of machines, Y, is fixed at level Y_1. If Y is fixed at Y_1, Harry can increase his company's production only by increasing the number of workers, X. The cost of producing different levels of Q depends on the price of X and the amount of X needed to produce Q. For example, the cost of producing Q_2 in the short run is $P_X X_2 + P_Y Y_1$. Since Harry has already purchased the machines, $P_Y Y_1$ is fixed, regardless of whether he uses all the machines or not. At Q_3, the short-run cost is $P_X X_3 + P_Y Y_1$. The change in total cost is due to the change in the cost associated with input X.

The graph of the total-product curve (Figure 3-2) appears again here as Figure 4-4 (p. 98). Note that output is on the vertical axis and that X, the variable input, is on the horizontal axis. We can derive the total-product curve

FIGURE 4-3 ▪ **Short-run cost minimization.** In the short run, at least one input is fixed. In this case Y is fixed at Y_1. The cost-minimizing level of X will be the smallest amount of X needed to produce the desired level of Q. For example, the firm would choose X_1 to product Q_1, X_2 to product Q_2, and X_3 to product Q_3.

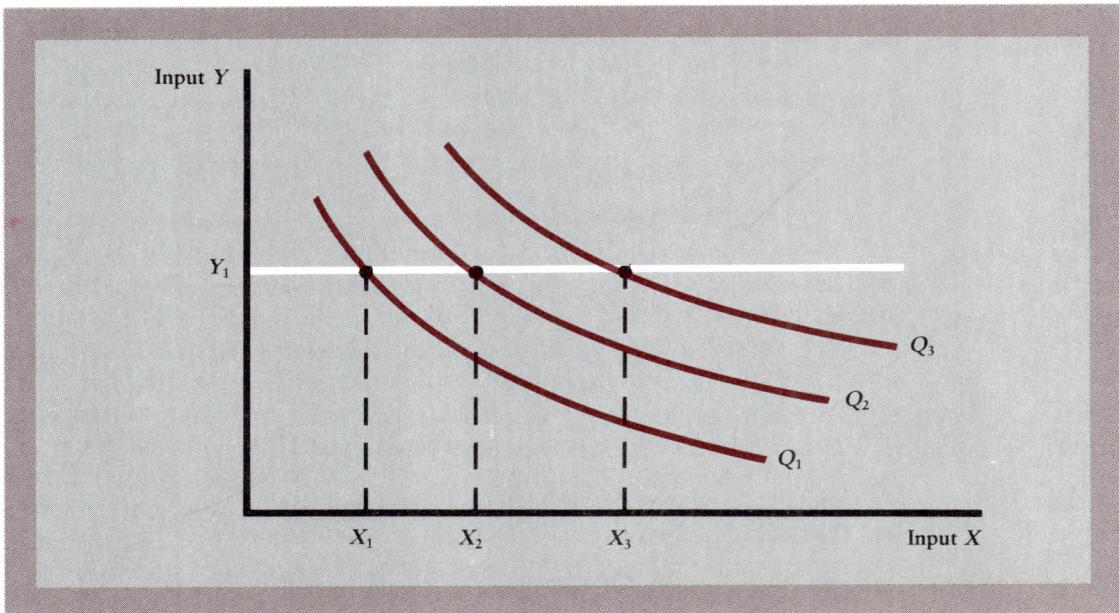

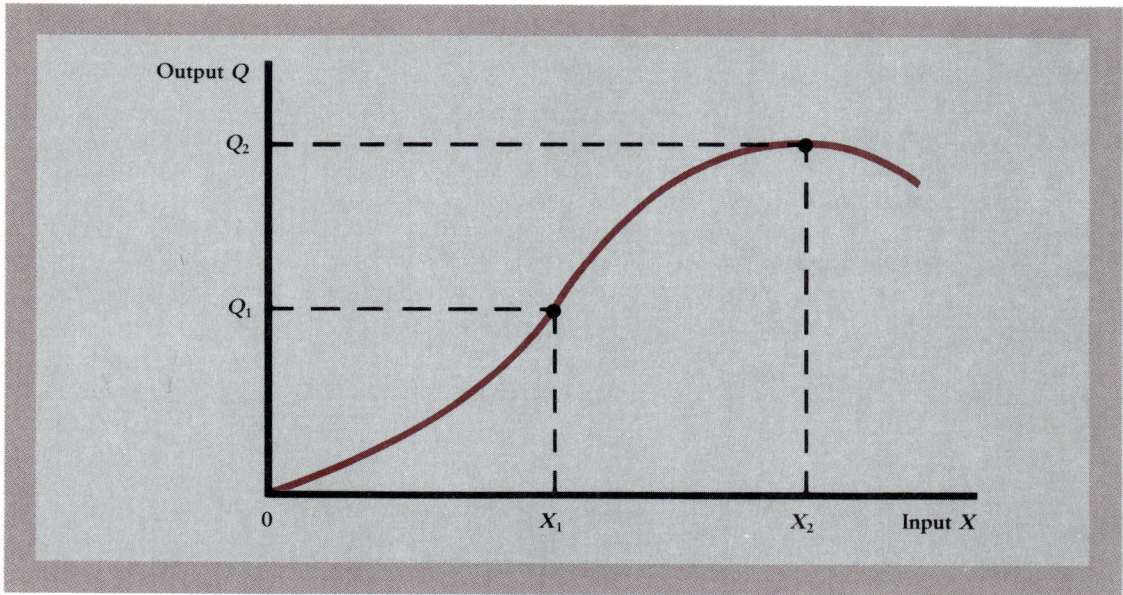

FIGURE 4-4 ▪ **Total-product curve.** This is the same curve as shown in the top portion of Figure 3-2. The curve shows the continuous relationship between the amount of output and the amount of input.

from the isoquant graph, Figure 4-3, by comparing the output generated at each value of X.

Assume that the prices of the two inputs are constant. If we multiply the values of X along the horizontal axis in Figure 4-4 by the constant price of X, the values on the horizontal axis become $P_X X$. The picture remains the same, but all the numbers on the horizontal axis are now P_X times greater than before.

By multiplying X by P_X, we have converted the number of workers, X, into total variable cost (TVC). The **total variable cost** is the total amount of money spent on inputs that the firm can vary during the short run as a function of the output of the firm. In this case there is only one variable input: workers, denoted by X. We now have TVC on the horizontal axis, while output is measured on the vertical axis. If we change Figure 4-4 so that total variable cost is on the vertical axis and quantity is on the horizontal axis, we create a graph like the one in Figure 4-5.

The relationship between Figures 4-4 and 4-5 is important because Harry must remember that the curve that relates cost to output depends on both the wages he pays his workers and the production function that converts the number of workers hired to the number of trees trimmed per day.

Figure 4-5 shows how cost varies due to changes in output. Since Harry cannot change the number of machines in the short run, his machine costs cannot vary. These are fixed costs. **Fixed costs** are committed payments for inputs that cannot be varied in the short run.

For Harry, fixed costs equal $P_Y Y_1$. Since fixed costs do not vary with changes in output in the short run, the total-fixed-cost curve (TFC) is a horizontal line. The **total-fixed-cost curve** is a graphical representation of the relationship between fixed cost and output. Figure 4-5 shows both fixed cost and variable cost together.

Figure 4-5 also shows the total-cost curve (TC). The **total-cost curve** represents the sum of fixed cost and variable cost for each output level. Since the fixed costs are constant, the total-cost curve and the total-variable-cost curve differ only by the constant fixed cost.

The top portion of Figure 4-6 (p. 100) reproduces the curves shown in Figure 4-5. The lower portion of Figure 4-6 shows several other short-run curves that one can derive from the curves in the upper portion. These curves

FIGURE 4-5 ▪ **Short-run cost curves.** The shape of the total-variable-cost curve is consistent with the shape of the total-product curve in Figure 4-4. At low levels of output any increase in output increases cost, but at a decreasing rate. At some point (Q_1) the slope of the variable-cost curve starts to increase. This point corresponds to the inflection point in Figure 4-4, because to the right of Q_1 there is diminishing marginal product of the variable input. The total-cost curve is the sum of the total-variable-cost curve and the total-fixed-cost curve.

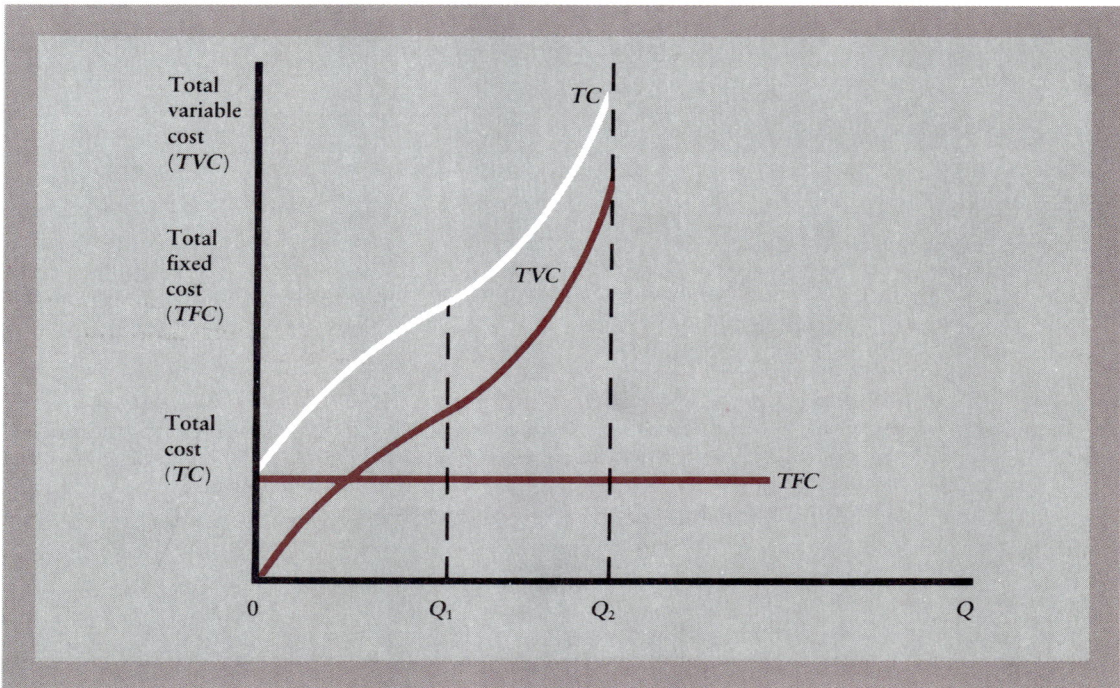

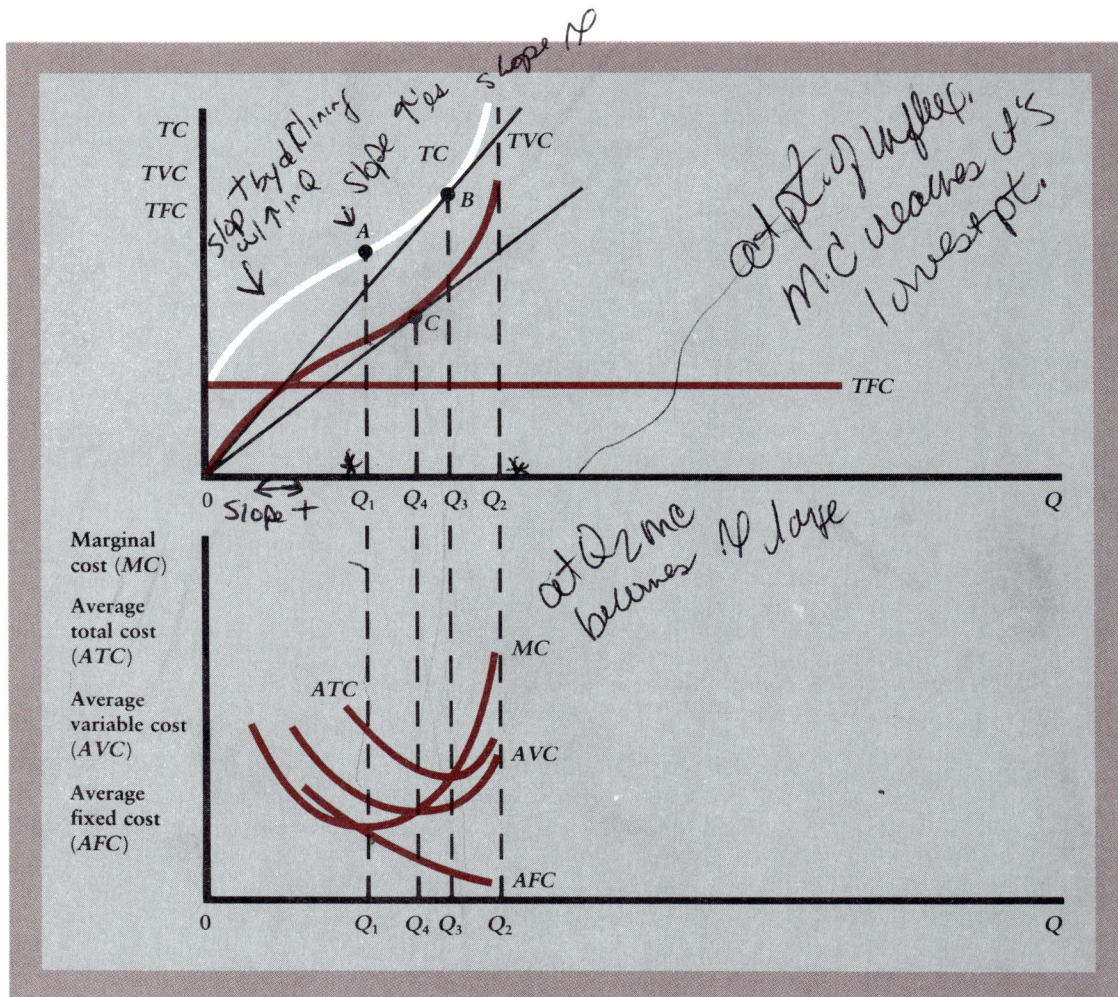

FIGURE 4-6 ▪ **Derivation of short-run marginal, average-variable, average-total, and average-fixed cost curves.** The shape of the curves in the lower graph are consistent with those in the upper graph. Since marginal cost equals the slope of the total-cost and total-variable-cost curves, marginal cost will reach its lowest value at the inflection point (Q_1) of the total-cost and total-variable-cost curves. The marginal-cost curve will cross the average-total-cost curve at the minimum point on the average-total-cost curve (Q_3). At Q_3 a line drawn to the total-cost curve will have the same slope as the total-cost curve. The marginal-cost curve will cross the average-variable-cost curve at the minimum point of the average-variable-cost curve.

represent marginal cost (*MC*), average total cost (*ATC*), average variable cost (*AVC*), and average fixed cost (*AFC*). **Marginal cost** is the change in total cost divided by the change in output, or

$$MC = \frac{\Delta TC}{\Delta Q}.$$

▶ ————— **Average total cost** equals total cost divided by output, or

$$ATC = \frac{TC}{Q}.$$

▶ ————— **Average variable cost** equals total variable cost divided by output, or

$$AVC = \frac{TVC}{Q}.$$

▶ ————— **Average fixed cost** is total fixed cost divided by output, or

$$AFC = \frac{TFC}{Q}.$$

4-3   **Derivation of the marginal- and average-cost curves**

GRAPHICAL Since marginal cost shows how total cost changes with a one-unit change in
EXPLANATION output, marginal cost is also the slope of the total-cost curve. There are two important benchmarks for the slope of the total-cost curve: Q_1 and Q_2. Between an output of zero and Q_1, the slope is positive but declining with increases in Q. Since, at Q_1, the slope starts to increase, Q_1 is the inflection point of the total-cost curve. The slope continues to increase until Q_2, where the slope is infinity.

The lower portion of Figure 4-6 shows that at Q_1, the inflection point of the total-cost curve, the marginal-cost curve reaches its lowest point. At Q_2, marginal cost becomes infinitely large. Notice that these two points correspond to the inflection point and the maximum-output point in Figure 4-4.

Since total fixed cost does not vary in the short run, average fixed cost must decline with increases in output. Given that Harry has already paid for the machines, the more trees he trims the lower the machine cost per tree.

We can derive his average total cost from the total-cost curve by noticing that a line drawn from the origin to the total-cost curve has a slope equal to average total cost at the point where the line crosses the total-cost curve. This is the same technique we used in the last chapter to derive the average-product curve for the Verte Tree Company.

For example, at Q_1, average total cost is TC_1/Q_1 by definition. A straight line drawn from the origin through point *A* has a slope equal to TC_1/Q_1. As one moves along the total-cost curve toward point *B*, the slope of a line drawn from the origin through the total-cost curve becomes flatter. At point B the line is at its flattest level. As Q increases, the line becomes steeper.

Since the line drawn from the origin has a slope equal to average total cost, average total cost must be at its minimum value at Q_3, which corresponds to point B on the curve. Note that one can represent the slope of the total-cost curve (that is, marginal cost) by the slope of a line drawn tangent to the curve. Notice that at B both a line drawn tangent to the curve and a line drawn to B from the origin have the same slope. At B, average total cost not only reaches its minimum point, but it also equals marginal cost.

You could derive average variable cost in the same manner by observing how the slope of a line drawn from the origin to the total-variable-cost curve changes with changes in Q. Since the only costs changing in the short run are variable costs, the slope of the total-variable-cost curve must also be equal to marginal cost. Another way of seeing this is to note that the slope of the total-fixed-cost curve is zero.

Marginal cost and average variable cost are equal at output Q_4, because a line from the origin to point C has the same slope as a line tangent to the total-variable-cost curve at point C. Since average variable cost equals marginal cost, average variable cost is at its minimum value.

| 4-3 | Derivation of short-run average-total-cost curve |

NUMERICAL EXAMPLE

A firm has the following production function:

$$Q = X^{0.5}Y^{0.5}.$$

Assume that Y equals 16 and that we are unable to adjust the amount of input Y in the short run. We know that the price of X is \$2 and the price of Y is \$1. From this information we can derive an equation for the short-run average-total-cost curve.

Since Y equals 16, the short-run production function is now

$$Q = X^{0.5}(16)^{0.5}$$
$$= X^{0.5}(4)$$
$$= 4X^{0.5}.$$

Total cost in this case is

$$TC = TFC + TVC$$
$$= P_Y Y + P_X X$$
$$= 16 + 2X.$$

By definition, a total-cost function must be a function of Q. Since we now have the production function as a function of the one variable, X, we can replace the X in the cost function in terms of Q as follows.

We know that $Q = 4X^{0.5}$. By squaring both sides of the equation and dividing by 16, X must equal $Q^2/16$. Replacing X in the TC equation we get

$$TC = 16 + 2X$$

$$= 16 + 2\left(\frac{Q^2}{16}\right)$$

$$= 16 + \frac{Q^2}{8}.$$

Since average total cost equals TC/Q,

$$ATC = \frac{TC}{Q}$$

$$= \frac{TFC}{Q} + \frac{TVC}{Q}$$

$$= \frac{16}{Q} + \frac{Q^2}{8Q}$$

$$= \frac{16}{Q} + \frac{Q}{8}.$$

For example, when Q is 8, average total cost is

$$ATC = \frac{16}{Q} + \frac{Q}{8}$$

$$= \frac{16}{8} + \frac{8}{8}$$

$$= 3.$$

ATC can be separated into its two components, AFC and AVC.[2] Since the cost of the fixed input, Y, is \$16, AFC is $16/Q$. AVC is the other term, $Q/8$. Note that a graph of AFC would look like the AFC curve in Figure 4-6, since we are dividing the constant 16 by Q. AVC would be a straight line in this case, with a slope of 1/8. Together they would form an ATC curve that would have a negative slope at small values of Q, and a positive slope at higher values of Q eventually.

---

[2] Since the total-cost curve is a nonlinear function of Q, we could determine the marginal-cost equation by taking the derivative of total cost with respect to a change in output: dTC/dQ. In this case, marginal cost is $MC = Q/4$.

APPLICATION

In Application 2-2 we found that the majority of British people prefer cremation to burial. Professor Martin Knapp measured the average variable cost of providing cremation services to the British public. Local authorities run the crematoria in Great Britain, which numbered 168 in 1974–75. Professor Knapp collected data on the operating costs of the crematoria and calculated the average variable cost at different output levels.

He found that there was a statistically significant, but fairly small, downward slope for the curve over the range of output for which he had data. He was unable to determine whether the average-variable-cost curve would be upward sloping at greater output levels.

Since there was a possibility that the service was not the same at all locations, he controlled for quality differences due to options such as organ music, recorded music, the presence of a minister, and a specially arranged scattering of the ashes following the procedure. All of these added to the cost of a standard cremation.

Source: Martin Knapp, "Economies of Scale in Local Public Services: The Case of British Crematoria." *Applied Economics* 14 (1982):447–53.

Long-Run Cost Curves

We will now turn to long-run cost curves, which can be derived using two different techniques. First of all, since we determined that Harry's expansion path looked like the one in Figure 4-2, we know how many workers and machines he should use at every output level.

Once we know his input prices, we can calculate the long-run cost of each output level,

$$TC = P_X X + P_Y Y.$$

▶ ———— **Long-run marginal cost** (*LRMC*) is the change in total cost divided by the change in output, or the change in long-run total cost resulting from a one-unit change in output. In notation, this is

$$LRMC = \frac{\Delta LRTC}{\Delta Q}.$$

▶ ———— **Long-run average total cost** (*LRATC*) is the ratio of long-run total costs to output, or

$$LRATC = \frac{LRTC}{Q}.$$

Since, by definition, there are no fixed costs in the long run, there is no average-fixed-cost curve, and the average-variable-cost curve is the same as the average-total-cost curve.

By following a second approach, Harry could derive the long-run average-total-cost curve from its corresponding short-run average-total-cost curves. Figure 4-7 shows several short-run average-total-cost curves with the corresponding long-run average-total-cost curve.

Since he wants to minimize the cost of producing any specific level of output, Harry should choose the amount of Y (the fixed input in the short run) that lowers the long-run average total cost of producing each amount of Q. Once he chooses an amount of Y, he must operate on the corresponding short-run cost curve in the short run.

By choosing the cost-minimizing amounts of X and Y at each output level, Harry would choose the lowest-cost, short-run average-total-cost curve. Thus, at Q_1, he would choose Y_1 as opposed to another value of Y. If output were to be Q_2, Y_2 machines would be the choice. Following this procedure for all output levels, we can create a long-run average-total-cost curve which envelops all of the short-run average-total-cost curves from below.

FIGURE 4-7 ■ **Long-run average-total-cost curve.** The long-run average-total-cost curve envelops (that is, encloses from below) all of the short-run average-total-cost curves. Each of the average-total-cost curves touches the long-run average-total-cost curve at one point.

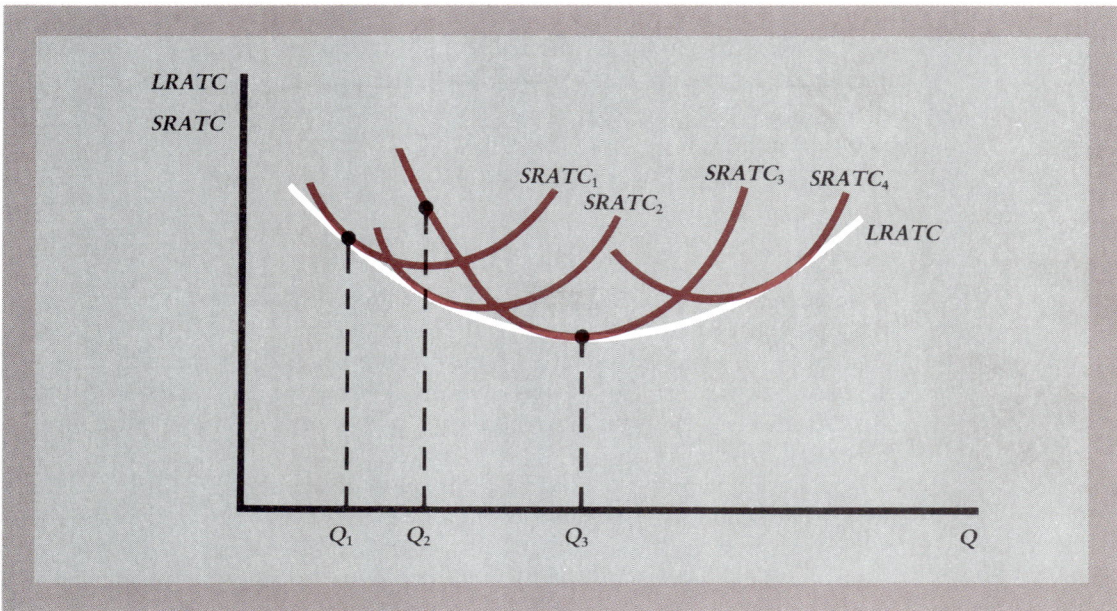

Scale Economies

In Chapter 3 we considered the effects of proportionate increases in all inputs on the firm's output. This was shown on a graph of the firm's isoquants. We will now extend this concept to the firm's long-run average-total-cost curve. The shape of the long-run average-total-cost curve will describe the nature of scale economies in the firm's production process. There are **economies of scale** (or **increasing returns to scale**) when the firm's average total cost decreases as output increases. When average total cost increases with increases in the output rate, or scale, there are **diseconomies of scale** (or **decreasing returns to scale**). With no change in average total cost, there are **constant returns to scale**.

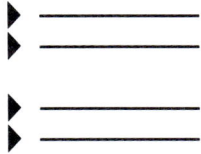

In Figure 4-7 average total cost decreases with increases in Q up to Q_3. To the right of Q_3 average total cost increases. As a result, there are increasing returns to scale up to Q_3 and decreasing returns to scale to the right of Q_3. If there were constant returns to scale at all output levels, the average-total-cost curve would be a horizontal line. In Chapter 16 we will see how to estimate scale economies using production data.

A firm can achieve scale economies by taking advantage of higher output per unit of input due to the nature of its production function. Some production processes allow workers to specialize and use their specific talents more fully rather than force them to master a large number of tasks. Such specialization was a main factor in Henry Ford's success with the assembly line approach to mass production. The assembly line process is suited to the production of large quantities of standard products.

A firm can also experience scale economies by becoming large enough to dictate lower prices for its inputs. These lower input prices may be due to economies passed on from suppliers experiencing economies in delivery or other transactions, or they may result from the market power of the large buyer.

Technological Change

Some economists argue that the cost advantages that some large firms have in a market are due to technological change and not to scale economies. In Chapter 3 we assumed that the nature of the production function does not change when the firm expands its operation. However, most empirical studies show that unless the technology changes, firms do not gain any advantage by increasing in size.

Figure 4-8 shows the effect of a change in technology on the firm's long-run cost function. A change in technology causes the long-run average-total-cost curve to shift downward at some output levels. In Figure 4-8 the long-run average-total-cost curve shifts downward at all output levels.

For any given state of technology, there is a range of output within which

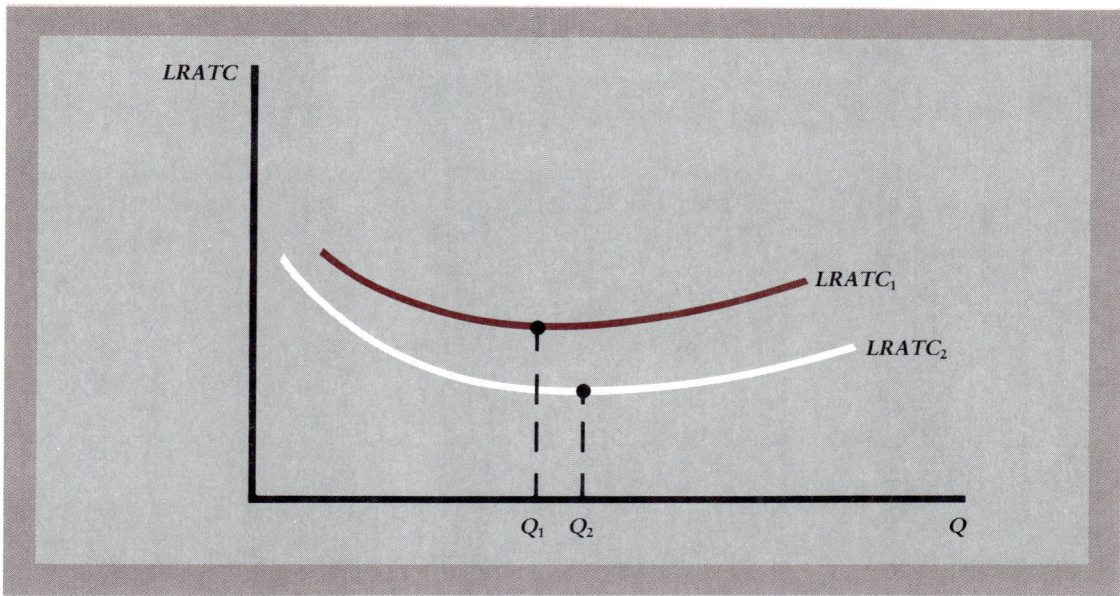

FIGURE 4-8 ▪ **A change in technology.** A change in technology lowers the long-run average-total-cost curve. Although the change in technology lowers the cost of producing all output in this example, it may affect cost more at different output levels. It may also affect the output level where the firm achieves minimum average total cost. In this case minimum average total cost occurs at Q_1 before the change in technology, and at Q_2 afterwards.

the firm can produce at the lowest average total cost. Unless there is a change in technology, the firm will experience higher average total cost by moving outside of this range of output. As a result, most significant changes in the size of firms over time are probably due to technological changes, not changes in scale using the same technology. Consider the following two examples.

4-4

Moving down lowers cost

APPLICATION Professors Laurits Christensen and William H. Greene found that most of the improvement in the average cost of producing electricity between 1955 and 1970 in the United States came from technological change rather than exploitation of scale economies. They used data on 114 electric utilities to determine the shape of the typical firm's long-run average-total-cost curve for this industry.

They found that in 1955 there were several firms that had not exploited all available scale economies. The typical firm had exhausted all scale economies by producing at an output level that was one-third less than that of the largest firm in their sample. In 1970 less than half of all firms had failed to exhaust all possible scale economies.

Between 1955 and 1970 the average firm tripled its output. Although average costs were substantially lower in 1970, Professors Christensen and Greene found that little of the savings came from exhaustion of scale economies. In fact, the long-run average-total-cost curve had essentially the same shape in 1970 as in 1955. The main savings in cost came from a downward shift of the curve. The researchers concluded that technological change, not the further exploitation of scale economies, led to the lower average cost of production.

Source: Laurits R. Christensen and William H. Greene, "Economies of Scale in U.S. Electric Power Generation." *Journal of Political Economy* 84, No. 4, part 1 (1976):655–76. © by the University of Chicago.

4-5 Not too big, not too small, just right

APPLICATION   Most studies of scale economies and technological change have been done on manufacturing industries. As Michael Daly, P. Rao, and Randall Geehan note, manufacturing accounts for only 20 percent of the output of their country, Canada. Using annual data from 1961 to 1977 for thirty-one Canadian insurance companies, these researchers estimated the impact of scale economies and changes in technology on the average costs of insurance firms.

They used a statistical technique that allowed them to determine the shape of the long-run average-total-cost curve, the shifting of the curve over time, and possible reasons for the shifts. They had data on three main inputs: labor, capital, and outside consulting services used by the firms. Output was a composite measure of insurance services.

They found that different-sized firms had different average total costs. Some small firms and also a few larger firms were operating at an average cost that was higher than that of the most efficient firms.

The firms experienced technical change during the period. Most of the technical change came from advances in capital equipment, which encouraged the firms to use a larger percentage of capital relative to labor and outside consultants. The researchers determined that the larger firms used a higher percentage of capital than smaller firms used, possibly due to indivisibilities in the capital innovations.

It is likely that the larger firms took advantage of the technological change and moved to a lower average-total-cost curve relative to the smaller firms, which were slow to adopt the new technology. They found that thirteen of the firms were too small to capture the scale economies enjoyed by the other firms. Only three firms were so large that they were operating at significantly higher average total cost due to diseconomies of scale.

It was found that unless the smaller firms were willing to adopt the technology of the larger firms, they would be unable to lower their average costs significantly by increasing their size. The biggest advantage to the firms' overall productivity during the time period was the change in technology.

Source: Michael J. Daly, P. Someshwar Rao, and Randall Geehan, "Productivity, Scale Economies and Technical Progress in the Canadian Life Insurance Industry." *International Journal of Industrial Organization* 3, No. 3 (1985):345–61.

Technological change may come in many forms. For example, it may mean a completely new production process that requires a more intensive use of machinery at higher output levels; or it may be simply an increase in knowledge, which lowers average cost without changing the proportion of inputs used in the production process.

Profit Maximization

Usually a firm wants to maximize its profits. We will approach profit maximization from two directions: the demand for the firm's inputs and the choice of the firm's output. As mentioned in Chapter 2, demand for products comes from two sources: final consumers and other firms. The demand that comes from another firm is called a derived demand, since it is derived from the demand for the firm's own product.

For example, our would-be restaurateur, Blanche Mayzone, would have no demand for flour if no one wanted to eat her bread and other baked goods. A landscaping firm would have no interest in Poobell plastic trash bags unless someone wanted its landscaping services. Using the Verte Tree Company as an example, we shall now see that when a firm chooses the profit-maximizing level of inputs, it simultaneously determines the profit-maximizing output level.

Derived Demand for an Input

Let us begin by assuming that the amount of every input except one is fixed. The one input—X, the number of workers—is available at a price, P_X. Harry determines how much of input X to use based on the value the input has to his company relative to its cost. From the previous section, we know that we can convert each incremental amount of the input into output, if we know the marginal product of X at each value of X.

Since marginal product equals the change in output divided by the change in the input, the dollar value of the input also depends on the additional revenue generated by each additional unit of input (that is, marginal revenue).

By multiplying marginal product by marginal revenue, we can determine the marginal revenue product of an input. The **marginal revenue product of an input** (such as X in our current example) is the change in total revenue divided by the change in the input X: $\Delta TR/\Delta X$. Denoted by MRP_X, the marginal revenue product of X is the monetary value of each additional unit of the input, as follows:

$$MRP_X = MP_X \times MR_Q = \frac{\Delta Q}{\Delta X} \times \frac{\Delta TR}{\Delta Q} = \frac{\Delta TR}{\Delta X}.$$

Harry measures the marginal product of labor as trees trimmed per hour of worker time. His marginal revenue is dollars per trimmed tree. The marginal revenue product is therefore in terms of dollars of revenue per hour of worker time.

4-4   Derived demand

GRAPHICAL
EXPLANATION

We can now derive the demand that Harry has for one hour of worker time. Figure 4-9 shows a marginal-revenue-product curve for input X. In addition, the price of X (the hourly wage) appears as a horizontal line, indicating that Harry can buy all the X he wants at the market price.

At this point we must make an assumption about the firm's behavior—namely, that Harry wants to maximize the company's profits. To do so he must maximize the difference between revenues and costs. To maximize its profits in purchasing input X, the firm must not reach a point where the value of additional units of X falls below the cost of these units. Harry will maximize profits where MRP_X equals the price of X.

In the figure the firm facing price P_1 does not purchase any more X than X_1. For X greater than X_1, the price of X exceeds its marginal revenue product. Purchasing an amount of X less than X_1 would mean passing up extra profits. The shaded area in the figure represents the amount of revenue earned by the firm in excess of its cost of purchasing X_1. This net revenue represents a return on the investment in the fixed input: machines.

If the price of X were to increase to P_2, the firm would face a new horizontal line at P_2 and would purchase the amount of X corresponding to the point where the next price of X equaled MRP_X. Since a firm always picks the profit-maximizing amount of X from the marginal-revenue-product curve, MRP_X becomes the firm's derived-demand curve for X. Note that a change in the demand for output Q or a change in the production function that affects the marginal product of X affects the derived demand curve.

If an employer does not pay a price equal to the marginal revenue product of its inputs, another employer may hire the services of the input instead. In

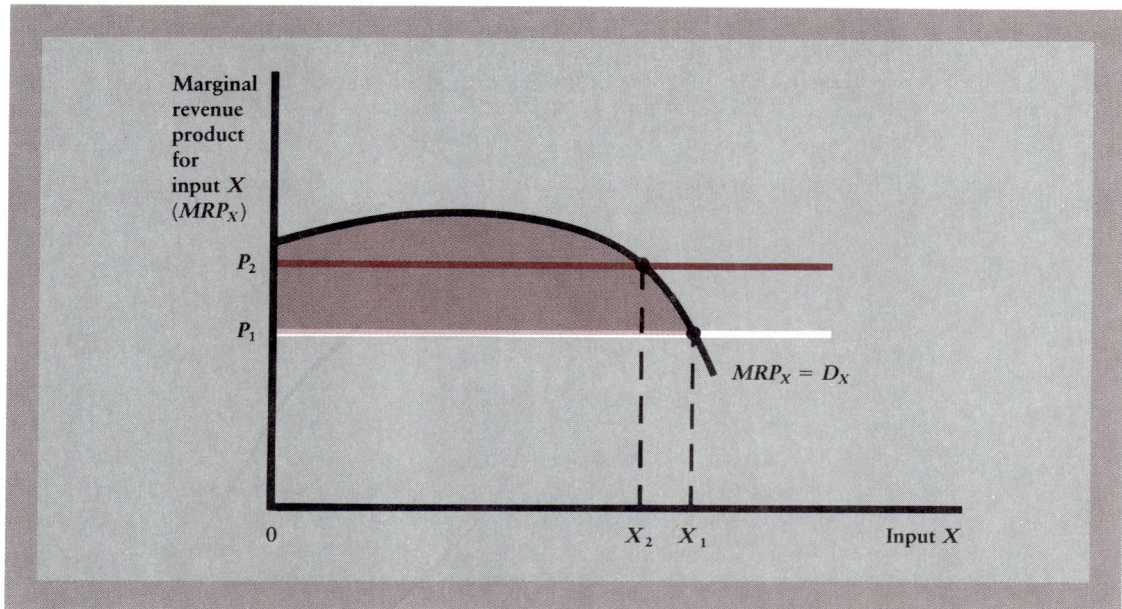

FIGURE 4-9 ▪ **Derived demand for an input.** The marginal-revenue-product curve (MRP_X) indicates the marginal value of an additional unit of input X. P_X represents the cost per unit of X. The difference in the area between the two curves (the shaded area) indicates the net gain to the firm of hiring X_1 units of the input. The firm should stop employing X at the point where MRP_X equals P_X. Any greater level of the input would cost more than the marginal value of the input to the firm.

some cases, though, there may be no alternative employer, as we see in the following example.

The value of one more home run: Marginal revenue products for baseball players

APPLICATION   Professional sports analysts have often contended that owners of the professional teams band together in setting salaries for players, and thereby keep salaries from getting too high. Despite relatively high salaries for players, some observers contend that they are really underpaid. Such assertions have encouraged some economists to evaluate the situation.

For example, Professor G.W. Scully analyzed data from the records of major league baseball players during 1969. Since the salaries of the players were available, Professor Scully needed only to determine the value of each player to his team. This is an application of the marginal-revenue-product concept. He was able to determine the performance of a player by using the following categories: the slugging percentage for hitters and the ratio of strikeouts to walks for pitchers.

He found that there was a correlation between a change in a team's winning percentage and a change in its revenues (marginal revenue). He then measured the marginal impact of an individual's performance on the team's performance (marginal product). By relating individual performance to the revenues generated by the team, he calculated marginal revenue products.

He concluded that the players' salaries were well below their marginal revenue products. For example, a hitter with a 0.490 slugging average was worth $350,400 to the team, but received only $60,500 per year, on average, in 1969. A pitcher with a ratio of strikeouts to walks of 3.54 was worth $479,700, and was paid $86,300.

The advent of free agency in the 1970s changed this story somewhat. Under the free agency system, a player is free to negotiate a contract with any team he chooses. Today a player can become a free agent after five years of major-league service. Although there have been claims made by the players of a conspiracy among owners to avoid the free-agent draft, a free agent can now make other teams bid for his services. It is interesting to note that free agents now hire consultants to do studies similar to Professor Scully's in order to convince potential employers of their own marginal revenue product.

Source: G.W. Scully, "Pay and Performance in Major League Baseball." *American Economic Review* LXIV, No. 6 (December 1974):915–30.

Profit-Maximizing Output

The preceding analysis was focused on the optimal level of a specific input. We can approach Harry's profit-maximization problem by considering the profit-maximizing output level. In the discussion on cost minimization, we did not ask which output level Harry should produce. To answer that question now, we must first know what the marginal revenue is for the firm's output.

Figure 4-10 shows an example of a short-run total-cost curve and a total-revenue curve. To maximize profits, a firm must find that output level where the difference between total revenue and total cost is greatest. This occurs at Q_1 in Figure 4-10.

At Q_1 lines drawn tangent to the curves have the same slope. At any Q on either side of Q_1 the curves will be closer to one another than the two parallel lines. Since the slope of the total-cost curve is marginal cost, and the slope of the total-revenue curve is marginal revenue, marginal cost equals marginal revenue at Q_1, the profit-maximizing output. The profit-maximization rule

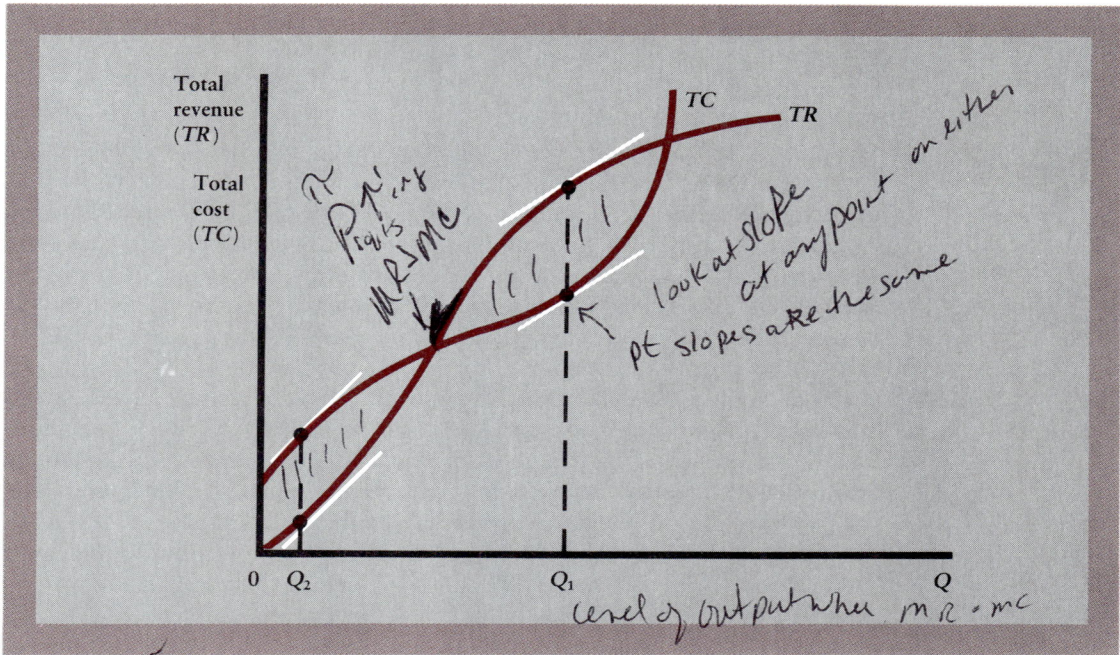

Handwritten annotations on figure:
- π = profits
- profits MR>MC
- look at slope at any point on either
- pt slopes are the same
- level of output when MR = MC
- (Relationship between) [left margin, vertical]

FIGURE 4-10 ▪ Profit maximization. The firm maximizes its profits by choosing an output level where the difference between the total-cost and total-revenue curves is the largest (Q_1). At this point the slopes of the two curves are equal. Since the slope of the total-revenue curve is marginal revenue and the slope of the total-cost curve is marginal cost, marginal revenue equals marginal cost at the profit-maximizing output level. At Q_2 the slopes are also equal, but the total-cost curve is above the total-revenue curve.

$$MR = MC$$

will be important to us in the chapters to follow.

Breakeven Analysis

Before we complete our discussion of cost analysis, let's return to Blanche Mayzone and her decision to open a restaurant. Blanche based her decision on a comparison of expected revenues and expected costs. In order to focus on the definitions of several important economic terms, we avoided many details of her decision. But now let's consider a technique, called breakeven analysis, which could have been especially useful to Blanche when she was making her decision to open the restaurant. **Breakeven analysis** is a technique designed to determine the number of units of a product or service that a firm must sell in order to cover all of its costs. Sales above the breakeven output level create economic profits for the firm.

Determination of the Breakeven Output

Through her earlier analysis, Blanche found that her expected revenues would exceed her expected economic costs by $50,200. We simplified Blanche's problem by assuming that she would earn a specific revenue per year. However, when opening a restaurant, one does not generally know exactly how many customers there will be. Rather than relying on an estimate, Blanche could have used breakeven analysis to decide how many customers she needed to have per day to make the venture worthwhile.

If she had used breakeven analysis, her first step would have been to distinguish between fixed and variable costs. Since she was planning to hire her staff on a part-time, on-call basis, depending on the number of reservations at the restaurant, she would incur no fixed cost for labor. Her food and liquor would also be directly proportional to the number of meals.

On the other hand she would have to pay for utilities, rent, equipment, and furniture. These costs would not vary significantly, regardless of the number of customers. She also would have fixed costs due to her lost rent, salary, and the opportunity cost of the investment made in the restaurant. Consider the following numerical example.

4-3	The breakeven output

NUMERICAL EXAMPLE

Blanche has determined that her opportunity costs will be $34,800 per year; her equipment rental, $15,000; and utilities, $30,000. The total of these fixed costs will be $79,800 per year. Since she expects to fill a void at the upper end of the market for continental cuisine and regional favorites, she expects that her prices will yield a revenue of $30 per customer, including food and drinks.

She determines that her food costs will account for 40 percent of the price of a meal on the average, liquor will be 20 percent, and labor, 15 percent. The labor cost is low, because she has not included tips in her revenue totals. All variable costs together will equal 75 percent of the price of the meal. She will use the remaining 25 percent to cover her fixed costs and to provide her with a profit.

Since 75 percent of each additional dollar will be for variable costs, the slope of the total-cost curve will be 75 percent of $30, or $22.50, per meal. Her total-revenue curve will be a straight line starting at the origin and having a slope, equal to the average revenue per customer, of $30.

Given this information, Blanche can determine how many meals she needs to sell per year to cover all her costs. She can construct a graph of her costs and revenues. In Figure 4-11, the total-cost curve is a straight line intercepting the total-cost axis at $79,800, Blanche's fixed cost. The horizontal axis measures the number of meals served at the restaurant per year.

In Figure 4-11 the total-cost and total-revenue curves intersect at 10,640 meals per year. Since Blanche plans to be open five days a week except for two weeks of vacation per year, she will be open 5 × 50, or 250, days per year. She must serve 10,640/250, or 42.56, meals per day to break even.

She plans to offer the same menu at lunch and dinner. She expects that she will be able to use a table at most twice during the evening and once during lunch. Since she has space for 40 customers at a time, she has a capacity of 3 × 40, or 120, customers per day. Based on her previous experience as a manager, she knows that she will be fortunate to average 60 customers a day. However, she is confident that she will surpass the 42.56 customers per day needed to break even.

FIGURE 4-11 ▪ **Breakeven analysis of opening a restaurant.** Since Blanche has a fixed cost of $79,800 and a constant marginal cost, the total-cost curve is a straight line. Total revenue is also a straight line, since Blanche is assuming that the price per customer is fixed, regardless of the number of customers. The two lines cross at 10,640 customers per year. At that point Blanche will receive total revenues that will equal her total costs. If she has more than 10,640 customers per year, she will make economic profits.

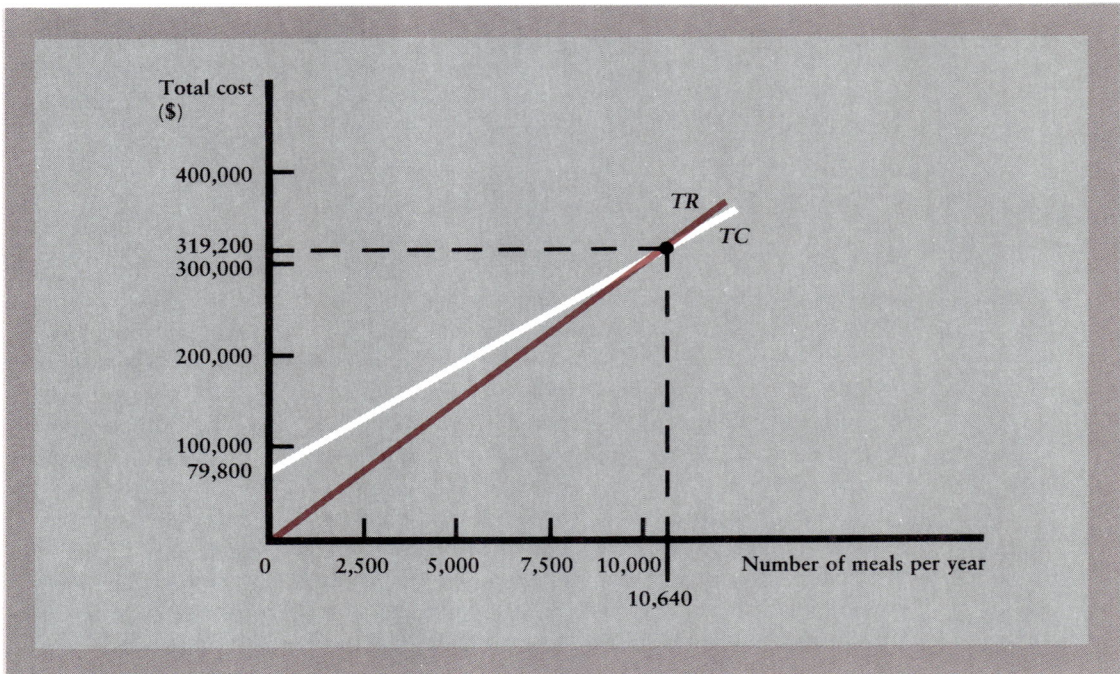

If she averages more than 42.56 customers per day, the difference between the total revenue and the total cost will give her some economic profits. For example, if she has 60 customers per day, the total number of meals per year will be 60 × 250, or 15,000. Her revenues per year will be $450,000. Her total costs will be $79,800 + ($22.50 × 15,000) = $417,300, and her economic profits will be $450,000 − $417,300 = $32,700. Since she has included the opportunity costs of her time and investment in the restaurant as part of her fixed cost, Blanche must add the $32,700 in economic profits to her lost salary, the opportunity cost of her investment, and her implicit rent, in order to determine her business profits.

We could make this analysis more sophisticated by assuming that the revenues per client were not fixed at $30. Based on our analysis of demand in Chapter 2, we would expect that a lowering of the price would encourage more people to come to the restaurant. This assumption would make the total-revenue curve look more like the one in Figure 4-11, and if Blanche's average variable costs were not constant, the total-cost curve also would be similar to the one in Figure 4-11. Blanche could now determine a price for her meals that would maximize her profits and determine exactly how many meals she should serve.

Unfortunately, the cost of calculating the exact nature of the total-cost and total-revenue curves may be too high to justify the effort for some firms. Also the firm may find that the nature of substitutes in the market does not provide much flexibility in pricing. Breakeven analysis is commonly used in these situations. Its main weaknesses are the assumptions of constant average variable cost and constant average revenue. Despite these weaknesses, however, breakeven analysis is helpful in making some economic decisions.

The Choice of Technology

Blanche could use breakeven analysis to consider some other options. For example, assume that a salesperson will rent a new scanning machine to Blanche for $26,600 per year. The machine involves the same technology found in automated check-out registers at supermarkets and security-scanning machines at airports. The company supplies dinner plates with magnetic tape embedded in them. The kitchen staff pass the filled plates under the scanner before sending them to the dining room. The machine analyzes the contents of each plate and calculates the size and weight of each component.

When the plates are returned to the kitchen, the staff once again pass them through the scanner for a post-meal analysis. The machine thus determines the popularity of each component of the meal. By entering the price of each ingredient into the computer that is attached to the machine, Blanche will automatically receive a detailed, per-plate cost analysis. The machine will also provide statistical advice regarding changes in the composition of these meals, based on the software's storage bank of over 100,000 recipes and its analysis of the customers' reactions. The machine also washes and dries the dishes!

The salesperson guarantees that Blanche will lower her per-meal food costs without lowering her revenues. In addition, she will no longer need anyone to wash dishes. The machine offers Blanche a new technology. Since the $26,600 represents a fixed cost, the intercept of the horizontal cost line in Figure 4-11 will increase by $26,600. Since the variable cost will decrease, the slope of the total-cost curve will be less than before. This change may result in a new breakeven point. Blanche would have to evaluate this option using the same analysis as before. Consider the following numerical example.

<table>
<tr><td>4-4</td><td>**New technology**</td></tr>
</table>

NUMERICAL EXAMPLE

If Blanche adopts this new technology, her fixed costs will increase by $26,600 per year, to $106,400. If her variable cost drops to $20 per meal from $22.50, her new total-cost curve will be TC_2, shown in Figure 4-12 (p. 118). (By coincidence, the new total-cost curve passes through the same breakeven point as before.) By using the new machine, Blanche will earn higher profits if she has more than 42.56 customers per day, but lower profits if the number of customers falls below 42.56.

If her marginal cost drops by only $0.50 per customer, to $22, her breakeven point will increase to 13,300 customers per year or 13,300/250, or 53.2 customers per day. However, at 53.2 customers per day, she will have the same cost with or without the machine. If Blanche thinks she will have more than 53.2 customers a day, she will be better off with the machine.

Blanche's dilemma about whether or not to rent the machine illustrates an important point. Firms need to continuously review new technology and consider adopting it. Often the decision represents an increase in fixed costs and a savings in variable costs. Whether the firm should adopt the new technology or not hinges on estimates of expected revenues. Breakeven analysis is especially helpful for firms facing these decisions.

<table>
<tr><td>4-7</td><td>**My workers never complain**</td></tr>
</table>

APPLICATION

In 1970 there were approximately 200 robots being used in U.S. factories. By the mid-1980s the number was greater than 16,000. The auto industry is the largest user of robots, most of which weld, paint, and assemble cars. For example, General Motors had 300 in 1980 and about 5,000 in 1985. It expects to have over 20,000 by the early 1990s.

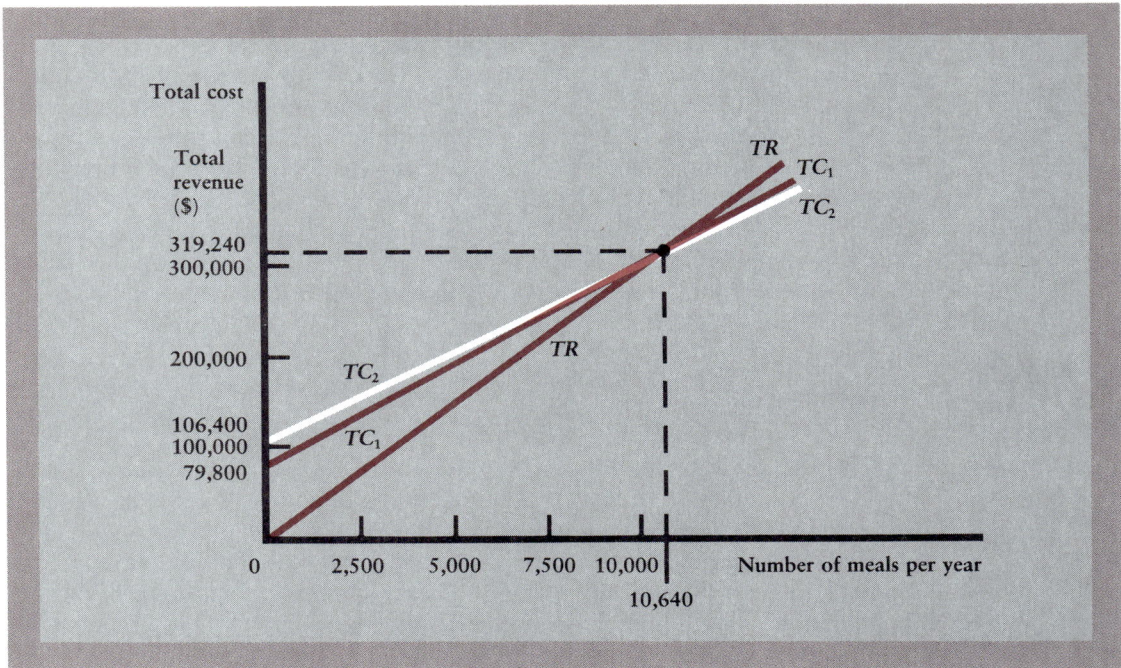

FIGURE 4-12 ▪ **Breakeven analysis of adopting a new machine.** The new machine increases her fixed cost but lowers marginal cost. By coincidence, the new machine results in the same breakeven point for both costs. However, the machine increases Blanche's losses for output less than the breakeven point, because TC_2 lies above TC_1. For output greater than the breakeven point, Blanche makes more profits by using the machine.

Firms that purchase robots lower their variable costs but raise their fixed costs. By 1985 General Motors was eliminating two jobs for every robot installed. West Germany's Commerzbank has estimated that the second generation of robots, which will incorporate sensors with increased versatility, could eliminate five workers for every robot. In California, robot-guided tomato pickers have led to a drop in the number of migrant workers from 40,000 to 8,000, and a tripling of output.

Whether a manager wants to purchase a robot or not will depend on the robot's cost and the size of the drop in variable costs. By using breakeven analysis, a manager can estimate how much output the robot would have to generate in order to cover the costs. Based on the rapid increase in the number of robots, it appears that the cost savings of using low-level production workers—that is, robots—is worth the switch.

Source: Roger Draper, "The Golden Arm." *The New York Review of Books* (24 October 1985). Reviewed in the *Wilson Quarterly* (New Year's 1986):19–20. Reprinted with permission from *The New York Review of Books.* Copyright © 1985 Nyrev, Inc.

Summary

In this chapter you encountered several cost concepts that will reappear often in the remaining chapters. You must be aware of the definitions of these terms and how to apply them. In addition, we derived the firm's short-run and long-run cost curves, based on cost-minimization behavior by the firm. These cost curves depend on the input prices and the production function of the firm. Changes in the production function or input prices affect the shapes and locations of these curves.

At the end of the chapter we added the assumption of profit maximization. When maximizing profits, the firm takes into account both costs and demand. We analyzed this decision in two ways. First the firm can focus on the profit-maximizing level of inputs. By determining the optimal input level, the firm simultaneously chooses its output level. Alternatively, the firm can determine its output level by finding where marginal revenue equals marginal cost.

In the following chapters we will use the "marginal-revenue-equals-marginal-cost" rule to find the firm's optimal output in several different market environments. While the environment will change, the principles developed thus far will not.

We ended the chapter by applying breakeven analysis to an entrepreneur's decision to open a new restaurant. We also saw how to use the technique in deciding whether or not to adopt a new machine. Breakeven analysis assumes that the firm's total-cost and total-revenue curves are linear. Since this is likely to be a realistic assumption for many managerial decisions, breakeven analysis is a useful tool for managers in evaluating new projects.

Important Terms

Opportunity Cost (p. 86)
Explicit Costs (p. 87)
Implicit Costs (p. 87)
Business Costs (p. 88)
Economic Costs (p. 88)
Business Profits (p. 88)
Economic Profits (p. 88)
Sunk Costs (p. 89)
Incremental Costs (p. 90)
Isocost Line (p. 91)
Expansion Path (p. 93)
Total Variable Cost (p. 98)
Fixed Cost (p. 99)
Total Fixed-Cost Curve (p. 99)

Total-Cost Curve (p. 99)
Marginal Cost (p. 101)
Average Total Cost (p. 101)
Average Variable Cost (p. 101)
Average Fixed Cost (p. 101)
Long-Run Marginal Cost (p. 104)
Long-Run Average Total Cost (p. 104)
Economies of Scale (Increasing Returns to Scale) (p. 106)
Diseconomies of Scale (Decreasing Returns to Scale) (p. 106)
Constant Returns to Scale (p. 106)
Marginal Revenue Product (p. 110)
Breakeven Analysis (pp. 113–114)

Selected References

Anthony, Robert N. "What Should 'Cost' Mean?" *Harvard Business Review* 48 (May–June 1970):121–31.

Baumol, William J. *Economic Theory and Operations Analysis,* 3rd ed. Englewood Cliffs, New Jersey: Prentice-Hall, 1972.

Hirschlifer, Jack. "The Firm's Cost Function: A Successful Reconstruction." *Journal of Business* (July 1962):235–55.

Johnston, J. *Statistical Cost Analysis.* New York: McGraw-Hill, 1960.

Roth, Timothy P. "Empirical Cost Curves and the Production-theoretic Short Run: A Reconciliation." *Quarterly Review of Economics and Business* (Autumn 1979):35–47.

Stigler, George J. *The Theory of Price,* 3rd ed. New York: Macmillan, 1966.

Walker, John L. "Tall Trees, People, and Politics: The Opportunity Cost of the Redwood National Park." *Contemporary Policy Issues* (March 1984):22–29.

Weiss, Leonard W. "Optimal Plant Size and the Extent of Suboptimal Capacity." In *Essays on Industrial Organization in Honor of Joe S. Bain,* edited by Robert T. Masson and P. David Qualls, pp. 123–41. Cambridge: Ballinger, 1976.

Problems

1. Assume that production of Val Holler's Customized Tombstones is governed by the production function

$$Q = X^{0.5}Y^{0.5}.$$

Assume that the price of X is 12 and the price of Y is 3. If Y is constant at 900, what is the short-run average total cost of producing 450 tombstones?

2. With the aid of a graph, explain how to derive both the firm's short-run and long-run marginal-cost curves. Assume that you know what the isoquants look like and that you know the input prices. The firm uses two inputs, X and Y, to produce output, Q.

3. Sal Minelli Desserts makes Obers Dairy Whip according to the following production function:

$$Q = 10X^{0.4}Y^{0.6},$$

where X and Y are the amounts of the two secret ingredients used to produce the dairy whip. Assume that the marginal products of X and Y are as follows:

$$MP_X = 4X^{-0.6}Y^{0.6} \quad \text{and} \quad MP_Y = 6X^{0.4}Y^{-0.4},$$

and that the prices of X and Y are both fixed at $2 per pound. Derive the long-run average-cost curve for Obers Dairy Whip.

4. Port Door Company has determined that it achieves its lowest average production costs by producing 100 doors per day at an average cost of $250 each. If marginal cost is a straight line intersecting the origin, what is the marginal cost of producing the 101st door?

5. Assume that Ray Gatt is considering opening his own marina, which he hopes to call the Sanzlow Marina. He asks you for some help in deciding whether he would be better off opening the marina or staying where he now works. He anticipates some of your questions by supplying the following information.

He currently works as the manager of Trocken Marina, earning $18,000 per year. This job is only part-time. He works additional hours as a Spanish tutor at the Sarah

Gosser Linguistic Institute, where he makes approximately $6,000 per year. If he opens the marina, he will have to give up both jobs. He has an old boat, which he was planning on selling for $3,000 before he got the idea of managing his own marina. Now he plans to keep the boat and use it as a sort of marquee to attract customers.

He will have to put $50,000 of his own money into buying the land and setting up the marina. He will not need to borrow any money in the foreseeable future, although he could do so at the market rate of 10 percent. To help him out, he will need to hire three people, at a total annual cost of $45,000. The remaining costs, for utilities and supplies, will come to $25,000 per year.

    (a) What are Ray's implicit costs?

    (b) What are his explicit costs?

    (c) How much will Ray need to make annually for him to consider opening the marina?

6. Assume that the Tosca Trampoline company makes its trampolines according to a production process that exhibits perfect complementarity between the two inputs, X and Y. Two X and one Y make one trampoline. Assume further that the price of one unit of X is $20, while the price per unit of Y is $50.

    (a) Graph this production function.

    (b) Determine the firm's expansion path.

    (c) Determine the long-run average cost function.

    (d) Determine the short-run cost function when Y is fixed at 5.

Answer questions 7–12 with true, false, or uncertain.

7. If two inputs are perfect substitutes and the marginal rate of technical substitution is greater (in absolute value) than the input price ratio, the firm's expansion path will be along the vertical axis.

8. If the firm is operating to the right of the inflection point of the total-product curve corresponding to the variable input, the firm will be on the increasing portion of the firm's short-run marginal-cost curve.

9. If Canio Cosmetics produces a facial uplift cream according to the production function

$$Q = 2X^{0.3}Y^{0.7},$$

it will minimize long-run average total cost at Q equal to 200.

10. The marginal product of input X is 2 and the marginal product of input Y is 4. If the price of X is 4 and the price of Y is 6, the firm should be using relatively more X.

11. If all the short-run average-total-cost curves reach a minimum at $2, the long-run average-total-cost curve will be perfectly elastic.

12. If a product is selling at $20 per unit and the price of the variable input is $4 per unit, the marginal product of the last unit must be 5.

MARKET STRUCTURE

5

In a modern economy the market environment fluctuates, and the profit-maximizing firm must adjust to these changes. In this chapter we will concentrate on two extreme market structures: perfect competition and monopoly. These two market structures are somewhat stylized and rarely seen in the pure forms presented here, but they will serve as important benchmarks for analyzing more realistic markets later. We will constantly refer to them when departing from the simplified assumptions made in this chapter. Without a thorough understanding of these market structures as a reference, you will be unable to understand what follows in later chapters.

At the end of the chapter we will turn to a more realistic example of a market environment: monopolistic competition. Monopolistic competition combines aspects of both perfect competition and monopoly. In Chapters 6–8 we will analyze a firm's pricing decisions in increasingly more complicated and realistic situations. Chapter 7, in particular, considers pricing strategies to deter one's competitors.

The structure of any market can be fluid and elusive. The structure depends on several factors: number and relative size of the firms and customers, homogeneity of the products included in the market, nature of information about the product's quality and price, and the ease of entry and exit from the market. Let's begin with perfect competition. In the perfectly competitive market the firm exercises no control over the market. It must passively react to market forces.

Perfect Competition

To avoid unnecessary complication of the firm's problem, we will again be following the fortunes of a small firm that produces only one product. This time we will consider the problems of Sam Frisko, who owns Frisko Flowers. Sam specializes in the year-round growing and sale of carnations. He wants to know what he can do to maximize his profits. He realizes that he is a very small producer of carnations in the overall market.

First let's look at the market forces that Sam faces. He sells his carnations to a wholesale market with many buyers and sellers. None of the buyers or sellers exhibit control over the setting of the market price. While firms strive to capture control over their market, there are markets in which no firm maintains control. As a simplification of the market that Sam faces, let's consider an extreme case: perfect competition. **Perfect competition** is an extreme situation in which firms are so small relative to the rest of the market that they exercise no direct influence on market prices.

We can summarize a perfectly competitive market by the following market-structure assumptions:

1. There are a large number of buyers and sellers of the product.
2. The output of any one firm in the market is indistinguishable from any other firm's output; that is, market output is homogeneous.
3. Information about the quality, location, and price of the product is perfectly known to everyone.
4. There is free entry into and free exit from the market.

A market is perfectly competitive when these assumptions are valid. Let's consider each of them separately.

1. While the number of buyers and sellers must be large, the importance of this assumption relates to the power that each buyer and seller has over market prices. The number must be large enough so that no buyer or seller has any influence over market prices. As a result, each buyer and seller is a price taker. **Price takers** are buyers or sellers who take the market price as given and who assume that their actions will have no influence on the price.

Because of the price-taking assumption, the perfectly competitive firm acts as though its demand curve were perfectly elastic, as in Figure 5-1 (p. 126). Since Sam's company produces a relatively small number of carnations, he assumes that he has no control over the market price. He feels that if he were to raise his price, he would lose all of his customers.

If he lowered his price, he could sell all he wanted to sell. However, he can sell all he wants now at the current market price. As a price taker with limited production capacity, he is resigned to the fact that he cannot alter his price, no matter how much he decides to produce.

2. By assuming that the products of all firms in the market are homogeneous, we make the output of any one firm indistinguishable from that of any other firm. If output were not homogeneous, there would not be a single market price. Each firm would have at least some control over its own price.

3. If information is perfectly available, all buyers and sellers have the same information. We will consider situations when all buyers and sellers do not have the same information in Chapter 9. Given the same information available to all buyers, no buyer will pay a price higher than some other buyer, and no seller will agree to sell at a price below the price received by some other seller. As a result, given perfect homogeneity of output and perfect information, all buyers and sellers face the same price.

4. The importance of the free entry and exit assumption will become more apparent later in this chapter. Free entry prevents firms already in the market from earning excessive profits over an extended period of time. As we will

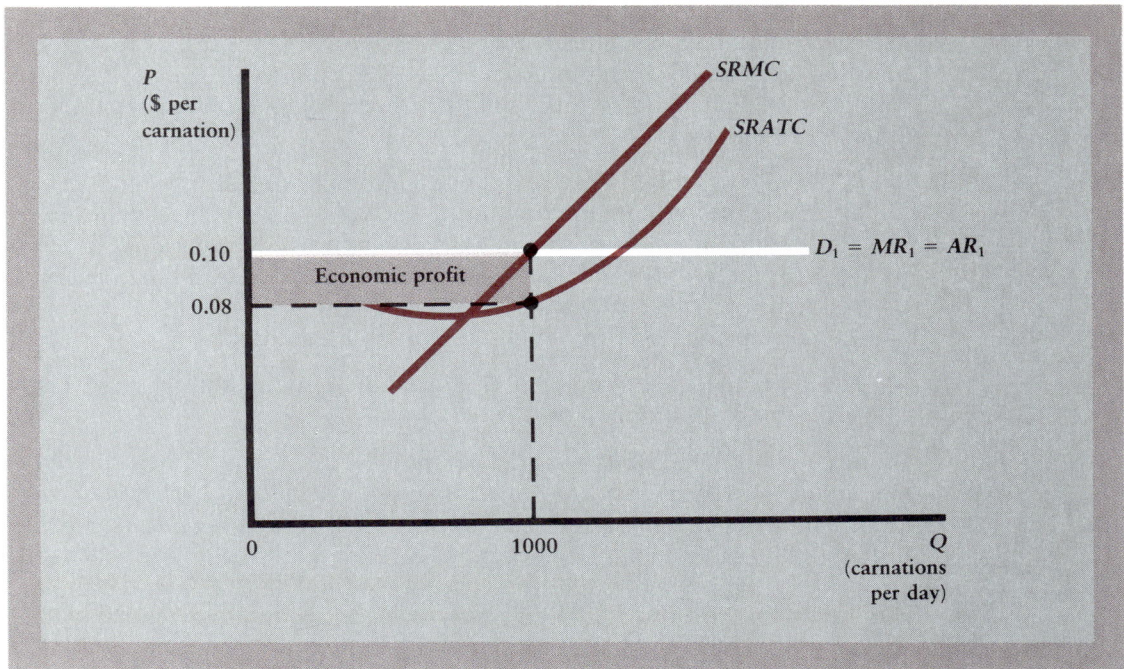

FIGURE 5-1 ▪ **Short-run profit maximization.** The perfectly competitive firm maximizes profits where marginal revenue equals marginal cost. In this case, price and marginal cost equal $0.10 at the profit-maximizing output level of 1,000 flowers. Average total cost equals $0.08 at an output level of 1,000 flowers. Since Sam makes $0.02 in economic profit per flower, his total economic profit equals $0.02 times 1,000, or $20 (the shaded area).

see, without restricted entry a company has little chance of making economic profits in the long run.

The Perfectly Competitive Firm's Level of Output

We start with Sam's short-run output decision. Remember that in the short run a firm does not have enough time to change the amount of all of its inputs. For example, Sam might not have enough time to increase the amount of land that he uses to grow carnations.

Sam's inability to influence the market means that he must be a price taker. Sam sells his carnations to wholesalers who, in turn, sell them to other people. Since he is a price taker, his demand curve is perfectly elastic, and the marginal-revenue and average-revenue curves corresponding to this demand curve look the same as the demand curve. **Average revenue** is total revenue divided by the quantity sold.

In Figure 5-1 the demand curve, D_1, is perfectly elastic at a price of $0.10 per flower; that is, if Sam Frisko sells one flower, he receives $0.10. For two flowers, he gets $0.20, and for three flowers, $0.30. Each additional unit increases revenues by $0.10, the price of one flower. Thus, marginal revenue equals $0.10, the price. Average revenue, or total revenue divided by quantity, also equals $0.10.

Figure 5-1 shows the demand curve and short-run marginal and average-cost curves for the company. Since the profit-maximizing, price-taking firm has no control over price, its only decision is how much to produce. Profit maximization occurs when marginal revenue equals marginal cost. Since marginal revenue equals price, price equals marginal cost at the profit-maximizing output level.

Since the price and marginal revenue are constant at $0.10, the profit-maximizing output occurs at Q equal to 1,000 carnations per day, where marginal cost is $0.10. You can determine average total cost by reading the corresponding value of average total cost on the $SRATC$ at Q equal to 1,000 carnations per day. Average total cost is $0.08.

The shaded area on the graph represents Sam's profits. Since the average revenue is $0.10 and the average cost is $0.08, the profit per flower is $0.02. Since Sam wants to sell 1,000 flowers at that price, economic profits will be 1,000 × $0.02, or $20. While $20 may not appear to be much money, remember that Sam's average total cost includes the opportunity cost of Sam's time and the use of all of his inputs. In his next best opportunity he would make an economic profit that would be $20 less.

If Sam were to choose any other output level, profits would be less than $20. Notice that an increase in Q by one flower would result in an increase in marginal cost above $0.10, while the marginal revenue of the extra unit would remain at $0.10. If costs were to go up more than revenues, profits would fall. On the other hand, if Sam were to produce fewer than 1,000 flowers, he could increase profits by selling up to 1,000 flowers. Only at 1,000 flowers does the marginal cost of the last unit sold equal the marginal revenue of that last unit.

The Perfectly Competitive Firm's Supply Curve

We can also use Figure 5-1 to determine Sam's supply curve. The **supply curve** is a graphical representation of the quantity that a firm is willing to supply at each price.

GRAPHICAL
EXPLANATION

If the price per flower were to jump to $0.15, Sam would have to adjust. There would be new demand, marginal-revenue, and average-revenue curves, all at $0.15. Look at Figure 5-2, where we see that Sam chose to produce 1,500 carnations per day. At an output of 1,500 carnations, price, marginal revenue and marginal cost all equal $0.15. We could continue this process for every possible price of carnations. At each price Sam would choose an output where price equaled marginal cost. Since the marginal-cost curve dictates Sam's output response, the marginal-cost curve is his supply curve.

The marginal-cost curve is his supply curve, with one exception. Price could be so low that Sam decides to produce nothing at all. This occurs when the price falls below minimum average variable cost. This is shown in Figure 5-3. Once the price falls below minimum average variable cost (AVC_1),

FIGURE 5-2 ▪ **A change in demand.** When the market price increases to $0.15, Sam increases his output to 1,500 flowers. At an output of 1,500 flowers, marginal revenue price, and marginal cost equal $0.15.

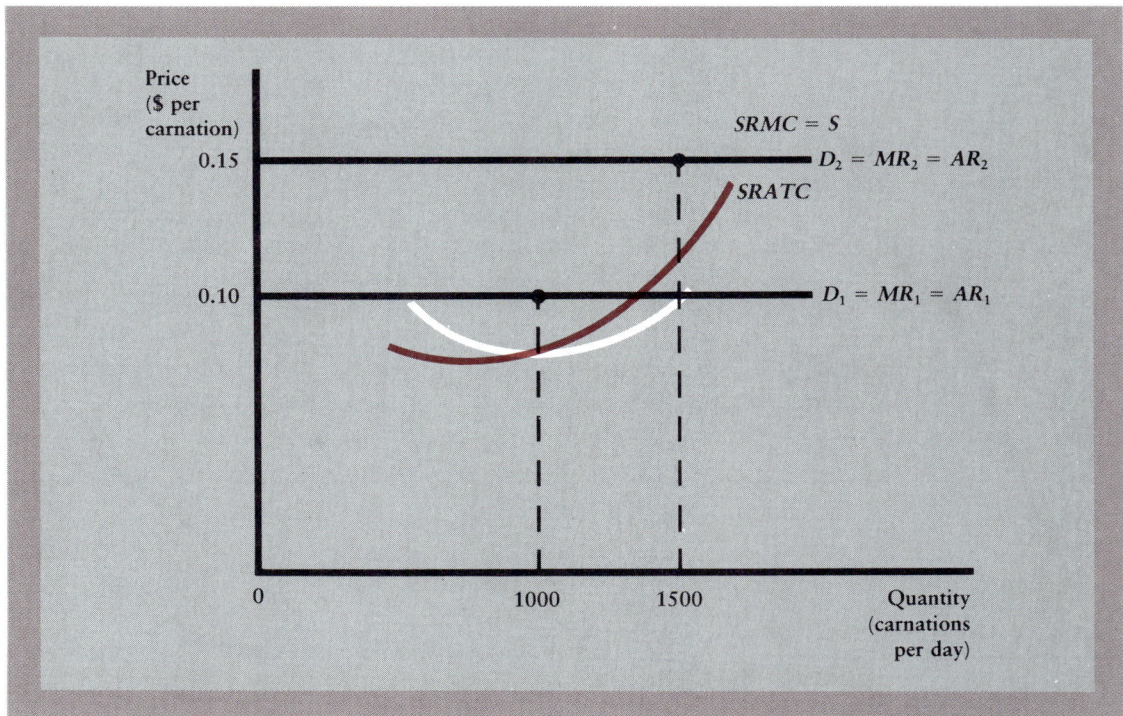

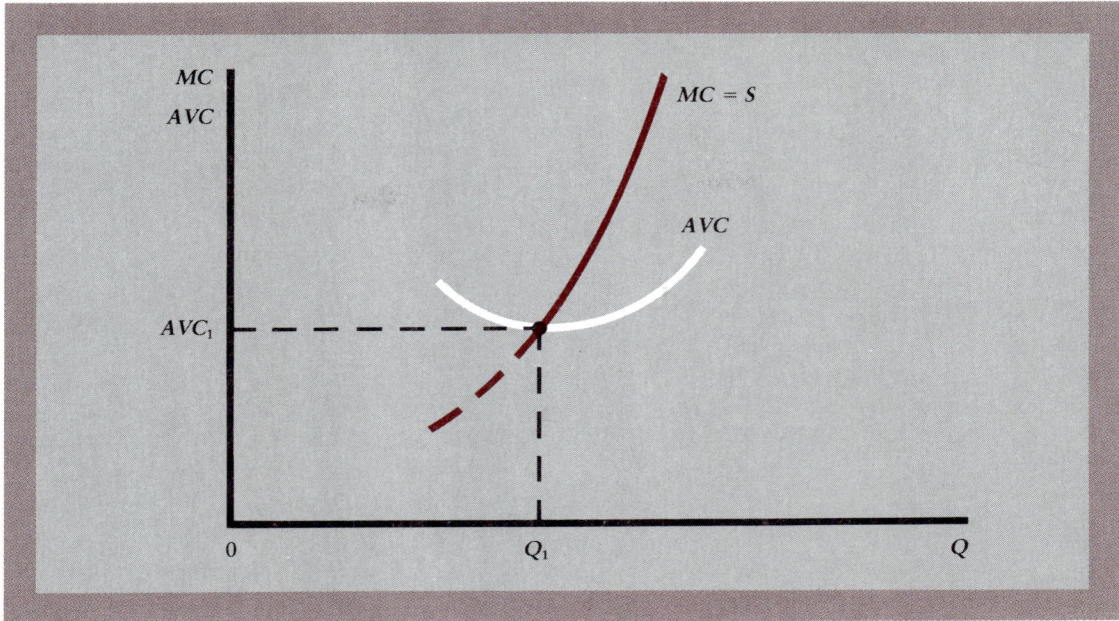

FIGURE 5-3 ▪ **Short-run supply curve.** The firm's marginal-cost curve is its supply curve as long as the price exceeds average variable cost. If the price is less than average variable cost, the firm is better off shutting down and producing nothing. Only the solid portion of the short-run, marginal-cost curve is the firm's short-run supply curve.

the firm receives revenues that do not even cover its variable costs. Recall that variable costs are avoidable costs, even in the short run.

The Market Short-Run Supply Curve

Once we know the supply curves of the individual firms, we can determine the **market supply curve,** which is the horizontal sum of the individual supply curves of all the firms in the market.

5-3	The market supply curve

GRAPHICAL EXPLANATION

Figure 5-4 (p. 130) shows the summation process. At each market price, each firm is willing to supply an amount of the product where the price equals its marginal cost. By summing these output responses, we can derive the total market output.

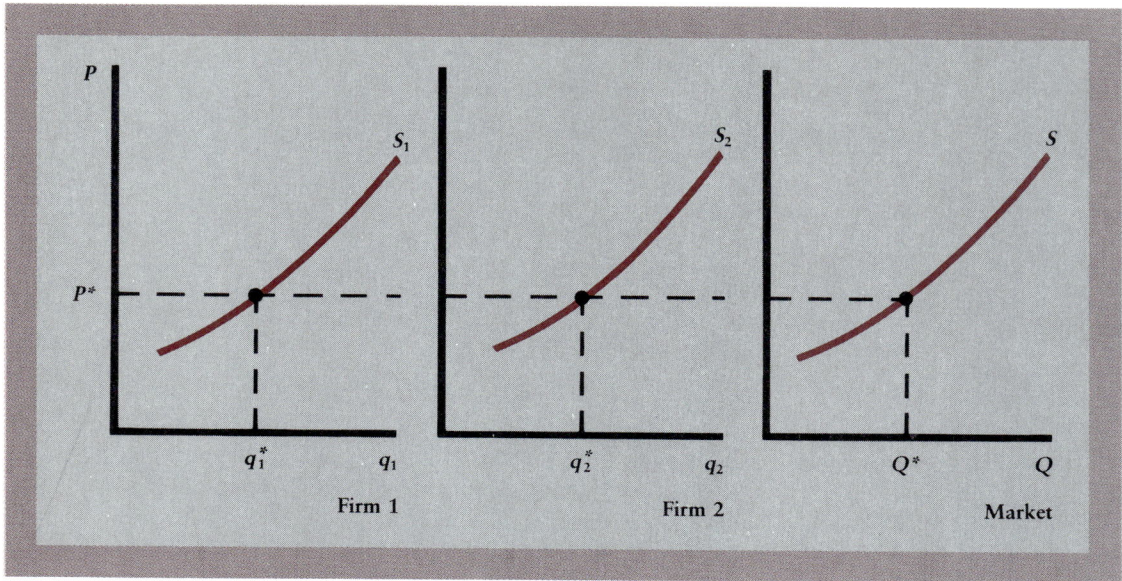

FIGURE 5-4 ▪ **Short-run market supply curve.** The short-run market supply curve is the horizontal sum of all of the firms' short-run supply curves. For example, at price p^*, Firm 1 produces q_1^* and Firm 2 produces q_2^*. If these are the only two firms in the market, market supply at price p^* is the sum of q_1^* and q_2^* (that is, Q^*).

For example, if there were only two firms in the market, firm 1 would supply q_1^* and firm 2 would supply q_2^* at price p^*. The marketing quantity supplied at that price is the sum of q_1^* and q_2^* or Q^*.

There are a large number of firms in a perfectly competitive market. Market output at each price would be the sum of the output of all the firms. If we assume that all firms are identical, then they have identical supply curves. For example, if there are 1,000 identical firms in the market, the market supply curve looks the same as the typical firm's supply curve, but the numbers on the quantity axis are 1,000 times larger.

The four assumptions for a perfectly competitive market are restrictive. We make these assumptions so that we can create supply curves for all firms and aggregate them on one graph, as a basis for analyzing more complicated market structures later. On the other hand, all of these assumptions do not have to be met before firms act in a typically competitive manner. The most important assumption concerns the inability of the firm to exercise control over price. This is a problem faced by many producers of basic commodities. For example, in the tire industry, costs apparently increased by 4 percent between mid-1981 and late 1985, while tire prices declined by 7 percent. Similar stories come from industries making steel, bearings, plastic resins, paperboard, paper, aluminum, and semiconductors that do not have significant brand-name recognition, patent protection, or technological innovations.

Some executives have sought alternative strategies, with mixed success, by attempting to create a unique identification or niche for their product. In other words, they wanted to gain some control over their demand curve by reducing the homogeneity of the market in which they participated. Since this strategy involves nonpricing behavior, we will turn to this strategy in Chapter 9 on nonprice competition.

As markets have become more international, commodity producers have discovered that prices in the world market are influenced very little by the small, individual producer. In the absence of government-supported commodity cartels, these markets behave much like the simplified perfectly competitive market. Sometimes governments attempt to intervene and control the destiny of commodity prices, which we will see in Chapter 15 on international trade policy.

Short-Run Market Price and Quantity

The interaction of the market demand and market supply curves determines the price and market output level of the product. Figure 5-5 (p. 132) shows how price and market quantity occur at the intersection of the market demand curve, D_1, and market supply curves. The market price will be $0.10 per carnation.

If the price were lower than $0.10, the quantity demanded by consumers would exceed the quantity supplied by the firms. This excess demand would cause the price to rise until there was no longer a difference between the quantity demanded and the quantity supplied.

| 5-1 | Short-run market equilibrium |

NUMERICAL
EXAMPLE

Assume that there are 1,000 identical, perfectly competitive firms growing and selling carnations. Each firm produces according to the following marginal-cost equation:

$$SRMC = 0.0001q,$$

where q is the firm's output level. Since the firm is a price taker, it sets the price equal to $SRMC$ to maximize its profits. This decision yields the firm's supply curve:

$$P = SRMC = 0.0001q$$

and

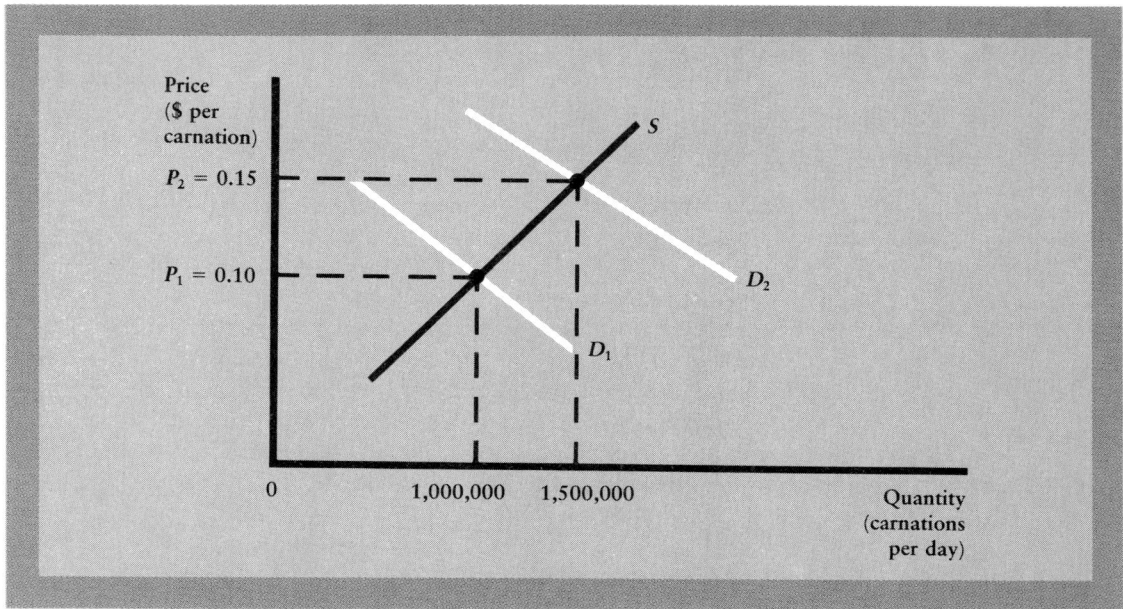

FIGURE 5-5 • **A shift in demand.** A shift in the market curve from D_1 to D_2 creates excess demand at the former price, P_1. Excess demand bids up the price until the market clears at the new short-run equilibrium price, P_2.

$$P = 0.0001q$$

or

$$q = 10,000P.$$

Since there are 1,000 identical firms in the market, the market output, Q, at any price equals

$$Q = 1000q$$
$$= 1000\,(10,000P)$$
$$= 10,000,000P.$$

This equation is the market supply equation. Since Q is now the quantity supplied, we can relabel Q as Q_s.

Assume that the market demand equation is

$$Q_d = 2,000,000 - 10,000,000P.$$

We now have the equations for both market demand and market supply. In order to have equilibrium, Q_d must equal Q_s. In this case,

$$Q_d = 2,000,000 - 10,000,000P = 10,000,000P = Q_s$$

and

$$2,000,000 = 20,000,000P$$

or

$$P = \frac{2,000,000}{20,000,000} = \$0.10.$$

Substituting the equilibrium price into both the market supply and demand equations, we find that the equilibrium quantity must be 1,000,000. Since there are 1,000 identical firms, each firm will produce an output of 1,000 carnations per day (that is, 1,000,000/1,000).

Short-Run Adjustments to Changes in Demand and Supply

Cost curves and demand curves shift whenever cost and demand factors, which had been constant, change. Recall from Chapter 2 that a change in a demand factor other than the price of the product results in a shift in the demand curve. For instance, a change in the average weekly rainfall would cause the demand for Poobell's trash bags to shift.

On the other hand, if the production function or an input price changes, there could be a shift in each firm's marginal-cost curve. For example, if the cost of seedling containers increases, carnation growers will pay more for this input, resulting in an increase in their average variable and marginal costs at all output levels. Since changes in demand or cost factors will cause these curves to shift, these changes will alter the equilibrium shown in Figure 5-5.

5-2 **Short-run adjustments**

NUMERICAL EXAMPLE

In Numerical Example 5-1, Sam's short-run equilibrium output was 1,000 and the market equilibrium price was \$0.10. Assume that there is now a shift in the market demand curve for carnations from

$$Q_{d1} = 2,000,000 - 10,000,000P_1$$

to

$$Q_{d2} = 3,000,000 - 10,000,000P_2$$

Assume that the short-run market supply curve remains at $Q_s = 10,000,000P$. Figure 5-6 (p. 134) shows that there will be a new equilibrium price, P_2, where quantity demanded, Q_{d2}, equals quantity supplied, Q_s:

$$Q_{d2} = 3,000,000 - 10,000,000P_2 = 10,000,000P_2 = Q_s$$

$$3,000,000 = 20,000,000P_2$$

$$P_2 = \$0.15$$

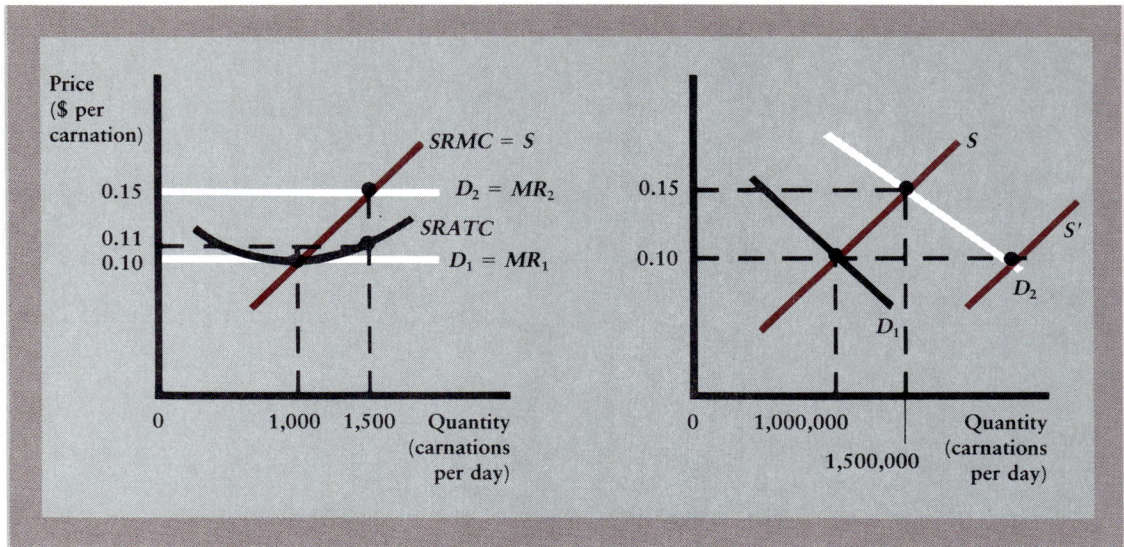

FIGURE 5-6 ▪ **Long-run adjustment.** If firms in the market earn economic profits at the short-run equilibrium price, $0.15, other firms will enter the market and force the price down to a level where no firm will be able to continue to earn economic profits. If there has been no change in any firm's long-run average-total-cost curve, the new equilibrium price will be the same as the original price, $0.10. At price $0.10, all firms are just covering their average total cost.

Substituting P equals $0.15 into both the supply and demand curves yields $Q_{d2} = Q_s = 1,500,000$. Since there are 1,000 identical firms, each firm will now produce 1,500 carnations per day (that is, 1,500,000/1,000).

Long-Run Equilibrium

In the long run there is enough time for firms already in the market to adjust all their inputs. There are no fixed inputs. There is also enough time for new firms to enter the market. With free entry there are no impediments for an entrepreneur who wishes to compete for the economic profits being earned by firms already in the market. We will now follow the effects of a shift in demand all the way through to a new, long-run equilibrium.

5-4　　**Long-run adjustments**

GRAPHICAL
EXPLANATION

After the shift in the market demand curve, shown in Figure 5-5, firms already in the market receive higher profits. For example, assume that prior to the shift in the demand curve each firm was making no economic profit. Remember that in Graphical Explanation 5-1 and Figure 5-1, Sam was making $20 per day in economic profits when the market price was $0.10 per carnation. We will now assume that the short-run, average-total-cost curve reaches a minimum value of $0.10 at an output of 1,000 carnations per day. In this case, Sam and the other growers would receive no economic profits when the price is $0.10 per carnation. Figure 5-6 shows this change in the location of the short-run, average-total-cost curve.

After the shift in demand from D_1 to D_2 the market price increased from $0.10 to $0.15. As shown in Figure 5-6, each firm responds to the increase in price by moving along its short-run supply curve until it reaches output 1,500 at price $0.15. Since $0.15 exceeds the average total cost of $0.11 per carnation at an output of 1,500 carnations, each firm will make economic profits. Economic profits provide a signal for potential entrants to the market. As new firms enter the market, the market supply curve shifts to the right. The rightward shift is due to the addition of the new firms' short-run marginal-cost curves.

Firms will continue to enter the market until there are no more economic profits to be made. In the long run, free entry and exit impose an equilibrium at which no firm expects to make additional economic profits in the future. Each firm will now produce at minimum long-run, average total cost. There will be no further change in this equilibrium unless a demand or cost factor changes.[1]

While the perfectly competitive firm may earn economic profits in the short run and during the adjustment to long-run equilibrium, it will not be able to earn any additional economic profits once the market reaches long-run equilibrium. Although few markets meet all four assumptions of a perfectly competitive market, perfect competition does provide a benchmark that will be useful to us in analyzing more realistic market situations.

5-1

Too many turkeys in the United States?

APPLICATION

The turkey market underwent a major adjustment in the mid-1980s due to changes in demand and supply factors. Food processors have substituted turkey for other meats in such products as turkey salami, turkey pastrami,

---

[1] If there has been no change in the individual firms' cost curves, the new long-equilibrium price will be the same as the original long-run equilibrium price, $0.10. In this case the entry of new firms would shift the supply curve to S′ in Figure 5-6. If, however, the entry of new firms forced some input prices to increase in the long run, each firm would now experience a higher cost for these inputs and higher marginal and average-total-cost curves. Since each firm must cover its costs to remain in the market in the long run, the new long-run equilibrium price would be higher than the previous long-run equilibrium price.

turkey bologna, turkey hot dogs, turkey ham, and turkey Canadian bacon. These new markets for processed turkey meat have increased the demand for turkeys. In addition, lower prices for fuel used to heat turkey coops and lower prices for grain used to feed the turkeys have lowered the marginal cost of raising the birds.

Despite stable prices from 1984 to 1986, outsiders discovered that turkey farmers were making economic profits. While turkey production was stable from 1981 to 1985 at a level of approximately 171 million turkeys (that is, 2.5 billion pounds), production rose to 240 million turkeys (that is, 3.8 billion pounds) by 1987 as competitors entered the market. Industry analysts indicated that so many firms had entered the market by 1987 that the total number of firms may have actually exceeded the number that would eventually survive once the market adjusted to its new long-run equilibrium.

The entry of firms to the market forced the market price to drop significantly. For example, the wholesale price per pound of a basic turkey that is already dressed and wrapped for sale at a store fell from \$0.93 in 1985 to \$0.88 in 1986 and \$0.51 in 1987. At these low prices, Americans started

FIGURE 5-7 ■ **Price controls.** If a government authority imposes a control on the price of a good or service, the market may not clear at an equilibrium price. For example, assume that the maximum allowable price is P_1 and market demand shifts from D_1 to D_2. There is now excess demand of $Q_3 - Q_1$. Normally the price increases in the short run to P_2 and the market clears. In this case, the market price does not increase. There must be an alternate mechanism for allocating the Q_1 units of the good that firms will produce.

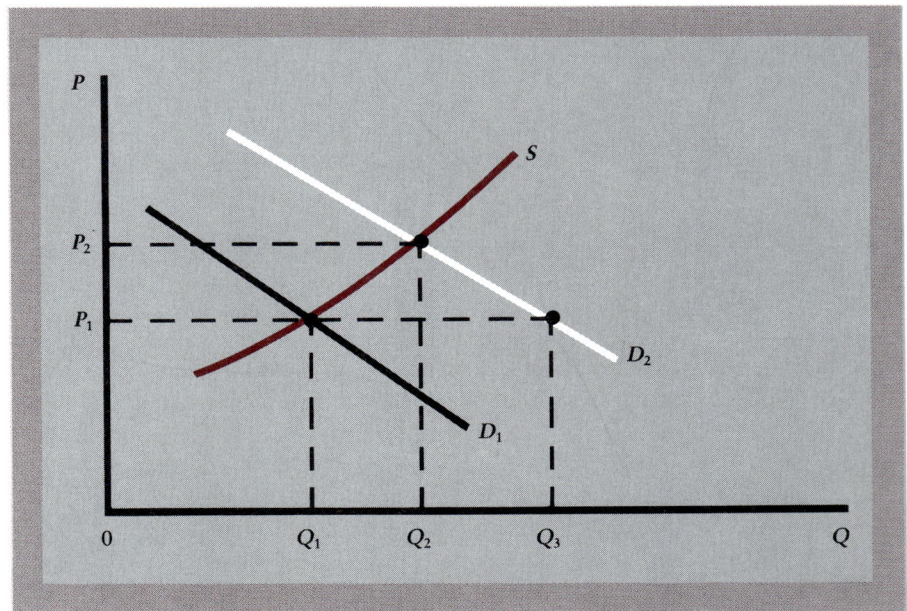

eating much more turkey—from 10.7 pounds per capita in 1985 to 13.4 pounds per capita in 1986 and 15.6 pounds per capita in 1987.

Price Controls

Governments do not always allow competitive markets to adjust by themselves. They often attempt to intervene when they feel that market prices are either too high, too low, or fluctuating too rapidly. The reasons for this intervention center on political concerns for fairness when prices are too high. If prices are high, poorer people may suffer. Rather than supplement the income of poorer people through income transfers or income tax adjustments, legislators often find it politically easier to treat the problem indirectly, through price controls. We will wait until Chapter 15 on international trade policy to consider the related issue of government support for firms that are receiving prices deemed to be too low. An example is agricultural price support programs.

Controls that limit price increases create inefficiencies in the market and can lead to even greater future problems. Although politically popular in many countries, price controls sometimes keep goods and services from those who need them most. Price controls impede the incentives of firms to invest in industries experiencing an increase in demand, and can lead to a rapid deterioration of the capital stock used in the production process. Figure 5-7 illustrates these problems.

5-5

GRAPHICAL
EXPLANATION

Price controls

Figure 5-7 reveals several problems with price controls. Assume that the market starts out in competitive equilibrium at market price P_1 and quantity Q_1. Demand increases from D_1 to D_2. In the short run, prices would jump to P_2. In the long run, prices would drop again to P_1, as new firms entered the market to capture the economic profits generated by the increase in demand.

By imposing controls on the market price, the government does not allow the market to allocate the available output. $Q_3 - Q_1$ represents an excess demand at the controlled price. If price does not allocate goods, then some other mechanism must do so. The alternative is a rationing of the available goods, or a system of illegal payments. Since everyone with a demand price as low as P_1 has a chance of obtaining the goods in a rationing scheme, those with the highest demand prices (that is, those who place the highest value on the goods) do not necessarily obtain the goods.

In the long run, as demand continues to increase, firms have an incentive to depreciate the value of their investment more rapidly than if they were receiving a market-determined (rather than government-determined) price. For example, when subject to severe rent control, landlords may abandon buildings altogether. Since firms cannot increase the price they receive, they have no incentive to increase output. If their average variable costs increase to the point where they exceed the controlled price, they will stop producing. In addition, unless there is the prospect of economic profits, no new firms will enter the market.

Nearly every government in the world has experimented with price controls for a wide range of goods and services. While the short-run benefits of lower prices make these policies popular among some citizens, the long-term effects often prove less popular. Rental housing is often subject to price controls. Consider the effects of over forty years of rent controls in New York City and Portugal.

| 5-2 | **Cheap apartments but expensive keys** |

APPLICATION New York City has maintained an elaborate system of controls over apartment rents. Advocates believe that the controls allow affordable housing for low-income people. Critics claim that landlords do not earn enough in rents to maintain apartment buildings. Landlords are moving out of the rental market by converting buildings into condominiums and cooperatives, since they have no incentive to create new rental units.

New York system has two main categories: rent-controlled apartments (218,000 units) and rent-stabilized apartments (943,000 units). The rent-controlled apartments generally have lower rents and have been under control since World War II. The New York state legislature determines annual increases in rents based on estimates of owners' costs. The rents are maintained well below market rates.

New York City has maintained very low availability rates relative to other major U.S. cities—for example, 2.04 percent in 1985. Long-time residents often live alone in large apartments because they cannot afford to move to smaller apartments that are not in the rent-control system. The shortage of apartments gives landlords an incentive to be lax in maintaining their buildings. Landlords leave many apartments vacant after tenants move out, in order to later convert the building from a rental unit to a condominium or cooperative. By law, landlords must give existing tenants an option to either buy or continue renting. In order to convert a building, the landlord must find a certain percentage of the current tenants who are willing to buy, and can then sell any vacant apartments to nonresidents at market rates.

The effect of rent controls on the value of buildings is difficult to measure directly. One indicator is the discount that landlords must give to existing tenants to get them to agree to purchase their apartments when the landlord converts the apartment to a condominium or cooperative. Once a tenant occupies a building under rent stabilization, the tenant implicitly shares in the appreciation of the apartment's market value. For example, landlords have offered as much as $100,000 in discounts to existing tenants to get them to buy their apartments. These discounts represent 35–50 percent off the prices paid by nontenants for vacant apartments.

Portugal appears to have an even more severe housing shortage due to rent control. Portugal ended a thirty-eight-year freeze on rents in 1986. Under the new law landlords can raise by as much as 300 percent those rents that were fixed before 1960, with annual adjustments for inflation thereafter. However, even a 300 percent increase may not help much. Landlords in Portugal have had little incentive to improve or even maintain rental units. One building a month collapses in Lisbon due to neglect, while 700,000 Portuguese families have no homes of their own. To evade the rent controls some landlords have demanded large, initial, illegal payments, called "key money." Some tenants have made fortunes by subletting parts of their apartments at market rates.

Monopoly

Up to this point we have considered only the firm that has no power over its demand curve. Since the firm is so small relative to the overall market, it must act as a price taker. If the firm operates in a market where all firms' products are homogeneous, entry and exit are free, there are no transportation costs, and information is freely available to all, the market is perfectly competitive.

However, two changes in the assumptions of a competitive market create a monopoly market: (1) there is only one firm in the market and (2) entry into the market is not free. A **monopoly** is a market with one firm producing a product for which there are no close substitutes.

Barriers to Entry

Given the large number of suppliers in the market, Sam Frisko is unable to prevent other firms from driving his economic profits to zero. He would like to maintain economic profits in the long run, but in order to do so he must establish a barrier to entry. A **barrier to entry** is a condition that prevents additional firms from entering a market where firms are earning economic profits.

Unless a firm can create a barrier to entry, it cannot prevent others from competing for its economic profits. By establishing a barrier, the firm keeps potential entrants from having access to the market and the firm's profits. For example, the major change in the structure of the airline, trucking, and long-distance telecommunications industries in the late 1970s and early 1980s resulted from a change in federal regulations, which allowed freer access to these markets. Prior to the change in regulations, the U.S. government limited the number of new entrants.

In the early 1970s the Organization of Petroleum Exporting Countries (OPEC) was able to raise prices significantly due to the limited number of suppliers in the market and the limited amount of proven oil reserves from non-OPEC members. By the late 1970s extensive exploration in other parts of the world resulted in substantial new oil reserves. By the mid-1980s oil prices had plummeted to levels that were below those of the early 1970s, with adjustments for inflation. Although the oil-producing countries reaped substantial profits during the 1970s, the development of fuel-saving technology, new sources of oil, and alternative fuels eventually reduced the profit-making potential of these firms.

Sources of Barriers to Entry

Considerable controversy surrounds the possibility that firms can block the entry of other firms to a market. Professor Joe Bain of the University of California at Los Angeles, a pioneer in this area of research, argued that barriers could result from absolute cost difference, economies of scale, capital-cost requirements, or product differentiation.[2]

A firm has an absolute cost advantage when it produces a product at an average cost that is always less than the potential competitors' average cost. In addition, an existing firm may have a cost advantage if it has exhausted the potential for additional scale economies, while a new firm must enter the market at a smaller scale. Capital cost barriers arise if a new firm must pay a higher interest rate than an existing firm due to the greater risk the new firm poses to lenders.

Professor Bain argued that product differentiation barriers, primarily due to advertising, were the most prevalent barriers to new entrants, but this conclusion has been the subject of extensive debate. We will explore the role of advertising and product differentiation in greater detail in Chapter 9.

Harold Demsetz, also of the University of California at Los Angeles, finds Bain's focus on production costs too narrow. Professor Demsetz sees barriers to entry as the result of a firm's investment in establishing its reputation. For example, existing firms may have established brand loyalty with customers. This loyalty may force new entrants to advertise more than existing firms at the same output level. Professor Demsetz argues that the true barrier to entry is the cost of information about products and firms. All firms must face this cost at some point.[3]

---

[2] See Joe S. Bain, *Barriers to New Competition*. Cambridge, Massachusetts: Harvard University Press, 1956.

[3] See Harold Demsetz, "Barriers to Entry." *American Economic Review* (March 1982):47–57.

If all customers had perfect information about products and firms, there would be no need for advertising or promotion. Complete information would eliminate the uncertainties about product quality. Firms create good will and brand loyalty to counter the effects of uncertainty about their product quality, and the more effectively they can convince customers, the more profitable they are.

Since new firms do not have the same history of providing a particular product, they must incur the cost of establishing their reputation. Large firms with long histories can provide more information to lending institutions about their future performance. Newer, and most likely, smaller firms are less able to convince lending institutions of their reliability. Since these firms offer a greater risk, they pay higher interest rates.

In order for a firm to face a negatively-sloped demand curve, regardless of the firm's profitability, there must be legal obstacles, such as trademarks, that prevent the complete imitation of a firm's product. If the government were to remove trademark protection, consumers would face the choice of lower prices and greater output already produced, but there would be a reduced incentive for firms to develop new products.

While there is debate about the ability of firms to establish barriers to entry, there is little doubt that governments limit the entry of new firms. By enforcing the right of firms to possess trademarks, governments impede the entry of imitators, and protect the asset value established by firms through their history of dealing with customers. Although patents allow firms to recover their investments in new products, regulations limiting market entry are not without cost. As we will see in Chapter 14, some government regulations lead to entry barriers that have potentially counterproductive results.

| 5-3 | **Make mine generic, please** |

APPLICATION The U.S. government awards patent protection for seventeen years. Drug companies have often used up as many as ten of the seventeen years waiting for approval of a new drug, before offering it for sale. In 1984 a new drug in the United States cost up to $100 million for testing and development, largely due to regulations imposed by the Food and Drug Administration (FDA).

Without patent protection, imitators could easily copy any new drug immediately and undercut the price of the company that developed it. The patent creates a monopoly for only a limited period of time, but without this protection the drug companies would have little incentive to invest in the development of new drugs.

In 1984, drug companies lobbied successfully for the right to extend their patents for up to five additional years to compensate for the length of time needed to test a new drug. In exchange, the drug companies agreed not to oppose a federal regulation permitting quicker FDA approval of generic drugs. The quicker approval and reduced testing requirements should lower the cost of bringing generic drugs to the market by nearly 96 percent.

Manufacturers of generics should experience a substantial increase in their share of the prescription market largely due to government-sponsored prescriptions. This is because most state governments require pharmacies to offer generic drugs when available. Blue Cross and Blue Shield, Medicare, and several other large insurance companies are also encouraging the use of generics. Generic drugs accounted for only 5 percent of prescription drug sales in the United States in 1984. This number is expected to exceed 20 percent by the 1990s.

Governments must decide how to regulate property rights and barriers to entry. Since firms have much to gain as a result of government decisions, they often invest substantial amounts of money in trying to influence these decisions. Because of the importance of these decisions to an individual firm's success, we will return to the subject several times later in the text. Consider next an example from Indonesia.

5-4   Indonesian plastic

APPLICATION   The government of Indonesia and its president, Mr. Suharto, have created several state-supported monopolies. For example, in March of 1985 the government announced that importers must use only one agent, Panca Holding Limited, which is based in Hong Kong. Formerly, firms purchasing unprocessed plastic purchased it directly from the foreign manufacturer.

Since Indonesia does not have its own plastics raw materials industry, the government's decree granted Panca Holding Limited a monopoly over the sale of plastics in Indonesia. By awarding the monopoly to Panca, the government created a legal barrier to entry. Incidentally, the principal director of Panca is Mr. Sudwikatmono, a cousin of President Suharto, and two other directors of the company are sons of the president.

According to the newspaper, the monopoly has added 15–20 percent to the cost of importing plastics raw materials and has raised the cost of plastic consumer goods by as much as 40 percent. An unnamed chief executive of a multinational consumer-products company complained that the monopoly raised his company's costs for plastic containers 20–25 percent.

In 1986 Panca charged $70 a ton plus 2 percent of the value of the transaction. In 1985 the company processed 324,000 tons of material valued at $321 million, according to government trade figures. Industry executives estimated that the company received as much as $30 million in commissions and fees for "handling the paperwork."

Source: Steven Jones, "Monopoly on Plastics Enriches Indonesian Leader's Kin." *Wall Street Journal* (26 November 1986):24. Reprinted by permission of *The Wall Street Journal,* © Dow Jones & Company, Inc., 1986. All Rights Reserved.

The Monopolist's Profit-Maximizing Output

Consider another one-product company: Mayard Stomach Balm, Inc. Its stomach balm revolutionized the market when it was introduced. By taking the balm, people with even the most painful stomachaches get instant relief with no side effects. The formula is a closely-held secret. The owner, Monica Mayard, is the only one who knows all of its components.

5-6   **The monopolist's output**

GRAPHICAL EXPLANATION

Since Mayard Stomach Balm, Inc. is the only supplier of this product, it is a monopolist. As a monopolist, Mayard faces the market demand curve for the good. Recall from Chapter 4 that the marginal-revenue curve corresponding to a negatively sloped demand curve will also have a negative slope. If the demand curve is a straight line, such as the one shown in Figure 5-8 (p. 144), the marginal-revenue curve will also be a straight line but will have a slope that is twice that of the demand curve in absolute value.

In Figure 5-8 the monopolist will produce where marginal revenue equals marginal cost (that is, an output of 1,500 bottles per day) and will set price at the corresponding point on the market demand curve: $12.50 per bottle. Note that the price of $12.50 is greater than marginal revenue (that is, $5) at an output of 1,500 bottles. Unlike the perfectly competitive firm, the monopolist does not set price equal to marginal cost.

The profitability of Mayard depends on the location of the average-total-cost curve. In Figure 5-8 the price of $12.50 exceeds the average total cost of $8 at the profit-maximizing output of 1,500 bottles per day. The firm will make economic profits of $6,750 per day (that is, ($12.50 − $8) × 1,500). In the absence of a barrier to entry, other firms would be attracted by these profits and would enter the market.

Monica Mayard has been able to keep her formula secret. Without this barrier to entry, she would have to decide to either make as much profit as possible while other firms entered the market, or set a price equal to average cost. A

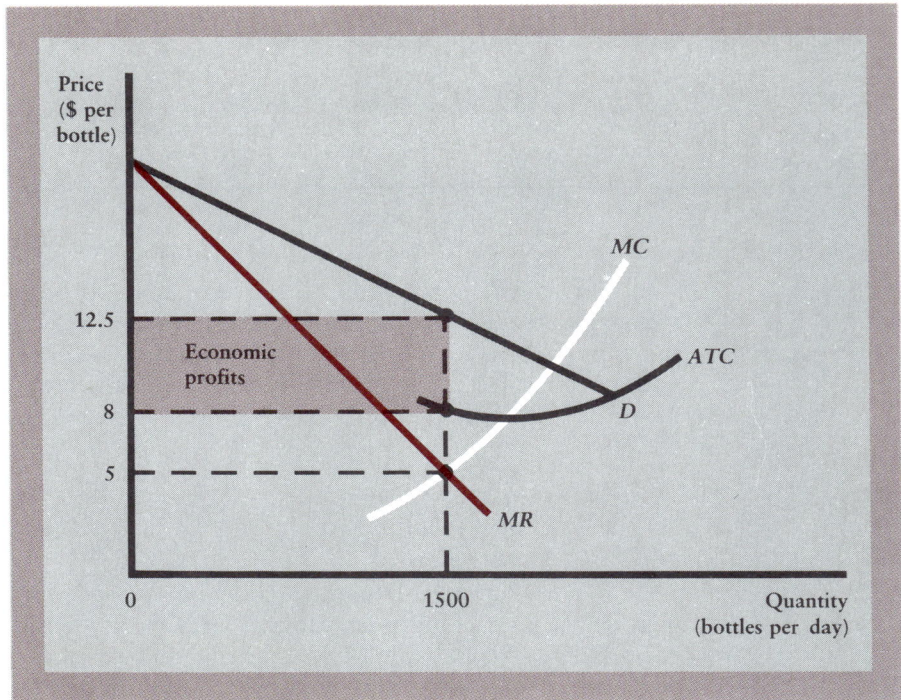

FIGURE 5-8 ▪ **Monopoly.** A monopolist produces output where marginal revenue equals marginal cost. In this case, output is 1,500 bottles per day and price is $12.50 per bottle.

price equal to average cost would prevent entry but would yield no economic profits. By keeping the formula secret, she maintains a barrier to entry. In Chapter 7 we will investigate the use of pricing strategies to bar entry by other firms.

Monopolistic Competition

Few real-world markets satisfy the assumptions necessary for a perfectly competitive or a pure monopoly market. Real-world markets usually fall somewhere in between these two extremes. For example, some markets are monopolistically competitive. **Monopolistic competition** is a market environment in which every firm in that market faces a negatively-sloped demand curve but has several close competitors and is unable to prevent long-run entry.

Let us now assume that Monica Mayard cannot block entry into the market for her type of stomach medicine. As a result, many companies make variations of Mayard Stomach Balm. The flight of customers to competitors that will occur if Monica raises her price results in a more elastic demand curve for this monopolistically competitive firm. By contrast, if a monopolistic firm raises its price, its customers have no alternative other than to go without the good or pay the higher price. In a competitive market, where the firm's demand curve is perfectly elastic, a slight increase in the firm's price leads to the loss of all the firm's customers.

The monopolistically competitive firm is unable to block entry into the market in the long run. Firms continue to enter the market until all potential profits are exhausted. Since output is no longer homogeneous, we cannot aggregate the output of all firms on one graph. Instead, we must focus on the demand and cost curves of individual firms.

<table>
<tr><td>5-7</td><td>Monopolistic competition</td></tr>
</table>

GRAPHICAL EXPLANATION

Figure 5-9 (p. 146) shows the effects of long-run entry on the output of Mayard Stomach Balm, Inc. D_1 is the demand curve faced by the firm prior to entry. The firm chooses output, Q_1, and price, P_1, where marginal revenue equals its marginal cost. This is exactly the same decision that a monopolist would make.

Unlike the monopolist, however, the monopolistically competitive firm faces entry, which forces customers away from the firm. If customers are bid away, the firm's demand curve shifts to the left. The firm continues to maximize profits where marginal revenue equals marginal cost. When there is no further entry into the market, profits must equal zero or else firms will continue to enter the market and compete for those profits.

In long-run equilibrium, the new demand curve for the stomach balm, D_2, must be tangent to its average-total-cost curve at the profit-maximizing output level. Recall that long-run entry forces the perfectly competitive firm to operate at minimum long-run average cost. The slope of the minimum point on the long-run average-cost curve is zero, the same as the slope of the perfectly competitive firm's demand curve.

Since the monopolistically competitive firm does not face a demand curve with a zero slope, its demand curve is not tangent to the long-run average-cost curve at its minimum point. As a result, Monica Mayard does not produce her stomach balm at minimum average cost in long-run equilibrium. Compared to the perfectly competitive firm, output by the monopolistically competitive firm is too small. This is a result of customers' preference for more variety in their products.

For example, at major road intersections, you can often find two, three, or even four gas stations, each offering a different brand of gas. If all customers were unconcerned about brand names of gasoline, there probably would be

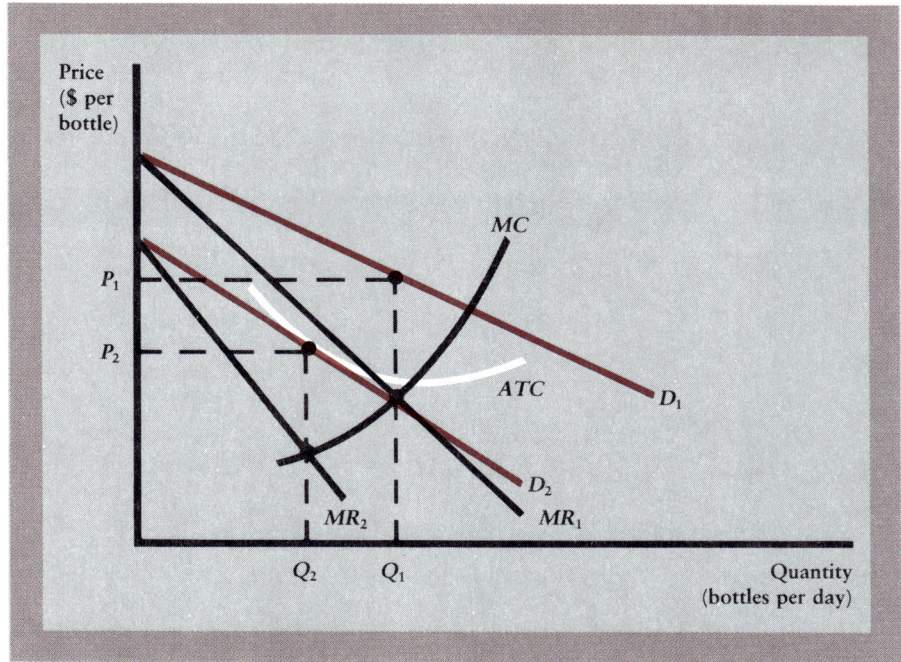

FIGURE 5-9 ▪ Monopolistic competition. The monopolistically competitive firm produces where marginal revenue equals marginal cost. When its demand curve is D_1, its profit-maximizing output is Q_1 and its price is P_1. Since the firm is making economic profit at this output level, other firms enter the market. Eventually the entry of new firms forces the monopolistically competitive firm to produce where price equals average total cost. In this case, entry forces its demand curve to D_2. While it maximizes profits at output Q_2, the firm makes no economic profits.

only one, much larger, gasoline station at each intersection. But such is not the case. Consumers' preference for variety leads to several different versions of the basic product, and smaller gas stations.

A monopolistically competitive market may be the result of firms entering a market that at one time was monopolized by a firm that was unable to prevent entry. The development of new products normally comes from one firm which has the market to itself for a limited time due to patent protection or time lags necessary for competitors to imitate the product. As imitators enter the market, that firm loses some of its share of the market.

For example, if Mayard's maintains the profit-maximizing price for its stomach balm, other companies will have a strong incentive to discover its secret formula. Eventually someone will develop a close copy of the balm and enter the market. Mayard's demand curve relative to the overall market will then decrease and become more elastic. Eventually, each firm will experience a demand curve such as D_2 in Figure 5-9, where it no longer makes economic profits.

In this discussion we have ignored the possibility that Monica might adjust her nonprice strategy to counter the influx of imitators. For example, by increasing her advertising budget, she might convince customers that her balm is worth a higher price than a competing brand. Although the advertising effort will raise the company's cost, it might also keep the demand curve from falling further towards the origin.

Regardless of its strategy, a company will continue to face entry as long as it remains profitable. In Chapter 9 we will return to the economics of nonprice competition in greater detail and consider nonprice strategies for slowing the entry of new firms.

Other Market Structures

Perfect competition, monopoly, and monopolistic competition are not the only possible market environments. A firm may compete with a small number of rivals, in which case the firm must acknowledge that rivals may react to any changes in the firm's prices, output, or marketing strategy. Such markets are classified as oligopolies. An **oligopoly** is a market that contains two or more firms producing similar products. In making market decisions, each firm in the market must consider the reactions of rival firms.

Many firms are aware of the other firms with which they compete for profits and market share. Throughout the remainder of this text we will be considering a firm's optimal strategy for this type of competition. Although each of the remaining chapters will consider this issue, Chapter 7, in particular, concentrates on pricing strategies in oligopoly markets, and Chapter 9 focuses on nonprice competitive strategies.

5-6   Market trends

APPLICATION   Professor William Shepherd of the University of Michigan classified markets in the United States according to their degree of competitiveness. He grouped markets into four general categories: monopolistic, competitive, tightly oligopolistic, and dominated by one large firm. He classified a market as a monopoly if one firm had more than 90 percent of the market. He considered a market to be dominated by one large firm if one firm had over 50 percent, but less than 90 percent, of the market and there were substantial barriers to entry. We will consider markets dominated by one large firm in detail in Chapter 7.

A market is oligopolistic if the combined market shares of the four largest firms exceed 60 percent, market shares have remained stable over time, and there are at least moderate barriers to entry. He classified the remaining markets as competitive. While these competitive markets are not necessarily perfectly competitive—that is, according to the definition at the beginning of the chapter—there is enough competition in the market, and enough potential competition from entrants to the market due to low barriers to entry, to insure that firms do not maintain economic profits in the long run.

Professor Shepherd determined that U.S. markets have become more competitive. In 1939 52.4 percent were competitive. By 1958 the number stood at 56.3 percent, and by 1980, 76.7 percent. Only 2.5 percent of markets were monopolies in 1980, down from 6.2 percent in 1939. Markets dominated by one firm amounted to only 2.8 percent of all markets in 1980, down from 5.0 percent in 1939. Oligopolistic markets represented 36.4 percent of all markets in 1939 and 35.6 percent in 1958. By 1980 this number was down to 18 percent.

Despite the restrictive assumptions of perfect competition, Professor Shepherd found that most firms exercised little control over their prices. The main reasons for the increased competitiveness of U.S. industries have been increased competition from imports, antitrust enforcement, and deregulation of industries. We will devote an entire chapter to each of these topics in Part IV.

Source: William G. Shepherd, "Causes of Increased Competition in the U.S. Economy 1939–80." *Review of Economics and Statistics* LXIV, No. 4 (November 1982):613–26.

Summary

Firms operate in a wide range of market environments. As a point of departure for the remainder of the text, we considered two benchmark market structures: perfect competition and monopoly. We also briefly discussed monopolistic competition and oligopolistic markets. We will return to these reference points several times later in the book.

While the perfectly competitive firm can make economic profits in the short run, it is unable to make additional profits once the market is in long-run equilibrium. To make economic profits in the long run, the firm must maintain a barrier to the entry of other firms. If it is successful in doing so, it becomes a monopolist. A monopolist is the only firm facing the market demand curve for a particular product.

Monopolistic competition differs from both perfect competition and monopoly. The monopolistically competitive firm does face a negatively-sloped demand curve, but it is unable to prevent entry to the market by imitators. Free entry keeps firms from making profits in the long run.

These market structures are oversimplifications of reality. Thus far we have not considered in any detail the possibility of a market containing only a few firms that compete with one another over a range of products. We have also ignored the problems of information, transportation costs, decisions about the future, and nonprice competition. The rest of this text deals with these and other important extensions. Feel free to pick and choose among the remaining chapters, according to your interests. While the remaining chapters do not depend on one another for background material, each chapter will constantly refer back to perfectly competitive and monopoly markets for purposes of comparison.

Selected References

Bain, Joe S. *Barriers to New Competition*. Cambridge, Massachusetts: Harvard University Press, 1956.

Baumol, William J. *Economic Theory and Operations Analysis*, 4th ed. Englewood Cliffs, New Jersey: Prentice-Hall, 1977.

Chamberlain, Edward. *The Theory of Monopolistic Competition*, 8th ed. Cambridge, Massachusetts: Harvard University Press, 1965.

Demsetz, Harold. "Barriers to Entry." *American Economic Review* 72(1)(March 1982):47–57.

Henderson, James M. and Quandt, Richard E. *Microeconomic Theory: A Mathematical Approach*, 2nd ed. New York: McGraw-Hill, 1971.

Shepherd, William G. "Causes of Increased Competition in the U.S. Economy." *Review of Economics and Statistics* 64 (1982):613–26.

Stigler, George J. "Perfect Competition, Historically Contemplated." *Journal of Political Economy* (February 1957):1–17.

Problems

1. Assume that each of 1,000 identical firms has a short-run marginal-cost curve given by the equation

$$SRMC = q - 5.$$

Market demand is $Q_m = 20,000 - 500P$.

(a) What is the equation for the market supply curve?

(b) Calculate the market price and quantity.

2. A perfectly competitive industry has a large number of potential entrants. Assume that each firm minimizes long-run average cost at an output of 40, where average cost is \$2 per unit. Market demand is given by $Q = 2000 - 100P$.

(a) Determine the number of firms in long-run equilibrium. Be sure to show your work.

(b) Assume that the short-run total cost associated with each firm's long-run equilibrium output is given by

$$SRTC = 0.25q^2 - 18q + 400.$$

Determine the short-run equilibrium market price and quantity, if demand increases to $Q = 3000 - 200P$.

(c) Calculate each firm's profits for parts (a) and (b).

3. Some people argue that there are too many gas stations located at major road intersections. Discuss the merits of this statement, assuming that the market for gas is perfectly competitive. How might your argument change if you were to assume that the market was monopolistically competitive?

4. Assume that the demand for X is given by the following equation: $P = Q/40 - 30$. Assume that X is produced by a constant-cost, perfectly competitive industry. Each firm has a long-run total-cost curve equal to $0.5q^2 - 10q + 200$ and a long-run marginal-cost curve equal to $q - 10$.

(a) Calculate the firm's long-run output.

(b) Determine the long-run equilibrium price.

(c) Calculate the market output and the number of firms in long-run equilibrium.

(d) What is the equation for the firm's long-run supply curve?

5. Assume that Flick Security Systems has a local monopoly providing security for special events. It faces a market demand curve that follows the equation $Q = 50 - 2P$. The marginal revenue curve is given by $MR = 25 - Q$. Assume that average cost is constant at 2. Calculate the profit-maximizing price-quantity combination for Flick Security Systems. What are the company's profits?

6. Assume that a perfectly competitive firm finds itself in the situations listed in (a)–(c). Discuss what the firm is likely to do in each case.

(a) It is making no economic profits.

(b) It is making no business profits.

(c) It is not covering its fixed costs.

Answer questions 7–12 as true, false, or uncertain.

7. The monopolist's long-run supply curve is less elastic than a corresponding competitive firm's supply curve.

8. If marginal cost is positive, a profit-maximizing monopolist would never produce on the inelastic portion of the market demand curve.

9. Since firms cannot make profits in long-run equilibrium, firms making short-run profits must expect that they will eventually experience a time when these profits will be offset by losses.

10. Assume that a group of liquor store owners agree to fix the price of their goods. Assume further that they make no economic profit. Since they make no profit, the market must have the same market equilibrium price and quantity as that in a perfectly competitive market in long-run equilibrium.

11. To make economic profits in the long run, a monopolist must set price equal to long-run marginal cost.

12. If a firm imposes short-run monopoly output and price on an otherwise perfectly competitive market, output will decrease and price will increase.

PRICING AND PRODUCT-PROMOTION STRATEGIES

Now that we have established a basic theoretical background for the study of managerial economics, we can pursue more specific areas in greater detail. In Chapter 5 we looked at two important benchmark market environments. In the extreme case of perfect competition, the firm was unable to exercise any control over the market. The perfectly competitive firm had to take the price as given and choose its output to maximize profits. At the other extreme was the monopolist, who took advantage of its market position and set both price and output to maximize profits.

In Chapters 6–9 we will change the market environment for our firm. We will see that changing the assumptions about market demand, the production function, information, or the nature of competition in the market alters the constraints that the firm faces. Once the constraints change, the firm must adjust its pricing and output strategy to make the most of its new situation.

In Chapter 6 we will look at more pricing possibilities for a firm that faces no direct competition for its product. If the firm can separate its customers into different segments of the market, it may be able to increase its profits. We will consider a range of possible ways of accomplishing this objective. This strategy will be applied to the pricing of a diversified group of services: classified ads, cosmetic surgery, theater tickets, tennis courts, and electricity. We will also discuss the use of metering devices and markup pricing rules, and we will review the importance of incremental pricing, which was first discussed in Chapter 4.

In Chapter 7 we will consider the constraint imposed by competitors. In particular, we will look at the threat of market entry in response to the firm's pricing decisions. We will also evaluate the likelihood of a pricing strategy that deters market entry by new firms and limits the competition from reselling the firm's own product, such as recycling aluminum. We will then consider the costs and benefits of colluding with one's competitors or of driving them out of business. Each of these situations involves a departure from the simplified market conditions discussed in Chapter 5.

In Chapter 8 we make our firm more realistic by allowing it to produce and sell

PART

II

more than one product. The principles discussed earlier apply to the multiproduct firm as well as to the single-product firm. The special nature of the production process or market demand may give the multiproduct firm an alternative for additional profits not available to the single-product firm. We will concentrate on advantages stemming from both demand and cost considerations.

In Chapter 9 we will concentrate on the problems posed by the cost of acquiring and disseminating information about product quality. In Chapter 5 we assumed that perfect information about product quality and price was available. Chapter 9 discusses more realistic assumptions about the availability of information. While consumers face costs in acquiring information about product quality, firms must find the lowest-cost and most effective methods for conveying messages about the quality of their products to consumers.

6

SINGLE-PRODUCT PRICING: THE CASE OF NO CLOSE SUBSTITUTES

Chapters 2–5 provided the basic tools for analyzing economically interesting problems. This chapter offers opportunities to apply these tools to commonly observed pricing problems. In this chapter we will consider pricing practices for a firm that produces a product with no close substitutes.

We will start with market segmentation, which economists call price discrimination. Although the firm facing a negatively-sloped demand curve for its product normally maximizes profits where marginal revenue equals marginal cost, occasions may arise when the firm may make even higher profits. In this chapter we will consider situations when the firm can increase its profits by dividing its market into groups and charging each group a different price.

We will then consider two related topics: metering and peak-load pricing. By using these two pricing procedures, a firm can increase its profits more than by charging each customer the same price. We will conclude the chapter with a discussion of two other common pricing practices: markup and incremental pricing.

Price Discrimination (Market Segmentation)

Price discrimination, metering, peak-load pricing, markup pricing, and incremental pricing are commonplace, as we will see by following one owner, Harry Sampson, and his economic consultant, Phyllis Steene, through the course of a normal day. In one day they will encounter all of the pricing strategies. Let's start with price discrimination. **Price discrimination is the procedure of charging different customers prices that differ by more than the costs of providing the product to the different customers.**

Perfect Price Discrimination

Let us start by eavesdropping on Harry and Phyllis as they are having lunch at a cafe near Harry's office. Although Phyllis was hired primarily as a consultant for Verte Tree Company, this time Harry has offered to pay her for personal advice about some facial surgery he is planning to have done. He is especially concerned about the fact that his nose is not directly centered between his eyes. He feels that everyone looks at his nose, rather than into his eyes, when he talks to them.

He has heard about a surgeon, Dr. Molly Podure, who specializes in nose adjustments. To avoid making an immediate response to Harry's question,

Phyllis warns Harry about the price discrimination possibilities available to this surgeon. She has heard that Dr. Podure requires all prospective patients to take personality tests that reveal how badly they feel about their looks (and thus how badly they want the operation) and to complete a financial statement that reveals how much they can pay. From this information, Dr. Podure can determine each customer's approximate demand price. The **demand price is the maximum price a customer is willing to pay for a product or service given a take-it-or-leave-it offer.**

By swearing customers to secrecy about the prices quoted them for the operation, the doctor proceeds to charge customers their demand prices. Note that some customers may pay more than the average price for the operation, while others may be offered an exceptionally low price. We call this pricing scheme perfect price discrimination. **Perfect price discrimination is the situation that exists when a firm charges all customers their demand prices even though the cost of providing the product or service to each customer is the same.**

6-1   Perfect price discrimination

GRAPHICAL EXPLANATION

In Figure 6-1 (p. 156) Dr. Podure has a long-run marginal cost of $LRMC_1$ per operation. The demand curve shows the various demand prices that the customers are willing to pay. Since performing additional operations does not result in a drop in the price, the demand curve becomes a marginal-revenue curve for the perfectly price-discriminating doctor.

If the highest demand price is $5,000, Dr. Podure can charge that person the full $5,000. If the next lowest demand price is $4,900, she can charge the second person $4,900 without having to lower the $5,000 price she charges the other person. The marginal revenue of the second operation will be the same as the price: $4,900. In the continuous case shown by the demand curve in Figure 6-1, the demand curve becomes the doctor's marginal-revenue curve. The marginal revenue of the last operation will equal the price charged the last customer. The doctor maximizes profits where the new marginal-revenue curve crosses the marginal-cost curve.

When compared to the simple monopolist, who charges everyone the same price, the perfectly discriminating monopolist receives considerably higher profits. Since Dr. Podure charges everyone their demand price, the market demand curve becomes the marginal-revenue curve. The area under the demand curve is the total revenue. Since the area under the long-run marginal-cost curve is total cost, the difference in the two areas, ABC, in Figure 6-1 is economic profits.

The monopolist who charges everyone the same price would instead receive economic profits $CDEF$ at P_1 and Q_1. The difference between the areas ABC and $CDEF$ represents the additional economic profits to be gained by discriminating perfectly in price.

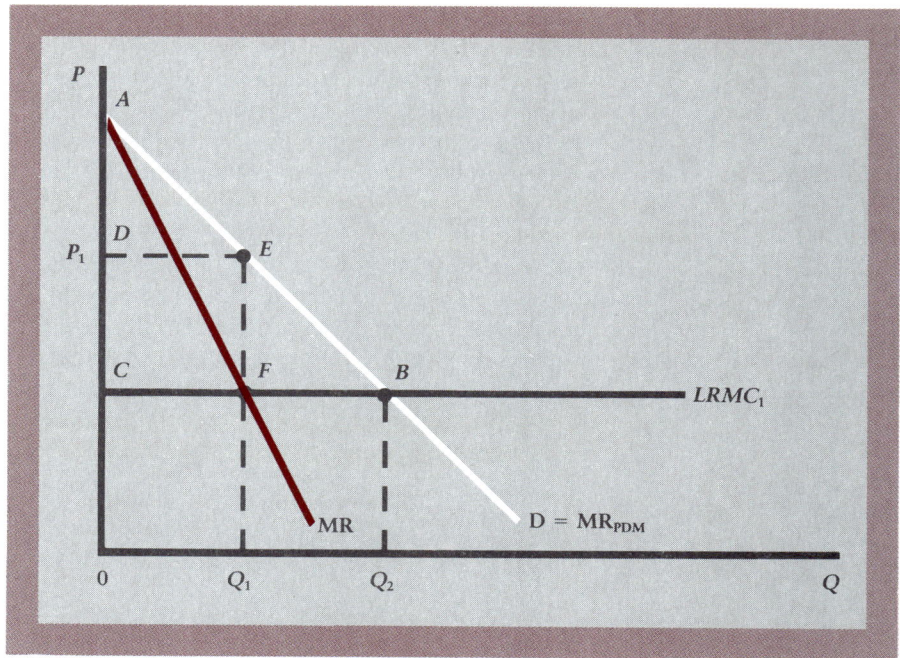

FIGURE 6-1 ▪ Perfect price discrimination. The demand curve becomes the marginal revenue curve for the perfectly discriminating monopolist. The perfectly discriminating monopolist will maximize profits at Q_2, the same output level chosen by a perfectly competitive industry. Unlike the perfectly competitive market, the perfectly discriminating monopolist will charge customers their demand prices and receive area ABC in economic profits. The monopolist who is unable to discriminate must charge everyone the same price, P_1. In this case profits equal $CDEF$.

6-1	Perfect price discrimination

NUMERICAL
EXAMPLE

Assume that Dr. Podure faces the following negatively-sloped continuous demand curve:

$$P = 500 - Q,$$

and that the marginal and average cost of an operation is $400. If she were to charge everyone the same price, she would set a price in the same way that the monopolist did in Chapter 5. She would set marginal revenue equal to marginal cost. In this case marginal revenue would be

$$MR = 500 - 2Q.$$

By setting *MR* equal to *MC*, Dr. Podure would perform fifty operations, as we see from the following.

$$MR = 500 - 2Q = 400 = MC$$

and

$$2Q = 100,$$

yielding

$$Q = 50.$$

She would determine her price by substituting *Q* equals 50 into the demand equation. She would set a price of

$$P = 500 - Q = 500 - 50 = \$450.$$

Since she would perform fifty of these operations at $50 over her average costs, she would make economic profits of $50 × \$50$, or \$2,500.

As a perfectly discriminating monopolist, she would charge everyone their demand price. In addition, she would not perform the operation for anyone with a demand price below \$400. For her cosmetic operation, there would be one hundred patients with a demand price greater than or equal to \$400. To calculate her profits, we would measure the area under the demand curve and above the marginal-cost curve. This area would be a triangle with a base of 100 and a height of $500 - 400$, or 100. The area of the triangle would yield the following profits:

$$\tfrac{1}{2}(100)(100) = \$5,000.$$

Price Discrimination in Two Submarkets

Although perfect price discrimination can be profitable, it is less common than price discrimination across a limited number of submarkets. There are three necessary conditions for successful price discrimination. First, the firm must be able to separate, or segment, the market. Secondly, the firm must prevent resales. Finally, the elasticities of demand must vary among the different groups.

Firms often use easily identifiable characteristics, such as age, gender, or geographical location, to segment the market. For example, young children often pay lower prices for tickets, while restaurants and pharmacies sometimes lower their prices for people over sixty-five.

6-1	Cheap seats

APPLICATION Theaters use price discrimination extensively. For example, people line up in front of the ticket office at the Guthrie Theater in Minneapolis for discounted tickets that go on sale fifteen minutes before the start of a performance if there are still empty seats. Students with valid international identification cards can appear at the ticket window at the Royal Shakespeare Theater in London five minutes before the start of a performance and purchase the best available seats for a fraction of the standard price. In New York City, there are several TKTS booths, where anyone can purchase tickets for Broadway and Off-Broadway shows for half price up to a day in advance. The Theater Development Fund, which is the same organization that runs the TKTS booths, maintains a mailing list of at least 100,000 students, teachers, performing-arts professionals, union members, and church members who may arrange in advance for low-cost tickets to performances that would not otherwise be sold out. These people must order tickets several weeks in advance and state at least three choices of dates. There is no guarantee that the order will be honored.

The inability to prevent resales limits the potential for this pricing practice. If the firm does not prevent resales, people in the low-price group can go into business selling to those who would otherwise have to buy in the high-price submarket.

For example, if children under twelve years of age could purchase a movie ticket for $1 that everyone else paid $2 for, these children would have an incentive to buy tickets for $1 and sell them to other people for a price between $1 and $2. This would be **arbitrage**, which is the process of buying a good at a low price and reselling it at a high price until there is only one equilibrium price for the good.

In the case of the movie tickets, arbitrage would lead to a single ticket price, unless the firm could stop the resales. To stop arbitrage, the theater could use different colors for the two types of tickets and hire someone to check identification cards at the door. In this way, they could be sure that only children under twelve were using the lower-priced tickets.

We will discuss the importance of the third necessary condition, concerning the elasticity of demand, later in the chapter. We will see that if the elasticities do not vary, the firm charges each group the same price.

Now back to the cafe where Harry and Phyllis are having lunch. Phyllis happens to notice that Harry has two large tomato slices on his hamburger, which reminds her of a recent trip to the country, where she stopped at a roadside stand that was selling tomatoes. She talked at length with the owner of the stand, a farmer by the name of Al Pomodory, who grew the tomatoes on his farm nearby.

Al grows tomatoes and sells them to a wholesaler who, in turn, sells them to canning companies. Although the wholesale price for tomatoes is determined nationally in a perfectly competitive market, Al has the option of selling tomatoes directly to passersby or tourists, such as Phyllis, and charging any price he wants. Since Al has been selling tomatoes to passersby for several years, and since he is aware that no one else in the area sells locally grown tomatoes, he knows what the demand curve is for this subgroup of customers. He has no control over the price he receives for his tomatoes from the wholesaler, but he does determine the price and quantity of sales to the tourists, as well as the quantity of tomatoes sold to the wholesaler. He is not worried that the wholesalers might set up competing tomato stands for sales to tourists even if he does charge the tourists more than he charges the wholesalers.

Figure 6-2 (p. 160) shows both demand curves and Al's marginal-cost curve. Consider the following graphical example based on Al's pricing problem. This example shows that Al will maximize his profits by selling where the marginal revenue of the last unit sold in both markets equals the marginal cost of the last unit produced.

<table>
<tr><td>6-2</td><td>Price discrimination in two submarkets</td></tr>
</table>

GRAPHICAL EXPLANATION

Assume that the wholesaler's price is $0.10 per pound. Since Al can sell all he wants to the wholesaler for $0.10 per pound, the opportunity cost of selling to the tourists is $0.10 per pound. Al wants to sell tomatoes to tourists up to the point where marginal revenue from the last pound sold to a tourist equals $0.10 per pound. This will occur at 400 pounds of tomatoes. As seen in Figure 6-2, the price paid by tourists is $0.30 per pound.

If Al were to lower his price to the tourists below $0.30, he would increase his sales, but his marginal revenue would be less than $0.10. This would happen because he would have to lower the price he charged all the tourists in order to make the additional sales. However, the number of tomatoes sold to the wholesaler would still depend only on his marginal cost of production.

You can calculate an overall marginal-revenue curve for Al Pomodory's tomatoes and compare it to his marginal cost. The marginal-revenue curve would look like the one in the right-most graph of Figure 6-2. Marginal revenue would be the same as that from the tourists, until it reached $0.10 per pound at an output of 400 pounds. For output greater than 400 pounds marginal revenue would be $0.10 per pound from sales to the wholesaler. Given the marginal-cost curve in Figure 6-2, Al would produce 900 pounds of tomatoes and sell 500 pounds to the wholesaler and 400 pounds to the tourists.

The previous example illustrates an important point: the profit-maximizing firm operates where the marginal cost of the last unit produced equals the marginal revenue of the last unit sold in both markets. Any deviation from

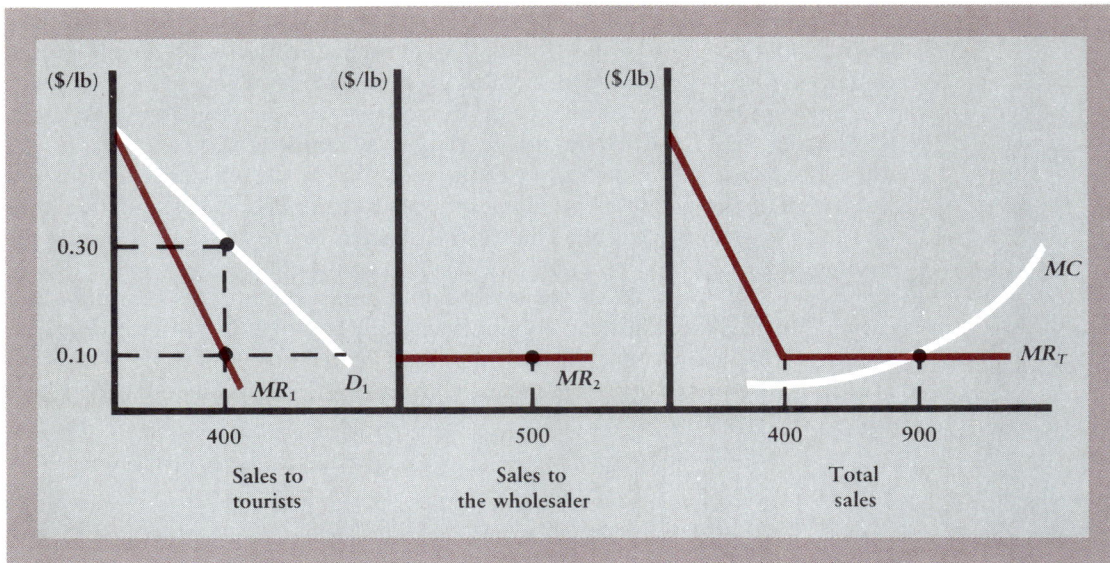

FIGURE 6-2 ▪ **Locally grown tomatoes.** Al faces a negatively sloped demand curve for tourists and a perfectly elastic demand curve for wholesalers. Since he can sell all he wants to wholesalers for $0.10 a pound, he sells to tourists at the point where the marginal revenue equals $0.10. Al chooses to produce at 900 pounds, where marginal cost also equals $0.10. He sells 400 pounds to the tourists at $0.30 a pound, and the difference between 900 and 400, or 500 pounds, to the wholesalers at $0.10 a pound.

this rule results in lower profits. If Al's marginal revenues were not equal, he could increase his revenue by transferring sales to the submarket with the higher of the two marginal revenues.

We can now see why the assumption about the elasticities of demand is important. Recall from Chapter 2 the results of the derivation of the equation linking marginal revenue to the own-price elasticity of demand:

$$ MR = P\left(1 + \frac{1}{e_d}\right), $$

where e_d is the own-price elasticity of demand, a number between minus infinity and zero. Since Al is selling in two submarkets, he sets the marginal revenue of one submarket equal to that of the other submarket. If the elasticity of demand were the same in both markets, the remaining variable in the equation—price—would also have to be the same. Since there are normally some costs associated with identifying and supplying two or more separate markets, it is not usually worth the effort to subdivide the market if the prices are to be the same.

In Al's case, the elasticities are different. Since in the perfectly competitive wholesalers' market the demand curve is perfectly elastic, price equals marginal revenue. The tourists' demand curve is less than perfectly elastic, resulting in a price greater than marginal revenue. Now let's consider the case when both demand curves have a negative slope.

The Case of Two Negatively-Sloped Demand Curves

After hearing Phyllis's explanation, Harry decides to leave lunch early to check with his secretary about some photocopies he needs. He wants to show Phyllis some of his company's production data that will be useful during their afternoon discussions. While Phyllis is finishing her coffee, she remembers another example of price discrimination, which she would prefer not to mention to Harry.

Before moving to the city, she lived in a small town. At one point she had a membership in Rural Dating Services, a company specializing in dates that are difficult to arrange. Since the firm has a special talent for matching people, it faces little competition for its unique service. Because of community pressure, it restricts its business to male-female dates.

Rural Dating Services determines that men and women do not have the same demand for its services. Figure 6-3 shows the demand curves for men

FIGURE 6-3 ■ **Demand for Rural Dating Services.** Rural Dating Services faces different demand curves for men and women. The marginal cost of providing dating services is the same for men and women. The firm adds the two marginal revenue curves horizontally and operates where the combined marginal revenue curve crosses the marginal cost curve. (that is, at 600 memberships). Marginal cost and marginal revenue for both men and women equal $7.

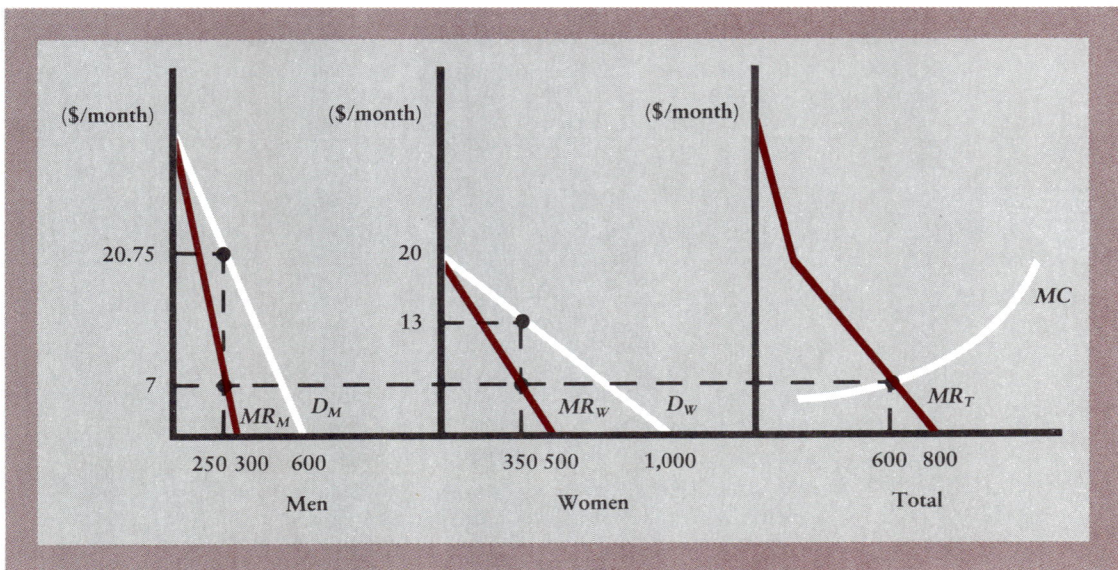

and women. The demand curve for men is more inelastic than the one for women. The firm is not sure why this is the case.

The firm sells monthly memberships for its service, guaranteeing members at least three dates per month. Rural Dating Services offers the same service to both men and women. The cost of making the dates and maintaining records is a function of the total membership cost and does not depend on whether the person is a man or a woman. From the solution to Al Pomodory's problem, we know that the marginal revenue of the last units sold in each market must be equal to marginal cost. The following numerical example shows how to solve for the output and prices with two negatively-sloped demand curves.

6-3   Two negatively-sloped demand curves

GRAPHICAL
EXPLANATION

In this case the product is a one-month membership. We can determine what the marginal revenue is at each membership level. For example, since the highest marginal revenue in market W (women) is $20, the aggregate marginal-revenue curve (that is, the horizontal sum of the two marginal-revenue curves) must be the same as that in market M (men) until marginal revenue falls to $20. When marginal revenue is zero, sales are 300 in market M and 500 in market W, totaling 800 in the aggregate.

The profit-maximizing number of memberships occurs when marginal revenue in each submarket equals the marginal cost of providing the last membership. This takes place at 600 in Figure 6-3. The optimal sales to both submarkets occur at the number of memberships corresponding to a marginal revenue of $7. Rural Dating Services determines the prices from the submarket demand curves. It charges each woman $13 per month and each man $20.75 per month. A total of 350 women and 250 men will be members in any given month.

6-2   Two negatively-sloped demand curves

NUMERICAL
EXAMPLE

Now let's assume that the demand curves for a dating service in the city are

$$P_M = 200 - Q_M \quad \text{and} \quad P_W = 100 - Q_W.$$

Assume that marginal cost is constant at $10. We know that marginal revenue equals marginal cost. Since marginal cost is constant in this case, we need only determine Q_M and Q_W, where marginal revenue equals $10.

In this case, MR_M is $200 - 2Q_M$, while MR_W is $100 - 2Q_W$. Setting both marginal-revenue equations equal to $10 yields

$$MR_M = 200 - 2Q_M = \$10$$

or

$$Q_M = 95$$

and

$$MR_W = 100 - 2Q_W = \$10$$

or

$$Q_W = 45.$$

Substituting these quantities into the demand equations, we find the prices to be

$$P_M = 200 - 95 = \$105$$
$$P_W = 100 - 45 = \$55.$$

Before leaving the restaurant, Phyllis takes a quick look at the classified ads in the newspaper that Harry left behind on his chair. Phyllis has been thinking of moving to a new apartment, and she is also looking for a piano. Given her neighbors' reactions to the noise at some of her recent parties, she knows that if she does buy a piano, she will have to find a new apartment. While looking at the paper, she notices that the classified ad rates vary according to the product or service sold or rented. She knows Harry will be surprised to hear how much these rates vary.

| 6-2 | It looks like either a house or a piano |

APPLICATION

Newspaper companies sell space in the classified ads section of their papers for the sale of a wide range of products and services. The cost of an advertisement to the newspaper company depends on the amount of space the ad occupies and the amount of effort it took to attract the advertiser.

Since most classified ad departments provide a central telephone number or mailing address for customers wishing to place ads, we would expect that a three-line ad for a piano would cost the newspaper company the same as a three-line ad for an apartment or house rental. While the cost to the newspaper company may be the same, however, the demand from individuals placing the ads is not always equal. Someone wishing to sell an old piano for $400 does not have as much to gain from an ad as a landlord offering an apartment with a one-year lease at a rent of $400 per month. In 1986, approximately 30 percent of U.S. newspaper companies charged different rates for these ads. The newspaper is the major source of current information for rentals and sales provided by private parties. People with higher-valued items or services to sell or rent will have a higher demand price for a space in the newspaper.

For example, Gannett Publishing Company publishes the *News Journal*, which serves the Wilmington, Delaware, market. Gannett also publishes *USA Today* and numerous other daily newspapers throughout the United States. You could have placed a seven-day, three-line advertisement for the rental of a house in the classified ad section of the *News Journal* for $38.85 during November 1986. At that time the newspaper did not allow ads of a shorter time duration. You could also have placed a four-day, three-line ad for the sale of a piano costing $500 or less for only $5. For sales valued from $501 to $1,500, the price was $8.

In the fine print of the newspaper's solicitation for these ads, the newspaper warns that the $5 and $8 rates do not apply to "dealers, breeders, etc." Since these dealers have more to gain from the business generated by an ad, they will have a higher demand price than the person selling a single item. The newspaper will want to exclude dealers from these special prices, so that it can charge the dealer a higher price.

By placing each ad in a special category that is a function of the value of the sale or rental of the advertised item, the newspaper attempts to segment the market as perfectly as possible. It deters resales easily, since it is hard to write an ad for the rental of a house disguised as the sale of a piano. Since the cost of printing these ads is nearly equal, the newspaper company generates unequal revenues in excess of variable costs across the different categories.

Although a firm facing a negatively-sloped demand curve can make more profits than a perfectly competitive firm, the potential for profits is even greater if the firm can separate the market into submarkets. The greatest potential for profits occurs when the firm can separate the market perfectly, creating a submarket for every customer.

More typically, however, the firm may be able to create a few submarkets and prevent resales among these submarkets. If the firm cannot prevent resales, someone will buy at the lower price and sell to those who would otherwise have to pay the higher price. This process would lead to one market price.

The last condition concerns elasticities of demand. If the elasticity of demand were the same in both submarkets, the price would be the same, negating any advantage of separating the submarkets. If the elasticities were not the same, the firm would charge a higher price in the more inelastic market.

Metering

In this section we will consider a related topic: metering. We will show that metering is an attempt to discriminate in price. Manufacturers must decide whether to sell their machines or offer them on a leasing basis. If manufacturers can accurately monitor the intensity of use by the lessee, they may prefer this alternative. For example, photocopier companies often lease their machines while requiring their customers to pay a fixed fee per page. Companies also lease computers based on a fixed charge per use.

Let us return to Harry and Phyllis. When Phyllis reaches Harry's office, Harry apologizes for the fact that his secretary has not been able to make the copies yet. After telling Harry about the price differences in the classified section, Phyllis helps him pass the time waiting for the photocopies by describing the price-discrimination possibilities related to machines with metering devices, such as photocopiers.

Fowse Copiers manufactures and leases the photocopying machine in Harry's office. Assume that Fowse Copiers faces a downward-sloping demand curve for its machines. The negatively-sloped demand curve for the machines is due to the variation in the intensity of expected use by Fowse's potential customers. For example, there will be one customer who will want to use this copier more than anyone else during the leasing period. If Fowse Copiers knows how much value the customer places on each copy, the number of copies multiplied by the value per copy will equal the customer's demand price for the use of the copier.

For example, assume that the machine makes special color copies. Fowse Copiers faces no direct competition for this machine and is protected for several years by patent laws. Assume that this machine results in a significant improvement in the quality of color copies. The alternative would be a more labor-intensive process involving photography at a substantially higher cost per copy for comparable quality.

| 6-4 | **Metering** |

GRAPHICAL EXPLANATION

Fowse produces its machine at constant marginal cost. Figure 6-4 (p. 166) shows the options available to Fowse. It could sell the machine at the monopolist's profit-maximizing output level, Q_1, and price, P_1. Or, alternatively, it could charge a fixed annual fee for renting the machine and a per-unit charge for each use of the machine.

For example, Fowse Copiers could charge the user no fixed fee for the machine but could require a fee for each page copied. The firm could install a counter that records usage. The charge per page copied would be the same for all customers. The price per copy would equal the value one receives from having a page copied on this particular machine. The value would be the cost of having it copied in the alternative manner.

Assume that before he began leasing the photocopier Harry had to pay a printing shop for copies, at $1 per page. If there are no other costs associated with the use of the photocopier, the value of a photocopied page to Harry is,

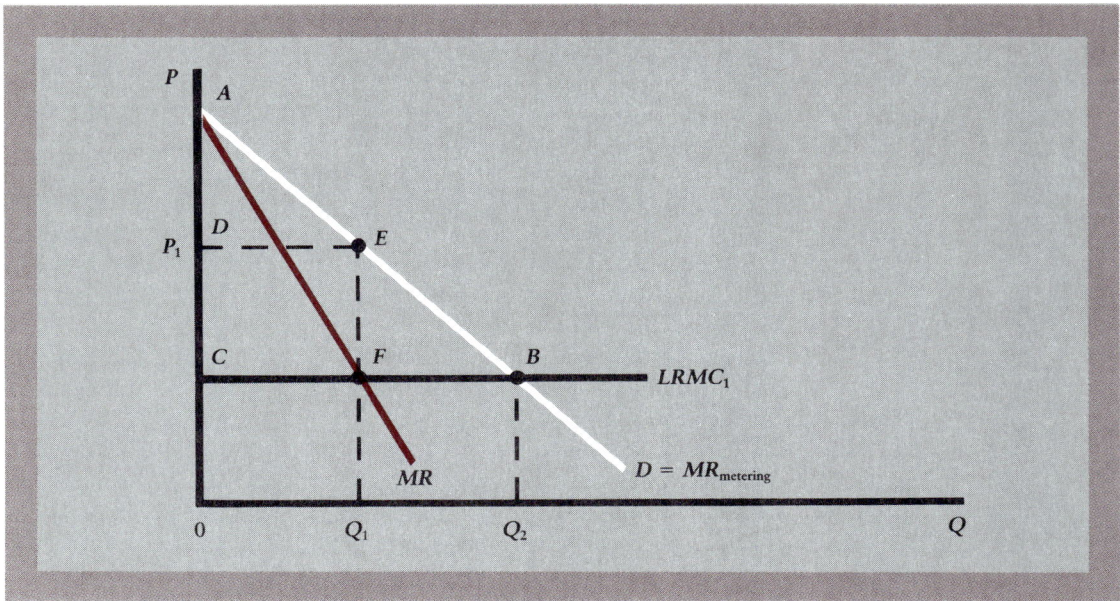

FIGURE 6-4 ▪ **Metering.** Metering accomplishes the same output and pricing decision as shown in Figure 6-1 for the perfectly discriminating monopolist. In this case the meter monitors the usage and allows the monopolist to charge customers their demand prices.

therefore, $1. A customer facing the same printing shop prices and planning to use the machine 1,000 times per year will have a maximum (that is, demand) price for the machine of just under $1,000.

If the rental price were $1,000, the customer would be indifferent about which of the two copying processes to use. A customer who needed only 500 copies would have a demand price of slightly less than $500. We will assume that the print shop picks up and delivers the copies so quickly that there is no other advantage, except price, in choosing the copier over the print shop.

Since customers differ in their intensity of use of the machine, the demand curve for the machine has a negative slope. By charging no fixed annual fee per machine, but a per-copy charge, the manufacturer can make all customers pay their demand prices for the use of the machine. Even if the manufacturer does not know in advance how often customers such as Harry plan to use the machine, this pricing practice will approximate perfect price discrimination, discussed earlier.

Fowse Copiers must add one stipulation: a minimum usage. Otherwise, some people might want a machine in their home to make only one or two copies per year. Fowse should charge for a minimum usage just large enough to generate revenue equal to the marginal cost of the machine.

By adopting this pricing scheme, Fowse produces at Q_2 in Figure 6-4 and generates revenue equal to the area under its demand curve, since the demand curve becomes the marginal-revenue curve for this perfect price discriminator. Since cost is the area under the marginal-cost curve, profit is the area *ABC*, the difference between total revenue and total cost. The firm is able to increase its profits by areas *ADE* and *EFB* relative to the monopolist who rents the machine to everyone at the same price.

As shown in Figure 6-4, Fowse Copiers can extract profits in excess of those earned by the monopolist who charges everyone the same price. By refraining from direct sales of the product, Fowse can charge customers by their intensity of use. This is especially important for equipment, such as specialized photocopiers, that may become technologically obsolete before reaching physical obsolescence.

Peak-Load Pricing

The services provided by such diverse firms as electric utilities, telephone companies, tennis clubs, golf courses, and other recreational facilities pose a unique pricing problem: peak-load pricing. **Peak-load pricing** is the charging of different prices because of fluctuations in a firm's demand at different times of the day or year. Unlike the manufacturer of products, a firm producing services cannot generally store its output to meet this fluctuation.

How each firm deals with the peak-load problem depends on the motive of the firm. We have been assuming that firms maximize profits. While managers of privately owned and unregulated firms facing a peak-load problem follow the profit motive, regulated firms, such as electric utilities, may not be permitted to price their output as they would choose to do. While we will analyze the peak-load problem from the viewpoint of the profit-maximizing firm, we will turn to the unique problems of the regulated firm at the end of this section.

Now back to Harry and Phyllis. After looking at the data for a couple of hours, Harry suggests that they stop early and go to his club, Hampton Courts, to play some tennis. Consider two problems faced by a company such as Hampton Courts:

1. how many courts to build and
2. what prices to charge at different times of the day.

The Number of Tennis Courts

Assume that Hampton Courts wants to build indoor tennis courts, which it will rent to groups of people in twelve-hour increments. The choice of twelve-hour increments is for mathematical simplicity. We will consider the more realistic possibility that demand fluctuates by the hour later.

Assume that tennis teams and independent clubs rent the courts for their members. Also assume that the manager of the firm, Hank Wheat, wants to maximize profits and adjust the size of the facility to meet his expected market.

He must decide what price to charge for each twelve-hour block of time and how many courts to build. As in all pricing decisions, he must know both the nature of the demand curve facing the firm and the firm's cost curves.

6-5   The number of tennis courts

GRAPHICAL EXPLANATION

Since the distinguishing feature of this problem is the nature of the demand curve, we will assume that the short-run marginal cost of providing the tennis courts is zero. We will also assume that demand varies by the time of day according to a simple schedule. Demand for a court per twelve-hour time block is $P_1 = 100 - Q_1$ from 8:00 A.M. until 8:00 P.M. During the rest of the time the demand is lower at $P_2 = 50 - Q_2$. You can see both demand curves in Figure 6-5.

Hank Wheat realizes that the value of a tennis court lies in the amount of money paid by everyone using the court. Since there are only two time periods, and since the same customers rent the court at the same time each day, he can compare the revenues and cost on a daily basis.

While the short-run marginal cost of providing a tennis court on a daily basis is zero, there is a capital cost associated with the courts. This includes all of the costs of either building or purchasing the courts and supporting facilities allocated on a per-court basis. Since the courts last for some time, the capital cost must be allocated on a daily basis in order to make a comparison of costs and revenues at the same point in time. Let us assume that the capital cost is $10 per day per court.

The value of a court per day is the sum of the prices paid by everyone using the court that day. To determine the value of providing an additional tennis court, Hank must calculate the marginal-revenue curves corresponding to each demand curve. In this case they would be

$$MR_1 = 100 - 2Q_1 \quad \text{and} \quad MR_2 = 50 - 2Q_2.$$

The overall marginal revenue per day associated with an additional court would be the sum of the marginal revenues from both time periods. Note that marginal revenue equals zero when Q_1 equals 50 and Q_2 is 25. The company would certainly not want to rent more than twenty-five courts during the off-peak time, because it would have to reduce its price to a point where marginal revenue would be negative.

Since MR_2 equals zero at 25, the only contribution to revenue for any number of tennis courts greater than twenty-five must come from time period 1. In Figure 6-5 the aggregate marginal-revenue curve is the vertical sum of the two individual marginal-revenue curves. For Q greater than 25, the aggregate marginal revenue is the marginal revenue from MR_1 alone. The profit-maximizing firm will build tennis courts to the point where marginal revenue equals marginal cost. In this case, this will occur at Q equal to 45.

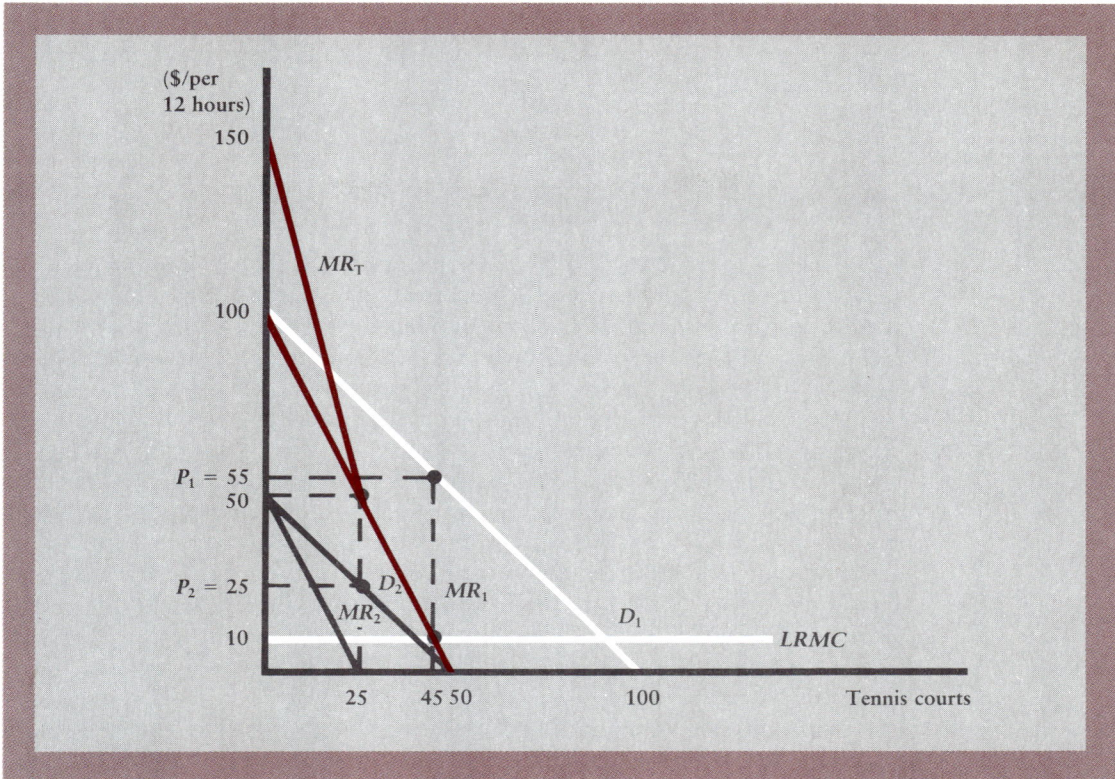

FIGURE 6-5 ▪ **Hampton Courts.** Hampton Courts faces different demand curves at two different time periods for its tennis courts. The marginal revenue curve per day is the vertical sum of the two marginal revenue curves. Hampton Courts maximizes profits by providing forty-five tennis courts, the output where marginal cost equals the marginal revenue per day. Hampton Courts does not rent a court if the marginal revenue of renting is less than the short-run marginal cost. Since short-run marginal costs are zero, it does not rent if the marginal revenue falls below zero. Since marginal revenue equals 0 at 25 during time period 2, Hampton Courts rents only twenty-five courts at that time. It rents all forty-five courts during time period 1.

Note that there is a significant difference between the technique used to construct the aggregate marginal-revenue curve for this problem and that used for the tomato and dating-service examples earlier. Since more than one group of customers uses a tennis court on any given day, the value of the court is the vertical sum of the values placed on the court by each of these customers. As a result, Hank adds the individual marginal-revenue curves vertically. In contrast to this, once a customer buys a pound of tomatoes from Al, Al cannot sell the same tomatoes to another customer later in the day. Al adds his marginal-revenue curves horizontally.

Peak-Load Prices

We will now calculate the prices that Hank should charge for each time period to maximize his profits.

Peak-load prices

GRAPHICAL EXPLANATION

The decision to build forty-five courts is due only to the demand during time period 1. The marginal revenue of the twenty-fifth court during time period 1 is $50, while the marginal cost of building the court is only $10 on a daily basis. Despite the lack of additional revenue coming from the off-peak time period (time period 2), it is worth building extra courts. The marginal revenue of the forty-fifth court during time period 1 equals $10, exactly the same as the marginal cost of that court.

Once the courts are built, Hampton Courts will equate marginal revenue to short-run marginal cost in the two time periods. In time period 1, marginal cost is zero up to forty-five courts, where marginal cost becomes infinite in the short run. The company will rent all forty-five courts during this time and charge the price which will ensure that they are all rented without excess demand. This will occur at P_1 equal to $55, since

$$P_1 = 100 - Q_1 = 100 - 45 = \$55.$$

In the off-peak time period Hank will rent twenty-five courts for $25 each. To rent more than twenty-five courts, he would have to lower his price below $25, which would result in negative marginal revenue and lower profits. Recall that Hank based his decision to build the forty-five courts solely on the marginal revenue coming from the peak time period. He would build forty-five courts even if there were no demand at all for the courts during the off-peak time period. Since there is a demand in this case, he will set output and price where marginal revenue in the off-peak time period equals short-run marginal cost in the off-peak time period.

We could make this problem more realistic by allowing the demand curve to vary at each hour of the day. In this case we would have to add vertically all twenty-four marginal-revenue curves to determine the aggregate-marginal-revenue curve. We would set this equal to the marginal cost of an additional court to determine the total number of courts to be built. To determine price for each time period, we would set price and output where marginal revenue equaled short-run marginal cost for each time period.

Peak-Load Pricing for a Regulated Utility

The behavior of a profit-maximizing firm can be contrasted with that of a regulated one. Normally, local governments do not allow a company having a monopoly to set whatever price it chooses. As a result, these companies must usually charge prices that just cover their average cost of production and distribution. The prices charged depend on the costs of providing service to customers at different times of day.

Government officials have granted monopolies to electric, telephone, and water companies in the belief that these companies produce and distribute electricity, telephone calls, and water subject to substantial economies of scale. While local governments want customers to benefit from the lower average cost of production and distribution due to scale economies, they do not want these companies to charge monopoly prices.

Assume that the city government decides to build the indoor tennis courts instead of Hank. The mayor of the city, Mary Scott, decides that the courts should be self-supporting. She wants the number of courts to account for the demand of the city's residents, but she does not want the courts to make a positive economic profit. Although Mayor Scott knows that her city would have a monopoly over tennis courts in the area, she is effectively seeking the equivalent of a perfectly competitive market solution: price equal to long-run marginal and average cost.

6-7 Regulated peak-load pricing

GRAPHICAL
EXPLANATION
Assume that the demand and cost curves remain the same as those in Figure 6-5. In this case we add the two demand curves vertically, instead of the two marginal-revenue curves, to determine the optimal number of courts to build. By adding the demand curves vertically, we determine the aggregate demand price associated with each additional court. The aggregate demand price is the value that all the city's residents place on each additional court.

In Figure 6-6 (p. 172) the aggregate demand curve has a kink at Q equal to 50, where the off-peak demand price is zero. Since the marginal and average costs of building a tennis court are both $10 per day, the city should build courts to the point where the aggregate demand price is $10 per day. Note that this occurs at Q equal to 90. Patrons would pay $10 per day for the use of a court. This would just cover the cost of the court and would be equivalent to a long-run competitive-market price.

Note that this would mean that those using the courts during the peak time period would pay the full $10 for the use of the court during that time period, while the off-peak patrons would pay nothing! At Q equal to 90, the demand price for the off-peak customers would be zero. They would pay nothing, because there would be no variable costs associated with their use of the courts.

If marginal cost were $60, both the off- and on-peak customers would pay something for the use of the courts. In Figure 6-6 the marginal-cost curve crosses the aggregate demand curve to the left of the kink. To the left of the

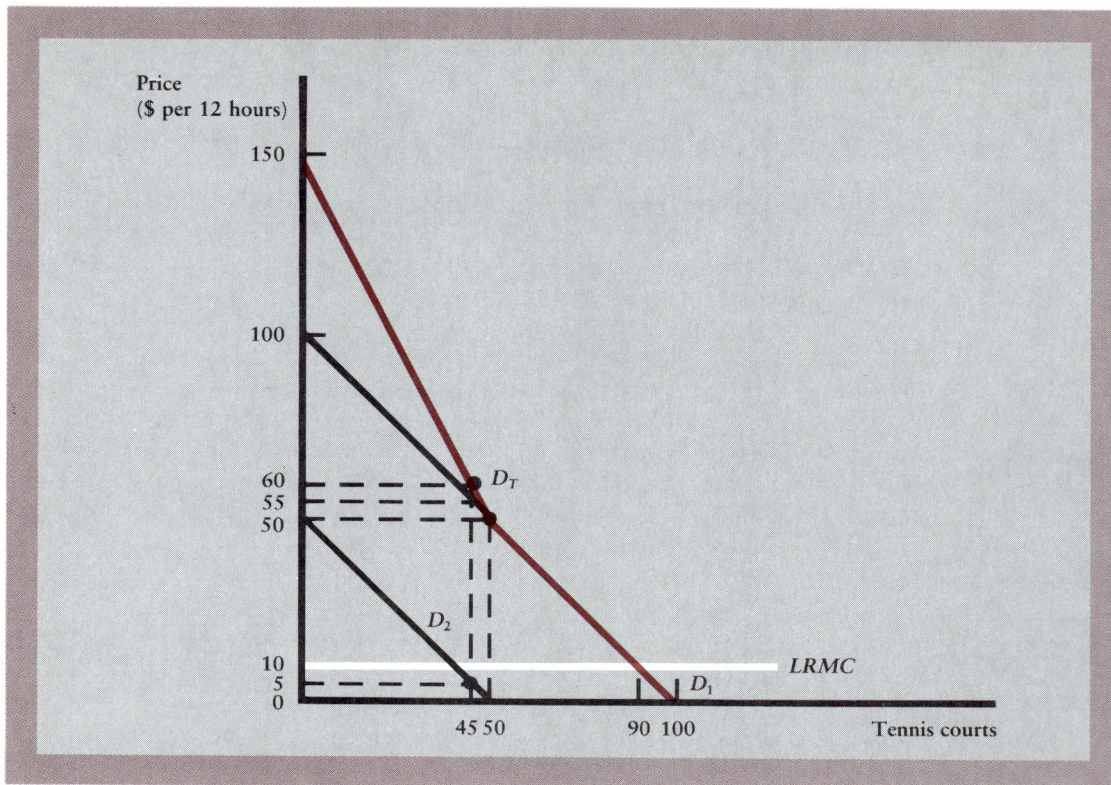

FIGURE 6-6 ▪ **Regulated tennis courts.** The city faces two different demand curves, which must be summed vertically. The city will build courts to the point where the marginal cost equals the demand price on demand curve D_T (that is, 90). Since the demand price in time period 2 is zero at 50, the city will allow people to use the courts for free at this time, while charging people in time period 1 $10 per court.

kink the aggregate demand curve is the vertical sum of the two demand curves. Since there would be the same number of customers during both the off- and on-peak times, Q_1 would equal Q_2. We could then add the two demand curves and derive an aggregate demand for tennis courts, Q_T.

$$P_T = P_1 + P_2$$
$$= 100 - Q_1 + 50 - Q_2$$
$$= 150 - Q_1 - Q_2$$
$$= 150 - 2Q_T.$$

Since marginal cost equals $60,

$$P_T = 150 - 2Q_T = LRMC = \$60$$

and

$$-2Q_T = 60 - 150 = -90,$$

yielding

$$Q_T = 45.$$

If the city were to build forty-five courts, it would charge each group its demand price. Group 1 would pay $P_1 = 100 - 45 = \$55$, and group 2 would pay $P_2 = 50 - 45 = \$5$. The sum of the two demand prices, $60, would equal the marginal cost of building the courts.

| 6-3 | Electric charges |

APPLICATION   We could now change the label on the horizontal axis of Figure 6-6 from "tennis courts" to "electricity-generating capacity" or "telephone-call capacity." For example, electricity is a nonstorable product subject to demands that vary considerably according to the time of day and season. Local and state governments regulate the prices that electric utilities may charge. Until the early 1970s most regulators required that the companies set a price per kilowatt hour (KwH) regardless of time of day and year. Due to concern that this pricing policy resulted in large amounts of excess capacity at off-peak times, the federal government passed a law in 1978 mandating that electric utilities consider peak-load pricing.

Pricing according to variation in demand has two advantages: it makes those who require extra capacity at peak times pay for this extra capacity, and it provides an incentive for those using the electricity at peak times to switch their demand to off-peak times. Any movement to the off-peak time uses existing capacity more fully and reduces the overall need for capacity. Unlike the manager of Hampton Courts, the electric-utility managers must set the price of electricity so that no economic profits can be made.

Instead of demand for tennis courts, let's assume that Figure 6-6 shows the demand for electricity capacity. The demand curve does not include the cost of the fuel (that is, variable cost) used in the production of electricity. Fuel, such as coal or oil, is a variable cost that must be added to the price charged for capacity to determine the price of electricity.

As in the case of the tennis courts, there may be such a significant difference in the demands at different times of the day that the full cost of capacity should be paid by the peak-period customers, and the off-peak customers should only pay for the fuel cost.

If the company is not constrained by the regulatory agency, it will charge prices in the same way that the manager of Hampton Courts did in the profit-maximization case. Note that unless Hampton Courts can maintain a barrier to entry, other companies will enter the market and force Hampton Courts' economic profits to zero in the long run.

<table>
<tr><td>6-4</td><td>The road to Singapore</td></tr>
</table>

APPLICATION

If you commute to work or school during rush hour, you know it can take much longer to get where you are going than during non-rush-hour times. You and your fellow rush-hour commuters impose a cost on one another by causing congestion on the highways. Traditional solutions to this problem have involved increased highway construction or creation of special lanes for car-poolers. Professor Stephen F. Williams of the University of Colorado noted that as early as 1963 the estimated cost of furnishing enough lanes to meet rush-hour traffic on some urban expressways was as high as $23,000 per regular commuter.

For political reasons, officials have ignored a more effective instrument for regulating traffic: peak-load pricing. In 1975 the Government of Singapore instituted a simplified peak-load pricing plan for traffic into its downtown area: commuters had to pay a fee and obtain a sticker that would authorize them to travel into the central downtown zone between 7:30 A.M. and 10:15 A.M. Car-pools of four or more people were exempt.

The effects were immediate and significant. Overall traffic dropped 40 percent, and car traffic, 65 percent. In response to the fee, people joined car-pools and took buses. Buses were able to travel much more quickly and reliably due to the reduced traffic. There were some unintended effects, however.

Since the system was simple, it did not take into account the possibility of people adjusting their time of arrival to just before or just after the restricted time. Traffic increased significantly at these times. People who used to travel through the zone to the other side of the city now circled the area and caused congestion on other streets. Officials could have controlled these side effects, but at the cost of greater monitoring.

Professor Williams suggests that a more sophisticated attempt to regulate demand with price would be worth the effort in the United States. He suggests that officials consider using parking charges that vary by time of arrival. This would simplify the monitoring of cars passing through checkpoints. If cars could not avoid tollbooths by switching to alternative routes, officials could use the tollbooths to collect tolls that varied by time of day.

The biggest obstacle is still politics. Despite Professor Williams's belief that nearly everyone would benefit from making people pay for the congestion cost they impose on others, voters have difficulty seeing these benefits, because the benefits are indirect: reduced taxes due to the toll revenues, saved time due to easier access to the city, more efficient use of automobiles and public transportation, reduced need for highway construction, and less pollution. Despite a few experiments in the United States, the idea has yet to catch on.

Source: Stephen F. Williams, "Getting Downtown: Relief of Highway Congestion Through Pricing." *Regulation* (March/April 1981):45–50. With permission of the American Enterprise Institute.

In this section we have considered the pricing of services when demand fluctuates during the day and year. Unlike other products, these services cannot be stored. If output cannot be stored, the firm can experience periods of time when capacity is idle. By varying the price by time of day and time of year, the firm can increase its profits.

Markup Pricing

After playing tennis, Phyllis and Harry decide to finish the day's business with an early dinner at the Ceiling Room, a restaurant located in a hotel on the outskirts of the city. On the way to the restaurant, Harry decides to stop at a convenience store and buy some aspirin for a headache that he suddenly got after losing the last set of tennis. He has not been in a convenience store for a long time and is somewhat amazed by the prices.

He mentions to the young clerk stocking the shelves that the prices of the pharmaceutical products are much higher than he is used to paying at his discount drugstore, while some of the other products, such as milk and bread, are closer to what he normally pays. The clerk merely says that he has been told to add a certain percentage to the wholesale price when assigning prices, and that he is not sure how the manager determines the markups.

Markup rules are common. Retailers who sell large amounts of merchandise of relatively low unit value often employ a pricing rule that appears to have little relationship to the demand for their products. Called by the various names of markup pricing, cost-plus pricing, and full-cost pricing, this pricing rule is simple in execution. **Markup pricing** is a pricing system which involves adding a fixed amount or percentage to the price a firm pays for the product when determining the price at which it sells the product to its own customers. In executing a markup pricing system, managers decide on a percentage markup and instruct all of their employees to add this percentage to the wholesale price paid by the retailer.

Retailers have been using the markup pricing rule for many years. For example, Hall and Hitch (1939) studied British firms, and found that more than 75 percent followed the rule. This decision rule is at odds with the theoretical development up to this point in the text. In Chapter 4 we noted that a profit-maximizing firm takes into account both revenues and cost in making its output decision. A markup rule implies that revenue, or demand, is not a factor. A markup rule may actually be an approximation to profit maximization, as illustrated in the following numerical example.

| 6-4 | **Markup pricing as a proxy for profit maximization** |

NUMERICAL
EXAMPLE

Assume that a firm does maximize its profits, where marginal revenue equals marginal cost. Furthermore, assume that the firm operates at minimum long-run average total cost, where marginal cost equals average total cost. As a result,

$$MR = MC = ATC \quad \text{or} \quad MR = ATC.$$

Recall that in Chapter 2 we derived the following identity:

$$MR = P\left(1 + \frac{1}{e_d}\right),$$

where e_d represents the own-price elasticity of demand, a number between minus infinity and zero. If MR equals ATC, then

$$ATC = MR = P\left(1 + \frac{1}{e_d}\right).$$

By rearranging terms,

$$ATC = P + \frac{P}{e_d}$$

and

$$P - ATC = -\frac{P}{e_d}$$

or

$$\frac{P - ATC}{P} = -\frac{1}{e_d}.$$

For example, if the elasticity of demand is -2, the markup above average total cost represents 50 percent of the price. If the elasticity of demand is -3 (that is, more elastic), the markup over average total cost is one-third of the price. As the demand curve becomes more elastic, the markup decreases.

Based on our discussion in Chapter 5 on market structure, we should not be surprised that more competitive markets allow firms smaller markups. For example, if the elasticity is minus infinity (that is, perfectly elastic), the markup of price over ATC is zero, while if the elasticity is zero (that is, perfectly inelastic), the markup is infinite.

A convenience store faces different elasticities of demand for its products. When people need aspirin or other over-the-counter medications, many of them go to the nearest place that sells the product. Thus, despite lower prices elsewhere, the convenience store is able to sell to some customers at a high price. By varying their markups to account for these different demands, the convenience store manager can determine the profit-maximizing prices.

Markup rules are particularly common among retailers who carry a large number of different products of relatively low unit value. For example, many liquor stores use a markup pricing rule for their wine. While the markup may be 30 percent initially, the store must lower its price when some of its wine does not sell as fast as desired. The markup for wine may not be the same as the markups for whiskey and beer. College bookstores also use different markups for textbooks than they do for travel guides, cookbooks, and novels. Their markups must be sensitive to the presence of competing bookstores near the college.

The use of markup rules does make sense as long as the rules are flexible. When a retailer employs several relatively unskilled and low-paid workers, it is simpler to use a standard markup for the store's products based on the retailer's experience of the nature of the demand curve. Workers need only consult a wholesale price list and add the set percentage to arrive at the retail price.

A firm can use information on how quickly its products sell at these markup prices to determine the elasticity of the demand curve for these products. By keeping track of these sales, the firm can get a better idea of the appropriate markup. In cases where products are relatively expensive, more unique, and sold less frequently, standard markups may not be the most appropriate method for pricing the product.

| 6-5 | **Adjustable markups** |

APPLICATION

There is extensive evidence that retail markups do vary in response to market forces. For example, Professor B. Nooteboom found substantial variation in markups for the retail grocery business in the Netherlands between 1957 and 1979. The markups varied in response to market forces. Markups were higher when the industry was growing and the firm's market share was increasing. During declining phases of the market, firms competed vigorously and markups dropped.

The markup also depended on the mix of services and the variety of products offered at the stores. For example, there were higher markups on luxury and durable goods due to their lower turnover rates. More basic foods and textile products had lower markups. As firms experienced scale economies, the markup again dropped. Apparently, competition within the market forced prices down to the lower average total cost of the larger firms.

Not surprisingly, those firms that did not take advantage of potential scale economies were unable to earn a markup to cover their opportunity cost. These smaller firms were among the first to leave the market during a contraction of the market. This study shows that while markup policies are common in retailing, the markup must adjust to the demand for the individual product and to changes in market conditions.

Source: B. Nooteboom, "A Markup Model of Retail Margins." *Applied Economics* 17 (August 1985):647–67.

Incremental Analysis

Due to the expense of accurately determining marginal-cost and demand curves, the principle of producing an output where marginal cost equals marginal revenue may be difficult to determine precisely in all cases. The profit-maximizing firm does benefit, however, by using the marginal-cost concept whenever possible.

In Chapter 4 we discussed several problems that Blanche Mayzone would have to face in operating a restaurant. One involved the decision to sell meals on a take-out basis to a guest planning a party for her parents. The solution to that problem involved incremental analysis. Let's return now to Harry Sampson and take a closer look at incremental analysis.

6-4	Incremental analysis

NUMERICAL EXAMPLE

Assume that a customer approaches Harry with the following offer: the customer will pay $500 for each of seven tree-trimming jobs. Harry normally charges $600 each, but he has a variable cost of $300 per job. The remainder of the price represents a return to his fixed cost. Although it may be worth Harry's time to negotiate for a price higher than $500, he may want to accept this offer.

If the sale at $500 does not affect his price to other customers, if he has sufficient excess capacity to meet this sale without affecting sales at their normal price, and if he perceives that it is a take-it-or-leave-it offer, he is better off making the sale. In fact, he is better off with any offer that exceeds the incremental cost of $300.

The preceding example used incremental analysis. According to this principle, a firm accepts all sales that generate revenues in excess of the incremental costs of the sale, even if average total cost is greater than average revenue. When a firm has excess capacity in the short run, the marginal cost of this capacity is zero. The only relevant production costs are the variable costs.

Firms selling large, set amounts of their product to certain customers may not be able to apply the marginal-revenue-equals-marginal-cost principle directly. Incremental analysis is useful in such cases. By blindly following a markup rule that includes an amount for average fixed cost, a firm may deprive itself of extra sales that could utilize its capacity more fully.

A firm must be careful to consider all costs when using incremental analysis. You can apply incremental analysis to a wide range of economic problems. For instance, consider the problem faced by the manager of the hotel where Phyllis and Harry are having dinner. The manager notices Phyllis and Harry having an after-dinner beer in the bar. Since Phyllis has done some consulting work for the hotel, the manager stops by to say hello.

The manager mentions that the hotel has always based its reputation on the quality of food served in its two restaurants: the Ceiling Room and the Panel Room. Unfortunately, however, he says that customers have been losing interest in the more expensive restaurant—the Ceiling Room—and he has decided that he should consider closing the Ceiling Room, at least temporarily.

He has been disappointed each time he has visited the restaurant, since over half of the tables have been empty. Before making the final decision, he says he conferred with the restaurant's maitre d', Dexter Hocknay. Well aware of the possibility of losing his job, Dexter offered the following advice to his boss.

Dexter suggested that they document all of the relevant costs associated with keeping the Ceiling Room open. He then pointed out some of the more obvious costs, including the salaries for the serving staff, and the food and drinks consumed by the customers. Since both restaurants use the same kitchen, the kitchen staff expenses are the net amount over the amount required to serve meals in the Panel Room.

Because of the unusual design of the Ceiling Room, Dexter noted that there was no immediate alternative use for the room, and this meant that its opportunity cost was zero. Since revenues from the restaurant exceed the remaining cost, he suggested that the restaurant remain open.

The manager mentioned to Dexter a less obvious effect that closing the Ceiling Room would have on the Panel Room. Since the hotel has many business guests who are generally unfamiliar with the city and who do not want to go too far from the hotel for meals, these guests are likely to choose one of the two restaurants within the hotel. By closing the Ceiling Room, the hotel would shift some of its revenues from one restaurant to the other without a net change. Since the Panel Room is not operating near capacity, it could absorb the extra business with no adjustment in seating capacity.

Dexter countered by suggesting an additional factor. Despite the reduced interest in the Ceiling Room, some out-of-town visitors come to the hotel simply for the opportunity of eating in the Ceiling Room. While they are at the hotel, they spend money in the hotel's shops and stay overnight at the hotel. The addition of these expenditures over incremental costs goes toward covering the fixed costs of the entire hotel.

Harry then suggests, contrary to what Dexter said earlier, that the Ceiling Room does have an opportunity cost. If it were not used as a restaurant, the room could become an auditorium, a theater, or a ballroom for special parties. The excess revenues over variable costs in its best alternative use would represent a part of the incremental cost of keeping the restaurant open.

Although impressed by Harry's contribution to the solution of this problem, Phyllis suggests that the hotel manager let her consulting firm work out the details. She needs to go home early to prepare for her next day's work. Secretly hoping that she might be assigned to this consulting job, she summarizes some of the important considerations while driving home.

First of all, if the hotel does not expect to earn revenues in excess of its incremental costs of preparing and serving the food and maintaining the dining room in an appropriate condition, the hotel should close the restaurant. Since the net revenues are positive, the hotel has a more difficult problem.

If the hotel does not have an alternative for the room, its opportunity cost is zero. If it could convert the room into a theater or ballroom, as Harry suggested, or into shops or seminar rooms, it should consider the lost revenues in excess of variable cost from these uses an additional incremental cost of keeping the restaurant open.

It should also subtract from its expected net revenues the net revenue that would be transferred to the Panel Room, since the hotel would earn this money whether the Ceiling Room stayed open or not. Admittedly, calculating precisely how many people come to the hotel only because of the Ceiling Room would be difficult. In the absence of exact information, the hotel should estimate this effect. The balance of these factors would determine the fate of the restaurant.

This example goes beyond the setting of output and price where marginal revenue equals marginal cost by considering all the effects that the restaurant's closing would have on the profitability of the entire hotel's operation. It shows the importance of considering all of the incremental costs in making management decisions.

Summary

In this chapter we considered several pricing problems. In each case the firm was able to maximize profits without immediate concern about competitors. We saw several possibilities for the firm to maximize its profits by segmenting the market demand. As long as the firm does not have to worry that a competitor will take away customers because of this pricing rule, the firm can charge customers different prices and increase its profits.

When segmenting the market the firm must be able to prevent resales. For this reason price discrimination (that is, market segmentation) is more common for services. The profit-maximizing firm sets prices so that the marginal revenue of the last unit sold in each market equals the marginal cost of the last unit sold.

A similar pricing opportunity exists when demand fluctuates over time. We looked at the pricing problem of a manager of a tennis-court complex. Since demand fluctuated by time of day, the manager had to determine the total demand for the tennis courts for the entire day. Since the manager could spread the cost of a tennis court among all of the customers who used the court, the manager added demand curves vertically. To maximize profits the manager would build courts to the point where aggregate marginal revenue equaled the marginal cost of the court.

We completed the chapter with discussions of markup and incremental pricing. Markup pricing may be a low-cost proxy for profit maximization when the firm faces stable demand for low-priced goods that are sold frequently. As long as the firm adjusts its markup to changes in the elasticity of demand, this procedure has some merit.

Incremental pricing is more appropriate for higher-valued and less frequently sold goods and services. Incremental analysis is much more general than its use for pricing products. Any economic decision involves some incremental costs and benefits. Blind reliance on markup rules or other arbitrary criteria may lead the manager to serious errors. It is worth the effort to consider the incremental costs before committing oneself to an economic solution to a firm's problem.

Price Discrimination (p. 154) Arbitrage (p. 158)
Demand Price (p. 155) Peak-Load Pricing (p. 167)
Perfect Price Discrimination (p. 155) Markup Pricing (p. 175)

Selected References

Adams, William J. and Yellen, Janet T. "Commodity Bundling and the Burden of Monopoly." *Quarterly Journal of Economics* 40 (May 1976):475–98.

Burstein, M.L. "The Economics of Tie-in Sales." *Review of Economics and Statistics* 27 (February 1960):68–73.

Frank, Ronald E.; Massy, William; and Wind, Yoram. *Market Segmentation*. Englewood Cliffs, New Jersey: Prentice-Hall, 1972.

Hall, R.L. and Hitch, C.J. "Price Theory and Business Behavior." *Oxford Economic Papers* 2 (May 1939):12–45.

Nagle, Thomas. "Economic Foundations for Pricing." *Journal of Business* 57 (January 1984): S3–S26.

Steiner, Peter O. "Peak Loads and Efficient Pricing." *Quarterly Journal of Economics* 71 (November 1957):585–610.

Williams, Stephen F. "Getting Downtown: Relief of Highway Congestion Through Pricing." *Regulation* (March/April 1981):45–50.

1. Assume that the Ernani All-Brass Band plays both at nightclubs and at weddings. The manager, Duke Alber, also plays lead horn and brings down the house with his solo at the end of each performance. His band plays essentially the same music at both weddings and clubs, and plays for the same length of time. Duke has determined that the demand curve for his band's services is not the same at weddings as at nightclubs. The demand and marginal-revenue curves at nightclubs (group 1) are given by

$$P_1 = 3600 - 20Q_1$$
$$MR_1 = 3600 - 40Q_1$$

and at weddings (group 2) by

$$P_2 = 2400 - 10Q_2$$
$$MR_2 = 2400 - 20Q_2.$$

The quantities are in performances per year, and the prices are in dollars. Short-run marginal cost equals $400. Calculate the prices and number of performances.

2. Explain and show graphically how price discrimination can increase profits for a firm selling a homogeneous good to two submarkets. Assume that the good is produced at constant marginal cost.

3. Assume that a movie theater, Visual Sensations III, is able to discriminate between patrons under twelve years of age and everyone else. The theater faces the following demand and marginal-revenue curves

Twelve years and younger: $P_1 = 10 - Q_1$ and $MR_1 = 10 - 2Q_1$
Everyone else: $P_2 = 10 - 2Q_2$ and $MR_2 = 10 - 4Q_2$
Marginal cost: $MC = 1.00$

Assume that there is a one-time cost of $50 to separate the two markets and to prevent resales. What should the theater manager do?

4. Assume that Ray-Zoe Electronic Systems faces the following demand curve for its machine:

$$P = 5000 - 0.2Q.$$

The company chooses to rent the machine on an annual basis. The marginal cost per machine per year is $200. If the owner can install a metering device, what will the owner's profits be relative to a perfectly competitive solution?

5. Assume that the owner of a stamping machine company, Will Frahpitt, decides to install a metering device in the machines and rent them out based on a fixed charge per unit used of the machine. Assume that Will's annual cost for each machine is $500, independent of the number of machines rented. Assume also that annual demand in dollars is given by $P = 10,000 - 0.1Q$, where Q is the number of machines. Calculate the additional profit made by the owner over and above the leasing price that would have been set without a metering device.

6. Assume that a local government is considering building a stadium to be rented to two professional teams whose seasons do not overlap. There will be no other tenants and no benefit to the government except for the rent. The government will set prices for the use of the stadium that will maximize the profits of the local government. Assume that the government knows what the demands of the two teams will be.

Determine the size of the stadium and the price each team should pay. The cost per unit of capacity is $5 million. The two teams' demand equations are as follows:

$$P_1 = 40 - 0.2Q_1 \quad \text{and} \quad P_2 = 20 - 0.1Q_2,$$

where the prices are in millions of dollars and the quantities are in units of capacity. The corresponding marginal-revenue equations are

$$MR_1 = 40 - 0.4Q_1 \quad \text{and} \quad MR_2 = 20 - 0.2Q_2.$$

7. Assume that Autovoll Guaranteed Parking rents parking spaces for two time periods during the day. Assume that demand for the parking spaces is

$$P_1 = 40 - 0.2Q_1$$

during normal working hours. For the rest of the day the demand is

$$P_2 = 10 - 0.2Q_2.$$

The corresponding marginal-revenue equations are

$$MR_1 = 40 - 0.4Q_1 \quad \text{and} \quad MR_2 = 10 - 0.4Q_2.$$

If the long-run marginal cost per day of supplying a parking space is $4, how many parking spaces should the firm supply, and what prices should the firm charge?

8. Loge Briquettes produces a line of instant-flaming charcoal briquettes, which it sells primarily to supermarkets. The company's pricing policy currently consists of a markup procedure. Prices are typically set at 200 percent of average variable cost; that is, the margin is 100 percent. The firm has a chance to sell 10,000 bags at a price of $1.80 each to a large supermarket chain located in New England. The production manager estimates production costs for this special order to be as follows:

Raw materials	$2,000
Direct labor	5,000
Other variable costs	4,000
Fixed overhead allocation	
(40 percent of direct labor)	2,000
Production setup costs for this run	500
Total cost	$13,500

The buyer specifies that Loge Briquettes must deliver the 10,000 bags within the next three months. To meet this schedule, the company will have to lose orders for 1,000 bags from regular customers at a price of $2.25 each because of the limited excess capacity currently available at the firm. This inability to supply regular customers will not affect future demand from them.

(a) Using this information, determine whether Loge Briquettes should accept the special order.

(b) What is the minimum unit price that Loge Briquettes should accept for the special order of 10,000 bags?

Answer questions 9–16 with true, false, or uncertain.

9. A firm facing two negatively-sloped demand curves for two well-identified submarkets maximizes profits by charging each group a different price.

10. When discriminating in price, the monopolist will raise the price in the relatively inelastic market and lower the price in the relatively elastic market.

11. By using a metering device, the manufacturer charges everyone the same price for the use of the machine.

12. Customers with higher demand prices value a product more than those with lower demand prices.

13. An unregulated firm facing a demand curve that varies according to the time of day will produce more output than a regulated firm.

14. To determine the total demand for a service that varies with time, one adds the individual demand curves vertically, as opposed to horizontally.

15. Markup pricing practices are inconsistent with profit maximization.

16. When facing a perfectly inelastic demand curve, a profit-maximizing firm will use an infinite markup.

7

PRICING WHEN FACING COMPETITION

This chapter extends the study of pricing strategies. In the previous chapter, the firm set output and price without concern for the reaction of other firms in the market. We simply assumed that the firm was able to block entry into the market. In this chapter the firm must be more mindful of the reactions of other firms, both those already in the market and those likely to enter the market.

We will start with a market structure that has much in common with the monopoly market of Chapter 5: the dominant-firm market. The firm dominating this market must contend with a group of price-taking firms when choosing its profit-maximizing output and price. We will consider the market for physicians as an example.

Following this, we will observe a firm that starts with a monopoly but then must face a used-product market. This problem is similar to the one faced by the dominant firm. We will see why this problem may have been relevant to ALCOA's (Aluminum Company of America) pricing decisions prior to World War II.

A dominant firm may be content to share a market with other firms. We will analyze the options available to a dominant firm that wants to deter entry into its market. We have been assuming that the firm sets its price to maximize its short-run profits. We will move from that assumption to long-run profit maximization. We will consider market structures where the firm must relate future entry into its market to the price and quantities it sets for its product.

We will then propose strategies for eliminating existing competitors. There have been several court cases involving alleged attempts by large firms to use low predatory prices to force smaller firms to leave the market or sell out at distress prices. We will consider both the economic and legal effects of a predatory-pricing strategy.

Finally, we will evaluate the prospects for avoiding competition with rival companies. In particular, we will look at the economics of collusive arrangements, such as cartels, with special attention given to the fate of air-travel and sugar cartels. We will also analyze the possibility of implicit price collusion.

All of these pricing strategies depend on the presence or the threat of competitors. These examples do not exhaust all of the possible scenarios faced by a firm. They do provide an extensive set of common pricing situations faced by most firms and a solid base for analyzing other more specialized environments. The references at the end of the chapter include examples for those interested in further study. In Chapter 13 we will encounter most of these pricing practices again when we consider the antitrust implications in more detail.

Dominant Firm

Let's return to the problems of Harry Sampson of the Verte Tree Company. Harry has many competitors. He has determined that his company currently has more than half of the local market, and each of the other firms are small compared to the size of his company. They are so small that they all take his price as the market norm. He wants Phyllis's advice concerning his pricing and output decisions given this competition.

▶ —————
Harry's firm is the dominant firm in this market. A **dominant firm** is a firm that sets the market price for a type of product or service while taking into account the supply response of a group of small firms that are acting as price takers. The small firms are **fringe firms**, since they form a fringe around the large firm, and are price takers, since they take the dominant firm's price as the market price.

Harry should conceptualize his strategy first. Assume that all the competing small firms offer the same service: a standard tree-trimming job. Since they are price takers, each of these firms has a supply curve. By observing the quantities supplied by the fringe firms at different prices, Harry can determine the supply curve for all of these firms. For the moment, assume that we know the nature of this supply curve. Assume further that Harry has estimated the market demand curve for tree trimming. With this information he can now determine his profit-maximizing price.

7-1	The dominant firm

GRAPHICAL EXPLANATION

Assume that Figure 7-1 (p. 188) represents the following market condition: a dominant firm (that is, Verte Tree Company) with knowledge of both the market demand curve and the fringe firms' supply curves. If Harry sets the price for a standard tree-trimming job at $150, both the quantity demanded in the market and the total quantity supplied by the smaller firms would be fifty tree-trimming jobs.

For all prices greater than $150, the quantity supplied by the small firms would exceed the quantity demanded by the consumers in the market. Since equilibrium solutions occur at prices where quantity demanded equals quantity

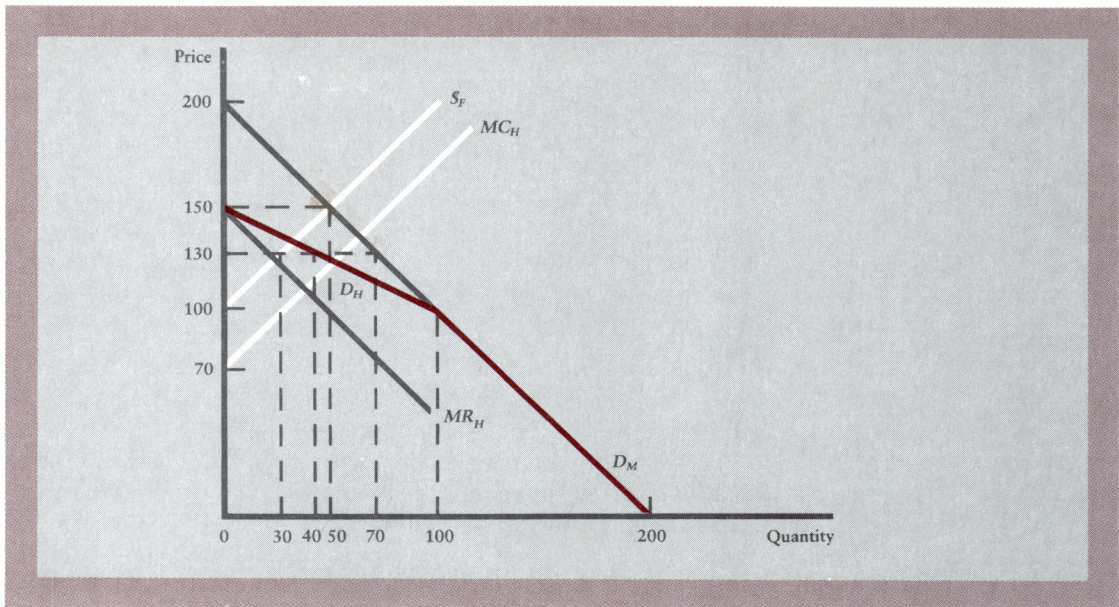

FIGURE 7-1 ▪ **The dominant firm.** The fringe firms are price takers and will supply according to supply curve S_F. The dominant firm (Verte Tree Company) derives its demand curve, D_H, by subtracting the quantity supplied by the fringe firms from the quantity demanded by the market at each price. Harry will produce forty tree-trimming jobs (that is, at the output level where his marginal-cost curve, MC_H, equals the marginal-revenue curve, MR_H). He sets his price at $130. The fringe firms will produce thirty tree-trimming jobs. The market quantity demanded will by seventy tree-trimming jobs.

supplied, Harry could not set the price higher than $150. To keep the price at $150 Harry must produce nothing! At and below $100, he must supply the entire quantity demanded by the consumers, since the other firms would not want to supply anything.

For prices between $100 and $150, Harry must supply the difference between the quantity demanded in the market and the quantity supplied by the fringe firms in order to maintain whatever price he sets. As a result, he can derive a demand curve, D_H, for his output as the residual between the quantity demanded by the market and the quantity supplied by the fringe firms at each price.

Figure 7-1 shows the demand curve derived in this manner as D_H. The demand curve begins at $150 and zero quantity demanded. At a price of $100, the quantity demanded is the entire market quantity demanded of one hundred units. Below a price of $100, Harry's demand curve is the same as the market demand curve, since the fringe firms find the price too low for them to supply any tree-trimming jobs.

Recall that a straight-line demand curve has a straight-line marginal-revenue curve corresponding to it. The marginal-revenue curve has the same intercept term on the vertical axis and a slope twice that of the demand curve in absolute value. Figure 7-1 shows Harry's marginal-revenue curve, MR_H. If Harry's marginal cost is MC_H, he will maximize profits at a quantity of forty, where his marginal revenue equals his marginal cost.

At a price of $130 the quantity demanded in the overall market is seventy. Since the fringe firms are price takers, they will react to the price of $130 by supplying a total of thirty tree-trimming jobs. The difference between the quantity demanded in the market (70) and the quantity supplied by the fringe firms (30) equals Harry's quantity demanded of forty jobs.

7-1	Dominant firm

NUMERICAL EXAMPLE

Assume that the market demand for tree-trimming services shown in Figure 7-1 is

$$P = 200 - Q_M,$$

where Q_M is the market quantity demanded. The equation for the fringe firms' supply curve is

$$P = 100 + Q_F,$$

where Q_F is the quantity supplied by the fringe firms. Figure 7-1 shows that if Harry did not participate in this market, the market equilibrium would occur where the two curves crossed. In this case Q_M would be the same as Q_F (both relabeled as Q) and

$$P = 200 - Q = 100 + Q$$
$$2Q = 100$$
$$Q = 50.$$

At Q equal to 50, the market price would be $150.

Assume that Harry does plan to sell in this market and that Verte Tree Company is the dominant firm with a marginal-cost curve equal to

$$MC_H = 70 + Q_H$$

where Q_H is Harry's quantity. We must now determine the equation representing Harry's demand curve. If the market price is $150, Harry will produce nothing. If the market price is $100 or less, the fringe firms will produce nothing. When the fringe firms produce nothing, Harry must supply the entire market. For example, when the price is $100, the market quantity demanded is one hundred units.

Harry's demand curve will be a straight line passing through the (P, Q) coordinates (150, 0) and (100, 100). Note that in moving from (150, 0) to (100, 100) on Harry's demand curve, the change in price is 50, while the change in quantity demanded is 100 in the opposite direction. For this reason, the slope of the demand curve will be $-50/100$, or -0.5. Harry's demand equation will be

$$P = 150 - 0.5Q_H.$$

Since the marginal-revenue curve will have a slope that is twice the slope of the demand curve in absolute value, the equation of the marginal-revenue curve will be

$$MR_H = 150 - Q_H.$$

Harry will determine his profit-maximizing output by setting MR_H equal to MC_H as follows:

$$MR_H = 150 - Q_H = 70 + Q_H = MC_H$$

$$80 = 2Q_H$$

$$Q_H = 40$$

and

$$P = 150 - 0.5Q_H = 150 - 0.5(40) = \$130.$$

Harry will set the market price at \$130, and the fringe firms will act as price takers. Since their combined supply curve is $P = 100 + Q_F$, they will supply thirty units at the market price of \$130.

$$P = 100 + Q_F = \$130$$

and

$$Q_F = 30.$$

Harry's pricing strategy would result in short-run profit maximization. Harry may not be able to maintain this dominant position in the long run. While a firm may be in a dominant position in its market at some point in time, it must maintain a barrier to entry to keep others from entering the market. It must also be able to keep the fringe firms from increasing their market share over time. If it is unable to do so, it will see its share of the market decline.

7-1   **The American Medical Association and the physician epidemic**

APPLICATION   According to numerous analysts and critics, the American Medical Association (AMA) has pursued policies aimed at limiting the number of physicians practicing in the United States. Despite a stable ratio of physicians to population from the end of World War II until 1965, the ratio rose from 1.4 per thousand to 2.0 per thousand between 1965 and 1981. This change prompted Monica Noether, Ph.D., of the Federal Trade Commission to investigate the AMA's influence on physician supply.

The market for physician services has a dominant firm: the AMA and its member physicians. There is a competitive fringe made up of physicians who enter the market outside of AMA control. We can use Figure 7-1 to summarize Dr. Noether's findings. Earlier we discovered that no firm, whether monopolist or dominant-firm, can maintain economic profits unless there is a barrier to entry. In this case Dr. Noether argued that the AMA has had some success in preventing the fringe physicians' supply curve from shifting far enough to the right to drive the market price low enough to eliminate the economic profits of AMA-member physicians.

The AMA has controlled the number of medical school spaces in the United States by awarding accreditation on a size basis and making it difficult for new schools to receive accreditation. The AMA has also lobbied actively to install state licensing statutes that require graduation from AMA-accredited schools and to curtail entry of foreign-trained physicians through restrictive licensing laws and immigration policy.

The AMA's power to limit the supply of physicians has diminished since the 1960s. Non-AMA representatives now sit on accreditation boards. In the mid-1960s the federal government initiated subsidy programs to provide incentives to increase the number of physicians. There was also a relaxation of immigration requirements for foreign doctors.

For example, the government abolished the national origin quota system of the Immigration Act, which had favored Western Hemisphere countries. The government also authorized a special quota of 17,000 annually for people with skills in short supply. In 1971 the government broadened the Exchange Visitor program to allow anyone possessing an exchange visa to apply for immediate change to immigrant status. In 1973 the Supreme Court ruled that states could not limit physician licensing to U.S. citizens.

Dr. Noether estimated that the relaxation of licensing and immigration laws increased the number of foreign-trained physicians by 35,000–40,000 between 1965 and 1980. The efforts of the federal government to subsidize the expansion of U.S. medical schools resulted in the licensing of 13,000 physicians during the same time period.

Source: Monica Noether, "The Effect of Government Policy Changes on the Supply of Physicians: Expansion of a Competitive Fringe." *Journal of Law and Economics* XXIX (October 1986):231–62. © by the University of Chicago.

Pricing When Facing Competition from a Used Product

There is a connection between the dominant-firm pricing strategy and pricing given a used-product market. A company could start with a monopoly position in the market while facing the prospect that some of its own output might come back as a competing product.

7-2	**Back again?**

APPLICATION

The United States Department of Justice prosecuted ALCOA (Aluminum Company of America) for monopolizing the domestic aluminum industry in the 1930s and 1940s. In its argument, the Department of Justice said that ALCOA had eliminated effective competition by charging low prices and earning only a 10 percent return on its investments. The only competitors of ALCOA were importers and recyclers of aluminum. The supply of recycled aluminum produced by several small firms was a function of the price set by ALCOA for its newly produced aluminum. According to this line of reasoning, ALCOA could not set its price without acknowledging the potential supply of recycled aluminum. The higher the price set by ALCOA the greater the incentive for a small company to recycle aluminum.

The Supreme Court concluded that recycled aluminum should not be considered a competing product, since ALCOA controlled the amount of recycled aluminum available in the future by how much new aluminum it produced. Even though the Supreme Court agreed that ALCOA was earning only an average return on its investment, and that ALCOA most likely had a cost advantage over potential competitors, it ruled in 1940 that ALCOA had systematically attempted to monopolize the market.

Professor Valerie Suslow of the University of Michigan questioned whether ALCOA had as much control over the recycled market as the Supreme Court suggested. She noted that earlier analysts (including the United States Supreme Court) assumed that recycled aluminum appeared quickly and that it was the same as new aluminum. Recycled aluminum accounted for an average of 20 percent of the market before 1940, except in the mid-1930s, when it rose to 31 percent.

Professor Suslow discovered that recycled aluminum was used for automobile castings but was not generally suitable for making sheet and wire products because of higher purity requirements. Most scrap aluminum came from automobiles and aircraft. Lags between original sales and scrapping varied between an average of five years for motor vehicles and twenty-five years for cables.

Despite her finding that ALCOA was unable to exert much influence over the size of the recycled market, Professor Suslow concluded that ALCOA had substantial market power, because the current stock of recoverable aluminum was at least an imperfect substitute for ALCOA's new aluminum. She determined that recycling lags were long enough to reduce the importance of the recycled aluminum market as a factor in ALCOA's short-run decision making. Although she disagreed with the Supreme Court's reasoning, she agreed that ALCOA did have substantial market power.

Source: Valerie Y. Suslow, "Estimating Monopoly Behavior with Competitive Recycling: an Application to ALCOA." *Rand Journal of Economics* 17, No. 3 (Autumn 1986):389–403.

Pricing to Deter Entry

Harry finds Phyllis's warnings regarding the problems of limiting the output of competitors worrisome. He certainly wants to maintain his market position and would even like to drive his competitors out of business. Whatever he has in mind for his current competitors, however, he still has to worry about future competitors entering his market. If he expects to make economic profits in the long run, he must establish a barrier to entry. Without a barrier to entry he can expect other firms to want the same economic profits he is making.

Although we will offer several nonprice strategies in Chapter 9, we focus our attention now on pricing strategies for deterring entry. As a way of introducing the subject, we can extend the dominant-firm theory to include market entry. We will start with a firm which we will call the incumbent firm. The **incumbent firm** is a firm already in the market. When there is only one firm in the market, the incumbent firm is a monopolist. We will begin by considering the threat of entry from several small firms. The analysis will depend on the dominant-firm theory.

Deterring the Entry of Small Firms

Remember that the dominant firm must be able to block entry to maintain economic profits in the long run. Without a barrier to entry, new firms will enter the market in pursuit of economic profits. Any entry of firms to the dominant firm's market will force the dominant firm's demand curve to shift to the left. Eventually, the dominant firm would lose its dominant position in the market and become a price taker like all of the other firms.

As a dominant firm, Verte Tree Company faces several pricing options. We will start with two extreme possibilities. For example, Harry could set his price at the short-run, profit-maximizing level or he could set it at a price low enough to remove all incentive for new firms to enter the market. In the rare case that Harry had substantially lower average total cost relative to all potential rivals, these two prices would be the same. If the prices were not the same, Harry's choice between the two strategies would depend on their effects on his long-run profits.

By charging the short-run monopoly price, Harry would generate larger profits in the short run, but he would see these profits diminish over time as firms entered the market. If Harry had a cost advantage over his potential rivals, a price below their minimum average cost would yield lower short-run profits for Harry but would eliminate potential rivals' incentive for entry. By maintaining these lower prices, Harry would lock in a consistently lower level of economic profits for a longer period of time.

You should not be surprised that any analysis of long-run pricing behavior hinges on the nature of barriers to entry. While we discussed barriers to entry in Chapter 5, we will now review the main forms that these barriers take. For example, a dominant firm could have an absolute cost advantage due to its exclusive control over nonreproducible inputs or a patented or otherwise protected production process.

It could have effectively used nonprice competition to create a brand image or good will with customers that would force new entrants to pay relatively higher production and/or promotion costs to offset the incumbent firm's advantages. In cases where entry would come most likely from smaller firms, scale economies in production, distribution, purchasing inputs, raising investment capital, or advertising could place entrants at a cost disadvantage.

Without a cost advantage or barrier to entry, the dominant firm cannot expect to sustain its market position over time. The two extremes of no barriers to entry and insurmountable barriers to entry are not likely to include all scenarios that the dominant firm could face. We would have to develop a detailed analysis of the market before we could determine the appropriate strategy. In the case of Verte Tree Company, Harry would have to base his strategy on several factors, including his cost advantage relative to other firms and the speed of entry by fringe firms. The slower the rate of entry by other firms, the longer the dominant firm can keep its price above its minimum average total cost.

7-3   **Get your profits while you can**

APPLICATION The U.S. Steel Corporation has been a leading producer of steel and a leading supplier of iron ore in the United States during the twentieth century. Despite dominance in both of these markets in the early years of the century, U.S. Steel's pricing practices have not been the same for these two markets.

A series of mergers led to the formation of the U.S. Steel Corporation in 1901. The company had 65 percent of the steel-ingot production in the United States at that time. Apparently it had no cost advantage over the other firms in the market due to the expiration of all of its important patents. In 1907 it acquired a large competitor, and in 1911 it opened the world's largest steel works in Gary, Indiana. Despite its dominance in the market, its market share dropped steadily to 51 percent in 1915, 42 percent in 1925, and 24 percent in 1967.

According to Professor George Stigler of the University of Chicago, U.S. Steel's business was highly profitable in the earlier years of its existence. It charged prices close to the short-run profit-maximizing level. Yet, while this strategy yielded profits, it encouraged market entry.

Since any price it had charged which exceeded its average total cost would have encouraged entry into the market, the company chose to set the short-run profit-maximizing price. Due to the time that it took for a new firm to establish itself in the industry, U.S. Steel was able to earn economic profits during the transition period to a new long-run equilibrium.

U.S. Steel also controlled a large share of U.S. iron-ore deposits. After purchasing most of the remaining high-grade ore between 1910 and 1920, U.S. Steel left only low-grade ore to its rivals and potential entrants. With its ability to block entry to the market, the company maintained its market share in the 40–45 percent range for decades.

Since U.S. Steel had no obvious cost advantage over its rivals in steel production, it chose to maximize its profits with a high-price policy in the early years. In the case of iron ore, U.S. Steel used its cost advantage to maintain a relatively constant market share by blocking the entry of new firms to the market.

Source: George J. Stigler, "The Dominant Firm and the Inverted Umbrella." *Journal of Law and Economics* 8 (October 1965):167–72. © by the University of Chicago.

Deterring the Entry of Large Firms

While entry is normally made by smaller firms, it is not unusual for large firms to make a move into new product lines and directly challenge the market position of another large firm. Since the entrant is not likely to act as a price taker, the preceding analysis is not appropriate. Assume that the incumbent firm is interested in setting a price and quantity that will remove any incentive for potential entrants. Assume that there are scale economies associated with this production process that are the same for both the incumbent firm and any new large firm planning on entering the market.

| 7-2 | **Large-scale entry** |

GRAPHICAL EXPLANATION

As a simplification, let's assume that no firm can produce a product unless it produces an output of at least q^*. For any output greater than q^*, the firm will produce subject to constant returns to scale (that is, its long-run average-

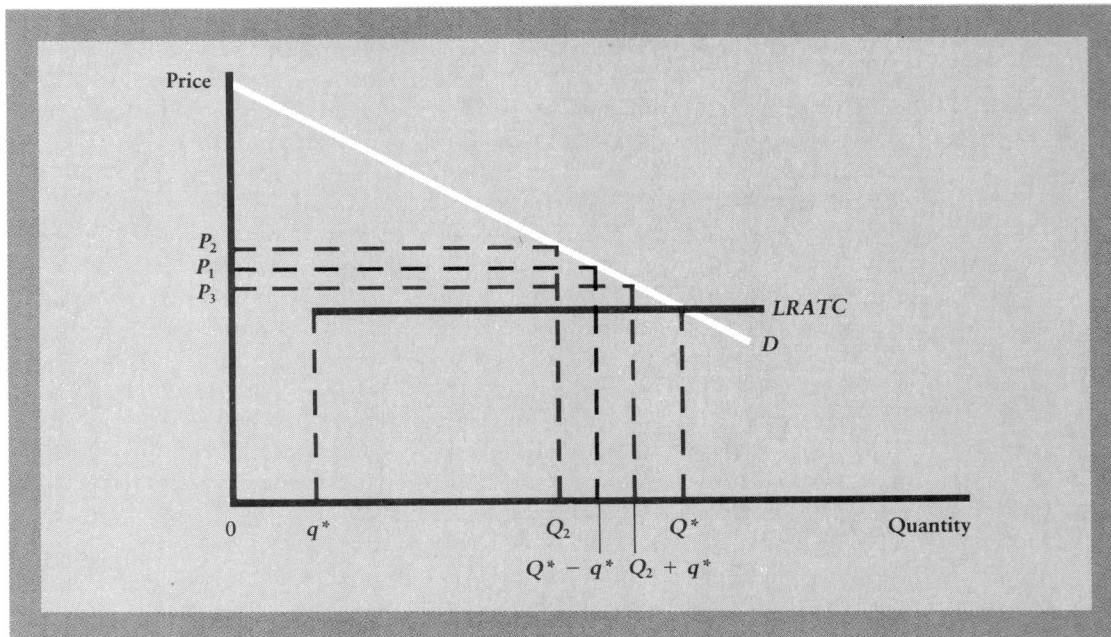

FIGURE 7-2 ■ Deterring large-scale entry. The incumbent firm can set its output as high as $Q^* - q^*$ without encouraging other firms to enter the market. A new firm must enter at size q^* or larger. By entering at size q^*, the new firm would drive the market price down to *LRATC*. Neither firm would make economic profits in this case. If the incumbent tries to gain more economic profits by raising price above P_1, new firms can enter the market and earn economic profits.

total-cost curve will look like the one in Figure 7-2). Later we will make the more realistic assumption that the average-total-cost curve has a negative slope between outputs 0 and q^*.

Given the average-total-cost curve in Figure 7-2, the incumbent firm can set a price greater than its long-run average total cost, while not encouraging entry. In order to do this, the incumbent firm must convince any firm planning on entering the market that it will continue to produce the same output regardless of the new firm's output. If this threat is convincing, the incumbent firm can set its output at $Q^* - q^*$, shown in Figure 7-2, and charge price P_1.

Any firm thinking of entering this market knows that the incumbent firm will continue to produce $Q^* - q^*$ as threatened. Even if the new firm produces the smallest amount possible, q^*, the total market output will be $(Q^* - q^*) + q^* = Q^*$, the quantity where the market price just equals long-run average total cost. At Q^* neither of the two firms will make any economic profits. If the potential entrant produces an output greater than q^*, the total market output will be greater than Q^* and the market price will fall below long-run average total cost. Both firms will suffer economic losses.

This strategy depends on the credibility of the incumbent firm's threat to maintain output at $Q^* - q^*$. Notice that any output smaller than this will result in a price that will allow a new firm to enter at output q^* without forcing economic profits to 0. For example, if the incumbent firm chooses output Q_2 and price P_2, a new firm will lower the market price to P_3 by adding output q^*. Since P_3 is greater than the firm's long-run average total cost, the new firm will find it profitable to enter the market even though the incumbent firm maintains its output at Q_2.

As mentioned earlier, it would be more realistic to assume that long-run average total cost declines for output between 0 and q^*. Figure 7-3 shows an example of this type of average-total-cost curve.

<table>
<tr><td>**7-3**</td><td>**Large-scale entry with declining average costs of production**</td></tr>
</table>

GRAPHICAL
EXPLANATION

A new firm can enter the market at a scale smaller than q^*, but it will have to operate at a higher average cost than if it produces at an output of q^* or greater. In this case the incumbent firm must choose an output and price that will make entry unattractive to potential entrants.

Figure 7-3 (p. 198) shows the average-total-cost curve of such an entrant. Once the incumbent firm chooses its output level, the entrant will compare its average total cost to the market price that it expects to receive by entering the market. By choosing Q_1 in Figure 7-3, the incumbent firm's output will be just large enough so that the potential entrant cannot select an output that will result in economic profits.

The best the new firm can do is produce q_1. With the incumbent firm producing Q_1 and the new firm producing q_1, the total market output of $Q_1 + q_1$ will drive the market price down to P_2. At P_2 the new firm will not make any economic profits. Without the prospect of economic profits, the potential entrant will not enter the market.

The incumbent firm will be able to charge price P_1 and produce at Q_1 without worry of entry. Since its price exceeds its average total cost, it will continue to make economic profits. To be successful it must be able to convince any potential entrant that it will not change its output despite the entrant's output decision. If a new entrant does not believe that the incumbent firm will maintain output at Q_1, this may not be a successful entry-deterring strategy.

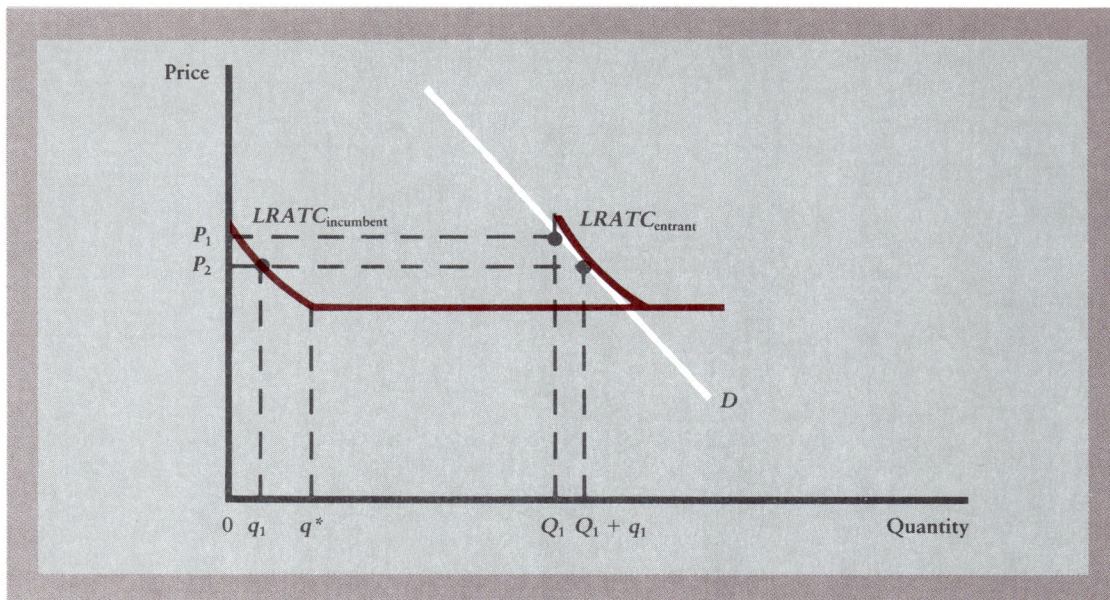

FIGURE 7-3 ▪ Deterring entry with declining average total cost. When new entrants produce subject to a declining average total cost curve, the incumbent firm deters entry by choosing a price and quantity combination, P_1 and Q_1, that offers the new entrant no opportunity for profitable entry. Since the new entrant's average-total-cost curve (starting at the incumbent firm's output of Q_1) never falls below the demand curve, there is no output level that will generate economic profits.

Contestable Markets

Some economists have challenged the notion that scale economies act as a barrier to entry against large firms. For example, it might not be rational for the incumbent firms to keep their output constant after large-scale entry into the market. Some economists have expanded the idea of scale economies by focusing on the importance of maintaining excess capacity as a threat to potential entrants. For example, if a new firm enters, the incumbent firm increases its output to lower the price to an unacceptable level for new firms. In order for these strategies to work, the incumbent firm has to convince new firms that it will not deviate from its stated position. Unless this threat is credible, the strategy will be unsuccessful.

The analysis of the preceding section also overlooks the possibility of an entrant taking away the entire market from the incumbent firm by convincing customers that the other firm's product is not worth buying. Faced with a threat from a potential entrant, the incumbent firm may be forced to maintain a price equal to its average total cost. This is the case with contestable markets.

A **perfectly contestable market** is a market that has at least one potential entrant that faces the same market demand and has access to the same technology as the incumbent firm, while facing no legal restrictions or sunk costs in entering or leaving the market.

The Threat of Market Entry   In a contestable market the incumbent firm must state a price for its product and maintain that price for some time period. The time period must be long enough for an outsider to offer consumers a lower price and take the incumbent's customers away. The basic feature of this market is that an outsider can rush into the market whenever an incumbent posts a price that is higher than the incumbent's average costs. This high price provides an incentive for the outsider to strike and capture the market. As long as there is no impediment to the outsider entering the market, the incumbent's only recourse is to charge a market price equal to its average cost to prevent entry.

Since the potential entrant to the market has no sunk costs, the potential entrant can leave the market without incurring a cost if the incumbent retaliates with a lower price. In this case economies of scale do not play a role in deterring entry, since the outsider can enter at the same scale as the incumbent firm.

In summary, if markets are perfectly contestable, the presence of an outsider ready to enter the market will force an incumbent to avoid taking economic profits even if it is the only firm in the market. The following conditions for perfect market contestability are demanding:

(a) There must be easy access to the market.
(b) There must be a second-hand market for the sale of whatever equipment and machinery an entrant may have utilized. (Without a second-hand market, the entrant may incur sunk costs if it decides to leave the market.)
(c) There must also be some delay before an incumbent can match the price of the entrant.

7-4

Air power

APPLICATION   Dr. Elizabeth Bailey reported the results of a U.S. Civil Aeronautics Board decision to support the merger of two airlines servicing the Houston-New Orleans market. Texas International wanted to acquire National Airlines. Before the merger the two largest firms had a 51 percent share of the market. With a merger the new company would be the largest firm in the market, and the two largest firms would have 75 percent of the market.

Although earlier decisions by the Supreme Court found market domination of this magnitude grounds for opposing a merger, Dr. Bailey argued that there was a pool of eleven carriers which had facilities already in place at both airports and which contested the route. The U.S. government decided that the routes were contestable and allowed the merger. Despite the large size of the newly merged firm, a small regional carrier, Southwest Airlines, soon entered the market and took a 25 percent share of the market.

Source: Elizabeth E. Bailey, "Contestability and the Design of Regulatory and Antitrust Policy." *The American Economic Review* 71 (May 1981):178–83.

The restrictive conditions necessary for a market to be perfectly contestable may limit the relevance of contestability. Consider the following study.

| 7-5 | **Somewhat contestable** |

APPLICATION

Professor Steven A. Morrison of Northeastern University and Dr. Clifford Winston of the Brookings Institution provided statistical evidence that the U.S. airline industry is not as contestable as suggested by Dr. Bailey. They used 1983 data for 769 randomly selected routes to show that the presence of a potential competitor did not always force the incumbent firm to keep prices equal to average total cost.

From a policy standpoint, this result is important. If the government believes that a market is contestable, it expects that potential competition from one large firm will keep incumbent firms from charging customers prices above average total cost. If the market is not contestable, the government must consider alternatives to keep the incumbent firms from maintaining economic profits in the long run.

These researchers suggested that the failure of airline markets to be contestable may be due to government restrictions on landing rights at airports and the computerized reservation systems that favor established airlines over new entrants. In addition, the "Frequent-Flyer" programs started by many airlines in the 1980s may deter business travelers from switching to a competing airline.

As additional support for their argument, the researchers provided statistical evidence showing that as more airlines compete on the same route, the difference between price and average cost decreases. Potential entrants also have a similar effect. The difference in this case is that the more firms that compete, or threaten to compete, the closer the price is to the average cost. Advocates of contestability argue that it takes only one potential entrant to force price to equal average cost.

As a result of the empirical evidence, Professor Morrison and Dr. Winston encouraged the U.S. government to free restrictions limiting the number of airlines with landing rights at airports and to investigate the effects that the computerized reservation system has on deterring entry.

Source: Steven A. Morrison and Clifford Winston, "Empirical Implications and Tests of the Contestability Hypothesis." *Journal of Law and Economics* XXX, No. 1 (April 1987):23–52. © by the University of Chicago.

Predatory Pricing

Now let's return to Harry and Phyllis. Harry wants Phyllis to take a closer look at his own market situation to determine how successful he might be in deterring entry to the market. He wonders, though, whether he should first consider a more aggressive strategy against his current competitors. He asks Phyllis to consider whether he could win a price war that would either drive his competitors out of business or force them to sell out to him at a distress price. Since his company is large relative to the other firms, Harry feels he could outlast them in a price war and intimidate them into selling.

Harry should consider both the economic and the legal effects of this strategy. There is an extensive debate within the economics profession concerning the merits and legality of an aggressive pricing policy aimed at the elimination of competitors. At the beginning of the century the U.S. Department of Justice prosecuted several firms for engaging in aggressive pricing practices and won.

While the number of cases citing this behavior is smaller today, a firm could be subject to prosecution. The courts would decide such a case under the Sherman Antitrust Act (1890), which forbids attempts at monopolization of a market. We will return to the Sherman Act and monopolization cases in Chapter 13. At this time we will focus only on the pricing strategy aimed at forcing competitors to sell at distress prices—namely, predatory pricing. **Predatory pricing** is a below-cost pricing strategy used by a firm to drive other firms out of the market. The predatory firm has the intention of raising prices once the other firms leave the market.

There has been substantial disagreement over what constitutes predatory pricing. For example, a firm's price may be

(a) above or equal to its average total cost,
(b) below average total cost but above or equal to marginal cost, or
(c) below marginal cost.

Some observers assume that a large firm is always able to dictate the price in the market. For example, some have argued that a price below average total cost constitutes predatory-pricing behavior if it causes other firms to leave the market. However, in Chapter 5 we showed that a decrease in demand in a competitive market results in the eventual departure of some firms from the market if the price does not cover long-run average total cost.

If the large firm acts as a price taker in a market, it must react to market forces in the same way as any other firm in the market. Just because price is below average total cost does not prove that the larger firm is attempting to drive out competitors. Likewise, if some of Harry's competitors were to leave the market when Harry charged a price that was above his average total cost, those firms must have been operating at a higher cost than Harry's firm. Government officials would have little need for concern in this case.

Many economists agree that setting a price below marginal cost may be grounds for alleging predatory behavior. By charging a price below marginal cost, a firm not only earns nothing towards its fixed cost, but it does not even cover its variable cost. Since firms normally do not keep records that reveal the marginal cost of each output level, the courts have resorted to average variable cost as a proxy for marginal cost.

Average variable cost has dominated the courts' interpretation of predatory pricing. For example, in a 1977 review of the lower-court decision in *Hanson* v. *Shell Oil Company* (1976), the Supreme Court ruled that one must show that prices are below average variable cost before establishing a case for predatory pricing behavior.

In an early article on this subject appearing in 1958, John McGee, an economist at the University of Washington, suggested that no rational firm would ever engage in predatory pricing to force competitors to sell out at distress prices.[1] He felt that a price war would be more expensive to the larger firm, since it would forgo a larger return on its investment during the price war than smaller firms.

Professor McGee suggested that the large firm would be better off buying other firms at their current value. Although the distress price would be lower, the negative effects of a prolonged price war would dominate any gain achieved by the lower buyout price. The longer the price war, the greater the cost to the large firm. McGee argued that any price reduction must be the result of market forces that dictate the market price, unless one can show that the savings due to buying at distress prices are significantly greater than the costs of the price war.

7-6

Tobacco companies at a bargain price

APPLICATION

Professor Malcolm Burns of the University of Kansas has argued that Professor McGee and others have underestimated both the cost of buying out a competitor peacefully and the potential effects of predatory-pricing behavior on acquisition prices. He provided evidence that distress prices may be significantly lower than Professor McGee and others may have expected.

Professor Burns analyzed the acquisition of forty-three companies by the American Tobacco Company between 1891 and 1906. The Supreme Court

---

[1] john S. McGee, "Predatory Price Cutting: The Standard Oil (N.J.) Case." *Journal of Law and Economics* (October 1950):137–169.

decided in 1911 that American Tobacco had gained a monopoly of the U.S. market largely through predatory pricing behavior and purchases of competitors at distress prices. As a result, the Court broke the company into several smaller companies.

Professor Burns argued that the peaceful acquisition of other companies may bid up the price of the last ones acquired. As firms are purchased, the large firm wants to lower market output. With a reduction in the number of competitors, profits increase due to the lower output imposed by the large firm. The remaining firms now benefit from increasing their own prices and output levels. The escalating purchase price of a successive buyout strategy makes this procedure expensive to the large firm.

Rather than absorb the higher buyout prices due to the upward valuation of the remaining firms, the large firm may initiate a predatory action. If it uses a disguised subsidiary as a bogus competitor, it may convince other firms that price reductions are due to competitive forces. The price reductions lead firms to downgrade their earnings projections erroneously and result in a lowering of the firms' market value. This behavior also results in a reduction in investment in the industry.

Even during periods of time when the large firm does not directly engage in predatory pricing, it may use the threat of a price war to negotiate a lower price when buying out a competitor. The large firm can use its reputation for predatory behavior in the past to make a credible threat.

Professor Burns has shown that predatory pricing by American Tobacco resulted in an average reduction in prices paid for the acquisition of competitors. American Tobacco paid approximately 60 percent of the price that it would have had to pay without the predatory behavior. He also showed that the company gained an additional 25 percent reduction due only to its reputation as a predatory firm.

He argued that these value reductions more than offset American Tobacco's operating losses during the price war. For example, he estimated that American Tobacco lost approximately $200,000 during its alleged predation of fine-cut tobacco companies. According to his calculations, Burns showed that American Tobacco saved more than one million dollars in the combined purchase price of two companies acquired at the end of the price war.

Source: Malcolm R. Burns, "Predatory Pricing and the Acquisition Cost of Competitors." *Journal of Political Economy* 94, No. 2 (April 1986):266–96. © by the University of Chicago.

Biologists, chemists, physicists, and other scientists do their research as much as possible in a laboratory setting under controlled conditions. In this way they can experiment with measuring the impact of changing one or a limited number of variables.

Natural and physical scientists have long criticized social scientists because of the lack of controlled experiments to support their theories. The study of economic phenomena does not lend itself as easily to the laboratory as do physics, chemistry, and biology. Despite limitations to this approach, however, several economists have attempted to answer this criticism by designing experiments that control for factors that introduce confusing results. The study described in the following application involves a controlled experiment of the predatory-pricing hypothesis that does not depend on measuring the costs of the firms.

| 7-7 | By the way, who owns these pumps? |

APPLICATION

Many economists feel that smaller firms use the emotional argument of predatory pricing whenever they do not fare well in the marketplace. According to Professors Barron, Loewenstein, and Umbeck of Purdue University, the oil industry has been a favorite "anti-big-business" target. Franchised gasoline dealers and independent jobbers have complained that the large oil refiners have used market power to engage in predatory pricing against them. As a result, several states have passed laws that forbid refiners from operating gas stations.

For example, Maryland passed a law in 1974 forbidding direct operation by oil refiners of gas stations. The refiners challenged the law in the courts, with the final appeal exhausted in 1978. The refiners were given one year to sell their stations or change them to independent franchise operations. The study compares prices charged by the refiners and the independents both before and after the final decision.

Professors Barron, Loewenstein, and Umbeck argued that the refiner would have no incentive to maintain prices below cost during the transition year. If the companies had engaged in a pricing strategy aimed at driving the independents out of business, they would have abruptly raised their prices after losing the final appeal in 1978 in order to earn as much economic profit as possible prior to conversion to franchises. A record of higher profits during that transition period would also have made the gas station more attractive to prospective buyers. Despite this possibility, the data suggested that the refiners' retail prices remained lower than those charged at the franchise stations both before and after the decision.

These researchers suggested that franchise station owners may have experienced the effects of a change in consumer demand following the oil embargo of 1973. Due to sharp increases in gas prices, consumers had become more sensitive to gas prices and less interested in the services provided at the franchised outlets. The refiners operated mostly low-service gas stations, while the franchisees continued to offer full services. Those stations offering lower prices but fewer services captured an increasing share of the market during this time. The researchers also noted in their study that after the refiners were no longer able to operate their own stations, the average price of gasoline rose in Maryland.

Source: John M. Barron, Mark A. Loewenstein, and John R. Umbeck, "Predatory Pricing: The Case of the Retail Gasoline Market." *Contemporary Policy Issues* III (Spring 1985):131–39.

In summary, there is disagreement over the extent of predatory pricing. To some observers predatory pricing is normal pricing aimed at maximizing profits. To others low prices that force otherwise efficient firms out of the market can be harmful to consumers in the future. Malcolm Burns's study suggests that there may be some support for the idea that a firm can use its size and reputation to intimidate firms into selling out at distress prices.

Firms that find themselves noncompetitive with a larger rival may try to claim that they are victims of predatory pricing in order to have the courts help them impede the market advantage of the larger rival. Given the sympathetic view of the courts to alleged victims of predatory pricing, there is a strong incentive for failing firms to make this claim. We will consider a more detailed legal view of predatory pricing in Chapter 13.

Collusion

Harry confides to Phyllis that he is afraid he might not be able to win a price war with his competitors. Besides, he is not sure he wants to take the risk of being prosecuted for predatory pricing. He wonders whether he would be better off trying to arrange a deal with his competitors to avoid price competition. He could get together with his competitors and agree on a monopoly output and price and then split the profits with the owners of the other firms.

Although Phyllis is aware that Harry is a hard worker and a confirmed profit maximizer, she is surprised that he is willing to risk going to jail for violating one of the antitrust laws. Price fixing in order to lessen competition is a violation of the Sherman Antitrust Act. In addition to the illegality of price fixing, there are other reasons for not considering it: price-fixing schemes are difficult to maintain and they do not necessarily offer any means of deterring entry.

The Incentive to Collude

We will start by outlining the potential gains from collusive price fixing. Figure 7-4 (p. 206) shows the cost curves of a perfectly competitive firm. If a firm forms a collusive agreement with the other firms, it creates a cartel. A **cartel** is a collection of firms that agree to determine their output and price

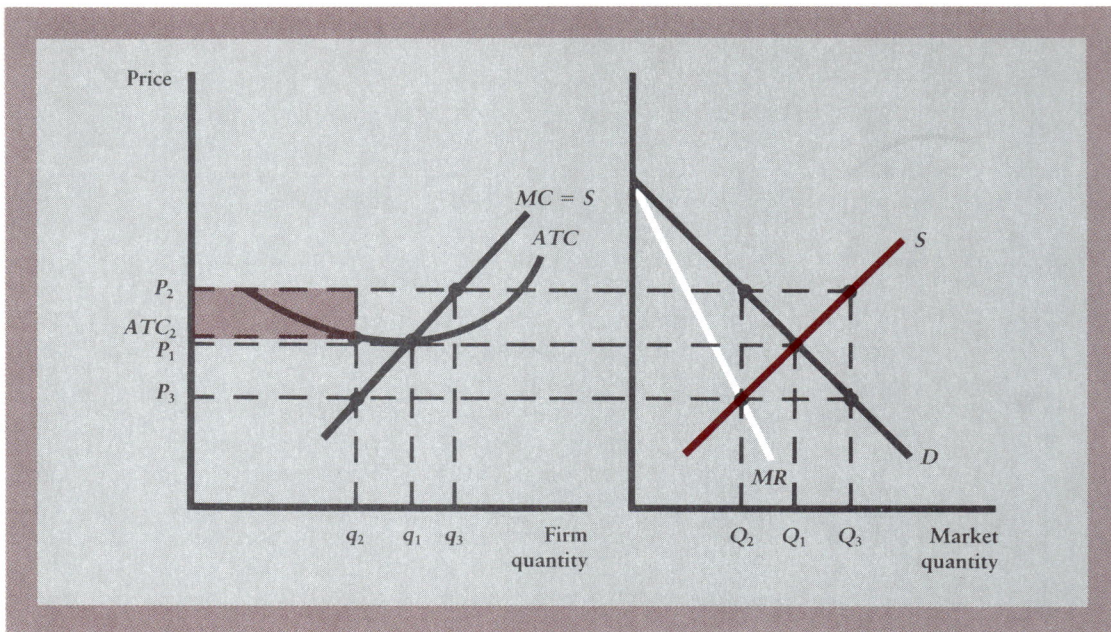

FIGURE 7-4 ▪ **Collusive pricing.** Firms can increase their profits by colluding. The market supply curve becomes the marginal-cost curve for the cartel. The cartel maximizes profits at Q_2, where marginal revenue equals marginal cost. Each firm produces at q_2, where its marginal cost equals the market marginal revenue, and receives price P_2. Each firm receives economic profits equal to the shaded area.

decisions collusively. OPEC (Organization of Petroleum Exporting Countries) is one of the best known cartels.

7-4	**Collusion**

GRAPHICAL
EXPLANATION

Figure 7-4 shows a typical firm's marginal-cost and average-cost curves. Since the firm is in a perfectly competitive market, its marginal-cost curve is also its supply curve. Figure 7-4 shows the short-run market supply curve representing the sum of the individual firms' supply curves. This market supply curve crosses the market demand curve at P_1 and Q_1.

In Figure 7-4 the market price, P_1, crosses the firm's supply curve at minimum average total cost. Assume further that long-run average total cost (not shown) and short-run average total cost reach their minimum points at the same output. At P_1 the firm makes no economic profits and has no incentive to enter or leave the market. We will use the long-run competitive equilibrium as a benchmark for comparing the effects of a collusive agreement.

Since the market supply curve represents the sum of the individual firms' marginal-cost curves, it becomes the cartel's marginal-cost curve. The cartel acts as a monopolist and sets its output where marginal-cost crosses the marginal-revenue curve corresponding to the market demand curve.

Since the cartel is maximizing profits, it must allocate output among its members so that there is no firm producing at higher marginal cost than any other firm. For example, assume that one firm produces at an output level where marginal cost of the last unit is $5, while another firm produces at a marginal cost of $4. The cartel should make the second firm produce more and the first firm produce less. Output should be reassigned within the cartel until there is no further gain from reassigning output. This occurs when all firms have the same marginal cost of production.

Since all firms have the same marginal cost of producing their last units of output, we can determine each firm's output by looking at each firm's marginal-cost curve. If the firms are all identical, they will produce the same output. In Figure 7-4 the typical firm would produce at q_2 and receive price P_2. Since average total cost would be ATC_2 at this output level, the typical firm would receive profits shown in the shaded area of Figure 7-4.

While each member firm in a cartel makes profits, a firm can do even better by cheating on the other members. At the cartel price P_2, it would maximize its profits by selling q_3. At q_3 the marginal revenue of the last unit sold would equal P_2 and the firm's marginal cost. Unfortunately for the cartel, if everyone attempted to cheat, every firm would want to sell q_3. If all firms offered to sell q_3, the market quantity would be Q_3. The market price would have to fall to P_3 before consumers would purchase all Q_3 units of output.

| 7-8 | Oil consumption exceeds production |

APPLICATION In 1978 an analyst for the Iranian government found that the nationalized Iranian Oil Company was exporting 10 percent more oil than indicated in official records. The analyst was soon given another job. Members of OPEC (Organization of Petroleum Exporting Countries) routinely produce more than their assigned quotas. For example, although OPEC's official ceiling output for the third quarter of 1987 was 16.6 million barrels per day, independent estimates of the actual production total ranged from a low of 18.5 to a high of 19.22 million barrels per day.

Analysts closely monitor OPEC's output to anticipate potential changes in market prices due to changes in the quantity supplied to the market. It appears that consumers purchase over a million barrels of OPEC oil per day in addition to the amount claimed by OPEC members. In an attempt to monitor the members, OPEC paid a consulting firm three million dollars in

1987 to make spot checks of production. Those countries most likely to cheat on the agreement did not cooperate.

Deterring Market Entry

While the incentive to cheat may undermine a cartel, the biggest threat may come from outside the cartel. The cartel must be able to prevent entry to maintain economic profits. While cartels are illegal within the United States and most other countries, several attempts have been made to form international cartels, mostly by producers of agricultural and other basic products. Few of these cartels have been successful for very long. The most successful cartels involve widespread collusive agreements sanctioned by governments.

| 7-9 | **Sweet subsidies** |

APPLICATION

The U.S. government, in cooperation with thirty-nine other countries, maintains quotas on sugar imports. The Department of Agriculture also sets the minimum price for raw, unrefined sugar in the United States. The price was $0.217 per pound in 1987, more than four times the world price. The 1987 quota was approximately 1.2 million tons, the lowest amount since the end of World War II. Without the quota, the U.S. price would fall to the world price.

Europe used to be one of the world's largest importers of sugar. After initiating a subsidy program for its farmers, it became a net exporter of 6 million metric tons per year by the early 1980s. With subsidies in many countries leading to a large increase in the quantity of sugar produced, unregulated world sugar prices dropped to $0.05 a pound by 1987. Governments supporting their domestic industries force their consumers to pay the higher regulated prices.

As a result of the high domestic minimum prices for sugar, artificial and corn sweeteners have captured a large share of the U.S. market. By 1986, corn sweeteners had a 44 percent share of the U.S. market, while artificial sweeteners had 11 percent. The annual per capita consumption of sugar in the United States fell from 102.1 pounds in 1971 to 63.4 pounds in 1985.

U.S. sugar producers have one of the most savvy, well-financed agricultural lobbies in Washington. The sugar companies and growers contributed over one million dollars to the election campaigns of members of the House of Representatives between 1983 and 1985. The House soundly defeated a proposal to reduce the subsidy to sugar in 1985.

Bilateral Sharing Agreements

Bilateral sharing agreements have a built-in mechanism for mitigating the effects of cheating on the cartel. A **bilateral sharing agreement** is an agreement between two firms to fix their price and share the market between them. For example, assume that two firms agree to share all revenues from their price-fixing agreement. Figure 7-5 shows how the firms would allocate output.

7-5	Bilateral sharing agreements

GRAPHICAL EXPLANATION

In Figure 7-5 the two firms' marginal-cost curves are MC_1 and MC_2. MC_t is the horizontal sum of these two curves. Since they are a cartel, the firms maximize profits by setting their total output where marginal revenue equals MC_t. Because of the sharing agreement, they have no incentive to increase output. Any increase in output would push their total output beyond Q^* and

FIGURE 7-5 ▪ **Bilateral sharing agreement.** Two firms will collude and set output where their aggregate marginal-cost curve equals marginal revenue. Since they share in the profits, any increase in output by either firm will increase costs by more than the increase in revenues. The sharing arrangement gives them an incentive not to cheat on the agreement.

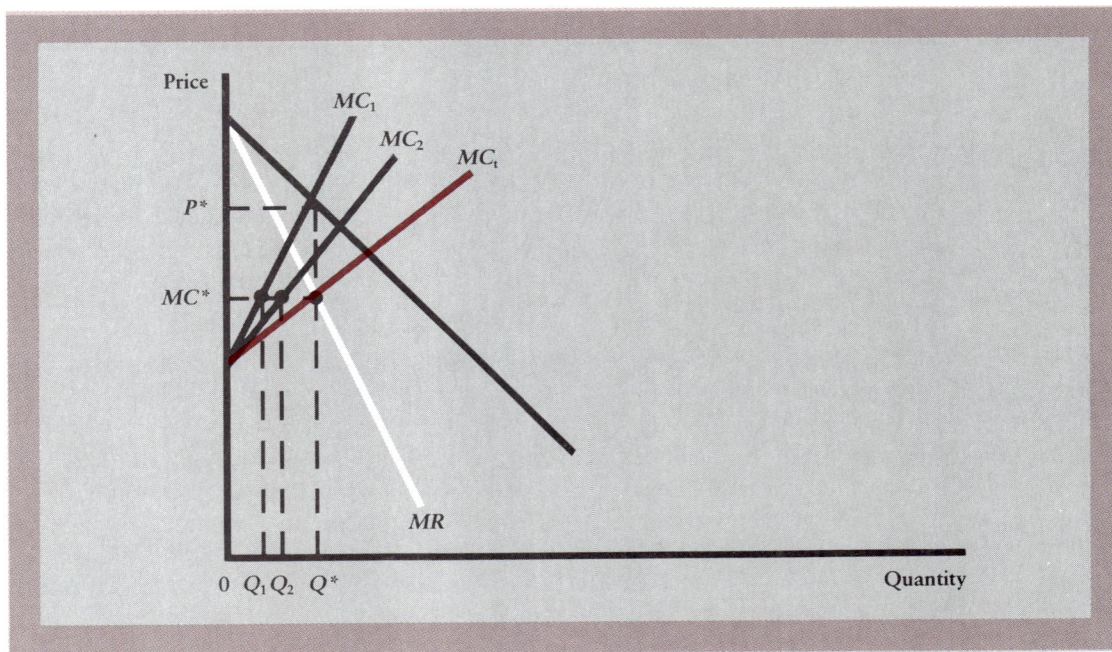

cause marginal revenue to drop below marginal cost. Since they both share in the profits, they would both lose.

<table>
<tr><td>7-10</td><td>A flying cartel</td></tr>
</table>

APPLICATION

The scheduled airlines of the world have an extremely effective cartel. Its origins go back to 1944. At the end of World War II, allied and neutral governments sent representatives to Chicago to reestablish the world's airline industry. While the U.S. government wanted a freely competitive market, the Europeans, led by the British, wanted to maintain national control. After failing to persuade the British, the United States signed the "Bermuda Agreement" with Great Britain in 1946. This agreement dictated fares, capacity, and routes between the two countries. Nearly all remaining countries sorted out their own bilateral routes on a 50-50 sharing basis.

Despite deregulation of air traffic in the United States since 1978, most of the rest of the world is governed by these cartel arrangements. Airfares in 1986 were typically 35–40 percent higher in other countries than fares for comparable routes in the United States. Although governments block entry into these markets by forbidding competition, there nevertheless has been some competition. For example, deregulated operators of package tours used charters to take over almost half of all air travel within Europe by 1986.

The Optimal Number of Firms for Successful Collusion

The threat of entry to a market can have a significant effect on a firm's ability and willingness to engage in cartel behavior. Economists do not know exactly how many firms are too many for a successful cartel. Increasing the number of firms can make it difficult for the cartel to remain intact.

<table>
<tr><td>7-11</td><td>Four seems about right</td></tr>
</table>

APPLICATION

Professor Robert Porter of the State University of New York at Stony Brook analyzed the importance of price wars as enforcement devices in maintaining a cartel agreement. He used data for the Joint Executive Committee railroad cartel (JEC) from 1880 to 1886. According to Porter, the railroad firms were price setters offering a product that was homogeneous in a market that faced limited entry.

Without uncertainty about prices, each firm can monitor its own market share. If its market share deviates from the agreed-upon level, the firm knows that someone has cheated on the agreement. If someone has cheated, the other firms will lower their prices in retaliation. They will revert to competitive behavior until they can reestablish their agreed-upon cartel arrangement. A firm considering cheating on a collusive agreement would weigh the advantages of short-run profits at the expense of the other firms versus a longer period of losses due to the response of the other member firms.

If there is uncertainty about the nature of the firm's demand, a decrease in demand could be due to an unexpected shock to demand or the cheating of another firm. The firm must distinguish the effects of cheating from the effects of unexpected shocks to demand.

The JEC was a cartel formed by the railroads controlling eastbound freight shipments from Chicago to the Atlantic coast in the 1880s. The railroads' cargo was mostly grain (73 percent). The companies agreed to market-share allotments. The JEC office monitored market shares on a weekly basis. Since total demand varied widely, a firm's market share was a function of both price and other unpredictable demand factors.

Professor Porter had access to weekly data on the quantity of grain shipped. During the first 139 weeks of the study there were four active firms in the market. During the remaining 142 weeks there were five active firms. He determined that there were three price wars in the first period lasting an average of 14 weeks. In the second time period there were seven price wars lasting an average of 11.6 weeks. Because of the increased number of price wars during the second period, a larger percentage of time was spent under competitive conditions.

The increased number of firms lowered the stability of the cartel, leading to more price wars of short duration. Professor Porter also determined that prices were, on the average, 9–10 percent lower during the second period. The time spent in competitive behavior increased from 26.6 percent to 40.1 percent. By controlling for other factors that could have accounted for this result, Professor Porter was able to conclude that the entry of the fifth firm made the cartel less stable, even though all five firms had openly agreed to follow the cartel arrangement.

Source: Robert H. Porter, "On the Incidence and Duration of Price Wars." *Journal of Industrial Economics* XXXIII, No. 4 (June 1985):415–26.

Implicit Price Fixing

The Department of Justice has not been successful in prosecuting firms that appear to be fixing their prices but do not leave sufficient evidence to establish a formal link among the firms. We showed in Chapter 5 that a competitive market forces all firms to charge the same price for products of the same quality. Even in a market with only a few firms, we can observe static prices without overt collusion. It is difficult to distinguish between the effects of collusive behavior and the power of a competitive market that forces all firms to offer the same price.

In the case of Harry's tree-trimming company, if there were only three other firms offering tree-trimming services in his area, and the other firms were about the same size as Harry's firm, each firm would be aware of the presence of the others and would make some decision concerning their response to his price changes. Each of the four firms would try to make its work appear to be of higher quality than their rivals'. They might promise faster service or outfit their workers in designer uniforms. These changes would make their services less homogeneous and their demand curves less elastic.

What might Harry expect in such a market environment if he were to change his price? He might expect that his competitors would likely follow any reduction in price, while resisting a price increase. They would be afraid to let Harry steal their customers with a price drop, but would be happy to see Harry lose his own customers with a price increase. Figure 7-6 shows these assumptions.

<table>
<tr><td>7-6</td><td>Implicit collusion</td></tr>
</table>

GRAPHICAL EXPLANATION

The demand curve D_1 in Figure 7-6 shows the assumption that all the other firms will follow Harry if he lowers his price below P_1. Demand curve D_2 shows what Harry expects if the other firms do not follow his price change. He cannot assume that his rivals will match his price change and not match his price change at the same time. He must assume one or the other, and he is more likely to assume that his rivals will match him if he lowers his price. If they do not match his price, they may lose a large number of customers to Harry. Note that if they all lower their prices, this will encourage new customers to buy some of each firm's goods. On the other hand, Harry may assume that his rivals will not match a price increase unless their costs increase significantly. If his rivals do not match his price increase, he will lose more customers to his rivals than he would if they matched his price increase.

If we were to follow Harry's assumptions about the other firms' behavior, we would ignore the dashed parts of D_1 and D_2. Harry's demand curve would look like D_1 for any price increase from P_1, and look like D_2 for any decrease in price from P_1. Figure 7-6 also contains the marginal-revenue curves corresponding to the two demand curves. The dashed part of each of the marginal-revenue curves corresponds to the dashed parts of the demand curves.

Notice that there is a discontinuous drop in the marginal revenue at Q_1. While the marginal revenue at Q_1 equals MR^*, the marginal revenue of selling an additional unit would drop sharply. Once he sold more than Q_1 units of output, Harry would determine the marginal revenue of additional units from the MR_1 curve.

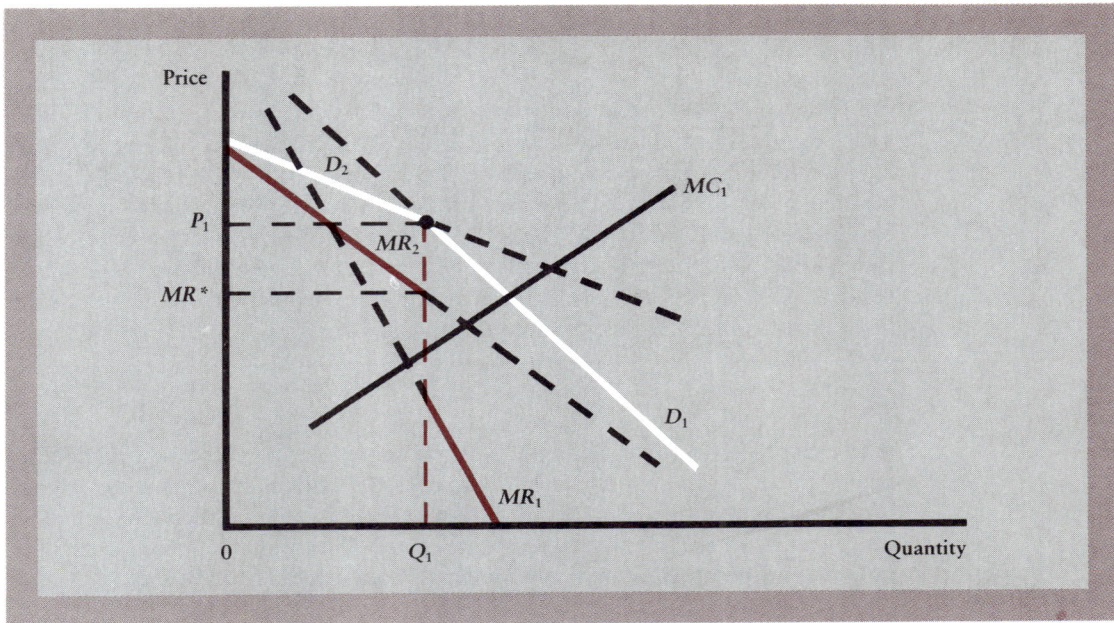

FIGURE 7-6 ■ **Implicit collusion.** Demand curve D_1 assumes that Harry's competitors will change their price if Harry changes his. Demand curve D_2 assumes that they will not match Harry's price change. If Harry assumes that his competitors will match a price decrease but ignore a price increase, he faces a demand curve with a kink at P_1. If he increases his output above Q_1, marginal revenue will drop from MR^* to the MR_1 curve. As long as the marginal-cost curve passes the marginal-revenue curve at a point on the vertical dashed line between MR_1 and MR_2, Harry will have no incentive to change his price or output.

Up to this point we have assumed that a profit-maximizing firm sets output where marginal revenue equals marginal cost. In this case marginal cost could be at several different levels and the firm would still produce Q_1 and charge price P_1. As long as the marginal-cost curve did not cross the solid line part of MR_1 or MR_2, Harry would maximize his profits at Q_1.

For example, assume that MC_1 was Harry's marginal-cost curve. If Harry were to lower his price below P_1, marginal revenue would be less than marginal cost and his profits would decrease. If he were to raise his price, the marginal-revenue curve would lie above the marginal-cost curve. When the marginal-revenue curve lies above the marginal-cost curve, the firm will increase its profits by producing more output. In this case if Harry were to produce more than Q_1, the marginal-revenue curve would be below the marginal-cost curve.

For Harry to change his output and price willingly, the marginal-cost curve would have to cross a marginal-revenue curve on the solid part of the curve. As long as the marginal-cost curve crossed the dashed vertical line connecting the two marginal-revenue curves, Harry would not change his price or output.

Harry's rivals would be likely to make the same assumptions about Harry as he made about them. Harry's and his rivals' reluctance to change price could lead to a static price in the market even if costs were changing in the market. Note that in a competitive market a change in the firms' marginal-cost curves would mean a change in the supply curve. A change in the supply curve would bring about a change in the market price and quantity. If markets were to follow the premise of this model, we would expect to see fewer fluctuations in the market price over time.

While successful implicit price fixing can increase a firm's profits, the difficulties facing more formal cartels apply equally to implicit arrangements. Unlike formal cartel arrangements, implicit price fixing is more difficult to prove. In Chapter 13 we will look at explicit and implicit collusive behavior and the evidence needed for a conviction under the Sherman Antitrust Act.

Summary

In this chapter we considered several situations when a firm must consider the presence of other firms either already in the market or capable of entering the market. Specifically, we considered the firm which starts in a dominant position in the market, surrounded by a large number of small, price-taking firms. We determined that the dominant firm must account for the supply response of these smaller firms in setting the market price and its own output level. We used the same graphical model to consider the possibility of a used-product substitute for the firm's product. If the firm knows the likely response of the used-product suppliers, it can determine the price that would maximize its profits.

We then assumed that it was likely that large firms would enter the market. We started with a firm's optimal behavior, given that it could convince potential entrants that it would not alter its output if they entered the market. We then considered a situation when this assumption was not likely: contestable markets. Although there has been extensive debate about the practical relevance of the contestable-market theory, there is evidence that it is currently being used as the basis for government policy in some markets—notably, airline routes.

We next considered the legal and economic merits of collusive arrangements among firms. We focused on collusive price fixing. While collusive arrangements can be profitable, their success depends on the ability of firms to prevent violation of the agreement and entry into the market by firms which are not parties to the agreement. Historically, the more successful collusive agreements have involved the concerted support of several countries' governments.

Selected References

Areeda, Phillip, and Turner, Donald F. "Predatory Pricing and Related Practices under Section 2 of the Sherman Act." *Harvard Law Review* 88 (February 1975):697–733.

Bailey, Elizabeth E. "Contestability and the Design of Regulatory and Antitrust Policy." *American Economic Review* 71 (May 1981):178–83.

Barron, John M.; Loewenstein, Mark A.; and Umbeck, John R. "Predatory Pricing: The Case of the Retail Gasoline Market." *Contemporary Policy Issues* III (Spring 1985):131–39.

Burns, Malcolm R. "Predatory Pricing and the Acquisition Cost of Competitors." *Journal of Political Economy* 94, No. 2 (April 1986):266–96.

Issac, R. Mark, and Smith, Vernon L. "In Search of Predatory Pricing." *Journal of Political Economy* 93, No. 2 (April 1985):320–45.

McGee, John S. "Predatory Price Cutting: The Standard Oil (N.J.) Case." *Journal of Law and Economics* (October 1958):137–69.

Noether, Monica. "The Effect of Government Policy Changes on the Supply of Physicians: Expansion of a Competitive Fringe." *Journal of Law and Economics* 29 (October 1986):231–62.

Parsons, Donald O., and Ray, Edward J. "The U.S. Steel Consolidation: The Creation of Market Control." *Journal of Law and Economics* 18 (April 1975):181–220.

Pindyck, Robert. "Cartel Pricing and the Structure of the World Bauxite Market." *Bell Journal of Economics* (Autumn 1977):343–60.

Porter, Robert H. "On the Incidence and Duration of Price Wars." *Journal of Industrial Economics* XXXIII, No. 4 (June 1985):415–26.

Schmalensee, Richard. "Economies of Scale and Barriers to Entry." *Journal of Political Economy* 89, No. 6 (1981):1228–38.

Stigler, George J. "The Dominant Firm and the Inverted Umbrella." *Journal of Law and Economics* 8 (October 1965):167–72.

Suslow, Valerie Y. "Estimating Monopoly Behavior with Competitive Recycling: An Application to ALCOA." *Rand Journal of Economics* 17, No. 3 (Autumn 1986):389–403.

Problems

1. Assume that a firm is very large relative to the other firms in the market. The other firms are so small that they act as price takers. Assume that on a graph the short-run marginal-cost curve of the large firm looks exactly the same as the combined supply curve of the remaining firms. Using a graph as part of your answer, describe how the short-run profit-maximizing output and price would be determined in this market.

2. Construct a graph showing the following situation:

There is a market with a dominant firm and a large number of fringe firms that are price takers. The fringe firms all have positively-sloped marginal-cost curves. The market solution leaves the dominant firm with less than 50 percent of the overall market share.

3. Assume that a large firm is unable to maintain a barrier to entry. What would the firm gain by charging a price below its own average total cost?

4. The United States government deregulated the trucking industry in 1980. From what you know about this industry, would you consider trucking to be a contestable market?

5. With the aid of a graph, show why the incentive to cheat is less in a bilateral profit-sharing agreement than in a price-fixing cartel.

6. With the aid of a graph, show how much additional profit a firm can make by joining a cartel.

7. Assume that Hal Tuna is the manager of a firm that dominates the market for mouthwash. All firms produce a homogeneous mouthwash: Q. Hal knows that the equation for the market demand curve is

$$P = 400 - Q_M.$$

There is a fringe of price-taking firms. Hal knows that the supply curve of the fringe firms is

$$P = 200 + Q_F.$$

Assume that Hal's marginal-cost curve is

$$MC_H = 150 + 0.5Q_H.$$

Determine the quantities produced by Hal and the fringe firms, as well as the market price.

8. Show how an incumbent firm may use scale economies to deter the entry of a firm that produces subject to a declining average-total-cost curve up to some level of output. What must we assume about the incumbent firm's behavior if the new firm enters the market?

Answer questions 9–16 with true, false, or uncertain.

9. If the marginal cost curve of a dominant firm lies above the supply curve of the competitive fringe firms, the dominant firm cannot have a market share in excess of 60 percent of the market.

10. Since all firms are receiving the same price, the fringe firms are colluding with the dominant firm.

11. To be a dominant firm, a firm must have a marginal-cost curve that is below the supply curve of the fringe firms.

12. If the MC of the dominant firm is the same as the supply curve of the fringe firms, the fringe firms will not be able to sell anything in the market.

13. A firm facing potential entry will never produce at the short-run profit-maximizing output level.

14. Any output in excess of the agreed-upon bilateral profit-sharing level will increase cost by more than it increases revenues.

15. Predatory pricing occurs when the market price decreases and some firms are forced to leave the market.

16. In the implicit-collusion pricing model, an increase in marginal cost will not cause the firm's price to increase.

MULTIPRODUCT PRICING

8

Most firms produce and sell more than one product. In this chapter we will determine the multiproduct firm's profit-maximizing output and price. The firm must take into consideration both the demand and the cost structures that it faces when making these decisions. We will focus on demand and cost considerations separately.

We will start with demand. If consumers consider the multiproduct firm's goods to be substitutes or complements for one another, the firm will price its goods differently than would the single-product firm. We will see how the multiproduct firm prices its goods based on the degree to which its goods relate to one another.

Even if the firm's goods are not directly related to one another, the firm can take advantage of differences in its customers' demand prices to increase its profits. We will see how the bundling of goods together as a package can increase the firm's profits. We will begin with the case in which the customer has no option but to buy the package or to buy nothing at all.

We will then consider offering the customer the option of buying the package or each component separately. Under certain circumstances the firm can raise its profits by offering both of these options. We will also see how tying the sale of a product can provide a metering device for the use of another product. The effect on profits will be the same as that shown for the metering example in Chapter 6.

The multiproduct firm's production function and cost structure can also dictate its choice of output and price. We will consider specialized production relationships that lead to multiproduct production and sales. We will spend most of our time on the simplest case: fixed proportions. In this case the firm produces more than one product from the same production process. At the end of the chapter we will briefly expand this analysis to the multiproduct firm that can vary the proportion of the output of its different goods.

Demand Relationships

If products are interrelated as either substitutes or complements, a change in the price of one product will have an effect on the sales of the other. Although the proper pricing of a company's products is a difficult task, it will be worth the effort to consider the interrelationship between the company's products. We can make the demand interrelationships more formal by looking at an expanded version of the marginal-revenue interrelationship.

$$MR_A = \frac{\Delta TR_A}{\Delta Q_A} = \frac{\Delta TR_A}{\Delta Q_A} + \frac{\Delta TR_B}{\Delta Q_A}$$

$$MR_B = \frac{\Delta TR_B}{\Delta Q_B} = \frac{\Delta TR_A}{\Delta Q_B} + \frac{\Delta TR_B}{\Delta Q_B}$$

The first term of each equation shows the marginal revenue directly due to the one-unit change in the output of the product. The second term represents the impact of a change in quantity on the revenue of the second product. The second term can be either positive, negative, or zero, depending on the relationship between the two goods.

If Rocky Sanders of Poobell Plastic Trash Bag Company decided to offer a second type of plastic trash bag, he would have to account for the effect that sales of the new bags would have on his original product. Since customers might perceive these two types of bags as substitutes for each other, he might find that most of the expected interest in the new bag would be at the expense of sales of the original trash bag.

Companies such as camera manufacturers are aware that customers purchase complementary products from them. Since overall profits depend on the success of the company's entire line of products, the company must determine the full impact of each product's price and output on company profits as a whole. For example, if a camera and film manufacturer can retain loyalty to its products through effective advertising or a barrier to entry, it may decide to lower the price of cameras to encourage initial sales in expectation of selling film at prices high enough to justify the lower price of the camera.

We will now consider pricing strategies when there is no direct demand interrelationship between the two products of the firm (that is, where the cross-product terms in the two equations above are zero). In this case the firm must exploit the difference in demand prices that customers have for the products.

Tied Sales

Firms may sell products in bundles. For example, you can purchase a suit of clothes that consists of a jacket, one or two pairs of trousers, and a vest. You can buy a single ticket for a concert peformance that consists of two segments, or for a baseball game with nine or more innings. Such sales, where products are sold in packages for one price, and where customers are not permitted to buy any one of the goods separately, are called **tied sales**.

There are two main reasons for using tied sales: cost reduction and price discrimination. Although we will consider production costs later as a separate issue, we will discuss cost reductions in marketing due to a tied sale. The firm may find that it can achieve both a cost-reduction and a price-discrimination objective simultaneously.

Tying Sales to Reduce Costs

We can justify many tied sales on the basis of a cost savings in the marketing and distribution of goods. Consider the following examples.

8-1 A penny for a song

There are two U.S. companies that sell the rights to perform copyrighted songs. These two companies, BMI and ASCAP, each represent about half of all the songwriters and act as their agent. A bar, nightclub, or television station must make arrangements with these companies before anyone can perform copyrighted music in their bar or club or on their television station.

Because of the substantial costs of negotiating for each song to be performed, these two companies sell the rights to all their songs, usually for a fixed percentage of the revenue generated by performances of their music. Since songs are not sold individually, this is an example of a tied sale. The arrangement reduces the potentially high cost of setting prices and negotiating for the use of individual songs.

8-2 I'll take an entire box of them

DeBeers Diamond Company controls most of the sales of diamonds in the world. Through their Central Selling Organization (CSO), DeBeers had control of between 80 and 85 percent of world sales of gem-quality, uncut diamonds in the mid-1980s. Most of the rest apparently come from stolen merchandise. Most of DeBeers's diamonds come from independent mine owners who sell to the CSO subject to long-term contracts with production quotas. DeBeers Company's own mines account for approximately 40 percent of total sales.

The CSO sorts the diamonds by six categories of shape, seven categories of quality, eight categories of color, and finally by weight, yielding a total of more than two thousand categories. There is still substantial variation in value within each category. The company creates presorted boxes of diamonds according to each buyer's requested specifications. DeBeers assigns a set price for each box of diamonds. Buyers cannot choose among boxes or among diamonds within a specific box. They either accept the box assigned to them as is or they do not buy anything.

The buyers consist of approximately three hundred traders and cutters with average annual sales per buyer of $10 million. Every five weeks buyers come to the CSO's office in London to inspect the boxes they have ordered. While buyers can complain that certain diamonds in the box are not consistent with the specifications, they rarely reject the boxes. If they do, they are deleted from the list of buyers and may not be invited back. The CSO does not include stones weighing more than 14.8 carats in boxes. These are sold on an individual, negotiated basis. If buyers reject these individual stones, they do not endanger their future relationship with the CSO.

Professors Roy Kenney and Benjamin Klein have argued that tied selling minimizes the search cost for buyers. Without tied selling buyers would be compelled to search through the stones and reject those below the average quality, even though all diamonds were in the posted quality range. If all the diamonds are sold, the customers will still get the same average quality. They suggest that economies of scale permit DeBeers to sort these diamonds at a more efficient cost. By relying on its reputation to supply an average quality box of diamonds, DeBeers reduces the customers' search costs.

If buyers search each box, there are two costs: buyer inspection costs and increased seller-sorting costs. By providing the inspection and sorting functions in advance, the CSO reduces these costs for the buyers. Since the buyers have lower search costs, they will be willing to pay more for the diamonds. Chapter 9 provides additional evidence of the value to buyers of having the sellers sort certain goods by quality and then guarantee the results of their sorting efforts.

Source: Roy W. Kenney and Benjamin Klein, "The Economics of Block Booking." *Journal of Law and Economics* XXVI (October 1983):497–540. © by the University of Chicago.

Tying Sales to Discriminate by Price

There could be another price discrimination, or market segmentation, rationale for tied sales. Let's return to Phyllis and Harry for an example. This rationale occurred to Phyllis one night when she and Harry were at the movies. Phyllis asked Harry to assume that a motion picture distributor has two movies available. One is the country-action film they are watching, "Mid-sized Truck Convoy," and the other, set in New York City, is called "Central Park Condo." Since these two movies are likely to appeal to different audiences, their relative value to a theater owner in a New York City neighborhood may be different than their value to a theater owner in a city such as Greensboro, North Carolina. The leasing of two or more films to a theater owner at the same combined price is known as **block booking**. By block booking these two movies, the distributor can maximize profits relative to charging the theater owners for each movie separately.

TABLE 8-1 ■ Tied sales

Theater	Demand Prices for Each Movie		
	"Mid-sized Truck Convoy"	"Central Park Condo"	Block Value
Joe Blittmann New York City	$1,000	$2,000	$3,000
Jewel Floyd Greensboro, NC	$1,600	$1,200	$2,800
Total revenue per film when sold separately	$2,000	$2,400	

8-1   Block booking

NUMERICAL EXAMPLE

Assume that Table 8-1 shows the maximum rental (demand) prices that each theater owner is willing to pay for the right to show each movie, given a take-it-or-leave-it offer. The New York City theater owner, Joe Blittmann, may value the New York–based movie relatively more than the country-based film. The situation may be reversed for the Greensboro, North Carolina theater owner, Jewel Floyd.

Joe has a maximum price of $2,000 per day for "Central Park Condo" and $1,000 per day for "Mid-sized Truck Convoy." Jewel values "Central Park Condo" at $1,200 per day and "Mid-sized Truck Convoy" at $1,600 per day. Assume that the distributor has multiple copies of both movies and that all of the distributor's costs are fixed. To maximize profits the distributor will want to maximize revenues, since marginal costs are zero.

Pricing each film separately, the distributor maximizes profits by charging $1,000 per day for "Mid-sized Truck Convoy" and $1,200 per day for "Central Park Condo." Total revenues will be $2,000 for "Mid-sized Truck Convoy" and $2,400 for "Central Park Condo," for a grand total of $4,400.

The distributor can increase profits by selling both movies as a tied sale. Without offering the option of leasing either film separately, the distributor will charge both theater owners a set price for both movies. In this case the optimal price is $2,800. Note that the value that Joe places on the two movies as a package equals $2,000 plus $1,000, for a total of $3,000. Jewel will pay a maximum price of $1,200 plus $1,600, for a total of $2,800.

By charging both theater owners the same price, $2,800, the distributor gives the impression that there is no price discrimination. In fact, both theater owners are forced into paying much different prices for each film. At the price of $2,800, the distributor makes $5,600 per day for the leasing of both films to the two theater owners, compared to revenues of only $4,400 if the movies are priced separately.

Loew's costs not low enough

APPLICATION   Although block booking is legal in most other countries, the United States Supreme Court essentially made block booking of motion pictures illegal in the United States with its decision in the Loew's case (1962). In that case a film distributor named Loew's maintained a library of old movies, which it rented in blocks of fifty to television stations.

The Justice Department argued that the distributor was using its market power to force television stations to purchase more films than they wanted while keeping other distributors from entering the market. While the Supreme Court was concerned about the monopolization effects of the block sales, it is possible that Loew's was more concerned with minimizing the cost of distribution than with price discrimination in this case.

The stations used the movies to fill the late evening hours when the number of viewers was substantially lower. These movies were of similar appeal to viewers; they were all of the grade-B variety. To the television stations, the movies were essentially perfect substitutes for one another. By offering movies in a block, Loew's eliminated the cost of separate negotiations for each movie.

The precedent set by this and other decisions made tied sales legal as long as the sales did not lead to monopolization of a second market. Historically, the courts have allowed tied sales as long as defendants can justify them as a means of lowering costs. Loew's was not successful in making this argument.

Tied Sales as a Metering Device

Tied sales may serve the same purpose as a meter in determining the usage of a leased piece of equipment. A firm holding patent rights for a specific type of equipment may offer a tying arrangement with another product to monitor the use of the leased equipment. The following example illustrates this possibility and considers the legality of tied sales as metering devices.

I lost count

APPLICATION   In 1936 IBM (International Business Machines) lost an antitrust case initiated by the Department of Justice. The Supreme Court sided with the Justice Department on grounds that IBM had attempted to monopolize the computer-

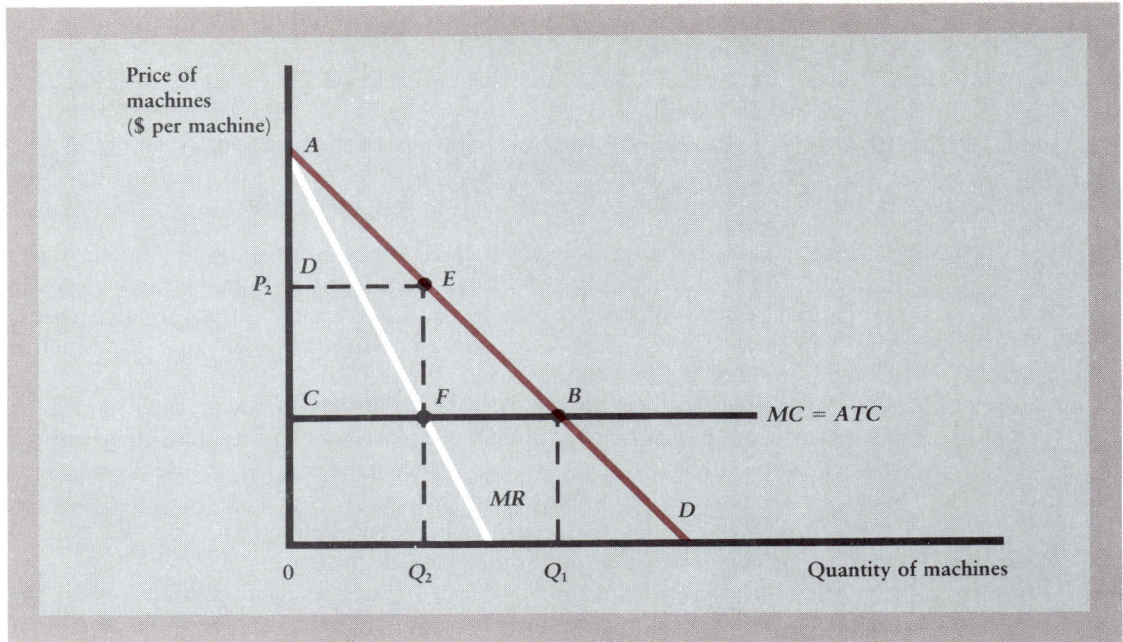

FIGURE 8-1 ▪ **Metering.** By tying the sale of machines and computer cards. IBM created a metering device for the use of its machines. By charging a premium for the cards over and above the competitive price. IBM could extract the value each customer places on the use of the machine. Since customers who use the machines more intensively purchase more cards at the premium price. IBM can force all customers to pay their demand prices for the use of the machine. Output will be Q_1 and profits will be ABC.

card industry by tying the sale of its business machines to the computer cards used by the machines. While IBM may have had monopolization in mind at the time, a more plausible reason was price discrimination through metering.

Figure 6-1 in Chapter 6 showed the advantages of metering the usage of a machine as an alternative to leasing the machine at a fixed fee. A meter on the machine monitored each consumer's usage. In the absence of a meter, we could monitor use by requiring the customer to purchase computer cards.

Figure 8-1 shows the demand from customers who wished to lease an IBM machine. The demand curve has a negative slope, because there were some customers who had higher demand prices than others. Those with the higher demand prices used the machine more intensively. IBM could have placed a meter on the machine and charged each customer by the number of uses. Alternatively, it could have required customers to buy computer cards at a premium equal to the per-use price that it would have charged with a meter.

For example, assume that the perfectly competitive price for a card had been \$0.01; no one would have been willing to buy computer cards from IBM for any price greater than \$0.01. IBM could have leased its machines at the profit-maximizing price P_2, and customers would have purchased cards in the competitive market for \$0.01 each.

IBM could have earned even greater profits. It could have determined intensity of use by each of its customers by requiring customers to buy cards from IBM. If IBM had known the value to the typical customer of each use of the machine, it could have added a premium to the perfectly competitive price of a computer card to capture this value from the customer. Since no one would have bought the computer cards from IBM at the higher price without some incentive, IBM could have charged no fee for the use of the machine, but forced customers to purchase cards.

It could have used the premiums paid for cards by its customers to compensate for use of the machine. Since those companies using the machine the most would have paid IBM a higher overall premium by using more cards, IBM could have charged customers different prices for the use of the machine. IBM might also have set a minimum number of cards to be purchased by each customer in order to insure that no one using the machine paid less than the marginal cost of providing the machine. The additional profits from this procedure would have been the same as those shown in Figure 8-1.

The monopolist using the tied sale as a metering device captures all of the revenue under the demand curve up to output Q_1. Total cost is the area under the average-total-cost curve. The triangle ABC represents economic profits. If everyone were to pay the same price for the use of the machine, the rental price would be P_2 and output would be only Q_2. Profits would be area $DEFC$. By tying the sale of the second good, the monopolist can increase profits substantially.

The Department of Justice filed the IBM case under Section 3 of the Clayton Act, which considers tied sales a violation of antitrust law if they endanger competition. IBM lost this case, but not because of the attempt to use price discrimination. The Supreme Court argued that the tied sale was an attempt to monopolize the computer-card industry.

IBM's ability to raise the price of computer cards was not a reflection of market power in computer cards, but market power in business machines. By installing meters IBM could have accomplished the same objective. After losing this case IBM installed metering devices and eliminated the tied-sale requirement. IBM maintained close to a 90-percent share of the computer-card market even after having complied with the court's decision. Although the courts consider each tied-sale case individually, the IBM case did set a precedent which remains today.

Mixed Bundling

By offering the tied sale the firm prevents anyone from buying individual products separately. If the firm instead offered both a tied sale and the option of buying each good separately, this would be mixed bundling. **Mixed bundling** is a sales strategy in which a firm offers its good for sale as a package with another good at a single price, while offering the same goods for sale separately. In this section we will determine the necessary conditions for a profitable mixed-bundling strategy.

We will help Harry decide whether this strategy would work for him in his latest venture. Harry is considering abandoning the tree-trimming business to sell trucks. He wants Phyllis's help with a plan to make more profit on a new, imported pickup truck, the Torrido, which he hopes to be selling soon. Since he would be the only dealer with the right to sell the truck in his immediate area, he would face a negatively-sloped demand curve.

Although there are other pickup trucks available to compete with Harry's product, the Torrido is so unique that Harry would have a virtual monopoly on that type of truck. For example, among its many features are three gears in reverse and an expandable cab. The cab can expand in variable amounts to displace the storage bed of the truck. By converting the storage bed into a minivan with seats that pop up with the flip of a switch, the driver can accommodate four extra passengers.

Because of these features, Harry knows that he would make substantial profits selling this vehicle. He wonders if he could tie the sales of the truck to some other product to increase his profits. Since he does not have exclusive rights to the sale of any other products, the previous movie example would not apply in Harry's case.

In the movie example we assumed that the theater owners had to rent the bundle of films as a package. The theater owners did not have the choice of renting films separately. We will explore the possibilities of increasing profit by bundling together (that is, tying the sale of) the product of a single-product monopolist with a different product sold by a large number of firms in a perfectly competitive market. We will see that a monopolist can increase profits by tying the monopolized product to a good produced by a perfectly competitive market. This strategy also gives customers the option of buying the monopolized good separately. Mixed bundling may be the best option available to Harry.

For simplicity assume that there are only two goods—Good 1 and Good 2—that are produced at constant marginal and average total costs. Assume that a customer purchases only one unit of each good at a time, and all potential buyers have a maximum price that they are willing to pay for each good. In Chapter 6 we called this maximum price a demand price. Sometimes it is also called a reservation price. The **reservation price** (or demand price) is the maximum price a customer is willing to pay for a good, given a take-it-or-leave-it offer. If the price exceeds the reservation price, the customer will have no interest in purchasing the good.

Independent sales of a monopolized and a competitive good

GRAPHICAL
EXPLANATION

Let's begin with the separate sale of the monopolized good and the perfectly competitive good. This will provide us with a reference for comparison. In this case our monopolist is Harry, who has a monopoly on sales of the new Torrido pickup truck. Harry's truck is Good 2. Harry decides that if he were to sell the Torrido by itself, he would maximize his profits by selling each truck for $20,000. He has a constant marginal and average cost per truck of $15,000. To have determined this price ourselves we would have had to know the demand for Harry's truck at each price. We will assume instead that Harry chose the profit-maximizing price. Assume that several firms produce a standard utility trailer in a perfectly competitive market. The trailer will be Good 1.

Assume that each potential customer for Harry's truck and/or the trailer has a pair of reservation prices R_1 and R_2 for the two goods. The competitive industry sells the trailer for $4,000, which equals marginal and average total cost. By the definition of the reservation price, no one would buy the trailer (that is, the competitive good) unless the reservation price, R_1 (the maximum price the customer is willing to pay for the trailer), were equal to or greater than $4,000. Customers would not buy the Torrido unless their reservation price, R_2, were equal to or greater than $20,000.

Figure 8-2 (p. 228) shows the possible reservation prices for the two goods. Harry will sell a Torrido to everyone with a reservation price on or above the horizontal line where R_2 equals $20,000. Everyone with reservation prices to the right of the vertical line where R_1 equals $4,000 will buy the trailer. Those customers with reservation prices above and to the right of point *a* will buy both the truck and the trailer.

Tied Sale of a Monopolized and a Competitive Good

In order to offer another means of comparison, we will start with the case of a tied sale of a monopolized and a competitive good. One of the other firms selling the trailer is located across the street from Harry's truck lot. Harry could set a price for the tied sale of the truck with a trailer. For example, he could refuse to sell the truck alone by requiring all customers to buy both a truck and a trailer for $24,000. Since he does not make any trailers, he simply gives his customers a coupon, which they can take across the street to exchange

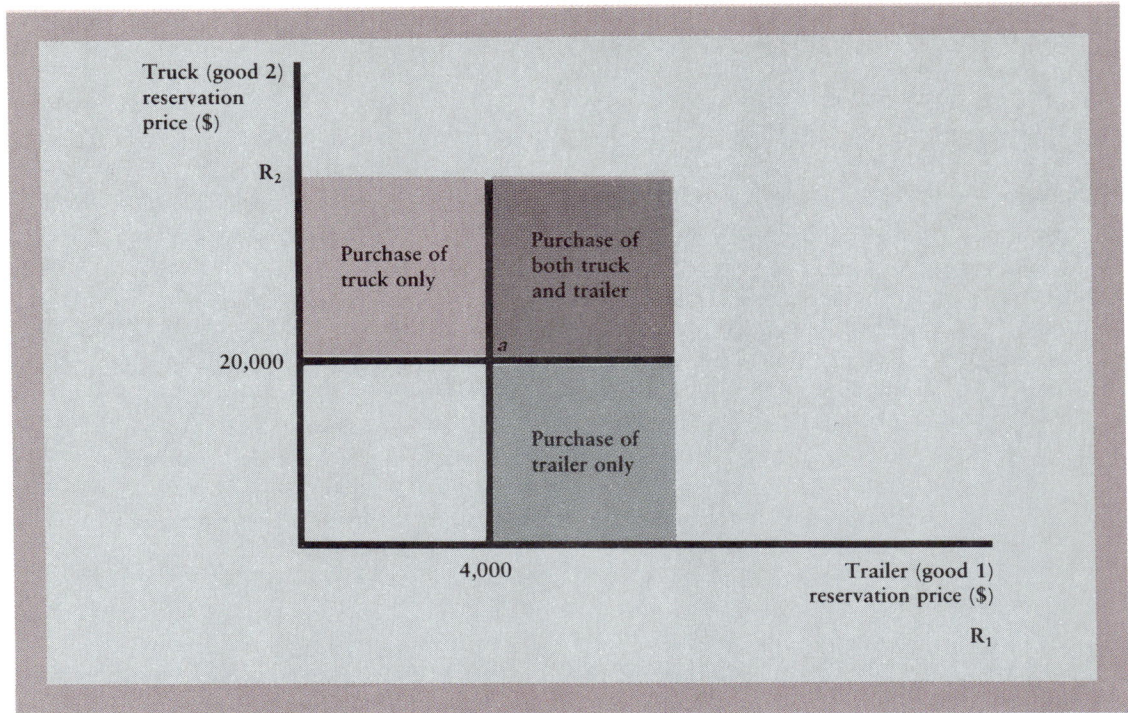

FIGURE 8-2 ▪ Reservation prices for Harry's truck and the trailer. Harry will sell his truck at $20.000 to all customers with reservation prices greater than or equal to $20.000. The competitive market will sell trailers to all customers with reservation prices for the trailer equal to or greater than $4.000.

for a trailer. Harry gives the trailer dealer $4,000 for the return of each coupon. Harry does not need to make profits on trailer sales. His goal is higher profits in selling his truck.

8-2 **Tied sale**

Figure 8-3 shows those customers who would be interested in buying both the trailer and the Torrido. Since the bundle price is $24,000, no one would be willing to buy the bundle unless their combined reservation price for the two goods were to exceed $24,000. Another way of stating this condition is

$$R_1 + R_2 \geq \$24{,}000.$$

$R_1 + R_2 = \$24{,}000$ is the equation of the diagonal line in Figure 8-3. If there were no alternative means of buying the trailer or the truck, all consumers with reservation prices to the right of the line would buy the bundle.

Since there is a competitive market available for the trailer, consumers with $R_2 \leq \$20,000$ do not want to buy the bundle. These people know that they can buy the trailer separately for $4,000. Since they would have to pay $24,000 for the bundle, they would be paying $20,000 extra to purchase the truck. If their reservation price for the Torrido were less than $20,000, they would not want the truck at that price. As a result, those consumers with $R_1 \geq \$4,000$ and $R_2 \leq \$20,000$ would buy the trailer separately and would not buy the bundle. They would find some other vehicle with which to pull the trailer.

The shaded area A represents all consumers who would buy the bundle. Shaded area B represents all those who would buy the trailer separately. Those consumers in shaded area C would have purchased the truck separately before, but would not buy the truck as a part of the bundle.

FIGURE 8-3 ▪ **Tied sale at $24,000.** By bundling the truck and the trailer, Harry no longer sells to those customers in area C. Those in area C have reservation prices for the truck that equal or exceed $20,000, but their combined reservation prices for the two goods is less than the $24,000 bundle price. Those customers in area A will buy the bundle, while those in area B will continue to buy only the trailer.

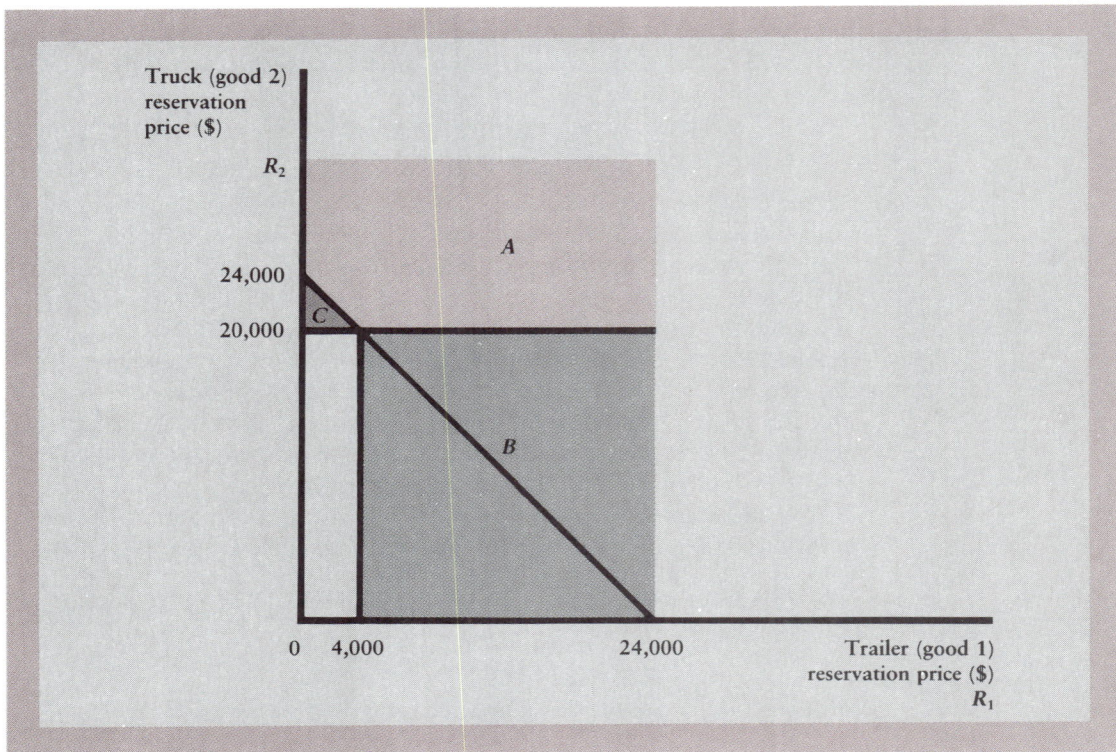

For example, a person with demand prices of $22,000 for the Torrido and $1,000 for the trailer would have a combined demand price of $23,000 and would be in shaded area C. Since this demand price is less than the bundle price of $24,000, this person would not buy the bundle. If Harry were to offer the truck for $20,000 instead, this consumer would buy the truck by itself.

By bundling the two goods, Harry would lose all those consumers whose reservation prices were in area C, without gaining any new customers. As long as there were customers in area C, Harry would lose profits by bundling. He would make more profits by selling the Torrido at $20,000 and by not offering the tied sale.

Mixed Bundling of a Monopolized and a Competitive Good

The potential for profit changes if the monopolist offers the monopolized good as a bundle with the competitive good at the same time that it offers the monopolized good separately.[1] Harry would have to set a price for the bundle that was less than $4,000 above the price of the truck. If the bundle price were $4,000 more than the truck price, customers would be better off buying the truck and trailer separately. If the truck price and bundle price differed by $4,000, there would be no difference between buying the two separately or as a bundle.

We will compare mixed bundling to selling the Torrido at the original price of $20,000. Harry has three pricing options.

1. He could continue to sell the Torrido for $20,000, while charging a price between $20,000 and $24,000 for the bundle. Since he has to pay the trailer dealer $4,000 for the trailer, he would earn the difference of the bundle price and the $4,000 for each truck sold in the bundle sale. He would receive two different prices for his truck: $20,000 from the unbundled sale and a net price below $20,000 from the bundled sale.
2. He could sell the Torrido for more than $20,000 but set the price of the bundle at $24,000. Again he would be selling the truck for different prices: $20,000 (net of the $24,000 bundle price) from the bundled sale and a price above $20,000 from the unbundled sale.
3. He could combine options 1 and 2 by raising the unbundled price above $20,000 and lowering the bundled price below $24,000.

We will now look at the effect each of these options would have on Harry's profits.

---

[1] Schmalensee (1982) provides a detailed theoretical analysis of this pricing problem.

GRAPHICAL EXPLANATION

Assume that Harry is charging $20,000 for his truck. Since his marginal and average cost is $15,000, he makes $5,000 in economic profits per truck. He now offers an additional pricing option: a tied sale of the truck and the trailer for $23,000. Since he must reimburse the trailer dealer $4,000 for every trailer he sells, he earns $19,000 in revenue per truck and $4,000 in economic profits for every truck that he sells in the bundle arrangement.

Figure 8-4 shows the potential for profits. Without the bundle option, Harry would sell only to those with a reservation price for the truck greater

FIGURE 8-4 ▪ Mixed bundling I. Harry sells his truck unbundled for $20.000 and offers a truck and trailer together for $23.000. Those customers in area C will now buy the bundle. Those in area B will also buy the bundle but will pay Harry an implicit price of $19.000 for the truck in addition to the trailer component of the bundle price. Customers in area A will buy the truck unbundled. and customers in area D will buy only the trailer.

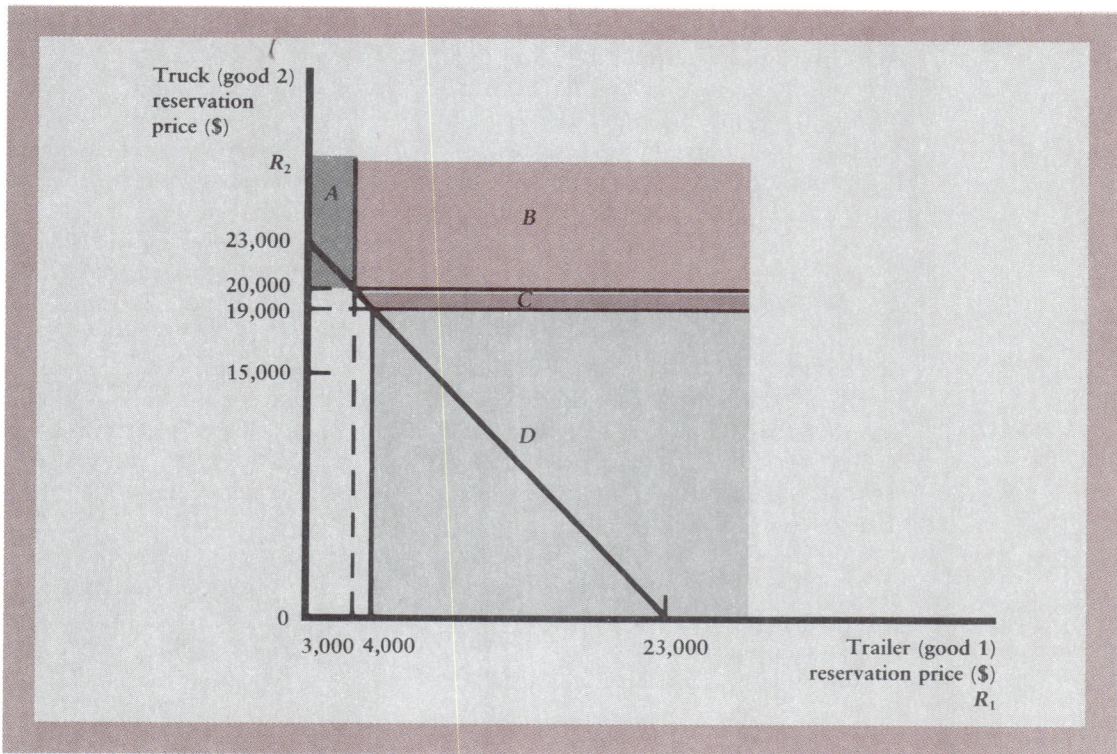

than $20,000. By offering the bundle for $23,000, Harry encourages more customers to buy his truck. All customers in shaded areas B and C will buy the bundle, while those in shaded area A will continue to buy the truck alone.

Those in shaded area A will not buy the trailer because they have a reservation price for the trailer that is less than $3,000. Since they can buy the Torrido for $20,000, they would have to pay $3,000 extra to purchase the trailer as a part of the bundle. Since $3,000 exceeds their reservation price, they will not buy the trailer.

Those in area D will continue to buy the unbundled trailer from the competitive industry. Since they can buy a trailer for $4,000, they would have to spend an extra $19,000 ($23,000 minus $4,000) to purchase the truck in the bundled sale. Since they have reservation prices for the truck that are less than $19,000, they will not be willing to buy the bundle.

Those in area B will buy the bundle and implicitly pay $19,000 for the truck. If Harry were not offering the bundle option, these customers would pay $20,000 for the truck and $4,000 for the trailer. These people will save $1,000 by purchasing the bundle.

Customers in area C would not buy the Torrido without the bundle option. They have reservation prices for the truck between $19,000 and $20,000. They are new customers of Harry's. He charges them effectively $19,000 for a truck that costs him $15,000.

To summarize, Harry can increase his profits by including the bundle option alongside the unbundled sale of his truck. He will lose $1,000 per truck sold to people in area B, but he will make $4,000 per truck from sales to customers in area C. Whether he makes additional economic profit depends on the number of people in areas B and C.

There is a difference between the type of person who would be in area B and the type of person who would be in area C. Area B contains people who have high reservation prices for both goods. They view both goods as important to them. Area C people value the trailer at least as high as $3,000, and some, more than $3,000. They do not value the truck above $20,000. The area C people are likely to view the trailer as a practical means of hauling things, and therefore they have little need for a fancy trailer. They also do not place as high a value as others do on all of the features of Harry's truck. In order for them to buy the truck, they must receive a price low enough to justify their purchase.

Since the success of this pricing strategy depends on the number of people in areas B and C, Harry should choose a good such as the basic trailer as the competitive good. If he were to choose a fancier trailer, he might find many of his customers to be in area B, not C, in which case he would make more profits selling his truck unbundled.

GRAPHICAL
EXPLANATION

We will now assume that Harry sells the bundle at the earlier bundled price of $24,000 but raises his unbundled price to $22,000. Figure 8-5 shows Harry's prospects for additional profits. Note that this graph looks similar to Figure 8-4.

By raising the price to $22,000, Harry reduces the number of unbundled sales of his truck to those customers in area E. These people have demand prices for the trailer that are less than $2,000. Since they can buy the Torrido for $22,000, they will not pay the $2,000 difference between $22,000 and the bundle price of $24,000 to get the trailer. Customers in area H will

• **Mixed bundling II.** Harry now raises the unbundled price of the truck to $22,000. Customers in area E buy the truck unbundled and pay Harry $2,000 more than they would have otherwise. Customers in area H continue to buy the trailer. Customers in area F buy the bundle. Customers in area G do not buy a truck or trailer, and thus Harry loses their business.

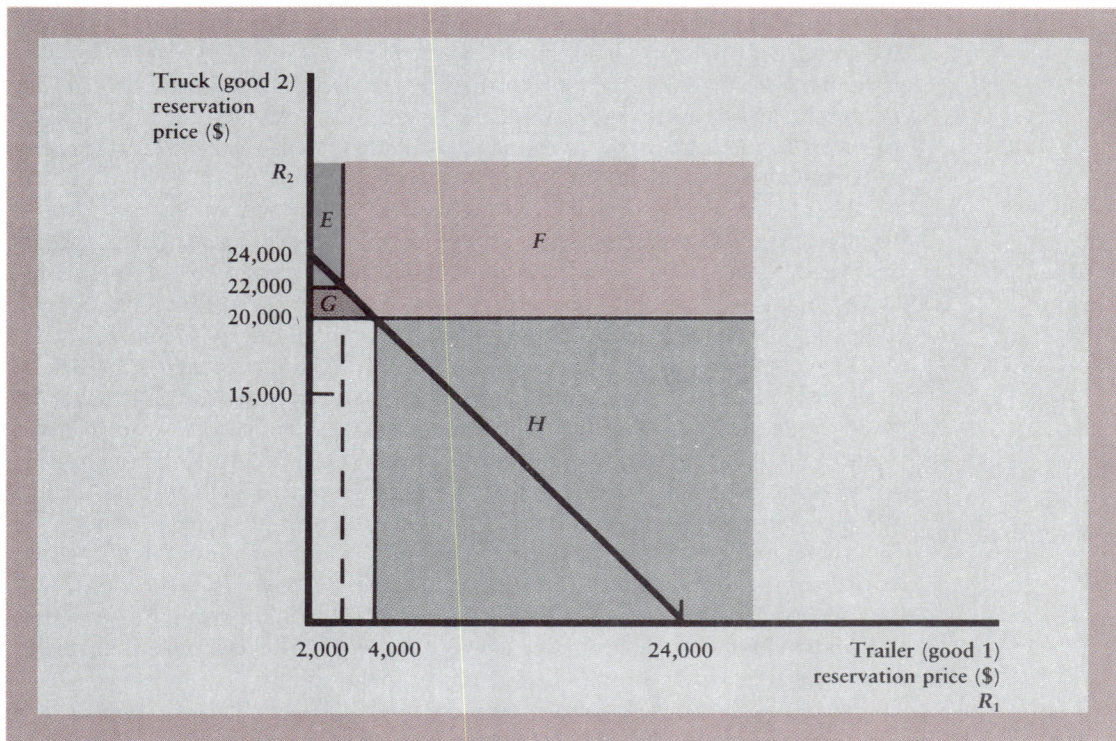

continue to buy only the trailer, since they have reservation prices for the truck that are less than $20,000.

Customers in area F buy the bundle and pay effectively $20,000 for the truck, as before. Those in area G do not buy either the truck or the trailer. If the unbundled price were $20,000, these people would purchase the truck. They have combined reservation prices below $24,000 and a reservation price for the truck below $22,000.

By raising the unbundled price for the truck to $22,000, Harry makes $2,000 more on each sale to people in area E. He loses $5,000 ($20,000 minus $15,000) for every customer in area G. The success of the price increase depends on the number of people in each of the two areas, E and G.

Customers in E and G do not have high reservation prices for the trailer. Customers in area E have relatively higher reservation prices for the truck. By offering the mixed bundling option, Harry can keep most of his customers (area F) while extracting higher profits from customers in area E.

We assumed that Harry had originally chosen $20,000 as the unbundled profit-maximizing price for his trailer. Now that Harry is considering the mixed-bundling option, he must consider both the marginal revenue and the marginal cost of changing his prices. We have seen that raising the unbundled price increases profits if the extra profits from sales to area E offset the profits lost by not selling to those in area G in Figure 8-5. Lowering the bundle price raises profits as long as the additional profits from sales to area C exceed the forgone profits from sales to area B in Figure 8-4.

There is a third option: Harry could combine the two previous strategies by raising the unbundled price and lowering the bundled price. The graph for this option would contain all the information from the two previous graphs. Mixed bundling would increase Harry's profits if he could tie the truck to a competitive good with a large number of customers in areas C and E.

He should not choose a good that would place too many customers in areas B (Figure 8-4) and F (Figure 8-5). Since customers in area E (Figure 8-5) value the features of the truck so highly, they are not likely to want to haul a drab-looking, basic trailer. Those who want a practical, no-frills trailer most likely do not want a fancy, multi-optioned truck with which to haul it. The no-frills trailer may be a good choice of a competitive good for Harry.

There are two additional considerations. First, resales of trailers and trucks at their original prices must be made costly. Otherwise, someone could buy the bundle and resell each good separately at the higher unbundled prices. In Chapter 9 we will see how used goods (no matter how new or old) normally carry a sizable discount due to uncertainty about quality.

Secondly, there are legal issues to consider. If Harry sells the bundle at a price lower than the combined unbundled prices, trailer dealers may complain that Harry is trying to force them out of business by selling trailers "below cost." Chapter 7 showed that the courts have been sympathetic to this complaint of predatory-pricing behavior. As long as Harry refrains from making or selling trailers on his own lot, he may be able to avoid this complaint. Note in Figures 8-4 and 8-5 that the number of trailers sold by all sellers increases with Harry's mixed-bundling pricing strategy. Harry might consider allowing his customers to redeem their coupons at any trailer dealer. In this way he would spread the extra sales around and diffuse potential legal challenges from trailer dealers not participating in Harry's sales program.

Multiproduct Production

We will now turn to cost considerations in production. In Chapter 4 we looked at the advantage that a large firm may have due to economies of scale. That discussion centered on the single-product firm. Since most firms produce more than one product, we must ask whether there is any cost advantage associated with large size for the multiproduct firm. If the firm has a cost advantage in producing more than one product, it must account for this advantage in determining the outputs and prices of its products.

The concept of scale economies is more complicated in the multiproduct case. As a starting point we will use a term that is complementary to scale economies for the single-product firm: economies of scope. There are **economies of scope** when the cost of producing two products jointly is less than the cost of producing them separately. Economies of scope occur when a single firm can produce two products more cheaply than can two independent firms, each of which specializes in the production of one of the two products. In notation,

$$C(Y_1, Y_2) < C(Y_1, 0) + C(0, Y_2),$$

where $C(Y_1, Y_2)$ is the cost of producing Y_1 (for example, 5) units of Good 1 and Y_2 (for example, 10) units of Good 2; $C(Y_1, 0)$ is the cost of producing Y_1 units of Good 1 but no units of Good 2; and $C(0, Y_2)$ is the cost of producing Y_2 units of Good 2 but no units of Good 1.

Economies of scope may occur when there is the possibility of sharing or joint utilization of inputs. For example, there are economies of scope in raising sheep for meat and sheepskins. A rancher who raises sheep for both meat and sheepskins can produce meat and sheepskins more cheaply than can two independent ranchers, one of whom specializes in raising sheep only for meat, and one, only for sheepskins.

There are many examples of economies of scope, two of which we will mention here. First, Amtrak (National Railroad Passenger Corporation) operates an electric-power generating plant in partnership with the United Illuminating Company in New Haven, Connecticut. Amtrak produces both steam and electricity. It uses the steam itself and sells the electricity to the United Illuminating Company.

Secondly, most of the helium in quantities available for storage is a byproduct of the production of natural gas. Helium is trapped underground with natural gas. Since helium is seven times lighter than air, it escapes into the air when natural gas is extracted.

The multiproduct firm must not only decide how large it will be but what its product mix will be. As long as the firm has a choice in varying the proportions of its outputs, it must consider not only its costs but the demand for its individual products. Now let's discuss the specifics of how a firm might solve a problem of this nature.

Starting with the simplest of the multiproduct problems, the case of fixed proportions, assume that the firm has to produce both products in a fixed ratio (that is, a fixed proportion), such as one unit of meat for every sheepskin. By making this assumption, we reduce the firm's problem to a determination of how many sheep to raise and what price to set for both meat and sheepskins. Later we will consider the possibility of varying the proportions of the two products.

Fixed-Proportions Production

Decisions concerning market prices and output for fixed-proportions production processes depend on the costs of production and the demand for the individual products. The important feature of this production process is the presence of shared costs that are difficult to allocate separately to each product. For example, how much of the cost of raising sheep is attributable to the production of sheepskin, and how much to the production of meat? We are about to meet some sheep and find out.

Barbie Tucker owns a sheep farm and raises sheep, which she sells for meat and sheepskins. Let's simplify her problem by ignoring the sale of wool and other sheep products. The sheep produce the two outputs, meat and sheepskins, concurrently. Barbie's main concern at this point is how many sheep to raise and what price to charge customers for sheepskins and meat. Assume that each sheep produces one sheepskin and one unit of meat. Barbie bases her output and pricing decisions on the demand for the two products and the marginal cost of producing sheep.

Figure 8-6 contains negatively-sloped demand and marginal-revenue curves for sheepskins and meat, as well as the marginal cost for raising sheep. Because of her location and the unique characteristics of her products, Barbie does not sell in a perfectly competitive market. Since one sheep produces both one sheepskin and one unit of meat in fixed proportions, the value to her of one more sheep is the additional revenue generated by the sale of one more unit of meat and one more sheepskin.

The profit-maximizing firm would raise sheep to the point where the combined marginal revenue of the last sheepskin and the last unit of meat equaled the marginal cost of raising sheep. You can see how to determine the quantities and prices in the following example.

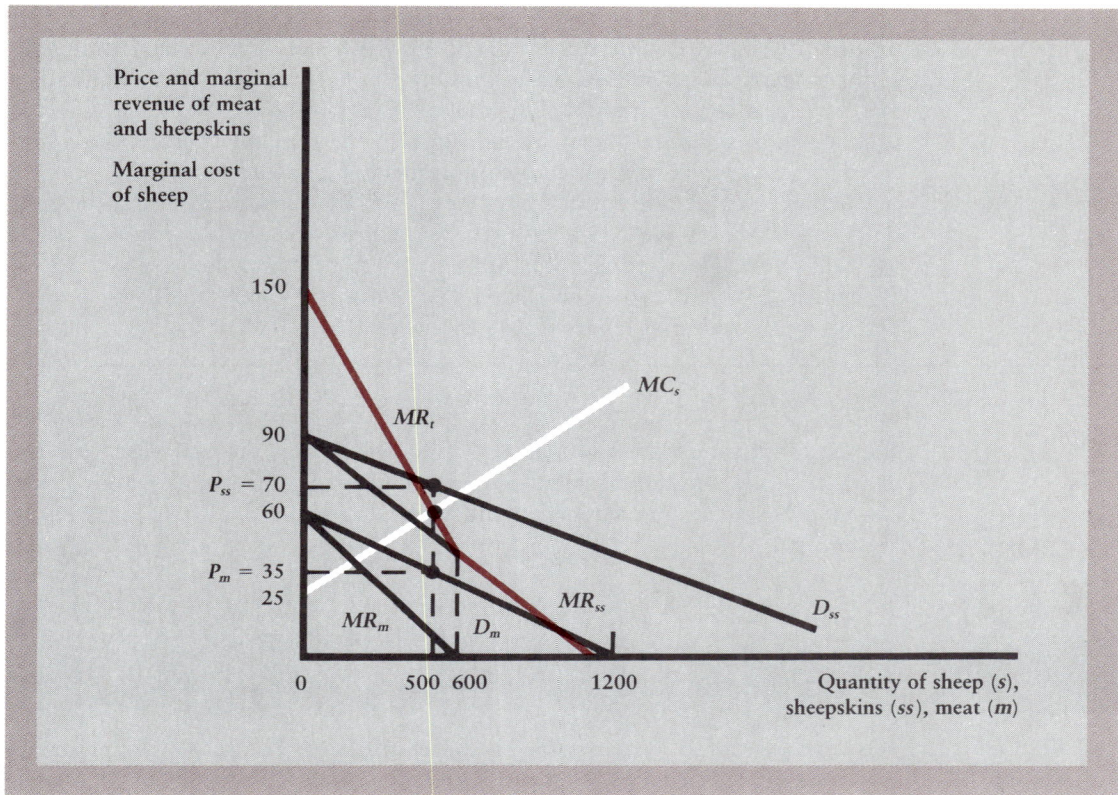

FIGURE 8-6 ▪ Fixed-proportions production. Since one sheep produces both one unit of meat and one sheepskin. we have to add the marginal revenue of meat and sheepskins vertically to determine the marginal revenue of a sheep. Setting marginal revenue of a sheep (MR_t) equal to the marginal cost of a sheep (MC_s). Barbie will decide to raise 500 sheep. She will sell the meat for 35 per unit and the sheepskins for 70 per unit.

8-5   Fixed-proportions production

GRAPHICAL
EXPLANATION
In this example the marginal revenue of the last sheep raised, MR_t, equals the vertical sum of the marginal-revenue curves, MR_{ss} and MR_M. MR_t has a kink at 600, where MR_M equals zero, since Barbie is not willing to sell more than 600 units of meat.

If Barbie were to sell more than 600 units of meat, marginal revenue would be negative, resulting in a decrease in revenues. Assuming there is no cost for disposing of excess meat, Barbie will sell only 600 units of meat, even if the optimal amount of sheepskin sales exceeds 600.

Once we have created MR_t by vertically summing the two marginal-revenue curves, we can determine the optimal number of sheep by setting MR_t equal to marginal cost, MC_S. The number of sheep equals both the number of sheepskins and the number of units of meat produced. We determine the price of sheepskins and meat by substituting the number of sheepskins and the number of units of meat into their respective demand curves.

In this example, the optimal number of units of sheep, meat, and sheepskins will be 500. The price of sheepskins, P_{SS}, will be 70, and the price of meat, P_M, will be 35. The average value of a sheep will be the sum of the two prices, P_{SS} and P_M, which is $70 + 35$, or 105. This is the same technique used to determine the value of tennis courts in Chapter 6.

We could calculate these prices and quantities using the equations for the demand curves and the marginal-cost curve. Consider the following numerical example based on the same demand curves and marginal-cost curve as in Figure 8-6.

| 8-2 | Fixed-proportions production |

NUMERICAL
EXAMPLE

We can determine the solution to the example in Figure 8-6 numerically. Assume that the demand for meat is given by

$$P_M = 60 - 0.05Q_M$$

and the demand for sheepskins, by

$$P_{SS} = 90 - 0.04Q_{SS}.$$

Recall that since these are linear demand curves, the corresponding marginal-revenue curves will have the same intercept terms, with slopes twice as steep. The marginal-revenue curve for meat will be

$$MR_M = 60 - 0.1Q_M,$$

while that for sheepskins will be

$$MR_{SS} = 90 - 0.08Q_{SS}.$$

Assume that the marginal-cost equation is

$$MC_S = 25 + 0.07Q_S.$$

Since one sheep yields one unit of meat and one sheepskin,

$$Q_{SS} = Q_M = Q_S.$$

The marginal revenue of raising one more sheep will be the sum of the two marginal-revenue equations for output to the left of the kink in the aggregate marginal-revenue curve:

$$MR_t = 150 - 0.18Q.$$

Since profit maximization occurs where

$$MR_t = MC_S,$$

$$150 - 0.18Q_S = 25 + 0.07Q_S.$$

Solving for Q_S yields Q_S, Q_{SS}, and Q_M all equal to 500. To determine the price of sheepskins and meat, substitute the quantities of sheepskins and meat into the demand equation. P_M equals 35, and P_{SS} is 70.

Fixed-Proportions Production with Excess Sales of One Product

It is possible that the market demand for two products will be sufficiently different to justify discarding some of the output of one of the two products. This is the subject of the next example.

As mentioned briefly in the previous example, Barbie Tucker will not sell one of her products beyond the point where marginal revenue equals zero. As long as she is free to do so, she will dispose of the excess rather than sell it. You can see the effect of this decision on the firm's profits in Figure 8-7 (p. 240).

8-6　　**Excess production of one product**

GRAPHICAL EXPLANATION

Now let's consider the effects of an increase in the demand for sheepskins. The new demand curve for sheepskins, D_{SS2}, crosses the vertical axis at 144 and is above and to the right of the previous demand curve for sheepskins. In this case everything is the same as before, except for the location of the demand and marginal-revenue curves for sheepskins.

Notice in Figure 8-7 that the marginal-cost curve now crosses the aggregate marginal-revenue curve to the right of the kink. At 600, where MR_M equals zero, MR_{SS} exceeds MC. By producing more sheep Barbie will add more revenue from the sales of sheepskins alone to justify the additional cost of raising sheep. Even without additional revenue from meat sales, it is worth raising more sheep for the sheepskins alone. In this case she will raise 700 sheep and sell 700 sheepskins at a price of 109 per unit. She will only sell 600 units of meat at a price of 30 per unit and will dispose of the difference between 700 and 600 units of meat.

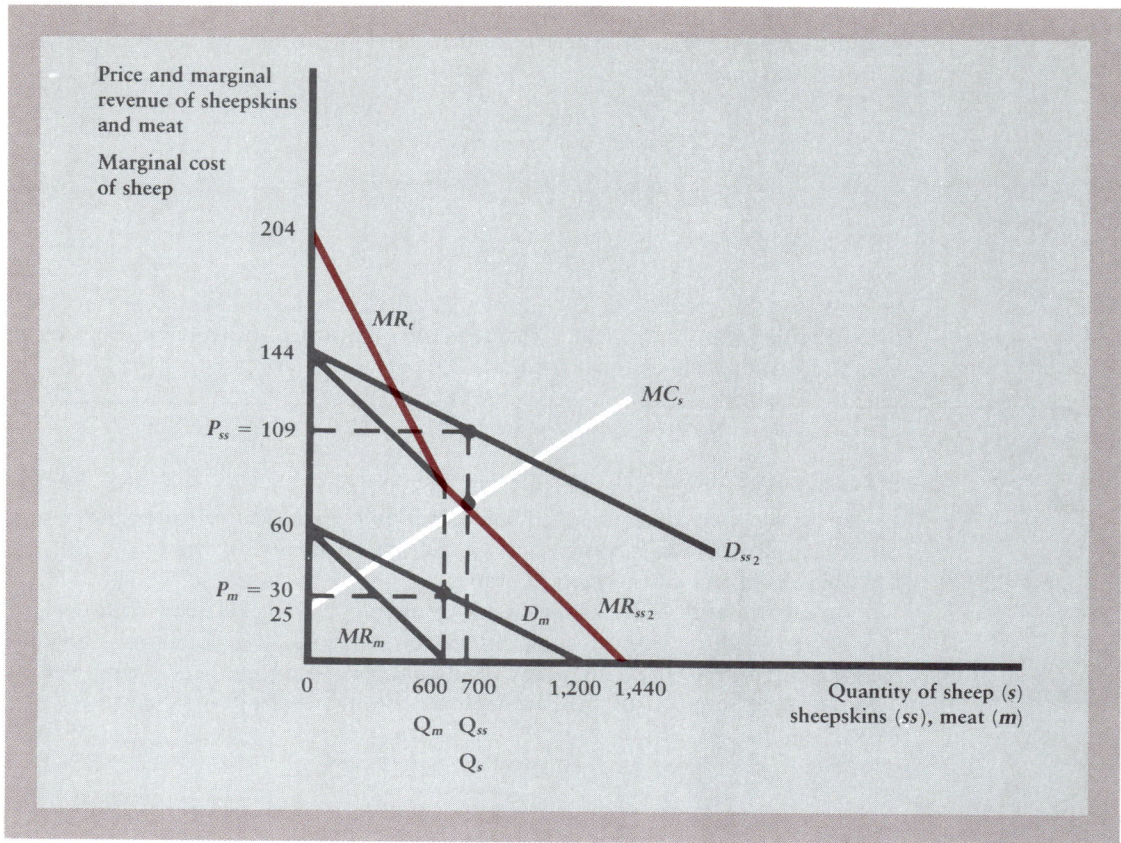

FIGURE 8-7 ▪ **Fixed-proportions production: excess output of sheepskins.** The demand curve for sheepskins has shifted to D_{SS2}. The marginal-cost curve now crosses the combined marginal-revenue curve to the right of the kink in the marginal-revenue curve. Barbie will maximize profits by raising 700 sheep. She will sell 700 sheepskins but only 600 units of meat. She will discard the difference of 100 units of meat to maintain the higher meat price and revenues.

We can extend the numerical approach used in Numerical Example 8-2 to include the case where a significant difference in demand for the two products dictates that the firm sell more of one product than of the other. The following numerical example is consistent with the previous graphical explanation.

8-3	**Fixed proportions with excess output of a product**

NUMERICAL EXAMPLE

Assume that the demand curve for sheepskins shifts to D_{SS2} as in Graphical Explanation 8-6. The equations for the demand curve for meat and the marginal-cost curve have not changed. The new demand curve for sheepskins has the following equation:

$$P_{SS2} = 144 - 0.05Q_{SS}.$$

The marginal-revenue curve for sheepskins will be

$$MR_{SS2} = 144 - 0.1Q_{SS}.$$

Before adding the two marginal-revenue curves, we should determine where marginal revenue equals zero for each of the two curves. Marginal revenue will equal zero when the quantity of sheepskins is 1,440, because

$$MR_{SS2} = 144 - 0.1Q_{SS} = 0$$

yields

$$Q_{SS} = 1,440.$$

The marginal revenue of meat will equal zero when the quantity of meat is 600, because

$$MR_M = 60 - 0.1Q_M = 0$$

yields

$$Q_M = 600.$$

If we were to add the two marginal revenue curves, we would find that the profit-maximizing quantity of sheep would exceed 600. In this case the marginal revenue of meat would be negative. Instead of adding the two marginal-revenue curves, however, Barbie should make her decision by using only the marginal-revenue curve for sheepskins, the product in greater demand at the time.

Recall that the marginal-cost curve has the equation

$$MC_S = 25 + 0.07Q_S.$$

Setting marginal revenue equal to marginal cost, Barbie would find the optimal number of sheep and sheepskins to be 700.

$$MR_{SS2} = 144 - 0.1Q_S = 25 + 0.07Q_S$$

and

$$0.17Q_S = 119$$

or

$$Q_S = 700.$$

Since the marginal revenue of meat will equal zero when the quantity of meat is 600 units, Barbie should sell 600 units of meat and dispose of the remaining amount. She will raise 700 sheep, sell 700 sheepskins, and sell only 600 units of meat.

APPLICATION   Professor John Hanner of the University of Chicago provided an economic
analysis of the rapid decline in the number of buffalo on the High Plains of
the United States during the nineteenth century. Between 1871 and 1883, the
number of buffalo decreased from eight million to near extinction. Most of
the hunters during this time killed buffalo only for their hides. Professor
Hanner analyzed this rapid depletion of buffalo as a natural result of the
changes in both the demand for buffalo meat and hides and the cost of
"harvesting" buffalo.

Prior to 1871, most hunters were Indians and settlers living on subsistence
diets. These people had a demand for both the hides and the meat provided
by the buffalo. In the early days of the westward expansion of the railroads,
some hunters harvested buffalo in the winter, sold hides locally, and arranged
for shipment of the meat to eastern markets by way of the railroads. The
railroads significantly lowered the costs of transporting buffalo products east
and of bringing settlers, hunters, and cattle ranchers west. Professor Hanner
argued that once the buffalo nearest the railroad tracks were depleted, the
cost of shipping meat increased dramatically due to the large overland cost
of bringing the carcasses to the railroads.

However, the cost of transporting only the hides remained low. The
marginal cost of obtaining hides was also low. Since no one owned the buffalo,
hunters had to kill them to establish ownership. The only costs to the hunters
were time, materials, and transportation. Due to the presence of competitors,
hunters had an incentive to kill as many buffalo as possible in the shortest
possible time.

The value of a hide did not fluctuate during this time period despite the
rapid increase in the number of hides obtained in the early years and the rapid
depletion of the number of buffalo in the later years. The price for a hide was
determined in the eastern market, where a buffalo hide was considered a close
substitute for a cow hide. Even at the height of buffalo hunting, buffalo hides
never exceeded 5 percent of the total sales of hides in the eastern market.

We can retell this story with the aid of Figure 8-7. Before 1871, the
demand for buffalo meat and hides was local and relatively small. Demand
curve D_M represents the demand for buffalo meat prior to 1871, and D_{SS}
represents the demand for hides prior to 1871. Starting in 1871, the significantly
lower transportation cost of sending hides east increased the demand that
traders had for hides. The increase in demand coming from these traders
caused the demand for hides to shift to D_{SS2}.

The profit-maximizing hunter facing marginal cost MC_S would have
harvested Q_{SS} buffalo, but would have discarded $Q_{SS} - Q_M$ buffalo carcasses.
While some have argued that the disposal of buffalo carcasses was wasteful,
Professor Hanner suggested that the buffalo was en route to extinction anyway,
due to the loss of its habitat to farms and ranches. The value of the buffalo

in terms of food and hides was not great enough to justify its preservation at 1871 levels due to the technological improvement offered by the railroad to both cattle ranching and agriculture.

Source: John Hanner, "Government Response to the Buffalo Hide Trade, 1871–1883." *Journal of Law and Economics* (October 1981):239–72. © by the University of Chicago.

Variable Proportions

Few firms are forced to produce joint products according to a fixed-proportions technology. They normally have some leeway in favoring the development of one product over the other. For example, by planning a special diet for her sheep, Barbie may be able to produce meatier sheep at the expense of the number of usable sheepskins.

Figure 8-8 (p. 244) illustrates the optimal decision rule for the variable-proportions case. The axes in the figure indicate the quantity of each output: meat and usable sheepskins. If output prices are constant, there will be a linear isorevenue curve. An **isorevenue curve** is a graphical representation of all of the combinations of output of two goods that generate the same total revenue. In addition, there will be an isocost curve that indicates the quantities of the two products equaling the same total cost. An **isocost curve** is a graphical representation of all of the combinations of output of two goods that have the same total production cost.

The shape of the isocost curve in Figure 8-8 demonstrates that there is an increasing marginal cost of shifting from one product to the other. That is, an increase in meat from the sheep would mean increasingly larger marginal losses of usable sheepskins.

Barbie will choose outputs of usable sheepskins and meat where she maximizes revenues for a given total cost. This will occur where the isorevenue curve is tangent to the isocost curve. While there will be one such point for each of the isocost curves, there will be one point overall that maximizes her profits. Figure 8-8 shows three possibilities. For example, at outputs Q_{SS2} and Q_{M2}, profits (π_2) equal $TR_2 - TC_2 = \$5,800 - \$4,950 = \$850$. Of the three examples shown, Q_{SS2} and Q_{M2} generate the most profit. As prices for Barbie's products change, the slope of the isorevenue line will change also. With a change in the slope, she will adjust the proportion of meat and usable sheepskins.

8-6	**We offer a better mix**

APPLICATION   Advertising agencies are multiproduct firms. According to Professors Richard Schmalensee and Alvin Silk of Massachusetts Institute of Technology and

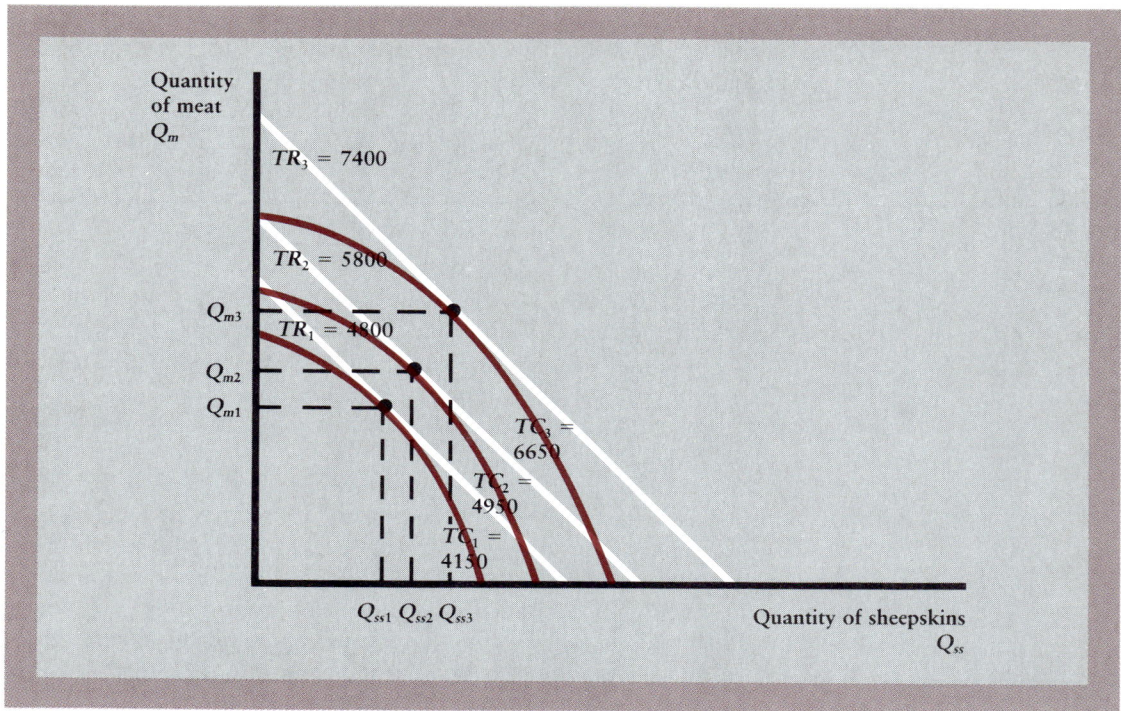

FIGURE 8-8 • **Variable proportions.** The firm will maximize profits by choosing a combination of the two goods where the isocost curve is tangent to the isorevenue curve. The firm must choose among these tangency points to determine the overall amount of the two goods that will maximize its profits. Profit (π) equals TR minus TC. In this case Q_{M2} and Q_{SS2} will give the firm the most profit of the three possibilities shown: $850.

Robert Bojanek of IBM, there is a considerable variation in the mix of media used by agencies. In their study, they used data from a sample of ninety-one agencies for the year 1977 to estimate the importance of economies of scale and media mix to the costs of advertising agencies. For the most part, agencies charge clients 15 percent of the total advertising costs as a fee for their services.

The larger agencies normally represent advertisers who compete in large markets and who use national media, such as television and large-circulation magazines. There are substantial economies from television and national magazine advertising for clients large enough to take advantage of them. Although larger agencies operate subject to costs lower than those of smaller agencies, the difference is due to the mix of media used by the clients of the larger agencies. The smaller agencies work for firms that have more limited markets and that focus their advertising in local media, such as newspapers, radio, and business publications.

These researchers found that most agencies took advantage of possible scale economies. As a result, any observed differences in average total costs between large and small advertising agencies were due to the type of media mix managed by the agency. The services provided by each agency reflected the needs of their clients and the prices for use of these media.

Clients with national markets were able to take advantage of the scale opportunities offered by television and national magazines, and preferred this form of advertising. As a result, agencies responded by offering more of this type of service. Depending on the demand for its services and the price of various forms of advertising media, the multiproduct advertising agency varied its mix of media to meet the demand for its services.

Source: Richard Schmalensee, Alvin J. Silk, and Robert Bojanek, "The Impact of Scale and Media Mix on Advertising Agency Costs." *Journal of Business* 56, No. 4 (October 1983). © by the University of Chicago.

Summary

Most firms produce and sell more than one product. In this chapter we considered the multiproduct firm given different assumptions about the nature of its products and its production processes. We started with the sale of more than one product by a single firm. We considered the possibility of bundling two goods. We observed two main reasons for bundling: cost reduction and price discrimination.

We considered the two related topics of metering and tied sales. Metering devices monitor usage and facilitate the use of price discrimination for equipment that is likely to become technologically, rather than physically, obsolete during its life span. The tying of the sale of one good to another may serve this same purpose.

In addition to the benefits of metering, tied sales may facilitate price discrimination if customers disagree on the relative merits of two or more products, as in the case of motion pictures. Another plausible reason for a tied sale is the potential for cost reduction in the production or marketing of the products. We expanded the bundling example to include the case of mixed bundling, where the tied good is produced in a competitive market.

We then focused on special relationships in the production process. Most of our attention was directed at firms whose outputs are in fixed proportion. The technique for analyzing this pricing rule is similar to that for peak-load pricing (Chapter 6). The firm sets output where aggregate marginal revenue equals marginal cost. As long as marginal revenue for each product is positive at this output level, the firm will sell all of each product.

If marginal revenue is negative for any of the products, the firm will sell only to the point where marginal revenue is zero. In the case of two products, the decision on how much to produce will be based only on the one product generating positive marginal revenue. In this situation the firm will increase its profits by discarding some of the product that is in lesser demand. We also briefly discussed the decision to produce products that are not in fixed proportions. This decision requires production information on the tradeoffs associated with shifting output levels of the various products.

<table>
<tr><td>

Important Terms

</td><td>

Tied Sales (p. 219)
Block Booking (p. 221)
Mixed Bundling (p. 226)
Reservation Price (p. 226)

</td><td>

Economies of Scope (p. 235)
Isorevenue Curve (p. 243)
Isocost Curve (p. 243)

</td></tr>
</table>

Selected References

Bailey, Elizabeth E., and Friedlaender, Ann F. "Market Structure and Multiproduct Industries." *Journal of Economic Literature* XX (September 1982):1024–48.

Epple, Dennis, and Lave, Lester. "Helium: Investments in the Future." *Bell Journal of Economics* 11, No. 2 (Autumn 1980):617–30.

Hanner, John. "Government Response to the Buffalo Hide Trade, 1871–1883." *Journal of Law and Economics* (October 1981):239–72.

Kenney, Roy W., and Klein, Benjamin. "The Economics of Block Booking." *Journal of Law and Economics* XXVI (October 1983):497–540.

Mulligan, James G. "The Economies of Massed Reserves." *American Economic Review* 73 (September 1983).

Schmalensee, Richard. "Commodity Bundling by Single-Product Monopolies." *Journal of Law and Economics* XXV (April 1982):67–71.

Problems

1. Assume that a firm raises sheep in order to produce two products: meat and sheepskins. The firm produces sheepskins and meat according to a fixed-proportions production process, with all costs shared jointly. Assume that the demand equation for meat is

$$P_M = 308 - 0.5Q_M$$

and that the demand curve for sheepskins is

$$P_{SS} = 172 - 2Q_{SS}.$$

The corresponding marginal-revenue equations are $MR_M = 308 - Q_M$ and $MR_{SS} = 172 - 4Q_M$.

The marginal cost for raising sheep is

$$MC = 20 + 5Q.$$

Assume that one sheep produces one unit of meat and one sheepskin. Determine the profit-maximizing quantities of sheepskins, meat, and sheep, and the prices of meat and sheepskins.

2. Change marginal cost in the previous example to

$$MC = 60 + 10Q$$

and derive the same quantities and prices.

3. Assume that a movie distributor faces the following demand prices for its two films from two theater owners:

		Movie	
		1	2
Theater Owner	A	$1,000	$2,000
	B	$800	$1,200

Assume that the marginal cost of distributing these two films is zero. Compare the profitability of setting separate rental prices for each movie with that of using a block price.

4. Block booking of products may be a form of price discrimination. Illustrate this argument by creating a numerical example. Indicate exactly why this pricing scheme is a form of price discrimination.

Answer questions 5–10 with true, false, or uncertain.

5. The multiproduct firm producing all outputs according to a fixed-proportions production process sets output where the sum of the marginal costs equals marginal revenue.

6. The firm producing two products subject to a fixed-proportions production process will charge the same price for each of the products.

7. The multiproduct firm producing subject to a fixed-proportions production process will produce equal amounts of all products.

8. In 1936 IBM was convicted of using its monopoly of business machines to monopolize the computer-card market. If IBM had not been convicted, IBM's tying of the sale of machines to the sale of computer cards would have led to monopolization of the computer-card market and an inefficient market solution.

9. If one theater owner likes each of two films more than another theater owner does, there will be no advantage to offering a block-booking price to the two theater owners.

10. Customers with higher demand prices value a product more than those with lower demand prices.

9

INFORMATION COSTS AND THE PROMOTION OF PRODUCT QUALITY

Although a principle focus of economic research in the past has been on pricing issues, economists have become increasingly interested in the nonprice behavior of firms. Nonprice competition includes both choice of the product's characteristics and promotion of the product. At the end of Chapter 5 we saw that differences in perceived quality give the firm more control over its demand curve, but may make demand curves interdependent. At that time we left unanswered questions concerning the firm's ability to differentiate its product from its rivals' products.

There is debate concerning the degree to which product differentiation is in the minds of consumers rather than in actual differences in the quality of products. While we will not be able to resolve this debate, we will acknowledge the importance of informational problems. People seek information because it is worthwhile. If perfect information were available, everyone would know a good's price and quality, and only one price would prevail for each type of good.

However, since information is not perfectly available, people will expend resources to acquire it. In this chapter we will discuss how a lack of perfect information constrains the firm. Our main emphasis will be on the firm's efforts to convince customers of the quality of their products. Consumers require information about prices, quality, and availability of products. Employers need information about the performance of their workers. Workers require information about employers, hoping to find the best job given their skills and interests. Firms need information about the demand for their product and their competitors' products.

While consumers have an incentive to obtain information about product price, quality, and availability, firms have an incentive to provide information to potential customers. We will look at these incentives and the market responses to them. We will also consider situations when the market may not perform adequately to meet the need for information. The failure of information markets has motivated governments to step in and enforce restraints on market activity to correct these failures. We will consider the government's role in addressing these issues throughout the chapter.

Although firms have many options for promoting the quality of their products, we will concentrate on the use of warranties, brand names, and advertising. Advertising plays two roles. For the new firm, advertising is a vehicle for alerting customers that a new product is available. For the firm with an established product, advertising may be a successful barrier against potential competitors. While the successful ad may often be the inspiration of an artist or psychologist, advertising does have an economic impact on the firm and the market. We will look at the economics of advertising, focusing on the importance of advertising as both information and a barrier to entry.

Consumer Search for Information

Consumers have an incentive to search for information about product price and quality. In the perfectly competitive market discussed in Chapter 5 there was perfect information in the market about product quality and price. In that type of market there is no need for consumer search. Although the market equilibrium results in a single price for each type of good, it is unlikely that a single price will prevail in markets when information is not perfect.

9-1	Spread out, please

APPLICATION

Even the price for standardized products may vary at any point in time. The degree of variation depends on the consumers' costs of obtaining information about these price differences. Professors John Pratt, David Wise, and Richard Zeckhauser of Harvard University surveyed the prices of thirty-nine standardized products available in the Boston area in the early 1970s.

They chose a specific brand and model number for each product and surveyed all sellers of each product advertising in the Boston *Yellow Pages*. The number of sellers per product ranged from four to twenty-two. The highest price was greater than twice the lowest price for eighteen of the thirty-nine products. For example, the price of a canvas cover for a pickup truck offered by fourteen sellers, and costing an average of $40.46, varied as much as 638 percent. A styling brush with an average price of $4.33 varied in cost by as much as 667 percent among twelve sellers. The price of home fuel oil offered by fifteen sellers and averaging $0.33 per gallon varied by 11 percent.

As the average price increased, the standard deviation (that is, relative dispersion) increased. For example, a doubling of the average price increased the standard deviation by 86 percent. According to the researchers, the higher dispersion of prices associated with the higher average price was most likely due to infrequent purchasing of the higher-priced products. The less-frequent purchaser had less information about the variation in prices and was more likely to purchase without extensive search. The standard deviation for the more frequently purchased goods was only 36 percent of that of the infrequently traded goods.

Source: John W. Pratt, David A. Wise, and Richard Zeckhauser, "Price Differences in Almost Competitive Markets." *Quarterly Journal of Economics* (May 1979):189–206. Copyright © 1979 by the President and Fellows of Harvard College. Reprinted by permission of John Wiley & Sons, Inc.

Since information search is costly, we would expect that people would seek information until the incremental cost of the search equals the incremental benefit. The more people search for information about price, the less dispersed prices will be in the market.

Information comes from many sources. Consumers determine product quality from an inspection of the product prior to purchase and from past experience. They may purchase information from experts. For example, publications and consultants inform buyers of product quality and provide comparative price information. Consumers may also seek recommendations from knowledgeable friends and relatives.

Consumers are not necessarily at odds with firms over information about the firms' products. Firms have two main incentives to provide information. First, firms compete for consumers and have an incentive to promote their own products at the expense of other firms' products. In the absence of a collusive effort to withhold information, firms will attempt to exploit the weaknesses of their rivals' products in their promotional efforts. Second, consumer search for information takes time and effort. Consumers face two costs when they buy goods: the purchase price and the time cost of searching for the good. If firms can promote their products in a way that reduces the total cost to consumers, consumers may compensate firms for their efforts by paying a higher price. Although the purchase price may be higher, the combined price to consumers is lower because of the reduction in search cost.

Possible Informational Problems

Before considering specific ways of promoting a firm's product, we will turn to some general informational problems that both firms and consumers must confront. The better informed can make better decisions, but there are costs that can get in the way of being better informed. First, there are costs associated with measuring product quality. These measurement costs make it difficult for the buyer to determine the true value of a firm's product. At the same time, the seller has difficulty convincing buyers of the product's quality.

Second, the problem is compounded when one party has more information about the product than another party. The seller must convince the buyer that it will not act opportunistically against the buyer. Without this guarantee, the market for the product may not exist.

Third, there are instances when a firm benefits from the promotional efforts of another firm without paying for the benefit. Because of this problem, firms may concentrate their promotional efforts on their product at the expense of other firms. This practice leads to an underprovision of information about the general product offered by all firms in the market.

These problems are of importance to Harry Sampson. In the last chapter, Harry was considering selling Verte Tree Company and becoming a dealer for the Awesome Truck Company. He would be primarily selling the company's new truck, the Torrido. While the next three chapters are devoted to analyzing the internal relationships and incentive structures of firms, we will assume in this chapter that both Harry and Awesome Truck Company work together to overcome the informational problems of promoting their new truck.

Measurement Costs

Since consumers purchase only what they believe to be worth at least what they are paying, they make an effort to measure the properties of goods, unless they are convinced that the costs of measurement exceed the benefits. However, consumers may not always be able to determine the quality of the product, even with a detailed investigation.

Recall that the Torrido's main features are three reverse gears and an expandable cab that converts the truck into a van with pop-up seats. While these features distinguish the Torrido from all other trucks in the market, consumers want assurances that the truck performs these functions properly. Even if the typical Torrido does perform as Awesome Truck claims it does, consumers cannot be sure that the specific Torrido they purchase will be as good as expected. Without assurances from the company, the consumer would have to invest in costly measurement of the truck's condition. Since this measurement cost would be over and above the purchase price of the truck, the total cost to the consumer would be higher than the purchase price alone.

For example, assume that a farmer has apples for sale. Consumers may inspect each apple prior to purchase if they wish to do so. If there is little difference in the apples, or if the consumer does not think there is much difference, then the consumer will have little or no incentive to search. The greater the variation in quality among the apples, the more consumers will search. By searching and finding the highest quality apples among those available, consumers will raise the average quality-to-price ratio of their purchases.

Knowing that consumers will search in this way, the farmer has an incentive to sort the apples into standard-quality groupings. Most consumers do not prefer to spend time searching and measuring the quality of apples. Since they have an opportunity cost attached to their time, they are usually willing to pay to save search time. The farmer has the incentive to sort the apples to the point where the consumer no longer has the incentive to search. In this way there is only one sorting of the apples.

If the farmer is more efficient at sorting (that is, sorts subject to lower average cost) than the consumers, the farmer will lower overall costs of the sorting process and will be able to charge higher prices than if the buyers had to sort. The net price to customers (that is, purchase price plus opportunity cost of sorting time) is lowest with the seller doing the sorting.

Awesome Trucks has a similar incentive to reduce variation in the quality of its Torridos. Unless it can prevent customers from sorting through the available trucks in order to find the one with above-average quality for the characteristics they prefer, customers will add the inspection costs to the purchase price in determining how much the truck will cost. Later in the chapter we will see how the use of a brand name and warranties may help Awesome Truck prevent buyers from excessive sorting prior to the purchase of a Torrido.

Asymmetric Information

When Harry sells a new Torrido, it is unlikely that he will know much more than the customer about whether that particular truck will be above average or below average in quality compared to all of the other Torridos in the lot. Since each truck is new, no one has driven any of them long enough to find all the possible defects.

This is not necessarily the case with a used truck. The person selling a used truck benefits from having owned the truck and most likely knows more about the truck's quality than prospective buyers do. This difference in information between buyer and seller is an example of asymmetric information. **Asymmetric information** is information relevant to a transaction that one party has but the other does not.

Asymmetric information may create the "lemons" problem.[1] Professor George Ackerlof of the University of California at Berkeley showed that a market might not exist for a product unless counteracting measures are taken to offset the effects of asymmetric information. As an example, he discussed the market for used cars.

Since sellers are likely to know more about the quality of their cars than buyers do, the seller has an incentive to sell "lemons" to unsuspecting buyers. Sellers sometimes offer for sale all those cars that have a value less than the market price. If buyers expect that sellers will sell only below-average cars, they will bid down the average market price to a lower level. At the lower price sellers will offer fewer cars: only those below the level of the new price. The end result is that the market may disappear.

---

[1] George A. Ackerlof, "The Market for 'Lemons': Quality Uncertainty and the Market Mechanism." *Quarterly Journal of Economics* 84 (August 1970):488–500.

APPLICATION   In 1976 the major league baseball players' association and the club owners agreed to give players the right to become free agents after six years of major-league service. Professor Kenneth Lehn of Washington State University studied the impact that free agency had on players' contracts. He noted that there may be a significant difference between the information that the owners of the team currently employing a player have about the player and that known by potential employers. He used data from the teams on the performances of 155 players to show that free agents do present risks to new employers.

Professor Lehn thought that a team would be unwilling to part with a player who was worth what he was asking for during negotiations. An owner unwilling to match an offer made by a competing team might have access to negative information about the potential performance of the player. Although statistical data on past performance is available to everyone, other teams might be unaware of a player's attitude about working hard in the future. This would be especially important for someone being offered a long-term contract in late career. Players might also be able to hide injuries from opposing teams for a period of time, while the seriousness of the injuries would be more obvious to those observing the player on a day-to-day basis.

Professor Lehn found support for these ideas. He observed the performances of free agents signed by their original clubs versus those signed by new clubs. He noticed that the post-contract disability rates for free agents signed by new clubs was significantly higher. The difference was most important for pitchers. Free-agent pitchers increased their disability rate by 448.24 percent compared to a 166.94 percent increase by those retained by their original teams. Free-agent pitchers pitched 15.92 percent fewer innings per season than before, while the innings pitched by retained pitchers dropped by 6.69 percent.

The number of five-year contracts involving pitchers signed as free agents was similar to the number signed by the original team from 1977 to 1980. The numbers of free-agent signings from 1977 to 1980 were four, three, two, and five, respectively, while the numbers retained by their original teams were five, three, four, and five. After a few years of experience with the free-agent process, owners apparently determined that there was something to be learned from the decision of the former club not to retain the players. Professor Lehn observed that the number of free-agent pitchers signed to five-year contracts decreased dramatically in the early 1980s.

In 1981 and 1982 there were no five-year contracts for free-agent pitchers, but there were six rehirings by the former teams in 1981 and four in 1982. The only free-agent pitchers signing five-year contracts after 1982 were Bruce Sutter by the Atlanta Braves and Ed Whitson by the New York Yankees. Sutter spent most of his first years with Atlanta on the disabled list, and

POSSIBLE INFORMATIONAL PROBLEMS

Whitson was eventually traded after pitching ineffectively for the Yankees. The owner of the Braves, Ted Turner, and the owner of the Yankees, George Steinbrenner, have been widely regarded as the biggest risk takers in professional baseball.

Source: Kenneth Lehn, "Information Asymmetries in Baseball's Free Agent Market." *Economic Inquiry* XXII, No. 1 (January 1984):37–44.

Free Riders

As mentioned earlier, firms have incentives to provide consumers with information about the goods they are selling. In addition, publications, such as *Consumer Reports*, and journalists compete with others to supply this information. Specialists, such as attorneys, termite inspectors, and house appraisers, offer advice to clients. The more generally applicable and the less specific the information to the buyer, the more likely there will be a problem of free riders. A **free rider** is someone who benefits from the actions of others without compensating them.

For example, free riders can obtain information about new truck prices and performance by reading publications at a newsstand or bookstore without buying the publication. They can team up with other interested persons to share the purchase price of publications. Although the publisher could raise the price to counter this behavior, the publisher would then lose those subscribers who find teaming with others too costly in time and effort.

Free riding decreases the incentive to supply information. Since publishers cannot recover the full value of their services, they sometimes underprovide information. They will provide information only to the point where the cost of producing extra information would exceed the extra revenue from producing the extra information.

Firms selling products also face free-rider problems. There are two components to their advertising and promotional efforts. Part of their advertisements promote their own products at the expense of competitors' products. On the other hand, some of their advertising promotes the general type of product that firms produce and therefore benefits all producers of the same type of product.

For example, a firm advertising that its light beer is less filling than a competitor's beer improves its image relative to other light beers, but it also improves the image of all light beers in comparison to higher-calorie beer or other drinks. Torrido ads that show it maneuvering through fields and dirt roads while hauling tree stumps and other cumbersome items encourage consumers to consider buying a truck. Since some of the consumers who are encouraged to buy a truck because of the ad may find the Torrido too expensive, the truck manufacturers who eventually do sell trucks to these consumers have benefited from the Torrido ad without compensating the Awesome Truck Company.

The more an advertisement promotes a general type of product (for example, trucks versus Torridos), the more opportunity for free riding by other firms. Given this problem, firms have an incentive to compare their product favorably to others or promote information relevant only to their own brand, rather than the general type of product. For example, Awesome Truck may decide to concentrate its advertisements on the Torrido's three reverse gears and its expandable cab.

The Promotion of Product Quality

We have already hinted at some of the possible nonprice strategies of firms. Firms must decide which characteristics to choose for their products, and they must determine the most effective way of informing customers of these characteristics. When a firm chooses characteristics that differ from those of other products, the firm has created a new product.

If the product is different enough from others, the firm might have a monopoly. Of course, unless the firm can protect the profits associated with the product by using barriers to entry, it will not have a monopoly for long. If the firm creates a product that is essentially identical to that of a large number of other firms and there is no cost in obtaining information about the product, then the market will be perfectly competitive, and the firm will have no control over its demand curve or price.

Between these two extremes are products that differ from other products in terms of certain characteristics. There are also differences that may be more in the minds of consumers than in the actual characteristics of the product. Firms transmit information that both informs consumers about the differences in their products and persuades them that there are differences that do not exist. We will start with a common practice for guaranteeing product quality: the issuing of warranties and money-back guarantees.

Warranties and Money-Back Guarantees

Awesome Truck can reduce search cost for its customers by using a warranty. A **warranty** is an offer of a satisfactory product at the posted price, with the stipulation that customers can return a defective good to the firm for a replacement or refund if they can show that the malfunction was the fault of the manufacturer. Since the customer can return a Torrido for one that meets the specifications of the manufacturer, the customer has less incentive to inspect the internal condition of the Torrido prior to driving the truck away from the dealer's lot. Warranties transfer the inspection process to the customer, who performs the inspection by driving the truck for a period of time after purchase. If it is relatively costly for the firm and the customer to make inspections prior to purchase, warranties may offer the lowest-cost alternative to detailed inspections prior to purchase.

While warranties and money-back offers may be effective in many cases, they may also be difficult to implement. For instance, buyers may be careless or act opportunistically, yet the seller may not always be able to prove that the damage was the fault of the buyer. For example, a lawnmower could malfunction because the operator tried to mow too tall and thick a patch of grass, or because of a defective piece of metal in the engine. Unless the manufacturer has some way of distinguishing between these two events, the manufacturer may find that warranties are not a feasible means of guaranteeing the quality of the product.

Brand Names and Bonding

We have already seen that manufacturers are less willing to use warranties the more an operator can mask negligence in reporting defects. In such cases the manufacturer may have to resort to alternatives for guaranteeing the quality of the product. A firm unable to offer cost-effective guarantees may emphasize its brand name as a means of insuring a consistent level of quality. According to Professors Benjamin Klein and Keith Leffler, the brand name is a bond that the firm offers customers as a guarantee.[2] The firm stakes the reputation of its brand on the consistent quality of its product.

For example, when Rocky Sanders sells Poobell Plastic Trash Bags, he is responsible for the quality of his trash bags. If the number of bags in the box does not correspond to the number listed on the box, or if the strength of the bags is not as advertised, Rocky will lose repeat customers. When customers buy trash bags again, they will intentionally avoid buying Poobell bags. Adverse publicity for his trash bags could mean a substantial loss in his investment in the Poobell brand name. If the name is significantly damaged, he may have to abandon it and start promoting an entirely new brand name.

| 9-3 | **I shouldn't have said that** |

APPLICATION

Professor Sam Peltzman of the University of Chicago has offered evidence that unfavorable news concerning the reliability of a brand does have a strong impact on the market value of the firm. He analyzed the behavior of the stock market value of twenty-three firms that the FTC (Federal Trade Commission) had investigated on charges of misleading advertising between 1962 and 1975.

Although the FTC is responsible for prosecuting antitrust cases, it uses approximately half of its resources to investigate and prosecute cases involving

---

[2] Benjamin Klein and Keith Leffler, "The Role of Market Forces in Assuring Contractual Performance." *Journal of Political Economy* 89 (October 1981):615–41.

misleading or fraudulent advertising. For example, the FTC challenged the makers of Blue Bonnet margarine for ads that claimed its product had "moisture buds" that made it taste more like butter than competing brands did. The FTC forced Blue Bonnet to remove the ads, because the margarine contained no flavor-enhancing additive.

At the time, the FTC had limited authority to penalize offending firms. Before 1975, the FTC could only order the firm to remove the advertisements. The substantial adverse publicity and the halt to the campaign appeared to be the only negative effects. He found that, on the average, a firm lost between 1 and 2 percent of its stock market value due to the public announcement of an FTC complaint. Since most of these firms produced many other products, the value of the brand name of one product was typically between 1 and 2 percent of the firm's total sales. According to Professor Peltzman, the drop in stock value appeared to cause "essentially a wiping out of the brand's advertising capital."

Source: Sam Peltzman, *Journal of Law and Economics* XXIV, No. 3 (December 1981):403–49. © by the University of Chicago.

Advertising and Competition

Up to this point we have emphasized the importance of informational problems and the firm's options in dealing with these problems. We now turn to the role of advertising. While advertising helps promote brand names, several researchers have also emphasized the effect of advertising on barriers to entry and on the extent to which firms compete by means of price.[3]

Since advertising expenditures are designed to influence the demand for a product, they may also affect both own-price and cross-price elasticities of demand. Some contend that advertising creates barriers to entry that lead to inelastic demand and low cross-price elasticities. Those who see advertising more as a means of entering markets argue that advertising makes demand curves more elastic while increasing cross-price elasticities of demand.

In order for advertising to have an adverse impact on competition, there must be asymmetries among firms in the market. With asymmetries, the firm that enters the market first may be able to continue to earn economic profits by matching any advertising on the part of entrants.

Those who see advertising as a barrier to entry emphasize the ability of advertising to artificially create differences in products and confuse consumers. Empirical support for this view comes from studies showing an association between high business profits and both high market concentration and

[3] William S. Comanor and Thomas A. Wilson, "The Effect of Advertising on Competition: A Survey." *Journal of Economic Literature* XVII, No. 2 (June 1979):453–76.

advertising intensity. These conditions appear to be common to only a small number of industries in the United States.

There have been challenges made to this empirical evidence. Since firms do not report economic profits, researchers have had to rely on a proxy: business profits reported by accountants. Accountants do not depreciate most advertising and promotional expenses even if these expenses create an asset with a useful life beyond one year. If advertising has a useful life beyond one year, the high profits reported by industries that advertise heavily will misrepresent their true profitability. The high business profits may reflect the normal return to an investment in advertising that was not depreciated over its useful life. Recent estimates by Professor Robert Ayanian suggest that the useful average life of advertisement may be seven years. According to Ayanian, a useful life of seven years would account for the high business profit rates in industries with heavy advertising-to-sales ratios.[4]

Professors Isaac Ehrlich and Lawrence Fisher showed that there is more advertising when consumers' wages increase.[5] They argued that the higher wages represent a higher opportunity cost for consumers' time. By advertising and promoting quality, firms reduce consumers' opportunity cost of search. The following two applications offer additional procompetitive evidence from two industries noted for high business profits and relatively large advertising-to-sales ratios: the pharmaceutical and cigarette industries.

| 9-4 | **Advertising opens the door** |

APPLICATION   Professor Keith Leffler of the University of Washington found that advertising for prescription drugs enhances market entry without raising prices to consumers. This industry has high advertising-to-sales ratios averaging 13 percent in the 1970s.

Professor Leffler selected a sample of 51 prescription drugs introduced between 1968 and 1977. The companies sold at least 75 percent of the quantity manufactured of each product to drugstores. His data confirmed the relative unimportance of the promotion of pharmaceuticals sold to hospitals. Since physicians make most of the drug choices for their patients, drug companies aim their advertising and promotional efforts at physicians.

Professor Leffler found that promotion was of two types. The firms promoted new products heavily, but also promoted older products to maintain the names of the products in the physician's memory. He compared the advertising for these 51 products to that of the largest competitor's product

---

[4] Robert Ayanian, "The Advertising Capital Controversy." *Journal of Business* 56, No. 3 (July 1983):349–64.

[5] Isaac Ehrlich and Lawrence Fisher, "The Derived Demand for Advertising: A Theoretical and Empirical Investigation." *American Economic Review* 72, No. 3 (June 1982):366–88.

and the competitor with the closest comparable market share one year after the introduction of the drug. He found that the advertising for the new product exceeded that of the largest competitor. Also, more of the promotion costs were for direct promotion to physicians.

There was no significant change in the promotional budgets of established products in anticipation of or after the introduction of the new products. The most important factor predicting the success of the new product was whether it represented an important therapeutic advance. Success of the market entrant was also dependent on promotional expenses. According to Professor Leffler, the entry-promoting aspects of advertising were greater than the entry-deterring aspects.

He also analyzed the effect of market entry on the prices of the competing products. Only 31 of the 102 competitors' prices increased during the first year after the entry of the new drug. The average price change for all drugs was a 5 percent drop. Since average prices drop with competitive entry, he concluded that advertising in this industry has been procompetitive.

While he argues that the government has been effective in eliminating fraudulent and misleading advertising by requiring proof of a drug's effectiveness prior to introduction of the product, he does not support restriction of nonfraudulent advertising. His results show that on balance advertising has speeded the introduction of new drugs and has helped consumers.

Source: Keith B. Leffler, "Persuasion or Information? The Economics of Prescription Drug Advertising." *Journal of Law and Economics* XXIV, No. 1 (April 1981):45–75. © by the University of Chicago.

| 9-5 | Fighting for a larger slice of a smaller pie |

APPLICATION

In the late 1980s, the American Medical Association tried to influence Congress to ban all remaining forms of advertising for cigarettes. Several studies done as early as 1950 showed a strong connection between smoking and a wide range of health problems. The FTC, in its role of regulating against false advertising, has issued several directives against the tobacco industry since the 1950s.

John Calfee of the FTC offered a review of the effects of earlier FTC efforts to control the industry's advertising. According to Calfee, these efforts were counterproductive. As we have already seen, advertising may serve not only the needs of an industry as a whole, but two additional groups: new entrants to a market and consumers.

He argued that advertising focused on the comparative advantages of one brand over another prior to the imposition of regulations by the FTC banning health claims. This form of advertising forced those manufacturers who were not improving the healthfulness of their cigarettes to lose market share and led to an overall decline in smoking. While the advertising was self-destructive from the industry's standpoint, it benefited smaller firms at the expense of the market leaders. When firms could not legally make comparative claims, they resorted to sanitized ads, which did not attack their competitors, and they stopped making improvements in their cigarettes.

For example, in 1950 two studies appeared that linked cigarette smoking to cancer. These studies received considerable publicity. In 1952 P. Lorilard, one of the smallest firms, with a 6 percent market share, introduced Kent cigarettes. Kent had a filter that reduced tar and nicotine considerably. Other companies followed suit within two years. Between 1950 and 1952, filter brands increased their market share anywhere from 2 percent to 10 percent. The companies advertised aggressively by promoting their cigarettes at the expense of other brands. While the two largest firms refused to use fear tactics in their ads, all the smaller firms did. Annual per capita consumption dropped by 3 percent in 1953 and by another 6 percent in 1954, despite a steady annual increase in smoking since 1931.

These decreases in consumption exceeded all others occurring later (even the decline following the Surgeon General's Report in 1964). During the fear campaign the smaller firms increased their market shares while the largest firms lost market shares. In 1954 the FTC required companies to stop using comparative health or effectiveness claims. Ads changed from pictures showing dark stains on the filters of competing brands to smokers walking through the woods or sitting beside freshwater streams.

Cigarette sales rebounded vigorously in 1955. In addition, test results appearing in *Reader's Digest* and *Consumer Reports* in 1957 showed that tar and nicotine in cigarettes returned to the higher levels of the early 1950s. For example, Kent had six times more tar in 1957 than in 1952. However, since the FTC's rule applied only to existing cigarettes and existing technology, some companies were able to work around the restrictions and introduce new, improved versions in the late 1950s to exploit this new information about the sharp rise in the tar and nicotine levels of competitors' brands.

Mr. Calfee reported similar evidence as FTC policy continued to change through the 1960s and 1970s. For example, in 1966 the FTC concurred with an appeal from the American Cancer Society and allowed tar and nicotine advertising again. By this time a group of cigarette firms had seen the benefits of preventing its members from engaging in comparative advertising, and they vigorously objected to the change. Two small companies broke from the group and began comparative advertising. The others had no choice but to follow.

Mr. Calfee did not disprove the claims that the removal of remaining advertisements in the print media and on billboards would have reduced smoking. Instead, he showed that firms compete against one another more vigorously than many believed. He found that, if left unchecked, cigarette firms show an eagerness to attack the claims of their competitors to increase their slice of a decreasing pie, while indirectly promoting both lower-tar and lower-nicotine cigarettes and market entry. According to Mr. Calfee, "restrictions on advertising have tended to undermine improvements in cigarettes while doing nothing to reduce smoking."

Source: John E. Calfee, "The Ghost of Cigarette Advertising Past." *Regulation* (November/ December 1986):35–45. With permission of the American Enterprise Institute.

The Choice of a Product's Characteristics

In Chapter 5 we introduced the notion of monopolistic competition. In that market there was enough variety in the types of products so that each firm faced its own negatively-sloped demand curve despite the presence of close competitors. That model does not explicitly account for the way in which products differ from one another. Firms enter the market by developing products with unique characteristics and force economic profits of all firms producing the same general type of product to zero in the long run.

We will now be more specific in describing the differences among different firms' products. We therefore move away from the assumption of a homogeneous product. Harold Hotelling in 1929 was the first person to attempt to formalize the effect that quality differences have on firms' competitive behavior.[6] In the simplified version of his argument presented here, we will concentrate on quality variations due to differences in just one characteristic. Since most products differ in terms of several characteristics, we will expand the logic of the argument to the multicharacteristic case.

Location of a Hot Dog Stand at the Beach   At some beaches you can buy ice cream, hot dogs, and other food items on the beach itself or at various shops along the boardwalk. Assume that one particular beach has an overorganized beach patrol, that requires all beachgoers to be spaced evenly in a line along the beach. On crowded days when no patch of sand is available, the crowd accomplishes this configuration without any outside help. The only hot dog vendor on the beach is Franky Hyster.

To simplify this scenario further, assume that everyone has the same demand function for a hot dog. Recall from Chapter 2 that this assumption implies that the mathematical equation representing one's demand for hot dogs is the same for everyone. Presumably, one demand factor will be how far the consumer has to walk to buy a hot dog. The price of the hot dog will also affect the quantity demanded. Since this chapter focuses on nonprice factors, let us assume that the hot dog price is set by the local beach authority. The price is high enough for Franky Hyster to cover his average total cost of selling hot dogs. We will assume that the average total cost is constant, and thereby ignore the role of scale economies.

[6] Harold Hotelling, "Stability in Competition." *Economic Journal* 39 (March 1929):41–57.

Given all of these assumptions, we can now determine what Franky may do. Since he cannot vary his price, he will maximize his profits by selling as many hot dogs as possible. The only variable that will create a difference in the quantity demanded of each beachgoer is the distance each must walk to the hot dog stand. To maximize profits, Franky must minimize the average distance that each customer must walk. This means he must locate the stand in the middle of the beach. By locating in the middle Franky makes the average one-way walking distance equal to one-fourth the length of the beach. While those located at the center of the beach have no walk, those at either end must make a one-way walk equal to half the length of the beach. Since customers are distributed equally along the beach, the average one-way trip will be one-fourth the length of the beach.

Now let's assume that a new vendor receives a license to sell hot dogs. Where should the new vendor locate? This will depend on whether Franky is free or willing to move. Assume that Franky cannot or will not move. Since the important factor in the demand function of consumers is the distance they must walk, the new vendor will want to minimize this distance.

Suppose the vendor chooses a location halfway between Franky and one end of the beach. Distance to the new vendor averages one-eighth the length of the beach, in one direction. You can see this by looking at Figure 9-1. The new vendor is at *B*, while Franky remains at *A*. Since *B* is 200 yards from the end of the beach and from *A*, the typical customer has to walk 100 yards each way.

Franky now faces a reduction in his share of the market. Since customers distinguish between hot dog stands based on walking distance, no one will walk to *A* if the distance to *B* is shorter. The halfway point between *A* and *B* (point C) divides the market between the two vendors. Franky's customers now come from point C to the other end of the beach, and Franky has more customers than the vendor at *B*.

FIGURE 9-1 ▪ **Locations at the beach.** Franky Hyster locates his hot dog stand at *A* in the middle of the beach. If another vendor locates at *B*, Franky will keep all the people to the left of *C* as his customers. The remaining customers will go to the hot dog stand at *B*. By moving closer to *A*, the vendor at *B* can increase his share of the market. He will move to the right of *A* in equilibrium and take all customers to the right of *A*. Franky will keep all customers to the left of *A*.

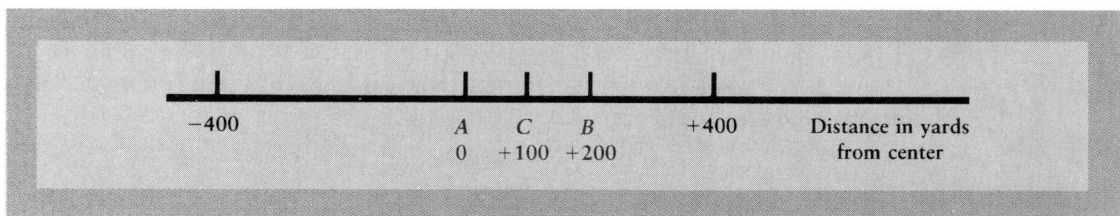

The vendor at *B* realizes that he can increase his profits by moving closer to *A*. By moving closer to *A*, he will keep all of his former customers, while taking away half of the customers located between him and point *A*. By moving to point *A* he will maximize his sales and take half of the market that Franky would have had if the new vendor had not entered the market.

Characteristic Space We can use the same logic to consider the choice of location in characteristic space. **Characteristic space** is a multidimensional representation of the amount or intensity level of each of a product's different characteristics. For example, candy bars may differ in terms of chocolate and sugar content.

We can see this by assuming that the position on a spectrum represents a specific preference for the sweetness of a soft drink. By way of illustration, assume that the demand for cola varies only in terms of the sweetness of the competing brands. Consumers located in the middle of the spectrum prefer an average amount of sweetness; those at one end prefer very sweet cola; and those at the opposite end prefer unsweetened cola. A firm's cola will appeal to those consumers whose preference for sweetness matches the sweetness of the firm's cola. The firm formulates its cola to attract as many customers as possible.

Assume that the total population of potential customers is spread uniformly along this sweetness spectrum. As long as there is no significant difference in price and the intensity of customers' preferences is strong, firms will compete to meet the demand of specific segments of this population. As in the case of the two hot dog vendors, two firms will have a tendency to locate near one another at the middle of the spectrum in order to maximize their profits.

Extensions of the Simple Hotelling Model When there are only two firms and one product characteristic, both firms will locate at the same point on the taste spectrum. Several economists have extended Harold Hotelling's simple example to account for more realistic assumptions about a product's characteristics. For example, there can be larger numbers of firms and product characteristics.

With four or five firms in the market there is a possibility of clustering near a specific set of characteristics. Professors Eaton and Lipsey found a tendency for clusters to occur when products have several characteristics.[7] The reason is that firms attempt to copy the characteristics of competitors in most respects but differ in a few characteristics enough to capture all those consumers who have a strong preference for a few distinguishing characteristics.

Clusters may also occur when there are economies from producing products similar to those already in the market. For example, new firms can free ride

---

[7] B. Curtis Eaton and Richard G. Lipsey, "The Principle of Minimum Differentiation Reconsidered: Some New Developments in the Theory of Spatial Competition." *Review of Economic Studies* XLII, No. 1 (January 1975):27–49.

on the information provided by makers of the existing products. They may also benefit from information about the production of the product and the market demand for that specific set of characteristics. There may be benefits to standardization. For example, a firm that produces a nonstandard type of computer disk may find that the disk does not correspond to existing computer hardware.

| 9-6 | **A pile of chips** |

APPLICATION

Professor Swann of the University of Bath in Great Britain analyzed the history of product competition in microprocessors (that is, microchips) between 1971 and 1981. He observed a strong tendency for firms to cluster their products. According to Professor Swann, the earlier microprocessors varied mostly by processing power, level of integration of functions, and a subjective measure of the status of the device called "generation."

He used these three characteristics to compare the products of 22 firms that made products of their own design. Most of these firms also made copies of existing products, while an additional 16 firms made only copies. In total, there were 203 separate products introduced between 1971 and 1981. Sixty-nine of them were original designs and the remaining 134 were copies.

While the copies were clear examples of clustering, there was evidence of substantial clustering in the new designs. For example, by 1974 there was significant clustering of second-generation microprocessors with 8-bit processing capacity. From 1975 to 1977 there was clustering of more integrated 4-bit and 8-bit processors, while 1978 and 1979 marked the appearance of a third generation of 16-bit processors.

Throughout this time period Intel was the market leader in new designs. Many of the other firms followed Intel's lead. The evidence generally suggested that the advantages of sharing technological change, feasibility information, and consumer interest in the product were a strong incentive for clustering.

In addition, Professor Swann concluded that since users of the microchips adopt standards that limit the variations of the characteristics of the newest products, producers of nonstandard variations may find limited interest for their products unless the variations represent a significant improvement over existing microchips.

Source: G.M.P. Swann, "Product Competition in Microprocessors." *Journal of Industrial Economics* XXXIV, No. 1 (September 1985):33–53.

Despite the evidence favoring clustering of products, there are situations when clustering may not occur. When there are large costs involved in moving an existing product to a different point in the characteristic space, firms may fear that their competitors will retaliate if they locate too close to the competitor's product. As a result, they may locate their products so as to minimize this reaction. Otherwise, firms can relocate their products to other points in the characteristic space with some cost of adjustment. When relocation costs are high, firms tend to spread out in characteristic space.

Product Location as a Barrier to Entry

Now let us look at the role that product location and scale economies play in keeping new firms from entering the market. By introducing scale economies we create a situation where the firm must sell enough of its product to cover fixed costs. Recall that scale economies occur when long-run average total cost decreases with increases in output. If the size of the market is not large enough to take advantage of falling average total cost, the new entrant may choose not to enter the market.

Unless there is a significant change in price, the only competitors directly affected by a competitor's actions may be those located to either side of the firm in the characteristic space. Researchers have shown theoretically that only two competitors are affected as long as there are no more than three distinguishing characteristics.[8] It is more difficult to prove this when there are more than three characteristics. You must rely on an empirical (that is, data-supported) argument for cases involving more than three characteristics.

| 9-7 | I can't fit in here |

APPLICATION

In the 1970s the Federal Trade Commission brought an antitrust case against the four major cereal producers in the United States: Kellogg, General Mills, General Foods, and Quaker Oats. Professor Richard Schmalensee of Massachusetts Institute of Technology worked with the FTC on this case and published a paper in 1979 outlining his argument that these companies had deterred the entry of new cereal brands to the market.

Professor Schmalensee suggested that customers' preferences for cereals vary according to such characteristics as sweetness, protein content, shape, grain base, vitamin content, fiber content, and crunchiness. Advertising-to-sales ratios in this industry have generally been greater than 10 percent since World War II. Despite a lack of entry by new firms, existing firms have increased the number of brands significantly. Many of a company's brands do not feature the name of the company.

Due to the fixed costs of start-up advertising, Professor Schmalensee assumed that there were economies to scale. With greater output, the average

---

[8] G.C. Archibald and Gideon Rosenbluth, "The 'New' Theory of Consumer Demand and Monopolistic Competition." *Quarterly Journal of Economics* 89, No. 4 (November 1975):569–90.

costs associated with advertising would be spread over larger output levels. His evidence suggested that the cost of relocating a brand to another point in the characteristic space would be very high. In addition, he assumed the market to be localized since companies focus their marketing efforts on at most two rivals.

He assumed that if there were two brands located along a one-dimensional characteristic space, and customers were distributed evenly along this dimension, a new entrant would choose to enter halfway between the two existing brands. The new entrant would take half of the market formerly shared by the two existing brands. If the scale economies associated with advertising were large enough, the new firm would not be able to charge a price that allowed it to cover its average fixed cost of producing the brand.

Professor Schmalensee argued that there were economies associated with the use of a brand name for more than one product that allowed an existing firm to introduce a new product at lower incremental cost than a new entrant. This advantage of an established position prevented new firms from entering the market.

The FTC eventually dropped the case against the cereal companies, based in part on the lack of evidence of overt collusion by the cereal makers and the entry into the market in the 1970s of companies making natural-grain cereals. This entry was largely unanticipated by the three largest firms. One of the established firms, Quaker Oats, did anticipate this new trend and increased its market share substantially as a result.

Professor Schmalensee argued that the established firms competed by new brand proliferation and advertising and avoided price competition. He supported the FTC's original proposal, which would force the companies to allow competitors to produce and sell the cereals using the same brand name. Under this proposal, competitors would not have had to pay royalties once the product had been on the market for five years; that is, they would have had royalty-free licenses. He argued that if all established firms could produce the cereal (for example, Cheerios or Wheaties), the original producer of the brand would not be able to use its reputation to charge higher prices. This would lead to stiff price competition and the erosion of profit margins on these brands. He noted that the quality of the product could be retained under the licensing of the trademark by subjecting licensees' quality to independent audit every five years.

Source: Richard Schmalensee, "Entry Deterrence in the Ready-to-Eat Breakfast Cereal Industry." *Bell Journal of Economics* (1979):305–27.

There is disagreement about the merits of royalty-free licenses for reducing barriers to entry caused by the successful promotion of a brand name. Consider the following example.

APPLICATION

Professor Clement Krouse of the University of California at Santa Barbara argued that a brand name's role as a bond (or guarantee) applied directly to a court case lost by Borden, Inc. in 1982.[9] Borden makes ReaLemon processed lemon juice. The FTC had filed a case against Borden after receiving a complaint from a competitor. The FTC claimed that Borden had used the "premium status" of its brand name as a barrier to entry and had engaged in predatory pricing.

Recall from Chapter 7 that predatory pricing is pricing below cost with the intent of forcing a competitor out of business. The competitor, Golden Crown, claimed that it had to charge between 10 and 15 cents per quart less than Borden in order to stay in the market. The FTC claimed that consumers become attached to a brand, forcing a new firm to charge a disproportionately low price to attract customers. This "habit" of consumers may give a firm monopoly power.

Professor Krouse did not agree with the FTC. He argued that the price premium was necessary because Borden was selling not only lemon juice, but information. Furthermore, consumers buying a processed lemon juice product were concerned about the variation in quality and required repeated samplings of the product to determine an estimate of the likely variation in the quality of that brand.

The court case revealed that the taste of processed lemon juice is very sensitive to small variations in the amount of preservative used. This sensitivity means that there must be stringent quality controls. Consumers use lemon juice in combination with other ingredients. If the quality of the lemon juice is not as expected, it may adversely affect the taste of the other foods. The cost of ruined ingredients is much greater than the cost of an ounce or two of lemon juice.

The price differential between ReaLemon and Golden Crown was 0.5 cents per one-ounce serving. Since the lemon juice amounted to a small but potentially important component of the final combination of ingredients, consumers may have been willing to pay 0.5 cents more to assure themselves of the quality of the product.

The ReaLemon trademark provided a bond with consumers that certified the quality of the product. If Borden betrayed its promise by deviating from the announced quality, consumers would retaliate by refusing to buy the product again. Professor Krouse noted that other firms began to realize the importance of quality assurance and began promoting brand names even

---

[9] See the earlier section, "Brand Names and Bonding," for a discussion of the use of a brand name as a bond.

before the FTC had initiated its case. ReaLemon found new competition from Seneca, Vita-Pakt, Minute Maid, and others.

Source: Clement G. Krouse, "Brand Name as a Barrier to Entry: The ReaLemon Case." *Southern Economic Journal* 51, No. 2 (October 1984):495–502.

Licensing

Firms may turn to other methods for communicating the quality of their goods and services. Earlier we noted that consumers have difficulty evaluating the quality of some products and services. The more sophisticated the service is, the more difficulty consumers have in evaluating it. For example, patients may not be able to determine whether a visit to their physician or hospital was responsible for an improvement or lack of improvement in their health. In such situations there is often political support for efforts to regulate the providers of these services in order to assure consumers of quality. Organizations representing professionals are usually enthusiastic supporters of self-regulation and requirements that prospective members meet specific standards before receiving a license to practice their specialty.

Licensing requirements affect two opposing parties: consumers and producers. Licensure can be a response to the asymmetric-information problem. Physicians know more about their skills than patients do, both before and after medical treatment. Those who support licensure contend that consumers benefit from the exclusion of those practitioners who have not met certain medical training standards.

Those who see licensure as benefiting physicians at the expense of consumers cite evidence of training requirements, restrictions on advertising, and constraints on hospital accreditation as attempts to raise physician income at the expense of consumers. Critics of licensure prefer certification as an alternative. Certification acknowledges a physician's qualifications but does not prevent others with different qualifications from practicing medicine. Consumers who prefer lower-cost, lower-quality service have the option to choose.

Licensure may benefit consumers by requiring physicians to make an investment in medical training. Physicians recoup their investment over their lifetimes by earning higher incomes in later years relative to their annual opportunity costs. If a medical board revokes a license, the physician loses an investment in a nontransferable skill and does not recoup the value of invested time. The investment of time offers consumers a bond or commitment of future high-quality service in the same way that a brand name is a bond guaranteeing the quality of a product. By failure to meet that commitment the physician sacrifices the investment.

APPLICATION

Professor Shirley Svorny of California State University developed a method for determining whether a specific licensing requirement benefited consumers or physicians. If consumers gain by physicians' investments, they experience lower costs in assessing physician quality, and their demand for physicians' services should increase. With a positively-sloped supply curve of physician services, the price for services should increase. Even though the price increases, the total price to consumers (including the opportunity cost of searching for the right physician) decreases as long as the reduction in the search cost is greater than the increase in the price paid to physicians.

If the price increase in physician services just offsets the reduction in search costs, there will be no difference in the quantity demanded of physician services. Figure 9-2 shows this result. Specific training requirements increase

FIGURE 9-2 ▪ Demand for physician services. The licensing requirements will shift the consumers' demand curve to D_2 because of the informational value of the licensing in reducing consumers' search costs. If the requirements restrict entry, the supply curve will shift to the left and reduce output of physician services. If the entry restriction exceeds the value consumers place on restricting entry, the market price will exceed P_3 and the quantity consumed will be less than Q_1.

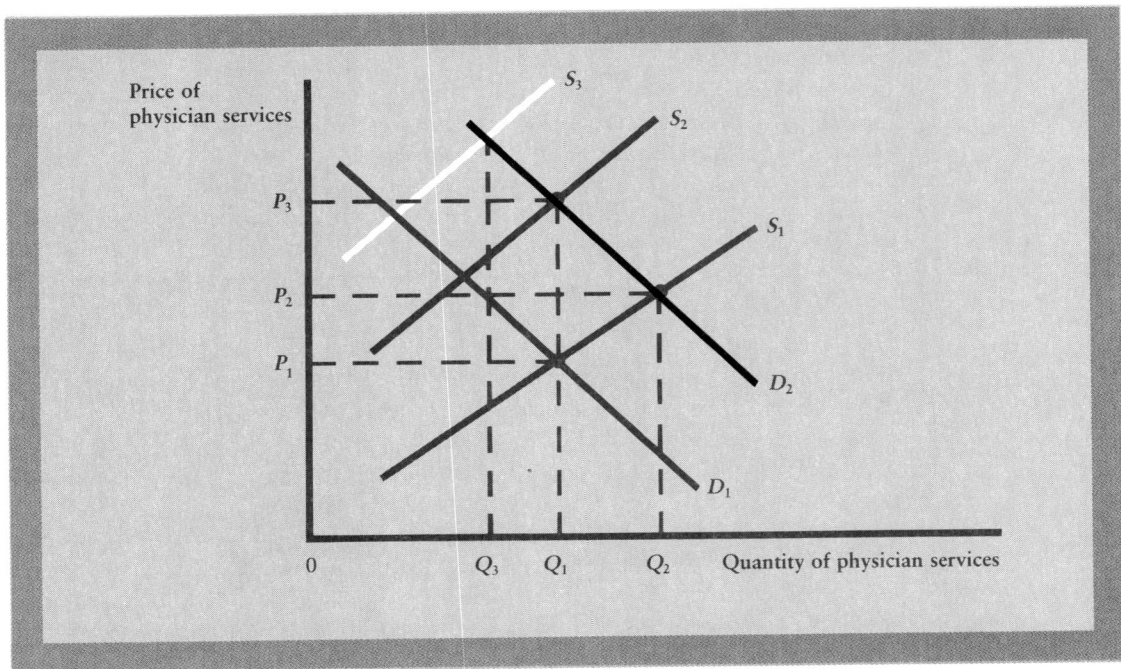

the costs of entering the profession and shift the supply curve from S_1 to S_2. The increased informational value of knowing that a physician has specific training shifts the demand curve for physician services, D_1, to the right to D_2.

Since the value of this information exactly equals the higher price paid to these physicians, consumers will demand the same quantity of services: Q_1. The difference between the higher price, P_3, and the former price, P_1, will reflect the benefit to consumers of knowing that these physicians have had specialized training. Although consumers pay a higher price for physician services, the higher price offsets the costs of their searching for information about the physician's quality of service and the higher costs to physicians of receiving training.

Professor Svorny analyzed data for the year 1965. In that year, twenty-three states required physicians to have basic science certificates, while twenty-four states restricted licenses to United States citizens. She estimated the effects that these restrictions had on the number of physicians working in the state. She had to control for other factors that could influence the number of physicians. These factors included age and size of the population, percent of the state population having medical insurance, the state's average educational levels, and public health care expenditure levels.

She found that together the two requirements for obtaining a license decreased the amount of physician services offered to consumers. This evidence showed that the restrictive nature of the licensing requirements dominated the consumer-interest aspects of the restrictions by shifting the supply curve to the left of S_2 (for example, to S_3). This resulted in a higher overall price (including both the price paid to physicians and the search cost for information) and a reduction in the quantity demanded. From this evidence she concluded that the restrictions served the interests of the physicians already having licenses more than they benefited consumers.

Source: Shirley V. Svorny, "Physician Licensure: A New Approach to Examining the Role of Professional Interests." *Economic Inquiry* XXV (July 1987):497–509.

Summary

Consumers face informational costs when deciding which goods and services to purchase. These costs increase for products that they buy less frequently or that carry higher price tags. Consumers are concerned with the combined price that they must pay for the product: the cost of the product itself and the cost of searching for the most appropriate product at the lowest cost.

There is considerable dispersion of prices for products of comparable quality. As price dispersion increases, consumers have an incentive to engage in a greater search for the lowest price. Since there is a cost to this search, consumers may be willing to pay for information that reduces the opportunity cost of search.

Firms have the incentive to lower a customer's search cost. By assuring customers of their product's quality, the firm can raise its price in exchange for information and assurances that lower the consumer's combined price. We considered the role of warranties, money-back guarantees, brand name promotion, advertising, and licensing regulations as means of providing consumers with information about product quality. Each of these has a role in reducing a consumer's search costs.

We also discussed the problems of measurement costs, asymmetrical information, and free riders, all of which may limit firms' efforts to provide an optimal level of information. Coupled with these problems is the possibility that firms may attempt to mislead consumers with their advertising so as to limit competition from firms wanting to enter the market.

Throughout the chapter we observed that governments often become involved when there is suspicion that firms may be trying to take advantage of unsuspecting consumers through misleading or harmful advertising. While the government may have a role in punishing firms that intentionally make fraudulent claims, we saw evidence that competitors often have sufficient incentives to seek out and expose unfavorable information about rivals' claims.

Important Terms

Asymmetric Information (p. 254)
Free Rider (p. 256)
Warranty (p. 257)
Characteristic Space (p. 265)

Selected References

Ackerlof, George. "The Market for 'Lemons': Quality Uncertainty and the Market Mechanism." *Quarterly Journal of Economics* 84 (August 1970):488–500.

Caves, Richard, and Porter, Michael. "From Entry Barriers to Mobility Barriers: Conjectural Decisions and Contrived Deterrence to New Competition." *Quarterly Journal of Economics* 91, No. 2 (May 1977):241–61.

Comanor, William S., and Wilson, Thomas A. "The Effect of Advertising on Competition: A Survey." *Journal of Economic Literature* XVII, No. 2 (June 1979):453–76.

Eaton, B. Curtis, and White, William D. "Agent Compensation and the Limits of Bonding." *Economic Inquiry* 20 (July 1982):330–43.

Hall, Christopher D. "Market Enforced Information Asymmetry: A Study of Claiming Races." *Economic Inquiry* XXIV (April 1986):271–91.

Klein, Benjamin, and Leffler, Keith. "The Role of Market Forces in Assuring Contractual Performance." *Journal of Political Economy* 89 (October 1981):615–41.

Lazear, Edward P. "Agency, Earnings Profiles, Productivity, and Hours Restrictions." *American Economic Review* (September 1981):606–20.

Lehn, Kenneth. "Information Asymmetries in Baseball's Free-Agent Market." *Economic Inquiry* XXII, No. 1 (January 1984):37–44.

1. Compare the likelihood of success in using warranties for the following products.
   (a) Closed-circuit television sets
   (b) Food blenders
   (c) Used cars
   (d) Small power saws

2. Assume that there are three hot dog vendors at the beach. Consumers choose among the three solely on the basis of the distance they must walk to the hot dog stand. In the absence of a collusive agreement among the three vendors, would you expect that there would be an equilibrium location for all three vendors?

3. Several states have inspectors who randomly test products sold in stores to verify the weight and volume of the contents listed on the containers. If the measured weight or volume is less than the listed weight or volume, the inspector can impose fines on both the store and the manufacturer. These states use the inspectors to protect consumers from fraudulent claims by manufacturers. If the penalized firms sell their products under a brand name, why might the inspectors' efforts work against the interests of consumers?

4. Compare the effects of a total ban on media advertisements for cigarettes with unrestricted advertisements in all media.

5. Assume that the Dommage Insurance Company introduces a new type of insurance for women to cover the costs of staying home from a market job during the first year after childbirth.
   (a) Assume that all women are eligible, as long as they do not have a child less than one year of age at the time they sign the insurance contract. There is no requirement for any other information. What is the likelihood of success of the new type of insurance?
   (b) Assume that there is a one-year wait from the time of signing the contract until one can start receiving benefits. What are the chances for success now?

6. Discuss the effect of a law that requires all candy bar manufacturers to provide royalty-free licenses to all interested companies seven years after the introduction of the candy bar.

Answer questions 7–11 with true, false, or uncertain.

7. High-income people are more likely to search for information about a product than lower-income people.

8. Price dispersion around the average price increases if consumers increase their search for information.

9. Consumers will pay a higher price for a product in exchange for more information about the dispersion of the product's quality.

10. Price dispersion is less likely for products that each consumer purchases frequently.

11. Licensure laws raise the quality of the services provided by the typical professional having a license.

THE ORGANIZATION OF
THE FIRM: INTRODUCTION

Most modern corporations produce several goods and often use some of them as inputs in the production of its other goods. In addition, most modern corporations produce their output at several plant locations and must decide how to allocate output among these plants. In the previous chapters we viewed the firm as a simple production process. We focused on the firm's reaction to market forces that affect the firm's price and output decisions. In the next three chapters we will go inside the firm and observe its internal organization and behavior.

Although most of us take for granted the fact that there are companies producing products, in this section we will be asking why firms exist. We will consider why firms choose to make some of their inputs rather than buy them from other firms. We will look at possible explanations: a desire for market power and an attempt to lower costs.

Chapters 10–12 focus on organizational issues and contractual alternatives. While these topics are interrelated, we will separate them into three principal categories: structure of the firm, internal pricing and output allocation, and contractual arrangements among buyers and sellers in the vertical distribution chain. The firm's concerns about uncertainty and the cost of information will be important to this analysis.

Before looking at the details, we need to consider the general reasons why firms exist. Up to this point in the text, we have seen the firm as a unit, or a little box, without having peered inside to examine its internal organization. For example, the previous discussions focused on the market as the force that insures that goods are produced in just the amount that customers want. We know, however, that firms do exist in a variety of sizes and offer a variety of products, while often producing many of their own inputs.

In an article published in 1937, Professor Ronald Coase attempted to define the nature of the firm. (Ronald H. Coase, "The Nature of the Firm," *Economica*, New Series, Vol. IV (1937):386–405.) He asked how firms ever manage to form. He suggested that anyone interested in developing a theory of the formation of firms must focus on what makes the market the more effective supplier of inputs in one case and the firm the more effective supplier in other cases.

He approached this problem in general terms. He could see that one reason for the formation of firms might be that the costs of determining market prices are too high. While this cost of acquiring information creates a need for advisors and consultants, there are also costs involved in negotiating market contracts. These costs may be high enough for the firm to justify producing the input itself rather than buying the input in the market.

Professor Coase focused on the difference between the firm and the market. More recently, other researchers have looked more closely at the firm and examined the importance of explicit and implicit contracts. Up to this point in the text we have seen the firm as a homogeneous decision unit driving for economic profits. Modern corporations are a collection of people with their own ambitions and talents. In order to mobilize these forces for the good of the corporation, managers and owners must design an effective organizational system.

In these three chapters we will look at attempts to answer Professor Coase's questions. We will focus on reasons for the formation of firms and the adoption of control mechanisms within the firm. In Chapter 10 we will look at specific reasons for the existence of firms as vertically integrated entities. We will pose two possible reasons for the existence of firms: enhanced market power and a reduction in transaction costs. We will also consider a related organizational issue: the relationship between the owners of the firm and management.

Although cost reduction will be the focal point of our analysis, we will contrast this approach with the possibility that a firm desires to monopolize a market. Because of the belief that firms were intent on monopolizing markets, the United States government followed an interventionist antitrust policy until the 1970s. Since that time academic and government opinion has shifted toward viewing markets as more self-policing. We will consider both views.

The survival of firms in their current structural form will also depend on whether the owners of the firm can maintain control over their managers and earn at least the opportunity cost of their investment. We will start by noting the possibility that the managers of the firm may pursue objectives that are inconsistent with the owners' goal of profit maximization. We will pursue this possibility by considering alternative behavioral assumptions for the firm. Since owners prefer to maximize profits, we will look at checks that owners can and do use to control their managers.

In Chapter 11 we will look at the internal pricing and output decisions of the firm. We will consider the internal pricing between divisions of the corporation and output allocation among different plants. We will see how the firm can use the theory of the first five chapters to design internal decision rules consistent with profit maximization.

In Chapter 12 we will consider alternatives to complete vertical integration of the firm. We will discuss the reasoning behind franchises, exclusive territories, exclusive dealing, resale price maintenance provisions, and functional discounts. All of these arrangements involve contracts and a reliance on the market to facilitate exchange. We will contrast these arrangements with the alternative of vertical integration described in Chapter 10.

THE ORGANIZATION
OF THE FIRM

10

In this chapter we will look at the internal structure of the firm. We will start by considering why some firms choose to produce their inputs rather than purchase them. We will evaluate the merits of competing explanations for the vertical integration of the firm. We will concentrate on two possibilities: the pursuit of market power and cost reduction.

The decision to organize as a firm and to perform activities within the firm is only one of many interesting aspects of a firm's organization. Since large corporations may have many shareholders with small stakes in the firm, ownership control over management is important.

Thus far in the text we have implicitly assumed that all parts of the firm work together to increase profits. In the small, owner-managed firm this may be a reasonable assumption. However, in a larger corporation, those who own the firm and those who manage it may not be the same people, and this separation of ownership and control may cause the firm to pursue objectives inconsistent with profit maximization.

For example, we have assumed that management works in the best interests of the owners of the firm. The owners of most modern corporations are shareholders who do not participate in the day-to-day operation of the firms. Some economists have argued that the separation of ownership and management may create incentives for management that oppose the interests of the shareholders. Unless managers' compensation reflects the impact that they have on the firm's profits, managers may pursue objectives that lower the firm's profits.

The Firm Versus the Market

Let us return to Harry Sampson and Phyllis Steene. Phyllis and Harry are having a coffee break. Phyllis happens to mention that she had to rely on a taxi to get to her last two consulting sessions because her car had finally failed to respond to her mechanic's efforts at resuscitation. As a favor to Phyllis, Harry offers to drive her to several new-car dealers on Saturday afternoon so that she can choose a new car.

It does not take Phyllis long to decide which car to buy. She chooses a metallic grey sports car with black leather seats made by the Triste Motor

Company. The unique exterior design of the car makes a big impression on her. The salesman notes that Triste Motor Company makes the car body that Phyllis likes so much, but purchases most of its other inputs, such as its tires, from other suppliers. The car manufacturer has decided to rely on the market for tires, but has chosen to produce its own car bodies internally.

There are two competing views as to why some firms choose to produce some of their own inputs rather than rely on the market: the pursuit of market power and cost reduction. In the first hypothesis, firms may seek market power in order to engage in monopoly-like behavior. In the second, firms may produce some of their own inputs because the costs of market transactions exceed the benefits of using the market. When a firm produces some of its own inputs, it is a vertically integrated firm. **Vertical integration is the consolidation of production of inputs and outputs under the control of a single firm.** The second hypothesis focuses on the cost-reduction potential of vertical integration. We will soon return to an example of an automobile manufacturer who avoided transaction costs by integrating vertically. First, though, let us consider the market-power hypothesis.

Vertical Integration to Gain Market Power

Firms may choose to integrate vertically to achieve market power. While this view was responsible for an active antitrust policy in the United States against mergers from the early 1950s to the early 1970s, today the United States government is less concerned that vertical mergers will result in increases in market power. You will find a detailed discussion of the government's role in merger policy in Chapter 13.

Market Foreclosure

The following Graphical Explanation shows how vertical integration can increase the costs of entry and lead to market foreclosure. **Market foreclosure is the result of a firm or group of firms erecting insurmountable barriers to market entry.**

| 10-1 | Foreclosing markets |

GRAPHICAL
EXPLANATION

Consider a market with five firms supplying an input to an industry that contains five firms using this specialized input. If the two groups of firms maintain their separate identities, there may be sufficient competition among the suppliers to insure a competitive price for the input. Figure 10-1 (p. 280) shows the possible patterns of trade.

The merger of a supplier and a buyer reduces opportunities for the remaining independent firms. If each of the firms supplying the input merges

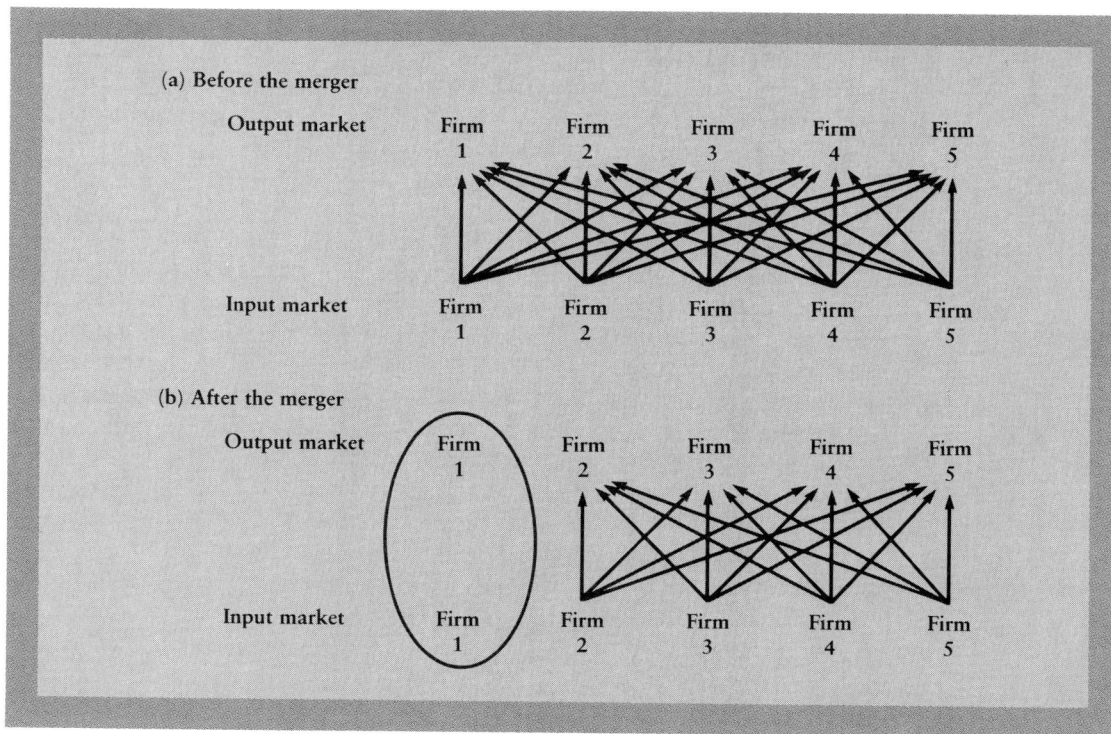

FIGURE 10-1 ■ **Market foreclosure.** When a firm supplying an input to another firm merges with the other firm, there may be fewer opportunities for nonintegrated firms to sell their goods. If all firms merge with a supplier, new entrants may have to be vertically integrated. The higher cost of entry may be a barrier to entry for these firms.

with a firm in the other industry, there are no independent suppliers or purchasers left in the market. A new entrant to the market may find it impossible to come in either as a supplier or as a buyer of the input. A new entrant will have to enter as a fully integrated firm operating at both levels in the vertical chain.

Since this larger-scale operation will involve a greater investment, some observers consider this added cost to be an increased barrier to entry. In addition to the higher investment cost, an entrepreneur with expertise in only one area of the vertical process may be reluctant to enter without expertise in the other area.

The United States Department of Justice issued merger guidelines in 1982 and 1984 acknowledging that most vertical mergers do not result in barriers to entry. Although it reserves the right to challenge any merger, the Justice Department has not actively opposed vertical mergers since the 1970s. Chapter 13 provides a more detailed analysis of the history of United States merger policy, but we will also consider one of the more important court cases involving market foreclosure in Application 10-1.

Bilateral Monopoly

▶ ——————— Consider the market structure known as bilateral monopoly. A **bilateral monopoly** is the situation that occurs when there is a sole supplier of a product that is purchased by a firm that is the sole buyer in the market.

When there are a sole supplier and a sole buyer there is no unique market-determined output or price. Instead, there is a negotiated market solution. While bilateral monopoly represents the purest form of market imperfection, the following analysis will be relevant as long as both buyer and seller have some market power relative to one another. We will assume that there are barriers to entry, since we have two firms with established monopoly positions. In the following Graphical Explanation you will see that the two firms have an incentive to coordinate their output levels.

| 10-2 | Bilateral monopoly |

GRAPHICAL EXPLANATION

Let us return to Phyllis and the Triste Motor Company. Phyllis discovered that Triste makes its own car bodies but buys its other inputs, such as tires, from other firms. To see why Triste has chosen to make its own car bodies, let us assume for a moment that Triste does *not* make its own car bodies, but buys them from another firm, Auto Foundations Limited. Assume that Auto Foundations has a monopoly on the sale of this type of car body, and that Triste Motor is the only buyer.

We will assume that Triste buys all of its inputs except car bodies in perfectly competitive markets. The marginal cost of producing the sports car due to all of these inputs, excluding the cost of the car body, is MC^*. Assume that MC^* is constant at all output levels and is equal to the average total cost, ATC^*.

In Figure 10-2 (p. 282) assume that Triste Motor faces demand curve D for its sports car. For purposes of comparison assume that Auto Foundations sells its car body to Triste at price P_{X1}, which equals the average and marginal cost of producing a car body. The marginal and average total cost of producing the sports car is the sum of MC^* and P_{X1}: MC_1. If Triste produces the car with marginal cost MC_1, it produces output Q_1 and charges price P_1.

Recognizing its potential market power, Auto Foundations is not content to charge a price that just covers its average cost of production. Assume that it decides to maximize its profits by raising its price. We will ignore the details of how Auto Foundations determines this price and simply assume that it

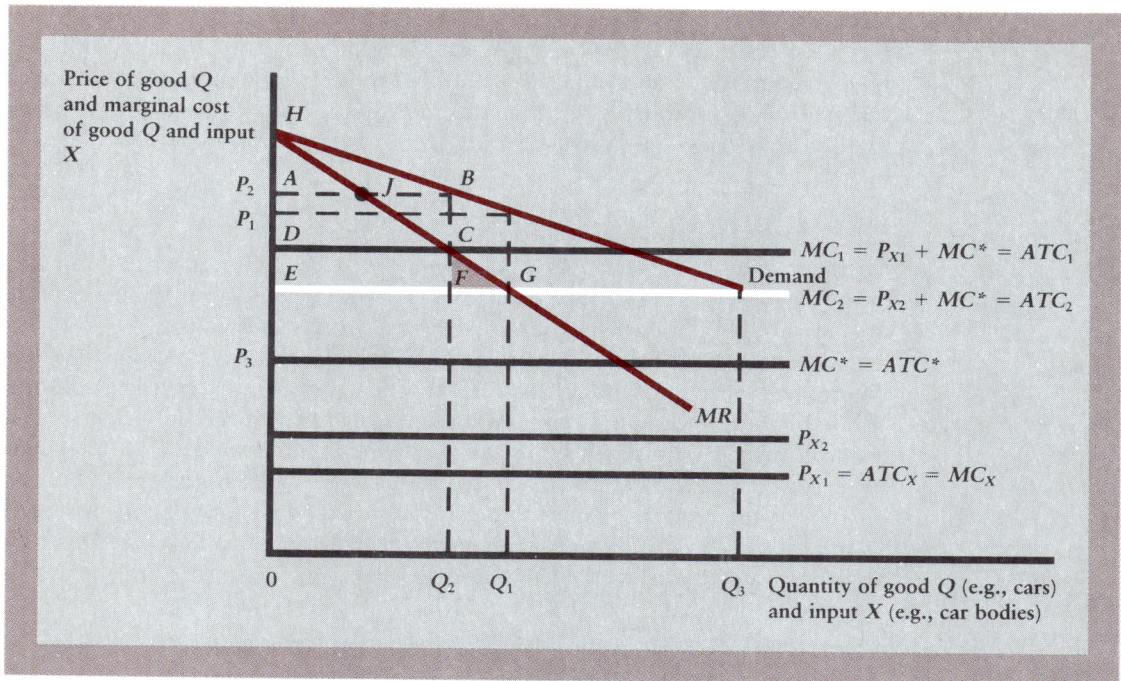

FIGURE 10-2 ▪ Bilateral monopoly. Auto Foundations Limited produces a car frame at marginal cost MC_X and ATC_X equal to P_{X1}. Triste Motor Company must buy the car frame from Auto Foundations at price P_{X2}. The cost of all other inputs is MC^*. The combined marginal cost of producing a car is MC^* plus P_{X2} or MC_2. Triste will produce Q_2 cars and sell them for P_2 each. It will earn profits equal to area HCD. Auto Foundations will earn profits equal to area $CDEF$. If the two firms were to merge, they would consider their actual marginal cost of producing cars to be MC_1: $MC_X + MC^*$. The new vertically-integrated firm would produce Q_1 cars and earn CFG more profits than before.

decides to raise its price to P_{X2}. The marginal cost of producing the car now increases to MC_2: $MC^* + P_{X2}$. Triste produces output Q_2 where marginal revenue equals the new marginal cost.

At output level Q_2 and price P_2, Triste receives area ABQ_20 in total revenue (that is, $P_2 \times Q_2$). Since the area under the marginal-revenue curve is also total revenue, area HCQ_20 equals total revenue at output level Q_2.[1] Since Triste has an average total cost of ATC_2, area DCQ_20 equals total cost.

---

[1] You can see the equivalency of these two methods of measuring total revenue by observing in Figure 10-2 that area CBJ equals area HJA. Note that area $AJCQ_20$ is a part of both HCQ_20 (the area under the marginal-revenue curve) and area ABQ_20 (the area equal to $P_2 \times Q_2$). By adding area CBJ to area $AJCQ_20$, we have area ABQ_20. By adding area AJH to area $AJCQ_20$, we have area HCQ_20.

Triste's economic profits equal the difference in the areas for total revenue and total cost. For example, since area HCQ_20 measures total revenue at output level Q_2 (the area under the marginal-revenue curve), profits will be area HCD (area HCQ_20 minus area DCQ_20). Auto Foundations receives $P_{X2} - P_{X1}$ in profit per unit and sells Q_2 units to Triste. Since $MC_2 - MC_1$ is equal to $P_{X2} - P_{X1}$, Auto Foundations' profits equal area $CDEF$.

If the two firms remain separate, their combined profits will be less than if they merge. By merging they will consider the true cost of producing the car to be MC_1: the actual production cost of the car body (P_{X1}) plus the cost of the other inputs (MC^*). Profit maximization will occur at Q_1. Since total revenue is the area under the marginal-revenue curve, the net gain in overall profits for the new vertically-integrated firm will be the triangle, FCG: the difference between the changes in total revenue (area CGQ_1Q_2) and total cost (area FGQ_1Q_2).

By merging, the two firms will eliminate the market imperfection caused by the market power of the two firms. The combined firm will produce cars where marginal revenue equals the true marginal cost of Q. The merger will benefit customers buying cars due to the fall in the market price of cars and the increase in the quantity sold. Note, however, that if neither firm has any market power, the markets for car bodies and cars will be perfectly competitive, with a much greater market output of Q_3 cars and a lower price equal to marginal cost MC_1.

In this section we have considered two reasons for vertical integration based on the assumption that firms have market power. Firms may want to integrate vertically to increase market power and foreclose the market. We also considered the case of bilateral monopoly, where two firms with market power find that they are unable to rely on the market to determine a price and quantity. By merging, the two firms may be able to maximize their combined profits.

The existence of the bilateral-monopoly market does not necessarily dictate that the firms merge, however. Recognizing their mutual interests, the two firms may be able to design a contract that insures that both firms agree to the same output levels and profit sharing that would result from a merger. In the next section we will discuss some of the difficulties in designing an optimal contract.

Vertical Integration to Avoid Transaction Costs

The primary alternative to vertical integration is an enforceable contract. Such contracts take one of two forms: (1) an explicitly stated contractual guarantee enforceable by the government or some other outside institution or (2) an implicit contract enforced by the threat of withdrawing future business.

Explicit contracts can be costly. The parties to the contract must specify all of the potential contingencies, monitor the agreement, and absorb the costs of litigation. Due to the difficulty in specifying each contingency, firms normally rely on an implicit, long-term contract. The harmed firm threatens to withdraw future business and damage the offending party's reputation as the main method of enforcement. In Chapter 12 we will concentrate on vertical arrangements governed by contracts.

Firms may find that the transaction costs of enforcing the provisions of a contract are too costly and may choose vertical integration as an alternative. **Transaction costs** are the costs associated with making contractual arrangements with individuals and firms.

Opportunistic Behavior

Given the nature of a firm's products and its inability to specify an adequately detailed contract, it may have little choice but to merge with a supplier, even if there is competition at both levels in the vertical chain. The source of the problem is the incentive to engage in opportunistic behavior at the expense of the other firm. **Opportunistic behavior** is any action on the part of firms or individuals where they use the threat of reneging on an explicit or implicit contract involving other firms or individuals in order to extract a higher payment for their services.

10-1

Pass the garlic salt, please

APPLICATION

In 1965 the U.S. Supreme Court ruled that the merger between Consolidated Foods Corporation and Gentry, Incorporated violated antitrust law, because the merger resulted in a lessening of competition due to the foreclosure of a market. Professor Stephen Walters of Loyola College in Maryland has argued that Consolidated Foods was not necessarily attempting to foreclose markets to competitors. He suggested that the merger was an attempt to avoid opportunistic behavior and increase the efficiency of sales within the vertical chain without resorting to complete vertical integration.

At the time, Gentry was one of only three domestic producers of dehydrated onion and garlic products. Consolidated Foods is a diversified food processor, distributor, and retailer. Acting on complaints that Consolidated Foods was requiring suppliers to use certain Gentry products as inputs for products, and that those products were later sold to Consolidated Foods, the Federal Trade Commission initiated an investigation in 1957, resulting in the 1965 Supreme Court decision.

The Supreme Court ruled that the required purchase of onion and garlic products by food suppliers in exchange for the willingness of Consolidated

Foods to sell the suppliers' goods in its stores eliminated from consideration those suppliers unwilling to make this agreement. According to the Supreme Court, it also hurt Gentry's competitors, who could have been closed out of the market for onion and garlic products.

Opportunistic behavior is possible whenever there are specialized assets that one or both parties to a contract can exploit. As a possible check on opportunistic behavior, the firms could post a bond or collateral that they would lose if they were to engage in opportunistic behavior. Professor Walters argued that the reciprocal-dealing arrangement amounted to collateral to discourage both Consolidated Foods and its suppliers from engaging in opportunistic behavior.

He offered extensive evidence to dispute the claim that Consolidated Foods was attempting to foreclose the market for onion and garlic products. For example, Consolidated Foods did not have market power to force suppliers to operate against their will. Consolidated's market share at the retail level was only 0.5 percent in 1958. Consolidated's wholesaling unit distributed products to other independent retailers, amounting to another 0.25 to 0.33 percent of total grocery sales in 1958.

Although the FTC alleged that twenty-three suppliers were vulnerable to pressure from Consolidated, none of these suppliers sold more than 7.5 percent of their output to Consolidated, and fourteen of them sold less than 1 percent of their sales to Consolidated. In the court testimony, there was no record of complaint from Consolidated's suppliers. Those who did testify felt that the reciprocal arrangement was in their best interest.

Professor Walters suggested that there is ample evidence of Gentry's need to avoid opportunistic behavior and insure reliable exchange. First, Gentry was required to invest in sufficient capacity to guarantee timely delivery to suppliers. Second, buyers incurred substantial sunk costs testing and evaluating products that they planned to use as inputs. Third, Consolidated was subject to quality deterioration through purchase of products for its own private label. Although it tested these products extensively, the presence of a deterrent helped. Fourth, interruptions in supply would impose a significant cost on a firm, due to its inability to complete a production process on time.

According to Walters, Consolidated's acquisition of Gentry helped resolve some of these potential problems. Sunk costs of authenticating Gentry's quality were duplicated. Both firms shared the costs of a delay in delivery. This sharing of the costs of any problem with Gentry's quality or reliability gave both Consolidated and its suppliers the same incentives for avoiding opportunistic behavior.

Source: Stephen J.K. Walters, "Reciprocity Reexamined: The Consolidated Foods Case." *Journal of Law and Economics* (October 1986):423–38. © by the University of Chicago.

Quasi-Vertical Integration

The possibility of opportunistic behavior may not be by itself a sufficient reason for vertical integration. A firm might prevent opportunistic behavior by choosing another organizational form. **Quasi-vertical integration** is a contractual agreement between two firms by which a firm owns a specialized piece of equipment that it leaves at a second firm's location for the second firm to use in making inputs for the first firm.

Let's return to Phyllis and Harry for an example of quasi-vertical integration. On the way home from the car dealer, Phyllis and Harry stop at a bookstore that sells books on tree-trimming techniques. The publisher, Movay Books, contracts the printing of its books to another firm, Turbo Press, a leading printer in the city. Since Turbo Press must print the books according to the specifications of the publisher, Turbo Press may have to purchase machinery that is highly specialized. Once Turbo Press purchases the specialized equipment, it may find itself at the mercy of Movay Books, which now has an incentive to renegotiate the original contract. Consider the following Numerical Example.

| 10-1 | **Quasi-vertical integration** |

NUMERICAL EXAMPLE

Assume that Turbo Press pays $5,000 per year to own the machine. Turbo Press had estimated that variable costs would be $3,000 per year. Movay Books had negotiated a competitive contract paying $8,000 per year to Turbo Press for the machine's services. As long as Movay Books pays $8,000, Turbo Press will make the competitive market return of no economic profits.

Assume that the specialized nature of the machine limits its flexibility in meeting the needs of other publishers. Assume that the next best offer for the machine's services from another publisher is $6,000. This suggests that once the machine is in place, Movay Books can force Turbo Press to renegotiate the contract to a price of just over $6,000 without losing Turbo Press as its printer.

By refusing to pay the agreed-upon price of $8,000, Movay Books could appropriate up to $2,000 of the returns to the machine ($8,000 − $6,000), and Turbo Press would be unable to do much about it. While Turbo Press could sue Movay Books, Movay Books could claim that there had been changes in the market environment that invalidated the original contract. A court case could be a lengthy and time-consuming process.

The power to operate opportunistically might also be in the hands of Turbo Press. If Turbo Press were to use the machine to print dated materials, Turbo Press could force a renegotiation of the terms upward by threatening to refuse to print the dated material on time. For example, Turbo Press could allege breakdowns or unexpectedly high maintenance costs. Movay Books would find it difficult to prove in court that Turbo Press was actually trying to act opportunistically. This example suggests that both parties may find themselves in a position to exploit the other party.

In this example, both Turbo Press and Movay Books are in a position to extract appropriable quasi-rents. An **appropriable quasi-rent** is the difference between the agreed-upon price and the price that a supplier of a good or service could get from the next best offer. While firms can sometimes avoid this potential problem by merging, Movay Books could resolve the issue by owning the machine and contracting Turbo Press to print the books on the press. This is an example of quasi-vertical integration. Consider another example in the following Application.

10-2

Somewhat vertically integrated

APPLICATION

It is common for automobile assemblers to own the specialized assets used by their suppliers. This is common in the plastics and steam turbine engine markets as well. The purchasing firm may forgo complete vertical integration in order to take advantage of economies associated with the supplier operating the machine.

Professors Kirk Monteverde and David Teece used a sample of twenty-eight components supplied by a major United States automotive supplier and determined that there was a positive relationship between the size of potentially appropriable quasi-rents and the decision of the assembler to own the specialized assets used by the supplier.

Source: Kirk Monteverde and David J. Teece, "Appropriable Rents and Quasi-Vertical Integration." *Journal of Law and Economics* XXV, No. 2 (October 1982):321–28. © by the University of Chicago.

We would expect that the lower the potential for appropriable quasi-rents, the more likely the two firms would rely on a contract. On the other hand, as appropriable quasi-rents increased, we would expect that contracts would not be as effective in stopping opportunistic behavior. In this case a merger would be more likely.

10-3

I have been framed

APPLICATION

General Motors now owns the subsidiaries that make the car bodies for their automobiles. This was not always the case. Opportunistic behavior by one of its suppliers forced it to integrate vertically in the 1920s.

In 1919 General Motors and Fisher Body entered a ten-year contract for the supply of closed auto bodies. Once Fisher had on line the dies needed to make these car bodies, the dies were of little use to other car companies. The highly specialized nature of this asset created the possibility of opportunistic behavior for both parties. Since General Motors agreed to buy these car bodies exclusively from Fisher Body, General Motors could not make a serious threat to purchase car bodies elsewhere.

Since Fisher was in a position to take advantage of General Motors, GM attempted to fix the price charged by Fisher. They agreed to a price that equaled Fisher's variable cost plus a payment of 17.6 percent of variable cost to compensate Fisher for its fixed costs. After they had originally negotiated the contract, GM had increased its orders for car bodies. Although the greater use of Fisher's capacity lowered its average fixed cost, there had been no renegotiation of the contract to reflect the effects of the increased volume.

In addition, GM wanted Fisher to relocate its plants closer to GM in order to increase production efficiency. Fisher refused. Frustrated with attempts to renegotiate the contract, GM finally purchased Fisher in 1926. The merger was a response to the problem of opportunistic behavior on the part of the supplier. Since the supplier had control over the specialized asset during a time of increased demand for its product, it could force GM to pay a much higher price for the use of its production capacity.

If General Motors had anticipated this problem, it might have been able to obtain ownership of the dies before initial production had begun. Although it could have contracted Fisher to make the car bodies at Fisher's facilities, General Motors would have maintained control of the specialized asset. In this way, General Motors would have established a quasi-vertically integrated production process. Unfortunately for General Motors, it did not anticipate this problem.

Source: Benjamin Klein, Robert Crawford, and Armen Alchian, "Vertical Integration, Appropriable Rents, and the Competitive Contracting Process." *Journal of Law and Economics*, 21 (June 1978):297–326. © by the University of Chicago.

Complete Vertical Integration

Quasi-vertical integration may not always be an option. A firm could act opportunistically by taking advantage of its access to specialized information. Consider Applications 10-4 and 10-5.

10-4

I would rather do that myself, thank you

APPLICATION Professors Monteverde and Teece studied the organization of Ford and General Motors to test the importance of transaction costs as a reason for vertical integration. They knew that the development of a new model design takes about five years. Each firm had to decide whether to make the components of the car themselves or rely on independent suppliers. Professors Monteverde and Teece hypothesized that there was the possibility for opportunistic behavior on the part of the supplier, if the supplier was able to benefit from specialized know-how in the process of designing the component.

Since the entire automobile and its components are designed concurrently, it is not always possible to identify exactly the specifications of a component in advance. The suppliers' participation in the design process gives the supplier specialized knowledge that it may use to extract higher payments, as the due date for the automobile arrives. The manufacturer cannot simply transfer the specifications for the production of certain components to another supplier in the event of opportunistic behavior.

In particular, the researchers hypothesized that the more applied engineering effort that goes into the development of a component, the greater the likelihood of appropriable quasi-rents. To test this hypothesis, they collected data on 133 components used by Ford and General Motors in the production of their automobiles in 1976. They used the data to determine which factors would add to the probability that the company would produce the component in-house rather than buy it from an independent supplier.

Since they were not given complete access to the companies' records, they had to use proxies for the important variables in the study. As a proxy for the degree of engineering effort incorporated in each component, they used an index of engineering effort supplied by a design engineer. They also asked company officials whether they would need to know the manufacturer, make, and model of the automobile to order a replacement for each component. Company officials responded "no" for 30 of the components. Since these 30 components were not specific to one model, there would probably be less incentive for vertical integration in this case.

They found that the degree of engineering effort and the specificity of the component were statistically significant predictors of the likelihood that the companies would make the component themselves. The substantial investment in developing the components made switching from one supplier to another supplier costly. It was concluded that, by vertically integrating the development process, the firms increased coordination in the production of the components and in the final assembly of the automobile and reduced the likelihood of opportunistic behavior on the part of otherwise independent suppliers.

Source: Kirk Monteverde and David J. Teece, "Supplier Switching Costs and Vertical Integration in the Automobile Industry." *Bell Journal of Economics* 13 (Spring 1982):206–13.

Professor Scott Masten of the University of Michigan provided additional empirical evidence supporting the transactions-cost explanation for vertical integration. While his study was similar to the one in Application 10-4, he found strong evidence that firms do choose to integrate vertically when they face potential opportunistic behavior.

10-5   An in-house job

APPLICATION

Professor Masten studied the "make-or-buy" decision of firms in the United States aerospace industry. He had information on 1,887 components, which a team of company representatives had determined to be either best made by the firm or by another firm on contract. He used these experts' classification system for analyzing their reasons for choosing between making or buying the components.

The components varied in terms of complexity and degree of specificity to the firm. He argued that a more complex and firm-specific component would offer a greater possibility of opportunistic behavior after all parties had agreed to a contract. He found that both complexity and specificity were statistically significant, as expected.

For example, if the component was complex, the probability that the firm would produce the component itself increased from 31 to 92 percent. The complexity of the design of the component made the writing and enforcement of a contract much more costly to the firm and offered too much opportunity for opportunistic behavior by another firm.

In addition, he found that the more specialized the machine making the complex component, the more likely the firm would make the component itself. When a more standard, readily-available machine made the component, the firm was more likely to have an outside firm make the component.

Professor Masten cited evidence showing the general reluctance of defense contractors to make the components in-house. Despite their predisposition toward buying components from others, the contractors generally found the potential transaction costs of the market large enough to produce the more complex and more specialized components in-house.

Source: Scott E. Masten, "The Organization of Production: Evidence from the Aerospace Industry." *Journal of Law and Economics* XXVII, No. 2 (October 1984):403–18. © by the University of Chicago.

While competitive markets rely on prices to insure the lowest-cost production of products, vertical integration replaces the market with managerial decision making. In this section we looked at two possible reasons for the vertical integration of two separate stages of the production process.

First we considered the pursuit of market power as a reason for vertical integration. Earlier antitrust cases dwelled on the prospects of market foreclosure as a motive. Today there is less fear that firms can foreclose a part of the market large enough to have an impact.

As a related issue, we looked at the problem of bilateral monopoly, where there is only one buyer and one seller in the market. Surprisingly, the merger of these two firms not only makes the two firms better off, but results in a lower price for consumers and a larger output as well.

Given the large number of mergers every year and the decline in the popularity of the market-power argument as a reason for vertical integration, economists have focused on the importance of transaction costs to explain the existence of firms. As an example, we considered the potential problem associated with specialized assets. Specialized assets at one stage in the vertical production process may place a firm in a position to renege on its original contract with another firm.

The inability of the courts to handle these breaches of contract inexpensively may lead to vertical integration. We considered two studies which showed that the complexity and specificity of the component could lead the firm to make the component in-house.

We also considered the possibility of an intermediate stage of vertical integration: quasi-vertical integration. In this type of arrangement, a manufacturer owns the specialized assets but has a contractual agreement with another firm that uses the assets to produce specialized inputs for the manufacturer.

The Role of Management

Up to this point we have continued to assume that there is no distinction between ownership and management of the firm. In the fictional examples the managers were the owners. We will now depart from this assumption for a short time. If the managers are not the owners of the firm, the owners may devise a method or system for insuring that the managers act in the owners' best interests. Without some safeguard, management may use the firm's revenues to enhance their own well-being at the expense of the owners.

There is a debate within the economics profession as to the degree to which managers can operate counter to the wishes of shareholders. In this section we will identify the potential problems associated with this separation of managers and owners. We will then consider alternative behavioral patterns that may result from this separation and possible ways of avoiding this behavior. Specifically, we will look at the role of corporate boards as overseers, the importance of hostile takeovers, and the use of compensation packages related to profit maximization.

Separation of Management and Ownership

In 1932 Adolf Berle and Gardiner Means offered the first serious study of the possible conflict between owners and managers.[2] Since then there has been a lively debate about the nature of this relationship. In the nineteenth century most top-level managers held at least substantial minority positions in the U.S. corporations that they managed. Companies are now much larger and have more diffused ownership. Berle and Means and many others have argued that the diffusion of ownership among many shareholders reduces the control that owners have over management.

Shareholders want to maximize the return on their investment. They expect managers to accomplish this objective by pursuing profit maximization to the best of their ability. Without direct control over management by the owners, managers may be free to pursue other objectives. As long as managers can increase their utility by pursuing objectives other than profit maximization, such as plush offices and expensive company cars, they will have a strong incentive to do so.

Throughout the remainder of this chapter we will consider several issues related to the possibility of a loss of owners' control of management. We will discuss the degree to which this condition exists and several methods for offsetting its effects. Among these possible methods are the threat of hostile takeovers, compensation plans consistent with profit maximization, and the use of a board of directors. We will consider some evidence on the effectiveness of these controls.

Let's start by considering alternatives to profit maximization that are possible when owners lose direct control over their managers. Since many analysts suggest that these alternatives are common, we should spend some time considering their impact on the long-term viability of the firm.

Alternative Behavioral Assumptions

There has been no lack of proposed alternatives to profit maximization behavior. These alternatives have in common the assumption that the management of the firm has an incentive to deviate from profit maximization. We will consider two main possibilities: sales maximization and entrenchment of management. While sales maximization is a clear operational rule, the other alternative does not yield complete predictions about a firm's reaction to a change in the constraints it faces.

Sales Maximization There is evidence to suggest that firms compensate executives according to sales levels and not economic profits. Executives may also derive power and prestige from being the head of a large corporation. Growth of the firm's assets and sales may enhance this prestige. We can

---

[2] Adolf A. Berle and Gardiner Means, *The Modern Corporation and Private Property.* New York: Macmillan, 1932.

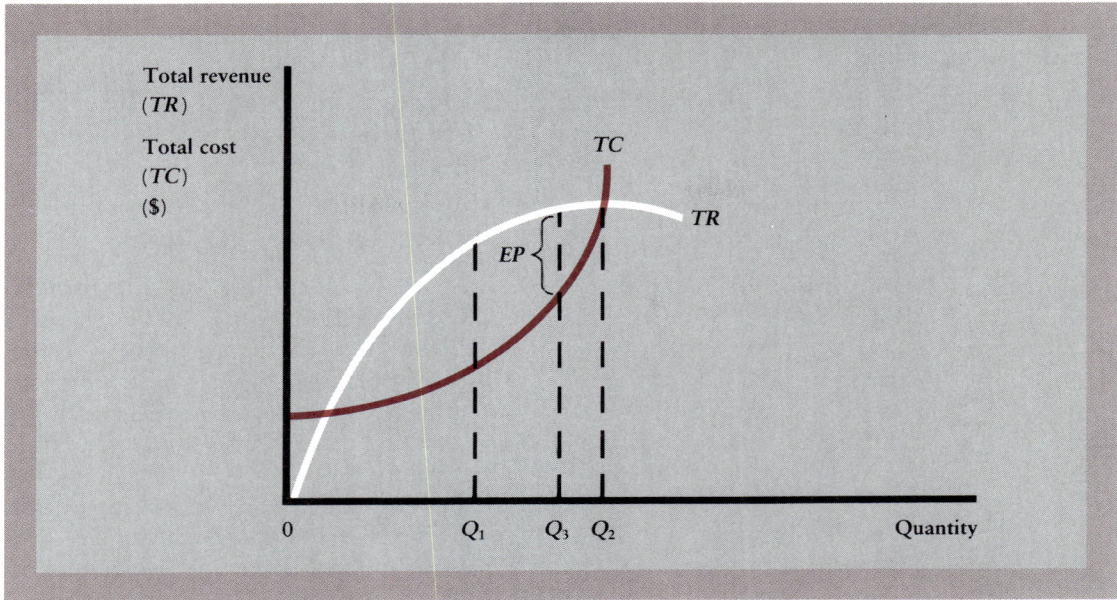

FIGURE 10-3 ▪ Sales maximization. The profit-maximizing firm would produce at Q_1. The sales-maximizing firm would produce at Q_2 if it were constrained by owners to make nonnegative profits (that is, no less than zero profits). If owners were to demand at least some economic profits, the firm would produce less than Q_2. For example, the firm would produce Q_3 if constrained to earn at least EP in profits.

compare the effects of a sales-maximization rule versus a profit-maximizing rule in the following Graphical Explanation.

10-3	Sales maximization

GRAPHICAL
EXPLANATION

Figure 10-3 shows a total-revenue curve and a total-cost curve for a firm. In Chapter 4 we used a similar graph to show that the profit-maximizing firm chooses the profit-maximizing output where marginal revenue equals marginal cost. This occurs at Q_1 in Figure 10-3. Profits are represented by the vertical distance between the two curves.

A sales maximizer generally chooses an output that is greater than the profit-maximizing firm's. Most advocates of this behavioral assumption assume that the firm operates subject to a minimum-profit constraint. For example, if the firm must not earn negative profits, the greatest output it can produce is Q_2. Any greater output would result in negative profits. If the firm chooses a higher minimum-profit constraint, such as EP, the firm reduces its output. In this case the firm maximizes sales while satisfying the constraint by producing Q_3.

Profit maximization and sales maximization occur at the same output if a minimum-profit constraint is the same as the maximum profits available. Since competitive pressure may force a firm to a long-run, zero-profit output, a perfectly competitive, profit-maximizing firm will choose the same long-run output as a perfectly competitive firm that maximizes sales subject to a constraint that it must earn at least zero economic profits.

Entrenching Management   Managers may also use separation of control to entrench their position within the firm. It would appear that this objective should not be in conflict with profit maximization. The manager who generates profits for the shareholders should be worth retaining. When there is difficulty measuring managerial performance, or when the time frame for exhibiting successful management is short, managers may adopt a strategy that, while safer, yields lower expected long-term profits.

For example, while shareholders may be happy when unexpectedly high profits result from a successful gamble taken by top management, they may be less patient when the gamble generates an unexpected loss. In the motion picture industry, there has been general consensus that chief executives avoid being fired by avoiding risky projects that may lead to a high-cost flop at the box office.

Management may also contest offers by outsiders to take over the firm even if, as a result, shareholders would receive a higher return on their investment. Most takeovers go through the target firm's board of directors. The board must approve the merger before submitting it to shareholders for a further vote.

Tender offers may serve as alternatives, however. A **tender offer** is a hostile bid by an outsider for control of a company's stock that bypasses the board of directors and goes directly to shareholders. Since a tender offer bypasses the board of directors, management has no way of blocking the merger.

10-6 We're staying put

APPLICATION   Professors Ralph Walkling and Michael Long offer evidence that managers do resist takeovers in order to entrench and enrich themselves. They analyzed ninety-five tender offers for U.S. companies between 1972 and 1977. Management contested fifty-seven of the ninety-five takeovers. This research supplied the first statistical evidence that managers do fight takeovers if they expect that they will be made worse off by the takeover. Professors Walkling and Long found three significant reasons for management's resistance to a hostile takeover.

First, the higher the probability that management would contest the takeover, the less management had to gain from the takeover in terms of increased personal wealth. Since most financial gain would have come from the exercising of stock options, those with more stock options were more likely to agree to the takeover. Secondly, managers of uncontested mergers were making lower than average compensation prior to the merger, while managers contesting a takeover were making higher than average compensation. Thirdly, 81 percent of managers who did not contest the takeover retained their jobs, while only 43 percent who contested mergers retained their jobs.

Source: Ralph A. Walkling and Michael S. Long, "Agency Theory, Managerial Welfare, and Takeover Bid Resistance." *Rand Journal of Economics* 15, No. 1 (Spring 1984):54–68.

Approximately 15 percent of U.S. industrial companies provided a "golden parachute" to top management in 1982. A **golden parachute** is a sum of money that is agreed upon in advance and paid to managers if they are forced out of their jobs due to a hostile takeover of the firm. Many observers suggest that the popularity of such arrangements is due to management's desire to maintain an entrenched position. Critics have found golden parachutes to be a deterrent to the efficiency-enhancing effects of hostile takeovers, because they increase the cost of removing existing management. There is some evidence that they may not be as harmful as suggested, however. Consider the following Application.

10-7 Pay up or else

APPLICATION Professor Charles Knoeber of North Carolina State University found that many executives receive delayed compensation from their companies to allow the board of directors sufficient time to evaluate the executive's performance. At the time the board hires an executive, it promises significantly higher annual income in future years if the firm does well under the executive's direction.

A golden parachute becomes part of the compensation package that the board and the executive negotiate. It protects the executive in case new owners take over the firm and renege on the existing compensation package. Often the contractual arrangement between the board of directors and an executive is implicit due to the difficulty of designing formal, explicit statements of future compensation. Without a golden parachute, an executive may be in danger of losing deferred compensation.

While members of a board could renege on their arrangement with an executive to pay compensation even without a takeover, they have little incentive to do so. Most directors derive a small proportion of their overall income from the firm. Of more importance is their reputation, which would be harmed by unfair practices. In addition, reneging on a set of promises to one executive would make the hiring of another executive more difficult.

A tender offer places the executive at the mercy of the shareholders and, if successful, the management of the buying company. Since neither the shareholders nor the new management made the implicit compensation agreement with the executive, they have less incentive to honor the deferred compensation. Unless a shareholder owns enough of the company to participate in negotiations with the executive, the shareholder remains anonymous and suffers no damage to his or her reputation.

Professor Knoeber analyzed data from a random sample of 331 United States corporations in 1982. He found support for the argument that golden parachutes are more common for executives who receive larger forms of compensation in deferred, implicit contracts. He determined that firms that are prone to hostile takeovers are not any more likely to offer their executives golden parachutes. While he added that the evidence does not assert that golden parachutes are used only to protect deferred compensation, he cautioned those claiming that the parachutes were used to shield inefficient managers to consider the alternative possibility.

Source: Charles R. Knoeber, "Golden Parachutes, Shark Repellents, and Hostile Tender Offers." *American Economic Review* 76, No. 1 (March 1986):155–67.

We have considered two alternatives to profit maximization: sales maximization and entrenchment of management. While managers may pursue other objectives, such as the maximization of the firm's growth or other indicators of the firm's performance, the common issue among all these alternatives is the incentive for management to deviate from profit maximization.

Few alternative operating rules are systematic enough to yield testable hypotheses concerning firm performance. Despite the presence of these alternatives to profit maximization, there is considerable debate as to their validity and usefulness. Many economists believe that there are sufficient checks on managers to justify the assumption that firms attempt to maximize profits.

Checks on Management

Even with a separation of ownership and management, there are potential checks on managerial behavior. We will consider three: the threat of a hostile takeover, corporate boards, and compensation packages tied to the firm's performance.

Threat of Takeover   We have already discussed some aspects of the threat of a hostile takeover. The threat of a takeover may be a strong deterrent to managers who deviate from a profit-maximizing path. Unless an inefficient management is able to block the takeover bid, new management could take over the firm and redirect its behavior. Professor Michael Jensen of the University of Rochester offers some evidence of the usefulness of a takeover threat to the firm's shareholders.

10-8	**Redirected cash flow**

APPLICATION

Professor Jensen argued that managers may choose to retain cash within the firm rather than pay it out to shareholders. By retaining cash, managers maintain more control and are less dependent on outside financing. With outside financing comes increased monitoring of the management and possibly higher costs of borrowing capital. In the United States, firms typically reward middle management with promotions rather than bonuses. Unless a company continues to expand, it becomes difficult to find positions within the firm for its better people.

Professor Jensen argued that companies with large cash flows have an incentive to reinvest, even if the investments generate returns that do not justify the investment. This is especially likely for firms that should be retrenching and forgoing further investment. Since this behavior is inconsistent with profit maximization, the firms become prime targets for a takeover.

Professor Jensen found several examples of this behavior with predictable results. For example, there were several mergers within the petroleum industry in the 1980s. The large increase in oil prices in the 1970s increased the cash flow of oil companies, while leaving the industry with excess capacity. Since crude oil reserves were too high, the industry should have been cutting back on exploring for new sources of oil. Instead of distributing a portion of the cash flow to shareholders, these companies spent heavily on exploration and development. Average returns on these efforts were below the opportunity cost of the capital to the shareholders. The firms also diversified into unfamiliar areas, with disastrous results.

Professor Jensen estimated large gains for shareholders after outsiders took over oil companies in the 1980s. These gains were approximately $17 billion for shareholders of Chevron, Texaco, and Conoco, and potentially $200 billion for shareholders of ninety-eight firms that had not been taken over as of December 1984.

A takeover is not necessary to increase shareholder value. Professor Jensen contended that the threat of takeover forced Phillips and Unocal to restructure their firms by abandoning losing projects and distributing cash to shareholders. This process led to an increase of 20 to 35 percent in the value of the shares of these companies.

This behavior, Professor Jensen argues, is not unique to the oil industry. Firms in the tobacco, forest-products, food, and broadcasting industries all fit the same mold. When a firm's management follows a path that deviates too far from profit maximization, a takeover is likely.

Source: Michael C. Jensen, "Agency Costs of Free Cash Flow, Corporate Finance, and Take-overs." *American Economic Review* 76, No. 2 (May 1986):323–59.

Corporate Boards Most corporations have a board of directors consisting of both management and nonmanagement (that is, outside) members. The board can and does perform different functions. It can be an advisory group or it can operate as a check on managerial decisions and plans. The board generally sets compensation for the top-level managers and can fire and hire managers on the shareholders' behalf. Corporate boards are not the same in all countries. Consider Applications 10-9 and 10-10.

| 10-9 | **As stiff as a board** |

APPLICATION

Shareholders leave much of the control over their interests to corporate board members, who are entrusted with supervising and approving major decisions of company management. There is still much variety in the structure of corporate boards worldwide. Boards in the United States spend much of their time protecting themselves from liability suits and their companies from takeovers.

The Japanese try to acknowledge everyone's opinions, in order to avoid unhappy board members, but because of this, it takes a long time to reach consensus. In Taiwan and Hong Kong most board members are family members, which does not preclude corruption and mismanagement. German attempts to incorporate workers as directors have not been especially successful, while boards in Great Britain remain "cliquey."

The typical U.S. board has fourteen members, although there are exceptions, such as General Motors, which had twenty-two in 1985. The Japanese firm has directors who concern themselves with the entire family, not only shareholders. Japanese boards comprise more executives than United States boards. For example, Nissan had forty-eight members on its board in 1986. Due to an increase in the number of large, individual shareholders in Japan, there is pressure for a change in the reliance on decisions coming from the bottom rather than the top of the firm.

In West Germany, large companies have both a supervisory and a management board. Due to legislation in 1976, half of the supervisory board must come from the work force. Nobody can be on both boards. The number of directors is prescribed by law and varies with the size and type of firm.

Great Britain's boards are similar to those in the United States in concerning themselves about personal liability. They are, however, more inbred, allowing fewer outsiders. The average board contains eight members, two of whom are nonexecutives.

The Delaware Supreme Court ruled in 1985 in *Smith* v. *Van Gorken* that the board of directors can be liable for decisions made by company management. This case concerned the decision made by Jerome Van Gorken, chief executive officer of Trans Union, to sell the company to the Pritzker family for $15 above the stock market price at the time. A shareholder sued the directors for moving too quickly to support this decision. The shareholder argued that Van Gorken could have received an even higher price for the company's stock. The shareholder won. Since the settlement exceeded the amount of liability insurance available for the directors, the decision reduced the incentive for becoming a director and forced a sharp increase in premiums for liability insurance. The Delaware legislature did pass a law in 1986 that allowed shareholders to reduce the personal liability of outside directors.

The composition of the board of directors—that is, the number of outsiders versus the number of insiders—may have an effect on the ability of shareholders to control management. For example, the board of directors could take on more responsibility for controlling management's behavior if the threat of a takeover were weaker.

10-10   Outsiders to the rescue

APPLICATION   Professors James Brickley and Christopher James analyzed the effects that the composition of the board has on firm profitability. They hypothesized that there would be a greater percentage of outside directors (that is, nonmanagement) in markets where takeovers were more costly or more difficult. Since some states have laws prohibiting or limiting corporate takeovers of banks, Professors Brickley and James measured the impact of this law on the composition of the corporate board. Their sample included 891 banks, of which 389 were in states forbidding acquisitions by corporations.

They found that the number of board members and the proportion of outsiders was greatest in the states allowing takeovers. This result was contrary to their hypothesis. They suggested the reason for the result was that in states where takeovers are frequent, corporate boards include outsiders more for their expertise in planning or loan development than for monitoring management.

In support of this argument they noted that there is a negative relationship between the number of outsiders and the degree of concentration of ownership in the no-takeover states. There is no such relationship in the takeover states.

Concentration of ownership acts as a check on the manager's discretionary behavior.

They also found that increased concentration of ownership and greater participation of outside directors reduces managerial perquisites. In the states where there is an active takeover market, there appears to be little evidence of consumption of perquisites by managers.

Source: James A. Brickley and Christopher M. James, "The Takeover Market, Corporate Board Composition, and Ownership Structure: The Case of Banking." *Journal of Law and Economics* XXX, No. 1 (April 1987):161–80. © by the University of Chicago.

Compensation Tied to Profit Maximization   Some researchers have suggested that executive compensation is not consistent with profit maximization. For example, if executives are paid based on other performance measures, such as sales, they do not have an incentive to maximize shareholder profits. If managers have large shareholdings in the companies they manage, they have much greater incentive to pursue profit maximization. Shareholders can also offer to the manager incentives that are tied to the manager's performance.

| 10-11 | I prefer cash |

APPLICATION

Professors David Flath and Charles Knoeber of North Carolina State University argued that shareholders attempt to control their managers by offering a combination of incentives and shareholding options. In designing an optimal contract between the shareholders and the manager, the shareholders choose the option that is least costly to themselves and most suitable to the managers.

A manager incurs potential costs by agreeing to either option. By increasing their holdings in one company's stock, managers reduce their ability to spread the risk of their investments through diversification. We would expect then that the more variation in the value of the stock from year to year, the less interested managers would be in compensation from shareholdings. On the other hand, if shareholders do not measure the performance of managers precisely, the manager incurs greater risk of lower compensation from the incentive arrangement.

Professors Flath and Knoeber analyzed data on manager shareholdings and incentives for thirty-seven department stores over an eight-year time period. Data of this type is difficult to obtain. They determined that these executives had significantly lower shareholdings in their firms if their firms had wider fluctuations in annual returns. On the other hand, those executives with lower shareholdings were more likely to receive larger compensation from incentives based on their performance.

Source: David Flath and Charles R. Knoeber, "Managerial Shareholding." *Journal of Industrial Economics* XXXIV, No. 1 (September 1985):93–99.

There have been many studies of the relationship between executive compensation and firm performance. Professor F. M. Scherer offers the following evidence.

10-12

If you want more money, increase profits or look for another job

APPLICATION

Professor Scherer lists three general findings from research on executive compensation.

1. Compensation does appear to be related more to sales than to yearly profits, but it is even more closely related to the size of the firm's assets. This suggests that executives of larger firms earn more because of the perceived difficulty of successfully managing a larger firm. Compensation does not increase linearly with size or sales; that is, firms twice the size of other firms do not pay their executives twice as much.

2. There is a strong relationship between compensation and firm profitability for firms of comparable size.

3. Executives are generally unable to make significant increases in their compensation during their tenure by a large change in the firm's size or sales. While executives might be able to increase their compensation significantly by finding a position with a much larger firm, they are more likely to increase their compensation at their current firm by increasing profits rather than the size of the firm.

Source: Paraphrasing from F.M. Scherer, *Industrial Market Structure and Economic Performance*, Second Edition, pp. 35–36. Copyright © 1980 by Houghton Mifflin Company.

Recall that Berle and Means implied that the ownership of large corporations is normally spread among large numbers of people. The more diffused the owners, the more likely that managers engage in activities that enhance their well-being at the expense of shareholders. While this behavior is possible, there are controls available to deter managers from behaving counter to the interests of owners. Professor Harold Demsetz of the University of California at Los Angeles and Professor Kenneth Lehn of Washington University provided evidence that the diffusion of ownership has not lead to lower profitability for United States firms. This evidence suggests that controls on management have been effective in deterring substantial deviation from the pursuit of economic profits.

| 10-13 | I am in charge here |

APPLICATION

Professors Demsetz and Lehn argued that the ownership of large corporations is diffuse because the cost of a few owners concentrating their assets in one firm is too risky. Although the diffusion of ownership encourages managers to indulge in some non-profit-maximizing behavior, there is a cost in maintaining control over the managers. According to Professors Demsetz and Lehn, if the non-profit-maximizing behavior of managers is excessive, owners place more of their assets in the firm and maintain more concentrated control.

Having analyzed data from a sample of 511 firms in 1980, they were able to determine the degree to which ownership was concentrated by shareholders. While controlling for other factors that could have influenced the rate of return of these firms, they determined that the concentration of ownership had no impact on the rate of return of the typical firm.

Source: Harold Demsetz and Kenneth Lehn, "The Structure of Corporate Ownership: Causes and Consequences." *Journal of Political Economy* 93, No. 6 (December 1985):1155–77. © by the University of Chicago.

Summary

In this chapter we considered some reasons for the existence of firms. Without firms, individuals would contract others to perform tasks for them or to produce inputs. The drafting and enforcement of contracts is costly. We saw several examples showing how costly contracting can lead to vertically integrated or quasi-vertically integrated firms. We contrasted this with the possibility that the quest for market power motivates firms to expand.

Most economists do not believe that the market-power argument is valid at current levels of market concentration in the United States. Sufficient checks exist within the market forces to stifle most attempts at gaining market power through merger. We only touched upon the legal aspects of this debate. A detailed discussion of the legal aspects is in Chapter 13.

The principal focus of this chapter was the cost-reducing rationale for vertical integration. Firms reduce costs by exchanging costly market transactions for less costly in-house production. The firm cannot avoid contract costs completely in this way, since the firm is itself a complex of explicit and implicit contracts among the owners, managers, and other employees.

We also considered the related problem of owner control. Shareholders do not invest in a firm if they feel they can do better by investing elsewhere. Since shareholders are interested in profits, the ability of the firm to attract investment depends to some degree on management's ability to convince investors of its successful pursuit of profits.

We discussed the possibility that a diffused ownership could encourage management to pursue other objectives, and we considered some of these alternatives. We also evaluated the merits of checks on managerial discretion. In particular, we found that corporate boards, potential hostile takeovers, and compensation plans tied to profit-maximization behavior can provide some check on alternative behavior.

Important Terms

Vertical Integration (p. 279)

Market Foreclosure (p. 279)

Bilateral Monopoly (p. 281)

Transaction Costs (p. 284)

Opportunistic Behavior (p. 284)

Quasi-Vertical Integration (p. 286)

Appropriable Quasi-Rent (p. 287)

Tender Offer (p. 294)

Golden Parachutes (p. 295)

Selected References

Berle, Adolf A., and Means, Gardiner. *The Modern Corporation and Private Property*. New York: Macmillan, 1932.

Coase, Ronald H. "The Nature of the Firm." *Economica*, New Series, IV (1937):386–405.

Monteverde, Kirk, and Teece, David J. "Supplier Switching Costs and Vertical Integration in the Automobile Industry." *Bell Journal of Economics* 13 (Spring 1982):206–13.

Scherer, F.M. *Industrial Market Structure and Economic Performance*, 2nd ed. Boston: Houghton Mifflin, 1980.

Simon, Herbert. "Theories of Decision-Making in Economics and Behavioral Science." *American Economic Review* 49 (June 1959):253–83.

Walters, Stephen J.K. "Reciprocity Reexamined: The Consolidated Foods Case." *Journal of Law and Economics* (October 1986):423–38.

Williamson, Oliver E. *The Economic Institutions of Capitalism*. New York: The Free Press, 1985.

Problems

1. When will quasi-vertical integration be more likely than complete vertical integration?

2. Assume there is one input, X, used to produce good Q. Assume that X is produced by a monopolist and Q is produced by the only buyer of X. With the use of the appropriate graph show why a merger between the two firms may increase the output of both X and Q.

3. Assume there are two firms that are identical, except that one maximizes profits and the other maximizes sales. Assume that the government imposes a tax equal to 50 percent of both firms' economic profits. How will each firm react?

4. Assume that the tax in Problem 3 was a fixed amount equal to $1,000 instead of a percentage of profits. How would the firms react? Would your answer change if the

sales-maximizing firm had to earn at least $500 in economic profits to satisfy its shareholders?

5. Discuss the conflicts of interest that top managers have when confronted by a hostile takeover. What might shareholders do to reduce these conflicts of interest?

6. What are the advantages of having a higher percentage of outside members on a company's board of directors?

Answer questions 7–12 with true, false, or uncertain.

7. Although the merger of a monopolist with a firm that is the only buyer of the monopolist's good results in greater output and a lower price to consumers, the merger increases the profits of the two firms.

8. The merger of a monopolist and the only buyer of its good results in an output of the final good that is the same as the competitive solution.

9. Formal contracts are more common than vertical integration when dealing with potential opportunistic behavior due to specialized assets.

10. Corporate boards consist mainly of nonmanagement outsiders, who monitor management behavior that may deviate from profit maximization.

11. A sales-maximizing firm produces more output than a profit-maximizing firm.

12. Executive compensation is more closely related to sales than profits.

11

INTERNAL PRICING AND
OUTPUT DECISIONS

In the previous chapter we focused on two important organizational issues. First, we sought reasons for the formation of firms. In particular, we considered why some firms produce their own inputs while others rely on the market for their inputs. Secondly, we considered the possibility that a lack of control by owners over management could encourage management to pursue objectives other than profit maximization.

In this chapter we probe more deeply into the organization of the firm and consider two additional issues: pricing and output allocation within the firm. A modern corporation that does not rely on the market for its internal output allocation and pricing decisions must create an efficient alternative. We will propose solutions to the pricing and output-allocation problems of the large firm.

We will start with the vertically integrated firm. Once the firm has chosen to economize on transaction costs by producing the input itself, it must adopt a policy for determining the level of its inputs and the prices it charges itself. The firm must decide whether or not to consolidate decision making or to allow for some decentralization. Centralized decision making may create unnecessary delays in the processing of important information within the firm. These delays could lead to significantly higher costs.

The company may want to make better use of lower management by establishing decentralized profit centers with incentives for the managers at these levels. It could establish an internal market based on prices for the goods produced and used as inputs by the firm. We will consider three possible situations: (1) no external market for the inputs, (2) a competitive external market, and (3) a monopolized external market.

We will then turn to the horizontally integrated firm and consider the firm's decision to produce output at more than one plant location. After a brief discussion of the possible economies of this organization, we will look at an optimal output-allocation rule for maximizing profits. We will focus on three possibilities: (1) no uncertainty about demand and input prices, (2) uncertainty about input prices, and (3) the presence of sizable transportation costs.

Transfer Pricing

The modern corporation must decide whether to centralize its decision making or rely on lower-level managers to make decisions. In this section we will explore some possible methods for choosing prices for products that are produced by the firm and also used internally by the firm. We will determine a transfer-pricing rule that will encourage managers within the firm to respond in the most economically efficient manner. **Transfer pricing** is the process by which a firm sets prices for the goods it produces itself and sells to itself. The alternative to a transfer-pricing rule is a directive from central management dictating the output of each level in the vertical chain. At some point the size of the firm becomes large enough to justify turning to a transfer-pricing rule to minimize inefficient delays in decision making.

This section considers three possible market environments for the firm:

1. the absence of an external market for the firm's input,
2. a competitive external market for the input, and
3. a monopolized external market for the input.

In each of these three cases the firm wishing to maximize profits should set an internal price for the input equal to the opportunity cost of the good to the firm.

No External Market for the Input

In the previous chapter Phyllis and Harry discovered that the manufacturer of Phyllis's new car made the body of the car but purchased tires from another supplier. Assume that the maker of Phyllis's sports car is vertically integrated and must decide how to price its inputs. Since the car body is unique to this type of sports car, the firm has no external market for the car body. In the following Graphical Explanation we consider the pricing decision of the car manufacturer, Triste Motor Company.

11-1

No external market

G R A P H I C A L
E X P L A N A T I O N

Assume that Triste Motor Company produces the car bodies for its sport cars according to a positively-sloped marginal-cost curve, shown in Figure 11-1 (p. 308) as MC_M. The demand for the car, Q, is given by the demand curve, D. The marginal-revenue curve, MR, corresponds to the demand curve, D. Assume that all additional costs of converting the car body into the sports car equal MC_A. In this case one unit of the input yields one unit of the output.

The marginal cost of a sports car would come from two sources: the marginal cost of producing the car body and the marginal cost of converting the body into a sports car. The marginal cost of the firm would be

$$MC_t = MC_M + MC_A.$$

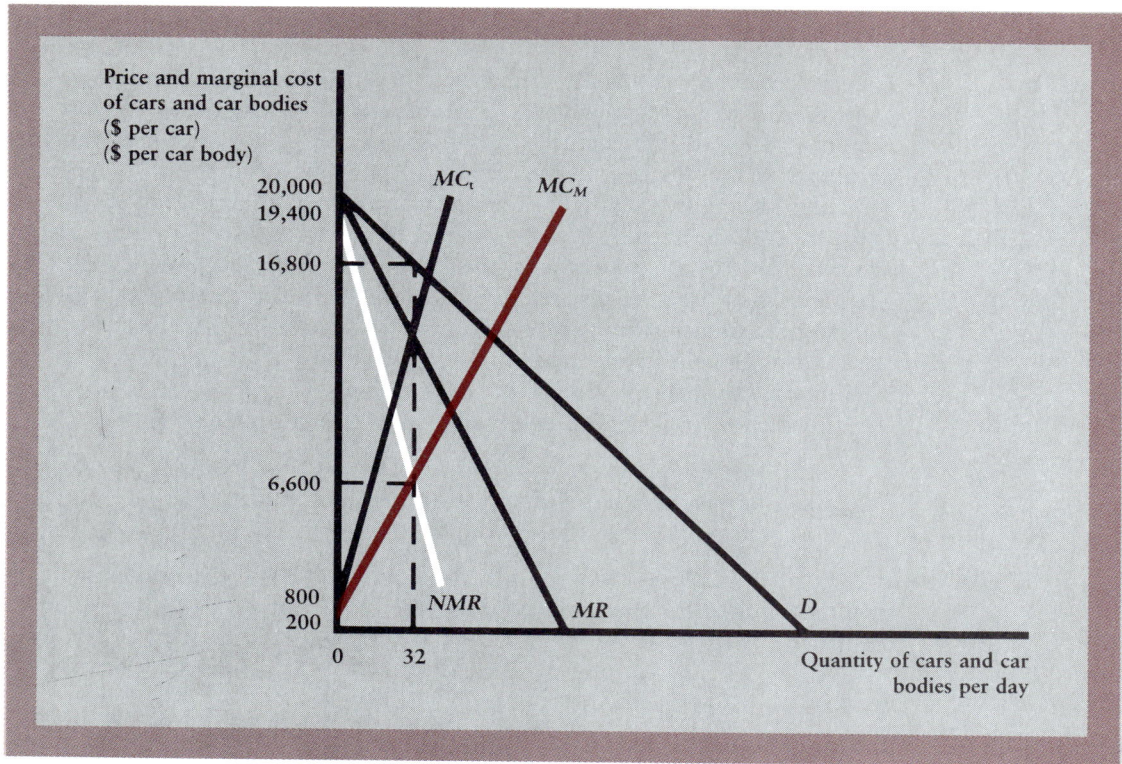

FIGURE 11-1 ▪ **No external market for the car body.** Triste Motor Company will maximize profits by producing 32 cars per day. At 32 cars per day. marginal cost MC_t equals MR. Since the total cost of producing a car consists of the cost of making the car body and the cost of converting the car body into a car. MC_t will equal MC_M (the marginal cost of the car body) and MC_A (the marginal cost of converting the car body into a car—not shown in the figure). NMR of the car body will equal MC_M at 32 car bodies. NMR becomes the derived demand curve for car bodies. MC_M will be the internal supply curve of car bodies if the producer of the car body is made a price taker. The internal price of the car body will be $6.600.

If top management were to choose to consolidate all production decisions at the central headquarters, it would need information on these marginal-cost and marginal-revenue curves. It would act as a monopolist in setting marginal revenue equal to marginal cost. Output of sports cars would be 32 and price would be $16,800, as shown in Figure 11-1.

If it were too expensive to determine these costs quickly enough to make timely output decisions, management might decide to decentralize. This would be especially important for complexly organized firms with several levels of vertical integration.

Triste Motor Company could set the price of the input but give the manager of the division producing the car body the authority to set the output level of the input. The central administration thus requires that the division manufacturing the car body act as a price taker. Since a price taker sets output where price equals marginal cost, the producer of the car body would use its marginal-cost curve as a supply curve.

Since Triste ultimately wants to produce the profit-maximizing output, it must provide an incentive for the manager of the assembly division to order the optimal number of car bodies. The value of the car body will be the net revenue it generates. We will soon see that a net revenue curve will become a derived demand curve for the input. In Chapter 4 we determined the derived demand curve for an input. In that discussion we assumed that the input was supplied in a competitive market at a fixed price.

We can determine the value of the car body to the assembly division in a similar manner. Since MR is the marginal revenue associated with the sales of the sports car, we can determine the net value of the car body by subtracting from marginal revenue the marginal cost of converting a car body into a sports car. This yields a net-marginal-revenue curve (NMR). **Net marginal revenue** is the marginal revenue attributable to a specific input and is derived by subtracting marginal costs due to all the other inputs from the marginal revenue of the firm.

Figure 11-1 shows the NMR curve for this example. The profit-maximizing firm produces where NMR equals the marginal cost of producing the car body. Note in Figure 11-1 that this is the same output that the centralized decision maker would choose. This should not be surprising. In Figure 11-1 the profit-maximizing monopolist chooses output where MR equals MC_t. By subtracting MC_A from both MR and MC_t, we have

$$MR - MC_A = NMR = MC_M = MC_t - MC_A.$$

Net marginal revenue must equal the marginal cost of car bodies at the same output level where marginal revenue equals marginal cost. In this case the NMR curve is the derived demand for the car body, while MC_M is the supply curve of the car bodies. The intersection of these two curves represents the number of car bodies produced (32) and the transfer price ($6,600) paid by the assembly division to the car body division.

11-1	No external market

NUMERICAL
EXAMPLE

Assume that the demand for the sports car is

$$P = 20,000 - 100Q_t.$$

From Chapter 2 we know that the marginal-revenue curve must have the same intercept term and a slope that is twice as large in absolute value:

$$MR = 20,000 - 200Q_t.$$

Assume that the marginal cost of producing a sports car is

$$MC_t = 800 + 400Q_t.$$

Since the firm maximizes profits where MR equals MC,

$$MR = 20{,}000 - 200Q_t = 800 + 400Q_t = MC_t$$

and

$$600Q_t = 19{,}200$$

and

$$Q_t = 32.$$

Triste Motor Company can achieve the same output level by setting the price for a car body and giving the division converting the car body into the sports car the authority to order the number of car bodies it wants at that price. The manufacturing division will take the price as given and consider its marginal-cost curve as a supply curve. Assume that marginal cost has two components: one for manufacturing the car body (denoted by subscript M) and one for converting this input into a sports car (denoted by subscript A):

$$MC_A = 600 + 200Q_A \quad \text{and} \quad MC_M = 200 + 200Q_M.$$

Since $NMR = MR - MC_A$,

$$NMR = 20{,}000 - 200Q - (600 - 200Q)$$
$$= 19{,}400 - 400Q.$$

Since

$$MC_M = 200 + 200Q_M,$$

the central administration should choose an input price equal to the marginal cost of producing the input:

$$P_M = 200 + 200Q_M.$$

Since the net-marginal-revenue curve represents the value of the car body to the assembly division, the manager will determine the number of car bodies needed at the point where

$$NMR = P_M$$

$$NMR = 19{,}400 - 400Q_M = 200 + 200Q_M = P_M$$

and

$$600Q_M = 19{,}200$$

and

$$Q_M = 32.$$

The transfer price will be

$$P_M = 200 + 200Q_M$$
$$= 200 + 200(32)$$
$$= \$6600.$$

A Competitive External Market for the Input

The firm may find itself in a situation where it makes an input that it can sell in a competitive external market. For example, a construction company, Appian Way Construction, makes its own asphalt material, which it uses in its highway construction jobs. It also faces a perfectly competitive external market for its asphalt. It could decide to sell asphalt externally or even purchase asphalt.

Appian Way's manager, Rex Nero, must decide how many construction jobs to complete and how much asphalt to produce. While these two decisions yield the same quantity when there is no external market, they are completely separate decisions when there is a competitive external market. The presence of a competitive external market makes the pricing of the asphalt a much easier task.

The internal price for asphalt should be the same as the external competitive price. If Rex decides to produce asphalt and use it all for his own purposes, he passes up the opportunity of selling it to others at the competitive price. The competitive price becomes the opportunity cost of using the asphalt. When deciding how much asphalt to produce, he should act like a competitive asphalt company by producing where marginal cost equals the competitive price.

He should base the decision of how much asphalt to use for his own construction jobs on the competitive price of asphalt. When there was no external market, the firm set output where net marginal revenue equaled the marginal cost of the input. However, in this case, the marginal cost of the input is its competitive price. Rex will produce construction jobs at the point where net marginal revenue equals the competitive price of asphalt. The solution to this problem is exactly the same as the case of derived demand for an input provided by a competitive market.

11-2   **A competitive external market**

GRAPHICAL EXPLANATION   In Figure 11-2 (p. 312), Appian Way Construction Company produces 24 units of asphalt and completes 36 construction jobs. Since the output of asphalt is less than the number of construction jobs, Rex purchases 12 units

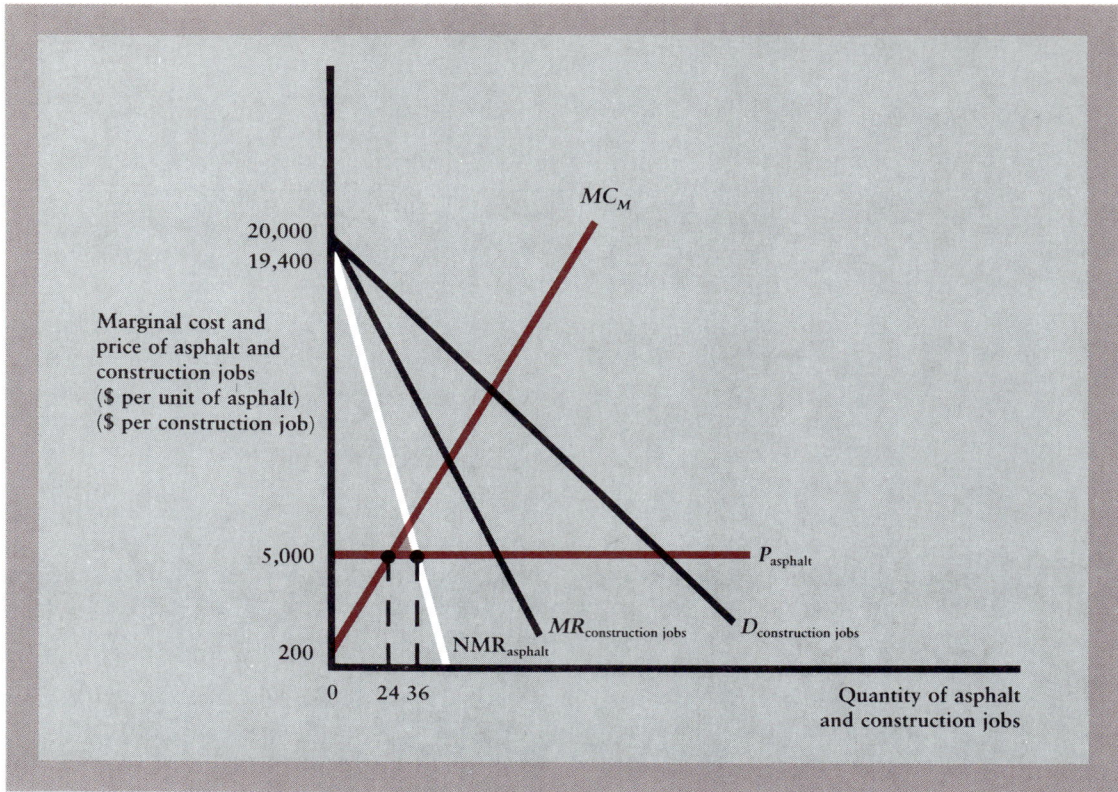

FIGURE 11-2 ▪ **Competitive external market for asphalt (net buyer of asphalt).**
With a perfectly competitive market for the asphalt, Appian Way will use the competitive
price of $5,000 as the opportunity cost of asphalt. MC_M equals $5,000 at 24 units of
asphalt. If Appian Way produces any more asphalt, it will cost Appian Way more to
produce than to buy the asphalt. It will determine that it needs 36 units of asphalt by
setting NMR equal to $5,000. The shaded area represents the extra cost of producing all
36 units of asphalt by itself rather than buying the difference of 12 units from the
competitive market.

of asphalt from the perfectly competitive asphalt market. If Rex decides to
produce all the asphalt himself, he incurs a greater cost. The shaded area in
Figure 11-2 shows this excess cost of producing the extra amount of asphalt
rather than buying it from others.

Figure 11-3 shows the opposite situation. In this case Rex faces a greater
external demand for asphalt. The higher market price of $9,800 will discourage
him from using as much asphalt himself as before, and encourage him
to produce and sell more asphalt to the competitive market. As shown in
Figure 11-3, he would sell 24 units of asphalt to the competitive market—the

difference between the 48 units he produces and the 24 units he needs internally. Any other output of asphalt would lower Rex's profits.

11-2

Competitive external market with excess output of construction jobs

NUMERICAL
EXAMPLE

Assume that there is a competitive market for the asphalt. The next marginal revenue of the asphalt is

$$NMR = 19,400 - 400Q_M.$$

FIGURE 11-3 ▪ **Competitive external market for asphalt (excess output of asphalt).** With the higher competitive price of $9,800, Appian Way will use less asphalt internally but will produce and sell more asphalt to the competitive market. Since NMR equals 98,000 at 24 units of asphalt, Rex will use 24 units of asphalt internally for his 24 construction jobs. He will produce 48 units of asphalt and sell 24 units to the competitive market.

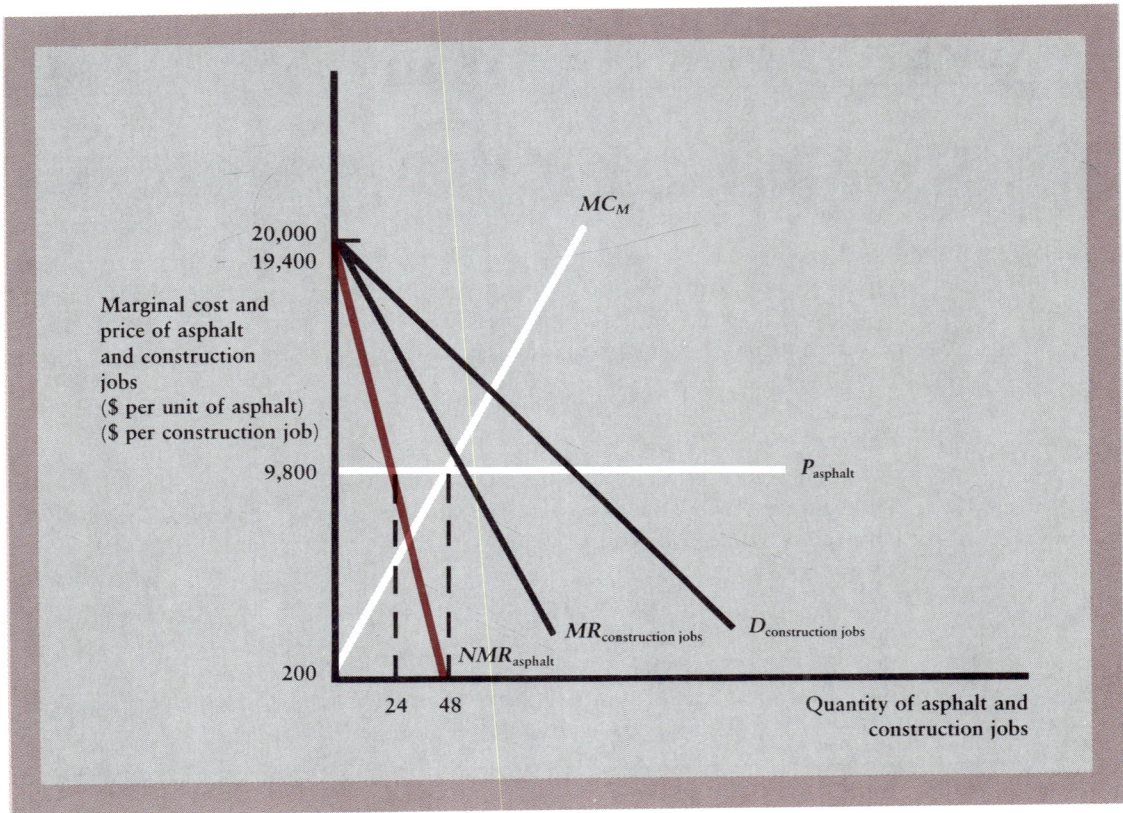

The marginal cost of producing the asphalt is

$$MC_M = 200 + 200Q_M.$$

Assume that the competitive price is $5,000. We can separate the firm's problem into two parts: how much of the input to produce and how much to use internally. To determine the amount of Q_M that the firm would use internally, we would set the competitive price equal to NMR.

$$NMR = 19,400 - 400Q_M = 5000 = P_M$$

yielding

$$Q_M = 36.$$

To determine how much to produce we would set the market price of $5,000 equal to MC_M.

$$MC_M = 200 + 200Q_M = 5000 = P_M$$

yielding

$$Q_M = 24.$$

Since Appian Way produces 24 units while requiring 36 internally, it will buy (36 − 24) or 12 units of asphalt from the competitive market.

11-3

Competitive external market with excess output of asphalt

NUMERICAL EXAMPLE

Now assume that the asphalt is in greater demand in the competitive market. The price jumps to $9,800. We solve this problem in exactly the same way as before. To determine the amount that Appian Way would use internally, set net marginal revenue equal to the market price.

$$NMR = 19,400 - 400Q_M = 9800 = P_M$$

yielding

$$Q_M = 24.$$

To determine the quantity that Appian Way should produce, set marginal cost equal to the competitive price.

$$MC_M = 200 + 200Q_M = 9800 = P_M$$

yielding

$$Q_M = 48.$$

Since Rex produces 48 units while using only 24 units internally, he will sell (48 − 24) or 24 units of asphalt to the competitive market.

Homemade chips

Although the transistor was invented in 1948, the first commercial integrated circuit did not appear on the market until 1964. Now companies etching small slivers of silicon made from sand (silicon dioxide) have created a business which generated over $30 billion in revenues in 1985. From 1975 to 1985 production more than doubled.

This market contains several vertically-integrated electronics firms which face an external competitive market for their main input: microchips. Despite the size of the microchip market, none of the big Japanese chip manufacturers (NEC, Hitachi, Toshiba, Fujitsu, Mitsubishi, and Matsushita) derives more than 5 percent of its revenue from the sale of chips on the open market.

On the average, electronics firms make three to four times as many microchips for their own internal use as they sell to others. The world electronics industry itself generated over $300 billion of goods in 1985. Because of the importance to electronics companies of having the fastest, most reliable chips available, these companies maintain their own production of chips.

On the other hand, many companies in the rest of the world are not vertically integrated. For example, European firms make few of the chips they use. In 1985 Europe imported about $1.5 billion more in chips than they exported. In the United States, IBM and AT&T produce chips for their own use. While IBM is the world's largest chip manufacturer, with $2.5 billion in sales in 1985, IBM also buys almost the same amount each year on the open market. AT&T sells some of the chips it produces, while both Hewlett-Packard and Digital Equipment Corporation buy more than they make each year.

The top ten firms control nearly 80 percent of the U.S. market for microchips. Hundreds of smaller companies divide the rest of the market. The price of microchips dropped dramatically during the 1970s and early 1980s, averaging a 50 percent or larger decrease per year. Price information in the market is nearly perfect and delivery costs are low. The entire, annual world chip production can be shipped in ten jumbo jets.

There is apparently little room for product variation. Most chips become components for standardized products. Many different suppliers produce nearly identical versions of every chip available on the market. Given this consistency with the assumptions for perfect competition in Chapter 5, it is not surprising that it has been virtually impossible to sell at anything other than the cheapest price obtainable anywhere in the world.

Smaller microchip companies, such as Intel, Motorola, Texas Instruments, and National Semiconductor, have left the microchip production market and have concentrated on service. These smaller companies were unable to survive exclusively on the production of microchips. The larger companies are able to sell in the competitive external market at close to marginal cost due to the sizable return from the use of microchips internally in the production of their own electronics products.

There is a solution for the smaller companies competing with the Japanese companies. They can either vertically integrate independently or merge formally or informally with existing firms. For example, IBM has purchased part of Intel. This argument suggests that the most efficient production structure dictates a vertically-integrated firm that faces an external competitive market for one of its important inputs: microchips.

A Monopolized External Market for the Input

The firm may be in a position to sell its transferable input to an external market that is not perfectly competitive. Several companies face this possibility. For example, companies that make manufactured goods choose to sell some

FIGURE 11-4 ▪ **Noncompetitive external market for Poobell trash bags.** Rocky faces a negatively-sloped demand curve for his trash bags from a supermarket chain that wants him to use the supermarket's private label in place of the Poobell brand name. The marginal revenue curve corresponding to this demand curve is MR_E. Rocky will also be allowed to sell bags carrying the Poobell label in the supermarkets. The NMR curve shows the value of the trash bags to Rocky net of the cost of marketing them with the Poobell brand name. Rocky must add NMR to MR_E to determine the overall value of his trash bags: MR_T. Rocky will produce at Q_T where MR_T equals the marginal cost of producing trash bags. He will sell Q_E private-label trash bags to the store at price P_E. He will sell Q_I trash bags that carry the Poobell label at a price P_F. The internal transfer price of trash bags will be P_T.

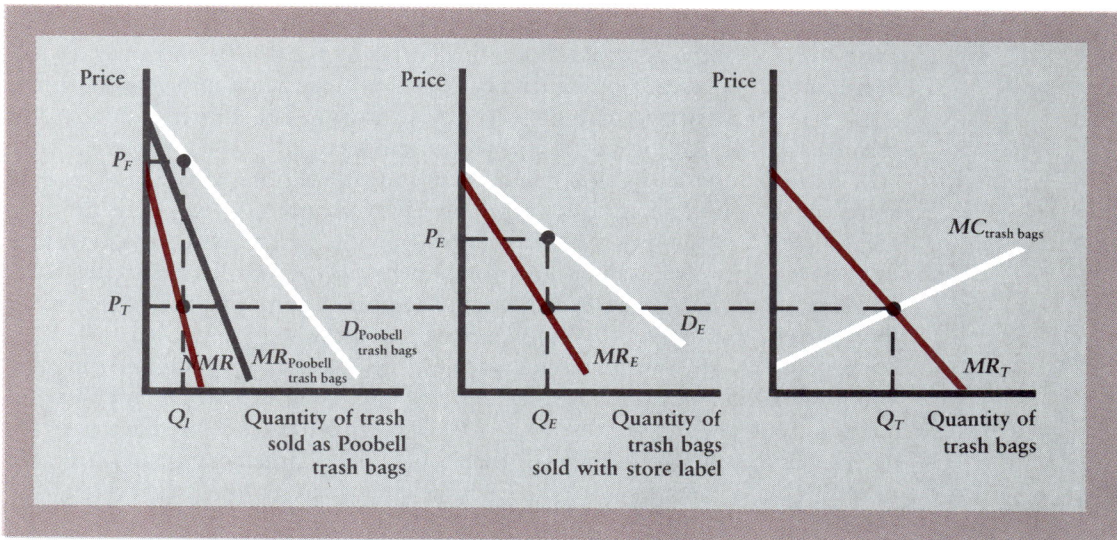

of their output through stores that affix the store label on their products. Whirlpool makes refrigerators for Sears, while other companies make a wide range of products carrying the Sears and J.C. Penney labels.

Companies making grocery products also sell some of their output to large supermarket chains. Companies whose brands are direct competitors make most of the products carrying the supermarket's own label. For years companies have sold their products under their own labels, while selling additional output to major chain stores. A chain store places its store label on the package and promotes the product along with the other products carrying the store label.

How much of the input to produce, utilize, and sell externally is somewhat more complicated than the competitive external market case. The technique for solving this problem is similar to the one used to analyze price discrimination in Chapter 6. Let us return to Rocky Sanders. Rocky has received an offer from a large supermarket chain, Gooters Supermarkettes, to sell his trash bags under the store's private label. Gooters will still sell Rocky's bags with his own Poobell label alongside his bags carrying the store's label.

If Rocky decides to sell the bags this way, he must make several related decisions. He must determine the total number of trash bags to produce, the number to sell with the store label, the number to sell with the Poobell label, and the prices to charge for the Poobell and private-label bags. He will actually have to place the store's private label on the boxes as a part of the production process. This last adjustment to the production process will involve the fixed cost of installing the machine for stamping the store's logo on the product box. Gooters will pay this cost.

11-3 A monopolized external market

GRAPHICAL EXPLANATION

To make an accurate decision, Rocky needs to know the store's demand curve for the store-label boxes, the market demand for boxes with the Poobell label, and his production and marketing costs. In this case the input is a box of trash bags. If Harry sells these bags with his own label, he must promote his label and assure customers that the bags are worth the purchase price.

If Gooters has its own label on the boxes, it must do the job of promoting the trash bags. Even though the bags are identical, Rocky and Gooters must convince customers of the bags' quality. We will assume here that both firms use the lowest-cost method for marketing the trash bags. Marketing costs will be the remaining costs that must be added to the production cost.

The net marginal revenue of the trash bags to Rocky is net of the costs of promoting his bags carrying the Poobell label. The value of sales to the grocery chain will be the marginal revenue associated with the demand curve in Figure 11-4. The marginal-revenue curve is a derived-demand curve. The store must also add marketing costs to the price it pays for the trash bags.

Since the marginal cost of producing the trash bags is upward-sloping, we must add the two marginal-revenue curves just as we did for price discrimination. Note here that we must use the NMR rather than the MR when determining the value of the trash bags to Rocky net of his marketing costs.

Figure 11-4 shows MR_T as the horizontal sum of NMR and MR_E, the marginal revenue from sales of private-label trash bags to the store. Rocky will produce Q_T boxes of trash bags, using Q_I internally to sell to stores as Poobell Trash Bags, and selling the balance, $Q_T - Q_I$, externally as private-label trash bags at price P_E. Internally, he will continue to price the trash bags at his marginal production cost, P_T. He will sell his trash bags carrying the Poobell label to stores at P_F.

| 11-2 | **How much did you say that label cost?** |

APPLICATION

In 1966 the Federal Trade Commission (FTC) successfully prosecuted Borden Milk for price discrimination. Borden sold its evaporated milk under its own label, while at the same time selling milk to supermarket chains who affixed their own store labels to the cans. The price paid by the supermarket chains for the unlabeled milk was less than that paid for the milk with Borden's label on it.

The FTC felt that this pricing practice was unfair to other milk suppliers, who could be run out of business by Borden, and to supermarkets which were not large enough to have their own private label. At that time large supermarkets were beginning to dominate the grocery store industry throughout the country, and there was significant opposition coming from the owners of smaller, traditional stores.

The court demanded that Borden prove that its difference in prices reflected a cost savings in the production of evaporated milk. All parties agreed that the milk was identical. Surprisingly, the court did not place any value on Borden's argument that there was a cost difference due to the marketing of the milk. Borden incurred marketing costs selling its milk under the Borden label that it did not face for the milk sold in unlabeled cans to the supermarket chains. The supermarket chains had to absorb the costs of marketing the milk and convincing customers of its quality.

Borden would have made its pricing decision as shown in Figure 11-4 if it had faced a negatively-sloped demand curve for its unlabeled milk. If the external market had been competitive, Figure 11-2 would have applied. In Figure 11-4 the net-marginal-revenue curve represents the value of the evaporated milk sold under the Borden label net of marketing costs. By selling to an external market, Borden could have increased its sales and profits.

Despite the Borden decision, the courts ruled in *FTC* v. *Anheuser-Busch, Inc.* (1961) that even though premium beers sold by the company under a regional label were technically the same except for advertising and imagery, they were to be considered different. The government is not actively pursuing this type of case anymore. The decision to stop was due to a realization that the marketing of products is not without cost.

The Allocation of Output

The previous section considered the pricing and output decision of the vertically-integrated firm. In this section we will consider the output allocation and pricing problems faced by the horizontally-integrated firm. **Horizontal integration** is the process of acquiring (via construction or purchase) and managing additional facilities that produce the same product that the firm is currently producing.

Since economies of scale may be limited at the plant level, a firm intent on expansion may resort to a multiplant operation. For example, there may be economies of scale in research and development. The multiplant firm may also utilize a central pool of financial, marketing, legal, and accounting personnel.

While these economies may require a concentration of personnel at a central location, the dispersion of customers and high transportation costs for the finished product may justify locating plants closer to customers. Many large corporations maintain several plants across the United States and in other parts of the world. We are not going to dwell on the economies of these arrangements here. Instead we will look at the optimal allocation of output among plants under three different sets of circumstances: certainty about input prices, uncertainty about input prices, and the presence of sizable transportation costs.

Output Allocation Among Plants with No Uncertainty

A multiplant firm has the option of choosing which of its plants it will use to produce its output. In this section we will consider the possibility that each of these plants employs different technology and depends on different types of inputs to produce the same type of good. We will discuss the general problem of output allocation in a multiplant firm. As an example, we will return to Rocky Sanders of Poobell Plastic Trash Bag Company. Rocky has expanded his operation and now has two plants producing his trash bags.

11-4   **Output allocation among plants**

GRAPHICAL
EXPLANATION

If one of Rocky's plants produces trash bags at a constant marginal cost of $0.40 per box of bags, while his other plant produces them at a constant marginal cost of $0.50 per box of bags, Rocky will want to use the $0.40-

per-box plant up to capacity before producing anything at the second plant. In the more typical case of increasing marginal cost at both plants, Rocky will allocate output between both plants.

When Rocky was producing at only one plant, he chose his output where marginal cost equaled marginal revenue. Now that he has two plants, he follows the same principle by allocating output so that the marginal costs of the last units produced at each plant are equal to one another and equal to the marginal revenue of the last unit sold.

In Figure 11-5 assume that Poobell is a price taker in the output market

FIGURE 11-5 ▪ Production at two plants. Rocky produces trash bags at two plants. The plants have different marginal cost curves. To determine his firm's marginal-cost curve, he must add the two marginal-cost curves horizontally. Rocky will produce where marginal-revenue equals marginal cost. In this case he will produce 30 boxes. Since the marginal cost of the last box is $0.40, he will produce 20 boxes at Plant 1 and 10 box at Plant 2.

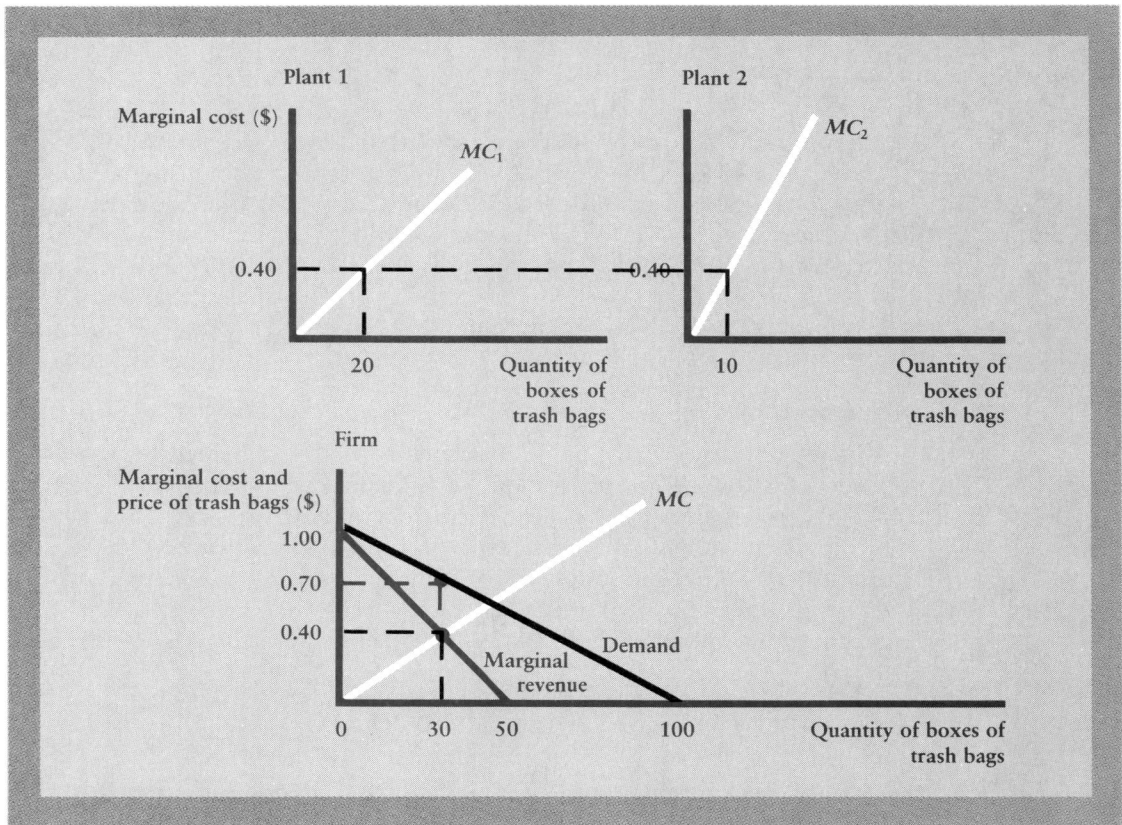

at a price of \$0.40. Its two plants have marginal-cost curves MC_1 and MC_2. Since Rocky knows that he can sell all of the bags he wants at a price of \$0.40, marginal revenue will also be \$0.40. Poobell will continue to make economic profits up to output levels of twenty at Plant 1 and ten at Plant 2.

Rocky produces many boxes of trash bags at his two plants. For mathematical simplicity, Figure 11-5 indicates Rocky's total output to be only thirty boxes per minute. Given the marginal-cost curves in Figure 11-5, Rocky will produce thirty boxes of trash bags by allocating twenty boxes to Plant 1 and only ten to Plant 2.

The marginal cost of the twentieth box at Plant 1 equals the marginal cost of the tenth box at Plant 2. If Plant 2 were to produce eleven boxes, and Plant 1, nineteen, the marginal cost of the last box at Plant 2 would be greater than at Plant 1. Rocky could increase the profits of producing the thirty boxes by shifting one box from Plant 2 back to Plant 1.

If Poobell were not a price taker, but faced a negatively-sloped demand curve, the operating rule would be essentially the same. In this case marginal revenue is no longer equal to price. To determine the output levels where marginal revenue equals marginal cost, we must determine the marginal cost of each unit.

To determine the optimal allocation graphically, we add the two marginal-cost curves horizontally in the same manner in which we created the aggregate supply curve in Chapter 5 for the competitive firm. As shown in Figure 11-5, the combined marginal-cost curves form the aggregate marginal-cost curve for the firm.

The firm determines output by setting marginal revenue equal to marginal cost. Output at each plant occurs at the quantity where marginal cost is the same as determined in Figure 11-5. Recall that if marginal cost were not equal at both plants, the firm could increase profits by shifting output to the plant with the lower marginal cost.

11-4 Multiplant production

NUMERICAL EXAMPLE

Assume that, as in Figure 11-5, the marginal cost at Plant 1 is

$$MC_1 = 2Q_1$$

and at Plant 2 is

$$MC_2 = 4Q_2.$$

Demand is

$$P = 100 - Q.$$

Marginal revenue will thus be

$$MR = 100 - 2Q.$$

To determine Rocky's overall marginal-cost equation we must determine his output at each level of marginal cost. First, we must solve both marginal-cost curves for output as follows:

$$Q_1 = \frac{MC_1}{2} \quad \text{and} \quad Q_2 = \frac{MC_2}{4}.$$

To find combined output, add Q_1 and Q_2 as follows:

$$Q = Q_1 + Q_2 = \frac{MC_1}{2} + \frac{MC_2}{4}.$$

Since Rocky produces where MC_1 equals MC_2,

$$MC_1 = MC_2 = MC.$$

Total output Q now becomes

$$Q = Q_1 + Q_2$$
$$= \frac{MC}{2} + \frac{MC}{4}$$
$$= \frac{3MC}{4}.$$

By rearranging terms we can determine Rocky's marginal cost to be

$$MC = \frac{4Q}{3}.$$

Profit maximization will occur where MC equals MR. As a result,

$$MR = 100 - 2Q = \frac{4Q}{3} = MC,$$

yielding

$$10Q = 300$$

and

$$Q = 30.$$

At Q equal to 30, marginal cost equals

$$\frac{4Q}{3} = \frac{120}{3} = 40.$$

At marginal cost equal to 40,

$$Q_1 = \frac{MC_1}{2} = 20$$

and

$$Q_2 = \frac{MC_2}{4} = 10.$$

While the cost of determining precisely the marginal cost of each output level at each plant may be too high for some companies, managers do increase their firm's profits by allocating output as closely as possible to the levels dictated by this decision rule.

Output Allocation Among Plants with Uncertain Input Prices

We will now extend the marginal-cost rule to the problem of fluctuating input prices. As an example, we will consider the generation of electric power. Rocky buys his electricity from the Tower Electric Power Company. Tower Electric uses oil, gas, and coal to generate electricity at several locations. Since Tower Electric faces fluctuating prices for these fuels, it must design a strategy for allocating production at its different production locations.

Before solving Tower Electric's problem we need to define some important terms. Electric utilities produce their electricity at several firing units. A firing unit is a production unit for electricity that normally uses one type of fuel, such as oil, coal, gas, or nuclear energy. Since an electric utility normally owns several firing units, it must decide which of these units to use at any given point in time.

While there are several factors to be considered in choosing among firing units, Tower Electric normally follows a procedure based on the marginal-cost principle. The marginal cost of producing electricity is dependent on the marginal productivity of the firing unit attributed to the unit's heat rate and the price of the fuel. The heat rate is the amount of BTUs (British Thermal Units) of heat needed to generate a kilowatt (KW) of electricity.

Since fuel varies in the amount of BTUs it generates, and firing units vary in their efficiency in converting BTUs into KWs, the marginal productivity varies considerably from one unit to the next. As evidenced by the wide fluctuations in oil prices since 1973, relative fuel prices also vary.

Electric utilities rank their firing units continuously by what is called a merit order. The merit order is a ranking based on the marginal cost of producing electricity. Those units with relatively higher marginal productivity and using relatively lower-priced fuels are high on the company's merit order.

APPLICATION   A unit's place in the merit order varies with changes in fuel costs. Tower Electric can minimize its overall costs by using the lowest marginal-cost firing units as close to capacity as possible before turning to the higher-cost units.

While the merit order forms the basis for the company's output-allocation decisions, there are at least three other factors that the company must consider.

1. Units break down unexpectedly and require repair. During a breakdown the unit is out of service and the company must go to a higher marginal-cost unit for its required output.

2. Tower Electric may also choose to perform preventative maintenance on a unit, temporarily removing it from the merit order.

3. The company must plan for unexpected surges in demand. Since most companies are regulated by local government agencies, companies do not normally have discretion over their output prices. They must maintain sufficient capacity to meet all demand at that price. Because of the time and cost involved in starting firing units from a cold start, Tower Electric must operate some units at less than full capacity in case of these unexpected surges. Adjusting the output of units already in operation is much less expensive than operating a firing unit from a cold start.

The cost-minimizing electric utility will incorporate adjustments such as these into its merit-order rule. The marginal-cost rule remains as the basis for the cost-minimizing company's output allocation decisions.

Tower Electric could lower its costs even further if it decided to join an electric power pool. By making a power-sharing agreement, firms can equate marginal cost at all firing units among the participating firms. Over 59 percent of U.S. electric capacity is managed through formal power-sharing agreements, which allocate output among all firms' firing units in the system. These sharing agreements essentially convert the member firms into one large firm for output-allocation decisions. The power pool creates a merit order for the entire pool and allocates output to the lowest marginal-cost firing units. The member firms share in the savings of production costs. The principal savings come from using firing units that have relatively lower marginal costs and that would otherwise be idle without the sharing agreement.

Source: Daniel E. Coates and James G. Mulligan, "The Cost-Reduction Potential of Electric Power Pools: Evidence from Firing-Unit Data." *Applied Economics* 18, No. 12 (December 1986):1323–34.

In summary, the cost-minimizing firm has an aggregate marginal cost that represents the horizontal sum of the firm's unit-level marginal-cost curves. The technique for adding these marginal-cost curves is the same as that used to create the industry supply curve in a competitive market. For industries with well-defined marginal costs at the unit level, such as electric power plants, this procedure is especially useful.

The common juice market

The potential for cost reduction extends beyond a country's borders. In 1986 a company began testing for the first time a new $1.1 billion undersea cable system designed to connect Great Britain to the European electricity grid. The full network is designed to transmit 2,000 megawatts of electricity in either direction at any given point in time. Estimates are that most of the flow will be from France to Great Britain in the early years. During the first two years (1986–88), Great Britain should have received electricity from France at a price 25 percent lower than the average cost of electricity in Great Britain.

France is a major seller of electricity because of excess capacity relative to domestic demand. In 1984, France produced 65 percent of its electricity from nuclear sources, while Great Britain and the United States produced less than 20 percent from nuclear sources. There were additional benefits from the new power line. Peak times in Great Britain lag those in France by an hour. In addition, Great Britain has endured many strikes and produces coal at protectionist prices. More competition from other energy sources makes the home market more competitive. Due to a greater reliance on the European grid, the quantity of electric power exchanged among France, West Germany, The Netherlands, Luxembourg, and Belgium doubled between 1970 and 1985.

Transportation Costs

Up to this point we have ignored transportation costs. Without transportation costs, firms could locate all their plants at one location and transport their goods to customers at no cost. In this section we will consider the firm's output allocation rule when it faces transportation costs. We will also discuss the firm's pricing decision.

The Allocation of Output As mentioned in the microchip example (Application 11-1), the entire yearly world production of microchips would fit into ten jumbo jets. Transportation costs are therefore not a major concern in this industry. Forest products, cement, steel, and other goods with high weight-to-price ratios have higher transportation costs per unit value of the good. A firm may offset some of these transportation costs by locating plants nearer to customers and purchasing inputs locally. Firms may lower costs by sending components for local assembly. For example, it may be less expensive to send the components of an automobile for local assembly than to ship cars already assembled.

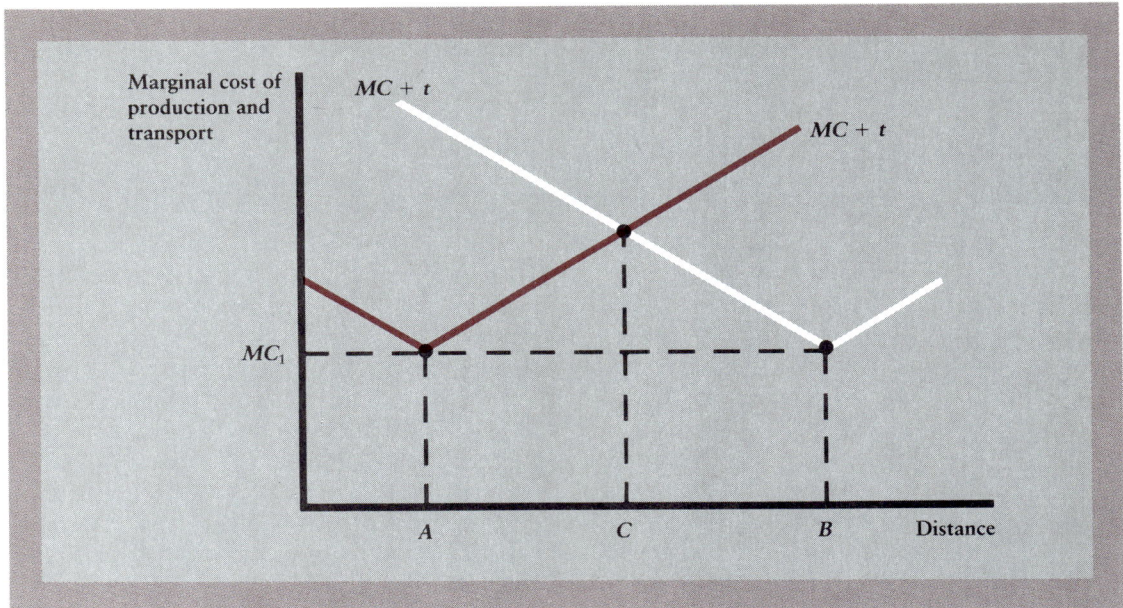

FIGURE 11-6 ▪ **Transportation costs.** Steiner Concrete Company has two plants located at A and B. Since marginal-cost and transportation cost are identical, Pete will use the plant at A to supply customers between A and C, and the plant at B to supply customers between B and C.

We now turn to an analysis of a specific firm's output allocation problem. Consider the problem faced by Pierre (Pete) Steiner of the Steiner Concrete Company. Steiner Concrete specializes in making a concrete mix of stones, sand, and cement. Since there is a high percentage of stones in the concrete mix, transportation costs are high. Pete has several plants making the concrete mix at different locations. He must decide how to allocate output among his plants and which plant to use to meet orders from customers located at varying distances from the plants.

We will consider two scenarios. First, we will assume that the costs of production are the same at all plants and that transportation costs are in constant proportion to the distance traveled. Later we will change these assumptions and assume that one plant has lower production costs and that average per-mile transportation costs decrease with increasing distances.

| 11-5 | **Transportation costs I** |

GRAPHICAL
EXPLANATION

Assume that Pete Steiner has one plant located at A and a second plant at B in Figure 11-6. For simplicity, assume that there is an identical number of customers located at every point along the horizontal axis. Also assume that

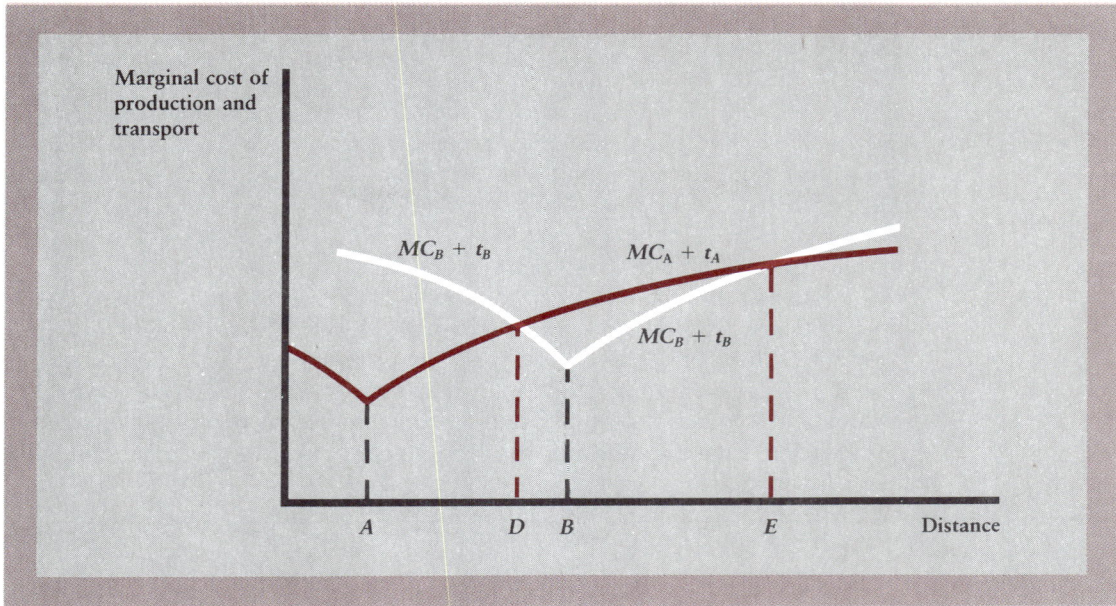

FIGURE 11-7 ▪ **Declining marginal transport cost.** The plant at *A* produces concrete mix at a lower marginal cost. Transportation costs per mile decrease with longer trips. In this case Pete will use the plant at *A* to supply customers between *A* and *D* and to the right of *E*. assuming he has no other plant located to the right of the one at *B*. The plant at *B* will supply customers located between *D* and *E*.

Pete can produce the concrete mix at constant marginal cost, *MC*, at both plants. Transportation cost equals t dollars per mile regardless of the distance shipped.

Pete will minimize his cost by using the plant at *A* to meet orders between *A* and *C*, where *C* is a point halfway between *A* and *B*. The plant at *B* will serve the customers between *C* and *B*. If Pete had plants on the other sides of *A* and *B*, he would allocate output in the same way: each plant would supply the half of the market closest to it.

There may be differences in production costs at any point in time due to the availability of materials or differences in the costs of hiring labor locally. While these differences may not persist for long, the firm may at any point in time experience differences in marginal cost, such as those experienced by Tower Electric Power Company earlier. Firms may also find that the per-mile cost of transporting their goods decreases as distance increases. This may be due to the spreading of fixed loading and unloading costs over longer distances.

GRAPHICAL EXPLANATION

Figure 11-7 (on p. 327) presents a slightly different situation from that in Figure 11-6. The plant at A has lower marginal cost than the plant at B. Transportation costs per mile decrease with increasing distance. The curve labelled $MC_A + t_A$ includes both the marginal cost of producing at A and the marginal cost of shipping the concrete mix. $MC_B + t_B$ represents the cost of producing and shipping from the plant at B.

If the cost difference were large enough at the two plants and the marginal cost of transportation were to drop enough, the two curves could overlap in two places. In Figure 11-7 the plant at A would have a cost advantage relative to the plant at B between A and D, and again to the right of E. Paradoxically, Pete would lower his costs by shipping concrete mix to points to the right of E from the plant at A, while shipping concrete mix in the other direction from his plant at B.

Summary

In this chapter we applied the basic economic theories of Chapters 2–5 to internal pricing and output allocation of the firm. We concentrated on developing some principles for the profit-maximizing firm. Since the firm that produces its own inputs or allocates output among several plants has decided to forgo the market for making these decisions, it must develop an alternative.

We began by discussing internal pricing among divisions of a corporation that sell to one another. The optimal price depends on the nature of the external market for the inputs produced by the firm. We considered three possibilities: no external market, a competitive external market, and a monopolized external market.

When there is no external market, the firm should adopt internal prices that encourage the division supplying the input to produce where its marginal cost is equal to the net marginal revenue of this input to the firm. With a competitive external market the situation is somewhat simpler. In this case the firm should use the external competitive price as its own internal price. In some cases it will be a net seller to the external market. At other times it will be a net buyer. In the last case, where a monopolized external market exists, the firm should sell where the marginal cost of the last unit it produces equals the net marginal revenue of the last input it uses itself and the marginal revenue of the last unit sold externally.

These examples of internal decision rules by no means exhaust the possibilities of applying economics to internal decision making. However, they do offer some guiding principles for designing decision rules in more complicated internal systems.

We then developed a decision rule for allocating output among several plants owned by the same firm. We showed that the cost-minimizing firm allocates output among its plants so that marginal cost is equal at all plants. We followed this analysis with an application to the generation of electricity. The electric utility must contend with fluctuations in the market price of the fuel it uses to generate electricity. Since fuel prices can fluctuate more quickly than the firm can adjust the fuel used by its firing units, the firm has an incentive to adjust its output according to the current fuel prices.

Since few firms can maintain sufficient capacity to accommodate all ranges of fuel prices, over half of U.S. electric capacity is managed through organized power-sharing arrangements, called power pools. The power pool allocates output among its member plants according to the marginal-cost rule and shares the cost savings with its member firms.

The costs of transporting electricity are small enough to justify transporting it long distances when there are differences in the cost of production. The cost of transporting other goods may be much higher. We modified our multiplant analysis to account for transportation costs. We found that the firm must allocate its output to account for both the marginal cost of production and the marginal cost of transportation.

Important Terms	Transfer Pricing (p. 307) Horizontal Integration (p. 319) Net Marginal Revenue (p. 309)

Selected References

Coates, Daniel E., and Mulligan, James G. "The Cost-Reduction Potential of Electric Power Pools: Evidence from Firing-Unit Data." *Applied Economics* 18, No. 12 (December 1986):1323–34.

Haddock, David D. "Basing-Point Pricing: Competitive vs. Collusive Theories." *American Economic Review* 72, No. 3 (June 1982):289–306.

Hirshleifer, J. "On the Economics of Transfer Pricing." *Journal of Business* 29 (July 1956):96–108.

Scherer, F.M. *Industrial Market Structure and Economic Performance*, 2nd ed. Skokie, Illinois: Rand McNally, 1980.

Scherer, F.M. et al. *The Economics of Multiplant Operation: An International Comparisons Study*. Cambridge, Massachusetts: Harvard University Press, 1975.

Problems

1. Assume that a firm makes an intermediate good, T, which it then uses to make good F. There is a perfectly competitive external market for good T with a market price of $40 per unit. Assume that one unit of T is used to make one unit of F. Assume that the demand for the final good is

$$D_F = 205 - Q_F$$

where D_F represents the demand for good F. The marginal cost of producing the intermediate good is

$$MC_T = 10 + Q_T$$

where MC_T is the marginal cost to the firm of producing good T. Assume that the marginal cost of producing F (excluding the cost of the input T) is a constant $15 per unit. Determine the profit-maximizing quantities of F and T produced by the firm.

2. Assume that a firm faces the following demand function for its final product:

$$P = 1100 - 0.001q.$$

It produces a component for this final product. There is no external market for the component. One component is used for each unit of the final product. Assume that the marginal cost of producing the component is:

$$MC_c = 20 + 0.007q.$$

The marginal cost of producing the final product in addition to the cost of the component is

$$MC_o = 40 + 0.004q.$$

If the firm adopts a transfer pricing policy, what will the transfer price be?

3. Assume that a vertically integrated firm produces an input X that is produced in a perfectly competitive market at price P_X equal to 2. The firm's marginal cost curve for X is given by

$$MC_X = 3 + 0.0001X.$$

Assume that the firm uses X as the only input in producing its product, Q. One X is used for every Q. There are no additional costs associated with producing Q. The demand for Q is

$$P_Q = 100 - 0.001Q.$$

Calculate the amount of X and Q that the firm should produce and the prices at which these products should be sold.

4. Assume that Musetta Momus, production manager of Left Bank Shoes, must decide how to allocate output among four plants under her control. Her company produces the patented Hi-Lo shoe for women. The shoe comes with both a high and a low heel attachment, which makes it convenient for travelers. The marginal cost of producing the shoe at each plant is as follows:

$$MC_1 = Q_1, \quad MC_2 = 0.5Q_2, \quad MC_3 = 2Q_3, \quad \text{and } MC_4 = Q_4.$$

All values of Q are in thousands of pairs of shoes. Assume that the marginal revenue curve is constant at $40. How many shoes will Musetta produce at each plant?

5. Now assume that marginal revenue in Problem 4 equals $MR = 63 - Q/9$. How much will be produced at each plant now?

Answer questions 6–13 with true, false, or uncertain.

6. The price set by the firm in an external monopoly market will always be greater than the internal transfer price.

7. The internal transfer price will equal the internal marginal cost at the internal output level.

8. The firm will produce more of the input than it will of the output as long as the external output market is perfectly competitive.

9. As long as the firm is capable of producing the input at a lower cost than the external competitive market price, it should produce the input itself.

10. Electric utilities allocate output according to a merit order, but would lower their costs if they ranked their units by marginal cost instead.

11. To calculate the marginal-cost curve for the multiplant firm, one must add the marginal-cost curves vertically.

12. A firing-unit's place in the company's merit order will depend on the production function at the unit and the price of fuel burned at the unit.

13. Assume that a company has two plants producing the same product according to the same marginal-cost curve. If all of the output is sold in the vicinity of the first plant and there is a transportation cost of shipping the output from the second plant to the vicinity of the first plant, the company will produce more at the first plant than at the second plant.

12

CONTRACTUAL ALTERNATIVES TO VERTICAL INTEGRATION

I n Chapter 10 we saw how the breakdown of contractual arrangements could convince some firms to make their own inputs. In this chapter we will look at alternatives to formal vertical integration. We will concentrate on the economic advantages of contractual arrangements to facilitate market exchange. Our main concern will be the manufacturing firm that must rely on distributors and/or retailers to place its product in the hands of the consumer.

Unlike the firm that produces an input that becomes a component of another firm's final product, the firm relying on others to distribute or sell its product shares responsibility for the quality of the product in the mind of the consumer. In this chapter we will concentrate on the efforts of manufacturers to insure the quality of the product, while at the same time seeking the lowest-cost means of meeting consumer demand.

The fear of opportunistic behavior can limit firms' efforts to achieve profit maximization through market exchange. Unless all parties to a contract can devise restraints on others' incentives to act in an opportunistic manner, vertical contractual arrangements will fail, and the firm may have no alternative but vertical integration.

We will begin by considering the coexistence of different distributional structures in the same market. Vertically-integrated firms often perform both distribution and retail functions in markets in competition with nonvertically-integrated distributors and retailers. We will look specifically at functional discounts for firms providing vertically-integrated distribution and retailing.

Next we will consider two common vertical contractual arrangements: exclusive territories and exclusive dealing. Both arrangements are attempts by the manufacturer to force retailers to sell the product in concert with the best interests of both the manufacturer and the retailer. Neither arrangement perfectly controls retailers and may provide incentives for the retailer to make decisions counter to the interests of the manufacturer.

We will also look at the reasons why manufacturers may want to control the retail price of their goods. The U.S. Supreme Court and the U.S. Congress have both singled out price as the one variable over which manufacturers cannot maintain control at the retail level. Despite this position, the executive branch has publicly affirmed its opposition to this policy and has hesitated to prosecute firms that require retailers to sell at fixed prices.

Next, we will discuss franchising. Over 38 percent of all goods sold at the retail level in the United States flows through a franchise system. In addition, more and more franchises are appearing throughout the rest of the world. We will consider reasons for the popularity of franchises and methods for insuring their success.

Functional Discounts

Let's return briefly to Rocky Sanders of Poobell Plastic Trash Bag Company. In the last chapter Rocky had started selling his trash bags through a leading supermarket chain, Gooters Supermarkettes, which used its own private store label on the box. Rocky still sells bags with the Poobell label to this supermarket chain and other distributors.

While Gooters is primarily a retailer of grocery products, it also distributes products for manufacturers to its own and other firms' retail outlets. It provides manufacturers with two levels of service, as opposed to firms that provide only distribution or retailing functions. Since nonvertically-integrated supermarkets must buy their products from distributors, they pay a higher price for products than Gooters Supermarkettes does. Gooters pays the same price to manufacturers that other distributors do.

The difference between the price Gooters pays the manufacturer and the price a nonvertically-integrated retailer pays a distributor for the same product represents a functional discount. A **functional discount** is compensation to the vertically-integrated firm for providing services at other levels of the vertical chain.

Despite the plausible claim that the discount covers the cost of providing the distribution function, the U.S. government has not always interpreted functional discounts in this manner. The relevant law is the Robinson-Patman Act, passed in 1935 by Congress to protect small firms against price discrimination by larger firms. We will consider this law more generally in the next chapter. Right now we will single out the provision concerning functional discounts.

Since the mid-1970s the federal government has not vigorously enforced Robinson-Patman cases. Since 1980 there has been only one such case filed. This case concerned functional discounts. The government's interest in pursuing this case seems inconsistent with its general position on vertical arrangements.

| 12-1 | Why are you so different? |

APPLICATION   The FTC issued an order in 1986 for the Boise Cascade Corporation to stop accepting functional discounts for office supplies that it purchased from over

1,000 different manufacturers. Boise Cascade purchased about 25,000 different goods, which it distributed through 27 distribution centers in the United States. Half of the goods went to stationery and office-supply retailers, and the other half was sold directly to customers through its own retail outlets.

Some of Boise Cascade's suppliers offered discounts for large-volume purchases and functional discounts for wholesalers who arranged their own distribution. Boise purchased all of its goods at the lower wholesale price, even goods sold at retail in competition with independents.

Regulation, a publication of the American Enterprise Institute, argued that Boise incurred the same distribution costs whether it sold to independent retailers or directly to customers. In either case, it performed a distribution function through its own distribution centers.

Working against Boise was evidence that it had received a larger discount than other integrated retailers. *Regulation* argued that the discounts were due to greater economies of scale. For example, other integrated retailers carried only 2,000–6,000 items, compared to Boise's 25,000, and relied on Boise and other distributors to stock the remaining items. Despite its size, Boise had only 2 percent of the market in 1986. Boise has appealed the FTC ruling.

Source: "Currents: Reagan FTC Fights Price Cutting on Pencils, Paper Clips." *Regulation* (September/October 1986):13–14. With permission of the American Enterprise Institute.

Exclusive Territories

In Chapter 8, Harry Sampson considered abandoning his tree-trimming business to sell trucks. At that time we focused on pricing options available to Harry to increase his profits. We did not consider the contractual relationship that Harry had with the truck manufacturer. In this section we will look at one contractual provision common to the sale of many manufactured goods, including trucks and cars: exclusive territories. An **exclusive territory** is a geographical area reserved by the manufacturer for the retailer in order to shield the retailer from competition from other retailers selling the same product.

Manufacturers grant exclusive territories primarily to provide incentives to the retailer to use local advertising and promotions without fear that another retailer will undercut prices. As noted in the beginning of the chapter, a manufacturer selling a product to the retailer cannot, under current antitrust law, dictate the final price of the product.

Harry receives the exclusive territory as an encouragement to provide the facilities and staffing required of a full-service dealer. Otherwise, anyone could set up an operation run from the back of a van across the street from Harry's lot. The shoestring operator would encourage potential customers to cross the street and test drive Harry's Torridos.

Once the customers decide that they want the Torrido, the budget dealer would guarantee a price below Harry's. Since Harry is a full-service dealer operating at higher cost, the budget dealer would always be able to offer a lower price. Given significant competition from budget dealers, full-service dealers lose their incentive to maintain the higher-cost services and inventories.

Since a reduction in these services ultimately hurts the manufacturer's sales, the manufacturer has an incentive to provide a sales revenue for the dealer high enough to cover these costs. Without exclusive territories, dealers would underprovide these services, resulting in decreased information and service quality.

If Harry has an exclusive territory, he does not face direct competition from other dealers selling the same truck. If the manufacturer, Awesome Truck, has been successful in establishing some market power over the sale of its Torrido, Harry will face a negatively-sloped demand curve at the retail level.

Once Awesome Truck has set its wholesale price, the wholesale price becomes a part of Harry's marginal cost. Harry can then act as a local monopolist and exploit the negatively-sloped demand curve. Since Awesome Truck must set a price for the sale of the Torrido to Harry, it does not benefit by any increase in Harry's price to final customers. The manufacturer would prefer that Harry sell as many Torridos as possible.

The exclusive territory may give Harry an incentive to reduce sales below the level desired by Awesome Truck. Figure 12-1 (p. 338) shows the difference between the incentives faced by Awesome Truck and Harry. The manufacturer would prefer that Harry sell Q_1 at price P_1. At Q_1 Harry would just cover his average total cost.

Harry would prefer to sell Q_2 at price P_2. If Harry sets his retail price higher than Awesome Truck's desired retail price, Awesome Truck will sell fewer trucks. Since Awesome Truck's price is set, the fewer Torridos Harry and the other dealers sell, the lower will be Awesome Truck's profits.

Without constraints on its dealerships, the manufacturer loses control over the pricing and output decisions at the dealer level. Unchecked, the dealer may take advantage of the situation and create a situation counter to the best interests of the manufacturer and the final customers. In order to decrease dealers' incentives to raise prices, the manufacturer could resort to threats of the following nature:

(a) *Removal of the exclusive territory.* While the manufacturer does not wish to eliminate exclusive territories without justification, the threat of termination or the opening of a new franchise nearby may keep the dealer's retail price within a range recommended by the manufacturer.

(b) *Setting of a maximum price, such as a list price.* Even though most car manufacturers do set list prices, actual sales prices vary considerably. For example, when Japanese cars have been especially popular, they have sold for above list price. More generally, dealers vary their prices by such practices as

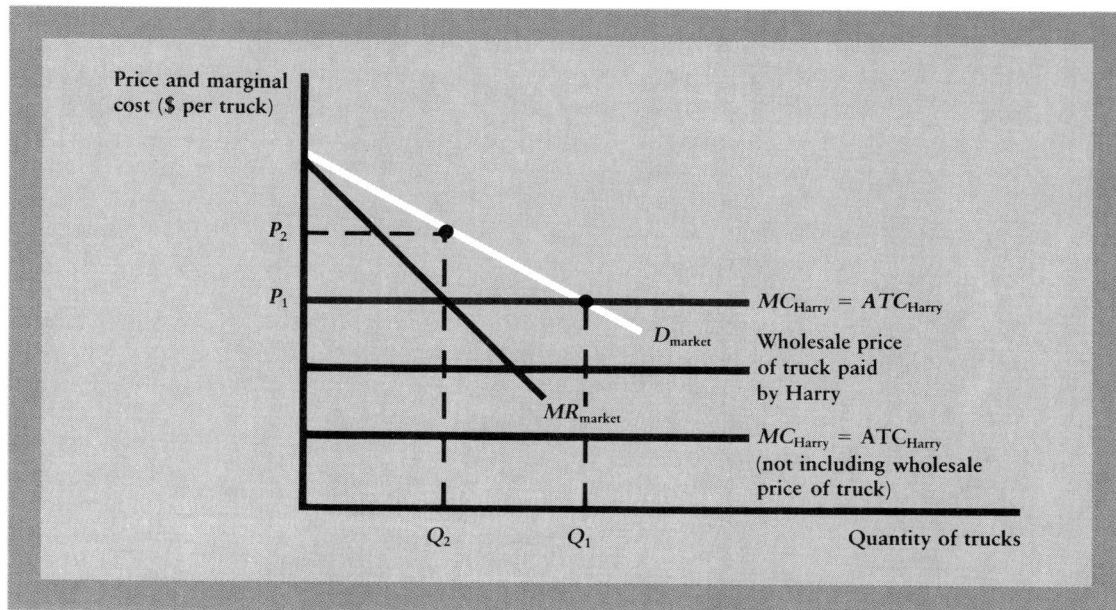

FIGURE 12-1 ▪ Exclusive territories. Harry's marginal cost is the sum of the wholesale price he pays Awesome Truck for each truck and the marginal cost of his remaining expenses. Since Harry faces a negatively-sloped demand curve, he would prefer to sell Q_2 trucks at price P_2. Since Awesome Truck makes more profit if Harry sells more trucks, it wants Harry to sell Q_1 trucks and charge price P_1, which just covers his average total costs.

trade-in prices, guaranteed delivery times, and variations in the prices on options. In addition, local differences in demand for specific car models make a national pricing policy difficult for manufacturers.

(c) *Sales quotas.* A manufacturer can force a dealer to set the appropriate price by sending unordered cars. The dealership must lower its price to sell everything in the lot. The manufacturer can also withhold more popular models.

The following Application describes the difficulties a manufacturer may have in keeping retailers from raising prices.

12-2

The best deal within a radius of seven miles

APPLICATION Several state legislatures have passed laws restricting the controls that automobile manufacturers have over their dealerships. Professor Richard Smith of Arizona State University has shown that there are higher-than-average car prices in those states that have passed laws restricting manufacturers' ability to impose threats and sales quotas and preventing manufacturers from opening new dealerships within a certain radius of an existing dealership selling the same make of car. Controlling for factors such as population and income levels, Smith found that dealers in those states have been able to raise prices to a level above that in states where manufacturers have more control over their dealers.

For example, he found that regulation accounted for an average price increase in 1972 of $524 per car, or 9.3 percent of the observed price, and an 8.3 percent decrease in the quantity of cars sold. Smith argued further that the increase in price may not be a pure price effect but may reflect partially the purchase of unwanted options. This practice amounted to between $3.9 billion and $6.7 billion in sales. The adverse effects of regulation were greatest in those states that had denied the manufacturer use of all of the controls listed earlier.

Source: Richard L. Smith, III, "Franchise Regulation: An Economic Analysis of State Restrictions on Automobile Distribution." *Journal of Law and Economics* XXV, No. 1 (April 1982):125–58. © by the University of Chicago.

Exclusive Dealing

Manufacturers sometimes have **exclusive dealing agreements** with retailers, whereby the retailers must agree not to sell the similar products of competing manufacturers. The manufacturer often combines an exclusive-dealing agreement with an exclusive territory. In this section we will consider the economic justification for exclusive dealing independently of the effects of the exclusive territory. We begin by considering an alternative explanation of the role of exclusive dealing: an attempt to erect barriers to entry. We then conclude with an argument based on efficient cost minimization.

Barriers to Entry

Since an exclusive-dealing arrangement requires a dealer to carry only one brand, some people have argued that such arrangements create barriers to entry. According to this line of reasoning, a manufacturer or group of manufacturers can control all retail outlets and prevent new manufacturers from entering the market. In order for this to work there must be a horizontal conspiracy at the manufacturing level.

We discussed the difficulty of maintaining conspiracies among large numbers of firms in Chapter 7. Despite the possibility of a conspiracy among manufacturers, there are aspects of exclusive-dealing arrangements that are inconsistent with the creation of barriers to entry.

Most exclusive-dealing contracts are of short duration, which means that a new manufacturer offering a better financial arrangement could still compete for existing dealers or encourage the entry of new dealers to the market. There are also costs associated with ignoring the alternative of a multiline operation that would place a retailer using exclusive dealing at a disadvantage relative to a multiline retailer. By offering several competing brands, the multiline retailer attracts a wider range of clients and can provide customers with choices.

Customers who do not know exactly what variation of the product they want can wait until they reach the store before making their final decision. With only one choice available, customers must increase their time costs of making store-to-store comparisons. In situations where the cost associated with maintaining large multiline inventories is too expensive, such as at gas stations, the dealer may voluntarily opt for an exclusive dealership.

Assuming that the dealer has not chosen the exclusive-dealer arrangement voluntarily, the dealer expects to experience an increase in average cost based on lower expected sales. To compensate the dealer, the manufacturer would have to accept a lower-than-usual percentage of total sales or offer some other form of compensation. Smaller manufacturers using multiline retailers could enter the market and drive the higher-cost dealers out of business.

12-3	Lining up the holes

APPLICATION

Standard Fashion Company sued Magrane-Houston Company, a Boston-based retail store, for switching to McCalls Patterns without giving sufficient notice. In 1922 the Supreme Court ruled that the original exclusive-dealing contract involving these two companies was illegal, because it could result in all retail stores carrying Standard Fashion's patterns to the exclusion of other brands. Although the Supreme Court has since treated this decision narrowly over the years and does not now frown on exclusive dealing, it is useful to follow the development of this industry in response to this court decision.

Before the Supreme Court's decision, Standard Fashion Company negotiated two-year contracts requiring three months' notice from either party if the contract were not to be renewed. The manufacturer supplied a new inventory every six months, provided pattern books, and bought back obsolete inventory. The dealer had to accept the exclusive-dealing provision, provide an attendant, and maintain a well-stocked inventory.

The asset that the manufacturer wanted to protect in this case was the investment in designing the clothes. Since the ready-to-wear market was in its infancy at the time of the court case, the pattern industry was the major source of new designs. The patterns could be easily copied by competitors by matching the holes of the perforated patterns.

Exclusive dealing gave the manufacturer a means of preventing the dealer from switching the customer to identical copies. In small communities manufacturers combined exclusive dealing with an exclusive territory. Despite the court's decision, the market structure remained similar for several years.

Without exclusive dealing the manufacturers developed second-best alternatives for payment. Manufacturers imposed fixed charges for the displays at the dealership. As the industry developed without exclusive dealing, it turned away from new designs and offered simpler fashions that followed the fashion lead of the ready-to-wear industry. For example, Simplicity entered the pattern market using a printed rather than perforated pattern and captured approximately 50 percent of the market.

Source: Howard P. Marvel, "Exclusive Dealing." *Journal of Law and Economics* XXV, No. 1 (April 1982):1–26. © by the University of Chicago.

Economic Efficiency

As mentioned earlier, we can base a more convincing argument for exclusive dealing on the manufacturer's concern for maintaining control over its potential customers. By preventing the dealer from carrying competing brands, the manufacturer prevents the dealer from switching customers from its product to that of a competitor. This is important when the manufacturer's advertising efforts have created a set of customers for the dealer.

If the dealer has the ability to persuade customers to switch to an essentially identical but lower-cost alternative, the dealer may gain at the expense of the manufacturer. This argument would not be valid if the promotional efforts were purely brand-specific. In this case intense brand loyalty may prevent the dealer from switching customers to other companies' goods.

For example, a manufacturer may promote a certain type of golf club through national advertising. The advertising may be effective enough to convince a golfer to go to a golf pro and try out the new club. Given the research and advertising effort involved in manufacturing and promoting the new club, the wholesale price to the pro would be higher than the price of a lesser-known brand. If the pro is able to influence the customer's choice once in the pro shop, the pro can direct the customer to the brand where he stands to gain the most profit.

Seen in this way, the exclusive-dealing arrangement is a way of insuring that the dealer cannot take away the customers that the manufacturer has brought to the store. Without this protection, the manufacturer will have to absorb the cost of attracting customers to a store without deriving the benefit of the sales.

The manufacturer is worried not only about initial sales; it does not want to lose repeat sales. If the dealer is able to influence customers to switch products, the dealer may switch to another brand name in a new exclusive-dealer arrangement. Customers initially attracted to the store by the original manufacturer may be persuaded to stay with the dealer.

The manufacturer may choose to handle this problem by negotiating a long-term contract with the dealer that effectively keeps the dealer from changing allegiance. However, while possible, this is not commonly done, primarily because of the reduced flexibility associated with long-term contracts.

Manufacturers often use warranties for products sold in exclusive dealerships, requiring customers to fill out forms with their names and addresses. Since these warranty forms are filed with the manufacturer, the manufacturer maintains a list of potential customers. If there is a change of dealers, the manufacturer can notify these customers of the change.

Exclusive servicing by the manufacturer removes the dealer from a long-term arrangement with the customer. In addition, most exclusive-dealing arrangements require the dealer to return unsold inventory and spare parts upon termination of the contract. Otherwise, old customers might continue to frequent the former dealer.

| 12-4 | **Does it include a piece of the rock?** |

APPLICATION

In the insurance industry new customers come from two sources: company advertising and the efforts of salespeople. The writing of policies is through either an exclusive agent or an independent agent. Generally, independent agents dominate the market for insurance sold to businesses, while exclusive agents sell almost all of the life insurance.

Independent agents receive higher commissions for initial sales and renewals. Upon the expiration of a contract, the customer belongs to the agent, not to the insurance company. The agent selling business insurance must spend time tailoring the insurance policy to the specific needs of the business. This may involve issuing policies from several competing companies. Direct advertising has less of an impact in this market due to the specialized needs of the customers.

Life insurance companies rely on direct advertising to influence customers. This advertising can appeal to consumer's concerns about the reputation of the company. Given the similar nature of most companies' offerings, there is little need for tailor-made policies. The insurance company retains the customer's account and the rights to renewals. Given the similarities between life-insurance companies, a multiline agent could switch customers over to less-advertised but comparable companies and make a higher commission.

Source: Howard P. Marvel, "Exclusive Dealing." *Journal of Law and Economics* XXV, No. 1 (April 1982):1–26. © by the University of Chicago.

Manufacturers' Control of Retail Prices

We now return to Rocky Sanders. Rocky has no interest in vertically integrating his trash bag business to the retail level. He knows that opening a retail outlet that would only sell Poobell Plastic Trash Bags would not be successful. While he has no intention of operating retail outlets, Rocky is considering the advantages of requiring retailers who sell his bags to charge a price that he determines in advance. Unfortunately for Rocky, though, he is unable legally to set the retail price for his trash bags.

Rocky sells his trash bags through independent retailers and prints a "suggested" retail price on the box. While many companies promote "suggested" retail prices, retailers are not bound legally to charge these prices. Control over retail price has moved back and forth between manufacturers and retailers often since 1911. When the manufacturer has control over the retail price, the practice is called resale price maintenance (RPM). **Resale price maintenance** is a stipulation made by a manufacturer requiring a retailer to sell the manufacturer's good at a specified price.

While manufacturers are generally free to establish detailed controls over retailers selling their products, they are not currently allowed to set retail prices. The special treatment given price is unusual. Throughout the remainder of this section we will consider why there is disagreement over the purpose of RPM. The decision in *Dr. Miles Medical Company* v. *John D. Park and Sons* (1911) established the legal precedent that resale price maintenance (RPM) arrangements constitute unreasonable restraints of trade and, as a result, are illegal.[1] The Supreme Court reasoned that RPM was the same as horizontal price fixing, because it resulted in no price competition at the retail level. The court argued that RPM provided no legitimate interest for the manufacturer. It ruled that once the manufacturer sells the product to a distributor, it should lose control of the product.

In 1931 California passed a "Fair Trade" law, which allowed RPM. After the Supreme Court upheld California's right to pass such a law, over forty other states issued similar statutes. By the late 1960s most of these laws had been repealed in response to consumer movement pressure. In 1975 the federal government repealed a law allowing the states to have fair-trade laws. While suppliers can still legally influence resale prices, they cannot use coercion to enforce a resale price. The Supreme Court reaffirmed this position in 1984.

The economic justification for RPM hinges on the options available to firms when competing in marketing their products. Although the practice is illegal in the United States, it is still worth analyzing. Laws change with time and create new opportunities for those prepared to react to the change. In addition, the Justice Department has shown little interest in prosecuting RPM cases.

---

[1] *Dr. Miles Medical Company* v. *John D. Park and Sons*, 22 U.S. 373 (1911).

As we have seen in Chapter 10, there have been two opposing views of why firms may desire a change in organizational structure: (1) the firm may want to gain more market power and (2) the firm may be trying to lower costs in response to changes in the market environment. Support for the first of these two explanations leads to a governmental role in correcting market imperfections.

The second explanation suggests a more relaxed attitude on behalf of government and more confidence in markets to control monopoly behavior. We will consider the arguments made by advocates of both views. The choice between these two views will depend on the assumptions we make about the market environment. By concentrating on the differences between these assumptions, we will have a better means of evaluating the merits of the two views.

Monopoly Power

There are two monopoly-based arguments: support of a retail cartel and reinforcement of a manufacturers' cartel. It is unlikely that a cartel could be maintained at the retail level. Retailing is not dominated by a few large firms. If the retail price is held at a high level, the manufacturer sells fewer units of the product and has an incentive to find retailers willing to sell at a lower price. Once the manufacturer sells the product to the retailer, the manufacturer wants the retailer to sell as many units as possible.

If the manufacturer could collude with other manufacturers, it could use RPM to reinforce its cartel at the retail level and legally punish those that did not comply. However, this arrangement would still give the retailers an incentive to join the cartel but then increase their market share by lowering their prices and reneging on the agreement. For example, a retailer could offer special sales that combined a product subject to RPM with one not subject to RPM at a lower combined price. The sale would be an indirect method for lowering the price of the RPM product.

A successful cartel would require the cooperation of a large number of manufacturers. When RPM was legal, often only a few manufacturers used it. Since all manufacturers of all sizes must comply in order for the cartel to work, the historical record does not lend support to its potential for widespread success.

Product Information

One of the strongest arguments in favor of RPM centers on the flexibility it offers manufacturers for minimizing distribution and promotion costs. Without RPM, manufacturers cannot guarantee that the dealers' margins will be large enough to cover the dealers' costs of providing the levels of consumer information and service recommended by the manufacturer. This may turn outlets into no-service dealers.

The manufacturer would have to choose an alternative method for providing consumer information. We have already considered one option, exclusive territories, but exclusive territories are not the best option for all products. Consumers not only pay the purchase price of a product, they also incur an opportunity cost for their time in finding and purchasing the product. If these opportunity costs are a significant part of the overall cost of buying the product, the manufacturer may not wish to use exclusive territories. Consider an example from the computer industry.

It comes with instructions

APPLICATION   Professor Frank Easterbrook of the University of Chicago provided the following examples of options available to computer manufacturers.

(a) Commodore sold its computers through discount stores, such as K mart. Commodore essentially put an instruction book and a machine in a box. The store provided little service, product information, or training.

(b) Companies such as Radio Shack sell through their own retail stores and franchised outlets. The salespeople provide customers with special information and training at the store, paid for through higher prices. This distribution technique is based on the appeal of the company's brand name. The main weaknesses are the higher inventory-to-sales ratios and the lack of alternative products. Knowing that there are no other computers in the store for comparison, customers may be less willing to shop there and trust the recommendations of the salespeople.

(c) IBM has used product centers to display machines and provide information. IBM charges for this service in its wholesale price. A manufacturer has to be large enough to justify using these information centers. If there are not enough conveniently located centers, consumers will face higher opportunity costs of information.

(d) Resale price maintenance (RPM) allows a fourth option. For example, a new company could place its computers in stores requiring dealers to display them and provide extensive information and support to customers. In order for dealers to be willing to provide this support, the manufacturer must provide some incentive. RPM provides the incentive by freeing retailers from price competition. In its place, retailers compete by providing information and services to customers. This is exactly what the manufacturer prefers. If successful long-term relationships between the manufacturer and the consumer depend on the consumer's proper and knowledgeable use of the manufacturer's products, the dealer's unwillingness to provide a suitable level of product information and services could hurt the manufacturer's sales.

Source: Frank Easterbrook, "Restricted Dealing is a Way to Compete." *Regulation* (January/February 1984):23–27. With permission of the American Enterprise Institute.

Certification of Quality

Professors Howard Marvel and Stephen McCafferty of Ohio State University offer a rationale for RPM for goods that are less complicated than computers. In their view, RPM can protect manufacturers and retailers who depend on their reputations for providing a certain quality or style. RPM protects these retailers from being undercut by those who copy them. With RPM, retailers who wait to copy the trendsetters cannot use lower prices to lure customers away.

12-6

It won't work unless we do it together

APPLICATION

After California adopted RPM in 1931, most of the other states considered adoption. Forty-four states adopted RPM within a span of one year in the mid-1930s. Professors Marvel and McCafferty analyzed retail drug pricing at that time. They concluded that the imposition of RPM did not lead to higher retail prices once all states had moved from no RPM to using RPM. They also followed the pattern of the price changes as the states began adopting RPM.

They did observe that prices were lower in non-RPM states during the transition period. Despite the lower prices in the transition period, they argued that the evidence was consistent with the theory that RPM facilitates the provision of services and higher quality at the retail level. By law the manufacturers could not charge different wholesale prices in different states during the transition period, even though they had higher costs in the non-RPM states. They had higher costs in the non-RPM states because they incurred the costs of offsetting the reduction in information and services by retailers at the point of sale.

They could not increase their wholesale price in non-RPM states to cover the additional cost at the same time that they were charging a lower wholesale price in the RPM states. Instead, they raised their wholesale price in all states to reflect the higher costs of replacing the retailer-provided services abandoned by retailers in the non-RPM states.

During the transition period retail prices in non-RPM states fell in areas where discounters had a larger share of the local market. The discounters were taking advantage of the informational services offered by the full-service dealers. Unable to control the retail price, the full-service retailers in these areas lowered prices and services to meet the lower prices of discounters.

Once RPM was in place in all states, prices actually dropped in areas that had switched to RPM earlier and at stores located in areas too small to support discounters when RPM was not in effect. The lower retail prices reflected the decrease in the manufacturers' and retailers' overall cost of promoting the products. Competition among manufacturers forced them to lower their retail prices to reflect the efficiency of RPM-protected point-of-sale services.

Source: Howard P. Marvel and Stephen McCafferty, "The Political Economy of Resale Price Maintenance." *Journal of Political Economy* 94, No. 5 (October 1986):1074–95. © by the University of Chicago.

Deterring Retailer Fraud

Critics of RPM contend that manufacturers used RPM for products such as boxed candy, pet foods, jeans, vitamins, hair shampoo, and shirts, none of which require detailed service. For example, there were complaints lodged with the FTC in the late 1970s and early 1980s involving Florsheim Shoes, London Fog raincoats, Levi-Strauss jeans, Gant shirts, and Mrs. See's candies.

As you will see in the following application, Professors Robert Springer and H.E. Frech III of the University of California at Santa Barbara suggested that RPM may be an effective method for controlling retailer fraud. Without RPM, retailers are free to increase the price of the lowest-quality items in a manufacturer's line of goods and trick customers into thinking that they are equivalent to higher-quality items.

This deception increases the retailer's profits as long as the deception is undetected. Eventually, consumers find that the products do not live up to the retailer's claims of quality and place the blame on the manufacturer. The harm to the retailer is spread among all of the retailers selling the manufacturer's product. RPM prevents this from happening by forcing retailers to maintain the manufacturer's desired price differences in a full product line. In this case RPM leads to lower retail prices and a closer relationship between the quality and the price of the goods.

12-7

APPLICATION

Can you tell the difference?

Professors Springer and Frech received data from the FTC relating to an investigation of a shirt manufacturing company's use of RPM. Because the investigation was in progress, they were not able to reveal the name of the company. The FTC data concern the pricing of four styles of shirts made by the company both before and after the manufacturer had to stop using RPM.

The data support the theory of Professors Springer and Frech. Three of the four types of shirts were similar in quality. Although the fourth shirt was inferior in quality relative to the others, it was still above average in the industry. The fourth shirt had a coarser weave, which made it more uncomfortable to wear, even though it was virtually indistinguishable from the others at the time of purchase.

When the manufacturer used RPM, it used a 92 percent retailer markup on its shirts. It also maintained a $1 difference between the retail price of the fourth type of shirt and the others. Other than the price difference, there was no indication of a quality difference to the customer.

After the end of RPM, eighteen of twenty-one surveyed stores were selling all four shirts at the same price. The average price difference was $0.19, compared to the expected difference of about $1.45 had RPM still been in effect. Despite the expectation that the removal of RPM would lower retail prices, retail prices actually increased. After RPM was no longer in effect, the stores used higher average markups than before. In one of the surveys, thirty-four of thirty-five stores used a higher markup than they would have with RPM.

Source: Robert F. Springer and H.E. Frech III, "Deterring Fraud: The Role of Resale Price Maintenance." *Journal of Business* 59, No. 3 (July 1986):433–49. © by the University of Chicago.

Resale price maintenance has been and continues to be a controversial topic. Although the courts and Congress have maintained their opposition to the practice on the grounds that manufacturers would use it to facilitate collusion and monopoly power, there is evidence suggesting otherwise.

We considered the possibility that RPM can protect retailers who have invested in informational and quality-enhancing services in conjunction with the manufacturer. If customers value these services, the investment pays off in greater sales. Without RPM, other retailers can free-ride on the services provided by others and increase sales by lowering prices.

RPM may also prevent fraud on the part of retailers intent on inflating the value of lower-quality products in the manufacturer's complete line of products. There is evidence that retailers do misrepresent the manufacturer's products when the law prevents the manufacturer from maintaining control over the prices charged by its retailers.

Franchising

Franchising accounts for more than 38 percent of total sales at the retail level in North America. A **franchising agreement** is an arrangement between a parent firm (the franchisor) and a franchisee that authorizes the franchisee to sell the franchisor's brand-name product or service in exchange for a share of gross revenues.

The typical franchise contract requires the franchisee to maintain quality standards and agreed-upon hours of operation and prices. However, franchisees must normally pay an initial fixed fee and then share the gross retail revenues with the franchisor. The franchisor normally provides national advertising and training programs. As a means of maintaining control over the franchisee, the franchisor monitors and inspects the franchisee's performance and may terminate the agreement in case of violations.

There was a significant increase in franchising in the United States in the mid-1950s for three reasons: (1) the development of television reduced the cost of promoting national brands; (2) increased travel placed more consumers in unfamiliar geographical areas and increased their demand for a guaranteed level of quality; and (3) higher incomes increased the opportunity cost of searching for quality.

In 1983 there were 46.3 franchised outlets per 100,000 people in both the United States and France and 48.9 in Japan. Great Britain had only 14.9 outlets per 100,000 people. While fast foods dominate the franchise business, there are franchises for cleaning and printing services, video stores, day-care centers, health care, optical services, and funeral parlors. The United States is the largest exporter of franchises. In 1983 there were 395 companies controlling 23,524 outlets around the world. Kentucky Fried Chicken was the largest franchise chain in Great Britain in 1985, with 350 franchisees and plans for another 350 by the early 1990s.

Franchisor-Franchisee Conflicts

In Chapter 11 we discussed the advantages of maintaining a decentralized system for decision-making. Franchising may be an efficient means of accomplishing this objective. Franchising exploits the advantages of relying on franchisees to respond quickly to changes in the local market. The franchisee makes decisions concerning prices, sales effort, servicing, and the use of inputs. All affect the perceived quality of the brand. The franchisor advertises nationally and promotes the product's quality.

Despite these advantages, the franchisor faces potential problems in its dealings with franchisees. As noted in Chapter 10, it is nearly impossible to specify all decisions in a contract. It is also impossible to monitor completely the actions of the franchisee. In the absence of a completely specified contract and complete monitoring, both parties to the contract have the incentive to pursue their own interests to the detriment of the other party. For example, the franchisee may not invest as much locally in promoting the quality of a product that is sold to a large proportion of one-time customers in the franchisee's area.

Given the difficulties of successfully enforcing franchise contracts, firms may be inclined to choose vertical integration instead. For example, Burger King decided to buy back its ten franchised outlets in Great Britain in the mid-1980s to attempt to raise standards. There are two main reasons for not choosing vertical integration: (1) there are costs involved in relying on a vertically integrated structure and (2) there are legal constraints. Consider the following application.

Father doesn't always know best

In a case study of a restaurant franchisor, Professor John Shelton of the University of California at Los Angeles showed that the firm had significantly higher costs at the restaurants it owned and managed directly than at those run by franchisees. Unable to mention the name of the company in order to gain access to the company's records, he noted that there was no significant difference in owner-operated and franchised outlets except for the type of management.

The parent company prescribed all items on the menu, dictated recipes, provided all ingredients, and standardized the entire operation by issuing service manuals with detailed instructions. Although the franchisor preferred to use franchisees instead of direct ownership and management, they had to take over restaurants when a franchisee quit for any reason. The franchisor used experienced managers to run the restaurants it owned.

Professor Shelton found that revenues in excess of all expenses, except the manager's salary and income tax payments, were higher for the franchised outlets than for the directly managed outlets. For example, the revenues averaged 9.5 percent for franchised outlets and only 1.8 percent for directly owned and managed outlets, even though sales were essentially the same.

Only two of twenty-nine franchised restaurants showed losses, while eleven of twenty-four directly managed restaurants were unprofitable. According to company executives, the franchises were more profitable because they supervised and scheduled their staffs better and made a more determined effort to reduce waste. In the absence of a systematic study, it is not clear whether the difference was due to problems in monitoring the performance of managers or to the greater incentives offered franchisees.

Source: John P. Shelton, "Allocative Efficiency v. 'X-Efficiency': Comment." *American Economic Review* (December 1967):1252–58.

Unless the franchisor can maintain control over the prices and hours of operation of the franchisees, the franchisees may have an incentive to deviate from the manufacturer's profit-maximizing output and price level. The following application illustrates this limitation of franchises.

Wanted: shorter hours, higher profits

Professors John Barron and John Umbeck of Purdue University provided evidence that some firms may find that the costs of franchise arrangements exceed their benefits. They studied the effects of a Maryland law that prohibited oil refiners from directly operating gasoline stations in the state of Maryland. The refiners had to choose either to sell the stations they had owned or to establish franchises. If the refiners chose the franchise option, they were subject to a federal law that prohibited them from dictating the franchisees' hours of operation and retail prices.

Professors Barron and Umbeck collected data for seven refiners who owned a total of 170 stations that were subject to the Maryland law. Four of the seven refiners chose the franchise option sometime between 1978 and 1981. Once the refiner switched from directly operating stations to using franchises, it faced the same problem that Awesome Truck and other truck and car manufacturers faced in the exclusive-territory examples. The franchisee had an incentive to decrease output and raise prices to take advantage of the negatively-sloped demand curve for the brand of gasoline sold at the station. Unless the franchisor (that is, the refiner) dictated the final price of gasoline or otherwise forced the franchisee to choose the price desired by the refiner, the franchisee charged a higher price and sold less gasoline.

Professors Barron and Umbeck determined that, on the average, the new franchisees raised their prices by 6.7 cents for full-service gasoline and 1.4 cents for self-serve gasoline. Prior to the change in the law, these stations sold their gasoline at prices below those of nonrefiner-operated stations.

Higher retail prices and lower output levels benefit the franchisee and not the refiner. Since the refiner could not dictate retail prices and hours of operation, the Maryland law made the refiners worse off. In addition, despite the legislature's intent of helping consumers, the opposite occurred: franchisees raised gasoline prices.

Source: John M. Barron and John R. Umbeck, "The Effects of Different Contractual Arrangements: The Case of Retail Gasoline Markets." *Journal of Law and Economics* XXVII, No. 2 (October 1984):313–428. © by the University of Chicago.

The Avoidance of Opportunistic Behavior

The most common method of paying the franchisor is with a franchise fee and a royalty payment. For example, when McDonald's changed from direct ownership to franchising in Great Britain in 1985, it received between 300,000 and 500,000 pounds sterling (approximately $400,000 to $650,000 at the time) for each franchise fee and took a royalty payment of 8 percent of gross sales. At the time it had 165 directly-owned stores there.

If there were perfect certainty about the future value of a franchise, the franchisor would simply sell the rights of the franchise to the highest bidder among those competing for the franchise. Bidders would equate the cost of acquiring the franchise to the present value of the future stream of net revenues of operating the franchise.

Since information about the future is not perfect, the franchisor must develop alternative methods for maximizing profits. Although there is uncertainty about future demand and costs, there is also considerable uncertainty about both parties' commitment to the agreement. The franchisor depends on the franchisee to maintain quality and effort. The franchisee depends on the franchisor to promote the brand name and regulate other franchisees' behavior.

The combination of a fixed franchise fee and a royalty payment is a compromise for insuring compliance by both parties. For example, Paul Rubin argued that the more the franchised operation depends on the franchisee's input for its success, the more the franchisor will use the fixed fee relative to the royalty. By decreasing the royalty payment, the franchisor leaves more of the profit from additional sales with the franchisee and gives the franchisee more incentive to improve the performance of the franchise. The franchisor gains by extracting a higher franchise fee at the outset, since the most productive of the prospective franchisees will outbid the others.[2]

We can characterize the franchise fee as a bond against a franchisee's failure to comply with the provisions of the agreement. If the franchisor removes the franchise from the franchisee for failure to comply with the agreement, the franchisee forfeits the fee and the profits expected from future years of operating the franchise. It is the same as giving a loan to someone who promises to pay you back in high yearly payments. The arrangement is attractive as long as you continue to receive the payments. Failure to comply with the contract may result in termination of the payments. The franchise fee provides a bond against this type of behavior.

The more influence the brand name has on sales, the more likely that the franchisor will rely on a royalty payment. Note that if the franchisor lowers the franchise fee, it must compensate itself with a higher royalty payment. As the royalty payment increases, the franchisee receives a smaller return from each additional sale and has less incentive to work towards additional sales. If the brand name is the main influence on sales, there is less danger of hurting sales by lowering the percentage of revenues received by the franchisee.

Additional Legal Considerations

All of the vertical agreements that we have considered in this chapter obligate both parties to the contract. In the past, the United States government has considered several of these obligations anticompetitive. We have seen some examples already in this chapter. While we will concentrate on antitrust law in the next chapter, we will consider the legal aspects of vertical restraints now. While there has been a long and varied record on these issues in the United States, the position of the government and the Supreme Court today is relatively consistent and simple: only vertical restraints that fix the retail prices of independent retailers are likely to be illegal.

[2] Paul Rubin, "The Theory of the Firm and the Structure of the Franchise Contract." *Journal of Law and Economics* (April 1978):223–33.

On January 23, 1985, the Justice Department issued guidelines supporting most of the restraints that manufacturers impose on distributors and wholesalers. It indicated that it would not prosecute exclusive-dealing and exclusive-territory arrangements. It advised judges to follow the same guidelines in ruling on cases brought by private parties. The Justice Department has not pursued nonprice vertical constraints since the 1970s and has not filed any new cases in this area since 1980.

The National Association of Attorneys General does not share the federal government's favorable view of most vertical restraints. It voted unanimously in 1985 to combat vertical restraints to trade. It not only promised to prosecute violations of RPM, but it opposed nonprice restraints, such as exclusive territories to distributors and the tying of the sale of a manufacturer's products (discussed in Chapter 8). In addition, while the Justice Department might approve RPM as a means of forcing retailers to maintain lower prices when a retailer has an exclusive territory, the Association would consider it illegal.

Summary

In this chapter we analyzed some contractual arrangements between manufacturers, distributors, and retailers. We concentrated on alternatives to full vertical integration. We emphasized an economic efficiency justification for these practices, in opposition to the view that they are a means of increasing monopoly power in the market.

We started with situations faced by a vertically-integrated distributor-retailer in a market with many nonvertically-integrated distributors and retailers. Despite the United States government's position in support of most vertical restraints, we found that the FTC remains suspicious about functional discounts for distribution services.

Next, we turned to exclusive territories. Manufacturers grant exclusive territories to retailers to protect them from low-service competitors. Exclusive territories are important when the manufacturer depends on the retailer to provide information and services to potential customers. Unfortunately for the manufacturer and possibly the consumers, retailers with exclusive territories may have an incentive to raise prices and reduce sales to levels unacceptable to the manufacturer.

Since manufacturers cannot dictate final sales prices, an exclusive territory gives a retailer an incentive to charge a higher price to customers than the manufacturer desires. As a result, manufacturers may add other stipulations to the exclusive-territory arrangement to diminish this incentive. We concluded the section with an example concerning automobile sales.

We also discussed the reasons for requiring retailers to adopt exclusive-dealing arrangements. Despite some claims that exclusive dealing provides an incentive to promote the product, or that it facilitates an entry-blocking conspiracy, exclusive dealing protects the manufacturers. By using exclusive dealing, the manufacturer prevents a retailer from convincing customers to switch to another manufacturer's product. The argument depends on the ability of the retailer to convince customers of the advantages of a switch.

We then considered the control over the retail price of a manufacturer's product: resale price maintenance (RPM). Supporters of RPM argue generally as follows: while a manufacturer can prescribe territories, customers, and quality standards, it cannot dictate price. If the outlets are owned by the manufacturer, it can set the price.

Supporters contend that RPM is just one of the options available to the manufacturer in marketing its product. There is little incentive for the manufacturer to establish a system that overly favors the dealer. In effect, the manufacturer buys distribution services for its product. If the manufacturer could integrate manufacturing and distribution services more cheaply, it would do so. Both the manufacturer and the customer want distribution costs to be as low as possible. RPM can protect retailers, provide important informational and quality-enhancing services, and also help the manufacturer prevent retailer fraud.

In closing the chapter, we reviewed the U.S. government's overall policy concerning vertical restraints to trade. With the exception of price-fixing provisions, the government has generally accepted the remaining vertical restraints that firms impose on one another to insure compliance with implicit and explicit contracts. The debate on price-fixing restraints is likely to continue.

Important Terms

Functional Discounts (p. 335)
Exclusive Territory (p. 336)
Exclusive Dealing Agreements (p. 339)

Resale Price Maintenance (RPM) (p. 343)
Franchising Agreement (p. 348)

Selected References

Barron, John M., and Umbeck, John R. "The Effects of Different Contractual Arrangements: The Case of Retail Gasoline Markets." *Journal of Law and Economics* XXVII, No. 2 (October 1984):313–428.

Blair, Roger D., and Kaserman, David L. "Optimal Franchising." *Southern Economic Journal* 49, No. 2 (October 1982):494–505.

Marvel, Howard P. "Exclusive Dealing." *Journal of Law and Economics* XXV, No. 1 (April 1982):1–26.

Mathewson, G. Frank, and Winter, Ralph A. "The Economics of Franchise Contracts." *Journal of Law and Economics* XXVIII, No. 3 (October 1985):503–26.

Rubin, Paul. "The Theory of the Firm and the Structure of the Franchise Contract." *Journal of Law and Economics* (April 1978):223–33.

Shelton, J. "Allocative Efficiency v. 'X-Efficiency': Comment." *American Economic Review* (December 1967):1252–58.

Smith, Richard L., III. "Franchise Regulation: An Economic Analysis of State Restrictions on Automobile Distribution." *Journal of Law and Economics* XXV, No. 1 (April 1982):125–58.

1. Assume that the Don Fatalli Electrical Company has developed a new short wave, AM-FM radio. This radio has higher-quality reception than the other radios available but is relatively complicated to operate. When operated improperly the reception will be poor. Discuss the wisdom of using exclusive territories, exclusive dealing, and resale price maintenance to market Don Fatalli's new radio. Assume that the firm will not be prosecuted if it uses resale price maintenance. If there is important information that you would need to know before making these decisions, be sure to mention this in your answer.

2. Assume that you are the owner of the Awesome Truck Company and are interested in establishing a contractual arrangement with a dealer. Discuss the possibilities for opportunistic behavior on the part of the dealer and what efforts you might be able to make to control this behavior.

3. Assume that the United States government makes all functional discounts illegal in markets having both vertically-integrated distributor-retailers and independent retailers. What impact would this law have on retail prices?

4. The State of Delaware passed a law in the early 1980s that requires any automobile manufacturer considering opening a new dealership within seven miles of an existing dealership to obtain permission from a state regulatory agency. The existing dealer can appeal the decision of the agency in court. What is the likely effect of this law? Compare the effects of the law in the following two cases: (a) there is little growth in the state's population and (b) there is substantial growth in the state's population.

5. Discuss the likelihood that a manufacturer would use resale price maintenance, if it were legal, in selling the following products. Discuss the reasons for using it in these cases.

(a) Computers
(b) "Designer" clothes
(c) Washing machines
(d) Typewriter paper

Answer questions 6–12 with true, false, or uncertain.

6. If manufacturers could set the final retail price, they would have little incentive to use exclusive territories.

7. Exclusive territories are illegal, except where specifically permitted by state law.

8. Dealers are likely to react to the forced delivery of unordered cars by raising car prices.

9. The U.S. Justice Department has given RPM cases a high priority.

10. Without RPM, a manufacturer has less incentive to use exclusive territories.

11. If RPM were allowed, nearly all manufacturers would use it.

12. A manufacturer would be able to control any dealer who had an exclusive territory by imposing an exclusive dealership.

GOVERNMENT POLICY: INTRODUCTION

We have seen how the market imposes constraints on firms. To be free of others' influence a firm must have a monopoly position and an effective barrier to entry. Unfortunately for the monopolist, these are the market conditions most likely to encourage government intervention.

In previous chapters we saw some examples of the influence of government in the marketplace. In Chapters 13–15 we will look at the government's role more systematically. Regardless of the intentions or effectiveness of government policy, governments do impose constraints on firm behavior that supercede the forces of the market. As with any constraint, government regulations and laws provide incentives for firms to alter their behavior in the pursuit of profits.

We will concentrate on three major areas of government influence on economic activity: antitrust, regulation, and international trade policy. Since governments evaluate and change policy constantly in these areas, managers should be aware of the main forces and economic principles behind these political decisions. Often the policies have more political and social objectives than economic objectives. No matter what the principal objective of the policies, each law and regulation has an economic impact and influences firms' decisions.

In Chapter 13 we will start with antitrust law. After discussing the problems with monopoly, we will follow with a summary of the principal antitrust laws of the United States and how they compare with those in effect in Canada, Western Europe and Japan. We will finish with an analysis of the deterrent effects and economic impact of these antitrust laws.

Chapter 14 covers a wide range of regulations enacted by state and federal legislatures. We will see that the publicly-stated objective of these regulations is not always consistent with their impact on the market. We will discuss the principal reasons for regulation, including the more widely-known reasons as well as the lesser known and less altruistic motives. We will close the chapter with an analysis of some regulations in force today.

PART

IV

Chapter 15 will offer an analysis of international trade policy. Large fluctuations in the exchange rates between the U.S. dollar and other currencies and record U.S. trade deficits have focused much attention on trade policy, starting in the mid-1980s. There has been no lack of recommendations for government action.

Governments can affect international trade in many ways. They can and do use quotas, tariffs, export taxes, and subsidies to influence trading patterns. World trade has become a major component of all countries' business. No country and few firms can ignore the international aspect of their markets. We will focus on the implications of the major policy tools used by governments in regulating international trade. Throughout the chapter we will compare the impact of these restrictions to that of a policy of unrestricted trade.

13

EFFECTIVENESS OF U.S. ANTITRUST LAWS

Penalties and
Punitive Damages

Triple Damages

Standing

I n previous chapters we encountered the application of economic principles in several antitrust cases. In this chapter we will consider antitrust more systematically. In the latter half of the nineteenth century there was considerable concern regarding the market positions of several large firms, most notably railroads. Backed by a coalition of farmers, consumers, and small business owners, the U.S. Congress passed the first antitrust law in 1890: the Sherman Antitrust Act. This law directs the U.S. Department of Justice to prosecute firms that either restrain trade in a way that lessens competition or attempt to monopolize a market.

Since 1890 Congress, the courts, and the executive branch have wrestled with the problem of making and enforcing laws designed to maintain a competitive market environment for firms. Congress has added other antitrust laws aimed at promoting a general environment of competition in the marketplace. The primary concerns of Congress have been limiting the economic and political power of firms in the market and elimination of "unfair" competitive practices. The wording of the earlier laws is somewhat vague, even though Congress attempted to be more specific in later laws.

The body of antitrust law in the United States empowers the Justice Department and the Federal Trade Commission to prosecute violators. Since some laws are vaguely worded, the courts have the principal role in determining the objectives of the country's antitrust policy. When we consider each of the major areas of antitrust enforcement, we will see how important the judiciary's role has been in the evolution of U.S. antitrust policy.

Monopoly and the pursuit of monopoly appear to be the main focus of government antitrust and regulatory law. We will begin with the problem of monopoly. We will concentrate on efforts to measure the impact of monopoly on efficiency and the distribution of wealth and then offer a brief description of the most important antitrust laws.

Before discussing the enforcement of antitrust laws, we will consider some important preliminary issues: the definition of the market in antitrust cases and the choice between a rule of reason or a per se rule for settling cases. We will then consider each of the major antitrust areas: monopolization, price fixing, price discrimination, and mergers.

While you can find a discussion of the economics of each of these areas in previous chapters, we will concentrate here on the development of the U.S. government's current policy in regard to each of these issues. We will see how the courts and the government have moved away from an activist position on antitrust matters to more reliance on market forces. Throughout the chapter we will compare the antitrust policy of the United States to that of other countries.

At the end of the chapter we will discuss the effectiveness of the antitrust laws. We will concentrate on the deterrent effects, the use of triple damages as a means of punishing violators of the laws, the merits of limiting rights of harmed parties to sue for triple damages, and the wisdom of using the antitrust laws to protect specific industries experiencing market downturns.

The Problem with Monopoly

Before elaborating on enforcement and effectiveness, let's discuss the principal concern of antitrust law: monopoly and the pursuit of monopoly. In Chapter 5 we considered monopoly as a polar extreme of the perfectly competitive market. However, we did not emphasize the potential harm that monopolists can impose on a country's citizens. Monopolies can impose losses in efficiency due to higher prices, lower output, and diversion of resources into less socially desirable uses.

Politicians often focus on two additional concerns: the concentration of political power and increased inequality of wealth and opportunity. As firms become larger they may exercise more control over the political process and capture special benefits at the expense of citizens. Monopolization of markets may lead to greater wealth for the monopolists, while limiting the opportunities of others to earn a living. We will not dwell on the problem of political power here, however. The next two chapters, "Regulation" and "International Trade Policy," will devote more attention to these issues and concentrate on both the economic and political effects of government policy.

Before turning to the potential economic effects of monopoly, let's review some related issues that we considered in earlier chapters. In Chapter 7 we discussed pricing rules for firms facing competitors and potential competitors. We noted the difficulty that firms have in impeding entry to a market when government support is absent. We must not forget that monopolists have to maintain effective barriers to entry in order to maintain their market positions. Without effective barriers the firm will find that the market provides an effective constraint on their long-term behavior.

The distinction between a monopolist and a large firm should not be ignored. A monopolist is large relative to its own market but is not necessarily large relative to firms in general. More importantly, large firms are not necessarily monopolists because they are large. Firms may be large in absolute size because of scale economies in production, marketing, or research and development. For example, firms competing in several countries may require extensive marketing support, which, in turn, requires large firm size. As markets become more international, the definition of the market changes, and the calculation of market share changes.

FIGURE 13-1 ▪ **Consumer surplus.** The consumer surplus is the sum of the differences between each customer's demand price and the market price. At a market price of $3, the consumer surplus will equal the shaded area.

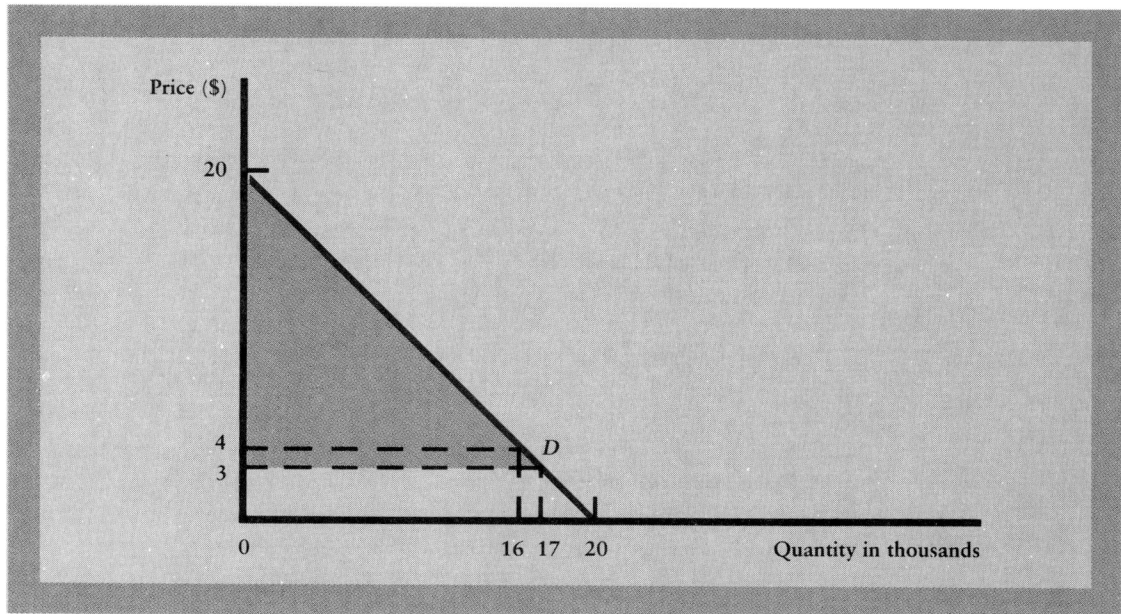

With these considerations in mind, we will look at two problems often associated with monopolies: inefficiency and potentially undesirable distribution of wealth. Both of these problems have provided justification for an active U.S. antitrust policy. Before turning to these problems, however, we will consider the issue of consumer surplus. The loss of consumer surplus is a measure of the efficiency loss due to monopoly.

Consumer Surplus

We will compare perfect competition and monopoly in terms of **consumer surplus**, which can be defined as the difference between the consumer's demand price and the market price. Consumer surplus measures the extra benefit a consumer gets by purchasing a good at a price that is less than the consumer's demand price. Consumer surplus for all consumers purchasing a good is the sum of the individual consumers' consumer surpluses.

In Chapter 6 we defined the demand price as the highest price a consumer would be willing to pay for one unit of a good when given a take-it-or-leave-it offer. Since consumers are not always required to pay the demand price, they gain something by paying the lower price. We can calculate the consumer surplus for all the consumers buying a product by adding up the individual consumer surpluses. We can use Figure 13-1 to show this procedure.

13-1   **Consumer surplus**

GRAPHICAL EXPLANATION

Figure 13-1 shows a straight-line demand curve with price indicated on the vertical axis and quantity demanded noted on the horizontal axis. Recall that the demand curve shows how many units the consumers will buy at each price during a specific period of time. If the price is $4, consumers will want 16,000 units of the good. If the price is $3, the number increases to 17,000. The one-dollar drop in price increases quantity demanded by 1,000.

Since the demand curve has a negative slope, only the last customer pays his or her demand price. All other consumers benefit by paying a market price, such as $3, that is less than their demand price. Since each customer's demand price varies, the overall market measure of consumer surplus is the area under the market demand and above the market price. At a market price of $3, consumer surplus would equal the shaded area. The shaded area forms a triangle with a height of 17 (that is, $20 - 3$) and a base of 17. Consumer surplus would be

$$\frac{1}{2}(17 \times 17) = 144.5.$$

Deadweight Loss

In Chapter 5 we determined that a monopolist produces a smaller output and charges a higher price than competitive firms do. Consider the monopolist's price and output in Figure 13-2. The monopolist chooses output Q_1 and price P_1 at the output level where marginal revenue equals marginal cost. This output and price will maximize the firm's short-run profits.

A competitive market producing the same output produces where marginal cost equals price. Recall that the competitive firm's marginal-cost curve is its supply curve. The market output occurs where the market supply curve crosses the market demand curve. Both of these explanations indicate that the competitive solution will be Q_2 and P_2.

The overall consumer surplus for a good will be a measure of the extra benefit that consumers get from purchasing the good at the market price. Since the market prices for a monopoly market and a competitive market differ, we should expect the consumer surplus of the two markets to differ also. We can now use Figure 13-2 to show the impact of the monopoly decision on consumer surplus. We will see that the monopolist imposes a deadweight loss on society. A **deadweight loss** is the consumer surplus that is

FIGURE 13-2 ▪ Deadweight loss. The perfectly competitive price and quantity are P_2 and Q_2. Consumers will receive area *abc* in consumer surplus. If a firm monopolizes the market and charges price P_1, consumers will receive only area *ade* in consumer surplus. The remaining consumer surplus will go to the monopolist as a transfer (area *decf*). Area *dbf* is the deadweight loss.

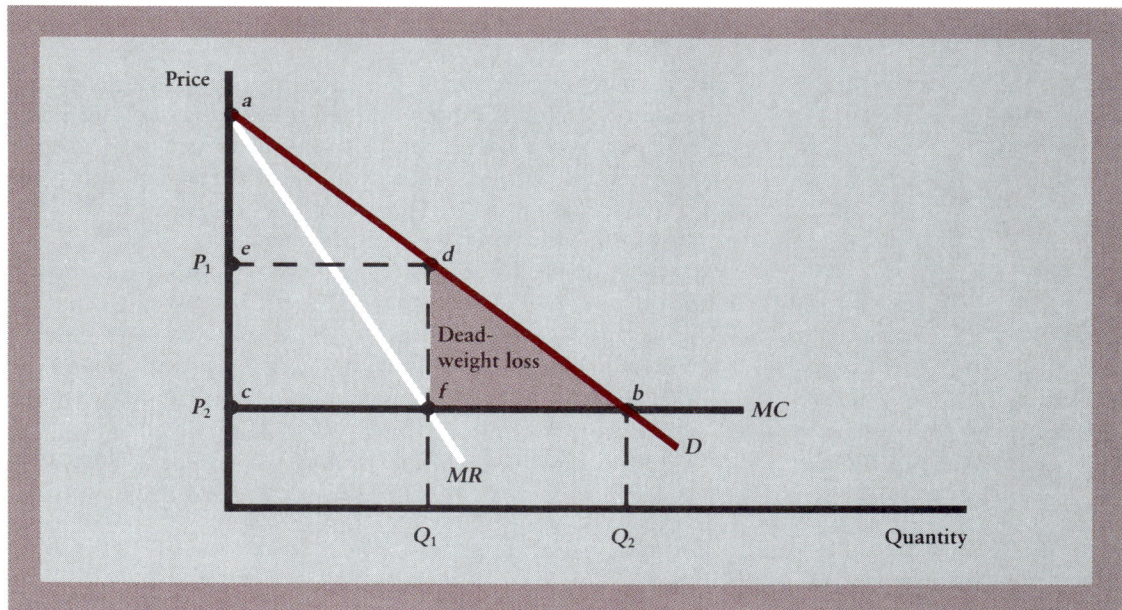

not recovered by any member of society when the monopolist imposes a higher price and lower output than a competitive market would impose.

GRAPHICAL EXPLANATION

Recall that the demand price is the highest price that each consumer is willing to pay given a take-it-or-leave-it offer. Since individual consumers differ in their demand prices, the market demand curve in this case will have a negative slope. Consumer surplus, as defined earlier, will be the difference between the demand price and the market price of each consumer.

At the competitive price of P_2 in Figure 13-2, consumers will purchase Q_2 units of the good. Those consumers with the highest demand prices will receive the greatest benefit from the competitive price, because they will experience the largest difference between their demand price and the market price. Consumer surplus for all the consumers will be the difference between the area under the demand curve and the area under the price line at P_2. Consumer surplus in this case will be the area *abc*.

Since the monopoly price is higher, the consumer surplus will be less. The area between the demand curve and the new price P_1 is *ade*. The difference in consumer surplus is the area of the trapezoid *decb*. The loss in consumer surplus has two components: area *decf* and area *dbf*. The losses of these two areas represent two different consequences of monopolization. Area *decf* represents a transfer of consumer surplus from consumers to the monopolist. When the price was P_2 consumers received the consumer surplus associated with this area. Now the monopolist takes this area as economic profits. The area *dbf* is different. It represents a deadweight loss—that is, a loss to society that no one recovers.

The triangle *dbf* represents the consumer surplus that consumers would have received by consuming the additional $(Q_2 - Q_1)$ units at price P_2. Since the firm only produces Q_1 units of the good, no one can receive consumer surplus for output greater than Q_1 units.

Several researchers have attempted to measure the size of this deadweight loss for the U.S. economy. The following Application summarizes these efforts.

APPLICATION

Professor Arnold Harberger of the University of Chicago was the first to measure the deadweight loss imposed by monopoly power in the United States. He studied the profitability of seventy-three U.S. manufacturing industries from 1924 to 1928. These industries represented 45 percent of all U.S. manufacturing at the time. He determined that the total deadweight loss for these industries was $26.5 million.

By applying these results to the entire U.S. economy, he concluded that the deadweight loss would not have exceeded 0.1 percent of the U.S. gross national product (GNP). In the late 1980s this would have equaled approximately $22 per person—enough for a complete steak dinner at a good restaurant. In Professor Harberger's opinion, the deadweight loss was not large enough to justify the effort of a vigorous antitrust policy.

Several researchers have attempted to extend Harberger's study. Some have made adjustments to the procedure by relaxing one or more of his assumptions. Although some have found higher estimates for later years, the order of magnitude is in the same general range as these earlier results. In the most recent of these studies, Professor Micha Gisser of the University of New Mexico used a larger sample of data and a more sophisticated methodology to conclude that the deadweight loss was only 0.114 percent of the GNP.

Sources: Arnold C. Harberger, "Monopoly and Resource Allocation." *American Economic Review* 44 (May 1954):77–87.

Micha Gisser, "Price Leadership and Welfare Losses in U.S. Manufacturing." *American Economic Review* 76, No. 4 (September 1986):756–67.

Rent Seeking

There are economic costs in addition to the deadweight loss. For example, we have treated the consumer surplus going from consumers to the monopolist as a pure transfer. Some observers have argued that there may be additional costs associated with this transfer of consumer surplus. As we have seen already, people do not sit idly waiting for economic benefits. Those most likely to benefit from economic transfers invest resources to the point where the expected marginal cost of obtaining the benefits equals the marginal benefit. This activity is called rent-seeking behavior, since those doing the seeking are pursuing economic gains or rents over and above their costs. **Economic rents** are returns to assets that exceed the opportunity costs of these assets. **Rent seeking** is the process of finding and attracting economic rents.

In Chapters 14 and 15 we will see several examples of rent-seeking behavior on the part of firms attempting to influence regulatory and trade policy to their advantage. In this chapter we will also see examples of firms using the antitrust laws to their own benefit. The part of the transfer that represents the cost of seeking the transfer could be significantly greater than the deadweight losses.

Distribution of Wealth

Loss of efficiency may not be the only effect of monopoly. While economists normally focus on efficiency, others, including politicians, emphasize fairness and the distribution of wealth. The following Application offers evidence that monopoly power has substantially affected the distribution of wealth in the United States.

13-2

How did you get your wealth?

APPLICATION

Professors William Comanor and Robert Smiley measured the effect of monopoly on the distribution of wealth. They noted that the main beneficiaries of monopoly are those who create the monopoly, not necessarily those who currently own a firm with monopoly power. If the current owners did not create the monopoly, they had to purchase it from someone who did. Since both the original owner and the prospective owners can anticipate a future stream of economic profits after the sale, prospective owners will compete with one another and bid up the purchase price.

The higher purchase price will most likely incorporate the value of the expected future benefit of having the monopoly position. For example, seats on the New York Stock Exchange are limited. These seats are sold from time to time at high prices. The scarcity of seats makes having one valuable. While the value may increase over time, the current selling price reflects the expected future value of owning the seat. Someone buying the seat will most likely not earn economic profits unless there is an additional unanticipated restriction that further limits the availability of seats.

Based on the results of others' research, Professors Comanor and Smiley assumed that monopoly profits net of taxes represent 3 percent of the annual gross national product. Using data from 1890, the year of the passage of the Sherman Antitrust Act, to 1962, they concluded that a substantial amount of the assets of the wealthiest people in the United States came from the creation of monopolies.

For example, the wealthiest segment of households (those having net worth exceeding $500,000 in 1962) represented 0.27 percent of the number of households but held 18.5 percent of total wealth. Professors Comanor and Smiley determined that without the power to create monopoly this group's share of total wealth would drop to between 3 and 10 percent.

Source: William S. Comanor and Robert H. Smiley, "Monopoly and the Distribution of Wealth." *Quarterly Journal of Economics* LXXXIX, No. 2 (May 1975):177–94. © 1975 by the President and Fellows of Harvard College. Reprinted by permission of John Wiley & Sons, Inc.

The Antitrust Laws

In 1890 the U.S. Congress passed the Sherman Antitrust Act in response to the alleged monopolistic behavior of the railroad, tobacco, steel, and oil trusts of that time. A **trust** is a combination of firms that form to set price and output as a single, monopolistic firm. Following is a brief description of the three principal antitrust laws. We will expand our discussion of these laws later.

The Sherman Antitrust Act

The Sherman Antitrust Act of 1890 prohibits firms from restraining trade to lessen competition. There are two substantive sections of the act. Section 1 prohibits collusive combinations and conspiracies that lessen competition. Section 2 prohibits firms from monopolizing or attempting to monopolize a market.

There are also important procedural sections. Section 4 authorizes the Attorney General to initiate court cases to stop violations of the act. Section 7 permits private individuals to sue for triple the damages that they may have incurred due to a violation of the act. Congress gives the Justice Department the authority to enforce the Sherman Act through either criminal or civil law.

The Clayton Act

After twenty-four years of experience with the Sherman Act, the U.S. Congress decided that the focus of antitrust law should be on restraining the growth of monopoly at an early stage. In 1914 it passed the Clayton Act. The Clayton Act addresses the potential anticompetitiveness of price discrimination, tying arrangements, exclusive arrangements, and mergers. The Clayton Act also makes it easier for individuals to sue for triple damages by allowing the results of government victories in antitrust cases to be used as evidence in triple-damages suits.

We discussed the economics of each of these practices (that is, price discrimination, tying arrangements, exclusive arrangements, and mergers) in earlier chapters. In each case we mentioned the relevant antitrust laws in an Application. The Clayton Act prohibits these practices when they lead to anticompetitive behavior. Later in this chapter we will return to them in more detail and assess the impact of the Clayton Act.

There have been two important amendments to the Clayton Act: the Robinson-Patman Act and the Celler-Kefauver Act. Congress created the Robinson-Patman Act in 1936 in response to charges that large, national retailers were forcing small, independent retailers out of business by price discrimination practices. The Robinson-Patman Act was an amendment to Section 2 of the Clayton Act. Although the Clayton Act prohibited price discrimination as a tool for anticompetitive behavior, Congress used the

Robinson-Patman Act to document more specifically the type of behavior it found unacceptable.

Neither the Federal Trade Commission (FTC) nor the Department of Justice had much success in prosecuting merger cases under the Clayton Act. There were legal loopholes that the companies found to avoid prosecution. In response to this problem Congress passed the Celler-Kefauver Act, amending the Clayton Act, in 1950. The Celler-Kefauver Act gave the FTC and the Department of Justice the authority to prosecute any merger that lessened competition.

The Federal Trade Commission Act

Congress also passed the Federal Trade Commission (FTC) Act in 1914. The FTC Act created the FTC. Section 5 of this act prohibits "unfair methods of competition." This vague mandate leaves the task of interpreting the extent of unfair methods to the Supreme Court. The act essentially gave the FTC joint responsibility with the Justice Department for enforcing U.S. antitrust law.

Background Issues

We will now consider two preliminary issues that pertain to all of the antitrust laws: the choice of either a rule of reason or a per se rule and the definition of the market. We will refer to both of these issues when we discuss enforcement.

Rule of Reason versus a Per Se Rule

The courts use one of two criteria in deciding cases: a rule of reason or a per se rule. A **rule of reason** requires the prosecution to show that the defendant committed the offense and that there were no mitigating circumstances to justify the defendant's actions. Even if the defendant committed the offense, (s)he can avoid conviction by showing that his or her actions were reasonable considering the circumstances at the time. With a **per se rule**, if the defendant committed the act, the defendant is guilty. Whether the action was reasonable or not is not an issue in the case.

The U.S. courts use a rule of reason to interpret most of the antitrust laws. A notable exception, however, is price fixing. Price fixing is illegal per se in the United States. In nearly all other countries the courts use a rule of reason for price-fixing cases. In the United States the prosecution only has to establish that the defendants conspired to fix prices. The rationale or ultimate successfulness of the price-fixing agreement is not a relevant issue in deciding the outcome of the case.

Per se rules simplify the legal process. Questions concerning the motives of the offenders or the effectiveness of price fixing are irrelevant. While this simplification leads to quicker trials and lower-cost enforcement, it ignores the possibility of extenuating circumstances. Because of the complexity of the issues involved in most antitrust decisions, the courts have had to resort to a rule of reason in other areas of antitrust. This process can lead to long delays and costly trials.

Definition of the Market

Throughout the text we have been discussing the nature of the market. The definition of the market plays an important role in the outcome of many court cases. The definition of a market has been especially important in monopolization and merger cases. In Chapter 2 we saw that cross-price elasticities were factors in the Du Pont and Brown Shoe cases (see Applications 2-8 and 2-9). The secondary aluminum market was an important factor in whether ALCOA had a monopoly of its market (see Application 6-2).

With markets becoming increasingly more international, the conventional notion of a national or even regional market is changing. By international standards, few firms would be large enough to dominate the world market. Compounding the problem of an international market is the network of restrictive trade practices that limit entry to many countries' domestic markets. In Chapter 15 we will elaborate on these problems.

The Department of Justice has tried to add precision to its methods for determining markets. It issued merger guidelines in 1982 and revised them in 1984. In 1984 it altered its definition of the market by defining regional markets according to the likelihood that price increases in the regional market would not encourage market entry. A separate regional market would exist if firms in the market could raise their prices by colluding permanently, without encouraging entry from firms located in other regional or foreign markets. By defining a regional market in this way, the Justice Department would then determine whether a merger would impair competition in the market, by calculating the market power of firms both before and after the proposed merger. Both the Justice Department and the FTC look at the impact of a merger on international, national, and regional markets within the United States. As a result, they have often approved mergers once the merging companies have agreed to sell assets to avoid unacceptably high levels of market power in specific regional markets.

13-3

APPLICATION

What's left over for us?

In two oil mergers involving refinery and distribution operations—Texaco's acquisition of Getty and Chevron's acquisition of Gulf—the Justice Department treated the northeastern region as a distinct market. As a condition for allowing these mergers to proceed, the Justice Department demanded that the firms sell off some of their assets in the region (for example, gas stations) to avoid unacceptably high levels of market power.

The northeastern region is one of four regions for refining petroleum products located east of the Rocky Mountains and is concentrated mostly near Philadelphia. Another region is concentrated near New Orleans, and a third in the Midwest. There is also a smaller Appalachian region. Imports come into the area primarily from the Caribbean and Europe.

Since the time of those two mergers, David Scheffman of the FTC and Pablo Spiller of the Hoover Institution have developed a statistical technique to aid the Department of Justice in determining relevant markets. They suggest that the Justice Department should calculate the demand facing the regional market. In this way they can determine the elasticity of demand faced by the producers in the market.

If the elasticity of demand faced by producers has been elastic, price increases in the market that have been greater than price increases outside the market increase the sales by refiners located in other markets. Unless the elasticity of demand faced by those in the market has been inelastic, a collusive agreement among the producers in the market to raise prices invites refiners in other regions to enter the market.

By concentrating on the elasticity of this residual demand (that is, net of the demand faced by refiners located outside the region), Scheffman and Spiller can determine the extent to which average price can increase in a region without encouraging entry by refiners outside the region. They considered four possible market definitions for oil refining east of the Rockies: (a) the whole area east of the Rocky Mountains, (b) the Gulf Coast and the East Coast, (c) the Northeast and the Appalachian region, and (d) the Northeast by itself. They calculated the demand faced by the producers in each of the four possible markets as a function of the prices received by producers in the excluded regions. Then they were able to determine elasticities of demand due to changes in prices both within the region and outside the region.

They determined that the market east of the Rockies would meet the Justice Department's definition of a market, because an increase in the price of refined oil in the region would not have encouraged a significant change in imports coming from the Caribbean and Europe. Market area (b), which excludes the Midwest and imports from the market definition, would also satisfy the conditions necessary for being a separate market.

According to their results, market (c) also constitutes a separate market, while the Northeast alone does not. They found that if refiners in the Northeast colluded and raised prices above competitive levels, refiners from the Appalachian region would enter the market in significant numbers. The Justice Department did not have the statistical technique proposed by Scheffman and Spiller at its disposal at the time it decided that the Northeast was the relevant market.

Source: David T. Scheffman and Pablo T. Spiller, "Geographic Market Definition under the U.S. Department of Justice Merger Guidelines." *Journal of Law and Economics* XXX (April 1987):123–47. © by the University of Chicago.

Enforcement

We now look at how the courts have interpreted the antitrust laws and consider the main enforcement areas of monopoly, price fixing, price discrimination, and mergers. We have already looked closely at the legal ramifications of other more specialized areas of antitrust law in earlier chapters: tying arrangements (Chapter 6) and resale price maintenance and exclusive arrangements (Chapter 12). Since these are self-contained analyses within their respective chapters, we will not repeat them here.

Price Fixing

Despite a general inaction in the enforcement of antitrust statutes since the late 1970s, the Justice Department has continued to prosecute price-fixing cases. The department has been primarily successful against contractors bidding for government contracts. Except in cases where the buyer is the federal government or one of the state governments or agencies, price-fixing agreements have been unstable or largely ineffective. In Chapter 7 we discussed the difficulties of maintaining collusive agreements among producers of most products.

The U.S. courts prosecute price fixing according to a per se rule. The courts established this precedent in the Trenton Potteries decision of 1923 and reaffirmed it in the Socony Vacuum Company case of 1940. In order to establish a violation of antitrust law, the prosecution only has to show that a conspiracy to fix prices took place.

13-4

It depends on the country

APPLICATION

Nearly all industrialized, Western countries have antitrust laws. As in the United States, antitrust policy is in constant evolution throughout the world. The United States has had the most stringent antitrust laws, with Great Britain being the next most stringent.

The United States is one of the few countries with a per se provision for price fixing. By contrast, Great Britain does allow defendants to offer evidence justifying their actions. The British courts have accepted a defense based on a need to compete more effectively in export markets by colluding with one's compatriots. While Canada's first antitrust law preceded the Sherman Act by one year, and an amendment in 1976 made the collusive rigging of bids illegal per se, enforcement in past years has been largely ineffective.

West Germany permits exceptions that promote efficiency among small firms, promote joint research, or help stagnating industries adjust. France allows firms to show that there are gains in efficiency or technological change due to the collusive agreement. Until 1977, there was little effort in France to

---

enforce price-fixing statutes. Although Japan prohibits price fixing, it condones cartels. Japan had 175 export cartels in force in 1972. Japan's Fair Trade Commission is responsible for antitrust policy but works closely with the Ministry of International Trade and Industry in evaluating cases for prosecution.

Source: Paraphrasing from F.M. Scherer, *Industrial Market Structure and Economic Performance*, Second Edition, pp. 504–508. Copyright © 1980 by Houghton Mifflin Company.

Monopoly

The Justice Department had to wait until 1911 to score its first major successes under the Sherman Act. In 1911 it won monopoly cases against the tobacco and oil trusts. As a result of these victories, the defendants were split into several smaller companies. (See Application 7-6 for background information on the tobacco trust.)

In its opinion against the Standard Oil Trust, the Supreme Court established two elements necessary for conviction: monopoly power and the intent to monopolize the market and keep rivals out of the market. While the Supreme Court awarded the Department of Justice several victories in the intervening years, the Department of Justice lost a case in 1919 against U.S. Steel despite the firm's dominant position in the market (see Application 7-3 for additional details). The court ruled that U.S. Steel had not exercised monopoly power, even if it had possessed it. Working in the company's favor was the supportive testimony of its competitors who stated that U.S. Steel's pricing policies did not harm them in any way.

The decision in the 1945 Aluminum Company of America (ALCOA) case is in sharp contrast to the decision in the U.S. Steel case (see Application 7-2). There were two primary issues in this case: ALCOA's market share and ALCOA's intent to monopolize the market. As a result of this decision, the Supreme Court set guidelines for future prosecutions. A firm must have a sizable market share to be considered a monopoly, and it has to establish an intent to monopolize the market.

ALCOA had a sufficiently large share of the market to meet the Supreme Court's criterion for monopoly power. Curiously, the court claimed that ALCOA had the intent to continue to monopolize the market. ALCOA had maintained a return on capital of approximately 10 percent per year. While the court did not consider this rate of return excessive (that is, ALCOA earned profits comparable to firms in a competitive market), the court convicted ALCOA of noncompetitive behavior. With this decision the Supreme Court left doubt as to whether it was defending the competitive process or the competitors.

Despite a temporary upsurge in monopolization cases in the late 1960s and early 1970s, the Justice Department and FTC have now shied away from monopolization cases. For example, the Justice Department abandoned cases pending against IBM and American Telephone and Telegraph in the early 1980s, after spending nearly thirteen years without successful prosecution. While the principles set by the ALCOA case remain in force, neither the Justice Department nor the FTC sees the merits of prolonged court cases trying to establish intent to monopolize. They have instead focused on enforcing merger guidelines to prevent monopolization through merger.

Price Discrimination

Most of Chapter 6 dealt with the economics of price discrimination. Section 2 of the Clayton Act, as amended by the Robinson-Patman Act, prohibits price discrimination that impairs competition. The law prohibits price differences on goods of similar quality unless the defendant can show that the difference in price was due to the disposal of perishable goods, cost differences, or a response in good faith to the low price of a competitor. Economists have generally criticized the interpretation of this law. The courts have tended to protect competitors rather than the competitive process. Consider the following evidence.

13-5	**Winning is all that matters**

APPLICATION

Professor Scherer questions whether or not the main beneficiaries of the Robinson-Patman Act are attorneys. Despite the intent of protecting small firms, small firms have been the main targets of Robinson-Patman cases. Only 6.4 percent of the defendants in cases brought by the FTC between 1961 and 1974 had sales greater than $100 million a year. Sixty percent had sales below $5 million.

Of the cases involving firms with less than $10 million of annual sales, 84 to 95 percent ended in settlements before the start of litigation. Only 37 percent of the cases involving the larger firms ended this way. While none of the smaller firms ever succeeded in having charges against them dismissed, 23 percent of the larger firms did. Professor Scherer argues that in the 1960s and early 1970s FTC lawyers preferred "to run up their success tallies bullying small companies unlikely to fight back vigorously." The FTC decreased the number of these cases from an average of 74 per year between 1960 and 1965 to 5.6 between 1966 and 1970. The FTC does not prosecute these cases today.

Source: Paraphrasing from F.M. Scherer, *Industrial Market Structure and Economic Performance*, Second Edition, pp. 580–581. Copyright © 1980 by Houghton Mifflin Company.

Despite this lack of federal enforcement of the Robinson-Patman Act, private suits are still occurring. In addition, most states have laws against price discrimination and some states go even further by limiting firms' flexibility in setting prices.

Robert Fenili and William Lane analyzed state laws that limit firms' flexibility in setting prices for gasoline. In 1982, twenty-eight states either had laws specifically controlling gasoline pricing or had general laws that also pertained to gasoline pricing. Fenili and Lane examined weekly retail prices for gasoline in 1982 for forty-three metropolitan areas in the United States. Nineteen were in states that had no law affecting gasoline pricing.

They controlled for the effects of wholesale prices, income, costs of labor, weather, land values, number of cars in the area, and number of gas stations. They found that prices were consistently higher in states that limited price flexibility. For example, prices averaged 2.67 cents higher per gallon at full-service pumps and 0.9 cents higher at self-service pumps. While these differences may appear small, the estimated cost to consumers per year on sales of regular gasoline was more than $640 million.

Fear of legal action can inhibit firms with cost advantages from using price as a competitive weapon. They note that in Idaho a brief price war ended as soon as one gasoline retailer threatened legal action under the state law. This threat is not confined to gasoline marketing. The authors of the study suggested that gasoline amounts to only 9 percent of all merchandise sold at the retail level. Since the general pricing laws cover the entire retail market, an extrapolation of the effects of these laws to all retail trade could have amounted to a $6.7 billion cost to consumers in 1982.

Source: Robert N. Fenili and William C. Lane, "Thou Shalt Not Cut Prices! Sales-Below-Cost Laws for Gas Stations." *Regulation* (September/October 1985):31–35. With permission of the American Enterprise Institute.

Mergers

Although the Clayton Act of 1914 made mergers that lessened competition illegal, there were loopholes in the law that made it ineffective. In 1950 Congress closed the loopholes by passing the Celler-Kefauver Act.

We can place mergers in five categories: horizontal, vertical, product-extension, market-extension, and pure-conglomerate. A **horizontal merger** is a merger of two or more firms producing similar products in the same market area. A **vertical merger** is a merger of one firm with another firm that supplies a good that the first firm buys as an input. A **product-extension conglomerate merger** is a merger of two firms that produce related but not similar products in the same market area. A **market-extension conglomerate merger** is a merger of two firms producing similar products in different market areas. A **pure conglomerate merger** is any merger not covered by the other four definitions.

The Historical Record The courts have treated product-extension, market-extension, and pure conglomerate mergers differently from horizontal and vertical mergers. Despite some victories by the Justice Department in the 1960s (see Application 9-1 for an example), the Justice Department and the FTC have had little success against conglomerate mergers since the early 1970s. Despite earlier concerns that conglomerate mergers would foreclose markets or increase overall consolidation of economic power, research has shown no apparent negative effects of these mergers on competition.

Through the 1950s and 1960s the Supreme Court found the horizontal mergers of even relatively smaller firms anticompetitive. The Von's Grocery case is an example.[1] Von's Grocery was the third largest grocery retailer in the Los Angeles area, with a 4.7 percent share of the market in 1958. It merged with Shopping Bag Food Stores, the sixth largest retailer, which had a 2.8 percent share. The market leader, Safeway, had an 8 percent share.

The Supreme Court found this merger anticompetitive, citing trends to unacceptably high levels of concentration of market power. It noted that the number of independent, single-unit grocery stores dropped from 5,365 to 3,818 between 1950 and 1961. The market share of the top twenty chains went from 44 percent in 1948 to 57 percent in 1958.

In response to requests from businesses seeking guidance on future mergers, the Justice Department issued formal guidelines in 1968. Although the Justice Department reserved the right to challenge any merger it deemed anticompetitive, it specified market shares and levels of market concentration in line with the precedent established in the Supreme Court cases.

For example, the Justice Department challenged mergers involving firms with as little as 4 percent of the market when the combined market share of the four largest firms exceeded 75 percent. In less concentrated markets, it challenged mergers between firms with 5 percent market shares. If there was a trend toward increasing concentration in the market, it challenged the merger of one of the eight largest firms with a firm having as little as 2 percent of the market. The Department of Justice also considered challenging a vertical merger between a firm that supplied 10 percent of the market with a firm that bought 6 percent or more of the good.

The 1960s marked the peak of U.S. government activity against mergers. Since the mid-1970s it has been less willing to challenge mergers other than horizontal mergers. The Justice Department issued new guidelines in 1982 and revised them in 1984. The FTC acknowledged that it would follow the

---

[1] *U.S. v. Von's Grocery Co. et al.*, 384 U.S. 270 (1966).

Justice Department's guidelines. While the guidelines specify a wider range of more acceptable horizontal mergers, they essentially permit all vertical and conglomerate mergers that do not have anticompetitive horizontal effects.

The Herfindahl Index   We have already discussed the definition of the market used by the Justice Department. The difference from the 1968 guidelines concerns the measure of market concentration. The new guidelines rely on a measure of market power called the Herfindahl Index. The **Herfindahl Index** (H) is a measure of the concentration of the market for a product according to the following formula:

$$H = (S_1)^2 + (S_2)^2 + \ldots + (S_n)^2,$$

where S_i indicates the market share of the ith firm, where i is a number from 1 to n. A firm will have a market share of between 0 and 100 percent.

13-1	Herfindahl Index

NUMERICAL EXAMPLE

The Herfindahl Index ranges from 0 to 10,000. For example, if there were only one firm in the market, the Herfindahl Index would be

$$H = (100)^2 = 10,000.$$

If there were n equal-sized firms, each with a $(1/n) \times 100$ percent share of the market, the Herfindahl Index would be

$$H = n\left(\frac{1}{n} \times 100\right)^2$$

$$= n\left(\frac{10,000}{n^2}\right)$$

$$= \frac{10,000}{n}.$$

If n were infinitely large, the Herfindahl Index would be zero. If there were ten equal-sized firms, the index would be 1,000. Most markets have indexes between the two extremes of 0 and 10,000.

The Justice Department will consider challenging a merger between two firms if the Herfindahl Index increases by 50 or more points and the market Herfindahl Index is 1,800 or greater. If the index is between 1,000 and 1,800 and the index increases by more than 100 points, the Justice Department will also consider challenging the merger. Below 1,000 the Justice Department is not likely to challenge the merger.

Note what happens to the Herfindahl Index when two firms merge. Assume that Firm 1 has a market share of A percent and Firm 2 has a market share of B percent. Prior to a merger, the Herfindahl Index is the sum of the squares of the firms' market shares. In this case the Herfindahl Index, H_1, includes A^2 and B^2 in addition to the contribution made to the index by the market shares of the remaining firms.

$$H_1 = A^2 + B^2 + \ldots.$$

After a merger, the new firm has a market share of $A + B$. The new index, H_2, is

$$H_2 = (A + B)^2 + \ldots.$$

The difference in the two values is $H_2 - H_1$, or

$$(A + B)^2 - A^2 - B^2 = A^2 + 2AB + B^2 - A^2 - B^2$$
$$= 2AB.$$

For example, if A is 7 percent and B is 8 percent, $2AB$ is $2(7)(8)$, or 112. Since the change in the index exceeds 100, the Justice Department might challenge a merger between these two firms provided the market Herfindahl Index is greater than 1,000.

The U.S. government's policy on horizontal mergers loosened considerably in the 1980s. After denying two bids by Heileman to take over Pabst and a bid to take over Schlitz in the early 1980s, the Justice Department allowed Heileman's takeover of Pabst in 1984. The combined national market shares of the two firms actually increased during the time of the takeover attempts. For example, Heileman had a 4.3 percent share in 1978, 9.7 percent in 1983, and nearly 10 percent in 1984. Pabst's share dropped from 9.3 percent in 1978 to 7.1 percent in 1983.

Although a Herfindahl Index based on 1983 national market shares would have been close to 2,000, and the index would have increased by approximately 68 points with the merger, the Justice Department was primarily concerned with the merger's impact on regional markets. As we noted earlier when discussing the definition of the market, the Justice Department and the FTC have resolved most contested mergers by requiring regional restructuring of the companies. In this case, Heileman had to sell part of Pabst to others. Included in the sale were Olympia, Hamm's, and two other smaller brands.

Rivals' Use of the Antitrust Laws to Block Mergers   The Supreme Court has always been suspicious of competitors' attempts to use the antitrust laws to gain an advantage. In December 1986, the court made it more difficult for companies to use the antitrust laws to block mergers involving a company's rivals. The ruling came in the case of an acquisition by Cargill, Incorporated of Land O'Lakes' Spencer Beef division. A competitor challenged the acquisition and forced a halt to the merger in 1983. The court ruled that the competitor must show a real anticompetitive threat, rather than a deteriorating position in its own market share due to an increase in competition in the market.

The Justice Department testified in the case before the Supreme Court seeking the court's ban on all private suits contesting mergers involving possible predatory or other below-cost pricing. While the court agreed that harm was rare in such cases, it refused to grant the Justice Department's request. While the Supreme Court was unwilling to stop all private challenges to mergers, it has made it more difficult for these private suits to succeed in stopping a merger.

Merger Policy in Other Countries   After World War II the U.S. Occupation Forces forced the breakup of several large Japanese and German companies to prevent a recurrence of military buildup in these countries. The United States soon found that this policy was counterproductive to the countries' efforts to rebuild their economies. Except for this experience, there appears to be no other example outside the United States of efforts to break up large firms having monopoly positions in the market.

In contrast to this, the U.S. Supreme Court resolved the 1911 case against Standard Oil of New Jersey by splitting the company into thirty-three components. The court diminished ALCOA's market share by awarding wartime aluminum plants to ALCOA's competitors. In its case against IBM during the 1970s, the Justice Department threatened to split the company into as many as ten separate companies.

13-8	**Another way of doing it**

APPLICATION   The governments of other countries have been less willing to use their antitrust laws to make large corporate structural changes. Although the British Monopolies Commission has had the authority to recommend such remedies since 1965, it has been reluctant to exercise this power. Instead it has focused on reducing entry barriers. Great Britain has also taken a more direct role in regulating the behavior of large, dominant firms.

For example, the Monopolies Commission tried to force Procter & Gamble and Unilever to lower their prices by 20 percent on household detergents. It settled instead for an agreement requiring the two companies to introduce nonadvertised detergents at 20 percent discounts from their advertised brands. The opposition Labor Party has proposed banning any merger unless the companies can prove that the mergers are in the public interest. While Great Britain has allowed mergers of some large firms to make them competitive internationally, it has considered challenging others that would not be large in international markets.

West Germany has also preferred to regulate the behavior of large firms rather than alter their structure. Under a change in the law in 1974, the West German Federal Cartel Office started forcing large firms to lower prices. For example, in 1977 it forced the three largest automobile makers to forgo a contemplated price increase.

In 1986, France tightened its control over mergers in anticipation of tighter rules proposed by the European Economic Community (EEC). The government must approve mergers that will generate sales in excess of seven billion Francs per year (approximately $1.2 billion) or that will create a firm with a share of the French market greater than 25 percent. France seems more concerned than most countries about takeovers by foreign companies. The only merger formally blocked between 1977 and 1986 was a proposed takeover by an American company of a French firm.

Despite efforts to make the Common Market countries one market by the early 1990s, there has been reluctance on the part of the member countries to think beyond the limits of their own borders in devising merger policy. Countries have imposed limits on takeovers by companies from other countries and have not acknowledged the impact of foreign competition on markets.

Europeans have adopted the U.S. practice of requiring merging firms to sell parts of the firms if there is a fear of decreased competition in parts of the market area. For example, the West German Cartel Office permitted the Daimler-Benz and AEG merger after the companies agreed to sell interests in five other companies.

Since 1923, Canadian law has banned mergers that operate to "the detriment of society." Several court decisions have limited the scope of this legislation to cases involving virtual monopolies. There were no convictions in contested merger cases through 1978. By 1984 there had been eight merger or takeover cases in court, with one prohibition and one guilty plea.

Japan's Anti-Monopoly Law requires the registration of sizable mergers with the Fair Trade Commission. The first test of this law came in 1969 when the FTC challenged a merger between Fuji and Yawata steel companies. Yawata had 18.5 percent and Fuji had 17.0 percent of Japanese steel capacity. Due to protests from other government agencies, a compromise agreement allowed the merger. During a transition period, the new company agreed to supply competitors with the knowledge of certain production processes and to divest itself of its holdings in another smaller company. Despite the registration of over a thousand mergers every year in the mid-1970s, the FTC did not contest another merger in the 1970s.

Source: Paraphrasing from F.M. Scherer, *Industrial Market Structure and Economic Performance*, Second Edition, pp. 504–508. Copyright © 1980 by Houghton Mifflin Company.

Effectiveness of U.S. Antitrust Laws

In this section we will consider evidence of the effect that antitrust policy has had on firms' behavior. Antitrust law permits the federal government, state governments, and individuals to initiate civil cases seeking damages. In addition, the federal government can impose criminal charges while simultaneously suing for damages.

We will begin with an outline of the criminal penalties. We will then concentrate on the effect of the triple-damages provisions of the law. While triple damages offer an inducement to bring a private case against firms violating the law, not everyone has the right to sue for triple damages. We will determine who can sue and what effect limiting the right to sue has on the deterrence of antitrust violations.

Penalties and Punitive Damages

It is difficult to determine what deterrent effects antitrust laws have on firm behavior. Without the laws firms may pursue monopolistic objectives. Until 1955 the maximum fine for a violation of the Sherman Act was $5,000 per count. Congress increased the penalty to $50,000 in 1955. In 1974 it became $100,000 for an individual and $1 million for the firm. Price fixing became a felony in 1974. Before that time it was a misdemeanor.

Violations can also lead to prison sentences of up to three years. Until 1940 only twenty-four cases involved jail sentences, and the average sentence was 90 days. Judges have been less reluctant lately to impose sentences. In 1978, twenty-nine individuals received sentences totalling 2,921 days as a result of conviction in collusion cases.

13-9

Get your profits while you can

APPLICATION

The Justice Department dropped a thirteen-year-old antitrust case against IBM in 1982. It had filed the case alleging that IBM was monopolizing the general-purpose mainframe computer market in violation of the Sherman Act. Professors David Levy and Steve Welzer argue that the antitrust case did alter IBM's behavior. Unfortunately, it appears that the behavior was not as intended by the Justice Department.

According to Professors Levy and Welzer, IBM feared that the Justice Department might win its case. If IBM had lost, the Justice Department would have sought court approval for a breakup of the company into smaller components. As we have seen before, firms must take into account the effects that their current prices will have on their future profits. IBM was no exception. Faced with a possible constraint on its future market share, IBM changed its low-price policy to a short-run, high-price strategy.

Although high prices encourage entry and erosion of market share, the process was relatively slower in the computer industry of the 1970s. Existing customers delayed switching to alternative companies because of the cost of converting software and retraining their staffs. New customers may have found it difficult to make an accurate comparison of price and quality. Despite these factors IBM would still have lost market share with a high-price strategy.

Throughout the 1970s, IBM charged higher prices relative to their prices prior to the filing of the case. Once the prospects for the case started to change in IBM's favor in 1980, IBM reversed its strategy and lowered prices. IBM maintained a market share of between 50 and 52 percent in electronic data processing between 1961 and 1968. Between 1968 and 1972 its share dropped to 37 percent and continued to decline to 31 percent by 1979. Between 1980 and 1983 its share increased to 37 percent.

Professors Levy and Welzer conclude that the antitrust case encouraged IBM to take short-run profits despite loss of market share in the long run, due to fears of a forced loss of market share at the hands of the government. Once prospects improved, IBM returned to a more aggressive position and competed for market share and long-run profitability.

Source: David Levy and Steve Welzer, "System Error: How the IBM Antitrust Suit Raised Computer Prices." *Regulation* (September/October 1985):27–30. With permission of the American Enterprise Institute.

Triple Damages

Triple (treble) damages became a part of the antitrust law with the passage of the Sherman Antitrust Act. Senator Sherman, who sponsored the bill, turned to the Bible when deciding the size of the penalty to impose. The Old Testament says that the Lord will punish offenders threefold for their misdeeds. Triple damages have been a mainstay of U.S. antitrust law ever since.

The size of the damage award has caused some concern. There have been allegations that firms willingly go along with price-fixing schemes involving their suppliers in hopes of joining a triple-damages suit at a later date to reap benefit. Unfortunately, these firms' own customers are not allowed to sue for triple damages resulting from the higher prices passed on to them.

Standing

Triple damages provide a strong incentive for a harmed party to consider suing for damages. In order to sue for damages a harmed party must have legal **standing**—that is, it must establish that it was harmed by the defendant. The courts have limited the extent to which a harmed party has standing. In *Illinois Brick* v. *the State of Illinois* (1977), the Supreme Court required that a plaintiff suing for damages must demonstrate that it dealt directly with the antitrust wrongdoer. The plaintiffs were the State of Illinois and 700 local government entities, all of whom charged the defendants with price fixing.

The defendants were manufacturers of concrete blocks who sold to masonry contractors who, in turn, placed bids with general contractors. The general contractors bid on governmental building projects sponsored by the plaintiffs. The plaintiffs sought $3 million in damages. In an earlier case, the Supreme Court ruled that a firm could not sue a company that unwittingly passed along the higher prices of a supplier.

The Supreme Court ruled that the plaintiffs did not have standing. They decided that granting standing would present a serious risk of multiple liability for the defendants, make the proof of liability an insurmountable problem, and impede the enforcement of antitrust policy.

Critics of this decision note that the direct purchasers of goods may fear future retaliation from suppliers and refrain from initiating cases. Even though they may receive triple the damages from a successful suit, the firms may pass on most of the cost to their customers and have less incentive to sue.

While this ruling appears to limit the enforcement potential of the antitrust laws, there still may be a strong incentive for harmed parties directly affected by a conspiracy to sue. Consider the following example.

13-10 | **Just pass it on**

APPLICATION Professor Edward A. Snyder of the University of Michigan measured the effect that the Illinois Brick decision had on the number of triple-damages suits initiated by firms. He analyzed data on private triple-damages suits between 1963 and 1982. He had to control for the fact that government cases against collusive practices declined during this time. If the government won a case, a private company suing for triple damages had only to show standing to claim damages. Without a prior conviction of a colluding firm, the plaintiff had to establish the guilt of the colluding firm.

He also noted that in a 1968 case, *Hanover Shoe, Inc.* v. *United Shoe Machinery Corp.*, the Supreme Court ruled that a direct buyer still has standing to sue for triple damages, even though it has passed the cost of the higher prices on to its customers. He determined that the combined effect of the two court decisions was neutral on the number of private suits for triple damages. Unfortunately, he was not able to obtain data on the size of damages collected by the firms in these suits. The size of damages would be a better measure of the effectiveness of limiting standing to direct purchasers.

Professor Snyder claimed that his results show that limiting standing to direct purchasers is efficient. Although indirect purchasers (that is, customers of direct purchasers) receive no compensation for paying higher prices, there would be higher costs of litigation by allowing indirect purchasers to sue for damages without any gain in the number of suits likely to be effective in assessing damages against price fixers.

Source: Edward A. Snyder, "Efficient Assignment of Rights to Sue for Antitrust Damages." *Journal of Law and Economics* XXVIII, No. 2 (May 1985):469–82. © by the University of Chicago.

Triple damages do not apply to cases decided out of court. Thus, paradoxically, the most likely to be guilty settle out of court to avoid triple damages, while the least culpable force the case to a court decision. If those firms that do not settle outside of court lose their cases, they are liable not only for their damages but for the damages of all their coconspirators who settled out of court.

13-11

APPLICATION

You are the only one left

In 1982, Mead Corporation agreed to pay $45 million to settle several thousand lawsuits seeking triple damages for an alleged fixing of the price of cardboard boxes. Mead was one of several companies indicted for price-fixing in the late 1970s. Thousands of industry customers filed civil triple-damages suits in 1978 against Mead and thirty-three other companies.

The other thirty-three companies settled out of court for a total of $330 million. Since Mead was the last company left, it would have been liable for as much as $750 million despite being accused of $15 million in overcharges. Rather than face the prospect of paying $750 million, it settled out of court.

In 1985 the National Association of Manufacturers and the U.S. Chamber of Commerce pushed passage of a bill that would limit the liability of a firm convicted of violating the antitrust laws to triple the damages due to the firm alone. Supporters of the proposed legislation argue that smaller and, likely, less-guilty firms will persevere in their defense, only to be liable for damages attributed to another firm that settles out of court.

The Reagan administration opposed the bill, because it would reduce the incentive of private firms to initiate cases and therefore reduce deterrence. As shown in the ruling in the Illinois Brick case, deterrence is the objective of the antitrust law at the expense of equitable compensation for past harm.

Summary

In this chapter we considered the major antitrust laws of the United States. In passing these laws, Congress indicated its interest in preventing a concentration of economic and political power. We looked closely at the problems normally attributed to market power. Market power allows firms to raise prices and reduce output while imposing deadweight losses and inefficiencies.

After listing the major laws, we looked at some preliminary antitrust issues: definition of the market and the use of either a rule of reason or a per se rule. These issues are relevant to each of the antitrust laws mentioned in this chapter.

In closing, we considered the recent enforcement of the laws. After an activist period extending through the early 1970s, the U.S. government now confines most of its activity to the areas of price fixing and mergers. In response to a perception of inactivity on the part of the Justice Department, state governments are taking a more active role. This has created a pattern of mixed enforcement across the country.

Important Terms

Consumer Surplus (p. 363)
Deadweight Loss (p. 364)
Economic Rents (p. 366)
Rent Seeking (p. 366)
Trust (p. 368)
Rule of Reason (p. 369)
Per Se Rule (p. 369)
Horizontal Merger (p. 375)

Vertical Merger (p. 375)
Product-Extension Conglomerate Merger (p. 376)
Market-Extension Conglomerate Merger (p. 376)
Pure Conglomerate Merger (p. 376)
Herfindahl Index (p. 377)
Standing (p. 382)

Selected References

Choi, Dosoung, and Philippatos, George C. "The Financial Consequences of Antitrust Enforcement." *Review of Economics and Statistics* LXV, No. 3 (August 1983):501–6.

Gisser, Micha. "Price Leadership and Welfare Losses in U.S. Manufacturing." *American Economic Review* 76, No. 4 (September 1986):756–67.

Harberger, Arnold C. "Monopoly and Resource Allocation." *American Economic Review* 44 (May 1954):77–87.

Levy, David, and Welzer, Steve. "System Error: How the IBM Antitrust Suit Raised Computer Prices." *Regulation* (September/October 1985):27–30.

Neale, A.D., and Goyder, D.G. *The Antitrust Laws of the U.S.A.*, 3rd ed. New York: Cambridge University Press, 1980.

Scheffman, David T., and Spiller, Pablo T. "Geographic Market Definition Under the U.S. Department of Justice Merger Guidelines." *Journal of Law and Economics* XXX (April 1987):123–47.

Scherer, F.M. *Industrial Market Structure and Economic Performance*, 2nd ed. Hopewell, New Jersey: Houghton Mifflin Company, 1980.

Snyder, Edward A. "Efficient Assignment of Rights to Sue for Antitrust Damages." *Journal of Law and Economics* XXVIII, No. 2 (May 1985):469–82.

Problems

1. Assume that there are eight firms in the market with the following shares of the market:

Firm	Share of the Market
1	25
2	25
3	10
4	10
5	10
6	10
7	5
8	5

(a) Compute the Herfindahl Index for this market.

(b) Assume that Firms 7 and 8 decide to merge. What is the Herfindahl Index now?

(c) What position would the Justice Department take concerning this merger?

2. Discuss the advantages and disadvantages of using a per se rule to evaluate price-fixing cases.

3. Assume that the Alberwreck Copper Company is able to monopolize the U.S. copper market. The market demand curve is as follows:

$$P = 50 - 2Q,$$

where the price is denominated in dollars per ton and Q is in thousands of tons.

(a) Assume that the Alberwreck Copper Company produces copper with a constant short-run marginal and average cost of $20 a ton. Calculate the deadweight loss and transfer of consumer surplus in comparison to a competitive market solution.

(b) Assume that Alberwreck has gained its monopoly by merging with other firms and achieving scale economies that have lowered its marginal cost per ton from $30 to $20. If the government decides to disallow the merger, the firm will lose the advantages of the scale economies. Discuss the consequences of allowing the merger to take place.

4. Evaluate the impact of limiting damage claims in antitrust cases to actual damages rather than triple damages.

5. Assume that all the coal-mining companies in the Appalachian region of the United States want to fix their prices in order to keep from going out of business. Assume that they are able to raise their prices just high enough to keep from defaulting

on their outstanding bank loans but low enough to prevent the sale of coal in the region by outside mining companies. How would you evaluate the companies' argument that they all would have gone out of business unless they had fixed their prices?

Answer questions 6–11 with true, false, or uncertain.

6. A monopolist imposes an inefficient market solution on society because of the large transfer of consumer surplus to the monopolist.

7. The Justice Department would directly contest the merger of a firm with a 10 percent market share and a firm with a 20 percent market share.

8. Price fixing is a per se offense in most countries having antitrust laws.

9. As a result of the Illinois Brick decision, there is now less deterrence of price-fixing arrangements coming from the private sector.

10. The U.S. government actively enforces price-fixing, merger, and monopolization cases at this time.

11. The Robinson-Patman Act supports competitors but not competition.

REGULATION

14

In the previous chapter we considered the impact of antitrust laws that apply generally to all firms. These laws are concerned mostly with the problems of monopoly and collusive practices. In this chapter we will consider the regulation of specific firms and industries.

The constraint that regulations impose on firms varies according to the type of regulation. For example, while local and state authorities dictate that local telephone companies must earn a regulated rate of return, environmental regulations may deal only with the pollution devices that a company must install or the allowed level of pollutants discharged at its plants.

The regulatory environment changes constantly. The pace of change accelerated in the late 1970s in the United States with the start of deregulation in several industries: telecommunications, airlines, trucking, trains, and buses. The deregulatory trend has been spreading to other countries and to local governments in the United States. Rather than list the regulations in force and the principal agencies enforcing these regulations, we will focus on the rationale for regulation and the reasons for the controversy that has always been associated with regulatory policy.

We will start with an analysis of the reasons most commonly offered in support of regulation. These reasons have in common the desire for an economic and social improvement in society. Despite these good intentions, regulations may also have unexpected effects. In fact, those most likely to gain from some regulations may be the regulated companies. We will consider why this may be possible.

After a general discussion of the main objectives of regulation, we will look at some regulations. Since the list of regulations far exceeds the space that we can devote to it here, we will focus on a sampling. From this sample you will get an appreciation of the complexities and the competing interests involved in most attempts to regulate.

Governments use regulations to correct or offset a failure of the market to produce an economically efficient amount of goods and services. Markets may fail when there are natural monopolies, externalities, or informational problems. Some economists have advocated regulations to correct these failures.

We will also consider less altruistic motives of the regulated firms and other interest groups. Despite the good intentions of many who sponsor regulations, the effects of these regulations are not always as intended or as advertised. Since regulation results from the political process, firms have an incentive to influence politicians to pass regulations that benefit them. While we have already seen examples of this in some of the previous Applications, we will analyze the problem more systematically in this chapter.

Market Failure

Markets may fail to insure that firms produce goods in the most economically efficient manner. We will concentrate on three principal reasons: natural monopoly, externalities, and information costs. While we will emphasize the economic justification for regulations to correct these market failures, we will want to see how special interests can use these arguments to mask other intentions.

Natural Monopoly

In Chapter 5 we emphasized the importance of barriers to entry in maintaining the monopoly position of the firm. Without barriers to entry, new firms would enter the market and drive economic profits to zero in the long run. The new equilibrium number of firms would be greater than one. However, natural monopoly is an exception to this story. A **natural monopoly** is a type of monopoly that occurs when the technology of providing a product or service makes it cheaper for only one firm to produce the market output. In this case there are increasing returns to scale at all output levels. A natural monopoly is "natural" because the decreasing average costs of production result in only one firm in a long-run competitive equilibrium. Figure 14-1 (p. 392) shows why this happens and why we might want to regulate a natural monopolist.

14-1	Natural monopoly

GRAPHICAL
EXPLANATION

Figure 14-1 shows the market demand curve and the long-run average-cost curve of a natural monopolist. If new firms were to enter the market and drive the price down, there would only be one firm left at minimum average cost. In Figure 14-1 the firm could lower average cost further by producing beyond Q_1, the output where average cost equals price. To the right of Q_1 average cost would be greater than the market price, so the firm would suffer economic losses.

The government faces two conflicting objectives: a competitive environment and the lowest possible cost of production. Since average costs decline

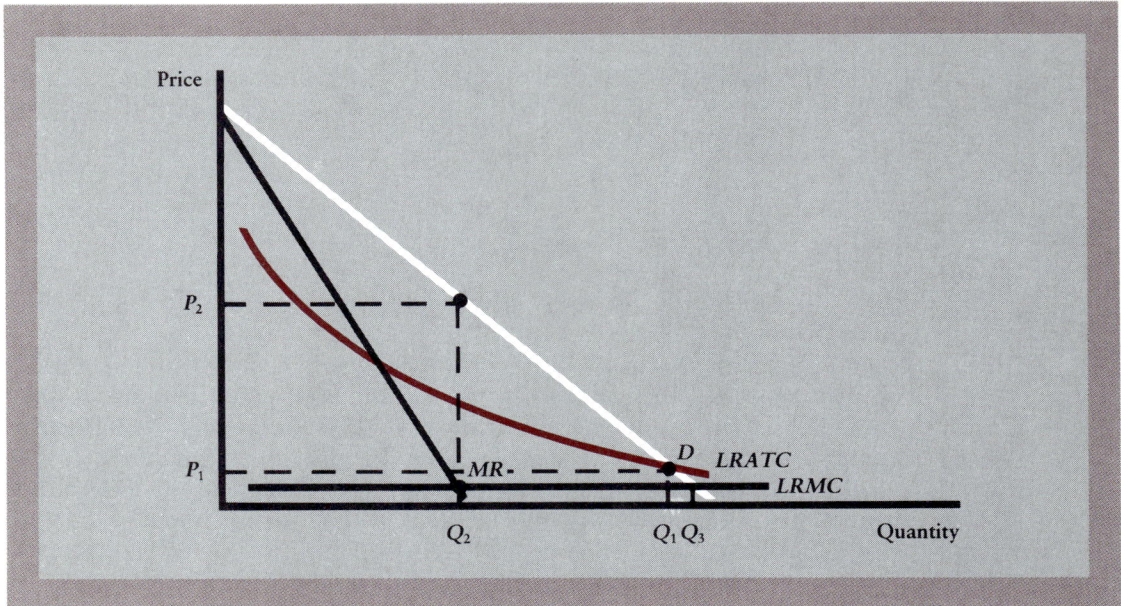

FIGURE 14-1 ▪ **Natural monopoly.** A natural monopoly has a declining average-total-cost curve at all output levels. If the firm were to charge a price equal to its marginal cost, it would produce Q_3 units of output and suffer economic losses. If left unregulated, it could charge the monopoly price of P_2 and produce only Q_2 units of output. Regulators often attempt to make regulated firms produce where average total cost equals price. At Q_1, the firm would cover its costs of production while maximizing consumer surplus.

with increases in output, the lowest cost of production requires only one firm. If the government does not regulate the firm, the firm has an incentive to maximize its profits by setting output at Q_2 where MR equals MC.

While a price above average total cost might provide an incentive for entry, the firm may be able to intimidate potential entrants by a threat of price reductions. We will not consider the entry problem here, since we discussed this issue in detail in Chapter 7. Some experts do claim that the barrier to entry posed by the natural monopolists is sometimes overstated. We will see examples of this in Applications 14-1 and 14-5. For further examples, you may want to review Applications 7-4 and 7-5.

Regulators could force the regulated firm to set its price equal to its marginal cost in order to achieve the output level Q_3, which is comparable to that of a perfectly competitive market. Unfortunately, however, the firm would have economic losses because marginal cost is always below average total cost. As a compromise between the monopolist and the competitive solutions, regulators could require that the firm set price equal to its long-run average total cost. This would be at output Q_1 and price P_1. P_1 would be the lowest price consistent with the firm being able to cover its costs. Most regulatory agencies adopt a pricing rule that attempts to achieve the average-cost pricing rule. This pricing rule maximizes consumer surplus while insuring that the natural monopolist earns revenue sufficient to remain in business. We will soon see some of the difficulties with the practical details of this approach.

In the United States, regulators have decided that certain services have natural-monopoly features. Regulatory commissions actively oversee electricity, gas, water, and telephone companies for this reason. There is now evidence that some of these industries are more competitive than was previously thought.

Prior to divestiture in the early 1980s, the U.S. government considered AT&T's entire operation to be a natural monopoly. The federal judge who ordered the divestiture of AT&T's local telephone services concluded that AT&T did not have a natural monopoly providing its other services and products. Now that AT&T has divested its regulated local telephone companies, it competes directly with several other telecommunications companies for long-distance service and sales of telephones, office communication systems, and computers.

| 14-1 | Megatruck |

APPLICATION

The natural-monopoly assumption has been extended to industries where the application is more doubtful. Until 1980 the Interstate Commerce Commission (ICC) restricted entry into the trucking market and normally ratified the rate schedules set by the carriers. While economists have argued that motor-carrier regulation encouraged collusion and helped truckers earn economic profits, the trucking industry countered with the specter of monopolization and higher profits after deregulation.

Professor Nancy Rose of Massachusetts Institute of Technology used a statistical model and data on the share prices of thirty-two publicly-traded trucking firms to distinguish between these positions. She collected data on share values from 1977 to 1981. During that time there were nineteen events that could have had an effect on share value. There were three categories of events: (1) announcements or decisions by the ICC concerning possible changes in regulatory policy, (2) Congressional decisions, and (3) post-law events that suggested a return to regulation.

Her empirical work suggested that the anticipation of policies promoting greater entry into the market reduced expected profits greatly. For example, the entry-enhancing announcements and decisions by the ICC had the cumulative effect of decreasing the share value of the typical common carrier by 19.2 percent. According to Professor Rose, the results allow her to reject the hypothesis that there is a natural monopoly in trucking. After deregulation of the industry, new firms entered the market and service expanded. At the same time, prices and profits fell to more competitive levels.

Source: Nancy L. Rose, "The Incidence of Regulatory Rents in the Motor Carrier Industry." *Rand Journal of Economics* 16, No. 3 (Autumn 1985):299–318.

Externalities

Firms do not always take into account all of the benefits and costs that their activities impose on society. For example, coal-firing electric utilities may impose costs due to pollution, while a government space program may encourage the commercial development of miniaturized circuity that will benefit companies that did not participate directly in the space program. These are examples of externalities. An **externality** is a cost or a benefit imposed by a transaction on someone who was not a party to the transaction.

There may be times when it is difficult to resolve possible externalities. For an example, let's check in with Phyllis Steene and Harry Sampson. After seeing a movie the other night, Harry complained to Phyllis about the noisy couple sitting behind them in the theater. Harry remarked that if he had wanted a running commentary of the film, he would have invited his uncle to join them. Phyllis's comment that the couple was having a good time and meant no harm did not do much to soothe him. As a means of distraction, she mentioned a recent problem involving the theater owner Jewel Floyd, who was discussed in Chapter 8. Both Harry's and Jewel's problems involve externalities.

Jewel and her husband, Buster, own a house in the country. One day their neighbor, a retired bank teller and avid butterfly and wildflower collector, decided to sell his house and move to a mobile home park in Florida. Soon after he left, the new neighbors, a local affiliate of the Sons of Satan, moved in and opened a twenty-four-hour motorcycle and lawnmower repair and swap shop. Although Jewel's house used to be worth approximately $85,000, she is sure that it is now worth much less. However, since her new neighbors are not breaking any laws by their behavior, Jewel has no legal recourse.

Jewel's new neighbors have imposed an externality, or what is sometimes called a spillover, on her and her husband. An externality occurs whenever a transaction, such as the purchase of a house or a ticket at a movie theater, imposes a cost or benefit on someone else who was not a party to the transaction. For example, home owners may see the value of their houses go up when their neighbors make improvements on their property, even though the neighbors take no account of this benefit when making their decisions.

APPLICATION

The problem of externalities is not confined to the purchase of houses or seats in movie theaters. Coal-firing electric utility plants produce electricity but also emit sodium dioxide and nitrogen oxides, which react with water in the air to produce acid rain. Acid rain coming from the United States is one of Canada's most unpleasant imports and the source of constant debate between the two countries. If this acid rain were to fall only on the power plant or the utility's customers, the customers would bear the cost of this negative effect of electricity production. However, when the acid rain falls on other people, these people bear a negative externality cost of electricity production without any offsetting benefit.

Social Marginal Cost   Figure 14-2 (p. 396) shows how an externality affects the output of a competitive market. In the figure, S represents the supply curve of the firms, since it consists only of the firms' private costs—those costs borne only by the producers. SMC is the social marginal cost. The **social marginal cost** is the marginal cost that includes all costs to society—those borne by the producer as well as those borne by the rest of society.

GRAPHICAL
EXPLANATION

The social marginal-cost curve includes both the externality and the firms' production costs. For example, assume that the externality is pollution imposed by a firm on others. In cases in which the SMC curve has the same slope as the S curve, as in Figure 14-2, each extra unit of output imposes the same additional amount of pollution per unit. If the incremental cost of pollution per unit were to increase with each additional unit of output, the SMC curve would be steeper than the S curve.

If the firms causing the pollution do not have to bear the cost of it, the equilibrium in the market will be at price P_1 and quantity Q_1. If each firm in the industry had to pay the cost of its pollution, the equilibrium would be at P_2 and Q_2. The benefit to consumers (and to society as a whole) of the extra output ($Q_1 - Q_2$) is shown by the area under the demand curve (acQ_1Q_2). The cost to society of the extra output is the area under the SMC curve (abQ_1Q_2). The difference in the two areas, abc, shows the cost to society over and above the value of the additional output.

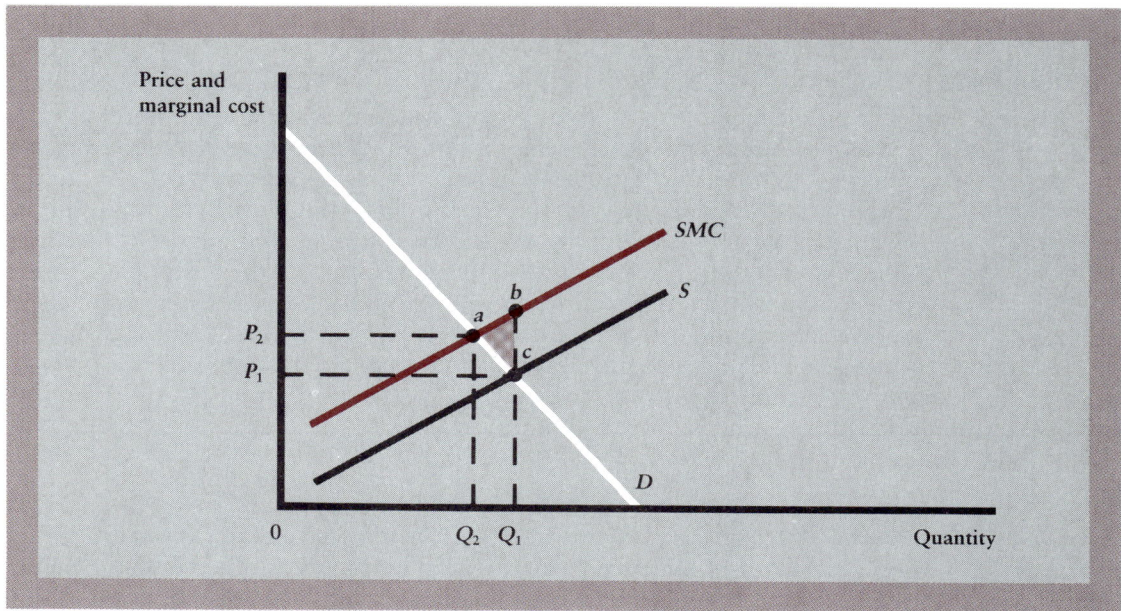

FIGURE 14-2 ▪ **Externalities.** *S* represents the private costs of the firms. *SMC* includes the cost of the externality. If the firms do not internalize the externality, market output is Q_1 and price is P_1. If the firms must account for the *SMC*, they produce only Q_2. The shaded area, *abc*, shows the additional cost to society of producing Q_1: the difference between the area under the *SMC* curve and the market demand curve.

14-3

You clean it up

APPLICATION

The government may attempt to offset the costs of an externality by imposing penalties. There have been several studies of the effects of pollution fines on firms' behavior. To be effective, the fines should force the firm to take responsibility for the cost it imposes on others; that is, it should internalize the cost of the externality. We would expect the firm to adjust to the pollution fines in the least-cost manner. It may install machinery and/or hire additional labor to reduce or eliminate the pollutants, or it may find that continuing to pollute while paying the fees is the lowest-cost alternative.

Professors J.B. Smith and W.A. Sims of Concordia University in Montreal studied the Canadian beer industry's reaction to pollution fines. Beer companies emit wastes into the sewer system which the sewer authority must neutralize. The main pollutants in the beer industry's wastewater are yeast left after fermentation, liquor left over from the straining process, spent grain husks, and products used in the filtering process.

Several local jurisdictions in Canada levy fines on emissions that exceed predetermined levels of waste. The fines levied by sewer authorities vary between 1 and 3 percent of the total charge for processing the firm's wastewater.

Professors Smith and Sims used detailed data from 1971 to 1980 from four plants. They determined that the own-price elasticity of wastewater was -0.48; that is, a 1 percent increase in the fine resulted in a 0.48 percent reduction in the amount of wastewater emitted at the plant. They also determined that a 1 percent increase in the fine resulted in only a 0.034 percent decrease in the yeast and liquor contaminants and only a 0.007 percent decrease in the amount of grain husks and other solid particles in the wastewater.

These results suggest that the firms' response to the fines was not large. Also, the fines resulted in only a small increase in the amount of labor and machinery used by the firms to reduce the pollutants. More importantly, Professors Smith and Sims found that the fines had a significant, negative effect on the productivity of the firms. They determined that firms not subject to the fines experienced growth rates of 1.6 percent in output per unit of inputs during the time period, while the regulated firms had no growth in productivity.

While the fines affected the firms' productivity and costs, the firms chose to absorb most of the added costs without altering their polluting behavior significantly. In effect, they chose to pay the sewer authority to clean the polluted wastewater. If the sewer authority were the more efficient processor of pollutants, this would be an efficient solution. Missing in this study was the expected benefit of maintaining the wastewater of the plants below the predetermined levels of contamination.

Source: J.B. Smith and W.A. Sims, "The Impact of Pollution Charges on Productivity Growth in Canadian Brewing." *Rand Journal of Economics* 16, No. 3 (Autumn 1985):410–23.

Property Rights Assume for a moment that Jewel's externality problem is due to inconsiderate neighbors who play their music too loudly. The neighbors enjoy benefits from loud music, while she bears a cost. One solution would be for Jewel to pay her neighbors to lower the volume of the music. While the payment might make everyone better off, such solutions are not common. The solution to this problem concerns property rights. A **property right** is the exclusive ownership of specific goods or the exclusive privilege to behave in a certain manner.

If the neighbor has the right to make noise, Jewel would not necessarily find it odd to buy this right from her neighbor to keep him/her quiet. If the neighbor is not allowed to make noise, (s)he might consider paying Jewel for the right to make noise. In reality the rights to make noise are not usually well established, especially in a country location such as Jewel's. Jewel and her neighbor are unlikely to come to an agreement, since they will spend most of their time arguing over who has the right to make noise.

This same problem is present in the pollution example. It is not important from an efficiency standpoint whether a polluter receives a payment to stop polluting or whether the polluter pays to pollute. Unless someone can establish property rights concerning the right to pollute, the market might not guarantee an efficient output level. For example, polluters normally feel that they have the right to pollute, while others feel that they have a right to unpolluted resources.

When individual property rights are not clearly established, governments often intervene. For example, whether or not anti-smoking laws are passed depends on the government's view of whether nonsmokers have property rights to clean air or smokers have the property right to smoke in public areas. Since the market normally does not resolve this problem, governments become involved.

Free-Rider Problem While Jewel might be able to work out an arrangement with a noisy neighbor, the Sons of Satan pose a more difficult problem. One solution would be to buy the house from the new neighbors and resell it to someone with more similar cultural values. Since there would be a large transaction cost involved in doing this, Jewel and Buster would want to encourage their other neighbors to participate in the buyout. If there were many neighbors, it would be difficult to organize them all. Since each neighbor would perceive the gains from relocating the Sons of Satan differently, they would not agree on their fair share of the costs of the relocation.

There is an additional problem, having to do with free riders. A **free rider** is someone who benefits from the concerted actions of others without paying for this benefit. For example, someone who watches public television programming without responding to the periodic appeals for contributions free rides on the generosity of others who do make contributions. In Jewel's case her neighbors would prefer that someone else bore the cost of removing the Sons of Satan, even though every neighbor would benefit. Unless Jewel could overcome this problem, she would probably be unable to raise enough money to buy the house and resell it.

Internalizing Externalities The presence of externalities may lead firms to internalize them. For example, beehive owners may realize that their bees are providing a service for nearby farmers who grow flowers outdoors for commercial sale. In turn, the farmers may notice that the bees are using their flower nectar to generate honey. These mutually beneficial exchanges may lead to an arrangement between the two owners that removes the externality. Because of the potential for a positive externality, both have an incentive to combine forces.

APPLICATION

Professor Steven Cheung investigated the prospects of externalities in the honeybee and honey markets. Prior to his study several observers used the bee and honey markets as an example of an unresolved externality. Since honeybees pollinate flowers on fruit trees, the bees provide a service to the owners of the fruit trees. Although the honeybees produce at least some honey by storing the nectar from the flowers, there is a possibility that the beekeepers could be providing pollination services without adequate compensation.

Professor Cheung is skeptical that there are substantial unresolved externalities involving firms. Guided by greater profits, firms have an incentive to internalize externalities. He found that owners of honeybees and owners of fruit trees do establish contracts that compensate them for their services. He focused on the honey and fruit industries in the state of Washington.

He determined that spring is the primary season for the pollination of fruit. Midsummer and fall are the peak honey seasons. Prior to 1910 most orchards relied on wild insects to pollinate fruit. Since 1910 orchards have been purchasing pollination services. He investigated the records of nine beekeepers having at least 10,000 colonies of bees. These beekeepers moved their hives to different sites between two and four times during 1971.

He found that in the spring beekeepers earned between $9 and $10 per hive for pollination services. In the late spring the bees were able to store some nectar to make honey in addition to the nectar they must consume in order to live. In these cases the fee for pollination services reflected the income to be earned by the beekeepers from the honey.

For example, pollinating blueberries in late spring yielded forty pounds of honey per hive. At $0.14 per pound, the honey yielded a revenue of $5.60 per hive. This was coupled with an average pollination fee of $5.00. The combined price was close to the average pollination fee paid when there was no excess honey for commercial sale. Honey from pollinating cabbage plants amounted to $1.95 per hive. The pollination fee was, on the average, $8.00.

In the summer when the bees swarm and collect substantial amounts of honey, the beekeepers pay farmers growing alfalfa, cloves, and fireweed mint for the right to let their bees swarm in the farmers' fields. When grown for hay, these plants do not require pollination. Since the bees provide the farmers no service, the beekeepers must pay the farmers for the right to use the fields.

Source: Steven S. Cheung, "The Fable of the Bees: An Economic Investigation." *Journal of Law and Economics* (April 1973):11–34. © by the University of Chicago.

Informational Costs

Since markets do not always provide a socially optimal level of information, the government may have a role in providing this information. For example, consumer magazines that conduct extensive tests of new products and warn consumers about potential problems cannot charge everyone who uses their information. People who read these magazines do not always purchase them. This allows some people to free ride on others and leads to a lower level of information than would be provided if all those who directly benefited paid for the information.

Information cost is an important issue. Some observers claim that providing information is the only function that governments should provide in offsetting externalities and other regulatory-related problems. We have already discussed information costs in Chapter 9, where we saw how the firm adjusts to increased costs of processing and producing information. A part of that discussion was concerned with the government's role in providing information and regulating the information provided by others.

Equity Considerations

Economists focus mostly on the efficiency of markets and the effect that government-imposed constraints have on efficient market performance. We have seen how a regulatory commission strives to increase social welfare by forcing natural monopolies to offer the lowest possible price while insuring that the company stays in business. Regulators also attempt to increase social welfare by offsetting negative externalities that private parties do not internalize.

While economists emphasize efficiency, politicians often emphasize fairness. Many political decisions involve a redistribution of income among people. When economists evaluate redistributions of income, they start with a concept called Pareto optimality. **Pareto optimality** is the market condition that exists when it is not possible to find another solution that could make at least one person better off without making someone else worse off.[1]

Markets impose solutions that do not necessarily benefit all parties equally. Many politicians consider Pareto optimality to be too weak a criterion for guiding economic policy. For example, assume a poor person has $1 in annual income and another person receives $1,000,000 per year. If the government were to tax the wealthier person $1,000 a year and give it to the poorer person, there would be no net change in overall income. Since the richer person is worse off, this redistribution fails the Pareto criterion.

While most economists have an opinion about the social merits of such a redistribution, they do not find support for their view in economic theory. Suppose we change the story slightly. Assume that the government passes a law changing the market environment. The new law provides an incentive for the poorer person to earn $1,000 a year but provides a disincentive to the

[1] This concept is due to the Italian economist Vilfredo Pareto (1848–1923).

richer person. With the disincentive the richer person earns $600 a year less. Overall, the total income increases by $400, but the richer person is worse off.

This new law would again fail the Pareto criterion. In this case economists could counter by suggesting that the poorer person could bribe or encourage the richer person not to oppose the new law. For example, with a payment of $600, the poor person could make the richer one as well off as before while still retaining an extra $400 (that is, $1,000 minus the $600 payment).

Most economically-based arguments rely on the Pareto criterion as a benchmark for acceptability. This criterion does not go far enough for many politicians, however. Faced with voters who have different income levels and economic situations, many politicians are willing to impose solutions that do not satisfy this criterion. By deviating from this criterion, politicians are willing to attach weights to the value of certain segments of the affected population.

A nation's people establishes its own criteria of fairness by its laws and the representatives it elects. Economists cannot determine what is fair or equitable for any group of people. This is the people's right. When economists argue against the merits of legislation involving issues of equity, they feel that the specific regulation may not be the least-cost means of accomplishing the stated objective.

Self-Interest Considerations: The Capture Theory of Regulation

Throughout this text we have emphasized the importance of the economic behavior of individuals and firms in response to changes in the constraints they face in the market. As you have seen in several of the Applications, people find ingenious ways of working around constraints in order to pursue their own self-interests. This is the behavior that Nobel Laureate George Stigler of the University of Chicago identified in 1961 when he wrote about the capture theory of regulation.

According to Professor Stigler, firms recognize that laws can adversely and positively affect them. While the return from investing in a new machine or hiring a new employee has an expected value to the firm, investing in efforts to affect legislation also has potential benefits to the firm. We should expect firms to invest in efforts to affect legislation up to the point where the expected marginal costs of the effort equal the expected marginal benefits.

According to Professor Stigler, the main beneficiary of regulation may actually be the regulated industry. Firms may use their influence to lead well-intentioned legislators into passing laws for their benefit. This is not a general rule, however. There are some industries which see themselves as harmed by specific laws and rules. The capture theory merely focuses attention on the possibility of less-than-altruistic motives for regulation.

APPLICATION   Professor Lawrence Shepard of the University of California at Davis considers the California-Arizona orange industry to be a classic example of the capture theory of regulation. Without government enforcement, the industry would be unable to maintain its market-allocation program. According to Professor Shepard, the industry uses the power of the U.S. government to enforce price discrimination between the fresh and processed orange juice markets.

There are more than 4,000 growers and 100 packers in the California-Arizona orange industry, which provides approximately two-thirds of the fresh orange crop in the United States. The industry attempted a voluntary cartel arrangement in 1932, but it lasted only a month after nonparticipating growers increased their output levels. With the passage of the Agricultural Marketing Agreement Act of 1937, the federal government gave producers of agricultural commodities the authority to determine collectively the amount of output allowed to reach the market and to allocate the output among existing suppliers.

The primary function of the marketing order is the allocation of output between fresh and processed oranges. The demand for fresh oranges is more inelastic than that for processed oranges. Professor Shepard concludes that when the size of the crop increases, the share of the crop going to the fresh market decreases in order to maintain high prices. The industry also uses minimum size specifications to block oranges from the fresh market. The minimum size fluctuates from year to year. He estimates that the amount of fruit suitable for the fresh market is far greater than that allowed in the fresh market.

By increasing the profits of growers initially, the marketing agreement increased entry into the market. The addition of more growers led to a greater diversion of oranges to the processed market. Professor Shepard estimates that the return on processed oranges was actually negative starting in 1969. Growers absorbed these costs as a way of maintaining the agreement. The agreement has resulted in a reduction in the average earnings of growers, relative to a nonregulated market situation, due to the distortions mentioned earlier and the inability to restrain entry to the market.

In the long run, free entry will eliminate the growers' economic profits. Under the marketing agreement, the prices of fresh oranges are much higher than they would be otherwise, while processed orange prices are lower than the marginal cost of harvesting and processing.

Source: Lawrence Shepard, "Cartelization of the California-Arizona Orange Industry, 1934–1981." *Journal of Law and Economics* XXIX(1) (April 1986):83–124. © by the University of Chicago.

We will now turn to some general types of regulations. We will consider the motives for these rules according to the three general categories mentioned earlier: economic considerations, political considerations, and special interests. Sometimes there will be overlapping reasons from two or all three of these areas. After a general discussion of each type, we will consider some specific applications.

Rate-of-Return Regulation

Local and federal agencies regulate several industries, including electricity, telecommunications, transportation, water, gas pipelines, and postal services. These industries do not all receive the same degree of regulation. The degree of government participation is subject to continual debate and change. Each of these industries has operated or still does operate under some form of rate regulation.

Fair Rate of Return

According to decisions by the U.S. Supreme Court, regulators must allow the utilities to earn a "fair rate of return" on their invested capital. The Supreme Court considers a **fair rate of return** to be the return on a firm's invested capital that is in keeping with comparable returns on investments in other industries facing similar risks.

Regulators implement this policy in the following way. First, a regulatory commission determines the percentage rate of return based on information supplied at a public hearing by the regulated firm and other interested individuals. The commission multiplies the percentage rate of return by the asset value of the firm to determine the amount of money the firm may earn on its investments. The capital assets of the firm form the **rate base**, which is the value of the capital investment of the firm.

Secondly, the commission adjusts the allowed return on investments to account for taxes that the firm will have to pay on its earnings. The commission then adds estimated operating costs to the return on the firm's investments to compute the overall revenue that the firm can earn.

After the commission determines the total revenue that the firm can earn, it must then decide how the firm will generate this revenue. The firm will propose a schedule of prices with estimates of sales at these prices. Even the regulated firm producing a single product may have a schedule with different prices. For example, in Chapter 6 we discussed how companies, such as electric utilities, telephone companies, and transportation firms, charge different prices at different times of the day and year due to fluctuations in demand.

APPLICATION

There has been considerable research showing that we do not necessarily require regulation to insure efficiently produced, low-priced electricity. Although regulators appear reluctant to open the market for the generation of electricity to competition and unregulated prices, they differ in how they attempt to ensure that the price of electricity approaches the competitive equivalent.

In all countries, price increases are unpopular. Regulators may respond by attempting to smooth out increases over time, even if present costs do not correspond to electricity prices. While attempting to achieve prices that equal the long-run marginal cost of generating electricity, regulators must rely on forecasts of future input prices, such as oil, coal, natural gas, and generating facilities. The uncertainty in these estimates gives the regulators substantial leeway in determining a firm's costs.

By way of contrast, consider the regulatory procedures used in France and the United States. Electricité de France maintains low electricity prices through subsidies, in anticipation of future sizable cost reductions due to a heavy reliance on nuclear power. In the United States, most state commissions use the historical costs of the firm's assets as the rate base. As a result, firms cannot usually add the costs of new construction to the rate base until the new plant is operating. Rates tend to jump when the new plant is operational.

Special Problems with Rate-of-Return Regulation

Regulators must contend with several potential problems associated with the rate-of-return process. First, if the firm can cover its operating costs and earn an average rate of return, it has no incentive to keep costs low. Rather than vigorously pursuing cost cutting, executives could mask activities such as expensive business trips, donations to favorite charities, and luxurious company cars as ordinary business expenses. If these expenses are necessary for the normal conduct of business and likely to exist at competitive firms, there may be little concern to regulators. If they represent instead a padding of the costs, they are inefficiencies that the customers must bear in the form of higher prices.

Second, there is an imbalance in the resources available to the regulators. Regulated firms can hire consultants and employees to design convincing arguments at rate hearings. These costs become a part of operating expenses. Regulatory budgets are limited, and the expertise of local regulators does not always match that of the industry representatives. This imbalance leads to a general tendency for regulators to rely on the information supplied by the representatives of the firms that they must regulate.

Third, the rate determination process takes time. Decisions depend on public hearings, with detailed information made available to all parties interested in the proceedings. The time needed to collect data and present a case before the regulatory agency leads to regulatory lag. **Regulatory lag** is the delay that occurs when regulators adjust rates at a slower pace than changes in costs and the rate base.

Regulatory lag can affect the firm in a positive or negative manner. For example, in the 1960s, electric utilities were able to lower their operating costs by adopting technological advances in their generating equipment. The reduction in costs coupled with the delay in the drop in prices to customers generated profits for these companies. In the 1970s, regulatory lag worked against the utilities. Rapidly increasing fuel costs linked to the OPEC price hike caused costs to increase faster than electricity prices did. Electric utilities were not profitable investments in the 1970s.

Fourth, despite the trend towards flexible pricing policies, the rate-of-return process often ignores the possibility of both competitive and monopoly aspects of a regulated industry's business. By focusing only on costs, the regulators ignore the importance of demand. Consider the following example from railroad regulation.

14-7 Flexible rail lines

APPLICATION

In 1987, Professors Robert Willig and William Baumol of Princeton University offered a favorable assessment of regulators' efforts to move toward a more flexible pricing rule for railroads. They not only reported on the success of the flexible pricing rule for railroads but encouraged the use of the rule in regulating other industries.

Since 1980, railroads have been subject to less regulation than during the previous fifty years. Before 1980, railroads had little flexibility in adjusting their prices to changes in demand. Railroads face competition along many of their routes from trucks, airplanes, and barges. While they have near monopolies along some routes for large, bulky shipments, such as coal, they face stiff competition elsewhere, such as from trucks hauling highly perishable fruits and vegetables.

Railroads had to set rates based on an arbitrary measure of costs. In addition to operating expenses (a proxy for average variable costs), they had to prorate their fixed costs by mileage on all parts of a trip. This pricing rule ignored the possibility that a train might make a round trip even if on the return trip the train is empty. The income generated on the outgoing segment of the trip might have made the entire trip worthwhile.

Forced to price artificially low on the profitable part of the trip, the railroads lost revenue. By charging too high a price on the less profitable return trip, they lost business that could have generated revenues in excess of the variable costs of the return trip. If the railroad faced a change in demand along any route or from any type of shipper, it had to adjust its rates in the same proportion that it adjusted all of its other rates.

According to Professors Willig and Baumol, railroad regulation had impoverished the U.S. railroad system. By the late 1970s the industry had delayed needed maintenance of tracks and equipment amounting to more than $5 billion. The inability of the firms to earn the opportunity cost of capital stopped essentially all new investment in the industry. Throughout fifty years of regulation, the industry has steadily lost its share of the transportation market.

In 1980, things changed. The Interstate Commerce Commission (ICC), which regulates the industry, gave the railroads more freedom in setting rates. They could now set rates without approval where they faced competition. In those areas where they faced no direct competition, the ICC set a ceiling and a floor for their rates based on the competitive market standard. The ceiling price reflected the price at which an outside firm could have offered the same service.

The ICC could not rely on potential entrants to force the railroads to maintain prices voluntarily below the ceiling because of the large fixed costs in the industry. As we saw in Chapter 7 in the discussion of contestable markets, large sunk costs can be used as a weapon to threaten potential entrants with losses if they enter the market. The ICC had to determine what an independent company's costs would be if it entered the market. This dictated the maximum price.

The ICC bases the floor price on the incremental costs of providing the service. Between the floor and ceiling prices, the firm is free to choose its price based on its estimate of demand. In the areas where it faces direct competition, the railroad is free to charge whatever price it chooses.

Professors Willig and Baumol credit substantial improvement in the industry since 1980 to the change to a more flexible regulatory environment. Between 1980 and 1985 coal freight rates rose 27 percent, while the charge for shipping farm products dropped by 26 percent. Railroads have arranged in excess of 50,000 contracts with shippers to design transportation arrangements specially suited to the shippers' needs.

A move to a pricing rule more suited to the variation in demand for this industry and more aware of the competitive and monopolistic aspects of the industry has increased the productivity and competitiveness of the industry. The railroads' share of the transportation market has recovered to 37 percent. Operating expenses have dropped by 26 percent in the first five years of the changed environment. Between 1981 and 1985 railroads spent approximately $27 billion on maintenance and improvements of the rails, while spending an additional $30 billion on equipment.

Based on several studies of this industry, Professors Willig and Baumol claim that prior to the change, more than $1 billion per year was wasted by using trucks to haul freight better suited for trains. Long routes and under-utilized shorter routes added another $1 billion in waste. An additional $1.5 billion was lost due to unused train capacity.

Source: Robert D. Willig and William J. Baumol, "Using Competition as a Guide." *Regulation* 1 (1987):28–35. With permission of the American Enterprise Institute.

Grants

Governments award grants that give firms exclusive rights to a national resource or to the production of a good or service. Recall in Chapter 5 how the Indonesian government awarded exclusive rights to administer imports to Panca Holding Limited (see Application 5-4). Governments award cable television, car phone, television, and radio franchises as well as landing rights at airports to firms for no more than the application cost. By doing this the government is releasing control over scarce resources technically owned by the entire country's citizens.

For example, the radio frequency band is a scarce resource. Since it is a common resource owned in principle by all of a nation's inhabitants, governments become involved in granting its use to private companies. In contrast to this, countries use international agreements to determine what part of the short-wave frequency band they can use for worldwide informational broadcasts. Even with international agreements there is difficulty accommodating all of the requests for space. Current crowding leads to interference and muddled transmissions.

Governments regulate access to other frequency bands for use within their own country. Technological change has led to the promise of a more intensive use of the frequency bands. Cable, satellite, and fiber-optic technologies also offer promise for accommodating the growing demand for communications channels.

14-8   **And the winner is . . .**

APPLICATION   The frequency-granting process does not necessarily result in frequencies going to the highest-value use. According to one study, the value of a place on the frequency band in Great Britain is only 75,000 pounds sterling when used for telephone traffic, but up to four million pounds (approximately $6 million) if used for broadcasting or mobile communications systems, such as car phones. Despite this discrepancy, the British government has allocated the largest share of microwave frequencies to the two major long-distance telephone companies.

Great Britain reelected Prime Minister Margaret Thatcher for a third term in June of 1987. Prime Minister Thatcher and her Tory government have championed a more free-market, less regulatory economic policy. Her government is pursuing the option of selling access to the airwaves. She sees this as a means of allocating the frequencies to those who value them most. Those who value them most will be the ones willing to pay the most. An auction for the frequencies will also raise revenues that will reduce the country's tax burden.

The U.S. Federal Communications Commission (FCC) used a lottery to allocate cellular-phone franchises worth billions of dollars. Under the system, the FCC awards two franchises for each of 700 markets. The local telephone company gets one, while the other is open to applicants in a lottery. Although the FCC had originally planned to award the second franchise to the best candidate, initial hearings dragged on for years. In 1984 the FCC instituted the lottery.

The FCC received approximately 300,000 applications for the lottery in 1988. Applications are usually fifty pages long at a cost of between $500 and $5,000 each. The expected payoff varies by the size of the market. One Dallas businessman spent about $5 million to acquire parts of seven franchises from lottery winners. He sold his shares eighteen months later for $34 million. Since the FCC has been concerned lately that it is giving away these franchises for nothing, this experience with cellular-phone franchises may encourage the government to consider using the market for future franchise sales.

Subsidies

Governments often decide to favor some firms and entire industries relative to others. This support may come in the form of a subsidy. A **subsidy** is a payment to a firm in the form of a tax reduction or a fixed amount of money, or a payment based on the output of the firm. The subsidy lowers the firm's production costs.

A government subsidizes a firm when the firm would not otherwise produce output at the level the government desires. A government can use subsidies to encourage production of firms that create positive externalities. In the next chapter we will see several examples of subsidies used by governments to offset the effects of international trade on the fortunes of domestic firms.

Governments subsidize a wide array of firms and industries: opera and ballet companies, museums, public television and radio stations, bus and passenger train service, public parks and recreational areas, highways and bridges, and universities. In offering subsidies, governments lower the direct costs to those consuming the goods and services and increase the quantity consumed.

Growing larger by becoming smaller

Nearly every European country maintains a public monopoly for bus transportation. Although governments may subsidize private firms to help out, they maintain control over fares. Costs generally exceed revenues, so the buses run with the help of subsidies. In some countries the government restrains competition from other sources.

For example, the Danish government does not allow a commuter-pool system that allows motorists to share a car and gas expenses, because it is "unfair" to taxis and buses. Local governments use their control to further other objectives by subsidizing the fares of students, retirees, and the handicapped. Local governments also subsidize the fares in large cities to reduce congestion from car traffic.

Contrary to the trend in other European countries, Great Britain is moving toward privatization of the busing industry. The one exception is likely to be London. In the rest of the country, Great Britain is moving toward private companies that rely on minibuses to complement the larger buses. Minibuses can go to less populated areas and still make a profit.

In Buenos Aires, Argentina, when a public company failed using large, traditional buses, about fifty privately owned companies entered the market operating minibuses with twenty-one to twenty-five seats. The new companies prospered offering frequent and dependable service. In Calcutta, India, unsubsidized private bus companies took on the state-subsidized company and captured two-thirds of the market by 1986.

Direct Compliance

Most firms must contend with regulations requiring that they meet certain standards of health and safety for their workers, their customers, and the environment. Failure to comply may lead to initial fines and escalating penalties for recurring noncompliance. While the intentions of these regulations are noble, there have been considerable debate and research as to their effectiveness and value. As an example of the issues raised in the debate, we will concentrate on one of the best-known regulatory agencies: the Occupational Safety and Health Administration (OSHA).

Unexpected guests

OSHA began operations in 1971. OSHA mandates workplace health and safety standards (such as composition of surface areas to avoid accidental falls) and conditions (for example, maximum allowable noise, or decibel, levels). OSHA enforces compliance with unannounced inspections and fines. Eighty-six percent of inspections are general, unannounced visits based on a program of random selection. The second highest category of inspections—responses to worker complaints—accounts for 9 percent of inspections. These worker complaints are generally ineffective and lead to few substantiated violations.

In 1978 the U.S. government began eliminating some of the standards and shifted their inspections toward hazards considered the most serious. It has also reduced the size of punitive fines, preferring to use escalating schedules of fines for recurring noncompliance.

While research on the first few years of OSHA's existence has shown that OSHA had little effect on accidents and lost worker days, a more recent evaluation has shown that OSHA has had some effect. Professor W. Kip Viscusi of Northwestern University analyzed the impact of OSHA's inspections and fines on the incidence of work-related injuries, illnesses, and lost worker-days between 1973 and 1983.

Professor Viscusi found that injuries, illnesses, and lost worker-days increased until 1977, fell slightly in the next two years, and then dropped significantly in the early 1980s. The drop in the 1980s was due not only to OSHA. He found that injuries, illnesses, and lost worker-days were correlated with changes in overall employment. The economic downturn of the early 1980s accounted for much of the drop.

Professor Viscusi concluded that OSHA has had no measurable effect on the accident rate but has influenced the total number of lost work-days. The unannounced inspections and the threat of escalating fines for noncompliance have had the most impact. Punitive fines following initial visits had little effect. OSHA prevents between one and two injuries involving the loss of at least one work-day per 1,000 workers annually. The biggest impact is on the more serious accidents that involve more than one lost day per incident.

An overall evaluation of OSHA must include both the costs and the benefits of compliance with the OSHA standards. No one has systematically calculated the cost of compliance. Professor Viscusi estimates that it must be billions of dollars. By comparison, the positive effects of the OSHA program have been modest at best. Opponents of OSHA and of similar federal and state programs argue that the threat of lawsuits from employees following work-related mishaps and employer concerns about the costs of lost worker time are the more cost-effective methods of insuring employer compliance with worker health and safety standards.

Source: W. Kip Viscusi, "The Impact of Occupational Safety and Health Regulation, 1973–1983." *Rand Journal of Economics* 17, No. 4 (Winter 1986):567–80.

Direct compliance to one set of standards may sometimes violate another standard. For example, the Food and Drug Administration (FDA) prefers smooth floor surfaces in meat-packing and other food-processing plants to reduce the chance of contamination spreading from improperly cleaned floors. However, OSHA favors textured floor surfaces to prevent accidental falls. In the early years of this type of regulation, there were conflicts that were eventually resolved by compromise. There are other effects that are neither anticipated nor intended.

| 14-11 | Large plants grow with less pollution |

APPLICATION

Government regulations can have unintended effects. We have already seen how pollution imposes externalities on others. Professor B. Peter Pashigian of the University of Chicago noted that direct compliance with pollution controls would force firms to install capital-intensive equipment to control the pollution. He tested the effect that the regulation would have on plants of different sizes.

He concluded that the environmental regulation reduced the number of plants and increased the size of the average plant. While some plants remained unaffected, firms in the copper industry had to absorb costs exceeding 8 percent of the value that they added to the inputs they used in their production processes.

He observed two different time periods: 1963 to 1967 and 1972 to 1977. In 1970 Congress passed the Clean Air Act and in 1972, the Clean Water Amendments. While statistically controlling for the effects of rising energy costs and the passage of health and safety regulations in the first half of the 1970s, Professor Pashigian found that the environmental regulations reduced the number of plants, increased the capital intensity, and increased plant size in the high-polluting industries.

The regulations forced a higher proportion of plant closings among the smaller plants and reduced the market share of the smaller plants. To economize on the environmental constraint, firms exploited the scale economies inherent to antipollution devices and consolidated production in larger plants.

Source: B. Peter Pashigian, "How Large and Small Plants Fare under Environmental Regulation." *Regulation* (September/October 1983):19–23. With permission of the American Enterprise Institute.

Entry Restrictions

Throughout this text we have emphasized the importance of free entry to keep firms from earning economic profits in the long run. In Chapter 5 we saw that a monopolist cannot maintain a monopoly without a barrier to entry. In Chapter 7 we analyzed the effects of barriers to entry in detail. In some of the Applications in Chapters 5 and 7 we saw how governments can impose barriers to entry that reinforce the market position of firms in the market.

According to Professor Stigler's theory of regulation, firms do not sit idly waiting for governments to impose legal restrictions on entry. Firms actively seek favorable legislation to the point where the marginal cost of pursuing legislation equals the marginal cost of obtaining it.

| 14-12 | Taxi, lady? |

APPLICATION

In 1937 the New York City government authorized the sale of slightly more than 13,500 licenses to operate taxis in the city. The licenses, given in the form of medallions, cost $10 each. The number dropped to 11,787 because of deaths and departures from the industry soon after 1937. The number of medallions has remained fixed at 11,787 despite the increase in the New York City population.

Mayor Koch has tried repeatedly to increase the number of taxis but has continually met resistance from taxi owners who fear increased competition. A medallion was worth approximately $100,000 in 1986. About 600 medallions change hands each year. The city also regulates taxi fares. Fares have not kept up with the cost of other forms of transportation, especially for shorter rides.

The freeze on medallions has lead to some results that are not surprising. Taxi owners concentrate their efforts in the more affluent areas of New York City and largely abandon heavily residential and outlying areas. During rush hours, bad weather, and the time before and after evening theatrical and musical performances, an unoccupied cab is hard to find. Limousines charging three times the taxi rate do a brisk business at these times.

There is a growing number of "gypsy" cabs, which are unlicensed and often underinsured, in areas that the licensed cabs ignore. Despite the rationing of cabs that results from this regulation, there are other unwelcome externalities. The lack of cabs encourages more people to use private automobiles in New York, crowding street traffic and parking facilities.

Self-Regulation

In the previous section we saw two examples of the effects of a government's policy of restricting entry. While the government may wish to protect a specific industry from competition, it may also hope that removal of the threat of entry will increase the quality of the service provided by the protected firms.

Many professional associations have successfully received legal limitations on entry into professions. They argue that legal restrictions to entry maintain the quality of the service provided by the profession. They further claim that unless professional associations maintain standards through restrictive entry, the general public will suffer. While quality may increase, prices and profits will likely increase as well. We have already seen an example involving the American Medical Association (see Application 7-1). The following is another example.

| 14-13 | **Now I can see the benefits of these regulations more clearly** |

APPLICATION

Professor Deborah Haas-Wilson of Smith College investigated the possibility that regulation of optometrists may have raised prices to consumers. According to Professor Haas-Wilson, most optometrists claim that regulation will raise the quality of eye care. Otherwise, they feel unscrupulous optometrists will consciously lower quality at the expense of consumers.

Regulation at the state level takes several forms. For example, states may regulate the following four areas: (1) limits on the employment of optometrists by nonprofessional corporations, (2) location of optometrists' offices, (3) branch offices, and (4) the use of trade names by nonprofessional corporations. The specific restrictions vary widely by state. Generally, they limit competition between self-employed optometrists and those employed by companies, such as Pearl Vision, that are primarily concerned with the sale of optical products.

In 1980, thirty-seven states placed restrictions on employment of optometrists in nonprofessional corporations. These restrictions usually prohibited an optometrist from working for a company whose owners were not all professional optometrists. There were twenty-eight states limiting the location of optometrists' offices. Usually in these states an optometrist must locate in a building designed exclusively for optometry services. This precludes locating in a shopping center or department store. Twenty-two states restricted the number of branch offices that an optometrist could operate. Forty-one states restricted optometrists from working under the trade name of an organization.

According to Professor Haas-Wilson, optometrists regulate themselves. In most states the professional optometry association plays a dominant role in the selection of the regulatory boards. Since these associations are controlled by self-employed optometrists, they are able to tailor regulations that favor themselves at the expense of optometrists employed by nonprofessional corporations.

Professor Haas-Wilson used data collected by the FTC during November and December 1977. The FTC sent interviewers to purchase eyeglasses and an eye exam from 280 optometrists (189 self-employed optometrists and 91 optometrists employed by nonprofessional corporations) in twelve metropolitan areas of the United States.

She concluded that in 1977 the four restrictive regulations had increased the price of a pair of glasses and an eye exam by at least 5 percent, holding quality constant. This would amount to at least $4.7 million more for exams and glasses in 1977. She also concluded that there was no statistical evidence that quality improved in the states having the restrictions.

Source: Deborah Haas-Wilson, "The Effect of Commercial Practice Restrictions: The Case of Optometry." *Journal of Law and Economics* XXIX (April 1986):165–86. © by the University of Chicago.

Overall quality may actually decrease when a profession regulates entry through licensing new entrants. Consider the following examples.

14-14	He had a license to do it

APPLICATION Sidney Carroll and Robert Gaston found that people who face both the higher prices and the smaller numbers of licensed practitioners are more likely to turn to dangerous self-help methods or to neighbors and friends claiming competence. For example, accidental electrocutions occurred ten times more often in states with the most restrictive licensing of electricians. They studied six other professions and found no evidence of increased overall quality in the heavily regulated states.

While licensing boards restrict entry as a means of insuring high standards of quality, they do not generally apply the same standards to those holding licenses. State medical boards disciplined only 0.14 percent of physicians in 1981. Narcotics violations were the major causes. Fifteen states did not discipline even one doctor. Even when cases involving serious crimes appear before disciplinary boards, doctors are usually unwilling to testify against each other.

Andrew Dolan and Nicole Urban have found that state medical boards become more active in disciplining doctors as the percentage of doctors on the board decreases. Jerome Carlin has found that disciplinary boards in the legal profession increase the degree of disciplinary action in response to the publicity that the case receives. While consumers may assume that the licensing process has guaranteed the quality of practitioners, licensing may be shielding incompetent practitioners from closer scrutiny.

Source: "Perspectives on Current Developments: Professional Licensure—One Diagnosis, Two Cures." *Regulation* (September/October 1983):11–13. With permission of the American Enterprise Institute.

Summary

In this chapter we considered the economic and political reasons for regulation of the marketplace. While most proponents of regulation may be well-intentioned, the regulations do not always have the desired effects. We concentrated on regulations that have unintended economic effects to emphasize the need for a careful analysis of the regulatory process. We saw how regulation may actually benefit the regulated firms to the detriment of society.

There may be an economic justification for regulation. We considered the case of natural monopoly. The natural monopolist has substantial economies of scale that preclude the possibility of several competing firms in a long-run competitive equilibrium at minimum average total cost. Governments may also use regulations to offset the problems caused by externalities and information costs.

We also considered the political goals of limiting excessive concentration of economic and political power. We have seen how firms can use their influence to persuade politicians to pass legislation favorable to firms' causes. We also considered a major political concern: equity. Equitable treatment of citizens is an admirable but difficult goal. The definition of an equitable solution is not the least of these problems, as everyone has his/her own definition of equity. The solution becomes a political, not an economic, solution. We saw, however, that economics can play an important role by measuring the cost in terms of efficiency for the various solutions possible. By focusing on efficiency, economists can offer politicians a lower-cost means of accomplishing their objectives.

Throughout the chapter we emphasized the importance that self-interest plays in the regulatory process. Firms do not passively accept whatever regulators decree. The capture theory of regulation predicts that firms will expend resources on affecting regulations to the point where marginal costs of effort equal the expected marginal benefits of the regulations. The lessons from the capture theory show the importance of looking beyond the surface of the regulations into the economic incentives that the regulations pose.

Important Terms

Natural Monopoly (p. 391)

Externality (p. 394)

Social Marginal Cost (p. 395)

Property Right (p. 397)

Free Rider (p. 398)

Pareto Optimality (p. 400)

Fair Rate of Return (p. 403)

Rate Base (p. 403)

Regulatory Lag (p. 405)

Subsidies (p. 408)

Selected References

Cheung, Steven S. "The Fable of the Bees: An Economic Investigation." *Journal of Law and Economics* (April 1973).

Eckard, E.W., Jr. "The Effects of State Automobile Dealer Entry Regulation on New Car Prices." *Economic Inquiry* XXIV (April 1985):223–42.

Haas-Wilson, Deborah. "The Effect of Commercial Practice Restrictions: The Case of Optometry." *Journal of Law and Economics* XXIX (April 1986):165–86.

Pashigian, B. Peter. "How Large and Small Plants Fare under Environmental Regulation." *Regulation* (September/October 1983):19–23.

Peltzman, S. "Toward a More General Theory of Regulation." *Journal of Law and Economics* 14 (1976):109–48.

Rose, Nancy L. "The Incidence of Regulatory Rents in the Motor Carrier Industry." *Rand Journal of Economics* 16, No. 3 (Autumn 1985):299–318.

Shepard, Lawrence. "Cartelization of the California-Arizona Orange Industry, 1934–1981." *Journal of Law and Economics* XXIX(1) (April 1986):83–124.

Stigler, George. "The Theory of Economic Regulation." *Bell Journal of Economics and Management Science* 2 (Spring 1971):3–20.

Stigler, George, and Friedland, Claire. "What Can Regulators Regulate? The Case of Electricity." Reprinted in *The Crisis of the Regulatory Commissions*, edited by Paul MacAvoy. New York: W.W. Norton (1970):39–52.

Willig, Robert D., and Baumol, William J. "Using Competition as a Guide." *Regulation* 1 (1987):28–35.

Problems

1. Discuss the political difficulties of eliminating the requirement that taxi drivers in New York City must have a special license to operate a cab in the city. Compare the effect of instituting this change in policy today versus 1937.

2. When the U.S. government deregulated the airlines in the early 1980s, several observers complained that more remote areas would not receive the type of service that they had received in the past. After deregulation the major airlines decreased service to these areas. What market response would you expect as a result of the airlines' decision?

3. As long as property rights are clearly established, why should there be no problem with externalities? In your answer, refer to the economic criterion of Pareto optimality.

4. Assume that a firm emits pollutants into a river. Although the river authority may impose water-purity standards on the wastewater of the plant, why might it be more economically efficient to impose fees on the levels of pollutants emitted?

5. The electricity industry has three major functions: generation of electricity at power plants, transmission of electricity through power cables, and distribution of electricity through local power lines. How appropriate is the natural-monopoly justification for regulation of each of these three functions?

6. Most local authorities award cable franchises after reviewing applications from all interested applicants. Compare the efficiency of this procedure with two alternatives: a lottery and direct sale to the highest bidder.

7. Discuss the advantages of using a flexible pricing rule versus a uniform rate for railroad cargo.

8. If OSHA did not exist, how might employers respond to health and safety hazards in the workplace?

Answer questions 9–14 with true, false, or uncertain.

9. Professional licensing regulations raise the quality of the services received by consumers.

10. Regulatory agencies should require natural monopolies to produce where price equals marginal cost.

11. Self-enforcing regulations by professional organizations ensure a uniform standard of quality among their members.

12. Deregulation of the United States trucking industry has led to increased profitability and concentration of market power in the industry.

13. Regulatory lag hurt electric utilities during the sharp increase in oil prices in the early 1970s.

14. A firm producing a product or service that creates a positive externality will not produce the socially desirable level of output.

15
INTERNATIONAL
TRADE POLICY

U p to this point the principles we have discussed apply directly to the economics of international trade, but there are features of international trade worthy of special consideration. First, since there is no international currency, we must deal with the problem of exchange rates. Secondly, countries can and do impose restrictions on trade or barriers to trade that individual companies would be unable to impose without government support. Examples are tariffs, quotas, and subsidies. Thirdly, inputs, especially labor, are not as mobile internationally as they are domestically. Finally, there are differences in demand patterns and marketing considerations across countries.

In this chapter we will consider each of these issues. Since a complete analysis of exchange rates would require a background in macroeconomic theory and finance, we will be unable to devote extensive time to it here. Trade restrictions, immobile inputs, and differences in demand across nations represent logical extensions of the material covered in Part I of this text. They receive considerable attention from politicians and the news media. Managers must be aware of these factors and their impact on their market environment.

We will start with the reasons why nations trade with one another, focusing on the gains from trade due to each nation's special attributes, such as natural resources, educational levels, and transportation networks. The international immobility of certain inputs and the differences in demand patterns among nations will be especially important factors in this discussion.

Next, we will turn to the restraints on trade imposed by governments. We will consider tariffs, quotas, "voluntary" export restraints, and international commodity agreements. We will discuss arguments for and against the use of these restraints and will compare each of them with the alternative, free trade. We will consider the principal arguments in favor of protectionist policies: support for infant industries, national defense, temporary relief from imports, and retaliation for dumping of foreign goods and "unfair" trade practices.

Why Nations Trade

Let us return to Rocky Sanders of Poobell Plastic Trash Bag Company. Rocky is back from his first vacation in Europe. The thing that impressed Rocky the most about his trip was the potential for international sales of his all-purpose trash bag. Until now Rocky had not sold any bags outside the United States. He is concerned about the impact on his own profits of expanding his market. However, we will start by considering what entire nations gain from international trade.

Nations trade with one another for the same reason that individuals trade with one another: mutual gain from specialization. Today, few individuals and few nations produce all of the goods that they consume. Individuals have different abilities and domestic environments, and all learn special skills that permit them to earn an income to buy goods and services provided by others. This specialization leads to higher levels of consumption for everyone.

Some people may excel beyond all others in more than one category. For example, John Elway, formerly of Stanford University, is playing professional football for the Denver Broncos even though he had another offer to play baseball with the New York Yankees. Danny Ainge, formerly of Brigham Young University, is playing basketball for the Boston Celtics rather than third base for the Toronto Blue Jays. These athletes have an absolute advantage in playing two professional sports relative to those of us who watch our baseball, basketball, and football games from the grandstands or our lounge chairs. A person or a nation has an **absolute advantage** in the production of a product or service when that person or nation can produce more units of the product or service than another person or country while using the same amount of inputs (such as time). The opposite of an absolute advantage is an **absolute disadvantage**.

These athletes made a choice between two sports because they could not play both during the same year. While few people and nations have an absolute advantage in the production of goods or services over others even for just one product or service, everyone faces a choice of how to use their skills and abilities. Fortunately, an absolute advantage is not necessary to gain from trade. You need only determine what you do best relative to the options available to you. Nations make the same choices. These decisions depend on the nation's endowments of labor, natural resources, and infrastructure.

Comparative Advantage

Individuals and nations maximize their potential well-being and consumption by producing goods and services that they are especially well-suited to produce. To gain from trade, nations do not need an absolute advantage relative to other nations. They can gain from trade as long as they have a comparative advantage. A **comparative advantage** is the production of those goods and services that individuals and countries produce more efficiently relative to other possible goods or services. The opposite of a comparative advantage is a **comparative disadvantage**.

The definition of the comparative-advantage concept requires elaboration. The following example shows how a country can have a comparative advantage in producing a good without having an absolute advantage.

NUMERICAL
EXAMPLE

Economist David Ricardo used the comparative-advantage concept to persuade the British parliament to overturn the protectionist Corn Laws in the nineteenth century. These laws protected aristocratic landowners in Great Britain from the imports of foreign agricultural products. While the British landowners were gaining from the protectionist policies, consumers and exporters were not. Ricardo argued that Great Britain had a comparative advantage in manufacturing but not in agriculture.

The following example provides the substance of Ricardo's argument. Assume that only two countries exist: Great Britain and Portugal. There is only one input: labor. The two countries can each produce only two goods: textiles and wine. The countries can trade the two goods freely with one another but labor is immobile internationally. We will assume that technology does not change as a result of trade, and that the only difference in the cost of producing the two products is the amount of labor used.

Table 15-1 shows specific production functions for the two countries. Note that in our simplified example it takes one worker-day in Great Britain to produce 45 gallons of wine and one worker-day to produce 60 yards of textiles. In Portugal, wine production is 30 gallons per worker-day and textile production is 30 yards per worker-day.

Note that this example assumes that labor in Great Britain is more productive than labor in Portugal in producing both products. You might expect that trade between the two countries would lead Great Britain to produce both goods and Portugal to produce nothing. This, however, ignores comparative advantage.

By comparing the relative productivity of labor in the two countries, we can see that Great Britain has a comparative advantage in textiles. For example, a worker in Great Britain can produce twice as many textiles (60 yards versus only 30 yards) as the Portuguese worker can, while the British worker's advantage in wine production is only 45 gallons to 30 gallons, or 3 to 2. Compared to the Portuguese worker, the British worker is relatively better at

TABLE 15-1 ■ Comparative advantage

	Textiles (yards per worker-day)	Wine (gallons per worker-day)
Great Britain	60	45
Portugal	30	30
Productivity (Great Britain/Portugal)	2/1	3/2

making textiles than wine, even though the British worker has an absolute advantage in producing both wine and textiles.

Given these production functions, Great Britain has a comparative advantage in textiles. Portugal has an absolute *dis*advantage in both products but a comparative advantage in wine production. Portugal must choose between the production of wine and textiles. Since Portugal's absolute disadvantage relative to Great Britain's is less when producing wine, Portugal has a comparative advantage producing wine.

As another example, as a manager you may be better at managing the company than anyone else is. You may also be the best typist in the company. While you have an absolute advantage in both, you have a comparative advantage in managing others. You would be better off hiring someone who had an absolute disadvantage to you in both categories but who had a comparative advantage as a typist. In the next section we will see how a nation can improve itself by exploiting its comparative advantage.

Mutually Beneficial Trade

We can now demonstrate the advantage of trade by looking at the opportunity cost of having both Portugal and Great Britain produce both wine and textiles. We will show that the two countries will be able to increase their levels of consumption of both goods by specializing. Great Britain will use its comparative advantage and specialize in producing textiles. Portugal will use its comparative advantage to specialize in producing wine.

| 15-2 | Mutually beneficial trade |

NUMERICAL EXAMPLE

Assume that the supply of labor is fixed in both countries. Each country must allocate its labor to maximize its overall production and consumption possibilities. Since one worker-day in Great Britain yields either 60 yards of textiles or 45 gallons of wine, Great Britain must give up 60 yards of textiles for every 45 gallons of wine it produces. The 60 yards of textiles is the opportunity cost of producing 45 gallons of wine.

Note that while there is no known way of converting textiles directly into wine, the use of labor to produce wine reduces the amount of labor available to produce textiles. The internal ratio showing the trade-off of yards of textiles to gallons of wine in Great Britain is therefore equal to 60 yards/45 gallons, or 4/3.

In Portugal this ratio is 30 yards/30 gallons, or 1/1; that is, the opportunity cost of 1 gallon of wine in Portugal is 1 yard of textiles. Portugal would be willing to trade some of its wine for British textiles as long as it would receive more textiles by trading wine for textiles than by producing textiles itself.

Great Britain would use the same reasoning in deciding whether to trade textiles for wine. By producing textiles and selling some of them to Portugal for wine, it could increase its overall consumption of wine and textiles. The incentive to trade will depend on the rate at which the countries trade wine for textiles.

Consider what happens if the price ratio for trade is 1 gallon of wine for 1.2 yards of textiles. Table 15-2 summarizes the following situation. Assume that at full capacity Great Britain can produce 1,000 yards of textiles and Portugal can produce 600 gallons of wine. Great Britain can convert textiles to wine by producing wine while reducing its output of textiles. The trade-off is 4/3 yards for 1 gallon. For example, at a production level of 700 yards, it would have 225 gallons of wine. If it instead produced 1,000 yards of textiles and sold 300 yards to Portugal, it would have 700 yards left over and 250 gallons of wine.

Portugal could produce 600 gallons of wine at full capacity. It could instead produce 300 gallons of wine and 300 yards of textiles. By producing 600 gallons and selling 250 to Great Britain, it would have 350 gallons of wine and 1.2 × 250, or 300, yards of textiles. By trading, both countries have done better than they would have done without trade. In this example, they have produced an extra 75 gallons of wine with the same total output of textiles.

We know that within Portugal the trade-off between wine and textiles is 1 to 1. In Great Britain, it is 1 to 4/3. Portugal would never trade 1 gallon of wine to Great Britain for less than 1 yard of textiles. Great Britain has to give up 4/3 yards of textiles for every gallon of wine it produces. Great Britain would not be willing to give up more than 4/3 yards of textiles to purchase a gallon of wine from Portugal.

This suggests that the limits to mutually beneficial trade are between a minimum of 1 yard and a maximum of 4/3 yards of textiles for every gallon of wine. At a trading ratio between these two limits both countries would be better off with trade than without trade.

TABLE 15-2 ■ Mutually beneficial trade

| | No Trade | | With Trade | | | |
| | Production and Consumption | | Production | | Consumption | |
	Wine	Textiles	Wine	Textiles	Wine	Textiles
Great Britain	225	700	0	1,000	250	700
Portugal	300	300	600	0	350	300
Total	525	1,000	600	1,000	600	1,000

Demand Considerations

The previous example shows that countries with different cost advantages have an incentive to trade. The price at which they trade also depends on demand conditions in each country. As long as the price ratio lies between the limits set by comparative advantage, both countries gain from trade.

In our previous example both countries increased their consumption of wine. If the trading price of textiles for wine were lower than 1.2 (that is, fewer textiles in exchange for 1 gallon of wine), Portugal would have to give up more wine to consume the same amount of textiles. The lower price would reflect Portugal's stronger demand for textiles.

We should note that even if the comparative advantages were the same in both countries, there still might be an incentive to trade. Actual markets are not as homogeneous as suggested by this simple example. For instance, people have different preferences for French, Italian, American, and Portuguese wine, which induces international trade among these countries even if the comparative advantage is the same in each country.

There are differences in tastes not only between countries, but within countries. The differences in tastes within countries may be greater than differences across countries. For example, there may be little difference in comparative advantage among European countries in the production of luxury automobiles. Differences in tastes within each country will lead to both a variety of automobiles purchased in a country and two-way trade in automobiles among such car-producing countries as Germany, France, Great Britain, and Sweden.

Rocky Sanders's success in selling trash bags in other countries will depend on the reception he receives for his product. Trash cans in West Germany are generally smaller and more standardized than in the United States, because they are designed to fit the automatic lifting machines attached to West German municipal garbage trucks. Rocky will have to modify the size of his bags to accommodate the smaller size of these trash cans. He may also find that the strength of his bags or even the color may be more important in one country than another. Tailoring the characteristics of a product to the concerns of potential customers is the focus of marketers, which we considered in detail in Chapter 9, "The Costs of Information and the Promotion of Product Quality."

Incomplete Specialization

In the wine and textile example we concluded that both countries should specialize in producing only one product. Actually, we do not see complete specialization in the real world. We had complete specialization in this example because of the assumption of a constant marginal productivity of labor in both countries. Recall from Chapter 3 that we expect that eventually there will be diminishing marginal productivity of an input.

With diminishing marginal productivity we may see incomplete specialization. **Incomplete specialization** occurs when a country produces several goods, some of which it also imports. With diminishing marginal productivity the country needs increasingly greater amounts of the input to increase output at the same marginal rate. This means that the marginal cost of each additional unit of output is increasing. Figure 15-1 shows how increasing marginal cost will affect the production of both products in a country. Each country will decide to produce an output level where marginal cost equals marginal revenue.

15-1   **Incomplete specialization**

GRAPHICAL   Figure 15-1 shows marginal-cost curves for wine and textiles in Portugal and
EXPLANATION   Great Britain. The figure indicates the pretrade outputs and an international trade price between the two extremes of marginal cost set by output levels prior to trade. After the two countries begin to trade, they will face the same prices. Great Britain will increase its production of textiles to the point where

FIGURE 15-1 ▪ Incomplete specialization. Once trade begins both countries will choose an output where marginal cost will equal the new price. Great Britain will increase its output of textiles and decrease its output of wine. Portugal will increase wine production and decrease textile production. Q_1 is the output of each good prior to trade. Q_2 is output with trade.

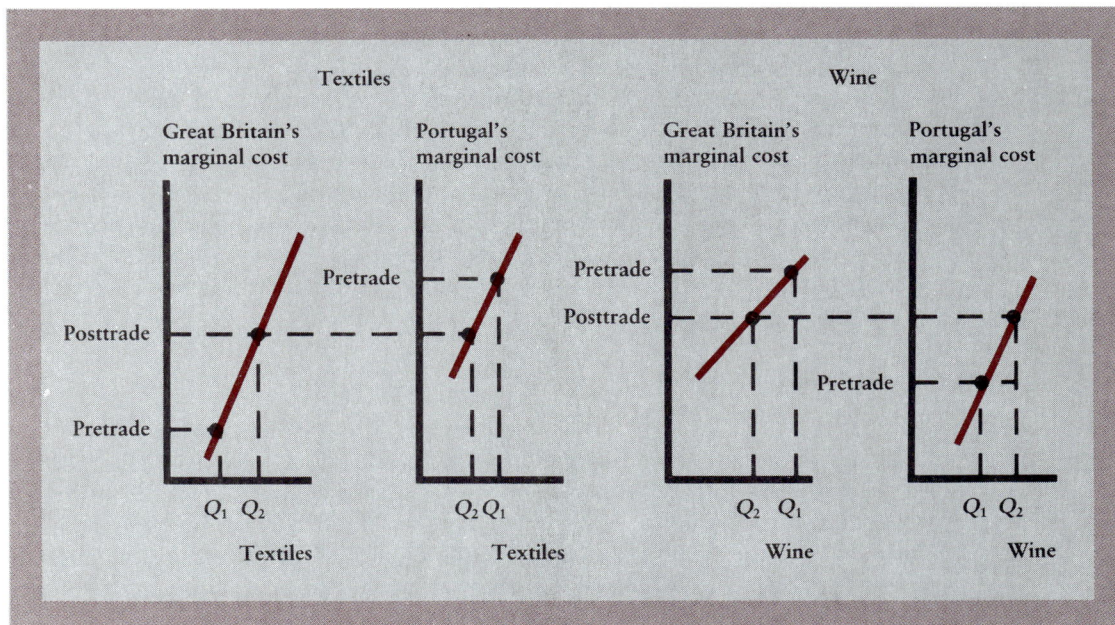

the trade price equals its marginal cost. It will lower its production of wine. The opposite will occur in Portugal: increased wine production and lower textile production.

We do not need to limit this analysis to two goods. Countries produce a wide range of products subject to different production functions. We expect that a country will export those goods in which it has the greatest comparative advantage and import more of the goods in which it has a comparative disadvantage. If the country has no effect on the world price, it will set its output level where the marginal cost equals the world price. Countries with a comparative advantage will have relatively lower marginal-cost curves and will produce more output at world prices.

15-1 How much do you make

APPLICATION

Professor Mordechai Kreinin of Michigan State University argues that we should rank all industries within a country in order of production costs to determine comparative advantages. By observing how an industry's labor cost changes relative to the manufacturing average within the country over time, we can determine whether an industry is gaining or losing its comparative advantage. Direct comparisons of the same industry across countries without accounting for the industry's relative position within the country are sensitive to fluctuations in exchange rates and methods used in the different countries to calculate costs.

By analyzing an industry's position within a country, we could conclude that a rise in wages in one industry relative to the average increase of wages in all industries in the country would lower that industry's comparative advantage in world trade. Professor Kreinin has determined that the United States, Great Britain, and France lost comparative advantage in steel production in the 1980s. Wages in the steel industry increased at a faster rate relative to the rest of those countries' manufacturing industries than they did relative to the manufacturing average in the other countries. There was no loss in comparative advantage for Japan and West Germany, because their wage increases were in line with increases in the rest of the country.

Compensation for U.S. automobile workers also increased during this time period, while Japanese auto workers received increases in tandem with the rest of Japanese manufacturing workers. As of 1980, wages in the U.S. auto industry exceeded the U.S. manufacturing average by 57 percent. Wages were 42 percent higher than the average in the iron and steel industry. By comparison, Japanese iron and steel workers received 93 percent of the Japanese manufacturing average and auto workers made only 7 percent more than the average.

In 1980 the United States had a comparative advantage in many high-technology industries, such as chemicals, computers, and medical instruments. Wages in these industries were lower in the United States relative to the manufacturing average. According to Professor Kreinin, an increase in wages that exceeds growth in labor productivity and inflation will lower an industry's international competitiveness. High wages in the U.S. auto and iron and steel industries have had much to do with the decline of these industries.

Source: This discussion is based in part on Mordechai E. Kreinin, *International Economics*, 5th ed. New York: Harcourt Brace Jovanovich, 1987.

Trade Policies

Despite the expected benefits of increased trade among nations, there is strong international sentiment in favor of restricting trade to achieve specific objectives. In this section we will turn our attention to the most common form of restrictions, concentrating at first on their effects on markets and the constraints they impose on firms' behavior.

Let us return to Rocky Sanders. While Rocky is considering selling his trash bags in Europe, he must also contend with European-made trash bags in the United States. He may one day find that firms in other countries can manufacture trash bags identical to his at lower average total cost. If imports of trash bags force the market price down, Rocky may be unable to cover the opportunity cost of his investment in the trash bag business.

Rocky might consider convincing the government to restrict imports of foreign-made trash bags. Several industries have sought and received some form of protectionist help from the U.S. government to counter an increase in imports. These include the automobile, textile, dairy product, steel, shoe, and canned mushroom industries. Protectionism takes the form of subsidies, export restraints, quotas, and tariffs.

Both quotas and tariffs increase the price paid by American consumers. In addition, more resources are used to produce these products than would be if they were produced by the most efficient suppliers. After looking at the effects of each of these policies, we will turn to the most common arguments in favor of protectionism and the most common rebuttals.

Tariffs

A country can impose a tariff on imports or exports. A **tariff** is a tax added to the price of a good when the good crosses the boundaries of the importing country. Export tariffs are relatively rare. The U.S. Constitution does not allow export tariffs. The U.S. government regulates exports by imposing bans or quotas. While import tariffs do generate revenue, the principal reason for their use today is protectionism.

There are three different types of tariffs: ad valorem, specific duty, and compound duty. An **ad valorem tariff** is a fixed percentage of the price of the good. A **specific duty tariff** is a fixed sum of money per unit of the good (for example, $10 per television set). A **compound duty** combines an ad valorem tariff and a specific duty on the same good.

While the United States uses specific duty and ad valorem tariffs in approximately equal proportion, European countries generally rely on ad valorem tariffs. The specific duty tariff is easier to administer because it is quantity-specific and does not depend on determining the appropriate price of the product. The two types of tariff differ only in the ease of administering them. They have essentially the same economic effects.

In the following example we will use the specific duty tariff to show graphically the impact of a tariff on an industry that would otherwise compete in a world market.

| 15-2 | Tariffs |

GRAPHICAL EXPLANATION

Figure 15-2 (p. 430) shows the effects of a tariff on an otherwise competitive industry. P_1 is the prevailing world price for good Q. S is the U.S. firm's supply curve, and D is the demand curve for good Q from U.S. consumers. If there were no world trade, U.S. suppliers would meet their country's demand at price P_2. With trade, the U.S. domestic price is the same as the world price. If the world price is P_1, U.S. consumers purchase Q_1, and domestic suppliers supply Q_0. The difference between Q_1 and Q_0 is net imports.

If the United States imposes a tariff of t equal to $P_3 - P_1$ on imports, the tariff would raise the effective domestic price to P_3. For a foreign company to be willing to sell to the United States, it must receive a price from consumers that covers the world price plus the tariff. Otherwise, it would sell its output elsewhere. The higher price of P_3 encourages U.S. firms to produce a greater output level since they do not pay the tariff. The higher U.S. price due to the tariff forces U.S. consumers to reduce their quantity demanded of the good to Q_3. The U.S. government receives the amount of the tariff times the number of units sold as revenue.

U.S. output of the good increases. The additional output is not without an opportunity cost to U.S. citizens. Recall that the market supply curve represents the horizontal sum of the marginal-cost curves of all of the U.S. firms in the market. The area under the supply curve represents the sum of the variable cost of producing a given level of output. In Figure 15-2 the area under the U.S. supply curve and above the world supply curve shows the additional cost of producing the extra amount of output domestically rather than purchasing it from other countries. That extra cost comes from resources

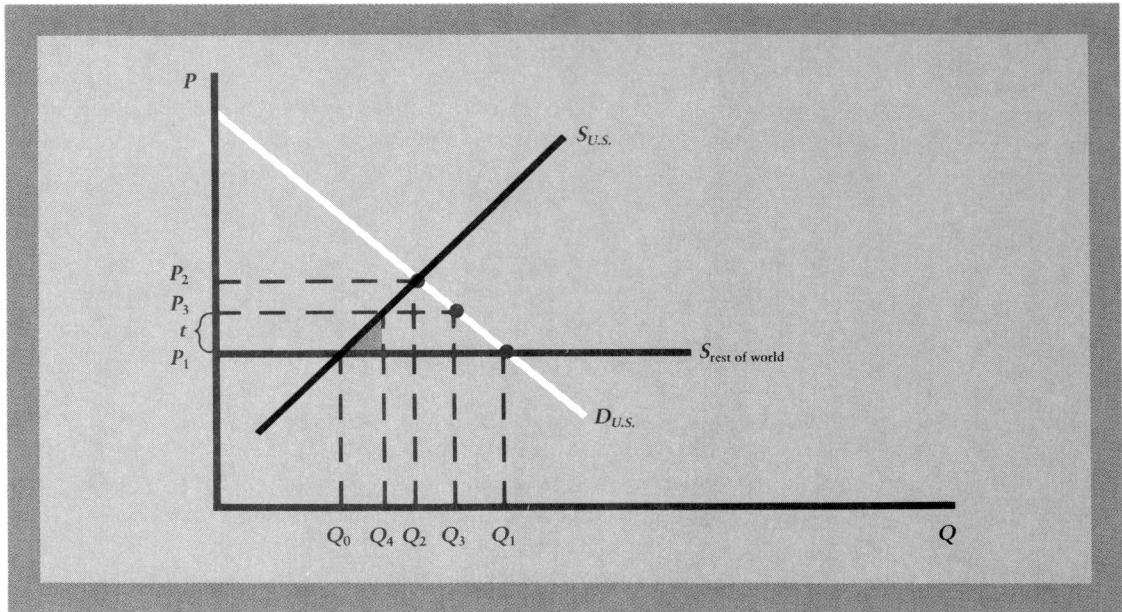

FIGURE 15-2 ▪ Tariffs. A tariff of t dollars per unit will raise the U.S. domestic price to P_3 (that is, $P_1 + t$). The domestic quantity demanded will drop from Q_1 to Q_3, while domestic output will increase from Q_0 to Q_4. U.S. consumers will have to pay a higher price and will be worse off. Although U.S. producers of the good increase output, the additional output costs more if produced domestically than if bought from foreign firms. The shaded area represents the additional production cost.

that have been pulled away from other industries that would use them more efficiently. These other industries must rank higher on the country's list of comparative advantage. Otherwise, the resources would already be in the protected industry.

Quotas

A quota is an alternative to a tariff. A **quota** is a physical limit on the amount of a good that a country can export to another country during a specified time period. Quotas can have essentially the same effects on domestic prices and output as tariffs have. One of the main differences, however, is the lack of tax revenue for the government imposing the quota. While the quota raises domestic prices, the benefits of the higher price go to the foreign firms. Consider the following Graphical Explanation.

In Figure 15-3 we have the same demand and domestic-supply curves as in Figure 15-2. At the world price, imports equal $Q_1 - Q_0$. If the government imposes a quota of less than $Q_1 - Q_0$, the domestic price will rise above the world price. For example, in Figure 15-3 a quota of q will result in a domestic price of P_3. Consumer demand will decrease to Q_3, while domestic output will increase to Q_4 (that is, $Q_3 - q$).

The government could have set the same domestic price by imposing a tariff of t equal to $P_3 - P_1$. With a tariff the shaded area in Figure 15-2 would represent the revenue going to the government. With a quota the shaded area would show the additional profits earned by the importers due to the higher domestic price.

FIGURE 15-3 ▪ **Quotas.** A quota of q will raise the domestic price to P_3. There is a quota q that will raise the U.S. domestic price by t: the tariff shown in Figure 15-2. With the quota, the foreign firms will sell fewer units of the good to the United States but will receive the shaded area as additional economic profits.

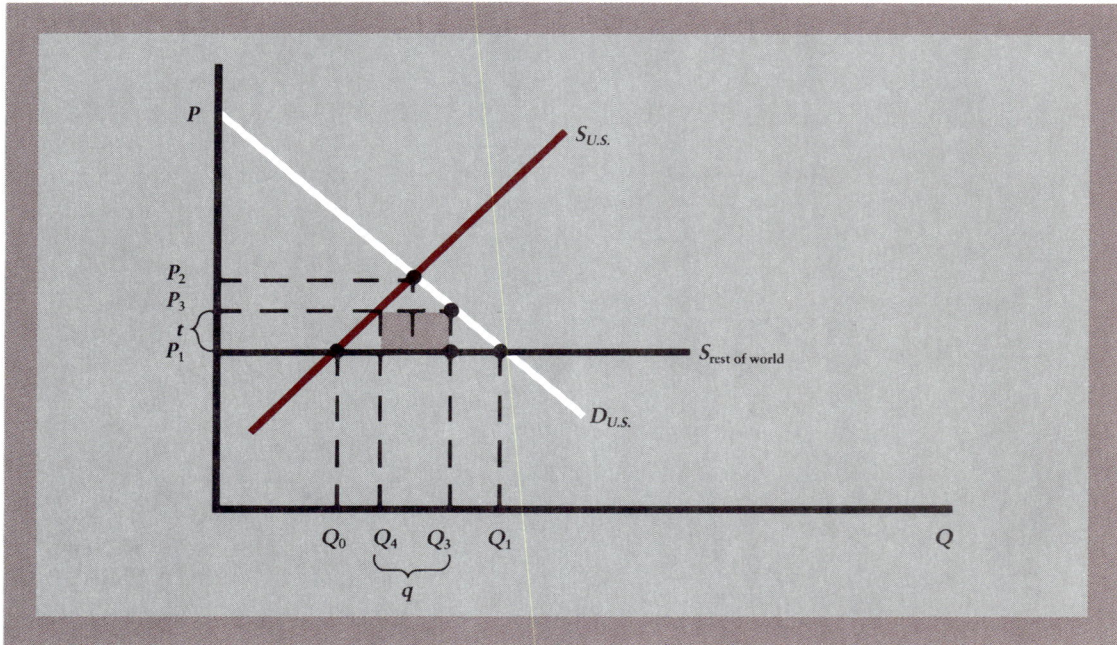

The effect on government revenues is not the only important difference between quotas and tariffs. When there is an increase in demand, quotas impose greater distortions on domestic prices than tariffs do. Consider the following Graphical Explanation.

An increase in demand

GRAPHICAL
EXPLANATION

In Figures 15-2 and 15-3 the tariff t raises the domestic price above the world price by the same amount as a quota of q. Despite this equivalent effect on domestic price, an increase in demand from D_1 to D_2 will have a different impact on the domestic price depending on whether the country has imposed a tariff or a quota. Figure 15-4 shows the effects of an increase in demand with a quota and a tariff.

FIGURE 15-4 ▪ **A shift in demand.** A shift in demand from D_1 to D_2 will affect both the domestic quantity supplied and the domestic price. With a tariff of t dollars, the domestic price will remain at P_3. Domestic output will remain at Q_4, while imports will increase from q to q^*. With a quota of q, the shift in demand will raise the domestic price to P_5. Domestic output will increase to Q_6, while imports will remain fixed at q. Domestic demand will now be Q_5 (that is, $Q_6 + q$).

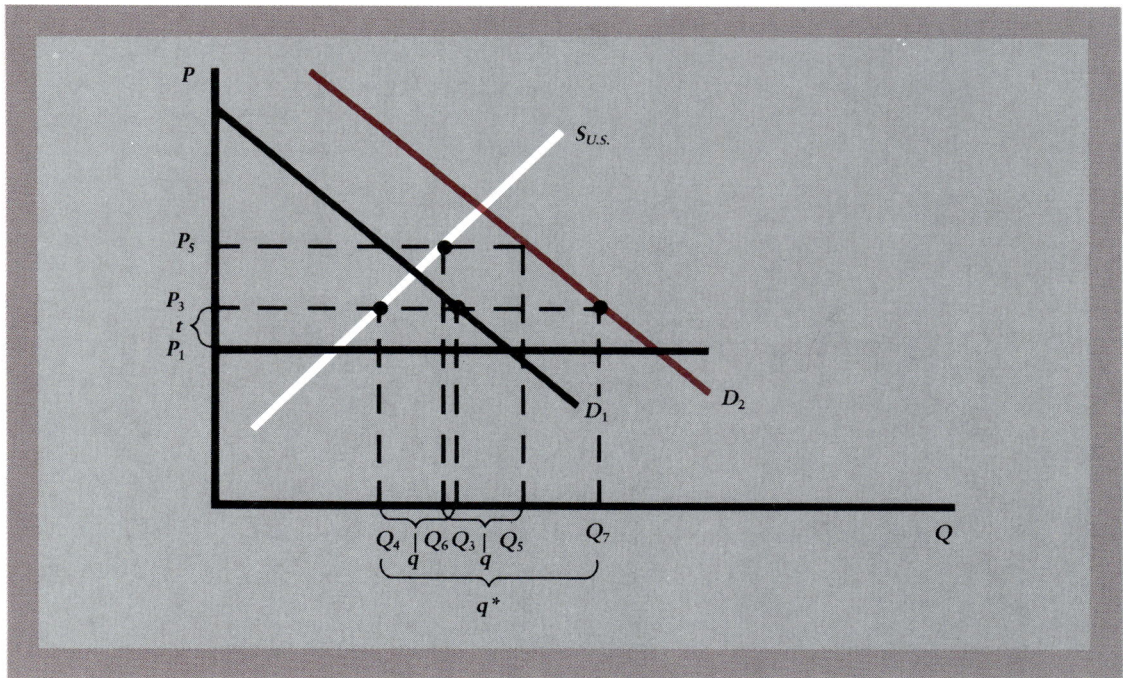

With a tariff of t the domestic price remains at P_3 regardless of the location of the demand curve. The additional quantity demanded due to an increase in demand from D_1 to D_2 will be met by increased imports. Imports will now be q^*.

The same increase in demand to D_2 will increase the domestic price if the quota remains unchanged. In Figure 15-4 a quota of q creates the same domestic price as the tariff t when the domestic demand curve is D_1. When the demand curve shifts to D_2 the domestic price has to rise to encourage domestic producers to produce more. Without greater domestic firm production there would be a gap between the quantity demanded and the quantity supplied. In this case the new price would be P_5. Domestic output would increase to Q_6. The quota fixes imports at q.

| 15-2 | Exotic cheeses |

APPLICATION

When George Wallace was campaigning for President of the United States in 1976, he told audiences in Wisconsin that he would work to keep out of the United States those "exotic cheeses" that were threatening the livelihood of Wisconsin dairymen. Since most industrialized countries restrict the importation of dairy products, this is not an unusual campaign promise.

According to the World Bank, if all subsidies and protectionist legislation for agriculture were removed, consumers and taxpayers would save $100 billion a year, while farmers would be $50 billion worse off. Instead of devising ways to compensate farmers while removing these trade restrictions, governments continue to support their domestic agriculture indirectly by manipulating world trade.

For example, the Japanese government reportedly gives its farmers as much as three times the world price for rice and then feeds the rice to pigs at half the world price. Japanese consumers pay as much as twenty times what it costs to feed the pigs. The European Economic Community (EEC) pays its farmers twice the world price for dairy products. As of 1986, the EEC countries had nearly 1.5 million tons of butter in government storage. Storage imposes additional costs while the butter gradually deteriorates.

Farm support in the United States increased from $2.7 billion in 1980 to $25.8 billion in 1986. The EEC's total was $21.5 in 1986. Only 2.5 percent of Britons farm or work directly for farmers. France, which is one of the biggest supporters of the EEC's subsidy program, has only 8 percent of its workers on the land compared to 22 percent in 1960. Despite their relatively small share of the population, farmers have been able to convince the rest of their compatriots to subsidize their businesses.

Voluntary Export Restraints

Due to international trade agreements, the developed countries do not use quotas to restrict imports of manufactured goods. Despite the ban on quotas, countries often demand "voluntary" export quotas in place of a threatened tariff or other nontariff barrier. These arrangements are bilateral agreements between two countries and are enforceable by the exporting country.

Export restraints are not as effective as quotas because of the difficulty of controlling imports. For its part, the exporting country does not usually want to control its exports. Companies in that country can often evade the restraints by selling through another country not subject to the agreement.

15-3	Any volunteers?

APPLICATION

Governments have spent large sums of money supporting troubled car manufacturers rather than suffer the political consequences of bankruptcies. The European companies Alfa Romeo, Seat, Fiat, British Leyland, and Renault might not have stayed in business without government subsidies. Because of the companies' political influence, they were able to attract enough protectionist support to survive.

Starting in 1981 the United States persuaded the Japanese government to impose voluntary export restraints (VERs) to allow U.S. car manufacturers enough time to adjust to Japanese competition. The limit was 1.68 million cars in 1981. The limit increased to 1.8 million, and then to 2.3 million in 1985. While the number of cars allowed into the country does not reflect the underlying U.S. demand for Japanese cars, some Japanese firms benefit.

The largest exporters, Toyota and Honda, earn a share of quotas in proportion to their share of the Japanese domestic market. They thus do not have to fear competition from newer growing Japanese firms. In addition, the underlying U.S. demand for Japanese cars allows Toyota and Honda to raise their prices in the United States above what they would be able to charge with no restrictions.

International Commodity Agreements

Countries dependent on one or two commodities, such as coffee, tin, cocoa, and sugar, may experience significant swings in earnings from the export of these goods due to unexpectedly large or small harvests or changes in production by other countries. For many agricultural products an unexpectedly large harvest should lead to sharp drops in market prices. A small harvest should send prices higher.

Dependence on export revenues and wide fluctuations in market prices have led many export countries to form international commodity agreements with the buying nations. Unlike a cartel, which contains only the producing firms and countries, a commodity agreement also includes the buying nations.

A commodity agreement can take one of several forms. First, there may be a provision to adjust price to compensate for a change in the quantity demanded. In Chapter 2 we saw that the own-price elasticity of demand gives us an indication of the effect on total revenues of a change in the price. Some agreements attempt to utilize this information to adjust price to maintain relatively stable total revenues.

A second form of agreement involves buffer stockpiles that a central agency buys and sells to smooth out the wide swings in the market price. By buying output and storing it, the central agency keeps the price from dropping. The guiding principle is that the agency sells from the stockpile during years when the quantity supplied is low. In this way the agency is acting as a speculator.

A third type of arrangement sets minimum and maximum prices. Within the limits the market price prevails. When the market price goes beyond the limits, the limits become the transaction price.

Each of these forms of managing the market interferes with the market forces pushing the market to an equilibrium price. The opportunity for distortion is great. Since the members of the agreement are operating on an assumed long-run equilibrium price, they can create distortions that may have graver consequences than if they left the market to its own devices. Consider the plight of the following international agreement.

<table>
<tr><td>15-4</td><td>A hole in the cocoa mug</td></tr>
</table>

APPLICATION The international cocoa agreement has not fared well. In the early 1970s prices were set at too low a level. After countries withheld production, market prices soared and made the agreements unworkable. The 1980 agreement failed for other reasons. The prices were too high, and not all of the principal countries in the market went along with the agreement to restrict output to keep prices high.

Due to world recession and oversupply at the high prices, cocoa prices dropped by half between 1979 and 1982. The person who is responsible for maintaining buffer stocks had spent all of the $230 million available to purchase excess demand at the controlled price. Unfortunately, he had only purchased 100,000 tons of the 250,000 tons needed to maintain the artificially set price. Once he could no longer prop up the price by stockpiling, the price fell dramatically. Despite some poor harvests since then, the price stayed below the minimum price through the mid-1980s.

Compounding the problem of maintaining the agreed-upon price was the absence from the agreement of the Ivory Coast, the world's biggest supplier, and the United States, the world's largest consumer. Malaysia refused to join as well, and has been expanding its production. By 1985, Malaysia had become the sixth largest producer. With these large buyers and sellers outside the agreement, there was little chance of maintaining control.

As the cocoa agreement shows, it can be difficult to determine the long-run equilibrium price for a commodity. Although at times private speculators appear to accentuate the swings in prices, they absorb much of the risks of these price swings by buying and selling on speculation in an unrestricted market.

When an agency enforcing the agreement stockpiles the commodity in anticipation of a higher long-term equilibrium price, it runs the risk of eventually having to sell these goods. If its estimate of the price was too high, it might have to sell when the price is low, leading to an even wider drop than would have been the case otherwise.

Artificially high prices give signals to producers to produce more. This can only add to the pressure on market prices to fall. Even if the group can discipline its members to curtail output, there will be countries that do not belong to the agreements and that will produce as much as is profitable for them.

Protectionist Proposals

There have been arguments made in favor of protectionism. During the remainder of the chapter we will consider four of them: initial support for an infant industry, national defense, anti-dumping and retaliation against unfair trade practices. Behind most of these proposals is the fear that there will be a loss of jobs due to an increase in imports. We will discuss the arguments for and against these proposals for protection while emphasizing the expected impact on employment and national income.

Infant-Industry Argument

There is support, especially in developing countries, for new firms seeking protection from larger, established, foreign companies until the new firms can support themselves. While the ultimate success of a new firm depends on its long-term profitability, there is fear that the firm may not be able to convince creditors of its long-term viability without this initial protection. Proponents of this argument stress that firms in the industry will experience significant decreases in their operating costs as time passes.

The infant-industry argument depends on special assumptions about the market environment that do not apply to as many situations as some would suggest. At times the argument appears in defense of declining industries hoping to protect their market position. Automobile manufacturers and steel companies have argued at times that they need support to change over to a new product line despite having had an established presence in the market for years.

Historically, it has been difficult to remove protectionist measures once the industry has become competitive. Firms not only become accustomed to the protected environment, they find it more profitable with barriers to competition than without them. Resources that could be used to improve their competitive position are used instead to pressure politicians to maintain the protection.

15-5

Milk made in New York

APPLICATION

Countries do not have a monopoly on protectionism. State governments also attempt to protect some of their producers. Consider the milk market in New York. New York enacted a milk licensing law in 1937 in reaction to claims that large national producers were using low prices to drive smaller New York dairies out of the market. Fearing that a monopoly would be the end result of this price war, the state legislature gave the Agriculture Commissioner the power to regulate the industry through licensing.

A potential entrant to the market must now show county-by-county that its entry into the market will not cause "destructive competition," a term never defined by the state. There were 60,000 people working in the New York milk industry in 1986. The New York trade associations argue that their wages and rents are higher than those in New Jersey, so that they would be run out of business if the market were open to dairies from out of state.

By 1986, five New York dairies controlled the New York City market, where prices generally range about $0.35 per gallon more than prices in neighboring areas. In January 1986, a New Jersey dairy, Farmland Dairies, received the first out-of-state license to sell milk on Staten Island. The price soon dropped by $0.40 a gallon on Staten Island.

It may be more efficient to use a subsidy to protect an infant industry than to rely on quotas or tariffs. A subsidy acts oppositely to a tax by lowering the production costs of the firm. Subsidies only affect production costs without affecting consumer choice. Consumers do not face higher prices for the good and do not alter their consumption patterns by switching to substitute goods. After a specified time period, the government can end the subsidies. If the firm cannot survive by then, it may never be viable.

National Defense

Many industries claim that their products are essential for national defense purposes. They claim that if the country does not have a viable industry producing the good, it might not be able to obtain the good in times of war. While military experts must decide which products are essential for national defense, there are important economic considerations.

The national security argument suggests that a good would not be available from other countries in time of need, such as during war. Few products would not be available from at least some nonhostile countries. For any country to be cut off from supplies of essential goods, it would have to be isolated from most of the world. Even if it were difficult to find the good in time of war, alternatives such as stockpiling might be more economical than supporting high-cost producers indefinitely.

15-6	A security deposit for the Soviet Union

APPLICATION

The world increased wheat production dramatically between 1976 and 1986. The Common Market's output went from 41 million tons to 72 million tons. Production in Asia went from 119 million to 189 million tons. Only Africa and the Soviet Union did not increase production.

African production suffered due to droughts and administrative disincentives. The Soviet Union decreased the land allocated for wheat production by 20 percent but did not achieve a change in productivity per acre. Technological changes in other countries have pushed yields higher. For example, Great Britain saw an increase of 75 percent in yields during this time period.

All of this growth in output has led to overproduction at current state-supported prices. European countries pay their farmers twice the world price for their wheat. High-cost producers have driven the world price down for those who choose to buy rather than export.

Despite low world prices, some countries see self-sufficiency in wheat production as essential to national security. For example, Saudi Arabia increased its production of wheat from 187,000 tons in 1981 to 2 million tons in 1986. The government paid approximately $1,000 a ton to its farmers in 1986. The world price in 1986 was $80 a ton. While a fear of destabilizing famines in other countries may make the more developed countries feel secure with stockpiled surpluses, farmers' lobbies encourage the large subsidies that this industry receives.

While the Common Market countries may feel more secure with a payment of twice the world market price for its wheat, it has seen its world market share increase from 9 percent to 17 percent from 1976 to 1986. Since these countries have to sell the wheat eventually on the world market at low prices, their taxpayers are subsidizing these sales.

While other countries tax their people to subsidize their farmers, there is one major beneficiary of the subsidized wheat that appears to have little interest in self-sufficiency and national security in wheat—namely, the Soviet Union. The major buyer of wheat on the world market at these heavily subsidized prices is the Soviet Union. Why produce wheat yourself when someone else is essentially giving it away?

Control of Foreign Dumping of Goods

▶ ——————— Via the media we often hear complaints of dumping by foreign firms. **Dumping** is the selling of goods to a foreign country for a price below that charged to customers in the home country. It is somewhat difficult to assess the extent of this practice. At one level price differences can reflect a difference in marketing and distribution costs. There are also costs of packaging and adjustments in product specifications. Dumping is actually an application of price discrimination, which we discussed in Chapters 6 and 8.

Dumping as a Form of Price Discrimination   In Chapter 6 we saw that a firm that has a monopoly can increase its profits by selling to two different submarkets at different prices. For example, a movie theater can charge children a ticket price that is different from the price paid by adults. Price discrimination is most suitable for services since it is difficult to prevent resales of manufactured goods. Unless the firm can prevent resales, it will not be able to maintain a difference in the market price.

| 15-7 | It pays to shop around |

APPLICATION

In the early 1980s, when the dollar was reaching record highs against European currencies, Americans saw little change in the dollar price of European cars sold in the United States. Despite 40 percent or more appreciation in the dollar, the new car prices did not drop. Americans interested in purchasing a European car had to arrange the purchase through U.S. dealers or representatives in order to buy a car with U.S. safety and environmental specifications.

To circumvent this situation, some Americans went to Europe to purchase cars with European specifications. After shipping the cars back to the United States, the owners arranged to have the specifications changed. Depending on the exchange rate at the time, the European traveler could earn a substantial reduction on a European vacation with the savings in the car price.

Until the early 1980s Britons paid, or the average, 40 percent more for automobiles purchased in Great Britain than for identical cars bought across the English Channel in Belgium. Belgian prices were somewhat lower due to price controls, but the main difference was British protectionism. Although car manufacturers sold fewer cars, the higher prices increased their profits.

Britons discovered the advantages of crossing the Channel and buying a car in Belgium.

Faced with a significant drop in sales within Great Britain, the car manufacturers attempted to stop sales in Belgium by reducing the availability of right-hand-drive cars there. Great Britain is one of the few countries in the world where drivers drive on the left side of the road and cars have steering wheels on the right side of the car.

Great Britain is a member of the Common Market. Since the Common Market countries are slowly moving towards economic integration, they have adopted some rules for intercountry trade. In response to the wide variation in car prices among the member states, the Common Market decreed in the mid-1980s that car prices could not vary by more than 12 percent in the member countries.

Dumping as Predatory Pricing A related argument against foreign dumping hinges on alleged predatory pricing by foreign firms. In Chapter 7 we discussed predatory pricing as a strategy for driving rivals out of the market. A predatory firm can lower its price and force less financially solvent firms out of the market. After the departure of these firms, the predator raises prices to recover losses. This argument hinges on the assumption that the firm can maintain a barrier to entry after it eliminates its competition. We have discussed in several parts of this text the difficulty in maintaining barriers to entry without government support.

15-8

APPLICATION

Excuse me, where do I dump this stuff?

The world sugar market is in disarray. In 1985, farmers in Common Market countries received 20 cents per pound, U.S. farmers received 17.75 cents per pound, and Colombia paid its farmers 21 cents a pound. All this was going on when the world price was less than 4 cents a pound.

High sugar prices have encouraged farmers in these and other countries to increase production. European farmers increased output from 10.8 million tons to 13.3 million from 1977 to 1985. Since the European countries guarantee the price, they must purchase the sugar and then either store it or resell it at the world price. To avoid adding to the mountains of butter and sugar, these countries have sold the sugar at a loss of $350 per ton.

These high prices have had the perverse effect of encouraging buyers to shift to alternative sweeteners. For example, in the United States, high-fructose corn syrup has taken over half of the sweetener market. Not surprisingly, corn farmers are strong supporters of legislation to protect the high price of sugar.

These government-backed policies have led to the dumping of sugar on the remaining nonregulated world market. While European taxpayers have allowed their politicians to impose a $2 billion cost on them with the sugar program, the most efficient producers have been driven from the market. Unable to compete with other countries' subsidies, Fiji, Brazil, and Australia have curtailed their operations due to a lack of buyers.

Retaliation against the Foreign Dumping of Goods In the United States a firm or industry must initiate a complaint of dumping by a foreign firm under the provisions of the 1974 Trade Act to the Commerce Department for its consideration. If the Commerce Department concurs with the complaint, it passes it on to the U.S. International Trade Commission. If both agencies agree that dumping of goods has taken place, they can levy a tax equal to the difference between the foreign country's price and the U.S. price of the imported product.

The crux of a policy against foreign dumping is the expectation that retaliation will have positive effects. Retaliation may have a direct effect once a government imposes a retaliatory tax. There may also be an impact due to the threat of a retaliatory tax against the importer. Consider the following example.

15-9

Are you threatening me?

APPLICATION Professors Mark Herander and J. Brad Schwartz of the University of South Florida estimated the effect of the threat of an antidumping complaint on the differences between the home and U.S. prices of imported goods. They used data from 1976 to 1981. They measured the threat by calculating the percentage of an industry's sales that was subject to complaints lodged with the Commerce Department.

They determined that as the number of complaints increased, foreign firms decreased their margins between home and U.S. prices. Surprisingly, they did not find the same response when there was an increased probability that the Commerce Department would rule against the foreign firms.

Professors Herander and Schwartz found, however, that in the latter part of the time period of the study, the increased probability of a successful case against the foreign firm led to a decrease in the price margins. They contended that foreign firms gained experience with the inner workings of the process as time passed and became better informed of the impending effects of an adverse decision. From this evidence it appears that the threat of retaliation does have an impact on foreign firms.

Source: Mark G. Herander and J. Brad Schwartz, "The Impact of the Threat of U.S. Trade Policy." *Southern Economic Journal* 51, No. 1 (July 1984):59–79.

Under provisions of Section 201 of the 1974 Trade Act, U.S. industries can also request temporary protection from imports, if they can establish that they have been injured by an increase in imports. If successful, the industry might receive protection in the form of a quota or tariff for as much as five years while it adjusts to the increased competition.

The U.S. International Trade Commission (ITC) makes an initial ruling on the appeal, but the President must make the final decision. While there is little difficulty establishing that an industry has been hurt by decreased profits, plant closings, or reduced sales and employment, proving that imports have caused the decline of an industry is more difficult. Consider the following example.

15-10 Not the right kind of decline

APPLICATION

Professors Robert Pindyck and Julio Rotemberg of Massachusetts Institute of Technology argue that the ITC does not have a systematic method for evaluating these appeals. They offer a technique that allows them to unravel the separate effects of a shift in demand and a shift in domestic supply from the effect of increased imports. Their statistical technique is based on a slight variation of Figure 15-1.

As an illustration of their technique, they reviewed the case of the U.S. copper industry, which requested relief from imports in 1984. In the early 1980s there was a significant contraction of the U.S. industry. Prices dropped significantly and many mines closed. Between 1982 and 1983, imports increased sharply. Although they agreed that the industry had suffered during the 1980s, they showed that the injury was due to shifts in demand and domestic supply, not imports. They used data from 1950 to 1983 to determine the causes of the problem.

They concluded that increases in wages in excess of inflation had the greatest impact on the industry in 1981. If wages had not increased relative to the average wages of all manufacturing, domestic output would have been more than 350,000 tons higher. If there had been no increases in imports, domestic output would have increased by no more than 100,000 tons. Together with a decline in demand due to a general recession in the early 1980s, the increased wages lowered potential output between 650,000 and 1,000,000 tons and employment by 20,000 workers.

The two researchers presented this evidence to the ITC at the time of the appeal. The ITC voted 5 to 0 in favor of rewarding relief to the industry, although they disagreed as to the method that should be used. In 1984 President Reagan decided not to grant relief.

Source: Robert S. Pindyck and Julio J. Rotemberg, "Are Imports to Blame? Attribution of Injury under the 1974 Trade Act." *Journal of Law and Economics* XXX, No. 1 (April 1987):101–22. © by the University of Chicago.

Retaliation for Other Countries' Subsidies and Unfair Trade Practices

There is little doubt that most countries use an array of subsidies and special policies to protect specific industries. These practices are based mostly on politics. Political leaders inherit policies backed by special interests. Few leaders have strong enough popular mandates to pursue the free-market policies suggested in this chapter. Despite a politician's personal convictions to serve the interests of the entire country, politicians must attract funds and support in order to gain reelection.

15-11	We will tell you what we want

APPLICATION

Professor Cletus Coughlin of the University of Georgia sought empirical evidence for factors that influenced legislators' votes for or against protectionist laws in the U.S. Congress. Many economists contend that legislators react strongly to the special interests in their districts. An opposing view suggests that legislators follow their own convictions even to the detriment of some of their constituents.

Professor Coughlin looked at the voting for a 1982 House of Representatives bill regulating the minimum quantity of automobile components made in the United States and sold by foreign companies in the United States. The proposed percentage would have been an increasing function of the number of cars sold by the firm in the United States.

Professor Coughlin explained 81 percent of the voting pattern with the following information: the importance of the auto and steel industries to the economy of the legislator's district, the unemployment rate, campaign contributions from labor unions, and party affiliation. While party affiliation was a statistically significant factor, the remaining factors were more influential. According to Professor Coughlin, the vote reflected the powerful effect that special interests have on Congressional voting patterns.

Source: Cletus C. Coughlin, "Domestic Content Legislation: House Voting and the Economic Theory of Regulation." *Economic Inquiry* XXIII, No. 3 (July 1985):437–48.

The success of a trade policy based on retaliation depends on two assumptions. First, the country targeted for retaliation must be using "unfair" trade practices. Second, the retaliation must be successful in forcing the country to change its policies. In Application 15-9 we saw that retaliatory threats sometimes do force foreign firms to adjust their behavior. There may be limits to the success of this policy.

Pressure by one country on another country's trade policy invites further retaliation. Despite the fact that most leaders of developed countries recognize the value of free trade, these leaders must acknowledge the political situation they face at home. A confrontational approach that angers the electorate in another country is more likely to encourage retaliation from that country.

For example, Japan has been the political target of U.S. and European politicians and special interest groups because of Japan's large trade surplus with these countries. These critics of Japan attribute their own countries' problems to Japan's trade surplus and Japanese protectionism. While Japan does protect some of its industries, consider the following evidence detailing the extent of this protectionism.

15-12 Getting to know you

APPLICATION

Japan protects some of its industries. According to the Organization for Economic Cooperation and Development (OECD), protectionism in Japan is not very different from that in other developed countries. Consider the following comparisons.

Japan's average tariffs in 1983 were 4.5 percent for dutiable imports and 2.5 percent for all imports. Both percentages were lower than those for the United States and European Common Market. The tariff on textiles was 13.8 percent, compared with 22.7 percent in the United States and a comparable figure for Europe. While quotas are almost nonexistent for manufactured goods in most developed countries, Japan does use them extensively in agriculture. Japan has twenty-two quotas for farm products, compared with only one in the United States. France has nineteen.

In 1982 the International Monetary Fund concluded that Japan's 1.5 percent of gross domestic product subsidies of private and public firms fell between the 0.5 percent in the United States and the Common Market average of 2.8 percent. Nearly all of Japan's subsidies go toward the national railway system and some coal mines. According to the OECD, no important industrial sector receives a large subsidy. Research in Japan receives less government support than research in other countries. The Japanese government provided 22.2 percent of total research spending in 1983; the U.S. government, 45 percent; the German government, 42 percent; and the British government, 50 percent.

Nontariff barriers are hard to measure. While Japan has made efforts to adjust to international standards, methods of doing business in Japan are historically and culturally determined. Difficulties in using the Japanese system of distribution exist for Japanese and foreign firms alike. Foreign firms have to decide whether it is worth making the effort to learn the language and marketing system of a country with over 120 million people.

The notion that the Japanese do not like foreign goods does not appear to be valid. The Japanese buy foreign brands that do not show up in the trade statistics because the goods are produced or assembled in Japan. If we were to include these products in the trade figures, we would find that Japanese consumers purchase more foreign goods per capita than U.S. consumers do.

The trade flows between Japan and other countries are due to fluctuations in exchange rates, relative competitiveness, and differences in savings rates. The removal of all trade barriers would have little significant impact on the balance of trade. While Japan has a unique distributional system, it does not appear to be more protectionist than other industrialized countries.

Summary

While changes in demand and cost factors will make entire industries contract and expand over time, attempts to counter the changes artificially through restrictive government trade policies only inhibit the long-run flexibility of an economy. There is no question that the owners of firms adversely affected lose money and some workers experience periods of unemployment.

Although spokespersons for industries may dwell on the unfairness of someone selling products at a cost below their own, we should investigate arguments in favor of protectionism closely. Lurking behind the arguments are special interests pursuing preferential treatment. Protectionist trade policies reduce special interests' incentive to compete with lower-cost firms.

These practices violate the concept of comparative advantage. Every person has a comparative advantage. One has to choose among the available options and select the best. A country as a collection of individuals is no different. A country's comparative advantage comes from its land, climate, and transportation system and the education level and mobility of its workforce.

This comparative advantage changes as technology and consumers' tastes change. Businesses experience birth, death, accidents, and good fortune as markets evolve. When a country protects some of its firms at the expense of others, it selects one group for favored treatment and lessens the chances for constructive change. By exploiting its comparative advantage, a country increases the efficiency and consumption levels of its citizens. Protectionist policies impede this development.

In this chapter we considered some of the principal methods used by countries to influence international trade patterns. We also discussed some of the principal proposals made in support of protectionism. Due to the strong special interests and political factors involved in trade issues, protectionism is likely to continue.

Important Terms

Absolute Advantage and Disadvantage (p. 421)

Comparative Advantage and Disadvantage (p. 421)

Incomplete Specialization (p. 426)

Tariff (p. 428)

Ad Valorem Tariff (p. 429)

Specific Duty Tariff (p. 429)

Compound Duty (p. 429)

Quota (p. 430)

Dumping (p. 439)

Selected References

Coughlin, Cletus C. "Domestic Content Legislation: House Voting and the Economic Theory of Regulation." *Economic Inquiry* XXIII, No. 3 (July 1985):437–48.

Greenway, David (ed.). *Current Issues in International Trade.* London: Macmillan, 1985.

Herander, Mark G., and Schwartz, J. Brad. "The Impact of the Threat of U.S. Trade Policy." *Southern Economic Journal* 51, No. 1 (July 1984):59–79.

Kreinin, Mordechai E. *International Economics*, 5th ed. New York: Harcourt Brace Jovanovich, 1987.

Norton, R.D. "Industrial Policy and American Renewal." *Journal of Economic Literature* XXIV, No. 1 (March 1986):1–40.

Pindyck, Robert S., and Rotemberg, Julio J. "Are Imports to Blame? Attribution of Injury under the 1974 Trade Act." *Journal of Law and Economics* XXX, No. 1 (April 1987):101–22.

Problems

1. Assume that you must respond to the following letter written to the editor of your newspaper.

> We must stop believing the myth that imports cost the consumer less. Imports cost the consumer about the same as domestically produced goods. The only beneficiary is the middleman. We in the shoe industry recommend a rollback of imports to 1980 levels. This plan, combined with a restriction of 2 percent growth of imports per year, will let the domestic shoe industry maintain a reasonable profit and will help keep workers in their jobs.

Assume that the editor asks you to write a reply of less than one hundred words. What would you write?

2. Recently, several people have argued that the United States is losing its manufacturing base and turning into a nation of fast-food chains and low-paid technicians. Discuss the major points made by these people in support of their position and evaluate the evidence available in support of and in contradiction to these points.

3. Discuss the differences between quotas and voluntary export restraints (VERs).

4. With the aid of a graph, show why tariffs and quotas have different effects on domestic prices when the domestic demand curve shifts to the right.

5. Assume that the two small, isolated, island countries of Valhalla and Erda decide to open trade with one another. The two countries employ their people in the production of two goods: grapefruit and bananas. Output per day prior to opening trade was as follows:

	Grapefruit	Bananas
Valhalla	400	300
Erda	600	400

In what price range would both countries gain from trade?

6. Discuss alternatives to protectionism for creating jobs.

Answer questions 7–11 with true, false, or uncertain.

7. The imposition of a quota affects the domestic output without affecting the price.

8. If Japan removed all of its nontariff barriers, the United States would not have a trade deficit with Japan.

9. A tariff increases the domestic price more than a quota does.

10. Although the U.S. steel industry is competitive worldwide, unfair trade practices have negated the industry's comparative advantage.

11. Foreign firms dumping goods in the United States raise their prices after the U.S. firms go out of business.

MANAGERIAL TECHNIQUES

In the preceding chapters we emphasized the application of economic theory to managerial problems. We approached problems with a theoretically consistent logic. We have seen several applications of economic principles to actual business problems.

In Chapters 16–18 we turn to techniques for implementing these economic principles. Many firms employ economists or hire economic consultants to make analyses and predictions about the firm's market environment. Chapter 16 summarizes some common statistical techniques used by economists to estimate demand and cost functions and to forecast the future.

We have often mentioned uncertainty in the book. Managers must have a technique for making decisions in an uncertain environment. Chapter 17 provides techniques for making decisions when the outcome of these decisions is uncertain. This chapter also offers an extensive case study involving the opening of a restaurant.

Chapter 18 focuses more closely on the firm's strategy for the future. Firms must decide which investment projects to pursue and how best to fund these projects. We consider techniques for comparing competing investment projects and conclude with a discussion of the use of debt and equity to finance these investments.

P A R T

V

STATISTICAL ESTIMATION

16

I n this chapter we will consider statistical techniques useful for estimating demand and cost functions. We will also consider techniques especially suited to forecasting future levels of demand and costs. This chapter is too brief to provide adequate training for anyone interested in becoming a specialist in these statistical methods. It provides only a summary of some of the techniques commonly used by economists to help firms analyze statistical information.

Managers can either rely on staff members more thoroughly trained in these techniques or devote time to learning these techniques themselves. Even those managers who choose to rely on others should at least be aware of the strengths and limitations of each technique.

We will emphasize statistical issues related to topics covered in the earlier chapters. Our emphasis will be on the intuitive rationale for and the importance of techniques, rather than on the mechanics. We will begin with some statistical issues directly related to the estimation of demand. We will then consider the estimation of a firm's cost function. Since there are similarities in the estimation of cost and demand functions, we will concentrate only on new material in the cost-estimation section. At the end of the chapter we will discuss the role of statistical estimation in forecasting (predicting) the future level of the demand for a product or the cost of a product.

Demand Estimation

We will start with the estimation of a demand function. In Chapter 2 we assumed that we knew the coefficients of the demand equations used in our examples featuring Rocky Sanders and his Poobell Plastic Trash Bag Company. In this section we will concentrate on determining, or estimating, these coefficients. There are four major ways of empirically determining the coefficients of demand equations: (1) interviews (surveys), (2) market studies, (3) experiments, and (4) regression analysis based on historical observation. You should not be surprised to find a trade-off between the precision and cost associated with each approach.

Interviews (Surveys)

Rocky could interview some of his customers or potential customers. Marketing researchers often use this technique. For example, Rocky could ask people how many cartons of trash bags they would be likely to buy at various prices or rainfall levels. Also, by collecting background information on the incomes, ages, and other characteristics of people, he could infer what a larger group of people might do given changes in his price. Despite the potential value of this approach, there are several practical problems related to sample bias, validity, reliability, and cost.

Sample Bias Since cost considerations often prevent firms from interviewing all potential customers, the firm may have to interview a sample of the intended market population and extend the results of the sample to the entire market population. Firms must use a representative sample when selecting the people to be interviewed. Otherwise, the results of the interviews will not be representative of the targeted population; they will be biased. For example, by confining his interviews only to the people walking into a downtown hardware store, Rocky may limit himself to a specialized segment of the population (for example, people who do their own repair work) without even knowing it.

The bias problem can be even subtler. Even if people are selected randomly, some of the people selected for the study may decline to participate. For example, we would expect that those people with a higher opportunity cost attached to their time would be less likely to take the time to participate in a study. People with a higher opportunity cost usually have higher incomes. Even if one starts with a random sample, one may find that a disproportionate number of higher-income people will not participate, and the results will consequently be biased.

Validity Even if the sample is unbiased, respondents may provide inaccurate information. Many people are reluctant to reveal information about themselves, especially if they feel it may reflect poorly on them. For example, people have a tendency to overstate their income when talking to strangers. Incorrect responses will make the survey results an invalid guide to predicting behavior.

In addition, what people *say* they will do is not always what they will do, even if they are trying to be honest when answering the interviewer's questions. This is especially true when the question involves the amount of money someone would be willing to spend for a product. Consumers have difficulty reacting to proposed prices in hypothetical situations, since their actual decisions involve only whether or not to buy any of the product at a given price.

Reliability   Even if the sample is unbiased and valid, there must be enough participation to ensure that any one observation in the sample does not dominate the results. A survey procedure is reliable if repeated applications of the procedure yield the same results. The general reliability of a sample survey's results depends on the size of the sample. The larger the sample size the less the impact of any one extreme case. The sample size needed for a study ultimately depends on the complexity of the study. If you are attempting to determine the independent effects of a large number of demand factors, you need a large sample to obtain reliable results.

Cost   Cost is a major problem in many surveys. To assure validity, lack of bias, and reliability, you must design a set of interview questions directly suited to your concerns. You need to select questions that pose realistic choices for the people being interviewed. Once you choose questions for the survey, you need to test the questions with a preliminary sample to insure that the questions are not invalid, misleading, or otherwise inappropriate.

You must train interviewers and decide whether to use mailings, telephone calls, or personal interviews to collect the information. If you sell your product nationally, you should find a group of people statistically representative of the entire country. The cost of meeting all of these criteria may be high enough to deter all but the largest companies.

Market Studies

While Rocky is somewhat concerned about the cost of an extensive survey, he is especially worried about the validity of his sample. He is worried that survey responses might not accurately reflect the way they would actually behave in a store. There is an alternative that reduces the risk of this happening: companies can, instead, use market studies of actual consumer behavior to test consumer reactions to changes in demand factors.

If we were to design a market study, we would select two or more test sites where the shopping populations had similar demographic characteristics, such as age, income, and education level. We then would experiment at one test site by changing the price of Poobell's trash bags. By not making the changes at the other test sites, we would be controlling, at least to some degree, the other factors that could affect the quantity demanded.

While this approach does reduce the problems associated with relying on what people say rather than what they do, there are still some things to worry about. First, market studies can be expensive. Secondly, it is sometimes difficult to generalize the results of a market study to a wider population. Since companies using market studies successfully are often large and sell their products throughout the country, they use test sites that approximate the average community in the country. While this approach may not reveal the effects on communities that differ significantly from the average community, it may offer an understanding of the effect on the average customer.

A third problem with market studies concerns the duration of the study. The results of a short-term study only reveal short-run reactions to a change in a product characteristic. For example, decreasing the price of trash bags might result in a substantial increase in sales as Poobell's regular customers stock up on the trash bags. The long-term effect might be much less substantial unless the lower price attracts new customers or increases the long-term use of the bags by Poobell's regular customers.

| 16-1 | **I do all my shopping in a van** |

APPLICATION

Many U.S. companies are switching from the standard methods to other methods of test marketing new products. In 1986 test marketing a new product in three or four typical cities cost approximately $1.5 million and took nine months to complete. A company called Management Decision Systems has developed an alternative, the "Mall Intercept" method, which has been used by over 100 companies, including Procter & Gamble, L'Oreal, and Unilever.

The company using this method gives shoppers a $2 gift certificate to spend in a van at a shopping mall. The van contains a simulated supermarket with the new product located on the shelf with other products. The company follows up with a telephone call three weeks later to customers who bought the product to see if they would buy the product again. The company can get results in three months at a cost of $50,000 for 300 test consumers at each of three different sites.

Lab Experiments

We could arrange a lab experiment for Rocky by setting up a supermarket environment, giving people some money to spend in the store, and seeing how they respond to the company's products. This is essentially the same as the mall intercept method and suffers from the same problems: it is costly and small-scale. In addition, the fact that people know they are participating in an experiment may affect their behavior.

Economists have used laboratory experiments to test some of their basic theories. Critics of this approach have argued that there is insufficient proof that the results carry over from the laboratory to the marketplace. Despite this criticism the following Application shows that there is some evidence of carryover.

16-2

Laboratory-tested strawberries

APPLICATION

Professors David Brookshire, Don Coursey, and William Schulze have shown that laboratory experiments can parallel behavior in actual markets. They experimented with the sale of strawberries both in the lab and in the community of Laramie, Wyoming. They used twenty-eight randomly selected participants in the lab study. For the Laramie phase, they used three sales teams to sell strawberries door-to-door.

Not surprisingly, they found that consumers bought more strawberries as the price decreased. They determined the demand curve for strawberries by changing price and observing the quantity demanded. When they plotted the data from the two separate groups, they found that both sets of data could have come from the same demand curve. They concluded that whether the experiment took place in an actual market or in a laboratory setting made no difference.

Source: David S. Brookshire, Don L. Coursey, and William D. Schulze, "The External Validity of Experimental Economics Techniques: Analysis of Demand Behavior" *Economic Inquiry* XXV, No. 2 (April 1987): 239–50.

Regression Analysis

If we already have data on both quantity demanded and each demand factor, we can use a statistical technique commonly employed by economists: regression analysis. **Regression analysis (the method of least squares) is the statistical estimation of the coefficients of an equation, and is used to determine the marginal effect of each factor, holding the amount of the other factors constant.**

If we have several observations relating the quantity demanded of the product to several demand factors, we can determine the coefficients of the equation and the expected effect of changing one of the factors. Regression analysis is a relatively low-cost method as long as we already have collected the data. There is extensive literature on the methods and relative advantages of this approach because of its widespread use in economic studies.

Although there is no need to minimize the importance of other approaches by concentrating on regression analysis, regression analysis appears to be especially relevant to Rocky's problem because of the availability of data. Since Rocky's company has collected data for several years on its sales in different parts of the country, we can use regression analysis to estimate the demand for Poobell trash bags.

To be competent in the use of regression analysis you should start with a course in statistical analysis. Once familiar with the basic methods of regression analysis, you can apply them directly to economic problems. Before summarizing the main features of regression analysis, we will consider three general conceptual problems with applying regression analysis to the estimation of demand: (1) choosing the demand factors, (2) choosing the functional form of the demand equation, and (3) the identification problem.

The Choice of Demand Factors

In Chapter 2 we emphasized the choice of variables in the demand function. The dependent variable (that is, the left side) is the physical quantity of the good demanded (cartons of plastic trash bags). The independent variables (the demand factors on the right-hand side of the equation) include the price of the product and such factors as the prices of related products, consumer income, and advertising. In Rocky's case he included average weekly rainfall. A change in any one of these demand factors other than the price of the product makes the demand curve shift to the left or right.

Once Rocky decides which variables to include, he must assemble data for each of these variables for the same time period and location. Since Rocky indicates that he has already collected these data, we do not have a problem. In general, data are not always available. In addition, some data may have come from consumer surveys with the same problems mentioned earlier in the chapter.

The Identification Problem

Regression analysis is not appropriate unless the right-hand-side variables are exogenous. An **exogenous variable** is a variable having a predetermined value. In other words, the variable's value is not determined by the values of the dependent variable or the other independent variables in the equation.

The opposite of exogenous variables are endogenous variables. An **endogenous variable** is one that depends on the values of the exogenous variables in the equation. Unlike the exogenous variables, its value is not predetermined by factors excluded from the equation.

Both quantity demanded and price are generally endogenous variables.

When the demand curve has a negative slope and the supply curve has a positive slope, the market price and quantity depend on the intersection of the two curves. The supply factors determine the location of the supply curve, and the demand factors determine the location of the demand curve.

The exogenous demand and supply factors determine the value of the two endogenous variables: price and quantity. If we simply estimate a demand equation with price as a right-hand-side variable, we violate this necessary condition of regression analysis; that is, we include an endogenous variable, price, on the right-hand side without making an adjustment in the estimation procedure for controlling for its endogeneity.

Ignoring this problem can lead to some implausible statistical results. For example, despite an approximately 20 percent drop in the value of the dollar relative to the leading European currencies, the number of U.S. tourists traveling to Europe was substantially greater in the summer of 1987 than in the summer of 1986. The decrease in the value of the dollar meant that U.S. travelers could not purchase the same amount of goods and services in these countries as they could before. If we limit our analysis to this information, we have to conclude that an increase in the price of being a tourist leads to an increase in tourism! Does that mean that the demand curve for tourism is positively sloped? No.

As we know from earlier discussions, changes in demand factors other than price make the demand curve shift to the right or left, while changes in supply factors cause the supply curve to shift. These changes might even change the slope of the demand or supply curve. For example, let us assume that the number of hotel accommodations and other tourist-related facilities increases in the short run according to the supply curve S_{86} in Figure 16-1. In 1986 we might have observed that the demand for these facilities looked like demand curve D_{86}. The equilibrium price and quantity would have been P_1 and Q_1.

A decrease in the value of the dollar makes dollar prices more expensive in Europe for Americans. More specifically, a decrease in the dollar causes the supply curve of foreign hotel services to shift upward to the left; that is, hotel owners decrease the quantity of hotel accommodations that they are willing to supply at each dollar price. If demand had remained the same in 1987 as it was in 1986 (shown by D_{86} in Figure 16-1), the dollar price of foreign hotel accommodations would have increased from P_1 and P_2 and the quantity demanded would have decreased from Q_1 to Q_2.

In 1987 the number of terrorist attacks and related events dropped from their 1986 levels. In 1986 there was a significant decrease in the number of American tourists relative to previous years. Fear of terrorism was a shock to this market and caused a significant drop in the number of tourists. A relaxation of these fears led to a shifting of the demand curve to the right in 1987 to D_{87}.

Since both the supply curve and the demand curve changed in 1987, the

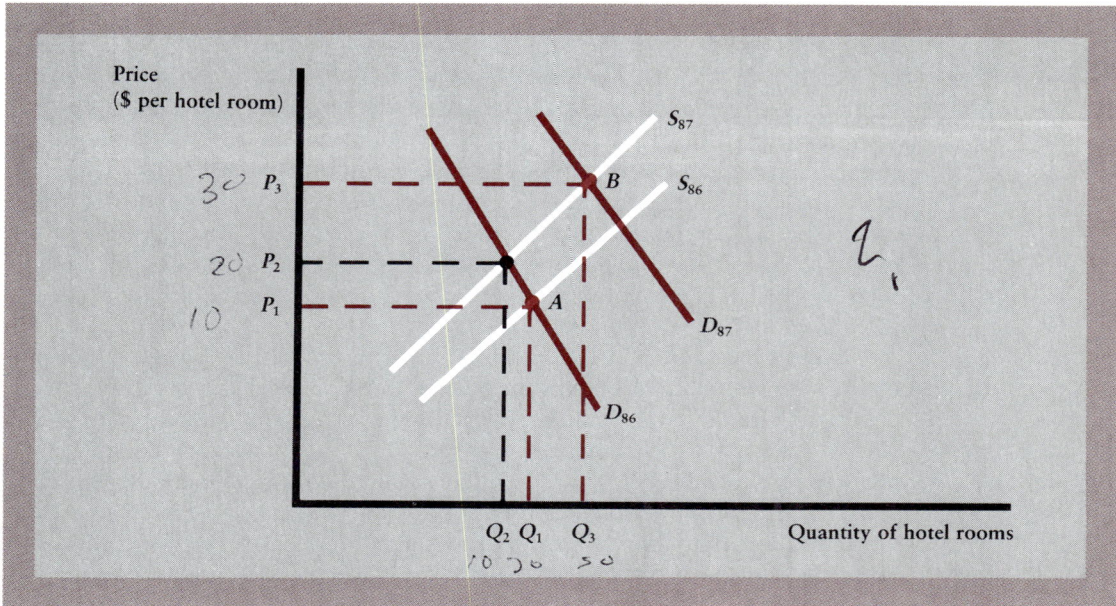

Price
($ per hotel room)

30 P_3 ---------------- B S_{87} S_{86}

20 P_2 -------------●

10 P_1 ----------- A

S_{87}

S_{86}

D_{87}

D_{86}

Q_2 Q_1 Q_3 Quantity of hotel rooms

10 20 50

FIGURE 16-1 ▪ Identification problem. Shifts in the supply curve create new equilibrium quantities and prices along a demand curve. This movement of the supply curve identifies the location of the demand curve as long as the demand curve does not shift. If the demand curve shifts, there will be an identification problem unless the shift of the demand curve is accounted for in the estimation procedure. For example, a shift in the demand curve and supply curve results in a new equilibrium at B. By connecting points A and B and ignoring the shift in the demand curve, we would conclude that the demand curve has a positive slope.

new market price would have been P_3 and the equilibrium output would have been Q_3. By simply connecting points A and B in Figure 16-1 and ignoring the shift in the demand curve, we could erroneously conclude that the demand curve had a positive slope—that is, that an increase in the equilibrium price was associated with an increase in the equilibrium quantity consumed. This is an example of what is known as the identification problem.

The **identification problem** is a problem concerning the proper location of the demand and supply curves. To identify a movement along a demand curve, we need to observe a change in the position of the supply curve. Changes in the location of the demand curve trace out the location of the supply curve.

To avoid the identification problem we must account for shifts in both curves. Consider an example of a successful effort to control for the identification problem.

APPLICATION

Professors John Bishop of the University of Alabama and Jang Yoo of Virginia Commonealth University show that it is important to control for both the supply and demand curves when estimating the effects of demand factors. They analyzed data from 1954 to 1980 from the U.S. cigarette industry. They were especially interested in the effects on the demand for cigarettes of the health scare of 1964 and the ban on broadcast advertising in 1971. The health scare of 1964 was the announcement by the Surgeon General linking cigarettes to cancer.

Noting that earlier studies of this industry focused only on the demand or the supply equation, Professors Bishop and Yoo argued that both of these equations should be estimated. They assumed that the quantity demanded was a function of cigarette prices, real disposable income, and cigarette advertising expenditures, while the quantity supplied was a function of cigarette price, federal and state taxes, and input prices. In addition, the Surgeon General's warning should have had a negative effect on the demand curve. Since the ban on broadcast advertising should have increased the industry's cost of reaching consumers, it should have shifted the supply curve higher.

Professors Bishop and Yoo determined that the demand curve was inelastic while the supply curve was elastic; that is, a 1 percent increase in the price of the good led to a greater than 1 percent increase in the quantity supplied of the good. Changes in taxes had a much greater effect on quantity demanded than did the health scare or advertising ban. While adverising did have an effect on individual market shares, it had little overall effect on total demand. The advertising ban actually resulted in an increase in advertising expenditures as companies switched from broadcast to print advertising. Since this medium is a less effective approach, costs increased.

Cigarette companies treated increases in taxes in the same way they treated an increase in the price of other inputs. The tax elasticity was only -0.387, which means that a 1 percent increase in the tax decreased the quantity demanded by 0.387 percent. An increase in the tax would have raised the supply curve and raised prices by less than the full amount of the tax.

Source: John A. Bishop and Jang H. Yoo, "'Health Scare,' Excise Taxes and Advertising Ban in the Cigarette Demand and Supply." *Southern Economic Journal* 52, No. 2 (October 1985):402–11.

Functional Form of the Demand Equation

Once past the hurdle of choosing the appropriate variables, we must face the problem of specifying the functional form of the equation. The chosen form should reflect the true relationship between the quantity demanded and the demand variables. In practice there is often no basis for deciding on the proper functional form in advance. We will limit our discussion to two functional forms: the linear form and the power function.

Linear Form In Chapter 2 we confined our numerical calculations to a linear form of the demand equation. The linear form has several appealing features. Statistical studies have shown that over small ranges of the quantity demanded, demand curves are generally linear. The linear form is easy to work with. With the linear form the coefficient shows the marginal effect of a one-unit change in the demand factor on quantity demanded. By selecting a value of the demand factor and the corresponding value of quantity demanded, we can calculate point elasticities.

A disadvantage of the linear form is its simplicity. By using this form, we must assume that the marginal effect of a one-unit change in the demand factor is constant regardless of the levels of the other demand factors. To remedy this problem we could use a power function.

The Power Function We could specify Rocky's demand function as follows:

$$Q = a P_0{}^b P_1{}^c I^d R^e,$$

where Q is the quantity demanded of cartons of trash bags, P_0 is the price of Poobell trash bags, P_1 is the price of Plenz trash bags, I is the average family income, R is average weekly rainfall in the summer, and a, b, c, d, and e are parameters, or constants. As written, this equation is a power function since each of the variables, or demand factors, is raised to a power. Although there are statistical techniques available for determining the value of the parameters directly, we can make a slight adjustment to this equation and convert it into a more familiar form.

By taking the logarithm (to any base) of both sides of the equation, the equation becomes linear. For example, the natural logarithm (to base e) would be as follows:

$$\ln Q = \ln a + b \ln P_0 + c \ln P_1 + d \ln I + e \ln R.$$

Let us simplify this equation by relabeling each of the variables as follows: Q^* is $\ln Q$, a^* is $\ln a$, P_0^* is $\ln P_0$, P_1^* is $\ln P_1$, I^* is $\ln I$, and R^* is $\ln R$. The equation now becomes

$$Q^* = a^* + b P_0^* + c P_1^* + d I^* + e R^*.$$

The transformation of each variable has created a linear equation that we can estimate with simple linear regression analysis. While we can estimate b, c, d, and e directly, we must use the antilog of a^* to determine the value of a.

The power functional form is common in applied studies. Consider the following example.

APPLICATION

As of December 1966, due to a papal decree, the Catholic Church no longer required Catholics to abstain from eating meat on Fridays, except during Lent. Professor Frederick Bell of Clark University estimated the impact of the decree on the demand for fish, a substitute for meat. He used data on fish sold at ports in the northeast area of the United States. In that region 45.1 percent of the population was Catholic at that time, more than double the percentage in any other region of the country.

Professor Bell collected data on the quantities and prices of seven species of fish for a ten-year period prior to the decree and for a year and a half after the decree. He used a power function to estimate the impact of the decree.

He specified the demand equation as

$$P = f(Q, Y, I, P_m, L, S, Z, PB),$$

where P is the price of the fish, Q is the quantity, Y is average personal

FIGURE 16-2 ▪ **The papal decree.** Since the quantity supplied of fish is not responsive to the price of fish in this case, the quantity of fish is exogenous and the supply curve is perfectly inelastic, or vertical. As the supply curve shifts from day to day, the equilibrium prices trace out the demand curve for fish. The figure shows three different supply curves representing three different days. The decree allowing meat on Friday lowers the demand curve from D_1 to D_2.

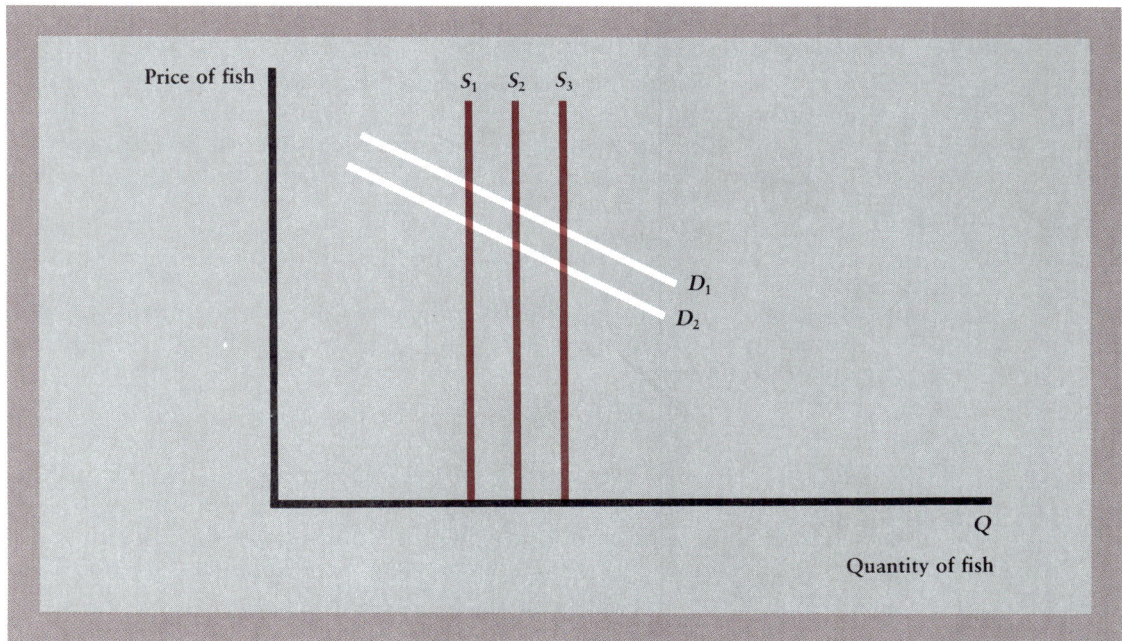

income in the Northeast, I is the quantity of imported fish of the same species, P_m is the average price of meat and poultry products, L is a control for the Lenten months, S is the capacity of cold-storage facilities available for storing fish, Z is the average price of competing fish products, and PB is a control variable indicating whether the decree had been issued or not.

To avoid the identification problem and still be able to estimate a single equation, all of the variables on the right-hand side of the equation must be exogenous to the determination of the price. Professor Bell was able to avoid the identification problem, since the supply of fish at any point in time is perfectly inelastic. He argued that the quantity of fish is due to fish migrations and weather in the short run. In the long run the size of the fishing fleet and the intensity of the fishing effort could change if both the fleets and their crews were not earning the opportunity cost of their investments of time and money.

Figure 16-2 shows the effect of the change in the quantity of fish supplied each month on the market price. Exogenous changes in quantity supplied cause a movement along the demand curve and trace out the location of the demand curve. He determined that the papal decree caused the demand curve to shift downwards. The average effect for all seven species was a price decrease of 12.5 percent. Figure 16-2 shows the effect of this decree as a decrease in the demand curve from D_1 to D_2.

Source: Frederick W. Bell, "The Pope and the Price of Fish." *American Economic Review* 58 (December 1968):1346–50.

Estimation Procedures

To help us understand the basic technique of regression analysis, let's start with a simple equation with just one demand factor. Table 16-1 lists some data for the quantity demanded of trash bags and the income of consumers. Assume that all other demand variables are held constant, including the price of the bags. We will confine the example to the determination of the parameters of a linear equation. The data also appear in Figure 16-3 (p. 465) as a scatter of points. Each point corresponds to an income–quantity-demanded combination in Table 16-1.

Since we are assuming that a linear equation represents the data in the best way, we can use a straight edge and attempt to draw a line that comes closest to representing the true relationship between the two variables. Regardless of how we draw the straight line, we cannot touch all the points on the graph. Once we draw this line we can calculate the intercept term and the slope of the line. Since we are assuming that the relationship is a straight line, we attempt to determine values of a and b in the equation $Q = a + bI$. The intercept term would be a, and b would be the slope, $\Delta Q / \Delta I$.

As an alternative approach, we could use regression analysis. We could

TABLE 16-1 ▪ Income and the demand for trash bags

Observation (Data Point)	Income (In Dollars)	Quantity Demanded (Cartons per Year)
1	20	20
2	22	25
3	25	24
4	18	21
5	30	28
6	27	27
7	35	34
8	32	33
9	40	38
10	28	30

also call regression analysis the method of least squares, because the technique finds the line that gives the smallest, or least, sum of the squared values of the vertical distances between the line and the data points. Table 16-2 (p. 466) shows the calculations for two possible lines shown in Figure 16-3: AA' and BB'. Suppose we draw a line, such as AA', and then calculate the vertical distances between the line and each of the points. We label these distances u_i, with the value of i corresponding to whichever of the ten points we are considering.

$$Q_i = a + b I_i + u_i.$$

Since line AA' has a much lower sum of squares (33, compared to 1,152), we can say that line AA' corresponds to the data better than line BB' does. If we use a computer, the computer program continues searching until it finds a line (that is, an equation) that makes the sum of the u_i^2 terms as small as possible.

With only one demand factor in the equation, we might be able to draw a line that fits the data well without using regression analysis. Regression analysis becomes essential when the number of demand factors increases. For example, Rocky knows that factors other than income affect the quantity demanded of his trash bags. Since he wants to account for the effects of all of these factors, he should use the regression procedures. With more than one demand factor, he cannot rely on the graphical technique.

Interpretation of the Estimated Equation

Regression analysis provides an estimate of the intercept term and the coefficient of each exogenous variable in the equation. The intercept term, a, simply shows the level of the dependent variable when all the independent variables equal zero. It usually has little meaning itself, because the independent variables are never zero all at the same time.

We do not want to use the results of the equation to interpret the effects of values of the independent variables outside the range of the data used for the estimation. While it may be true that the equation is valid outside the range of observations, you cannot guarantee it. For example, in the previous numerical example we had no observations for income below $18,000. It would not be meaningful to use the estimated equation to predict the quantity demanded of someone with a zero income.

The b coefficient gives Rocky an estimate of the effect of a one-unit change in income on the quantity demanded of trash bags. We can easily extend the two-variable equation as follows:

$$Q_i = a + b\,P_{0i} + c\,P_{1i} + d\,I_i + e\,R_i.$$

A computer program will provide estimates of a, b, c, d, and e. As before, a is the intercept term, while b, c, d, and e represent the independent effects

FIGURE 16-3 ■ Regression analysis. The figure shows the data from Table 16-1 and two lines, AA' and BB'. The u_i for each of the ten observations is the vertical distance between the line and each data point. Table 16-2 indicates that line AA' has a lower sum of squares than does line BB'. A computer regression analysis program continues to adjust the line until the average value of the u_is equals zero and the sum of the u_i^2 is the smallest possible value.

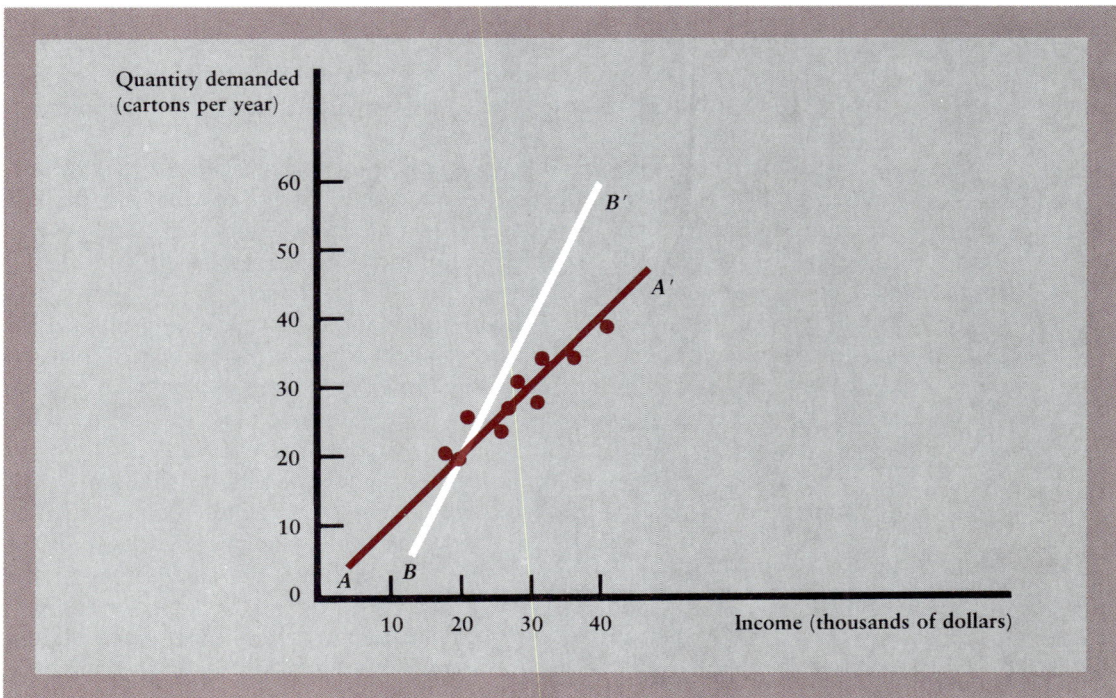

TABLE 16-2 ■ Calculation of u_i and u_i^2

Observation	Income	Quantity Demanded	Line AA' u_i	u_i^2	Line BB' u_i	u_i^2
1	20	20	0	0	0	0
2	22	25	3	9	1	1
3	25	24	−1	1	−6	36
4	18	21	3	9	5	25
5	30	28	−2	4	−12	144
6	27	27	0	0	−7	49
7	35	34	−1	1	−16	256
8	32	33	1	1	−11	121
9	40	38	−2	4	−22	484
10	28	30	2	4	−6	36
			+3	33	−74	1,152

on Q of a one-unit change in each variable, if all the others are held constant. For example, c is the effect of a one-unit change of P_1 on Q if P_0, I, and R are held constant. As long as the demand factors P_0, P_1, and R are important factors in explaining variations in Q, the sum of the squared distances between the actual values and the values predicted by the equation decrease by adding these additional factors to the equation. If you wish to review the statistics that a typical regression computer program will supply, you can find a summary in the Appendix to this chapter.

While managers may rely on experts to do the technical statistical analysis, they should at least be competent in interpreting most of what the experts report. Although we can choose a survey, a market study, or a lab experiment, economists have found regression analysis to be an especially useful and relatively low-cost method for analyzing historical data.

The survey approach is common and may be especially appropriate for local products sold on a small scale or for totally new products for which no data currently exist. The main disadvantages are the cost of a large-scale study, the reliability of the survey respondents, sample bias, and the need for a sufficiently large sample.

The market study is useful in testing new products or changes in the characteristics of existing products. Due to the cost of these studies, usually only large national companies use them. The main disadvantages, in addition to cost, are the short-run nature of the results and the small scale of the sample.

Laboratory experiments force consumers to make choices involving the company's product. They also suffer from the scale of the experiment and the cost. In addition, there is the added problem of participants knowing that they are in an experiment, which may alter their behavior.

Regression analysis is a relatively lower-cost method based on how consumers actually behaved in the past. As long as the level of future demand factors falls within the range of those observed in the past, the regression results may offer useful information. The main contribution of regression analysis is the determination of those demand factors that are the most significant contributors to the demand for the product.

Cost Estimation

We must now see what progress Phyllis Steene is having helping Harry Sampson. In Chapter 4, Phyllis provided Harry with a theoretical analysis of cost functions. Phyllis prefers to consider short-run and long-run cost curves separately. Knowledge of the short-run cost curves will help Harry decide his short-run price and output, while knowledge of his long-run cost curve will help him determine his long-term capacity requirements.

Since we have already reviewed some of the basic features of regression analysis in the previous section, we will not repeat them here. Instead, we will concentrate on those problems associated with cost functions that are distinct from those associated with demand functions. While most of what we plan to discuss involves regression analysis, we will have something to say about the use of two other approaches as well: the survivor method and the engineering approach to estimating long-run cost curves.

Short-Run Cost Functions

If we were to estimate Harry's short-run cost function, we would ignore fixed costs. Fixed costs do not vary with output and are not variables in the short run. The dependent variable in this case would be the variable cost. The independent variables would be those factors that affect the variable cost. For example, in Harry Sampson's case, the cost of his tree-trimming machines is a fixed cost and the cost of labor is a variable cost.

There are potential problems with using regression analysis to estimate short-run cost functions. The problems come from two sources: (1) collecting and modifying data and (2) specifying the functional form of the regression equation.

Data

Harry must be careful about the data he uses. First, he must be aware of the relevant cost. We discussed the issue of relevant cost in some detail at the beginning of Chapter 4. Harry must be able to match the cost to the change in short-run output. Some of his costs will not change when he changes his output. For example, if he were to buy his own tree-clipping machines he would not pay any more for them whether he used them or not. Time-series data are best for short-run cost functions. A **time series** is a set of repeated observations of the same variable at different points in time. For example, assume that Harry collected data on output for each of the past twenty-five months. With a time series for several variables, we can observe the variables' effects on the cost of output. Given a sufficiently short time, it would be reasonable to assume that Harry did not adjust his fixed costs significantly during the span of the time series.

As mentioned earlier, Harry must account for all factors that could significantly affect his costs. Sometimes these factors include unusual items.

Historical Costs While Harry has collected sufficient historical data on his variable costs for the study, his main concern is using the cost estimates to assist him in future decisions. Since Harry cannot get data on future costs until he incurs them, he must rely on the historical data as a first approximation. Since Harry's decision depends on this expectation of the future, historical data pose a problem. We will consider some more recent developments in statistical estimation designed to deal with these problems at the end of this chapter.

Opportunity Costs Harry, like other managers, normally depends on data provided by his accountants. Recall the discussion concerning opportunity cost in Chapter 4. Accountants do not normally document opportunity cost. Since opportunity cost is the most important cost concept for short-run decisions, accounting data may be inappropriate.

Harry must be able to account for the timing of costs. For example, once AT&T's central administration developed an incentive plan to reward its regional managers based on the profitability of their regions. For several years the regional company consistently outperformed the others. Suddenly, at a later date, the telephone lines and switching equipment deteriorated quickly, requiring unusually large expenditures for major repairs. Unfortunately, the profit criteria used by the company had been business profits. By not performing routine maintenance the managers in the one region had made their business profits look significantly higher. Over time they created a much less profitable situation.

Inflation Prices for inputs generally increase over time due to inflation. If Harry's output also increases and he does not adjust for these price increases, he might erroneously conclude that his average cost goes up with increases in output. To deal with this problem, he should use a measure of the change in price for each of the inputs to adjust for inflation. For example, Harry should use the inflation-adjusted wage rate as his measure of wages.

Period of Observation   A short-run cost curve is based on a specific amount of the fixed inputs and a fixed technology. To estimate the short-run cost function properly, we must use data during a period of time when Harry maintains the same fixed cost and technology. One difficulty is the need for a large enough number of observations to estimate the cost function over a range of output, while still remaining within a time period short enough for both technology and fixed cost to remain fixed.

Functional Form

The first problem we face in any statistical estimation is choosing the proper functional form of the equation to be estimated. When discussing demand we considered two examples: linear and power functions. We chose those two forms because of their simplicity and because of the likelihood that the true relationship is consistent with these functional forms over short ranges of the independent variables, or demand factors.

The functional form should be consistent with the theoretical relationship linking the dependent and independent variables. Since we discussed the theoretical relationship between total variable cost and output in Chapter 4, we can now see what we must assume about the functional form of the cost function. We will start with a linear functional form and proceed to quadratic and cubic functions.

Linear Cost Functions   Over a short range of output, a linear form may be accurate. The equation

$$\text{Total Cost} = a + bQ + \sum_{i=1}^{n} c_i X_i$$

represents a linear relationship between total cost (TC) and output (Q). The X_i terms are independent variables that Harry wants to include in the estimation. In Harry's case, one variable is the price of his inputs, such as the wage rate of manual workers. Input prices were constant when we constructed the graph of TC in Chapter 4. A significant change in any one of these factors may affect Harry's costs at each output level. By including these factors, Harry can account for their influence on the relationship between his cost and his output level.

A computer regression program would report estimates of a, b, and each of the c_i coefficients along with statistics indicating the statistical significance of each coefficient (that is, T-statistics) and the explanatory power of the independent variables as a group (that is, the coefficient of determination). A brief description of these statistics is included in the Appendix to this chapter. The intercept term would have little meaning in this case. We would expect total variable cost to equal zero at zero output levels. In fact, the equation would only be relevant over the range of output used in data sample, which would not include zero output. On the other hand, estimates of b would be important since b would be the best measure of marginal cost over the range of the data.

Figure 16-4 contains the total-cost (TC) curve from Figure 4-5 with a linear approximation to the curve superimposed. Assume that the true relationship is the curve from Figure 4-5. If the observable range of output were between Q_1 and Q_2, the regression software would assume that the true relationship is a straight line between Q_1 and Q_2 and would fit the line to the data, as in Figure 16-4.

Figure 16-5 shows the average-total-cost curve (ATC) and marginal-cost curve (MC) consistent with the equation

$$TC = a + bQ.$$

In this case

$$ATC = \frac{TC}{Q} = \frac{a}{Q} + b \quad \text{and} \quad MC = b.$$

As Q increases, a/Q approaches zero and AVC approaches b.

FIGURE 16-4 ▪ **Linear approximation of a total-cost curve using the equation** $\boldsymbol{TC = a + bQ}$. The linear equation $TC = a + bQ$ approximates the true total-cost curve. Unless the true total-cost curve is linear, this may be a misleading approximation of the true relationship between total cost and quantity.

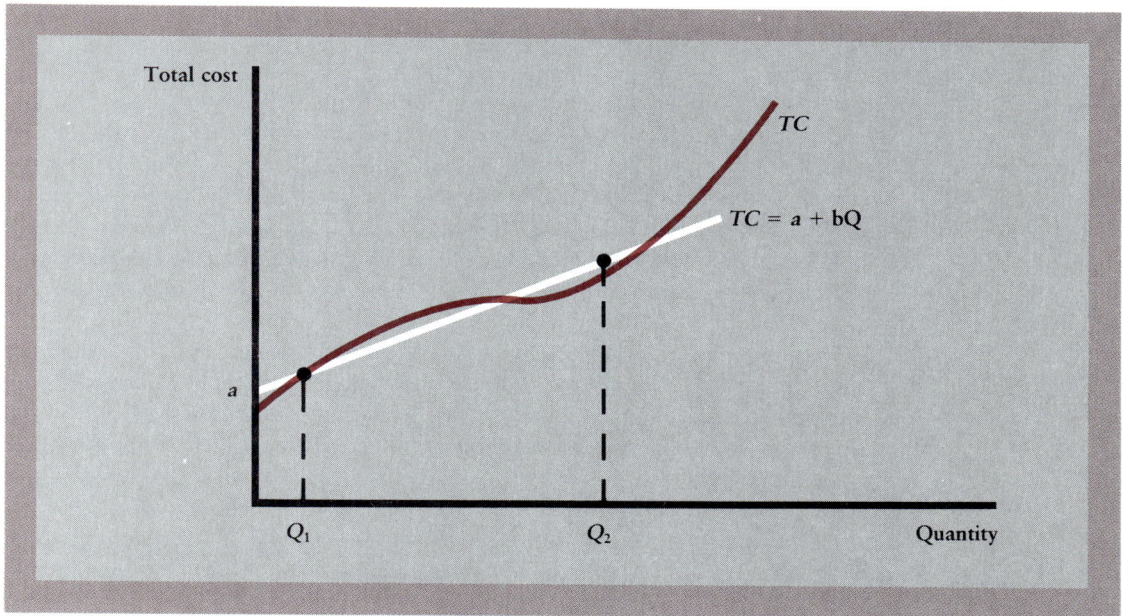

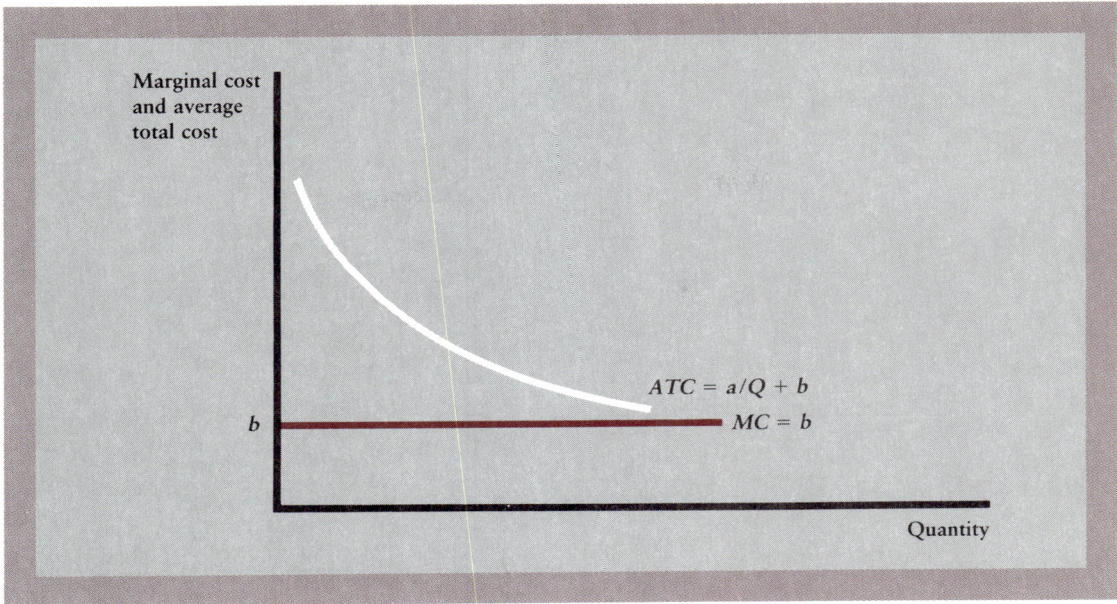

FIGURE 16-5 ▪ **Average total cost and marginal cost for** $TC = a + bQ$. The linear approximation assumes that marginal cost is constant and that average total cost falls exponentially as marginal cost approaches the limit.

Quadratic and Cubic Cost Functions We could generalize the form of the equation if Harry believed that his cost function was not linear over the range of output used in the sample. For example, with a quadratic form the equation would be

$$TC = a + bQ + cQ^2.$$

Figure 16-6 (p. 472) shows the average total cost,

$$ATC = \frac{a}{Q} + b + cQ,$$

and the marginal cost,

$$MC = b + 2cQ.$$

We can come closer to the MC and AVC of Chapter 4 by using a cubic form:

$$TC = a + bQ - cQ^2 + dQ^3.$$

Now

$$MC = b - 2cQ + 3dQ^2$$

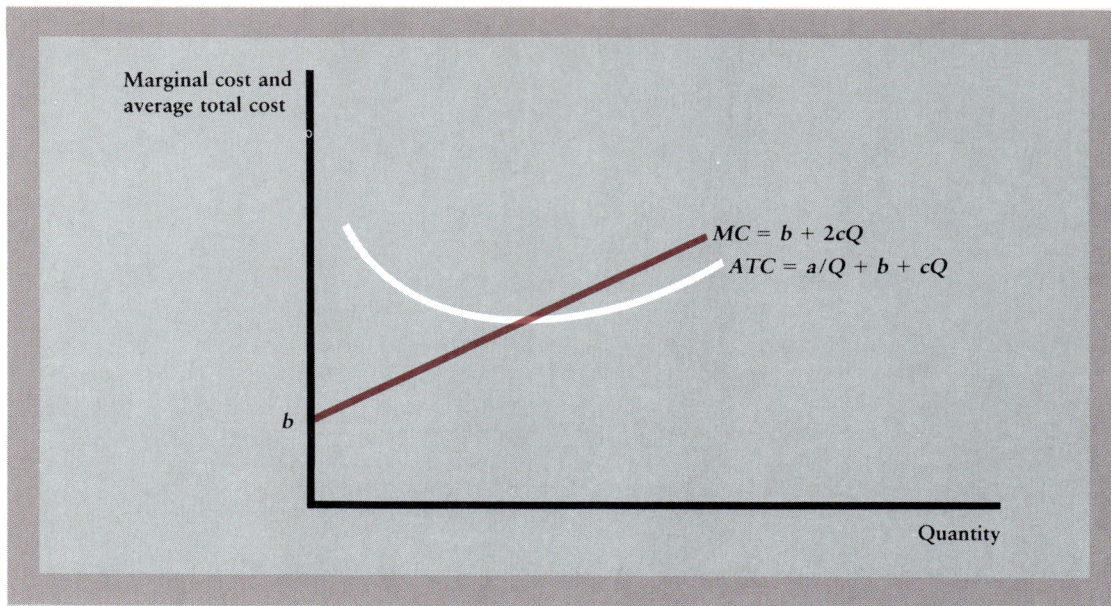

FIGURE 16-6 ▪ **Marginal cost and average total cost for** $TC = a + bQ + cQ^2$.
The quadratic approximation has a linear, positively-sloped marginal-cost curve. The MC
and ATC curves cross at the minimum point of ATC.

and

$$ATC = \frac{a}{Q} + b - cQ + dQ^2.$$

Figure 16-7 shows that the ATC and MC curves look much more like the
cost curves of Chapter 4.

Empirically Estimated Short-Run Cost Functions

Despite the generality offered by the use of quadratic and cubic functional
forms, many empirical studies reveal that short-run marginal cost is constant
over observable output levels. You might be surprised with these results,
especially given the theoretical development in Chapter 4, but there is an
explanation.

Although the costs of some inputs, such as machines, are fixed in the
short run, the use of these inputs might be variable and in proportion to the
amount of variable inputs up to the capacity of the fixed input. For example,
in Harry's case, he might normally use two workers for every one of his tree-
clipping machines, as opposed to using all of his machines all of the time and
varying only the number of workers in the short run.

For example, assume that Harry does not employ his workers on a permanent basis. Each day he hires workers for that day's work from a pool supplied by a local agency. Since he owns the machines, his costs for them are fixed in the short run. His variable costs include the workers' pay plus fuel for the machines. If business is slower, he will not use all of his machnes on those days and, as a result, will not hire as many workers. If he hires more workers, he will use more of his machines in the same proportion of two workers for every one of his machines. In this way marginal cost—the cost per unit of output due to the extra workers and fuel—will be constant with increases in output.

Long-Run Cost Functions

While the estimation of long-run cost curves is similar to that of short-run cost curves, the former is more complex. In the long run all costs are variable. The principal problem concerns the role of technology. We must collect sufficient data over a range of output to estimate the cost function. If a firm makes changes in its machinery over the long run, the new machinery may embody changes in technology. To avoid this problem we must either use a data set with observations of constant technology or find a means of controlling for changes in technology in the estimation equation.

FIGURE 16-7 ▪ **Marginal cost and average total cost for** $TC = a + bQ - cQ^2 + dQ^3$. The cubic cost equation has marginal-cost and average-total-cost curves that look like the ones derived in Chapter 4.

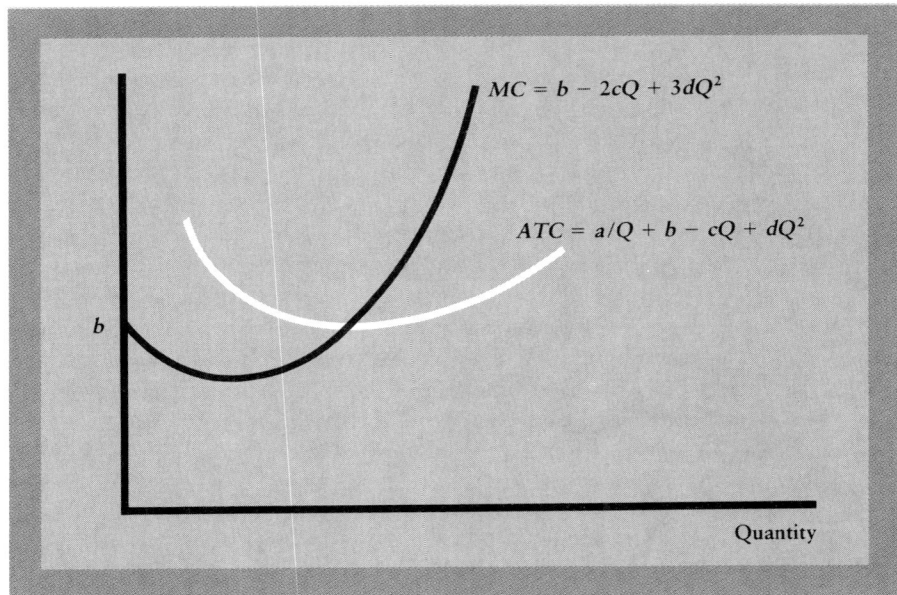

$$MC = b - 2cQ + 3dQ^2$$

$$ATC = a/Q + b - cQ + dQ^2$$

Quantity

Because of the problem of maintaining control over the changes in technology, researchers use **cross-section data**, which are observations from several production units or firms at the same point in time. If Harry were to estimate a long-run cost function, he would have to collect data from several tree-trimming companies that use the same technology that he uses. The regression equations would have total cost (*TC*) as the dependent variable and output as an independent variable. To account for the variations in factors affecting the different firms differently, he should add variables such as the firms' wage rates and fuel costs. For example, wages could vary by region due to cost-of-living differences. Because the data would come from the same point in time, inflation would not be a problem.

Some variations in cost may be difficult to detect. For instance, other firms might not use the same accounting procedures that Harry uses. They may use different depreciation schedules and report different costs for their machines. An estimate of a cost function that uses data from different firms can yield misleading results unless someone controls for this possible problem.

This technique also requires the assumption that all firms are operating efficiently and are located on the long-run average-total-cost curve. If firms are not operating efficiently, the average-total-cost curve is actually located below the estimated one, resulting in an overestimate of the long-run average-total-cost curve.

16-5 Lowering average costs by taking longer trips

APPLICATION

Economists have extended the generality of cost functions well beyond that of the quadratic and cubic forms. The more general the functional form, the less dependent the research is on assumptions about the shape of the cost curves. Professors Douglas Caves, Laurits Christensen, and Joeseph Swanson used a flexible mathematical expression of the cost function to estimate the cost relationship for railroads hauling both passengers and freight in the United States between 1955 and 1974.

They used cross-section data from a set of firms for three years: 1955, 1963, and 1974. Their statistical technique allowed them to estimate a series of short-run average-variable-cost curves corresponding to different levels of both the capital stock and the level of technology. Since the level of capital stock varied among the different firms, they were able to use the envelope procedure of Chapter 4 to trace the shape of the long-run average-total-cost curve and show how changes in technology make the long-run average-total-cost curve shift.

They found that by increasing the length of hauls there was potential for substantial scale economies in railroad transportation at that time. Many railroads were not taking advantage of the economies possible with longer hauls. They also found that the cost curve had shifted down at an average rate of 1.8 percent per year. Most of the gains in productivity came between 1955 and 1963, when the cost curves shifted downward at a rate of 3.5 percent per year. They noted that earlier studies had not properly controlled for the possibility that the average-cost curve could have been shifting downward at that time.

Source: Douglas W. Caves, Laurits R. Christensen, and Joseph A. Swanson, "Productivity Growth, Scale Economies, and Capacity Utilization in U.S. Railroads, 1955–74." *American Economic Review* 71, No. 5 (December 1981): 994–1002.

Alternative Estimation Procedures

There are two other approaches to the estimation of cost functions for situations where there is an absence of adequate data for a statistical cost estimation: the survivor technique and engineering cost functions.

Survivor Technique   In 1958, Professor George Stigler of the University of Chicago proposed a method for measuring economies of scale in the absence of detailed cost data for firms. He hypothesized that the more efficient firms— those with lower average costs—prosper and survive over time. Specifically, he proposed classifying firms in size categories and calculating the share of the industry captured by each size class. Professor Stigler looked at the steel industry between 1930 and 1950 and saw a steady decline in the share of the market captured by the smallest and largest categories, with a steady share spread across a wide range of class sizes in between.

However, this approach is limited by the definition of the market. If the market is defined too broadly, it is not surprising that small firms can coexist with larger ones. For example, some clothing manufacturers are small due to the need for flexibility in adjusting to rapid changes in clothing styles, while makers of jeans and other more traditional clothes tend to be larger. Lumped together as clothing manufacturers, these companies can coexist at significantly different sizes.

The problem of technology also resurfaces here. Changes in market share by class size may reflect changes in technology and product variation within an industry rather than a change in scale over time. Since most of these studies have been conducted for highly aggregated industries, there is a concern of some importance regarding the results.

Engineering Cost Functions   We could use an engineering-based production function for Harry's Verte Tree Company. Many firms use this technique. By asking engineers to supply data on the output ratios of each piece of equipment, Harry could determine the nature of his short-run and long-run production functions. By assigning current prices (opportunity costs) for each input he could determine the short-run and long-run cost functions.

In Harry's case if he always had to use exactly two workers per machine and each machine clipped four trees per day, he would have a simple cost function. Assuming that the numbers of worker-hours, machine-hours, and trees would be divisible into units of less than one, he would have a constant average variable cost per tree up to the capacity of his machines. Since the cost of a machine would be fixed regardless of use, he would minimize average total cost at capacity.

For more typical firms the production process is much more complicated, involving several stages. While several studies have been done using an engineering approach for determining the firm's production and cost functions, the following example of solar power costs is particularly interesting.

16-6 It prefers hot weather

APPLICATION

Professor G. Thomas Sav of West Georgia College used physical laws and engineering models to derive a production function for solar processes to determine the possible substitution between solar-produced energy and conventionally-produced energy. He used the engineering approach because a lack of historical data on solar-produced energy made statistical estimation impossible. Solar-produced energy was new at the time and is still not widely used today.

Professor Sav concentrated on solar energy used in producing hot water for residential and commercial buildings. He started with a general specification of the production function: energy output as a function of energy from solar processes and conventional sources. He then relied on engineering data and physical laws to relate energy output from solar processes to the level of inputs used in the solar process. The principal input is the size of the solar collectors used. In reaction with sunlight of high intensity and long duration, a solar panel generates enough heat to maintain a sufficient supply of hot water.

Professor Sav was able to construct isoquants showing the substitution possibilities between solar power and conventional energy at different output levels for different parts of the country. By using prices for conventional energy, such as electricity, and for the construction of solar processors, he was able to determine the prospects for solar processors. He found that the climate makes a substantial difference. In the United States, for example, a solar processor in the Northwest has to be $2\frac{1}{2}$ times as large as one in the Southwest to accomplish the same effect.

Source: G. Thomas Sav, "The Engineering Approach to Economic Production Functions Revisited: An Application to Solar Processes." *Journal of Industrial Economics* XXXIII, No. 1 (September 1984): 21–35.

Forecasting

Before leaving the subject of statistical estimation, let's return to Sam Frisko, the carnation grower of Chapter 5. Recall that Sam owns Frisko Flowers, a local company that supplies cut carnations to wholesalers in several parts of the country. Since Sam must plan ahead to anticipate future demand, he has to make decisions based on his own expert opinion. He needs some advice concerning options available to him to improve his forecasts.

While Sam is most interested in forecasting his own cost and sales, he may find that these variables follow changes in the national economy as a whole. For example, he may find that his input prices change with inflation and that demand for his flowers depends on average consumer income. This information may give him an indication of the future demand for his flowers. Most firms do not find it cost-effective to prepare their own forecasts of national income and inflation.

There are several sources of information about national income and inflation. Companies such as Wharton Econometric Forecasting Associates, Data Resources, and Merrill Lynch Economics sell this information on a subscription basis. These companies use large economic models of the United States economy to forecast changes in economy-wide variables. One can also purchase some of this information from publications, including the *Wall Street Journal*, the *Quarterly Survey of Economic Forecasts* from the American Statistical Association, and the *Journal of Business Forecasting*. In addition, banks and other large private firms sometimes produce their own forecasts and make them available to their customers.

While information on changes at the national level may be sufficient for Sam, he may wish to pursue a more detailed analysis instead, using his own data or data from the rest of the cut-flower industry. We will start with an overview of the techniques available for this purpose, without belaboring the details of each approach. Sam may have to rely on an expert to handle the details of the specific approach he chooses.

In planning for the future, Sam should consider several issues: he must determine the geographic and product markets where he can earn the highest profits and then forecast the level of demand in these markets given different possible prices. He should also forecast the cost of producing different output levels of his flowers under conditions of changing technology, wage rates, and materials prices. Once he has an idea about his future demand and cost, he can decide on a plan of action that will maximize his profits.

Methodology

Many economic forecasting techniques are available. They range from Sam's current simple and relatively inexpensive procedure to methods that are quite complex and very expensive. Some forecasting techniques are basically quantitive; others are qualitative. The most appropriate one for a particular task depends in large part on the following factors:

  a. The time into the future that must be forecast
  b. The degree of accuracy needed
  c. The lead time needed before making decisions
  d. The quality of data available
  e. The benefits expected from a successful forecast
  f. The costs associated with using a particular technique.

Some techniques work well for short-term projections. Others require more lead time and are more useful for forecasting into the distant future. The level of sophistication varies. Not surprisingly, the more sophisticated techniques are also more expensive. In choosing among techniques of varying degrees of sophistication, Sam should consider the benefits of greater accuracy versus the additional cost of achieving this accuracy.

For example, if Sam expects that an inaccurate forecast would leave him with a large number of expensive, fading, unsalable flowers, he should consider reducing the risk of suffering large potential losses by paying for greater accuracy. If greater accuracy saves him only small amounts in losses, he may find that greater accuracy is not worth the extra expense.

We will now consider some of the forecasting techniques. Sam must assess the strengths and weaknesses of each technique in order to choose the best technique for his particular problem. We will group the techniques into the following three categories: qualitative methods, time series analysis and projection, and econometric models.

Qualitative Methods

Up to this point Sam has relied on a qualitative approach to his forecasting problem. Sam's qualitative forecasts come from his expert assessment of the market. One may rely on qualitative forecasting as long as the forecasts are systematic and come from unbiased sources.

Expert Opinion Sam's approach has been the most basic of qualitative analyses: he has used his personal business experience to assess current events and forecast the future. Despite his concern that this approach is unscientific and highly subjective, his approach cannot be rejected out of hand. For a one-person business such as Sam's, there is only one person to convince and only one person who will suffer if the forecasts are inaccurate. If Sam's estimates have proved accurate enough without incurring the cost of obtaining greater accuracy, he should be content to continue relying on his own expert opinion.

More generally, expert opinion forecasts may come from committees within a much larger firm, with possible turnover in the key personnel making these forecasts. Since those who gain and lose from inaccurate forecasts include individuals not in the forecasting group, the firm may be less willing to entrust the committee with uncontrolled decision making. If decisions are to remain systematic, care must be taken to prevent elements of a group from dominating the group's decision.

Because of changes over time in the membership of these forecasting committees, the assumptions behind the forecasts should be explicitly stated. Otherwise, a change in the underlying conditions could make the basic forecasts totally unreliable. For example, once the price of oil dropped dramatically in 1986, state governments in oil states such as Texas and Oklahoma quickly realized that forecasts made in 1985 of tax revenues for the late 1980s were greatly overstated.

Survey Methods Sam could increase the cost of his forecasts by using a survey of the demand for carnations. Surveys are usually based on interviews or questionnaires that ask individuals to reveal their future plans. Since businesses normally plan and budget their purchases in advance, surveys may reveal the impact of these decisions on one's own company. While most consumers make many last-minute buying decisions, they often plan for major purchases of houses, automobiles, education, and trips in advance.

Surveys may offer useful supplementary material in addition to more highly quantitative techniques. As we will see, econometric forecasts depend on an underlying stability in the relationship between the demand factors and the quantity demanded. These techniques do not always capture the more emotionally and psychologically based swings in consumer behavior, but a carefully constructed survey may reveal this information.

Not surprisingly, the further into the future we must forecast, the much greater the chance of error. This is shown in the following Application.

16-7   **Who said that?**

APPLICATION   Conrad Berenson of Baruch College and Steven Schnaars of City University of New York argue that survey techniques designed to predict far into the future are not always useful. In their article they reported the result of a 1967 survey by a U.S. firm, TRW. The company asked twenty-seven top scientists to determine the new products that the world would want by 1987. Included in a list of 401 products were a 500-kilowatt capacity nuclear power plant on the moon, robot soldiers, and germproof plastic houses. In 1968 the National Institute of Dental Research predicted that by 1980 tooth decay and gum disease would be wiped out by plastic teeth and vaccines for tooth decay.

Professors Berenson and Schnaars followed ninety forecasts announced between 1960 and 1980. Of these forecasts, 53 percent failed. According to their research, the principal reason for failure was an overreaction to the glamour of new technology and a simplistic reliance on past trends. They suggested that managers be aware of the assumptions about the world that are behind their forecasts. If the assumptions change, managers must be flexible enough to adjust and be aware of the effect of the change in assumptions on their forecasts.

In the late 1960s, large oil companies had the idea of turning oil into food. Gulf Oil planned to make biscuits, soups, and cereals from petroleum. Exxon linked with Nestlé, the Swiss international food company. British Petroleum produced ham from pigs fed on protein made from natural gas. The companies made these assumptions: a booming world population, slow growth in traditional agricultural production, and the continued abundance of cheap oil. The last two assumptions proved wrong in the 1970s. While oil prices rose dramatically, traditional agriculture responded to higher food prices and increased technology.

Source: Conrad Berenson and Steven Schnaars, "Growth Market Forecasting Revisited." *California Management Review* (Summer 1986). © 1986 by the Regents of the University of California. Condensed from the *California Management Review*, Vol. 28, No. 4. By permission of The Regents.

Time-Series Analysis and Projection

The most frequently employed forecasting methodology has several different names: trend projection, curve fitting, and extrapolation. It is a quantitative technique based on the assumption that future events will follow an established trend from the past. This approach fails when there is a significant unexpected change in one of the underlying trends.

If Sam were to use this technique, he would focus on the historical pattern in the demand for carnations and then assume that this pattern would continue into the future. Since he would be using data collected at different points in time for a specific variable, he would be using a time-series data set. For example, weekly, monthly, or yearly reports on sales of carnations would be used for Sam's forecast.

Each one of these time-series observations has the following components:

a. A secular trend, which represents the long-term direction or average movement in the time series.
b. Cyclical fluctuations or rhythmic variations in the time series. For example, these may follow variations in the growth of the economy in general around a long-term, secular trend.
c. Seasonal variations caused by weather patterns and social habits, such as the need for cut flowers to remind people of warmer weather during the winter and to honor mothers on Mother's Day.
d. Unpredictable shocks and random variations, such as wars, natural disasters, and changes in fashions.

Figure 16-8 provides an example of the first two of these four characteristics. The simplest forecast involves the long-run secular trend. Superimposed

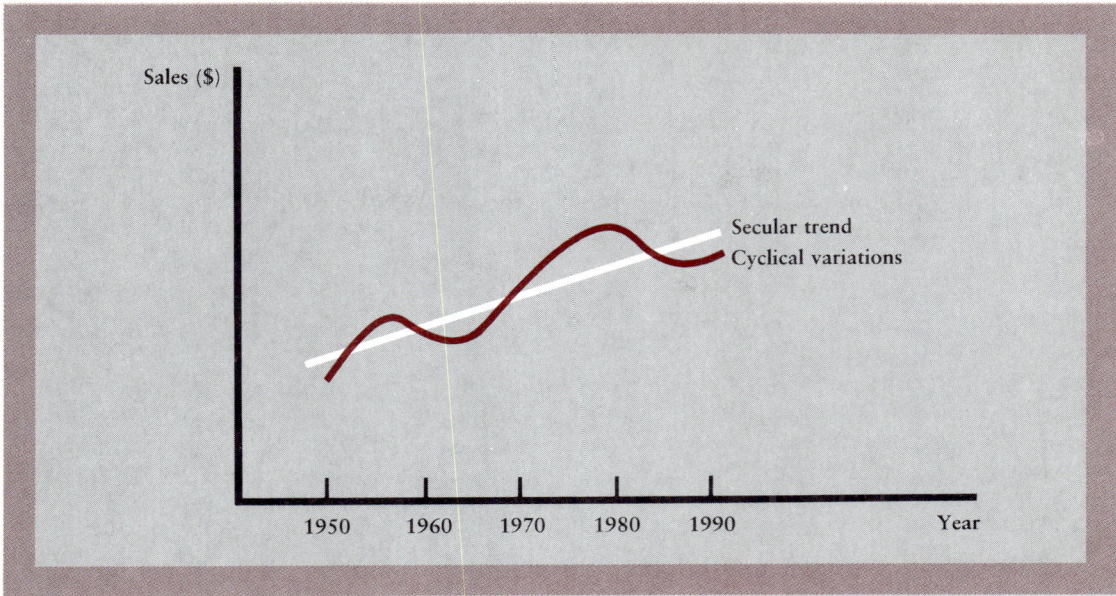

FIGURE 16-8 ▪ **Secular trends and cyclical variations.** The secular trend shows the long-term average movement in the time series of a company's sales. There may be cyclical variations during this time that correspond to outside forces, such as changes in the overall market for the product or in the entire economy.

on this trend is the effect of adding the cyclical patterns around this trend over a number of years. Figure 16-9 (p. 482) looks more closely at the trend over one year and includes seasonal variations. Superimposed on this curve are the effects of unpredictable shocks. By adding the effects of each of these four characteristics, we derive the actual historical movement of the variable.

Econometric Models

Time-series techniques depend on the ability of a functional form to fit a series of data and provide a useful forecast of the future. A potentially more appealing approach would draw on the theory in Chapters 2, 3, and 4. For example, in Chapter 2 we derived the relationship between the quantity demanded of Poobell Trash Bags and several demand factors. Although based on historical data, these estimated relationships provided a link between movements in the quantity demanded variable and the factors influencing these movements. If we could assume that this relationship would remain stable in the future, we could use the equation to estimate the future demand for a product.

Once we had estimated the coefficients of each factor included in the equation, we could substitute future estimates of the factors into the equation

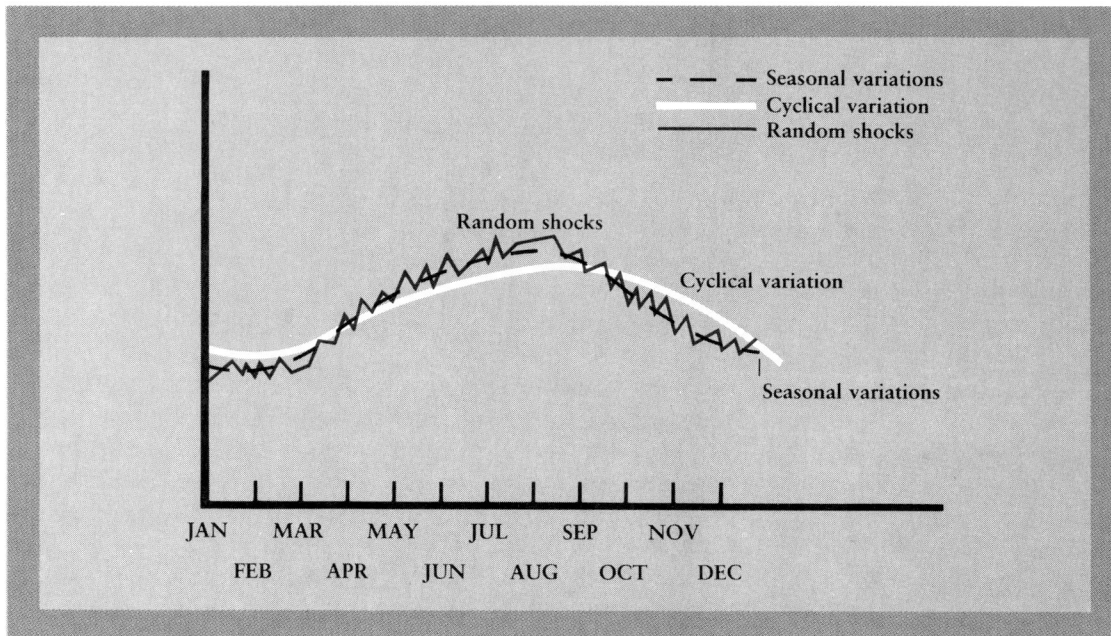

FIGURE 16-9 ▪ **Seasonal variations and random shocks.** During shorter time intervals, there will be additional fluctuations due to seasonal variations and unexpected shocks. The figure shows seasonal variations around the cyclical fluctuations. Once we add the unexpected shocks to the seasonal variations, we have a graph of the actual movement in the time series. The most sophisticated time series methods control for all but the unexpected-shocks component of the time series.

and calculate the future demand. This would be an especially useful technique if we had more reliable information on future values of the demand factors than on the quantity demanded variable.

16-8   More work for dentists

APPLICATION   Willard Manning and Charles Phelps of Rand Corporation estimated an econometric model of the demand for dental care in order to forecast the effect of a change in U.S. health insurance policies. Congress has often considered passing bills establishing national health insurance for U.S. citizens. The medical care included in these proposed bills has varied. Drs. Manning and Phelps estimated the impact that including comprehensive dental-care insurance would have on dental-care services and prices.

They used data from a cross section of 7,775 people in 1970. They had data on people's income, race, gender, and age, as well as on the price and consumption of ten different types of dental care. For example, they found that the price elasticities for teeth cleaning were high for both women and children, while the income elasticities ranged between 0.74 and 0.80. Men were less sensitive to price. The own-price elasticity was -0.14 for men.

Tooth extractions may be an inferior good. The researchers found that wealthier people used more preventative care, while poorer people used less preventative care and demanded more extractions as a result. Again, men were less sensitive to the price of examinations than women and children. Drs. Manning and Phelps suggested that the time cost of leaving work may have been a more important factor than the out-of-pocket cost of an examination for working men in 1970.

There was sufficient variation in the price and income data in their sample to forecast the effects of a change in health insurance coverage. They determined that providing insurance that eliminates the out-of-pocket costs of dental care increased the demand for dental care between two and three times for those people who did not have private dental insurance.

Their forecast indicated that the aggregate effect on demand would be an 11 percent increase in demand at the same prices. Eleven percent would be the expected increase, but there would be a chance for error in the estimate. They were able to predict that the true increase would be between 6.5 percent and 16.2 percent, with a 95 percent confidence level; that is, the probability that the true value would fall outside this interval would be less than 5 percent.

They cautioned that this was a long-term prediction. Since children and, to a lesser extent, women were highly sensitive to the price of dental care, a significant decrease in the out-of-pocket cost due to the insurance coverage would sharply increase demand for dental care. In the short run the relatively fixed supply of dentists would likely lead to equally sharp increases in prices. They suggested that the government should phase in any change in policy to allow the supply of dentists to adjust to the expected change in demand.

Source: Willard G. Manning, Jr. and Charles E. Phelps, "The Demand for Dental Care." *Bell Journal of Economics* 10, No. 2 (Autumn 1979):503–25.

16-9 Weather forecasts

APPLICATION

In the movie *Trading Places*, Eddie Murphy and Dan Aykroyd intercept the National Weather Service's weather forecast for the central Florida region and use it to make a fortune in the futures market for frozen concentrated orange juice. They make their money by convincing futures traders that the weather is going to be much worse than they had expected.

Professor Richard Roll of the University of California at Los Angeles has studied the effects of unexpected weather changes on the Florida orange crop.

As of 1984, 98 percent of frozen concentrated orange juice came from the central Florida area around Orlando. Weather is a major factor in growing oranges. Although frozen orange juice is not perishable, only a small amount is stored from year to year. Professor Roll found that cold temperatures do affect the price of orange juice futures. He also found a significant relationship between prices and errors in the National Weather Service temperature forecasts. Errors in rainfall had much less of an effect.

Source: Richard Roll, "Orange Juice and Weather." *American Economic Review* 74, No. 5 (December 1984):861–80.

Forecasting Turning Points

Economic forecasters are always searching for indicators of a change in economic activity. While no simple indicator has ever provided a consistent signal of change, there are well-known time series that have served as barometers of change. **Barometric forecasting** is the prediction of turning points in one economic time series through the use of observations on other time series called barometers or indicators.

Economists at the National Bureau of Economic Research and the Bureau of Economic Analysis at the U.S. Department of Commerce have classified economic time series into three general categories: leading indicators, coincident indicators, and lagging indicators. These indicators provide indications of changes in economic activity, such as gross national product or inflation. **Leading indicators** provide advance warning of a change. **Coincident indicators** change at the same time as the time series being studied. **Lagging indicators** confirm that a change has actually occurred.

Leading indicators are not perfect omens of a turn in economic activity. For example, the index of leading indicators used by the U.S. government predicted all ten turning points between 1948 and 1970, but also predicted twenty-four peaks that did not occur.[1] The indexes are also inaccurate in predicting the exact timing of the turning points. Despite these difficulties, however, extensive, promising research is being done in this area.

| 16-10 | **Things are going to turn our way soon** |

APPLICATION One of the most difficult tasks for forecasters is predicting turning points in a time series of data. For example, we would like to know when inflation rates will start rising after having been falling for a period of time, or when

[1] Saul H. Hymans, "On the Use of Leading Indicators to Predict Cyclical Turning Points." *Brookings Papers on Economic Activity* 2 (1973):339–84.

they will start falling after a period of rising. As late as 1987, forecasters have had difficulty predicting these turning points.

Professor John Kling offered a method that has had success in predicting turning points. The method involves statistical techniques well beyond the level of nonspecialists. Professor Kling noted that the leading-indicators index has been successful in predicting business cycle peaks and troughs but has not been able to predict specific dates. It is best at providing an indication that a turning point is imminent. Also, the leading indicators do not give a probability of the likelihood of their forecasts.

Professor Kling extended others' work by using time series of explanatory variables to increase the accuracy of predicting the turning point of a time series of principal concern, such as inflation. He also formalized the source of uncertainty in the time series and developed a method for assigning probabilities to the days likely to be turning points. He found that the method was effective in predicting the month of a change in the trend in Gross National Product and personal income.

Source: John L. Kling, "Predicting the Turning Points of Business and Economic Time Series." *Journal of Business* 60, No. 2 (April 1987):201–38. © by the University of Chicago.

The Choice of Forecasting Technique: A Summary

Despite the availability of sophisticated statistical techniques to forecast the magnitudes and turning points of economic activity, most company forecasters rely on simple linear or exponential curves to extend these trends to the future. While the cost of detailed forecasting is not practical for most small firms, there is evidence that the widely available summaries of professional forecasters may be sufficiently accurate sources of national income and inflation figures.

16-11   **It's a matter of opinion**

APPLICATION   Dr. R.W. Hafer of the Federal Reserve Bank of St. Louis and Professor Scott Hein of Texas Tech University have compared the successfulness of three of the forecasting methods. They compared a time-series approach, an econometric interest-rate model, and a survey of professional forecasters to predict the inflation rate for the United States from 1970 to 1984. They found that the survey of professional forecasters yielded the most accurate forecasts.

Since the late 1960s the American Statistical Association and the National Bureau of Economic Research have conducted quarterly surveys of thirty to fifty professional forecasters and used the average of their forecasts as an indicator of the future inflation rate. These experts do not always reveal the techniques they use to make their forecasts.

The interest-rate model is based on the assumption that the inflation rate follows the interest rate closely over time. The model assumes that deviations from the long-term trend relationship between the inflation rate and the interest rate are random. On the other hand, the time-series model relies on past levels of inflation as the best indicator of future inflation rates.

While these three methods of forecasting are simple compared to some sophisticated and more expensive methods being used now, they are commonly used by companies to predict inflation rates. Surprisingly, the survey average outperformed the other two by providing estimates that were 40 percent more accurate on the average. There was little significant difference between the other two techniques over the fourteen-year time period.

Source: R.W. Hafer and Scott E. Hein, "On the Accuracy of Time-Series, Interest Rate and Survey Forecasts of Inflation." *Journal of Business* 58, No. 4 (October 1985):377–98. © by the University of Chicago.

Summary

This chapter dealt with several statistical issues of importance to managers. Statistical estimation techniques increase in sophistication constantly. Profit-maximizing managers must be aware of the potential for a greater understanding of their market environments. Statistical analysis provides this opportunity. It also provides potential for confusion.

In this chapter we considered some basic principles associated with the estimation of demand and cost functions and the forecasting of future demand and costs. We emphasized that the search for meaningful information cannot ignore the basic economic theory behind the functional forms used in the estimation process. For example, estimation procedures for determining the demand for the firm's product must account for problems such as the identification problem. Ignoring the identification problem can lead to a confusion between a change in demand and a change in supply.

We compared the relative merits of consumer surveys, market studies, and laboratory experiments. While each of these techniques is useful, especially for new products, all three are often expensive and limited. We concentrated, therefore, on a fourth technique: regression analysis. Regression analysis is a statistical technique used extensively in economics and business. Regression analysis is relatively less expensive and less dependent on reconciling people's statements of intended behavior with actual behavior.

We then considered the estimation of cost functions. We focused on the estimation of both short-run and long-run cost functions. We emphasized the importance of generalizing the nature of the functional form that we choose to estimate. The functional form imposes explicit assumptions about the cost function that may not be true. We saw that a cubic functional form produces average-total-cost curves and marginal-cost curves similar to those that were derived in Chapter 4.

We closed the chapter with a brief discussion of some of the more important issues in forecasting. Forecasting of economic trends at the macroeconomic level has had mixed success. By comparison with the 1970s, the first half of the 1980s has not been the best for professional forecasters. Despite this track record, however, substantial resources and time are being devoted to improving the quality of predicting both the future magnitudes and the turning points of major economic trends.

While most firms are not large enough to rely on their own staffs to make accurate forecasts of the gross national product, inflation, or other aggregate measures of economic activity, they can avail themselves of the privileged nature of data based on their own operations to forecast their own costs and sales. While firms most likely are better off subscribing to services that provide information of national aggregates, they should consider devoting the talents of their in-house economic and statistical staffs to an analysis of their own firms' data.

Important Terms

Regression Analysis (p. 456)
Exogenous Variable (p. 457)
Endogenous Variable (p. 457)
Identification Problem (p. 459)
Time Series (p. 468)

Cross-Section Data (p. 474)
Barometric Forecasting (p. 484)
Leading Indicators (p. 484)
Coincident Indicators (p. 484)
Lagging Indicators (p. 484)

Selected References

Bell, Frederick W. "The Pope and the Price of Fish." *American Economic Review* 58 (December 1968):1346–50.

Berenson, Conrad, and Schnaars, Steven. "Growth Market Forecasting Revisited." *California Management Review* 28, No. 4 (Summer 1986):873–84.

Bishop, John A., and Yoo, Jang H. "'Health Scare,' Excise Taxes and Advertising Ban in the Cigarette Demand and Supply." *Southern Economic Journal* 52, No. 2 (October 1985):402–11.

Kaserman, David L., and Mayo, John W. "Advertising and the Residential Demand for Electricity." *Journal of Business* 58, No. 4 (1985):399–408.

Kling, John L. "Predicting the Turning Points of Business and Economic Time Series." *Journal of Business* 60, No. 2 (April 1987):201–38.

Manning, Willard G., Jr., and Phelps, Charles E. "The Demand for Dental Care." *Bell Journal of Economics* 10, No. 2 (Autumn 1979):503–25.

Sav, G. Thomas. "The Engineering Approach to Economic Production Functions Revisited: An Application to Solar Processes." *Journal of Industrial Economics* XXXIII, No. 1 (September 1984):21–35.

Problems

1. Assume that an entrepreneur, Earl Mazoo, is planning on marketing a new oil furnace that greatly reduces energy use for home owners who use large amounts of oil. These furnaces will be most appropriate for owners of large homes. They are expensive relative to other furnaces, but they are much more durable. Earl plans to determine the interest in his product by making a telephone survey with many detailed questions. What problems might Earl encounter using this approach?

2. Assume that Rocky Sanders has collected the following data about the relationship between annual income of his customers and the number of cartons of trash bags they bought during the past month.

Income (in thousands of dollars)	30	31	27	40	24	27	22	42	70
Purchases (in cartons)	2	3	3	4	2	2	2	5	0

(a) Plot this relationship on a graph and draw a straight line that comes closest to representing the relationship between the two variables.

(b) Eliminate the last observation and redraw the line.

(c) What might you do to reconcile the difference in your answers to parts (a) and (b)?

3. Orbal Force Consumer Products manufactures several consumer goods and is a major advertiser. The company's accountants treat advertising expenses as a current expense. If you plan on using cost data provided by the company's accountants to estimate cost functions, what effect will this procedure have on your estimates?

4. In Application 16-9 the researchers claimed that the range in the income and price variables was large enough to forecast the effects of a change in government-provided dental insurance.

(a) If the variation in these two variables had not been large enough, what problem would the researchers have had in using their estimates to forecast the effects of the insurance plan?

(b) Since prices of dental care and incomes are much higher now than they were in 1970, is it still possible to use the results of this study to forecast the effect of this policy now?

Answer questions 5–10 with true, false, or uncertain.

5. The U.S. government's leading indicators are the most accurate measures of turning points in inflation and gross national income.

6. An average forecast of independent professional forecasters may offer the best indicator of future economic activity.

7. Most firms should rely on outside experts for forecasts of national trends.

8. A small firm that relies on its owner's opinion about future events would be better off seeking outside forecasting help.

9. Cost functions based on engineering production functions may be best for new products.

10. Time-series data are best for short-run cost functions, and cross-sectional data are best for long-run cost functions.

Appendix

This Appendix describes some important statistics normally provided by computer regression packages. These statistics provide useful information concerning the ability of the equation to measure the relationship between the dependent and independent variables.

Coefficient of Determination

The coefficient of determination, R^2, indicates the explanatory power of the entire regression equation. It shows the proportion of the total variation in the dependent (endogenous) variable that is explained by the variation in the full set of the independent (exogenous) variables in the equation. R^2 ranges from 0 to 1. The closer it is to 1, the more the equation explains the variation in the dependent variable. If it is close to 0, the independent variables do not explain much of the variation in the dependent variable. It is often adjusted to account for the amount of information, or number of observations, used to calculate the relationship. If an adjusted R^2 is available, you should use it in place of the unadjusted R^2.

F-Statistic

The *F*-statistic is another measure of the explanatory value of the equation. The *F*-statistic is adjusted for the sample size used in the estimation procedure.

$$F = \frac{\dfrac{\text{Total explained variation}}{(k - 1)}}{\dfrac{\text{Total unexplained variation}}{(n - k)}}$$

where n is the number of observations in the sample and k is the number of independent variables in the equation. The *F*-statistic tests whether a significant proportion of the total variation in the dependent variable is due to the variation in the independent variables. If there is no relation between the independent variables and the dependent variable, the *F*-statistic will be zero. There are tables for the *F*-statistic that show how large the *F*-statistic must be to test the significance of the relationship.

Standard Error of Coefficients

The standard error provides a measure of the confidence that we have in the estimated values of the coefficients. The standard error approximates the range of probability of likely values for the coefficient. Although the estimated value provides the best prediction of the coefficient, it is possible that it is not the exact value. For example, with a sufficiently large sample, we can be 95 percent confident that the true value of the coefficient lies within 1.96 standard errors of the estimated value. The smaller the standard error is, the more confidence we can have in the estimated value.

We can also use the standard error to test whether the true coefficient is likely to be a specific value. The most common test is whether the true value is zero. For example, if the estimated coefficient is 2.0 and the standard error of this estimate is 0.5, it is unlikely that the true value of the coefficient is 0. Zero lies 4 (that is, 2.0/0.5) standard errors away from 2.0.

T-Statistic

The *T*-statistic provides another measure of the confidence that we can have in the estimated value of the coefficients in a regression equation. It can be used even for small sample sizes. The *T*-statistic is the ratio of the difference between the estimated value and a benchmark value and the standard error of the estimated coefficient. The most widely used test is the comparison of the estimated value and zero mentioned in the explanation of the standard error. In this case the *T*-statistic is the ratio of the estimated value and its standard error.

17

RISK ANALYSIS

Throughout most of this text we have analyzed problems by assuming that we knew the outcomes of our actions with certainty. Although most decisions involve the unknown and require an assumption about future events, we can improve our decision-making by analyzing problems at first as though we had perfect knowledge. Analyzing problems by assuming perfect certainty provides a basis of comparison when approaching the more complex problems that involve elements of uncertainty.

In Chapters 9–12 we considered indirect methods for dealing with a lack of information. In those chapters we were concerned with a lack of information about the intentions of buyers, competitors, employees, and parties to contractual agreements. In each case we discussed strategies and general procedures for coping with the lack of information about future events and the actions of others.

In this chapter we consider decisions where the likelihood of success is known in advance but the outcome is still subject to chance. These are decisions involving risk. We will focus on specific techniques for coping with risk.

For example, we can improve the usefulness of the present-value method by explicitly incorporating the risk of future events into the formula. There are two common ways of doing this. We could adjust the numerator to account for the uncertainty of each of the future outcomes, or we could adjust the interest rate used in the denominator to discount the value of future outcomes.

We begin by defining risk and determining methods for its calculation. We then discuss the two methods for adjusting the present-value formula to account for risk. At the end of the chapter we consider two additional techniques for improving our decision making in more complex and uncertain environments.

Risk

The decision maker may know about future events with certainty. For example, an investor purchasing a $10,000 U.S. Treasury Bill offering an annual 10 percent interest rate has little need to worry about whether the government will pay the required interest as planned.

Other decisions are less certain. In Chapter 4 Blanche Mayzone confronted the decision of whether or not to open a restaurant. We analyzed her problem in two ways. We started by assuming that she knew with certainty the future revenues and costs of opening and running a restaurant. Using that approach we were able to calculate the relevant costs of her decision and compare them to the future revenues. Based on this analysis, Blanche decided to open the restaurant.

At the end of Chapter 4 we used breakeven analysis to determine the number of customers Blanche would need on a daily basis to make the venture worthwhile. Rather than assume that we knew her future revenues with certainty, we compared her revenues and costs for different numbers of customers. Since Blanche expected that she would attract enough customers to make her revenues always exceed her costs, she made the decision to open the restaurant.

However, there is more to the story of Blanche and her restaurant. All investment decisions depend on assumptions about future events. While Blanche has had prior experience in the restaurant business, her new restaurant will be the only one of its kind in her town. Careful market research prior to making the decision to open the restaurant may give her more information about her chances for success, or the probability of success. The **probability** of an event is the chance, or odds, that the event will take place. For example, Blanche may find that others have opened similar types of restaurants in market areas similar to hers. She may discover that these restaurants succeeded 70 percent of the time, and that the remaining 30 percent failed. The market researchers may not have enough information to remove the remaining uncertainty about the restaurant's potential for success. Since Blanche now knows the probability of success, she knows the risks associated with opening her restaurant. **Risk** is the possibility of a gain or loss from an investment when the investor knows the probabilities of all possible outcomes.

If Blanche had to make her decision with no knowledge of the possible outcomes or the probabilities of a set of known outcomes, she would be making her decision in a state of uncertainty. **Economic uncertainty** is the state in which decision makers do not know the possible outcomes of their actions and do not know the probabilities attached to a set of known possible outcomes.

We considered several situations involving uncertainty in Chapters 9–12. For example, we analyzed the use of brand names, warranties, and advertising as means of reducing the degree of uncertainty that consumers have about the quality of a firm's product. We studied contractual arrangements among firms buying from and selling to one another. Potential for opportunistic behavior on the part of one or all parties to the contract could make these contracts untenable. We saw how firms may cope with the uncertainty imposed by this possible behavior.

In this chapter we will limit our focus to investment decisions involving risk. We will concentrate on techniques that decision makers can use to compare competing investment projects once the firm has knowledge of the probabilities attached to all possible outcomes. The basis of our analysis will be the present-value formula.

Probability Distributions

While Blanche may expect a specific number of customers per day, the actual number may be much different. The more the number of customers varies from the number she expects, the greater the risk she will experience. Once Blanche has been operating her restaurant for a few years, she will be able to predict the number of customers with greater accuracy, and any decisions she makes that depend on knowing the number of customers will involve less risk.

If Blanche knows the probability attached to each possible number of customers and lists both the nature of the event (that is, the number of customers) and the probability, she will have a probability distribution. A **probability distribution** is a complete list of both the possible outcomes and the probabilities of their occurrence. Table 17-1 shows a simplified probability distribution indicating the probability of the success of Blanche's restaurant. Let us assume that she does face the risk that her restaurant may not be a success. The table shows that she faces a 70 percent probability of success and a 30 percent probability of failure. Column 1 shows the probability in decimal form, while column 2 shows it in percentages. Since the sum of the decimals is 1.0 and the sum of the percentages is 100 percent, the probability distribution includes all possible outcomes.

TABLE 17-1 ▪ The probability distribution of opening Blanche's restaurant

Nature of the Event	Probability	
	(1)	(2)
Success	0.70	70%
Failure	0.30	30%
	1.00	100%

TABLE 17-2

State of the Economy	Annual Economic Profits from Blanche's Investment	
	Restaurant	Real Estate
Prosperity	$15,000	$12,000
Normal Times	$10,000	$10,000
Recession	$5,000	$8,000

Payoff Matrix

The decision to open the restaurant may be more complicated than this simple example suggests. Recall that Blanche invested $88,000 of her own money in the restaurant. If she had decided not to open the restaurant, she would have continued to rent her house to tenants and would have invested the $88,000 in another venture.

For example, let's assume she could have used the $88,000 to purchase more homes for renting to tenants. She now has to choose between investing in the restaurant business or in the real-estate business. Although the success of each venture will depend on several factors, assume here that success depends only on the overall strength of the local economy. If times are good, more people will be moving into the area and will be needing houses to rent. People will also be going out to eat more often. Table 17-2 shows Blanche's estimate of the impact of the health of the local economy on the annual profits from both ventures.

The table simplifies the problem by considering only three possible conditions for the local economy. In reality, the local economy could vary continuously between severe recession and prosperity. Note that she will earn the same annual return on her investment from either venture during normal times—$10,000. In times of prosperity the restaurant would be the best investment. During recession the real-estate investment would be the more attractive of the two choices.

Expected Values

Blanche must make a decision to either open the restaurant or go into the real-estate business. In many ways her decision is similar to flipping a coin. She knows that a normal, unaltered coin offers equal probability of landing on either side. Assume that she places a bet on the flip of a coin. She receives $10 every time the coin lands heads up, and nothing if the coin lands tails up. If she plays the game repeatedly, she expects to win $10 half of the time and nothing the other half of the time. On the average she expects to make

$5 per flip of the coin even though she will never receive exactly $5 on any one flip of the coin. Five dollars is the expected value of the coin toss. The **expected value** is the sum of all the probability-weighted outcomes possible due to a decision.

To determine the expected value of the profits for her decision, Blanche needs to know the probability of each of these three prospects for the local economy. Assume that there is a 0.25 (25 percent) probability of prosperity, a 0.5 probability of normal times, and a 0.25 probability of recession. Table 17-3 combines these probabilities with the outcomes shown in Table 17-2. Note that the probabilities of the three states of the economy add up to 1.0 (100 percent).

Table 17-3 shows how to calculate the expected value of the profits for each of the two investment possibilities. First, we multiply each outcome (that is, the annual profits) by the probability of each state of the economy. We then add these probability-weighted outcomes to determine the expected profits for each of the investments. In this case the expected value of profits is $10,000 for both the restaurant and the real-estate venture.

In general, we can use the following equation to calculate the expected value:

$$E(V) = \sum_{i=1}^{N} [(V_i) \times (P_i)].$$ (17-1)

V_i is the value of the ith outcome. In Blanche's case these are the different profits associated with each of the possible outcomes. P_i is the probability of each outcome occurring; N is the number of possible outcomes; and $E(V)$ is

TABLE 17-3 ▪ Expected values

	State of the Economy	Probability (1)	Annual Profits ($) (2)	(1) × (2) ($) (3)
Restaurant	Prosperity	0.25	15,000	3,750
	Normal Times	0.50	10,000	5,000
	Recession	0.25	5,000	1,025
		1.0		Expected Profits: 10,000
Real Estate	Prosperity	0.25	12,000	3,000
	Normal Times	0.50	10,000	5,000
	Recession	0.25	8,000	2,000
		1.0		Expected Profits: 10,000

the expected value of the investment. For example, the expected profit of investing in the restaurant would be

$$E(V) = \sum_{i=1}^{N} [(V_i) \times (P_i)]$$
$$= V_1 P_1 + V_2 P_2 + V_3 P_3$$
$$= 15,000(0.25) + 10,000(0.5) + 5,000(0.25)$$
$$= 3,750 + 5,000 + 1,250$$
$$= 10,000.$$

Discrete Probability Distributions

We could represent the information of Table 17-3 on a graph showing the probability and the possible outcomes. The vertical axis of Figure 17-1 shows

FIGURE 17-1 ▪ **Discrete probability distributions.** The graph on the left shows the three possible outcomes of opening a restaurant. There is a 0.25 (25 percent) probability of a $5.000 annual profit and a 0.25 probability of a $15.000 annual profit. There is a 0.5 probability of $10.000. The graph on the right shows the corresponding probabilities for the real estate business. There is a 0.25 probability of an $8.000 annual profit and a 0.25 probability of a $12.000 annual profit. There is a 0.5 probability of a $10.000 annual profit.

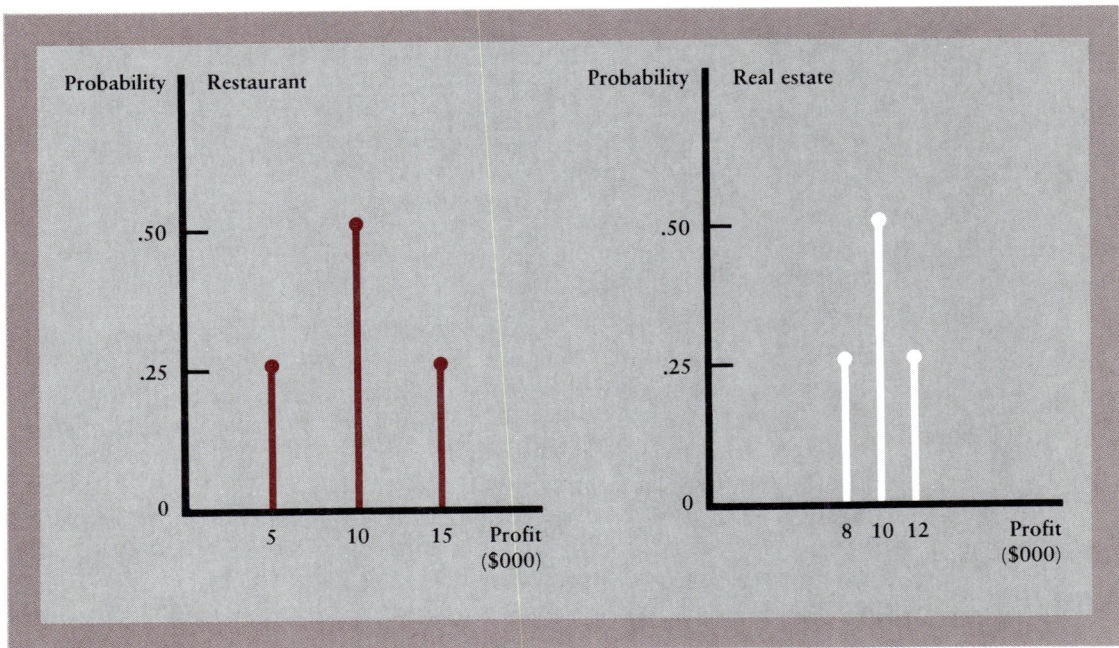

the probability of each outcome. The real-estate venture has the same expected return, but the range of possible profits is between $8,000 and $12,000. The restaurant yields the same expected return but the range is larger—between $5,000 and $15,000. The figure shows the possible outcomes as a discrete probability distribution. A **discrete probability distribution** is a graphical representation of the relationship between each outcome and the probability of its occurrence when there is a finite number of possible outcomes.

Continuous Probability Distributions

In Blanche's case it is unrealistic to assume that there will be only three possible states of the local economy. There will be an infinite number of possible states, each having an impact on the success of both investments. We can still represent the probability distribution on a graph. The continuous probability distribution allows us to determine the probability that the actual outcome will be within a range of possible outcomes. A **continuous probability distribution** is a graph of probability and outcomes where all outcomes are possible within a range of extreme values. The area under the curve between two outcomes shows the probability that the true outcome will fall between these two possible outcomes. The total area under the curve from one extreme outcome to the other extreme outcome is 100 percent.

Figure 17-2 shows continuous probability distributions for both of the two investment possibilities. We are assuming that all levels of economic profits between the extreme endpoints of the distributions are possible and that the annual returns follow a normal, bell-shaped distribution. The two distributions look similar to the graphs in Figure 17-1. They have the same expected values of $10,000. The flatter distribution for the restaurant indicates that the probability of outcomes is spread out over a wider range of possibilities. The distribution for the real-estate investment is more highly concentrated around the expected value of $10,000.

Measurement of Risk

We can use the probability distribution to indicate the risk associated with each of the investments. We can observe the flatness of the probability distribution as a rough indicator of risk. The flatter the probability distribution (that is, the less concentrated the distribution around the expected value of profits), the greater the risk. According to this criterion, the restaurant would be riskier than the real-estate investment.

We can determine the concentration of the probability distribution around its expected value more formally by using the following procedure. First, calculate the expected value of the outcome using Equation (17-1). Next, subtract the expected value from each of the possible outcomes to calculate a set of deviations from the expected value. Then square each deviation and

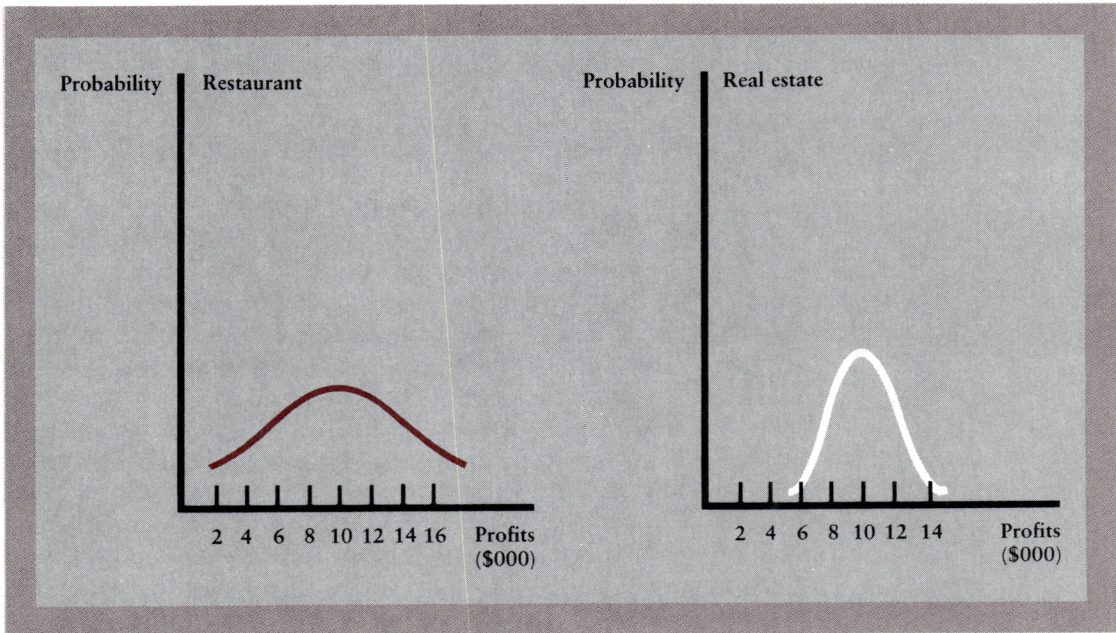

FIGURE 17-2 ▪ **Continuous probability distributions.** The two continuous probability distributions have the same expected value of $10.000. The flatter probability distribution for the restaurant indicates that the probability is spread along a wider range of possible outcomes, while the distribution for the real-estate venture indicates that the actual outcome is likely to be closer to the expected value.

multiply the squared terms by the probability of occurrence. The sum of these values is the variance of the probability distribution. The **variance**, σ^2, is the sum of the probability-weighted, squared deviations from the expected value of the distribution. The equation for calculating the variance is

$$\text{Variance} = \sigma^2 = \sum_{i=1}^{N} [V_i - E(V)]^2 P_i$$

where V_i is the value of the ith outcome, $E(V)$ is the expected value, and P_i is the probability of the ith outcome.

The variance is one measure of the risk of an investment. As the variance increases, the risk increases. Alternatively, we can calculate another measure directly related to variance: standard deviation. The **standard deviation**, σ, is the square root of the variance. The equation for calculating the standard deviation is

$$\text{Standard Deviation} = \sigma = \sqrt{\sum_{i=1}^{N} [V_i - E(V)]^2 P_i}.$$

We can calculate the variance and standard deviation for the restaurant investment. Recall that the expected value was $10,000.

Possible Outcomes (in dollars)	Deviation from Average Outcome (in dollars)	Deviation Squared × Probability
15	$15 - 10 = 5$	$5^2 \times 0.25 = 6.25$
10	$10 - 10 = 0$	$0 \times 0.50 = 0$
5	$5 - 10 = -5$	$(-5)^2 \times 0.25 = \underline{6.25}$
		$\sigma^2 = 12.5$

The variance is the sum of 6.25, 0, and 6.25, from the last column. The standard deviation is the square root of the sum:

$$\sigma = \sqrt{\sigma^2} = \sqrt{12.5} = 3.536.$$

Standard Deviations for the Normal Distribution

We can use the standard deviation to determine the range of probability to either side of the expected value. For such a distribution a range from one standard deviation to the left of the expected value to one standard deviation to the right of the expected value includes 68 percent of the probability of an event occurring. For example, if the returns on Blanche's investment in the restaurant are distributed normally, she can expect the true return on her investment to have a 68 percent probability of being within ± one standard deviation from the expected value.

Two standard deviations to both sides of the expected value will include 95 percent of the probable outcomes, and there is more than a 99 percent probability that the true value will lie between ± three standard deviations. As a result, the smaller the standard deviation, the less risk Blanche must take in investing in her restaurant. Figure 17-3 summarizes this relationship.

Coefficient of Variation

The standard deviation is not a perfect measure of risk. We have been assuming that both of Blanche's investments have the same cost and the same expected

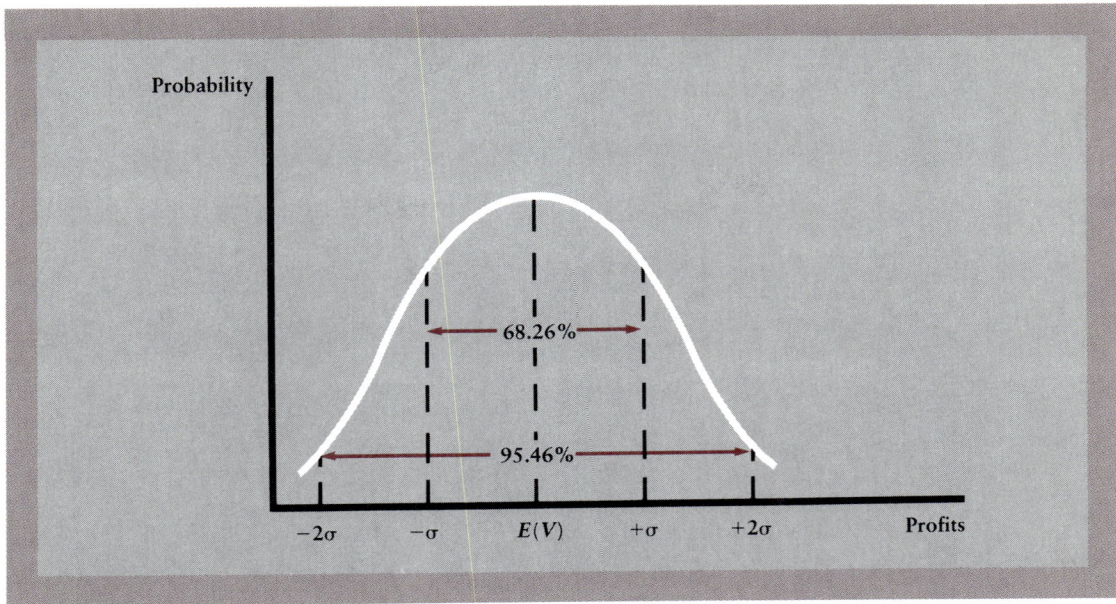

FIGURE 17-3 ▪ Standard deviation for the normal distribution. The area under the normal distribution equals 100 percent of the probability of all possible outcomes. The area under the curve between any two points on the horizontal axis represents the probability of the actual outcome being between the two points. For example, the probability (that is, the area) between ± one standard deviation (σ) equals approximately 68 percent.

return. If one of the two ventures involves a larger investment, the standard deviation is likely to be larger, even if the percentage return on the investments is the same. For example, expected profits of $1,000 per year from an investment with a standard deviation of $100 is less risky than an investment yielding expected profits of $200 with a standard deviation of $90.

We can correct for this problem by calculating the coefficient of variation. The **coefficient of variation**, v, is the ratio of the standard deviation and the expected value (mean).

$$\text{Coefficient of Variation} = v = \frac{\sigma}{E(V)}$$

As the coefficient of variation increases, risk increases.

When we are comparing two unrelated investment possibilities that are not of equal size, the coefficient of variation provides a better measure of relative risk than the standard deviation. In our example, the standard deviation for the restaurant investment is 3.536, while the expected value is $10 (that is, $10,000). Therefore, the coefficient of variation is

$$v = \frac{\sigma}{E(V)} = \frac{3.536}{10} = 0.3536.[1]$$

Risk Aversion and Utility Theory

Now that we have a method for measuring risk, we must adjust the expected values to account for this risk. If all individuals had the same attitude towards risk, this would be a much simpler problem. If the owners of the firm have different attitudes towards risk, the decision maker must take these attitudes into account. Before discussing methods for adjusting the values of outcomes for risk, we must consider differences in attitudes towards risk.

Attitudes Towards Risk

Individuals have different attitudes towards risk. In this section we consider three different possibilities: risk-seeking, risk-averse, and risk-indifferent, or neutral, behavior. Assume that we have two investments with equal expected profits but unequal risk or standard deviation. A **risk seeker** is one who chooses the riskier investment. A **risk-averse person** is one who chooses the less risky investment. A **risk-neutral person** is one who is indifferent and does not favor one investment over the other.

The popularity of insurance suggests that most people are risk-averse. Note that no firm will provide insurance to individuals unless the firm can earn the opportunity cost of its time and investment in providing insurance services. This means that the expected payout on insurance claims must be

---

[1] Note that we calculated the standard deviation using $10 as the expected value, not $10,000. When calculating the coefficient of variation, we must maintain the consistency of the units used in calculating both the standard deviation and the expected value. For example, if we had used $10,000 as the expected value, the standard deviation would be

$$\text{Standard Deviation} = \sigma = \sqrt{\sum_{i=1}^{N} [V_i - E(V)]^2 P_i}$$
$$= \sqrt{(5,000)^2(0.25) + 0(0.5) + (-5,000)^2(0.25)}$$
$$= \sqrt{(25,000,000)(0.25) + (25,000,000)(0.25)}$$
$$= \sqrt{12,500,000}$$
$$= 3,536.$$

The coefficient of variation in this case is

$$v = \frac{\text{Standard deviation}}{\text{Expected value}}$$
$$= \frac{3,536}{10,000}$$
$$= 0.3536.$$

less than the total insurance premiums paid by customers of the insurance company.

If the payout is less than the premiums, the cost of having insurance is greater than the expected dollar value of claim payments. Some customers are relinquishing premiums in exchange for coverage that, on the average, pays them back less than they pay. This is consistent with risk-averse behavior.

On the other hand, there are people who like to take risks. Consider racetrack betting and lotteries. Racetracks pay back less in prize money to bettors than they receive in bets. The difference covers the costs of operation and the racetrack's profits. There are additional revenues from concessions, parking, and admission fees at the racetrack, but these revenues do not compensate the track for its operating costs.

The cost of betting is not limited to the size of the bets. The more serious racetrack bettors invest time and money in acquiring information about the horses and jockeys and often spend a complete day at the track making their bets. Offtrack betting centers reduce these costs somewhat. Altogether the costs of betting are greater than the expected returns for the typical bettor.

A willingness to place bets on horses is due either to risk-seeking behavior or the entertainment value of having a horse for which to root. The dedicated trackgoer is most likely a risk taker, while the casual bettor is probably spending money for entertainment purposes. Consider the following example of company-sponsored sweepstakes contests.

17-1 Risk seeking and boredom

APPLICATION

Professors Edward Selby, Jr. and William Beranek of the University of Georgia studied sweepstakes contests to determine what type of person participates. They found that substantial numbers of people participate in sweepstakes despite the lack of information in the sponsor's advertisements about the probabilities and expected value of winning.

They argued that risk-averse and risk-neutral consumers do not participate in sweepstakes unless they receive an expected return that is greater than or equal to their costs of participating in the sweepstakes. They collected information on fifteen sweepstakes contests advertised in the *Reader's Digest* during 1976 and 1977. Only six of the contests completely revealed the value of individual prizes to participants. Three others provided enough information to calculate it indirectly. In eleven cases the sponsors were willing to indicate the number of valid entries that they had received during the sweepstakes.

Based on the information about the number of entries and the value of the prizes, Professors Selby and Beranek were able to calculate indirectly the expected value of an entry to each sweepstakes. They also calculated entry costs based on the average time involved in filling out the entry form, valued conservatively at the minimum hourly wage rate. Added to this opportunity cost of time were any out-of-pocket costs involved.

They determined that, at most, four out of the fifteen sweepstakes offered an expected return that exceeded the conservatively estimated cost of participation. This means that in the other eleven sweepstakes, risk-neutral and risk-averse people would not be adequately compensated for their participation time. Despite this evidence, 3,610,000 of the total 4,610,000 entries went to these eleven contests. From this evidence they concluded that the participants did not consider time a cost of participation in the sweepstakes. To these people, sweepstakes are a form of entertainment rather than an expression of risk-taking behavior.

Source: Edward B. Selby, Jr. and William Beranek, "Sweepstakes Contests: Analysis, Strategies and Survey." *American Economic Review* 71, No. 1 (March 1981):189–95.

Diminishing Marginal Utility of Money

One possible explanation for risk-averse behavior focuses on the assumption about the value to the individual of additional amounts of money. The **marginal utility of money** is the value to the individual of an additional dollar. Figure 17-4 shows three possible relationships between utility and an individual's wealth or income. Assume that each of the three graphs represents the relationship between utility and income for three different types of people. The vertical axis measures *utils* associated with the corresponding amount of money (such as income or wealth) measured on the horizontal axis. **Utils** are a measure of the level of satisfaction and well-being created by the amount of money that the person has.

Figure 17-4(a) demonstrates diminishing marginal utility of money, because the slope of the utility curve decreases as income increases. Since the slope of the curve shows the marginal change in utility, this curve represents diminishing marginal utility of money. Figure 17-4(b) shows a utility curve with a constant slope. In this case the marginal utility of money is constant. Figure 17-4(c) shows an increasing slope and increasing marginal utility of money. Since the utility attached to different levels of income differs for these three types of people, there is also a difference in their attitudes toward risk.

We can determine this relationship to risk aversion by proposing the following experiment. Assume that we offer each of these three people a choice. Each one may have $1,000 with certainty or may elect to forgo the $1,000 in exchange for a 0.5 probability of receiving $2,000 and a 0.5 probability of receiving nothing.

The expected value of the risky investment is 0.5 × $2,000, or $1,000. The expected utility of the risky investment is 0.5 times the utility of $2,000 plus 0.5 times the utility of $0. Figure 17-4(a) shows that since this expected utility is less than the utility of a certain sum of $1,000, a person would not

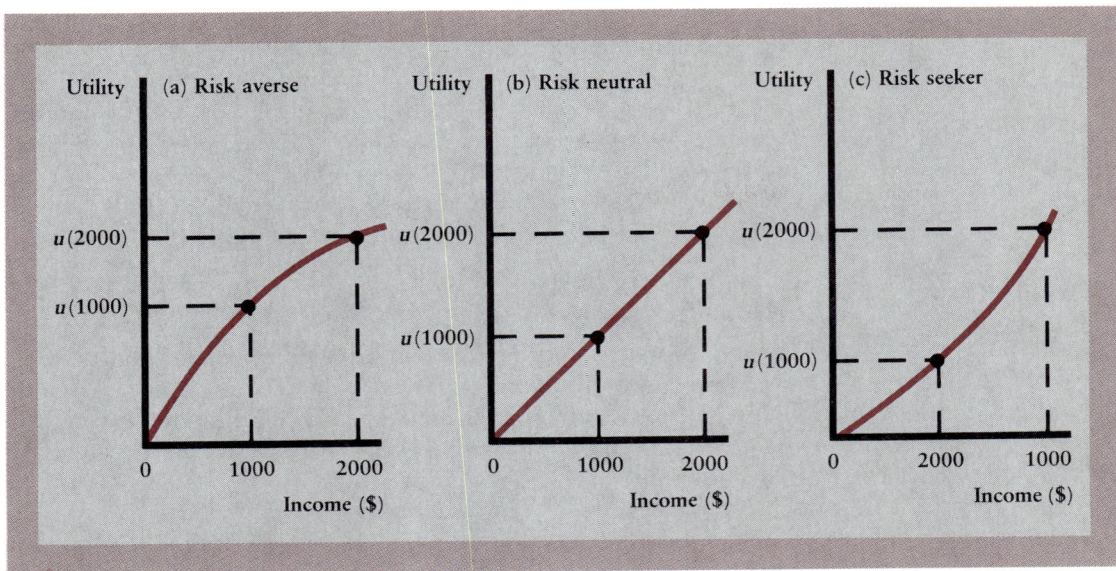

FIGURE 17-4 ▪ Utility and risk aversion. Part (a) shows diminishing marginal utility of income. In this case the utility of income increases at a slower rate than income does. This is consistent with risk aversion. Part (b) shows risk-neutral behavior, because the marginal utility of income is constant. Part (c) shows an increasing marginal utility of income and risk-seeking behavior.

take the risky offer and would be risk-averse. The person represented by Figure 17-4(b) is indifferent—that is, does not favor either the risky offer or the certain payment of $1,000. Figure 17-4(c) shows risk-seeking behavior. This person places higher value on a 0.5 probability of receiving $2,000 than on a certain payment of $1,000.

Adjusting the Present-Value Formula for Risk

Investors' attitudes towards risk affect their valuation of the future profits of the firm. The present value of the future stream of a firm's profits indicates the value of the firm to the owners.

$$PV = \sum_{t=1}^{T} \frac{\pi_t}{(1 + i)^t},$$

where π_t represents the expected profits in each time period t, i is the interest or discount rate, and T is the number of time periods in the life of the investment project.[2] If the investors are averse to risk, they may be willing to accept a lower expected profit in each time period in exchange for assurance of lower risk.

Risk seekers do not require the same inducement. They are willing to forgo a certain outcome that exceeds the expected value of a risky investment. If investors are indifferent to risk, they make their decisions based on the present value of expected profits and do not need to adjust the formula to account for risk.

Certainty-Equivalent Adjustments

We can use utility theory to determine an adjustment to the present-value formula. Decision makers determine how much they require in compensation for the added risk of undertaking an investment. This amount makes them indifferent—that is, they do not favor either a certain sum or the expected return from a risky investment.

Recall that Blanche had $88,000 to invest. Assume that the restaurant would produce a return on this investment in present-value terms of $300,000, with a probability of 0.5. There would also be a 0.5 probability that Blanche would lose her $88,000 and receive nothing in return. The expected return on the investment would be

$$(0.5 \times \$300,000) + (0.5 \times 0) = \$150,000.$$

If Blanche were indifferent about investing the $88,000 in exchange for the risky return of $300,000 with a 0.5 probability, the $88,000 would be the certainty equivalent of the risky investment. The **certainty equivalent** is the guaranteed sum of money that makes a decision maker indifferent about the choice between it and the expected value of a risky investment.

If the certainty equivalent equals the expected value of the risky investment, the decision maker is risk-neutral. In Blanche's case, if she were risk-neutral, she would be willing to invest as much as $150,000 in the restaurant in

---

[2] Present value measures the time adjusted-value of money. For example, by placing a dollar in the bank we can earn interest on the dollar. If the interest rate is 10 percent per year, we can convert a dollar today into $1.10 at the end of the year. In the same manner we could borrow $1.00 today by promising to pay back $1.10 next year. In this example the interest rate i is 0.1 (10 percent), and the present value formula is

$$PV = \$1.10/(1 + i)^1$$
$$= \$1.10/(1.1)$$
$$= \$1.00.$$

If we were to receive $1.10 at the end of the year and an additional $1.21 at the end of the second year, the present value of this future payoff would be

$$PV = \$1.10/(1 + i)^1 + \$1.21/(1 + i)^2$$
$$= \$1.10/1.1 + \$1.21/(1.1)^2$$
$$= \$1.10/1.1 + \$1.21/1.21$$
$$= \$1.00 + \$1.00$$
$$= \$2.00.$$

exchange for an expected return of $150,000. If her certainty equivalent were less than the expected value of $150,000, she would be risk-averse. If she were willing to invest more than $150,000, she would be a risk seeker.

We can summarize this comparison by calculating a certainty equivalent adjustment factor, β:

$$\beta = \frac{\text{Certainty equivalent amount}}{\text{Expected value of the risky investment}}.$$

The certainty-equivalent adjustment factor, β, provides a measure of a decision maker's attitude toward risk, as summarized by the following:

$$\beta < 1 \quad \text{for risk aversion,}$$
$$\beta = 1 \quad \text{for indifference to risk, and}$$
$$\beta > 1 \quad \text{for a preference for risk.}$$

Figure 17-5 shows a method for calculating the adjustment factor. The figure shows the relationship between risk, measured on the vertical axis, and the expected return, measured on the horizontal axis. The curve indicates all combinations of the risk and the expected return, which the decision maker

FIGURE 17-5 ▪ **Certainty-equivalent adjustment.** Individuals require a higher expected return to compensate for higher risk. The vertical axis measures the risk in terms of the coefficient of variation. The certainty-equivalent adjustment will equal $4.000/$8.000 or 0.5 at V_a and $4.000/$10.000 or 0.4 at V_b. The decline in the certainty-equivalent adjustment reflects this individual's risk aversion.

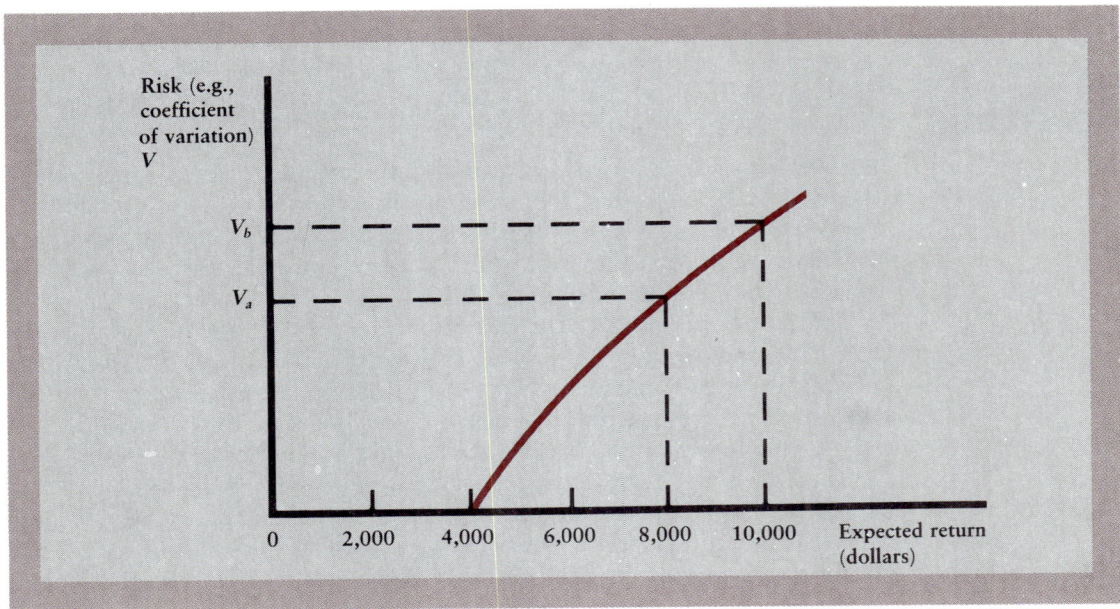

considers to be of equal value. To make this decision maker take higher risks, the expected return has to increase above the certain return of \$4,000. For example, at risk level v_a, the decision maker would expect at least \$8,000 in order to forgo the certain return of \$4,000. The adjustment factor would be

$$\beta = \frac{\$4,000}{\$8,000} = 0.5.$$

At risk level v_b, the adjustment factor would be

$$\beta = \frac{\$4,000}{\$10,000} = 0.4.$$

Since this decision maker requires a higher expected return in order to accept higher levels of risk, this person is averse to risk. If we could calculate the adjustment factors at each level of risk, we could use this information to adjust the expected returns for any investment. We would replace the expected value of profits (π_t) in each time period with its certainty equivalent $(\beta\pi_t)$. The present-value formula would now be

$$PV = \sum_{t=1}^{T} \frac{\beta\pi_t}{(1 + i)^t}.$$

By replacing the expected profits by their certainty equivalents, we adjusted for the effect of risk on future investments. To make this adjustment we must have an estimate of the adjustment factor for different levels of risk. In determining the adjustment factors, managers must take into account the aversion to risk of the owners and the risk of the proposed projects.

17-2

A big enough risk

APPLICATION

The usefulness of certainty-equivalent adjustments for expected future returns depends on decision makers' ability to process information on the probabilities of future events and the risk associated with each possible outcome. There has been concern that this problem may be more severe in cases where the probability of events occurring is small.

A team of four researchers, David S. Brookshire, Mark A. Thayer, John Tschirhart, and William D. Schulze, showed that individuals are capable of assessing these probabilities for financial decisions of importance to them. They studied the effect that the threat of earthquakes has on the prices of single-family houses in the San Francisco and Los Angeles areas.

There were 251 areas at high risk for earthquakes in California in 1979. The researchers compared the selling prices of houses in risk areas with those not in risk areas. In addition to the physical characteristics of the houses, they controlled statistically for the impact of other factors on house prices, such as the quality of schools in the area, proximity to employment areas and beaches, and the quality of the air.

A law passed in 1974 required that anyone selling a home in these risk areas had to give written notice to prospective buyers about the potential earthquake danger. The research team found that this information helped home buyers make rational decisions. For example, houses sold in 1978 in parts of Los Angeles not in the high-risk areas cost, on the average, $4,650 more than identical homes in the high-risk areas. The differential was $2,490 in the San Francisco area, since the risks of damage due to earthquakes are lesser in San Francisco than in Los Angeles. For homes sold in 1972, two years before the law requiring the disclosure of information on earthquake risks, there was no significant difference in the prices of houses sold in high-risk areas versus other areas.

The purchase of a house is a major investment for most people. This evidence suggests that individuals do process available information on risks and use it to adjust the value of their investment. People making significantly larger investments than the purchase of a house should have strong incentives to seek available information in order to assess the risks associated with their decisions.

Source: David S. Brookshire, Mark A. Thayer, John Tschirhart, and William D. Schulze, "A Test of the Expected Utility Model: Evidence from Earthquake Risks." *Journal of Political Economy* 93, No. 2 (April 1985):369–89. © by the University of Chicago.

| 17-3 | **The cost of staying alive** |

APPLICATION   There is a parallel between certainty equivalence in evaluating risky investments and compensating wage payments for employees engaged in risky jobs. The willingness of employees to accept life-threatening jobs in exchange for higher pay indicates the value that these people place on their own lives. Since they face an increased probability of death on the job, they implicitly indicate how much money it takes to compensate them for this higher probability of death.

Professors Stuart Low and Lee McPheters of Arizona State University analyzed data on the compensation and threat of death faced by 64,000 police officers in seventy-two U.S. cities in 1979. They noted that a common method for calculating the value of a human life in wrongful-death lawsuits has been the present value of the forgone market earnings.

This procedure only accounts for the market value of the person's life, not for the monetary value that individuals place on their own lives. Instead of using the present value of market earnings, Professors Low and McPheters determined the amount that police officers would be willing to pay to reduce their probability of death in the line of duty. This method is similar to the certainty-equivalent approach, because individuals are trading risk for income based on their preferences (that is, utility) for risk and income.

The two researchers determined that, on the average, an officer would be willing to accept a reduction in annual income of $516 (1979 prices) to avoid the expected killing of one officer in the line of duty in their city during the year. The typical city in their sample had 888 officers. Together these officers would be willing to pay $458,208 to avoid the expected death of one of them during the year.

The researchers determined these amounts by observing police officers' employment decisions in areas of different probabilities of death in the line of duty. After controlling for other factors that could have influenced differences in income levels, they determined that cities with higher risks of death had to pay more to attract police officers. The willingness of police officers to accept riskier jobs for higher compensation implicitly showed the monetary value they placed on their own lives.

The researchers concluded that this value of a human life ($458,208) is lower than that found in similar studies of employees in other lines of work. They suggested that the lower wage differentials needed to attract police officers to risky work might be due to the type of people who are attracted to police work in general. Since police work is riskier than most other lines of work, police officers are likely to be less averse to risk than most other people.

Source: Stuart A. Low and Lee R. McPheters, "Wage Differentials and Risk of Death: An Empirical Analysis." *Economic Inquiry* XXI, No. 2 (April 1983):271–80.

Risk-Adjusted Discount Rates

We could adjust the present-value formula by adjusting the discount rate, *i*. This method is similar to the certainty-equivalent method, since it adjusts for the relationship between risk and expected return. In this case investors demand a *risk premium* before they are willing to make a risky investment. A **risk premium** is the difference that an investor requires between a riskless interest rate and an expected rate of return on a risky asset before being willing to make the risky investment.

In this case the decision maker requires a risk premium as compensation for making an investment with a known degree of risk, such as the coefficient of variation or standard deviation. The risk-adjusted discount rate is the sum of the risk premium and the risk-free interest rate. The investor can now calculate the risk-adjusted present value of the investment by discounting the future expected returns by the risk-adjusted discount rate.

For example, assume that Blanche attached a risk premium of 5 percent to opening the restaurant. Since the risk-free interest rate is 10 percent, she would discount all future expected revenues by 15 percent (that is, 10 percent plus 5 percent). If the discounted present value exceeded the cost of her investment, she would make the investment.

Decision Trees

We will now increase the complexity of Blanche's restaurant venture. Assuming that Blanche does decide to open the restaurant, let's consider what type of restaurant she should have. She could decide to use her money to enlarge the house in order to add more seating capacity, or she could spend the money on more luxurious furnishings and tableware and keep the restaurant small. The larger restaurant would have a greater capacity but would attract a more family-oriented clientele, which would be less willing to pay high prices for her meals. The more luxurious and intimate restaurant would attract a more affluent and possibly older clientele. While the latter group would pay more on the average, there would be fewer of them.

The condition of the local economy would not necessarily have the same impact on the profits from the two types of restaurants. The more exclusive restaurant would probably do much better than the family-style restaurant in prosperous times, and worse during recessions. During a recession there would be less money available for luxurious dining. On the other hand, the need to work more to earn money would reduce time at home for home-cooked, family-style meals, thus creating the need for inexpensive, family-style restaurants.

We could complicate the problem further by adding the effects of competitive factors that respond to changes in the local economy. For example, when times are prosperous, there may be a positive probability that competitors will enter the market and compete with Blanche's restaurant. This probability may differ depending on what type of restaurant she chooses to open. Since Blanche is concerned about the present value of her investment, she must consider the effect that these events will have on the success of her restaurant.

Despite the increasing complexity of this problem, we can make Blanche's decision more tractable as long as she can assign probabilities to each of these possible events. In order to help her, let us use a decision tree. A **decision tree** is a graphical representation of the probabilities of a sequential set of outcomes that result from the initial investment decision, where each sequential level forms a new set of branches coming from a branch that represents the previous level on the decision tree.

Figure 17-6 (p. 512) shows a decision tree for Blanche's problem. Blanche must decide on either the family-style or the luxury restaurant. Since she will have to spend money on promoting either image for her restaurant, she will not be able to switch easily from one type of image to the other at a later date. Column 2 in the figure contains the probabilities of three possible states of the economy. Column 4 shows the probabilities of three types of competitive reactions in response to the general state of the local economy. Column 5

State of the economy		Competitive response		Present value of outcome	Expected value (2) × (4) × (5)
(1)	(2)	(3)	(4)	(5)	(6)
Luxury					
Prosperity	.25	New competitors	.6	200,000	30,000
		No change	.3	350,000	26,250
		Fewer competitors	.1	400,000	10,000
Normal times	.50	New competitors	.2	120,000	12,000
		No change	.6	150,000	45,000
		Fewer competitors	.2	180,000	18,000
Recession	.25	New competitors	.1	50,000	1,200
		No change	.4	70,000	7,000
		Fewer competitors	.5	90,000	11,250
					$160,700
Family-style					
Prosperity	.25	New competitors	.5	150,000	18,750
		No change	.4	250,000	25,000
		Fewer competitors	.1	300,000	7,500
Normal times	.50	New competitors	.1	120,000	6,000
		No change	.8	160,000	64,000
		Fewer competitors	.1	170,000	8,500
Recession	.25	New competitors	.2	80,000	4,000
		No change	.6	100,000	15,000
		Fewer competitors	.2	140,000	7,000
					$155,750

FIGURE 17-6 ▪ **Decision tree.** Blanche has to choose either the luxury or the family-style restaurant. The decision tree shows that there are several risk factors that she cannot control in advance. Although only one of the eighteen possible outcomes will take place, she must calculate an expected value to determine the best choice. She determines the expected value by weighting the present value of each outcome by the probability that it will occur. The sum of these weighted present values (column 6) is the expected value. The expected present value for the luxury restaurant is $160,700, while the expected present value for the family-style restaurant is $155,750.

indicates the present value associated with each of the eighteen possible outcomes.

Blanche can use this information to calculate the expected present value of opening a family-style or luxury restaurant. She must multiply the probability in column 2 by the probability in column 4 to determine the probability of earning the present value indicated in column 5. For example, if she opens the luxury restaurant, the probability of prosperity is 0.25. The probability that she will face no change in competition during the period of prosperity is 0.3 (that is, 30 percent of the time).

The overall probability of simultaneously having prosperous times and no change in the competitive response is 0.075 (that is, 0.25 × 0.30). Since she would earn a present value of $350,000 given these conditions, column 6 shows the contribution to expected value of 0.075 × $350,000, or $26,250. She would add $26,250 to each of the other eight values in column 6 associated with opening a luxury restaurant. This sum would be the expected value of opening a luxury restaurant.

The sum of the numbers in column 6 is the expected value for each of the two possible choices. Blanche would have a higher expected value by opening the luxurious-style restaurant. The expected value for the luxury restaurant is $160,700, while the expected present value of the family-style restaurant is $155,750.

Despite the higher expected present value, the luxury restaurant may be riskier. Note that there is a larger probability that the luxurious restaurant will have a present value that is less than Blanche's investment of $88,000. If there is a recession she will earn only $50,000 when there is new competition. She will earn only $70,000 if the competitive response remains the same. The probability of the first event is 0.025 (that is, 0.25 × 0.1) and the probability of the second event is 0.1 (or 0.25 × 0.4). The total probability of these two events is 0.025 + 0.100, or 0.125 (that is, 12.5 percent).

The family-style restaurant would earn less than the cost of her investment when there was a recession or new competition. The probability of this happening would be 0.25 × 0.2, or 0.05 (that is, 5 percent). If Blanche were risk-averse, she would want to adjust the expected present value to account for the risk. In order to make a final decision Blanche would have to adjust the value of these outcomes to account for her attitude towards risk. She could use either the certainty-equivalent method or the risk-adjusted discount rate.

Simulations

While Blanche's decision is not an easy one, investment decisions can be even more complicated. As we add more branches to the decision tree, we reduce our ability to analyze problems quickly. However, the rapid development of sophisticated computer equipment has increased the usefulness of computer-based analysis of complex investment decisions.

For example, the decision to build a nuclear power plant is a difficult one. It can take up to ten years to complete such a project. Along the way there may be threats of strikes, unanticipated cost increases, technical problems, and resistance from antinuclear groups. Revenues depend on future demand. Demand depends on population trends, income levels, energy use, and alternative sources of energy.

If we can determine probability distributions for each of these factors, we can program a computer to simulate the future. The computer randomly selects a value from each of these distributions and simulates its effect on the firm's demand and cost functions. After hundreds of these simulations, the computer generates a distribution on the expected rates of return from this decision.

If there is a choice of projects, the firm can use the simulated rates of return to calculate both the expected return and the degree of risk involved. Using the certainty-equivalent method or the risk-adjusted discount rate, the firm can compare these investments. Recall that the success of this approach depends on the quality of the probability distributions of a large number of variables.

As a similar but less-involved method, the firm can arbitrarily choose a best-guess value for each of the variables of importance. By recalculating the expected rate of return by varying each of these variables within a reasonable range, the firm can determine the sensitivity of the expected rates of return to changes in these variables. The firm can then concentrate on finding more precise estimates of those variables that have the greatest influence on the expected rate of return of the project.

| 17-4 | **Anticipated oil spills** |

APPLICATION Professors James Opaluch and Thomas Grigalunas of the University of Rhode Island showed how oil companies use simulation models to calculate the value of oil leases on the Outer Continental Shelf (OCS) of Georges Bank. They showed that firms use simulation studies to determine expected rates of return based on probability distributions for production, exploration, development, and operating costs.

They were specifically concerned about whether bidders took into account changes in the law that made them strictly liable for any environmental damages from oil spills. They analyzed bids for sixty-four tracts in December of 1979. They were all new tracts with no neighboring tracts under development at the time of the bidding. There was extensive litigation by environmental groups opposed to the leases, many of which would be near sizable fishing areas and heavily populated coastal areas.

Thirty-one companies made bids ranging from $200 thousand to $80.3 million. The total amount of accepted bids was $813 million. Although bidders accounted for the uncertainty about the value of the tracts, they were primarily concerned about the threat of legal action due to oil spills. The researchers estimated that bids on the most environmentally sensitive areas were between $1.67 million and $4.33 million less than bids on similar tracts in nonenvironmentally sensitive areas. The total of the winning bids was $236.7 million less than it would have been if there had been no liability for environmental damage. This was in excess of 25 percent of the actual total bids.

While the government estimated that the potential environmental damages would have been $101 million, the lower bids reflected other potential risks. Adverse publicity due to an oil spill could have affected the sales of their products. This adverse effect on demand would have been in addition to their legal liability for damages. The government could also have underestimated the environmental costs. The evidence showed that bidders do use simulations to evaluate the prospects of oil leases and assign a substantial risk adjustment to compensate for possible legal costs when there is a risk of oil spills.

Source: James J. Opaluch and Thomas A. Grigalunas, "Controlling Stochastic Pollution Events through Liability Rules: Some Evidence from OCS Leasing." *Rand Journal of Economics* 15, No. 1 (Spring 1984):142–51.

Summary

Decision makers must contend with uncertainty when making their decisions. In Chapters 9–12 we analyzed several options for the firm trying to cope with uncertainty about the reactions of other firms and consumers. In most of those situations the firm did not have a clear understanding about the probabilities associated with the possible outcomes of their decisions.

If decision makers know the probability of future outcomes, they can use this information to improve the decision-making process. In this chapter we considered some techniques for solving investment problems when prior experience or detailed market studies reveal probabilities about possible outcomes.

When decision makers know the risks attached to their decisions, they can use this information to choose the project that satisfies their criterion for expected profits and risk. We showed how we could modify the present-value formula to account for risk. We considered adjusting both the numerator with the certainty-equivalent method and the denominator by using a risk-adjusted discount rate. Both methods allow the decision maker to make comparisons among several possible investment decisions.

We finished the chapter by extending the complexity of the decision-making process to multiple sequential levels. We found that decision trees can provide a useful means of summarizing the prospects for an investment decision. In addition, advances in computer sophistication make computer-based simulations an increasingly attractive option for more complicated decisions. As an example, we discussed the use of these methods by oil companies in determining the size of their bids for leases of drilling rights on the Outer Continental Shelf.

In the next chapter we will approach investment decisions from a slightly different angle. We will emphasize the importance of time in making investment decisions. When deciding about the future, it is more difficult to disentangle time and risk. We will emphasize the time dimension while referring to the issues already raised in this chapter.

Selected References

Brookshire, David S.; Thayer, Mark A.; Tschirhart, John; and Schulze, William D. "A Test of the Expected Utility Model: Evidence from Earthquake Risks." *Journal of Political Economy* 93, No. 2 (April 1985):369–89.

Kihlstrom, Richard E., and Mirman, Leonard J. "Constant, Increasing and Decreasing Risk Aversion with Many Commodities." *Review of Economic Studies* 48 (April 1978):271–80.

Low, Stuart A., and McPheters, Lee R. "Wage Differentials and Risk of Death: An Empirical Analysis." *Economic Inquiry* XXI, No. 2 (April 1983):271–80.

MacCrimmon, Kenneth R., and Wehrung, Donald A. "The Risk In-Basket." *Journal of Business* 57, No. 3 (July 1984):367–88.

Opaluch, James J., and Grigalunas, Thomas A. "Controlling Stochastic Pollution Events through Liability Rules: Some Evidence from OCS Leasing." *Rand Journal of Economics* 15, No. 1 (Spring 1984):142–51.

Selby, Edward B., Jr., and Beranek, William. "Sweepstakes Contests: Analysis, Strategies and Survey." *American Economic Review* 71, No. 1 (March 1981):189–95.

Problems

1. Assume that Percy Tuppence, owner of Percy Thunder Wheels, is considering a new advertising campaign for his oversized truck tires. He is considering two principal options: radio and newspapers. His marketing consultant has given him the probabilities and present value of incremental revenues that Percy should expect from both campaigns. Each campaign would cost Percy $20,000. Since he does not want to use both mediums, he must make a choice between the two. The payoff matrix is as follows:

Radio		Newspapers	
Probability	Present Value	Probability	Present Value
0.1	$35,000	0.2	$50,000
0.2	$30,000	0.5	$30,000
0.5	$20,000	0.3	$10,000
0.2	$15,000		

(a) Calculate the expected present value of revenues from each campaign.

(b) Make a discrete probability distribution for each campaign. Which appears to be the riskier of the two?

(c) Calculate the standard deviation and the coefficient of variation for each campaign.

2. Murray Rivers, manager of the Adelaide Vintners, grows grapes and makes wines. His annual income depends on the quality of his grapes. The quality of wine grapes, in turn, depends on the weather. If the weather during the fall stays warm longer than usual he will earn a profit of $50,000. If the weather is normal, he will earn a profit of $10,000. His profit will be $-$20,000 if the weather is colder than normal. Assume that he knows that the probabilities of these three events occurring are 0.1 for warmer weather, 0.8 for normal weather, and 0.1 for colder weather.

(a) Calculate the expected value of Murray's profits.

(b) Construct a discrete probability distribution.

(c) Calculate the standard deviation.

(d) Calculate the coefficient of variation.

3. Melody Gavotte, owner of Turbo-Drive Electronic Organs, has made a series of investments in the past to expand her business. From this experience we know that she has implicitly used a certainty equivalent adjustment factor equal to 1.0 minus the coefficient of variation. Assume that her current project has a 0.5 probability of increasing net revenues by $40,000 and a 0.5 probability of increasing net revenues by $30,000 per year for each of four years. Assume that the risk-free interest rate is 10 percent.

(a) Calculate the expected present value of the revenues, the standard deviation, and the coefficient of variation.

(b) What is the maximum price she would pay for this project?

4. Meck's Garage is planning to expand its automobile repair business. It has enough space for one of two new projects. It could either do body work and painting of damaged cars, or it could convert foreign cars to United States specifications after the cars arrive in the United States.

Meck's thinks that the body work and painting operation has a 60 percent chance of earning $11,000 by the end of the first year. If the project fails the first year, Meck's will earn no economic profits that year. The conversion venture has a 0.5 probability of success with economic profits of $8,000 and a 0.5 probability of $2,000 in the first year.

There is the possibility of a market reaction during the second year. The following table indicates the probability of each type of possible reaction. The table also indicates the present value of profits for the second and all succeeding years. The present values are evaluated as of the end of the second year.

(a) Construct a decision tree for Meck's Garage.

(b) Use a discount rate of 10 percent and calculate the net present value for both projects.

(c) Which project should Meck's choose?

		Probability of Reaction	Present Value
Body Work and Painting	*Success*	0.5 (reaction)	$12,100
		0.5 (no reaction)	$121,000
	Failure	0.2 (reaction)	− $50,000
		0.8 (no reaction)	$1,000
Conversion	*Success*	0.8 (reaction)	$20,000
		0.2 (no reaction)	$99,000
	Failure	0.4 (reaction)	0
		0.6 (no reaction)	$22,000

5. Violette Browning has a new product that she wants to promote in a major metropolitan market area. She decides to choose among New York, Boston, and Philadelphia. She has completed an initial study on the potential success of an advertising campaign for her Tan House Umbrella. The umbrella lets tanning rays pass through it but blocks harmful rays and the glare of the sun. She will only choose one of the three cities for the promotional effort. The following table lists the probabilities for success and the corresponding incremental revenues from each campaign. Assume that all three campaigns would cost the same amount.

	New York		Philadelphia		Boston	
	Probability	Revenues (thousands of dollars)	Probability	Revenues (thousands of dollars)	Probability	Revenues (thousands of dollars)
Major Success	0.2	$300	0.3	$300	0.2	$400
Moderate Success	0.5	$200	0.3	$250	0.4	$250
Failure	0.3	$100	0.4	$60	0.4	$80

(a) Calculate the expected value, standard deviation, and coefficient of variation for each city.

(b) What advice could you offer Violette?

Answer questions 6–11 with true, false, or uncertain.

6. If the expected value of profits and the coefficient of variation is the same for two projects, the standard deviations of the two projects will be equal.

7. Individuals will have lower certainty equivalents for projects if they are more risk-averse.

8. The present value of an investment is higher for those people with higher certainty-equivalent adjustment factors.

9. The willingness of many people to participate in sweepstakes contests indicates that most people are risk-takers.

10. Given a choice between two investments yielding the same expected value, a risk-neutral individual will choose the investment with the lowest coefficient of variation.

11. The standard deviation is a more accurate measure of risk than the variance or the coefficient of variation.

18

DECISIONS OVER TIME:
CAPITAL BUDGETING

Up to this point in the text we have concentrated on the firm's short-run pricing and output decisions. Whenever we considered the firm's long-run choices of inputs and outputs, we ignored the time dimension of these decisions. Since firms must make investments that have payoffs and costs that occur at different times in the future, the timing of costs and revenues is vital. In order to maximize its profits the firm needs methods for evaluating competing investment projects.

In Chapter 17 our emphasis was on adjusting for the risk of making investment and other managerial decisions. In this chapter we will emphasize the time dimension of investments. We will consider the firm's decision to add to its stock of capital. Although we have used the term "capital" throughout the text, we will use it here in its broadest sense. **Capital** is the stock of assets that will generate a flow of revenues in the future.

Examples of capital outlays include purchases of land, buildings, and equipment, additions to inventories, and the cost of research and development. We would also include advertising and promotional expenses. Our focus is on all assets that have durability beyond one year. A one-year cutoff point is convenient, because data are often aggregated at one-year intervals. We could choose any other time period for assessing the profitability of investments.

The flow of revenues generated by capital contributes to the wealth of the firm. We must decide whether the additional revenue is worth the additional cost. If it is not worth the cost, the investment will lower the firm's wealth. We will look at techniques that the firm can use in evaluating possible investments. We call this process capital budgeting. **Capital budgeting** is the planning process for allocating all expenditures that will have an expected benefit to the firm for more than one year.

We will start with the estimation of future revenues and costs of a specific project. This is one of the more difficult parts of the process because of the need for accurate estimates of the future. Chapter 16 provided a summary of statistical techniques that may help make these estimates more accurate.

Next, we will focus on the use of net present value as a method for choosing among various investment projects. This technique allows the firm to compare competing projects more easily. We will show that the net-present-value procedure is consistent with marginal analysis. By using the net-present-value method, the firm will invest in projects until the marginal benefit equals the marginal cost of investing.

We will conclude with a discussion of the main sources of capital for funding the firm's investments. Our emphasis will be on the proper economic definition of the cost of each of these sources and the methods for determining the marginal cost of investment.

Evaluation of Projects

Each part of the firm has an effect on the success of the project-evaluation process. While control of capital-budgeting decisions normally rests with financial managers, members of all major departments become involved to some extent. The marketing department provides sales forecasts. Accountants and engineers provide cost estimates. The finance department must obtain funds at the lowest possible cost.

After evaluating the input of each department, higher-level management must choose among the possible projects. Capital budgeting utilizes a basic economic principle in helping with this decision: operate where the marginal benefit equals the marginal cost. In this case the marginal benefit of an investment is the incremental revenue it adds to the firm. We call the incremental revenue the return on the investment.

The process starts with proposals. Since proposals do not appear at zero cost, the firm must design incentives within the firm to encourage members of the firm to offer suggestions. Once the firm receives ideas for projects, it can simplify the process by classifying projects by type. Since detailed analysis is expensive, the firm may seek a preliminary screening of projects at lower levels of management. Firms normally place projects in the following categories:

1. Replacement and maintenance of old or damaged equipment.
2. Investments to upgrade or replace existing equipment.
3. Marketing investments to expand product lines or distribution facilities.
4. Investments for complying with government or insurance-company safety or environmental requirements.

Many projects, such as replacement of worn-out equipment, are at a low enough cost so that a detailed and expensive analysis is not required. Once the dollar amount increases, the opportunity cost of a failed project increases. Not surprisingly, the higher the opportunity cost of the decision, the more detailed and extensive the analysis required.

The firm must then estimate the expected revenues and costs of the project. Since the future is uncertain, the firm has to rely on its best forecast of these revenues and costs. As noted in Chapter 16 the firm must face the trade-off of greater forecast accuracy versus the greater cost of the forecast.

The Cash Flow of Investments

Determining the future cash flow is an important part of the capital-budgeting process. The **cash flow** is the net incremental change in revenues and cost at each time period.

There are two important points to remember in determining the cash flow. First, the cash flow is an incremental change in the net revenues associated with the investment. The incremental effects could lead to an increase in the revenues of the firm or reduce the firm's costs. Both would have a positive effect on the firm's wealth. An investment in labor-saving machinery might even lead to a decrease in the overall costs of the firm while not affecting revenues. In Chapter 4 we used breakeven analysis to show that by leasing a new meal-analysis machine, Blanche Mayzone could lower her food preparation and dishwashing costs without affecting her revenues.

Second, depreciation is not part of the cash flow. The firm does not pay for depreciation. Depreciation is an accounting concept used in determining taxes. Since the cash flow is an after-tax net revenue, depreciation is only a factor in the calculation of the tax effects of the investment.

We return to Harry Sampson of Verte Tree Company for an example of a cash flow from an investment. Harry is planning to purchase a new tree-trimming machine. He understands that the machine will last only four years given normal usage. Despite the short life of this new machine, he expects that it will be worth purchasing.

Table 18-1 shows the cash flow for this investment. There are incremental revenues in each of the four years. He will incur incremental costs in addition to the initial cost of the machine. These costs will cover the expense of additional workers and materials. The difference between the incremental

TABLE 18-1 ▪ Cash flow for Harry's new tree-trimming machine

	Year			
	1990	1991	1992	1993
Incremental Revenues (Net of Taxes)	11,000	12,100	13,310	14,641
Incremental Costs Due to Additional Workers and Materials	2,200	2,420	2,662	2,928.2
Cash Flow	8,800	9,680	10,648	11,712.8

revenues (net of taxes) and incremental costs will be the cash flow for each of the four years.

Harry must have a means of comparing the incremental costs and revenues to his initial cost for the new machine. Cash flow next year is not as valuable as cash flow today. The important feature of investment analysis is the need to evaluate cash flow at different periods of time according to a common time period. The general method for this evaluation is present value. We reviewed the present-value technique in Chapter 17. We used the procedure to discount the value of future revenues and costs to the present. By placing all costs and revenues at the same point in time, we had a method for comparing alternative options of the firm. In the next section we will apply a slight variation of the present-value technique to the capital-budgeting process.

Net-Present-Value Technique

Although we have discussed the present-value technique before, we will be applying it here to a slightly different problem. In this case we will have a project with an initial cost and an expected flow of costs and revenues over time. We must decide whether to choose the project or not. The process will involve the following mathematical version of the present-value formula:

$$NPV_i = \sum_{t=1}^{T} \frac{R_{it}}{(1 + r_i)^t} - C_i, \qquad (18\text{-}1)$$

where i represents the ith project and t denotes the time periods in which the project generates net revenues R_{it} (that is, revenues minus costs in each time period). T is the total number of time periods, r_i is the discount rate, and C_i is the initial cost of the investment project. This is the net-present-value formula. **Net present value** is the difference between the present value of a future cash flow and the initial cost of the investment project.

Estimation Procedure

To evaluate the project using the net-present-value formula we use the following procedure:

1. Determine the net cash flow of the project (R_{it}).
2. Estimate the expected cost of the project. As long as the project involves the direct purchase of equipment, the cost estimate will be accurate. For construction projects with future costs, cost overruns could make estimates difficult.
3. Choose an appropriate discount rate. The discount rate will depend on the riskiness of the project. While we will discuss this later, we also considered it in Chapter 17.

4. Calculate the *NPV* formula with each of the components added. If the project generates a positive expected *NPV*, the firm should adopt the project.

NUMERICAL EXAMPLE

Table 18-1 showed the following cash flow over four years for Harry's new tree-trimming machine:

Year	Cash Flow
1990	8,800.0
1991	9,680.0
1992	10,648.0
1993	11,712.8

Assume that the discount rate is 10 percent. We will also assume that the machine costs $34,000 and will have a scrap and parts (resale) value at the end of four years of $4,392.30. The net-present-value formula is

$$NPV_i = \sum_{t=1}^{T} \frac{R_{it}}{(1 + r_i)^t} - C_i.$$

The first part of the formula calculates the present value of the annual cash flow as follows:

$$\sum_{t=1}^{T} \frac{R_{it}}{(1 + r_i)^t} = \frac{8,800}{(1.1)^1} + \frac{9,680}{(1.1)^2} + \frac{10,648}{(1.1)^3} + \frac{11,712.8}{(1.1)^4}$$

$$= \frac{8,800}{1.1000} + \frac{9,680}{1.2100} + \frac{10,648}{1.3310} + \frac{11,712.8}{1.4641}$$

$$= 8,000 + 8,000 + 8,000 + 8,000$$

$$= \$32,000.$$

We must also discount the resale value of the machine. Since Harry will sell it four years after he purchases it, he will discount its value as follows:

$$\text{Present Value of Resale of Machine} = \frac{4,392.30}{(1.1)^4}$$

$$= \frac{4,392.30}{1.4641}$$

$$= \$3,000.$$

Since the machine costs Harry $34,000 in 1989, the net present value will equal the present value of the cash flow ($32,000) plus the present value of the resale value ($3,000) minus the initial cost of the investment ($34,000):

$$NPV = \$32,000 + \$3,000 - \$34,000$$
$$= \$1,000.$$

Since the *NPV* is positive, Harry should purchase the new machine.

Throughout the text we have emphasized the importance of making decisions using marginal analysis. Firms should estimate the effect that a decision has on both its marginal costs and its marginal revenues. We will now approach the problem of investment evaluation using marginal analysis. After this discussion we will show that the net-present-value method is consistent with marginal analysis.

The Internal Rate of Return

We could evaluate investment projects based on their percentage rate of return. The more profitable investments will generate higher rates of return. For example, when individuals save their money, they search for the highest savings rate consistent with their willingness to take risks. Firms will also search for the highest return on their investments. We call the rate of return on a firm's investment the internal rate of return. The **internal rate of return** (*IRR*) is the rate of return (that is, the interest rate) that will equate the present value of a multi-year cash flow with the cost of investing in a project. The internal rate of return shows the marginal gain in net revenues from an investment. We will soon see that firms can compare investment projects using either the internal rate of return or the net present value. Both methods yield equivalent results.

While the internal rate of return measures the returns on an investment, the marginal cost of capital is the cost of the investment. The **marginal cost of capital** (*MCC*) is the cost to the firm of each additional dollar that it obtains to make capital investments. The profit-maximizing firm will invest in projects until the incremental gain equals the incremental cost of the last project chosen. The following graphical explanation shows that this occurs where the internal rate of return equals the marginal cost of capital.

18-1	The capital-budgeting decision

GRAPHICAL
EXPLANATION

In Figure 18-1 (p. 528) the horizontal axis measures the amount of investment per year in dollars. The vertical axis measures the rate of return on each investment. Assume that Harry considers a total of five investment projects. He

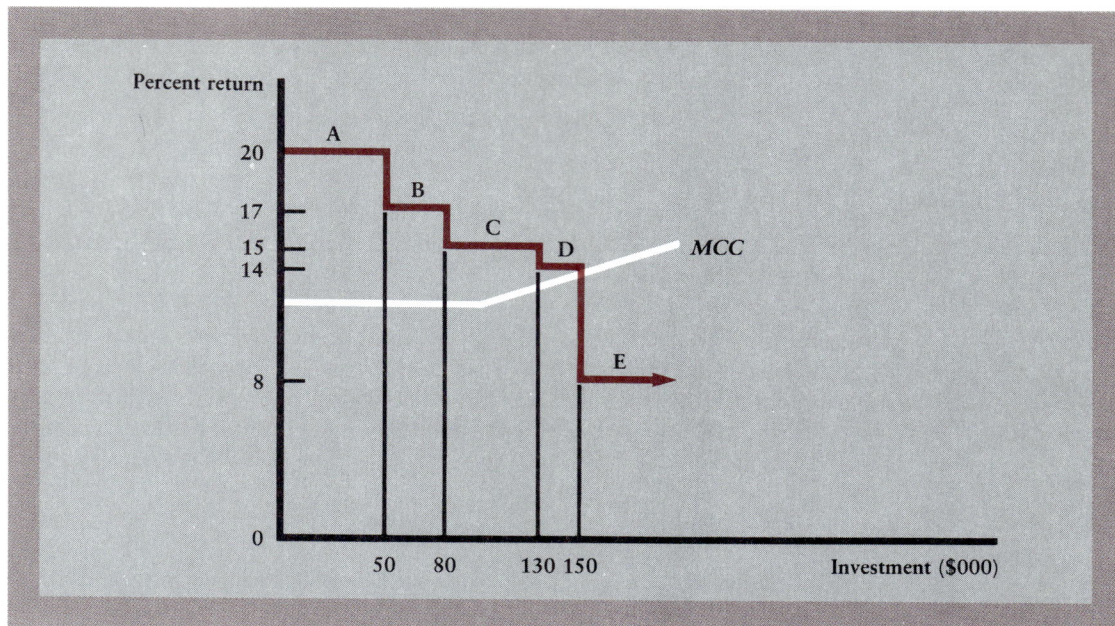

FIGURE 18-1 ▪ **Discrete investment prospects.** Harry has five possible investment opportunities. Projects *A* through *D* all yield a rate of return that exceeds the marginal cost of capital (*MCC*). Harry does not invest in Project *E* because the 8 percent return is below his marginal cost of capital.

does not have the option of a partial investment in any of the projects. He must either invest in the complete project or not at all.

The graph shows the five investments in descending order of rate of return. For example, Project *A* would cost $50,000 and offer a rate of return of 20 percent. The next highest-valued project is Project *B*. Project *B* would cost $30,000 and offer a 17 percent rate of return. The fifth, Project *E*, is an investment in a diversified government-bond mutual fund offering an 8 percent return.

The curve *MCC* shows the marginal cost of capital. Figure 18-1 shows that the marginal cost of capital is stable at 12 percent until there is a total investment of $100,000. For amounts greater than $100,000 per year, Harry must pay a higher cost of capital to attract funds. The higher marginal cost of capital will be due to the greater risk that Harry incurs by taking on additional new projects.

Harry must order the projects in descending order of their rate of return. Project *A*'s rate of return at 20 percent exceeds the cost of capital of 12 percent. Even Project *D*'s internal rate of return of 14 percent exceeds the marginal cost of capital. However, if Harry adopts Project *E*, he will make an investment with a marginal cost of capital that exceeds the internal rate of return of that investment. Harry should accept Projects *A* through *D*.

Figure 18-2 replaces the stepwise depiction of the rate of return in Figure 18-1 with a more general *IRR* curve. This *IRR* curve assumes that all investments are continuously divisible (that is, the firm can invest in parts of each project). Since we have again ordered the investments in declining order of the internal rate of return, we will be able to evaluate each investment on the margin. Figure 18-2 illustrates the general rule. The firm should invest to the point where the marginal cost of investing (*MCC*) equals the marginal gain from investing (*IRR*).

Net Present Value and Marginal Analysis

We started this chapter by noting that the firm should invest in new assets until the marginal revenues equal the marginal cost of the investment. Figure 18-2 showed that the firm satisfies this condition when it invests up to the point where the internal rate of return equals the marginal cost of investment. We will now see why the net-present-value rule also satisfies this condition.

FIGURE 18-2 ▪ **Continuous investment opportunities.** This firm has continuous investment opportunities. The firm will invest *I** at the point where the internal rate of return (*IRR*) equals the marginal cost of capital (*MCC*). The last investment project will yield a return of 10 percent.

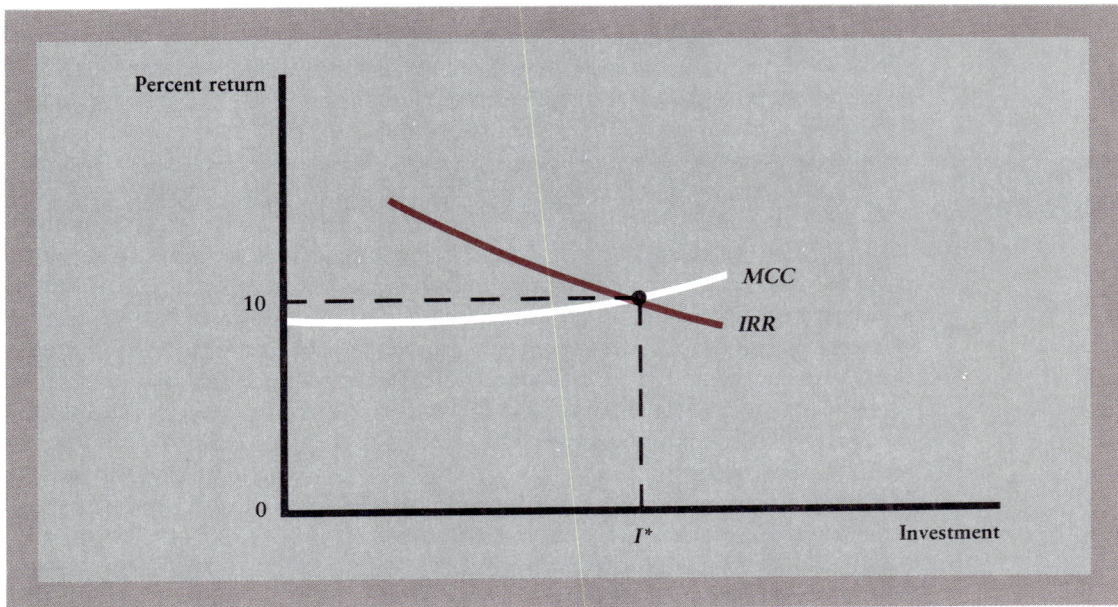

Recall that the internal rate of return is the discount rate that equates the future stream of revenues with the initial cost of the investment. We can solve Equation (18-1) for r_i^*, the internal rate of return, by setting NPV_i equal to 0.

$$NPV_i = \sum_{t=1}^{T} \frac{R_{it}}{(1 + r_i^*)^t} - C_i = 0. \qquad (18\text{-}2)$$

We can solve for r_i^* directly by rearranging the equation and isolating r_i^* on the left-hand side. This is usually difficult, because r_i^* appears as a polynomial raised to different powers of t. Although it is somewhat tedious if done by hand, you can use a trial-and-error approach. Start with a value of r_i^* that you expect to be close to the true value. If NPV_i does not equal 0 for this value of r_i^*, adjust r_i^* until you find the true value. Computers can make the trial-and-error process a fast and simple exercise.

In Equation (18-1) we used r_i, the marginal cost of capital, to evaluate the merits of a project. If the NPV_i were positive, we would adopt the project. This is equivalent to solving for r_i^*, the internal rate of return, in Equation (18-2) and comparing the internal rate of return of the project to the marginal cost of the investment. The firm should choose projects with a positive NPV_i (that is, projects with internal rates of return greater than the marginal cost of the investment).

Harry can evaluate all other possible projects in the same way that he evaluated the prospects for the tree-trimming machine. For example, he may be able to purchase equipment for cutting down and hauling away diseased trees or to buy land and equipment to open a tree nursery. He can determine either the internal rate of return or the net present value of these projects. As long as no two of the projects are mutually exclusive, he can invest in all the projects that give him a positive net present value—that is, an internal rate of return that exceeds his marginal cost of capital.

18-1   The value of a bicycle

APPLICATION   One day in December 1986, Professor Burton Abrams of the University of Delaware noticed a long queue in front of a bank in Tianjin, China. Although it appeared at first to be a run on the bank, the customers were actually waiting to purchase bonds offered by the Flying Pigeon Factory, a producer of over three million bicycles annually. The company was offering bonds with an annual return below that offered by bank savings accounts. The bonds had a two-year maturity, with payment of 28 yuan at maturity for a bond with a face value of 200 yuan ($60). The bonds yielded a compounded 6.8 percent return per year. One-year time deposits at the People's Bank of China yielded an effective rate of 7.44 percent.

In addition to the interest payment, each bond holder received the right to purchase a Flying Pigeon bicycle at the officially determined price. Most

Chinese citizens do not have the right to buy the bicycle at the official price, because the government rations bicycles. Those unable to obtain permission through official channels must turn to the black market to buy a coupon. A coupon authorizing the purchase of a Flying Pigeon bicycle costs between 40 and 60 yuan in the black market.

We can now reevaluate the merits of purchasing the company's bond. Assume that the coupon price remained at 60 yuan. Since the bond purchaser could immediately sell or use the coupon to purchase the bicycle, the effective purchase price of the bond was 140 yuan (that is, 200 − 60). Since the bond would pay 228 yuan in two years, the internal rate of return was 28 percent. At a value of 40 yuan per coupon, the internal rate of return was 20 percent.

Flying Pigeon's inability to raise the market price of its bicycles because of government price controls prevented it from selling enough bicycles to equal the market demand. The coupon arrangement allowed it to raise its price indirectly by offering a face-value interest rate below the market rate. The long lines of enthusiastic customers indicated that the coupon was worth more than the difference between Flying Pigeon's interest rate and the market bank rate. When Flying Pigeon raises money again, it may be able to borrow at an even lower rate.

Source: Burton A. Abrams, "A Tale about Peddling Bonds in China." *Asian Wall Street Journal Weekly* (16 June 1986):15.

Payback-Period Criterion

Despite the theoretical support for using net present value and internal rates of return, there is a popularly used capital-budgeting procedure that has received little academic support: the payback-period criterion. The **payback period** is the amount of time sufficient to cover the initial cost of an investment. The payback-period criterion ignores the time cost of money. The decision maker simply sets an arbitrary time period by which the investment must generate a nondiscounted flow of net revenue that equals the initial investment.

For example, assume that Harry spent $50,000 for land and equipment to open the nursery for trees and shrubbery. At the end of the first year, the nursery would have a net positive revenue (net of all costs other than the original investment) equal to $4,000. In the second year he would earn $6,000. By the third year the trees and shrubbery would be large enough to sell in greater quantity and he would earn $25,000. During the fourth year he could expect to have a cash flow of $40,000.

The cumulative cash flow by the end of the third year would be $35,000 ($4,000 + $6,000 + $25,000). By the end of the fourth year it would be $75,000 ($35,000 + $40,000). According to the payback-period criterion, Harry would have paid back the entire cost of the land and equipment at some point during the fourth year. If his criterion was that all investments should have a payback period of four years or less, he would make the investment.

This procedure ignores the time path and the magnitude of the cash flow. Although the payback criterion is a simple rule of thumb, the alternatives are not much more difficult. Despite the technique's disregard for the time value of money, there have been attempts to justify this commonly used practice.

Some analysts have shown that this criterion can approximate the internal rate of return when the internal rate of return is large and the useful life of the asset is short. On the other hand, there appears to be little need for this simplified procedure as a rule of thumb, since most firms that calculate it also calculate the internal rate of return.

Professor M.P. Narayanan of the University of Florida has argued that the payback criterion may be popular with decision makers in firms with a separation of control between owners and management.[1] In Chapter 10 we considered the problem that shareholders may have when they do not exercise complete control over the managers of the firm. Managers may take advantage of the situation to pursue their own interests at the expense of shareholders.

Professor Narayanan has argued that a manager may influence the shareholders' evaluations of the manager's performance by creating large initial returns on investments by approving only those investments that have high paybacks in the first few years of the payback period. If shareholders have difficulty evaluating the manager's performance, the manager can deceive the shareholders by choosing a shorter time horizon. This argument hinges on the assumption that the manager has more knowledge about the operations of the firm than the shareholders do and can continue to maintain this deception.

Other Investment Options

Investments imply a long-term commitment. If efficient resale markets are available, the firm can sell any fixed assets that are not needed if market conditions change unexpectedly. When there are sunk costs or imperfections in the market for used equipment, the firm may incur costs due to under-utilization of the assets.

In this section we consider two options available to the firm. First, the firm can choose to lease its durable assets rather than buy them. Secondly, it can purchase assets with shorter useful lives in order to gain flexibility in case of unexpected fluctuations in market demand. In both cases the firm may choose to limit its commitment to an asset in order to gain flexibility. This becomes a more important consideration as the uncertainty about the future increases.

[1] M.P. Narayanan, "Observability and the Payback Criterion." *Journal of Business* 58, No. 3 (July 1985):309–23.

Purchase or Lease

Firms do not have to buy all of the assets they use. In Chapter 4 Blanche considered leasing a machine rather than buying it. You can rent or own homes and lease or buy cars. Leasing gives a firm more flexibility but may be more costly.

In Chapter 10 we discussed contractual problems that may make leasing arrangements impractical and force a firm to own the assets it uses. That discussion focused on the opportunities for parties to a contract to renege on the provisions of the contract when changes in market conditions make it profitable to do so. We will not repeat the details of that discussion here. Instead, consider the following example of financial considerations important to the purchase-or-lease decision.

18-2

Purchase or lease

NUMERICAL EXAMPLE

Assume that Harry can either purchase or lease a new tree-trimming machine with a useful life of four years. In addition, Harry has a friend who is developing a new type of machine that will be available in two years and that promises to lower tree-trimming costs substantially compared to the available alternative.

Since Harry cannot wait for two years to find a new machine, he needs another machine until his friend's machine becomes available. One of his options would be to buy a machine that would incorporate the present technology and then sell it after two years. He might find that the appearance of his friend's new machine on the market would depress the resale price of the other machine even though there would still be two years of useful life remaining. Alternatively, he could lease a machine on an annual basis.

Harry can use the net-present-value formula to solve this problem. Assume that Harry can lease the currently available machine for $11,000 the first year and $12,100 the second year. The firm supplying the machine also includes as a part of the lease price all of the associated materials and maintenance that Harry would require to operate it. The discount rate is still 10 percent. The present value of the cost of leasing for two years is

$$PV = \frac{11,000}{(1.1)^1} + \frac{12,100}{(1.1)^2}$$
$$= 10,000 + 10,000$$
$$= 20,000.$$

If Harry buys the machine, his cash flow for the first two years will be the same as calculated earlier (see Table 18-1): $8,800 for the first year and $9,680 for the second year. Assume that if he sells the machine after two years, he will receive $22,285. The machine will cost him $34,000. The net present value of this investment will be

$$NPV = \frac{[\text{Cash Flow (Year 1)}]}{(1.1)^1} + \frac{[\text{Cash Flow (Year 2)}]}{(1.1)^2}$$

$$+ \frac{[\text{Resale Value after Year 2}]}{(1.1)^2} - \text{Purchase Price}$$

$$= \frac{8,800}{1.1} + \frac{9,680}{1.21} + \frac{22,285}{1.21} - 34,000$$

$$= 8,000 + 8,000 + 18,500 - 34,000$$

$$= \$500.$$

The present value of owning the machine and selling it after two years is $500. If, instead, Harry leases the machine for two years, the present value of the cost of leasing the machine for two years will be $20,000. To decide between leasing and owning, Harry must know the present value of the net revenue from using the leased machine. If the present value of the net revenue he would earn by leasing the machine exceeds $20,500 ($20,000 + $500), Harry is better off leasing rather than owning.

This problem is actually more complicated than this comparison implies. Harry should take a longer view than two years and consider other options. For example, he could lease machines each year; he could buy a new machine for four years and then lease or buy another machine after four years; or he could buy or lease a machine for four years and then buy his friend's machine. He should consider these and all other options and then choose the best one.

Regardless of Harry's decision in this case, there may be times when leasing is more profitable than buying. Leasing offers more flexibility and limits the time that the firm is obligated to a specific piece of equipment. When making this decision the firm should use the net-present-value technique to compare the various options.

Durability Versus Flexibility

Investment in capital goods represents a long-term commitment to an input of a specific capacity. The utilization of this capacity throughout the useful life of the input is a major determinant of the profitability of the investment. Although inputs are available in a wide range of capacities, once the decision maker chooses a capacity of a certain size, the decision maker is committed to that capacity.

Capacity utilization depends on the demand for the good produced by the input. If demand varies unpredictably, the firm may experience periods of excess capacity. The greater the unpredictability of demand, the less likely the firm is willing to commit to a durable input. Although we have already considered leasing as an option for the firm faced with uncertainty or other constraints on its buying decisions, the firm has an additional option. It can choose between assets of different useful lives.

| 18-2 | **Stay flexible** |

APPLICATION

Dr. Joel Gibbons of the American National Bank of Chicago has argued that increased uncertainty about the demand for a firm's products forces the firm to make investments in less durable capital. In order to maintain flexibility, the firm avoids locking itself into a long-term commitment to an asset that may not be useful to the firm after a period of time.

Again, this is not a problem if there are resale markets for these inputs that involve little or no costs of making transactions. In the absence of perfect resale markets, firms absorb the costs of having excess capacity. Dr. Gibbons tested this hypothesis with U.S. Census data for the major U.S. manufacturing industries between 1958 and 1972. He found that the durability or longevity of capital depends on the variability of market demand.

Source: Joel C. Gibbons, "The Optimal Durability of Fixed Capital when Demand is Uncertain." *The Journal of Business* 57, No. 3 (July 1984):389–403. © by the University of Chicago.

Cost of Capital

The cost of capital is an important consideration in evaluating new projects. We now offer some economic principles and potential problems associated with determining the cost of capital. Firms raise capital from a variety of sources: long-term and short-term debt, sale of preferred stock, sale of common stock, and retained earnings. The cost of each of these sources of capital is different.

To calculate the overall cost of capital we must determine the cost of each of these components, weight each cost by its share in the overall capital structure of the firm, and then sum the weighted costs. We will limit ourselves to the two main sources of capital: debt and equity capital. By concentrating on these two basic sources we will avoid veering off too sharply into legal, financial, and accounting details.

The Cost of Debt

The cost of debt is the interest rate paid to investors net of taxes. Since firms may deduct their interest payments to offset their tax liability, the after-tax interest rate is the true cost of debt to the firm. Since we are concerned with new investments, we must consider only the incremental cost of the new debt, not the average debt faced by the firm on its previous investments.

NUMERICAL EXAMPLE

Assume that a firm borrows $1,000,000 and has annual interest payments of $100,000. These interest payments amount to a 10 percent interest rate before taxes. If the firm is in the 28 percent marginal tax bracket, it will be able to deduct 28 percent of the $100,000 from its tax bill each year. Due to this $28,000 tax reduction, the government effectively pays 28 percent of the firm's interest payments. The effective interest rate must account for this tax benefit.

$$\text{After-Tax Cost of Debt} = \text{Interest Rate} \times (1.0 - \text{Tax Rate})$$
$$= 10\% \times (1.00 - 0.28)$$
$$= 10\% \times 0.72$$
$$= 7.2\%$$

The Cost of Equity

The cost of equity (that is, issuing common stock) is the rate of return that a firm must offer a stockholder to invest in the firm. Since the firm cannot deduct dividends from its revenues in determining taxes, there is no tax adjustment for the cost of equity. Dividends are not the only source of gain for shareholders; they also expect an appreciation in the value of their shares. Since appreciation in share value is not certain, there is risk involved in being a shareholder.

The cost of capital has a risk-free and a risky component. In general, we can characterize this relationship as follows:

$$r = R_f + P, \tag{18-3}$$

where R_f is the risk-free return and P is the risk premium to the cost of equity. The **risk-free return** is the cost of transferring money (that is, the interest rate) from one time period to another without losing the transferred money. The **risk premium** is the rate of return, in addition to the risk-free rate of return, that an investor requires as compensation for assuming the risk associated with the firm.

The risk-free interest rate is an important assumption used in financial economics. With a risk-free interest rate, individuals can transfer money to different time periods without incurring the risk of losing their money. The risk-free interest rate is available for both borrowing and lending.

Most observers think the U.S. Treasury bill rate is the best proxy for the risk-free lending rate and the stockbroker's loan-call rate is the best proxy for the risk-free borrowing rate. The loan-call rate is the interest rate charged investors who borrow money on a short-term basis from brokerage firms. In all market economies the borrowing and lending rates do not coincide perfectly. The difference between the two rates is the market cost of facilitating the matching of borrowers and lenders. If the financial market functions efficiently, the difference between these two rates should be small.

18-3	No risk

APPLICATION

Professors Menachem Brenner and Dan Galai of Hebrew University have shown that stock-option trading offers another implicit, risk-free interest rate. There are two basic options available: puts and calls. A put gives you the option of selling a stock to someone at a predetermined price, called the strike price. You would exercise this option if the market price were to fall below the predetermined price. This option provides a floor below the current value of the stock. The buyer of the put is betting that the price of the stock will not fall below the floor price.

A call works in the opposite direction. The call allows you to buy a stock from someone at a predetermined price. If the market price exceeds the predetermined price, you can exercise the call option and buy the stock at the lower strike price. You would gain the difference between the market price and the predetermined price, minus what you paid to purchase the call option.

By combining puts and calls you can effectively borrow or lend money at no risk. For example, by buying a stock and a put and selling a call on the same stock, you lend the dollar value of the stock. By selling a call and buying a put, you establish a box around the price of the stock that insulates you from the effects of changes in the stock price. If the stock price falls below the strike price, you still earn the strike price. If the stock price exceeds the call strike price, you receive the strike price.

The researchers compared the U.S. Treasury bill rate and the stockbrokers' lending rate to the implicit rate that you can earn by lending money using this option. They determined that the changes in the implicit rate occurred at the same time as changes in both the U.S. Treasury and the stockbroker lending rates. The actual value of the implicit rate was closer to the brokers' borrowing rate than the lending rate. They concluded that the introduction of option trading has likely increased competition in the market for borrowing money and has forced the borrowing and lending rates closer together.

Source: Menachem Brenner and Dan Galai, "Implied Interest Rates." *Journal of Business* 59, No. 3 (July 1986):493–507. © by the University of Chicago.

Analysts use a variety of methods for calculating the risk premium. We will now consider two methods used by financial analysts in calculating the cost of equity. In practice you may want to use both methods to check for consistency.

Capital-Asset-Pricing Model (CAPM) CAPM is a more sophisticated method of calculating the risk premium. The CAPM method assumes that the risk of a stock depends on the sensitivity of its return to changes in the returns of all the other stocks in the market. The risk premium has two components: systematic and unsystematic risk. **Unsystematic risk** is risk that investors can reduce by diversifying their investment portfolios. **Systematic risk** is risk that remains despite efforts to remove it with diversification.

Well-diversified investors are concerned only about systematic risk, since they are unable to diversify in a way that eliminates this risk. They cannot remove the systematic risk, because it moves directly with the overall movement of the stock market. In a modern, efficient financial market, investors do not invest in a company's stock unless they expect to earn enough to cover both the risk-free rate of return and the risk premium. According to the CAPM, the risk premium is the systematic risk of the company.

The following is a summary of the CAPM procedure that one should follow in calculating the rate of return required for a decision to invest in a firm.

1. Determine the risk-free rate of return, R_f. As mentioned earlier, most analysts use the rate on U.S. Treasury bills as a proxy for the risk-free rate of return.

2. Calculate the systematic risk. While the estimation of the systematic risk is complex and involves regression analysis, a systematic risk index, called the stock's beta coefficient, b, is available to the public for companies listed on national exchanges. The b index has a value of 1.0 when the stock has average risk. Low-risk stocks have betas less than 1.0, and high-risk stocks have indexes above 1.0.

3. Determine the average return of all publicly owned common stock. This information is widely available.

4. Estimate the cost of equity using the following modification to Equation (18-3):

$$r = R_f + b(R_m - R_f). \tag{18-4}$$

R_m is the average market rate of return. The difference between the average market return and the risk-free rate of return, $(R_m - R_f)$, is the risk premium for the average stock. The risk premium for the firm is the average market risk premium multiplied by the beta for the firm. The rate of return necessary to attract investment in the firm is the sum of the risk-free rate of return, R_f, and the firm's risk premium.

Capital-asset-pricing model

NUMERICAL EXAMPLE

Assume that R_f is 10 percent, R_m is 15 percent, and b is 0.75 for a specific stock. The cost of equity will be

$$r = R_f + b(R_m - R_f)$$
$$= 10 + 0.75(15 - 10)$$
$$= 10 + 3.75$$
$$= 13.75\%.$$

With an average beta of 1.0, the cost of equity would be

$$r = 10 + 1.0(15 - 10)$$
$$= 10 + 5$$
$$= 15\%.$$

Low-risk steel

APPLICATION

Professors C.Y. Baldwin, J.J. Tribendis, and J.P. Clark have used the CAPM to determine the risk-adjusted rate of return on new investments in the U.S. steel industry. Since the industry is not homogeneous, they placed firms into three groups: integrated producers, scrap-based producers, and specialty firms.

They used data from the Center for Research in Security Prices at the University of Chicago on monthly security information for twenty-two steel firms from 1955 to 1980. They selected only those firms whose principal business was steel-making, omitting all diversified firms with less than 70 percent of their sales in steel products.

Using data on rate of return, share prices, and number of shares for each of the companies, they calculated the rate of return from a portfolio of companies for each of the three industry subgroups. They used the monthly rate of return for each portfolio, the monthly rate of return of all publicly traded U.S. firms, and the risk-free interest rate (such as the return on ninety-day U.S. Treasury bills) to determine the systematic risk, beta (b).

They determined that the integrated and specialty companies had similar systematic risk premiums that declined significantly between 1955 and 1980. While the systematic risk in the scrap-based sector has generally been lower relative to the other two sectors, this risk increased during the time period. After removing the effects of inflation and taxes, they found that the rate of return (net of inflation and taxes) fluctuated between 5.4 and 9.0 percent for integrated companies, between 6.2 and 10.6 percent for specialty steel, and between 5.0 and 8.5 percent for scrap-based products.

The researchers noted that their estimates were lower than those of earlier studies. They argued that earlier studies used accounting rather than financial data. Accounting data can create problems, especially in times of inflation, because accountants do not continually update the value of the company's assets to control for inflation.

Earlier studies also did not measure the risk of the steel industry relative to other industries. Most other observers assumed that the steel industry was riskier than the average of all industries. Somewhat surprisingly, the steel industry between 1955 and 1980 had less systematic risk than the average for all U.S. manufacturing industries.

Source: C.Y. Baldwin, J.J. Tribendis, and J.P. Clark, "The Evolution of Market Risk in the U.S. Steel Industry and Implications for Required Rates of Return." *Journal of Industrial Economics* XXXIII, No. 1 (September 1984):73–98.

An Alternative Method A second method focuses on the expected growth rate of the company's stock. The method considers the combination of dividends and the growth in the value of the shares as the two sources of compensation to shareholders. The formula in this case is

$$\text{Rate of Return} = \frac{\text{Dividends}}{\text{Price}} + \text{Expected Growth Rate}$$

$$r = \frac{D}{P} + g.$$

Estimating the growth rate g is easier if the firm has been growing at a steady rate over time. If the value of the firm is more variable, analysts must develop forecasts along the lines mentioned in Chapter 16. The more variable the past growth rate, the more likely analysts will have to rely on their own assessment of the stock's future based on estimates of future sales and profits and expected market pressures. While determining the average growth rate for any one firm may be difficult, there has been a consistent pattern of growth for the average stock since 1871 in the United States.

18-5	Just as good as in the good old days

APPLICATION Professors Jack W. Wilson and Charles P. Jones of North Carolina State University analyzed the long-term returns on investing in the United States stock market since 1871 and have found that there is a stable, long-term, inflation-adjusted return to stock-market investments of 8.457 percent. They compared returns from 1871 to 1926 and 1926 to 1983 and found that inflation-adjusted returns were statistically identical in both time periods.

In calculating their indexes they assumed that investors maintained portfolios consisting of all stocks listed on the New York Stock Exchange and revised their portfolios on a monthly basis to reflect changes in the composition of the stock market. They determined both the return based on dividends and the appreciation in the value of the stock. They assumed that dividends were reinvested in the market portfolio.

While the average return was stable over long periods of time, the total return fluctuated from year to year. The lowest annual change in total return adjusted for inflation was −37.37 percent, and the highest was 57.46 percent. The arithmetic inflation-adjusted mean was 8.79 percent from 1926–1985. Inflation averaged 3.21 percent. For the earlier period the arithmetic mean was 8.10 percent, with an average inflation rate of 0.75 percent.

Source: Jack W. Wilson and Charles P. Jones, "A Comparison of Annual Common Stock Returns: 1871–1925 with 1926–85." *Journal of Business* 60, No. 2 (1987):239–58. © by the University of Chicago.

The Aggregate Cost of Capital

Since the firm normally seeks financing from several sources, it must aggregate the various components of its overall capital and weight each of the sources by the proportion of its contribution to the incremental amount of capital invested. For example, if 50 percent of the firm's incremental financing comes from debt with an after-tax rate of 8 percent, and 50 percent comes from equities at a 12 percent rate, the marginal cost of capital is 10 percent, or $0.5(8) + 0.5(12)$.

The firm must not ignore the opportunity cost of choosing one source of capital to the exclusion of others. For example, assume again that a firm faces an after-tax cost of debt of 8 percent and an equity cost of 12 percent. It appears that debt is the lowest-cost source of financing new investments, but the firm should not necessarily finance its new investments exclusively with debt.

A firm that finances its investments exclusively with equity capital can normally lower its marginal cost of capital by incurring debt. Since the cost of debt (in this case, 8 percent) is less than the cost of equity (12 percent in this case), the firm lowers its weighted cost of using both debt and equity financing by incurring some debt. Recall, however, that the marginal cost of capital eventually increases as the firm increases its debt. Lenders see the firm as a higher risk due to its increasing reliance on debt.

A relatively higher leverage makes it more difficult to meet cash-flow payments during times of recession. **Leverage** is the ratio of the value of the firm's external debt to the value of its assets.

Risk is generally lower on debt and higher on common stock. Holders of debt have first claim on the assets of the firm. As firms increase the percentage of total capital that comes from debt, there is also an increase in risk for the firm. If risk increases, firms must offer a higher-risk premium to investors to convince them to hold common stock. In this way there is an opportunity cost of increasing debt. The cost of debt must implicitly include its impact on the cost of common stock.

The firm must take into account the impact of increasing its leverage on its borrowing costs. Despite the appeal of lower borrowing costs of debt, there is an opportunity cost that the firm should not ignore. While accounting for this opportunity cost makes the investment problem more complex, it improves the accuracy of the capital-budgeting process.

The firm should also consider the timing of its investments. Assume that the firm borrows heavily in the first year at 8 percent to finance new projects, with a return of 9 percent. The next year it has projects available that yield a return of 11 percent. If the firm exhausts its capacity to borrow at 8 percent, its only option may be to borrow through issuing equity. Since the cost of equity capital exceeds 11 percent, the firm should not make these investments. At the end of the chapter we briefly consider techniques for analyzing the timing of projects.

Capital Rationing

Sometimes firms impose constraints on the amount of investments they make at any point in time. These constraints lead to investments at levels below those suggested by marginal analysis. In this section we will consider the rationale for these constraints. Many observers have questioned the validity of capital rationing. If markets are competitive, firms should be able to finance all projects that offer a positive net present value. Despite this argument there are those who claim that capital rationing is a common occurrence in business.

Following are the usual justifications given for capital rationing. The first two are rules of thumb for coping with the uncertainty about market reactions to the firm's investment strategy and insufficient information on the interdependence of the firm's complete set of investments. The third reason is the possibility of a lack of control by shareholders over the management of the firm.

First, the firm cannot ignore the impact its investments may have on the market. Any one project may lead to predictable results, assuming no reaction by other firms. A massive investment program may lead to a reaction by other firms that would alter the firm's assumptions about future revenues. A firm unable to forecast perfectly the impact of major changes in investment may be forced to adopt a conservative capital constraint. In Chapter 17 we discussed methods for calculating the risks of a market reaction. If the firm finds an extensive analysis of the risks too costly, it may choose to use capital rationing as a rule of thumb.

Second, we have been considering the value of each project in isolation. The management of the firm must account for the overall impact of undertaking several investment projects at once. If the investment program requires a large, rapid expansion in the size of the firm and its number of employees, the management must acknowledge the effect of these adjustment costs on the future stream of revenues of the firm. A careful account of these costs may lead to a lower level of investment than otherwise predicted. While we will soon discuss methods for analyzing this problem systematically, some firms decide to forgo the cost of this type of analysis and impose a capital constraint as a rule of thumb.

Third, the firm must consider the impact that high levels of borrowing have on the stability of the firm. If management is operating in the best interests of shareholders, it commits the firm to the level of risk desired by the firm's shareholders. On the other hand, if management is able to direct the behavior of the firm more to its own concerns, we may see some firms shy away from outside debt to finance investments. By reducing its dependence on debt management, the firm reduces the possibilities of outside scrutiny of its operations and minimizes the possibilities of large changes in its performance. While we considered the potentially conflicting concerns of management and ownership in Chapter 10, we note here that top management's concern for its own jobs may make it behave in ways that minimize both the firm's level of risk and the risk of losing top management jobs.

18-6 Plan your refinancing carefully

APPLICATION

Professor David Dubofsky of Texas A & M University provided some evidence that there are times when the market does ration credit. He argued that price is not the only factor that determines who borrows at any particular point in time; the riskiness of a firm may also be a factor.

He showed that riskier firms face a greater likelihood of not receiving refinancing at times when there is greater than usual demand for capital. Financing demands are greatest at the outset of a significant downturn in the economy. At such times firms are financing capital investment programs while their sales and cash flow are starting to decline. They are also accumulating larger than expected inventories that require financing.

Professor Dubofsky determined that bond offerings from the lowest-rated, or riskiest, firms are significantly lower during these time periods. Since these firms face the same refinancing needs as the higher-rated firms, there must be some market reaction. Using data from the 1970s, Professor Dubofsky concluded that there was greater variance in the stock market value of the firms facing this problem than of the average firm.

The additional risk associated with this phenomenon was greatest for the lowest-rated firms that faced the relatively largest needs to refinance maturing bonds. Investors anticipated that the firms' reduced chances of refinancing their debt would increase their risk of bankruptcy. As a result, the stock market systematically decreased the market value of these companies and increased the risk of owning the firms' stock.

Source: David A. Dubofsky, "Capital Market Credit Rationing and Stock Risk." *Southern Economic Journal* 52, No. 1 (July 1985):191–202.

More Complex Project Evaluation

Most firms initiate more than one investment project at any point in time and plan additional investments for future years. We can revert to our simplified decision rule if the marginal cost of capital is constant. If the marginal cost of capital remains constant, the firm will invest in all projects that offer an internal rate of return in excess of the marginal cost of capital. It is unlikely that the marginal cost of capital will stay constant as the firm increases the size and number of its investments.

We can complicate the problem by assuming that the firm faces several interrelated projects starting in different years. For example, the development of new production processes may depend on the firm's development of a new fabric to use in the process. This interrelationship imposes a constraint on the revenues earned by a specific project. The firm must select from the best projects while accounting for each investment's impact on investments in future years.

There are mathematical programs for handling these complications. If the projects are infinitely divisible, the firm can use linear programming techniques to model the problem. An infinitely divisible investment must pay out proportionately the same amount of revenue even if the firm only invests in part of the project. For example, if Harry could earn proportionately the same net revenue from purchasing any portion of the land available for the nursery, the investment would be infinitely divisible.

As another example, assume that a project costing $1,000 pays back $500 after one year and an additional $800 after the second year. To be infinitely divisible the firm could adopt a scaled-down version of the project for $500 and earn the same proportion of revenues in years 1 and 2: $250 after year 1 and $400 after year 2.

Since most projects are not infinitely divisible or divisible at all, there is an alternative technique called integer programming. While both linear programming and integer programming are beyond the scope of this text, note that both techniques seek solutions to the same problem—that is, selection of projects that maximize the *NPV* of the firm subject to a constraint.

Summary

Firms respond to changes in technology and expected demand by adjusting the size and composition of their assets. We have labeled as capital all those assets with a useful life greater than one year. Although the one-year criterion is arbitrary, it is often useful because of the manner in which firms and governments collect and report data. Capital budgeting is the process of making decisions concerning the firm's capital stock.

We concentrated on capital-budgeting methods. We showed how the net-present-value method provides a means of comparing projects that is consistent with marginal analysis. The profit-maximizing firm invests in all projects with a positive net present value or, equivalently, an internal rate of return in excess of the marginal cost of capital.

Next, we discussed the two principal sources of financing investments: debt and equity. The cost of equity is the more difficult to determine of the two. We emphasized the use of the capital-asset-pricing model in determining the rate of return that the firm must offer to attract equity financing. An important component of this rate of return is the systematic risk of the firm.

Important Terms

Capital (p. 522)

Capital Budgeting (p. 522)

Cash Flow (p. 524)

Net Present Value (*NPV*) (p. 525)

Internal Rate of Return (*IRR*) (p. 527)

Marginal Cost of Capital (*MCC*) (p. 527)

Payback Period (p. 531)

Risk-Free Return (p. 536)

Risk Premium (p. 536)

Unsystematic Risk (p. 538)

Systematic Risk (p. 538)

Leverage (p. 541)

Selected References

Baldwin, C.Y.; Tribendis, J.J.; and Clark, J.P. "The Evolution of Market Risk in the U.S. Steel Industry and Implications for Required Rates of Return." *Journal of Industrial Economics* XXXIII, No. 1 (September 1984):73–98.

Brenner, Menachem, and Galai, Dan. "Implied Interest Rates." *Journal of Business* 59, No. 3 (July 1986):493–507.

Dubofsky, David D. "Capital Market Credit Rationing and Stock Risk." *Southern Economic Journal* 52, No. 1 (July 1985):191–202.

Gibbons, Joel C. "The Optimal Durability of Fixed Capital when Demand is Uncertain." *The Journal of Business*, 57, No. 3 (July 1984):389–403.

Narayanan, M.P. "Observability and the Payback Criterion." *Journal of Business* 58, No. 3 (July 1985):309–23.

Wilson, Jack W., and Jones, Charles P. "A Comparison of Annual Common Stock Returns: 1871–1925 with 1926–85." *Journal of Business* 60, No. 2 (1987):239–58.

1. Assume that Harry Sampson can purchase a tree-trimming machine that offers the following cash flow at the end of each year:

Year	1	2	3	4	5
Cash Flow	10,000	12,000	13,000	16,000	20,000

Assume also that Harry uses a 10 percent discount rate. The machine will cost $40,000 at the beginning of the first year and will have a resale value of $16,105 at the end of the fifth year. Should he purchase the machine?

2. In the previous problem assume that Harry anticipated that he could resell the machine, if he wanted to, for $15,000 after the third year, or for $10,000 after the fourth year. What should he do now?

3. A series of mergers in the U.S. oil industry provoked criticism that oil-refining companies were investing their capital inefficiently by buying the assets of firms with large oil reserves rather than investing in the exploration of new oil reserves. Some critics of the mergers argued that borrowing money to finance takeovers of other companies would increase the marginal cost of capital for all companies in the market and decrease the incentives to explore for oil. At the time of the mergers, competition in the oil industry and the inability of the Organization of Petroleum Exporting Countries (OPEC) to maintain their cartel price of oil brought about a substantial decrease in the price of oil. Evaluate the claims of the merger critics.

4. Assume that the average rate of return in the market is 14 percent and that the rate on ninety-day U.S. Treasury bills is 8 percent. Calculate the rates of return for three firms that have betas of 0.5, 1.0, and 1.5.

5. Why is the net-present-value method consistent with marginal analysis?

Answer questions 6–10 with true, false, or uncertain.

6. Firms should use net present value to evaluate investment projects only when they do not have sufficient information to calculate internal rates of return.

7. The payback-period criterion is a better rule of thumb for projects with a low internal rate of return.

8. When there is a separation of control between shareholders and management, shareholders would prefer that management use the payback-period criterion instead of net present value.

9. The cost of debt should be the average of all of the firm's debts.

10. The effective cost of debt must include taxes in order to be comparable with the cost of equity.

Answers to
Odd-Numbered Problems

Chapter 2

1.

Price	Larry	Ann	Frank	Total
0	50	100	100	250
10	40	80	60	180
25	25	50	0	75
50	0	0	0	0
75	0	0	0	0

The market demand curve consists of two straight-line segments. One line goes from price-quantity coordinates (50, 0) to (25, 75). The second segment starts at (25, 75) and goes to (0, 250).

3. (a) $X = 5 - 1 + 5 + 2 = 11$. The elasticity equals $-0.5 \times 2/11 = -1/11$.

(b) Increases because P_X is on the inelastic portion of the demand curve.

(c) When $P_X = 3$, $X = 10.5$. When $P_X = 1$, $X = 11.5$. By the arc formula, the elasticity would equal

$$-0.5 \times ((1 + 3)/2)/((10.5 + 11.5)/2 = -0.5 \times 2/11 = -1/11.$$

Note that this is the same answer as in part (a). Why?

5. (a) Q_X equals 11,000 if you substitute the values of each variable into the equation. The point elasticities will be the coefficients of each variable times the value of the variable divided by Q_X (i.e., 11,000). The elasticity for P_X is $-200 \ (5/11,000) = -1,000/11,000) = -1/11$. The elasticity for Y is $0.1 \ (15,000/11,000) = 3/22$. The elasticity for A is $0.5 \ (5,000/11,000) = 5/22$. The elasticity for P_W is $-200 \ (10/11,000) = -2/11$.

(b) The equation would be $Q_X = 12,000 - 200 \ P_X$.

(c) The equation changes to $Q_X = 11,000 - 200 \ P_X$.

7. False. Since we could rewrite the equation as $PQ = 150$, all price-quantity combinations must yield the same total revenue of 150. If total revenue stays the same at all points on the demand curve, the demand curve must be unit elastic (i.e., -1) everywhere.

9. True. Since the arc method formula uses the average of the two prices and the average of the two quantities, it would give the same answer for the point elasticity at the midpoint of these values of price and quantity.

11. True. The elasticity is in the inelastic range. By increasing price, we would move closer to the unit elastic point. If we increase price too much, we may move into the elastic portion of the demand curve.

Chapter 3

1. (a) The production function has isoquants that are straight lines. Rearrange the equation as follows:

$$Y = Q/10 - 2X/10 = 0.1Q - 0.2X.$$

Since Q is constant along an isoquant, the only variables are X and Y. Since the coefficient of X is -0.2, the $MRTS$, $|\Delta Y/\Delta X|$, equals 0.2.

(b) Since the $MRTS$ will always be 0.2, there are no output levels where the $MRTS$ will be greater.

3. To the right of the inflection point, marginal product is decreasing with increases in the inputs. If both marginal products are decreasing, the $MRTS$ will approach zero with increases in the input read off the X axis. As a result, the isoquants will be strictly convex.

5. (b) $AP = Q/H = 100/H^{0.5}$

(c) The marginal product will always be one half of the average product.

(d) She experiences declining marginal product, which causes her average product to decrease with increases in H.

7. False. The $MRTS$ is both the absolute value of the slope and the ratio of the marginal products. Since the ratio of the marginal products must be constant for the slope to be constant, both marginal products must be constant.

9. False. They cross at the maximum point on the average product curve. To the right of this point the marginal product is less than the average product and causes the average product to decline.

11. True. You would want to show this with a graph of isoquants. Holding one input constant and increasing the level of the other input in equal increments, we could show that eventually marginal product would decrease. To determine the effect of a change in scale, increase the level of both inputs in the same proportion. Output could increase in the same proportion (that is, constant returns to scale).

Chapter 4

1. $Q = X^{0.5}Y^{0.5} = X^{0.5}(900)^{0.5} = 30X^{0.5} \rightarrow Q^2 = 900X \rightarrow X = Q^2/900.$

$\text{Total cost} = P_X X + P_Y Y = 12X + 3(900) = 12X + 2700 = 12Q^2/900 + 2700$

$= Q^2/75 + 2700.$

Average total cost $= TC/Q = (Q^2/75 + 2700)/Q = Q/75 + 2700/Q$. If Q equals 450, ATC must equal $450/75 + 2700/450 = 6 + 6 = 12$.

3. This is a difficult problem with many steps. Recall that in the long run, $MRTS = MP_X/MP_Y = P_X/P_Y$. In this case,

$MP_X/MP_Y = (4X^{-0.6}Y^{0.6})/(6X^{0.4}Y^{-0.4}) = 2Y/3X = P_X/P_Y = 2/2 = 1$

$\rightarrow Y = 3X/2.$

$Q = 10X^{0.4}Y^{0.6} = 10X^{0.4}(3X/2)^{0.6} = 10(1.5)^{0.6}X = 12.75X$

$\rightarrow X = Q/12.75 = 0.0784Q.$

$TC = P_X X + P_Y Y = 2X + 2Y = 2X + 2(3X/2) = 5X = 5 Q/12.75 = Q/2.55$

$\rightarrow ATC = TC/Q = Q/2.55Q = 1/2.55 = 0.392.$

5. Ray has an opportunity cost of $24,000 from his two jobs. He must also forgo the return to the next best investment of his $50,000 and the $3,000 he could get from selling the boat. If his next best investment equaled an annual return of 10% (the market rate of interest), he would forgo $5,300 per year. His implicit cost per year would then be $29,300. His explicit costs (i.e., the opportunity cost of the inputs he purchases directly) will be $45,000 plus $25,000. To open the business, he must expect to make more than the sum of the explicit and implicit costs: $99,300.

7. False. The marginal rate of technical substitution shows the ratio of the marginal product of the input on the X axis to the marginal product of the input on the Y axis. In this case, $MP_X/MP_Y > P_X/P_Y \rightarrow MP_X/P_X > MP_Y/P_Y$. This means that the X input is giving the firm more additional output for the dollar than the Y input. The firm would use only the X input regardless of the output level.

9. Uncertain. Since the exponents sum to 1, this production function exhibits constant returns to scale at all output levels. The firm will minimize long-run average total costs at every output level, not just at 200 units.

11. True. The production function will exhibit constant returns to scale, and the long-run average total cost curve will be a horizontal line at $2.

Chapter 5

1. $SRMC = q - 5 = P$ because each firm is a price taker. Solve for $q \rightarrow q = P + 5$. The quantity supplied by the market is 1000 times that supplied by any one of the identical firms. $Q = 1000q = 1000(P + 5) = 1000P + 5000$. Market equilibrium occurs where the supply and demand curves cross.

$$\text{(supply equation)} \quad Q = 1000P + 5000$$

$$\text{(demand equation)} \quad Q = -500P + 20{,}000$$

Subtract the second from the first $\rightarrow 0 = 1500P - 15{,}000$; $P = 10$. Substitute P equals 10 into both the supply and demand equations to find that Q equals 15,000.

3. If the market is perfectly competitive, the market ensures that the optimal number of firms is in the market. In long-run equilibrium, no firm will make economic profits, and consumers pay the lowest possible prices without forcing firms to leave the market. In a monopolistically competitive market, firms make no economic profits in long-run equilibrium, but firms do not exhaust all the potential for scale economies. If the products of all firms in a market were homogeneous, the market would force all the firms left in the market to exhaust all potential for scale economies. In a monopolistically competitive market, prices are higher, but firms provide more variety of products.

5. Since $MR = 25 - Q = MC = 2 \rightarrow Q = 23$. $P = 25 - 0.5Q = 25 - 11.5 = 13.5$. Profits $= TR - TC = PQ - (ATC)(Q) = 13.5(23) - 2(23) = 310.5 - 46 = 264.5$.

7. False. The monopolist does not have a supply curve. It uses both its cost curves and the market demand curve to determine its output and price. Unlike the perfectly competitive firm, it does not take the price as given.

9. Uncertain. In long-run equilibrium, firms will no longer make economic profits unless there is a shock to the market that creates new profits. Firms can accumulate profits in the short run as the market adjusts to long-run equilibrium.

11. False. The monopolist must set a price that exceeds its long-run average total cost while still preventing entry into the market.

Chapter 6

1. Since $P_1 = 3600 - 20Q_1$, $MR_1 = 3600 - 40Q_1$. Since $P_2 = 2400 - 10Q_2$, $MR_2 = 2400 - 20Q_2$. Since $MC = 400$, we would set $MR_1 = MC$ and solve for Q_1 and set $MR_2 = MC$ and solve for Q_2. In this case, $MR_1 = 3600 - 40Q_1 = 400$ and $Q_1 = 80$. $MR_2 = 2400 - 20Q_2 = 400$ and $Q_2 = 100$. Substitute the quantities into the demand equations and find that $P_1 = 2000$ and $P_2 = 1400$.

3. In this case, $MR_1 = 10 - 2Q_1 = 1 = MC$ and $MR_2 = 10 - 4Q_2 = 1 = MC$. Q_1 would equal 4.5, and Q_2 would equal 2.25. Note that the price would be 5.5 in both cases. If there is a cost for separating the two markets, the firm would be worse off by separating them. In fact, since the optimal price is the same in the submarkets, there is no reason to separate them anyway. The reason the prices ended up being the same in both submarkets is that the own price elasticities of demand are the same at these prices. Check this out for yourself.

5. In this case we would compare the profits of a perfectly discriminating monopolist to those of a simple monopolist (i.e., the same machine price to all customers). The output of the monopolist using a meter would be 95,000. The simple monopolist would set output where $MR = 10,000 - 0.2Q = 500$ or where $Q = 47,500$. Price would be 5,250 for the simple monopolist. The simple monopolist's profits would be $(5,250 - 500) \times 47,500 = \$225,625,000$. The metering monopolist would earn profits that are twice as large.

7. $MR_1 = 40 - 0.4Q_1 = 0$ when $Q_1 = 100$. $MR_2 = 10 - 0.4Q_2 = 0$ when $Q_2 = 10/0.4 = 25$. Since $MC = 4$ and $MR_1 > 4$ when $Q = 25$, the number of parking spaces will be dictated by the marginal revenue during time period 1. Since $MR_1 = 40 - 0.4Q_1 = 4$, $Q_1 = 90$. The firm will rent 90 spaces during time period 1 and 25 spaces during time period 2.

9. Uncertain. Recall that the firm would charge them the same price if there were no difference in the elasticity of demand.

11. False. They pay their demand prices, which will be different if the demand curve is negatively sloped.

13. Uncertain. The unregulated firm will produce the same output if both situations would produce the competitive output level. If the unregulated firm can act like a monopolist, it will charge a higher price and produce a lower output level.

15. Uncertain. Recall that they can be consistent as long as the markup varies with changes in the elasticity of demand.

Chapter 7

1. This is an application of the dominant-firm model. You would draw the fringe firm's supply curve in the same place as the dominant firm's marginal-cost curve. Since the dominant firm's marginal-cost curve crosses its marginal-revenue curve at an output that is less than that of the total output of the fringe firms, the dominant firm will have a market share of less than 50 percent.

3. If a firm is unable to maintain a barrier to entry, it accomplishes little by trying to force others out of the market by setting prices below its own average total cost. Since the firm would be taking losses during the time of this pricing strategy, it would need to make economic profits later to offset these losses. If it cannot impose a barrier to entry, it will be unable to earn economic profits without encouraging other firms to enter the market.

5. The bilateral profit-sharing arrangement makes cheating on the agreement unattractive because both firms share in the profits. By increasing output, a firm lowers overall profits. Cheating by a firm as a member of a cartel is more likely because the firms do not share aggregate profits and the number of participants is larger.

7. The market demand curve crosses the fringe firms' supply curve where $P = 400 - Q_M = 200 + Q_F = P$. Since Q_M equals Q_F at this point, we can solve for Q_M as follows: $2Q_M = 200$ or $Q_M = 100$. Note that if you substitute 100 for quantity in both the market demand equation and the fringe firms' supply equation, P will be $300. At a market price of $300, Hal would sell nothing. Since the supply curve for the fringe firms is $P = 200 + Q_F$ or $Q_F = P - 200$, the fringe firms would supply nothing if the market price were $200 or less. At a market price of $200 or less, Hal would be the only firm supplying output. At $200, Hal would face the market demand of 200 units. We now have two points on Hal's demand curve: ($300, 0) and ($200, 200). The equation of this demand curve will be $P = 300 - Q_H/2$. Note that in moving between these two points the change in P is $300 - $200 or $100. The change in Q is $0 - 200$ or -200. As a result, the slope of the demand curve, $\Delta P/\Delta Q$, is $-100/200$ or $-1/2$. Remember that a straight-line demand curve has a straight-line marginal-revenue curve with the same intercept on the vertical axis and a slope twice as large in absolute value as the slope of the demand curve. Hal's marginal-revenue curve has the corresponding equation $MR_H = 300 - Q_H$. Hal will set his MR curve equal to his MC curve as follows: $MR_H = 300 - Q_H = 150 + 0.5Q_H = MC_H$. $1.5Q_H = 300 - 150 = 150$ and $Q_H = 150/1.5 = 100$. The price will be $P = 300 - Q_H/2 = 300 - 100/2 = 300 - 50 = $250. At a price of $250 the fringe firms will supply $Q_F = P - 200 = 250 - 200 = 50$. The market quantity will be $Q_H + Q_F = 100 + 50 = 150$.

9. True. You should show that when the two curves are in the same place (see Problem 1 above), the dominant firm produces less than 50 percent of the market output. Thus if the marginal-cost curve is higher, the share of output for the dominant firm must be even less.

11. False. To be a dominant firm, the firm must be large enough that all the other firms act as price takers.

13. Uncertain. The profit-maximizing firm would not be likely to set output where marginal revenue equals short-run marginal cost when it does not have a barrier to entry or a cost advantage over potential entrants. If it did have a substantial cost advantage, it would set output where MR equals $SRMC$ as long as price is equal to or below the average cost of potential entrants.

15. Uncertain. If a firm lowers its price below its average cost to drive firms out of the market, we might consider this an example of predatory pricing. Recall, however, that price falls in perfectly competitive markets when there is a decrease in market demand. In this case, some firms may drop from the market.

Chapter 8

1. $MR_M = 308 - Q_M = 0$ when Q_M is 308. $MR_{SS} = 172 - 4Q_{SS} = 0$ when Q_{SS} is 43. The kink in the aggregate MR curve will occur at 43. At Q equal to 43, MR_M is $308 - 43$ or 265. Since $MC = 20 + 5Q = 235$ when Q is 43, the firm will produce an output greater than 43. $MR = 308 - Q$ to the right of the kink. In this case, $MR = 308 - Q = MC = 20 + 5Q$, yielding $288 = 6Q$ and $Q = 48$. The sales of

Q_{SS} will be 43 at a price of $86. Q_M will be 48 at a price of $284. The firm would destroy five sheepskins.

3. If the movie distributor set individual prices for both movies, the profit-maximizing prices would be $800 for the first movie and $1,200 for the second movie. Total revenue would be 2 × $800 + 2 × $1,200 = $4,000. The block-booking price would be $2,000 (that is, the smaller of the sums of demand prices for the two theater owners). The revenue from block booking would be the same as that from separate pricing of both movies. You will always come to this conclusion when one theater owner values both movies more than the second theater owner. In this example, theater owner A has a higher demand price for both films than does theater owner B.

5. False. It produces where the sum of the marginal-revenue curves crosses the marginal-cost curve.

7. True. Notice in Problem 1 above that the firm sold five more units of meat than sheepskins, but it did produce the same amount.

9. True. In this case the block price will be the sum of the demand prices of the theater owner who likes both films less than the other theater owner.

Chapter 9

1. The issues here are the measurement costs of determining product quality and the possibility of a consumer misusing or tampering with a product and complaining later that the product was defective. The closed-circuit TV appears to be the strongest candidate for a warranty. The possibilities of consumer abuse of a warranty for the remaining three products would limit the usefulness of the warranty. The used car would be the least likely choice for using a warranty, since customers might be able to replace working parts with defective ones without the dealer being able to detect the tampering.

3. To avoid paying fines, firms would likely institute tighter quality controls to ensure a smaller variation around the expected contents in the package. This additional production cost will increase the costs of all firms subject to the inspections and will result in higher prices for consumers. If consumers had wanted this degree of quality before, they would have forced the market to provide it.

5. (a) This could result in a "lemons" problem. Those who would benefit the most are those women who are already pregnant. All women would wait until they were about to give birth before seeking the insurance. The insurance premiums would have to rise to cover the costs of providing coverage. This type of insurance would disappear from the market.

(b) The chances are better, but those attracted to the insurance program would most likely be those planning to have a child soon (after a year or so). The high premiums necessary to cover the expenses of these people would drive out most people who would consider their pregnancy a surprise.

7. Uncertain. Higher-income people have higher opportunity costs to their search time. However, they are also more likely to have higher education levels and are better able to process information.

9. Uncertain. People will be willing to pay a higher price as long as the increased information results in an overall lower combined price that includes both the purchase price and the search costs.

11. Uncertain. To the extent that licensing screens out some people of lower than average quality, the average quality of those who qualify may be higher. However, as the last application in the text shows, overall service could decrease. Whether average quality increases or not is not the important issue. Whether the higher quality is worth paying for is the more appropriate issue.

Chapter 10

1. Quasi-vertical integration refers to the ownership of the specialized equipment by the firm that uses the input. As long as there is a possibility of opportunistic behavior, the user of the input has an incentive to prevent the supplier from operating opportunistically. If the supplier of the input can produce the input at lower average variable cost, the user of the input would be better off contracting the production of the input to the other firm while retaining ownership over the critical, specialized input. Complete vertical integration is more likely if the user of the input can produce the input at lower cost than the supplier or if the supplier can take advantage of specialized information to act opportunistically.

3. While the firm that maximizes profits would experience a decrease in its profits, there would be no other output level at which it could earn higher profits. As a result, it will continue to produce the same output level. The sales-maximizing firm may also maintain the same output level. However, if the sales-maximizing firm operates subject to a minimum profit constraint, such as the one shown by *EP* in Figure 10-3, the reduction in profits would force the firm to reduce its output and increase its profits in order to satisfy the profit constraint.

5. This question asks you to summarize the main points mentioned in the text concerning the problems that owners may have with management's desire to enrich itself at the expense of the owners. Application 10-6 shows that management has an incentive to oppose hostile takeovers. To check this type of behavior, owners should make takeovers easier, use the board of directors more effectively, and tie compensation more closely to performance.

7. True. There will be an increase in profits. The merger will produce the equivalent of the simple monopoly solution (that is, all consumers pay the same price for the product) seen in Chapter 5.

9. False. When there is a possibility of opportunistic behavior, firms are more likely to seek either quasi-vertical integration or complete vertical integration rather than rely on formal contracts.

11. Uncertain. This depends on the nature of the minimum-profit constraint faced by the sales-maximizing firm. For example, in the long-run a sales-maximizing firm operating subject to a zero economic profit constraint would produce the same output level as the profit-maximizing firm if they both faced free entry into the market.

Chapter 11

1. Since MC_F (excluding the cost of input T) = 15, NMR will equal

$$NMR = MR_F - MC_F = 205 - 2Q_F - 15 = 190 - 2Q_F.$$

Since the price of T is 40, $NMR = 40$ and

$$190 - 2Q_F = 40,$$
$$2Q_F = 150,$$

and
$$Q_F = 75.$$

Since $MC_T = 10 + Q_T = P_T$, $10 + Q_T = 40$ and $Q_T = 30$. The firm will produce 30 units of the input and purchase 45 units from the competitive market to produce 75 units of the output.

3. Since $P_X = 2$ and $MC_X = 3 + 0.0001X$, the firm's marginal costs are too high in relation to the market price. It should not produce any X at all. NMR and MR will be the same, since there is no other cost of production: $NMR = 100 - 0.001q$, $NMR = 2$, and $Q = 49,000$.

5. When the marginal-revenue curve has a negative slope, you have to add the marginal-cost curves together. Solve for Q. $Q_1 = MC$, $Q_2 = 2MC$, $Q_3 = MC/2$, and $Q_4 = MC$. Add the Q's to find that $Q = 9MC/2$. Solve for MC. $MC = 2Q/9$. Set MR equal to MC. $MR = 63 - Q/9 = 2Q/9 = MC$. As a result, $63 = 3Q/9$, and $Q = 189$. MC will be 42. $Q_1 = 42$, $Q_2 = 84$, $Q_3 = 21$, and $Q_4 = 42$.

7. Uncertain. This would be true if the firm had no external market for the input. If there is a competitive market for the input, the internal price should be the competitive price.

9. Uncertain. It should produce at least some of the input, but it may be a net buyer or seller of the input. It should produce where its marginal cost equals the competitive price.

11. False. You add them horizontally.

13. True. The firm would add the transportation cost to its marginal cost of production to determine the overall cost of the product. Since the plant located farthest away would have a higher overall marginal cost at each output level, it would produce a smaller amount.

Chapter 12

1. You should consider the importance of maintaining on-site services, advertising, and inventory when choosing an exclusive territory. Exclusive dealing will be important if dealers can use their influence to switch customers from the product to a lower-cost alternative. Resale price maintenance concerns the need to encourage retailers to promote the product without fearing price competition. You should summarize these points while referring to the material in the chapter. Of the three practices, only resale price maintenance is illegal according to antitrust law in the United States.

3. It would likely increase retail prices in the long run. If vertically integrated firms cannot receive discounts for the services they provide, they will cease offering these services. If vertical integration resulted from a firm's efforts to lower costs, the alternative of no vertical integration must be more costly.

5. (a) See Application 12-5.

(b) See Application 12-6.

(c) See Application 12-7.

(d) This would be an unlikely case for *RPM*. Since the product is relatively standard, there would be less need for monitoring the promotion efforts and pricing of retailers.

7. False. They are legal.

9. False. It does not actively prosecute these cases.

11. False. All manufacturers did not use it when it was legal. Besides, some manufacturers would prefer that dealers have more flexibility in adjusting price to changes in local market conditions.

Chapter 13

1. (a) $H = 25^2 + 25^2 + 10^2 + 10^2 + 10^2 + 10^2 + 5^2 + 5^2 = 625 + 625 + 100 + 100 + 100 + 100 + 25 + 25 = 1700$.

(b) $1700 + 2(5)(5) = 1750$.

(c) The industry Herfindahl index is in the 1000–1800 range. Since the change in the index would be less than 100, the Justice Department is unlikely to challenge it.

3. (a) If $P = 20$, $Q = 15$. The monopoly output would be 15/2 or 7.5, and the monopoly price would be $P = 50 - 2(7.5) = 35$. The deadweight loss would be $0.5(35 - 20)(15 - 7.5) = 0.5(15)(7.5) = 56.25$. The transfer of consumer surplus would equal $(35 - 20)(7.5) = 112.5$, or twice the value of the deadweight loss.

(b) If the government does not allow the merger, the average cost of each firm would be $30. The market price in a competitive market would be $30, and the market output would be 10. The relevant comparison now is a market price of $30 and a market output of 10 compared to a market price of $35 and a market output of 7.5. The monopolist will produce the 7.5 thousand tons at a lower cost of $10 per ton, yielding a cost savings of 75. However, there is a deadweight loss of $0.5(35 - 30)(10 - 7.5) = 6.25$ and a transfer of $(35 - 30)(7.5) = 37.5$. From an efficiency standpoint the monopoly would actually be more efficient. One should question, however, whether scale economies are important enough to justify only one firm in a national market.

5. Some might have gone out of business, but the competitive market would ensure that the optimal number of firms would survive.

7. Uncertain. The change in the Herfindahl index would be 400. However, we do not know whether the Herfindahl index is less than 1000 or not.

9. Uncertain. There is less incentive to sue for damages for someone purchasing goods from a firm that paid the higher prices in the first place. However, the firm paying the higher prices has an incentive to sue regardless of the court decision.

11. True. It prevents low-cost firms from driving higher-cost firms out of business.

Chapter 14

1. The people who now own the licenses are not necessarily the same people who owned them in the 1930s. Current owners probably purchased the right to drive a cab (that is, a medallion) in the same way that they would purchase any other asset. If there were more cabs, the value of the asset would drop, and the current license holders would take a loss. Since the medallions are sold in competitive markets, most cab owners are earning a normal return on their investment.

3. If there are clearly established property rights, one party would have to compensate the owner of the property right for infringements on that property right. For example, if Jewel owned the right to have peace and quiet at night, the Sons of Satan would have to pay her to compensate for any increase in the sound level. Externalities occur when one party can impose costs or even benefits on others without their permission.

5. It has become increasingly less appropriate for the generation of electricity. Studies show that scale economies are exhausted at output levels below the capacities of most modern firms. On the other hand, there may still be economies in transmission and distribution. For example, the cost of adding one more customer is much smaller than the average cost of distributing electricity to customers.

7. See Application 14-7.

9. Uncertain. They will likely raise the quality of those who meet the qualifications. However, since customers will also turn more often to alternative lower-quality sources of these services, the overall average quality could be lower. See Applications 14-12 and 14-13.

11. Uncertain. See Application 14-14. The regulations might create uniform standards, but they could also lead to entry restrictions that raise prices in excess of that justified by the increase in quality.

13. True. Their costs increased at a much faster rate than did the price they could charge for electricity.

Chapter 15

1. While imports and domestic goods will sell at the same price, this price will be higher with restrictions imposed on imports. See Graphical Explanation 15-3 and Figure 15-3 for an explanation of the effects of quotas.

3. In many ways they are the same. The VERs are imposed by the exporting country to head off potentially more restrictive quotas by the importing country. The difference is the enforcement of the restriction. The exporting country enforces the VERs, while the importing country enforces the quotas. There is more likelihood that the exporting country will be less attentive in enforcement than will the importing country.

5. 300/400 or 3/4 (bananas for grapefruit) to 400/600 or 2/3.

7. False. If the quota is binding, it must affect both the price and the domestic quantity.

9. Uncertain. It depends on the size of the tariff and quota. You could design a quota or tariff that would accomplish the same effect on price.

11. Uncertain. There is nothing to keep other firms from entering the market to drive prices down to minimum average total cost. The dumping-of-goods argument hinges on the assumptions about deterring market entry needed to justify a predatory pricing argument.

Chapter 16

1. The most likely customers are those with relatively higher incomes. Since individuals with higher income have a higher opportunity cost associated with their time, they are less likely to participate in surveys.

3. Any time accountants do not amortise assets over their economic life, they create a distortion in the cost data. You would have to adjust the data to account for this problem.

5. False. See Application 16-10.

7. Uncertain. Most small firms would be better off relying on others for these forecasts. There are several companies that specialize in making forecasts at relatively low cost.

9. True. New products do not have a history of cost information. Engineering estimates of the cost of each stage of production may be the only alternative.

Chapter 17

1. The expected value of the radio campaign is $22,500, while the expected value of the newspaper campaign is $28,000. The variance for the radio advertisements is 41.25, and the standard deviation is 6.426. The variance for the newspaper advertisements is 163.6 with a standard deviation of 12.791.

3. (a) The present value of the $40,000 per year for four years is $126,794. The present values of $30,000 per year is $95,096. The expected value is $110,945. The standard deviation is $15,849. The coefficient of variation is 15,849/110,945 or 0.14285.

(b) Since she has used a certainty equivalent adjustment factor, β, equal to 1.0 minus one-half of the coefficient of variation, β equals $1.0 - (0.1428/2)$, or 0.9286. Since β is less than 1.0, Melody is risk-averse. The maximum she would pay is $0.9286(110,945)$ or $103,023.

5. The New York investment yields an expected value of 190, a standard deviation of 70 and a coefficient of variation of 0.3684. The Philadelphia investment is less attractive, since the expected value is 189, the standard deviation is 107.09 and the coefficient of variation is 0.5666. The Boston investment has a higher expected investment (212) but a larger standard deviation (120.90) and a higher coefficient of variation (0.57027). She must weigh the trade-off of a higher expected revenue versus the greater risk.

7. True. Those investors with a greater aversion to risk will place a lower certainty equivalent value on a risky investment than will less risk-averse investors.

9. False. See Application 17-1.

11. False. The standard deviation is not more accurate. The variance is the squared value of the standard deviation and yields the same information. The coefficient of variation is more useful than the standard deviation for comparing investments with different expected values.

Chapter 18

1. Yes. The present value of the investment is $62,122, while the initial cost is $40,000.

3. By borrowing money to buy other assets the oil companies try to find the best investment opportunity for maximizing their profits. If they had believed that exploration for additional oil reserves was potentially more profitable than fuller use of existing reserves, they would have used the money for exploration. Once they purchase

the assets of the other companies, they give money to the shareholders of the takeover target. These shareholders are free to invest this money as they please. They will invest in the best opportunity available. The total amount of money available for investment does not decrease because the oil companies purchase existing assets rather than explore for additional reserves.

5. See the discussion in the section entitled "Net Present Value and Marginal Analysis." The net present value rule leads to the same investment decision as that used by a firm that invests to the point at which the internal rate of return equals the marginal cost of investment.

7. False. Since this method ignores the time cost of money, it is less inaccurate for projects with high internal rates of return and short payback time periods.

9. Uncertain. The firm should determine the opportunity cost of each component of the firm's overall debt and weight each component by its share of the debt.

AUTHOR INDEX

A

Abrams, Burton A., 531
Ackerlof, George A., 254
Alchian, Armen, 288
Archibald, G.C., 267
Ayanian, Robert, 260

B

Bailey, Elizabeth E., 200
Bain, Joe S., 140
Baldwin, C.Y., 540
Barron, John M., 205, 351
Baumol, William J., 407
Bell, Frederick W., 463
Beranek, William, 504
Berenson, Conrad, 480
Berle, Adolphe A., 292
Bishop, John A., 460
Blair, Roger D., 52
Bojanek, Robert, 245
Brenner, Menachem, 537
Brickley, James A., 300
Brookshire, David S., 456, 501
Burns, Malcolm R., 203

C

Calfee, John E., 263
Caves, Douglas W., 475
Cheung, Steven S., 399
Christensen, Laurits R., 108, 475
Christopher, James M., 300
Clark, J.P., 540
Clements, Kenneth W., 44

C

Coase, Ronald H., 275–276
Coates, Daniel E., 324
Comanor, William S., 259, 367
Coughlin, Cletus C., 443
Coursey, Don L., 456
Crawford, Robert, 288

D

Daly, Michael J., 109
Demsetz, Harold, 140, 302
Denton, Derek, 19
Draper, Roger, 118
Dubofsky, David A., 544

E

Easterbrook, Frank, 345
Eaton, B. Curtis, 265
Ehrlich, Isaac, 260

F

Feinberg, Robert M., 96
Fenili, Robert N., 375
Fisher, Lawrence, 260
Flath, David, 301
Forgionne, Guisseppi, 4
Førsund, Finn R., 79
Frech, H.E., III, 348

G

Galai, Dan, 537
Gattis, Donald R., 4
Geehan, Randall, 109
Gibbons, Joel C., 535

Greene, William H., 108
Grigalunas, Thomas A., 515

H

Haas-Wilson, Deborah, 414
Hafer, R. W., 486
Hanner, John, 243
Harberger, Arnold C., 366
Hein, Scott E., 486
Herander, Mark G., 441
Hjalmarsson, Lennart, 79
Hotelling, Harold, 263
Hymans, Saul H., 484

J

Jensen, Michael C., 298
Johnson, Lester W., 44
Jones, Charles P., 541
Jones, Steven, 143

K

Kaserman, David L., 51–52
Kenney, Roy W., 221
Klein, Benjamin, 221, 258, 288
Kling, John L., 485
Knapp, Martin, 104
Knoeber, Charles R., 296, 301
Kreinen, Mordechai E., 428
Krouse, Clement G., 270

L

Lane, William C., 375
Leffler, Keith B., 258, 261
Lehn, Kenneth, 256, 302
Levy, David, 382
Link, Charles R., 69
Lipsey, Richard G., 265
Loewenstein, Mark A., 205
Long, Michael S., 295
Low, Stuart A., 510

M

Manning, Willard G., Jr., 483
Marquis, M. Susan, 34
Marvel, Howard P., 341–342, 347
Masten, Scott E., 290
Mayo, John W., 51
McCafferty, Stephen, 347
McGuirk, Marjorie A., 50
McPheters, Lee R., 510
Means, Gardiner, 292
Mitchell, Bridger M., 30
Monteverde, Kirk, 287, 289
Morrison, Stephen A., 201
Mulligan, James G., 69, 324

N

Narayanan, M.P., 532
Naylor, Thomas H., 4
Noether, Monica, 191
Nooteboom, B., 178

O

Opaluch, James J., 515

P

Pareto, Vilfredo, 400fn
Park, Rolla Edward, 30
Pashigian, B. Peter, 411
Peltzman, Sam, 259
Phelps, Charles E., 34, 483
Pindyck, Robert S., 442
Porell, Frank W., 50
Porter, Robert H., 211
Pratt, John W., 252

R

Rao, P. Someshwar, 109
Roll, Richard, 484
Rose, Nancy L., 394
Rosenbluth, Gideon, 267
Rosenzweig, Mark W., 61
Rotemberg, Julio J., 442
Rubin, Paul, 352

S

Sav, G. Thomas, 476
Scheffman, David T., 371
Scherer, F.M., 301, 373–374, 380
Schmalensee, Richard, 230fn, 245, 268
Schnaars, Steven, 480
Schultz, T. Paul, 61
Schulze, William D., 509
Schwartz, J. Brad, 441
Scully, G.W., 112
Selby, Edward B., Jr., 504
Shelton, John P., 350
Shepherd, Lawrence, 402
Shepherd, William G., 148
Silk, Alvin J., 245
Sims, W.A., 397
Smiley, Robert H., 367
Smith, J.B., 397
Smith, Richard L., III, 339
Snyder, Edward A., 384
Spiller, Pablo T., 371
Springer, Robert F., 348
Steigler, George J., 195
Strauss, John, 68
Suslow, Valerie Y., 193

Svorney, Shirley V., 272
Swann, G.M.P., 266
Swanson, Joseph A., 475

T

Teece, David J., 287, 289
Tepel, Richard, 52
Thayer, Mark A., 509
Tribendis, J.J., 540
Tschirhart, John, 509

U

Umbeck, John R., 205, 351

V

Viscusi, W. Kip, 410

W

Walker, John I., 87
Walkling, Ralph K., 295
Walters, Stephen J.K., 285
Welzer, Steve, 382
Wetzel, Bruce M., 30
Williams, Stephen F., 175
Willig, Robert D., 407
Wilson, Jack W., 541
Wilson, Thomas A., 259
Winston, Clifford, 201
Wise, David A., 252

Y

Yoo, Jang H., 460

Z

Zeckhauser, Richard, 252

SUBJECT INDEX

A

Absolute advantage, defined, 421
Absolute disadvantage, defined, 421
Ad valorem tariff, defined, 429
Advertising, 47, 51–52, 259–263
  and competition, 259–263
Advertising elasticity of demand, 51–52
Aggregate marginal-revenue curve, 168–171
Alternative estimation procedures, 475–476
Antitrust laws, 368–385
  effectiveness of, 381–384
  enforcement of, 372–380
  mergers, 375–380
  monopoly, 373–374
  penalties and punitive damages, 381–384
  price discrimination, 374–375
  price fixing, 369, 372–373
  use by rivals to block mergers, 379
Antitrust policy, 360–385
Appropriable quasi-rent, 287–288
  defined, 287
Arbitrage, defined, 158
Arc method, 25–27
  defined, 25–26
Asymmetric information, 254–263, 270
  defined, 254
Average fixed cost, defined, 101
Average-fixed-cost curve, derivation of, 100–102
Average product, 65–69
  defined, 65
Average-product curve, 65–66
  defined, 66

Average revenue, defined, 126
Average total cost, defined, 101
Average-total-cost curve
  defined, 101–102
  derivation of, 100–104
Average variable cost, defined, 101
Average-variable-cost curve, derivation of, 100–102

B

Barometric forecasting, defined, 484
Barrier to entry, 139–143, 339–342, 411–414
  defined, 139
  and exclusive dealing, 339–342
  and product location 267–270
Behavior, opportunistic, 284–285
  defined, 284
Bilateral monopoly, 281–283
  defined, 281
Bilateral sharing agreement, 209–210
  defined, 209
Block booking, 221–223
  defined, 221
Board of directors, 288–300
Bonding and brand names, 258
Brand names, effects of unfavorable publicity
  on, 258–259
  and bonding, 258
Breakeven analysis, 113–118
  defined, 113
  and technological change, 116–118
Breakeven output, 114–116
Bundling, mixed, 226–235

Cost of capital, 535–542
    aggregate, 541–542
Cost of debt, 535–536
Cost of equity, 536–541
Cost-plus pricing, 175–178
Cross-price elasticity of demand, 45–48
    defined, 45
Cross-section data, defined, 474
Cubic cost functions, 471–473

D

Data
    cross-section, defined, 474
    and short-run cost functions, 467–468
Deadweight loss, 364–366
    defined, 364
Debt, cost of, 535–536
Decision trees, 511–513
    defined, 511
Decreasing returns to scale, defined, 106
Demand, 16–52, 109–112
    advertising elasticity of, 51–52
    change in, 22–24
        defined, 22
    consumer, 17–18
        defined, 17
    derived, 17, 109–112
        defined, 17
    effect of changes in income on, 40–42
    income elasticity, defined, 39
    linear functional form, 20–21
Demand curve, defined, 21–22
Demand equation, linear, 20–21
Demand estimation, 453–467
Demand function, 18–20
Demand price, defined, 155
Derivative of equation with one variable, 10–11
Derived demand for an input, 109–112
Deterring the entry of large firms, 195–201
Deterring the entry of small firms, 193–195
Diminishing marginal product, 63
Diminishing marginal utility of money, 504–505
Discount rates, risk-adjusted, 510–511
Discrete probability distributions, 497–498
    defined, 498
Diseconomies of scale, defined, 106
Distribution
    probability, defined, 494
    of wealth, 367
Dr. Miles Medical Company v. *John D. Park and Sons* (1911), 343
Dominant firm, 187–195
    defined, 187

Dumping of foreign goods, 439–445
    defined, 439
    and price discrimination, 439
    and predatory pricing, 440–442
    retaliation against, 441–445

E

Econometric models of forecasting, 481–486
Economic costs, defined, 88
Economic profits, defined, 88
Economic reasoning, 4–6
    impact of, 4–6
Economic rents, defined, 366
Economic uncertainty, defined, 493
Economies of scale, defined, 106
Economies of scope, defined, 235
Elasticity of demand, 24–52, 160
    advertising, 51–52
    cross-price, 45–48
    defined, 24
    gas-mileage, 52
    income, 39–44
    and marginal revenue, 35–39
    measurement by arc and point methods, 25–30
    own-price, 28–39, 43–44, 49, 160
        defined, 28
    and total revenue, 35–39
Endogenous variable, 457
Engineering cost functions, 475–476
Entrenching management, 294–295
Entry deterrence, 193–201
Entry restrictions and regulation, 411–412
Equilibrium
    long-run market, 134–137, 206–207
    short-run market, 131–134
Equity
    considerations, 400–401
    cost of, 536–541
Estimation, 452–487
    cost, 467–476
    demand, 453–467
    regression analysis, 463–467
Estimation of cost functions, 467–476
    alternative procedures, 475–476
    engineering technique, 475–476
    survivor technique, 475
Exclusive dealing, 339–342
    and barriers to entry, 339–342
    defined, 339
    and economic efficiency, 341–342
Exclusive territory, 336–339, 345
    defined, 336

Exogenous variable, defined, 457
Expansion path, 93–95
    defined, 93
Expected value, 495–499
    defined, 496
Explicit costs, defined, 87
Externality, 394–397
    defined, 394
    internalizing an, 398–399

F

F-statistic, 489
Fair rate of return, defined, 403
Fair trade law of California (1931), 343
Federal Trade Commission Act (1915), 369
Federal Trade Commission (FTC) v. *Anheuser-Busch, Inc.* (1961), 319
Firm, 2–4, 58, 187–191, 275–276, 292–295
    defined, 58
    dominant, 187–191
    fringe, defined, 187
    objectives of the, 2–4, 292–295
    theory of the, 275–276
Fixed costs, defined, 99
Fixed-proportions production, 236–243
    with excess sales of one product, 239–243
Forecasting, 477–486
    barometric, defined, 484
    correcting for seasonal variation, 482–483
    econometric models of, 481–486
    expert opinion, 478–479
    methodology, 477–486
    qualitative methods, 478
    survey methods, 479–480
    time-series analysis and projection, 480–481
    turning points, 484–485
Foreign dumping of goods, 439–445
Franchising, 348–351
Franchising agreement, defined, 348
Free entry, 125–126, 135
Free rider, 256–257
    defined, 256, 398
    problems with, 398–399
Fringe firms, defined, 187
Functional discount, 335–336
    defined, 335
Functional form
    in cost estimation, 469–475
    of the demand equation, 460–467

G

Golden parachute, 295–296
    defined, 295

Goods, 42–45
    complement, defined, 42
    inferior, defined, 43
    luxury, defined, 43
    normal, defined, 42–44
    substitute, defined, 45
Government policy on international trade, 428–436
Grants, 407–408
Graphing of lines, 7–11

H

Hanover Shoe, Inc. v. *United Shoe Machinery Corp.* (1968), 383
Hanson v. *Shell Oil Company* (1976), 202
Herfindahl index, 377–380
    defined, 377
Historical costs in cost estimation, 468
Horizontal integration, defined, 319
Horizontal merger, defined, 375
Hotelling spatial model, 265–266

I

Identification problem, 457–460
    defined, 459
Illinois Brick v. *the State of Illinois* (1977), 382–384
Implicit collusion, 211–214
Implicit costs, defined, 87
Implicit price fixing, 211–214
Income elasticity of demand, 39–44
    defined, 39
Incomplete specialization, 425–428
Increasing returns to scale, defined, 106
Incremental analysis, 178–180
Incremental cost, 89–90, 178–180
    defined, 89–90
Incumbent firm, defined, 193
Infant industries, 436–437
Inferior good, 42–44
    defined, 42
Inflation in cost estimation, 468
Inflection point, defined, 63–64
Information
    asymmetric, 254–256
        defined, 254
    consumer search for, 251–257
Information costs, 125, 140, 251–261, 399–400
Input substitution, 69–71
Integer programming, 544
Integration
    horizontal, defined, 319
    quasi-vertical, 286–287
        defined, 286

Interest rate model of forecasting, 485–486
Internal pricing of the firm, 306–329
Internal rate of return, 527–529
  defined, 527
Internal structure of the firm, 278–303
International commodity agreements, 434–436
International trade, 420–445
  and comparative advantage, 421–422
  demand considerations of, 425
  and foreign dumping of goods, 439
  and incomplete specialization, 425–428
  and infant industries, 436–437
  and international commodity agreements, 434–436
  mutual benefits of, 423–424
  and national defense, 438–439
  and protectionism, 436–444
  and quotas, 430–433
  and specialization, 421–428
  and tariffs, 429
  and voluntary export restraints, 434
International trade policy, 428–436
Interviews, 453
Isocost curve, defined, 243
Isocost line, 91–95
  defined, 91
Isoquant, 69–75, 78–80
  defined, 69
  kinked, 74–75, 78
  movement along an, 72
Isorevenue curve, defined, 243

K

Kinked demand curve, 211–214

L

Lab experiments, 203–205, 455–456
Lagging indicators, defined, 484
Leading indicators, defined, 484
Leasing or purchasing decisions, 533–534
Leverage, 541–542
  defined, 541
Licensing, 267–273, 412–414
  as a barrier to entry, 271–272
  and promotion of product quality, 271–272
  royalty-free, 267–270
Linear cost functions, 469
Linear form of demand equation, 461
Linear programming, 544
Long run, 62, 69–75
  defined, 62
  versus short run, 61–75
Long-run average total cost, defined, 104–105

Long-run average-total-cost curve, derivation of, 105
Long-run cost functions, 473–475
  empirical estimation of, 473–475
Long-run cost minimization, 91–96
Long-run costs, 90–91
Long-run marginal cost, defined, 104
Luxury good, 43–44
  defined, 43

M

Management, 291–302
  checks on, 296–300
  compensation of, 291–302
  separation of ownership and, 292
Managerial economics, defined, 2
Marginal analysis and net present value, 529–531
Marginal cost, defined, 101
Marginal cost curve, defined, 101–102
  derivation of, 100–102
Marginal cost of capital, defined, 527
Marginal product, 62–69
  defined, 62
  diminishing, 63
Marginal product curve, 64–69
  defined, 64
Marginal rate of technical substitution, 71–74, 78
  defined, 71
Marginal revenue
  defined, 35
  and elasticity, 35–39
Marginal revenue product of an input, 110–112
  defined, 110
Marginal utility of money, defined, 504
Market 2, 47–48, 124–148, 186–214, 370–371
  defined, 2, 47
  defining empirically, 47–48, 370–371
  perfectly contestable, defined, 198
  used-product, 192–193
Market entry, threat of, 199
Market-extension conglomerate merger, defined, 376
Market failure as a justification for regulation, 391–400
Market foreclosure, 279–280
  defined, 279
Market power and vertical integration, 279–283
Market segmentation, 154–167
  defined, 154
Market structure, 124–148
Market studies, 454–455
Markup adjustments, 177–178

Markup pricing, 175–178
  defined, 175
Mathematical review, 7–11
Maximization, wealth, 3–4
Measurement costs, 253–254
Measurement of risk, 498–502
Mergers, 375–380
  horizontal, 375
  market-extension conglomerate, 376
  product-extension conglomerate, 376
  pure conglomerate, 376
  vertical, 375–376
Metering, 164–167, 223–225
Methodology, forecasting, 477–486
Mixed bundling, 226–235
  and competitive good, 230–235
  defined, 226
Models and modeling, 4
Monopolistic competition, 144–147
  defined, 144
Monopoly, 13, 139–144, 360–367, 373–374
  defined, 139
  determination of profit-maximizing output, 143–144
  problem of, 361–367
Multiplant production, 319–323
  and transportation costs, 325–327
Multiproduct demand, 218–235
Multiproduct production, 235–246
Mutually beneficial trade, 423–424

N

National defense argument for protectionism, 438–439
Natural monopoly, 391–394
  defined, 391
Necessity good, defined, 43
Net marginal revenue, defined, 309
Net present value, 525–531
  defined, 525
  and marginal analysis, 529–531
Normal distribution, 501
Normal good, 42–44
  defined, 42

O

Objectives of the firm, 2–4, 292–295
  entrenching management, 294–295
  sales maximization, 292–294
  wealth maximization, 2–4
Occupational Safety and Health Administration (OSHA), 409–411
Oligopoly, 147–148
  defined, 147

OPEC (Organization of Petroleum Exporting Countries), 49, 140, 207–208
Opportunistic behavior, 284–285, 287–288, 351–352
  defined, 284
Opportunity cost, 85–87, 345, 468
  in cost estimation, 468
  defined, 86
Organization of the firm, 275–303
Output allocation among plants, 319–327
  no uncertainty, 319–323, 325–327
  uncertain input prices, 323–325
Own-price elasticity of demand, 28–39
  defined, 28

P

Pareto optimality, 400–401
  defined, 400
Payback period, defined, 531
Payback-period criterion, 531–532
Payoff matrix, 495
Peak-load pricing, 167–175
  defined, 167
  regulated, 170–175
Perfect competition, 13, 124–139
  assumptions of, 125–126
  defined, 125
  determination of output level, 126–127
Perfect complements, 74–75
  defined, 75
Perfectly competitive market equilibrium, 131–139
Perfectly competitive supply curve, 127–136
Perfectly contestable market, 198–201
  defined, 198
Perfectly elastic, 31–34, 37–39
Perfectly inelastic, 31–34, 37–39
Perfect price discrimination, 154–157, 166
  defined, 155
Perfect substitutes, 74–75
  defined, 75
Per se rule, defined, 369
Point method, defined, 27–28
Power function approximation of the demand equation, 461–463
Predatory pricing, 201–205, 440–441
  defined, 201
  and the dumping of foreign goods, 440–442
Present value, 505–511
  net, 525–527
Price
  demand, defined, 155
  reservation, 226–230
    defined, 226

Total-product curve, 63–68, 97–98
  defined, 64
Total revenue
  defined, 35
  and elasticity, 35–39
Total variable cost, defined, 98
Total-variable-cost curve, 99
Trade associations, 47
Transaction costs, 275–276, 283–291
  defined, 284
Transfer pricing, 307–319
  competitive external market for the input, 311–316
  defined, 307
  monopolized external market for the input, 316–319
  no external market for the input, 307–311
Transportation costs, 325–327
  and multiplant production, 325–327
Triple (treble) damages, 382–384
Trust, defined, 368
Turning points, forecasting, 484–485

U

Uncertainty, economic, defined, 493
Unit elastic point, 31–32
Unsystematic risk, defined, 538

U.S. v. Brown Shoe Company (1962), 48
U.S. v. E.I. DuPont de Nemours (1961), 47–48
U.S. v. Von's Grocery Company et al. (1966), 376
Utility, 17–18
Utility theory and risk aversion, 502–505
Utils, defined, 504

V

Variable
  endogenous, defined, 457
  exogenous, defined, 457
Variable-proportions production, 243–245
Variance, defined, 499
Vertical integration, 279–291
  complete, 288–290
  defined, 279
  to gain market power, 279–283
  and transactions costs, 283–291
Vertical merger, defined, 375–376
Voluntary export restraints, 434

W

Warranty, 257–258
  defined, 257
Wealth distribution, 367
Wealth maximization, 3–4
  constrained, 4–5

INDEX OF APPLICATIONS